W9-BLF-199

# EDUCATION AND NATIONALISM

An Historical Interpretation of American Education

FOUNDATIONS IN EDUCATION

Harold Benjamin, *Consulting Editor*

# Education and Nationalism

An Historical Interpretation of American Education

Gladys A. Wiggin, *University of Maryland*

McGraw-Hill Book Company, Inc. 1962

*New York      San Francisco*

*Toronto      London*

# EDUCATION AND NATIONALISM

70155

THE MAPLE PRESS COMPANY, YORK, PA.

# Preface

A nation is what its people are, and this nation is one of the richest in the world in terms of the number of kinds of people who have contributed to its development. It is this variation in Americans and the values of this variation, as they shine through the organization man, that have always appealed to the author's sense of high drama. She has wanted to explore—and has done so only in small part—the impact of cultural diversity on social institutions.

Another set of ideas has engaged the author's attention—ideas that have to do with why the American school system was established. If she has made her meanings on this subject clear, then readers may be astonished with her at current criticisms of schools. The public schools do not teach reading, say some; they are weak in mathematics and science, say others; the able are given short shrift; youth are not required to do homework. Most of these criticisms are, at least in part, unjustified. Schools do teach reading so well that the reading level of the American people rises substantially every decade; they teach mathematics and science to a higher percentage of youth of secondary school age than did schools of the 1890s; there have been a few programs for the able for many years and more are being established every year. The criticisms and their answers, however, are not the point. The fact that they are made often, with such venomous outrage, shows a vast ignorance of why schools were established in this country. No set of Americans in any generation in the past has ever argued for schools for such a puny purpose as the teaching of any set of specific subjects. The purposes were always more profoundly conceived and more broadly stated. Our first presidents and men of the American Institute of Instruction would be shocked at the lack of vision of some modern self-styled critics.

The author seeks to communicate these ideas and many others. There are undoubtedly blind spots that are a product of the author's

vii

biases.  She is a liberal in religion, being of the same persuasion as Thomas Jefferson, and is probably as liberal politically in her time as the third President was in his.  Her commitment to a public school establishment is also as deep as his.  She recognizes the fine contributions of some private colleges and universities and is in accord with the right of parents to choose their children's schools.  Yet she is firmly in accord with her New England ancestors, who believed that the proper place for a child or youth in a republican society is in a public elementary or secondary school.  She is happy to note that what research there is shows that public high school—as opposed to private school—graduates are better students in colleges and universities.

Whatever failings this book has are a reflection of the limitations of the author.  Whatever merit it has is due in part to many persons.  The author's colleagues have listened endlessly to the author's arguments. Students have sat patiently through dress rehearsals.  Her good friend Mrs. Serena Jane Lake has offered help and sympathy.  Librarians at the University of Maryland have been most patient and cooperative. Personnel at other institutions, such as the Library of Congress and the library of the Department of Health, Education, and Welfare, unbeknownst to themselves, have been of service.  Several publishers have kindly given permission to quote.  These include the Bureau of Publications, Teachers College, Columbia University; the Department of Health, Education, and Welfare, the U.S. Office of Education, formerly the Bureau of Education under the Department of the Interior; Harvard University Press; Henry Holt and Company, Inc.; The Macmillan Company; Robbins Music Corporation; Social Science Research Council; University of Chicago Press; University of Pittsburgh Press; and Yale University Press.  Last, Mrs. Ellen M. Behrens, Mrs. Elsie B. Steely, and Mr. Charles T. Stewart have given valiant service in typing and proofreading.

GLADYS A. WIGGIN

# Contents

ix

# List of Tables

# PART I

# Backgrounds of the American School System

# 1

# Education and Nationalism

> Education is also a . . . symbolic field of behavior. Much
> of its rationale cannot be tested as to direction or value. . . .
> For the social psychologist education, whatever else it may
> be or do, stands out as a peculiarly massive and well articu-
> lated set of symbols which express the needs of the individual
> in society and which help him to orient himself in his rela-
> tions to his fellow men. . . . Society has misgivings about
> the function of specific items in the educational process and
> has to make symbolic atonement by inventing such notions
> as the cultivation of the mind.[1]
>
> EDWARD SAPIR

Ernst Cassirer has suggested that we change the characterization of a
human being from the old Greek *animal rationale* to a modern world
*animal symbolicum*. The revised designation, Cassirer argues, more
aptly describes what is now known of the human being and at the same
time provides a framework for unifying the efforts to understand his behavior. Religion, the arts, and language are three among the symbol
systems which Cassirer proposes for study.[2] He might well have proposed education as a "well articulated set of symbols" which would
bear penetrating scrutiny; for the nature of schooling in the past or
present appears to be symbolic of the value system of a controlling
group.

In the twentieth century some of the educational symbols are a function of a force called *nationalism*. So pervasive is this force in deter-

---

[1] Edward Sapir, "Symbolism," in Edwin R. A. Seligman and Alvin Johnson (eds.),
*Encyclopaedia of the Social Sciences,* The Macmillan Company, New York, 1934,
vol. XIV, p. 494. Quoted by permission of The Macmillan Company.
[2] Ernst Cassirer, *An Essay on Man: An Introduction to a Philosophy of Human
Culture,* Doubleday & Company, Inc., New York, 1953.

mining the patterns of education that it is an unstated assumption in educational circles that an education system is expected to support nationalism. This assumption can be made whether the social institutions under consideration are of the Soviet, the Danish, the Indonesian, or the American variety. Yet the interrelationship between nationalism and education has been incompletely explored. Each day's paper sees the emergence or resurgence of some new and often aggressive nationalism; but the effect which this social upheaval has on the shaping of the attendant education system appears often to go unexamined.

This book is dedicated to an examination of the crucial twentieth-century educational question in one society, that of the United States. However, before exploring this special aspect of American education, the making of citizens, it is necessary to examine nationalism and education in general. For when the connection between the two has been made, the derivative statement next in order is that a particular education system supports a particular kind of nationalism. It is the *meaning* of nationalism in any designated society which sets the pattern for the role of schools in that society. An understanding of nationalism in general as well as of particular nationalisms becomes essential, therefore, to the understanding of all school systems, including the American.

## MAKING A NATION

Nationalism is of relatively recent origin. To be sure, in tribalism, which preceded the development of large civilizations, there was a kind of primitive nationalism. Among tribesmen there was a feeling of kinship to a group, which nevertheless did not prevent these early peoples from appreciating and occasionally getting along with other groups. A primitive nationalism and an equally primitive internationalism were not necessarily antithetical. It was not, however, directly on the foundations of tribalism that modern nationalism was built. The latter evolved in Europe, when the state systems emerged from "the ruins of Empire and the wreckage of Church."[3]

The state systems were not in their beginnings infused with nationalism, however. The absolute monarchies which were the first states were rather the forms into which the idea of nationalism could be later injected.[4] Ordinarily there were few of the accouterments of nationalism in the monarchical states which evolved from empire. The masses were not conscious of a common language and often spoke dialects or differ-

---

[3] Carlton J. H. Hayes, *The Historical Evolution of Modern Nationalism*, The Macmillan Company, New York, 1950, pp. 1–4.

[4] Hans Kohn, *World Order in Historical Perspective*, Harvard University Press, Cambridge, Mass., 1942, p. 100.

ent languages. Scholars might communicate in still another tongue. A bow was made to language only for the sake of understanding or for political advantage, as when Elizabeth I ordered the Bible and the Prayer Book to be put into Welsh so that her subjects might be weaned from "popery."[5]

The word "patriotism," with its roots in the Latin word for father, might better have characterized the loyalty which was given to the ruler.[6] Yet a modern nationalism did arise under the mild Joseph II, emperor of Austria and freethinker, who abolished religious oppression and serfdom alike, and established schools. Joseph's move toward nationalism was made when he tried to force the non-German population in Hungary to learn and use German in schools.[7]

National movements, however, were rarely ever initiated by the privileged classes that included wealthy merchants, noblemen, and generals, as well as kings. Rather, they were developed by teachers and their former students, literary men, and occasionally priests. These reformers, of mild or violent cast, helped to transfer loyalty from the person of a ruler to an impersonal state.[8] It is in these reforming movements, then, that one finds the seeds of modern nationalism.

Carlton J. H. Hayes isolates five kinds of European nationalism.[9] The first of these, the humanitarian variety, arose in the reforming zeal of the eighteenth-century Enlightenment, and some aspects of it spread to most countries of Europe as well as to America. This nationalism was designed to restrict the authority of government and, in the process, to ensure civil rights. It was based firmly on liberty of the individual.[10] In the eyes of the citizens of the "heavenly cities of the eighteenth century," nationalism was a means by which injustices could be rooted out by resort to consent of the governed. It was a democratic nationalism through which self-determining nations, uniquely different one from another, might come together to settle differences peaceably.

To return to Hayes's analysis, after the idylls of the eighteenth century came the violent French Revolution and fanatically idealistic Jacobin nationalism. Under this latter concept, the state as a servant to individuals was transformed into "a mystical entity . . . not only of classes but

[5] *Ibid.*, pp. 70–73.

[6] For a distinction between nationalism and patriotism, see H. Munro Chadwick, *The Nationalities of Europe and the Growth of National Ideologies*, Cambridge University Press, New York, 1945.

[7] *Ibid.*, p. 5.

[8] *Ibid.*, pp. 1–5, 12.

[9] Account of five nationalisms taken from Hayes, *op. cit.*, pp. 8–231, unless otherwise indicated.

[10] Hans Kohn, *Nationalism: Its Meaning and History*, D. Van Nostrand Company, Inc., Princeton, N.J., 1955, pp. 29–30 and throughout the book.

of individuals." A militant citizen army, patriotic societies, a new journalism, and an adapted education system underpinned a paternalistic state which was to regulate economic and social life in minutest detail.

The inevitable reaction to the violence of the Jacobins brought in its wake a traditional nationalism clothed in history and custom rather than reason and revolution. Aristocratic critics who embraced traditionalism had no rosy-eyed view of human beings as instruments of progress. Rather they relied on the lessons of the past and the revelation of human limitations as guides to a modestly happy present and future. To Edmund Burke, traditionalist, nationalism meant glorification of the British Constitution, continuity of peoples in time and space, and a hierarchy of loyalties, some of which were attached to objects other than the national state. To most traditionalists—whether in Germany, France, or England—nationalism meant historic rights, aristocratic privileges, and loyalty to state, class, and Christianity, in contrast to natural rights, democratic privileges, and the absolute sovereign state of the Jacobins, according to Hayes.

As the middle classes, and particularly the intellectuals, made gains in the nineteenth century, there was a modest return to and mild revision of the premises of the eighteenth-century Enlightenment. Jeremy Bentham, who put stress on the superiority of the English language, liberties, and mind, believed that every man serving his own interests would inevitably serve his fellows. He buttressed this stress on the individual with the concept of freedom to teach and study, and with a laissez-faire attitude in respect to government. Liberal nationalism in the form of an intellectual movement spread to the Continent, where it found expression in free popular education through national schools, universal military training, a popular press, and patriotic societies. In a somewhat more aristocratic vein, it was disguised in the 1848 Declaration of the Fundamental Rights of the German People, in which historic rights were substituted for natural rights and universal suffrage was skirted.

As wars bred militancy and as the struggle for power among the nation-states became more acute, there was spawned the idea of "exclusive pursuit of national policies" as expressed in an integral nationalism developed largely on the Continent but spreading even to the United States. A cardinal principle of this newest nationalism and one which set it apart from earlier forms was its reliance on brute force. In France this position was to be made tenable through emphasis on the French language and the Catholic religion, regionalism and syndicalism, hero worship and the necessity for overseas expansion, and hostility to the Germans, says Hayes. Integral nationalism triumphed, however, not in France, but in such countries as fascist Italy, Nazi Germany, and communist Russia. Steeped in a presumed historical tradition, anti-individualist and antidemocratic, these countries are examples of nations in which all loyalty is to be absorbed by the state and right is indistinguishable from might.

In the mid-twentieth century, nationalism is a highly complex phenomenon. In the countries of Western Europe, which have had their independence continuously for some hundreds of years, nationalism is on the wane as trading blocs encourage an incipient internationalism. The historic enmity of France and Germany is giving way before the necessity for economic health and well-being. Some of the people of the United States are becoming dimly aware of the fact that they may need help as much as they are prepared to give help; and if this concept gains wide acceptance, the eighteenth-century humanitarian nationalism which forms the basis for the American society may be well suited for a new kind of internationalism of the free and neutral worlds.

The new nations, nevertheless, and particularly those created since World Wars I and II, are still drunk with the potential power of independence, which is fed by a continuing revolt against the alien world of former imperial masters. The new national peoples tend to overemphasize "their selfhood and independence, their cultural particularities and self-sufficiency." In the wake of this determined difference follow violations of neighbors' rights and oppression of minorities as gross as any perpetrated by the imperial powers, according to Dr. Hans Kohn. The Asians and Africans have made human beings their victims before and since Western rule. "The Indonesian government has repressed" the natives in North Sumatra. The only period when Thailand has not been "threatened" by Burma was when Great Britain ruled the latter country. In the nineteenth century, Mohammedans in China were drowned in an "ocean of blood."[11] The formerly dependent peoples have often, unfortunately, borrowed the worst features of integral nationalism whilst professing the doctrines of the humanitarianism of the eighteenth century.

The nationalism of the twentieth century is a many-splendored thing. It is neither good nor bad in and of itself. Its manifestations can lead to good or bad results. If cultural freedom is an objective of all peoples, then that freedom has in the past, according to Kohn, been most threatened by "authoritarian and absolutized religion" and in the present is again threatened by "over-resentful or semi-totalitarian forms" of nationalism.[12] It can as aptly be promoted by the nationalism of the age of reason or of that of nineteenth-century liberal nationalism, either of

[11] Hans Kohn, "A New Look at Nationalism," *The Virginia Quarterly Review*, vol. 32, pp. 329–331, Summer, 1956.

[12] *Ibid.*, p. 332.

which can meld into an economic and social internationalism of a freeing and rewarding kind.

A native language, a preferred leadership, a symbol system, a designated territory, a common religion, and a common ancestry are props of many nationalisms. These props are not, however, as fundamental as is "a living and active corporate will." The latter is a "state of mind" which permeates the society.[13] It is the will—as symbolized in the props and as interpreted through such tools as patriotic societies, the press, and the schools—which determines whether nationalism is a limiting or freeing force. To one of those tools, the schools, we now turn for an introduction to their use in the cause of nationalism.

## THE ROLE OF THE SCHOOL

Education for support of a nation-state is a part of the process by which the young are fitted for living in their society. This kind of education, like nationalism itself, is of relatively recent origin—not more than two centuries old, as a matter of fact. It is coincidental with the development of a mass education system. In its inclusiveness and comprehensiveness it possibly has usurped some of the functions of the family, which has been the primary agency in the preparation of the young to live in their cultures.

The strikingly different character of education for nationalism cannot be properly understood unless reference is made to the primary socializing agency and to the schools which existed before nationalism was born. It is in the contrast with the tasks of these latter agencies that the tasks of nationalist education can be most clearly outlined.

### The Primary Agency in the Process of Socialization

Probably most sociologists and anthropologists would say that historically the family has had the major and often the sole responsibility for helping children to grow up and live successfully in their cultures. The sociologists call this process *socialization*. In recent years, anthropologists have coined the term *enculturation*, which distinguishes acquisition of culture by an otherwise cultureless child from adaptation of an adult to a foreign culture, which is ordinarily termed *acculturation*.

The family's role in the socialization process can be described functionally. For the helpless newborn and for the developing human being, the family members provide that minimum of physical care and comfort

---

[13] Kohn, *Nationalism: Its Meaning and History*, p. 10.

which will the better ensure physical survival. At the same time, through their positions in a society, family members give the child an appropriate status in the group. These two functions have been described as "controlling the environment of the child."

Another broad function of the family is to help the child to acquire the behaviors effective for and approved by the group in which he is to live. This is called "inculcating social values." In relatively complex societies where more than one kind of behavior in a specific circumstance may be approved, a highly important function of the family is helping the youngster to make appropriate choices.

A final broad function of the family is one which might be looked at in the twentieth century as a mental health service, providing regeneration for the family member. For the small child, who has so much to learn and so many demands upon him, home is the haven where he can be a little freer in his behavior without meeting with undue disapproval. Here he can get a second wind for his struggle to learn the ways of the tribe.[14] In short, the family is the social agency from which the child secures emotional security, economic and social skills, and social and political standards by which to live.

From the standpoint of roles of parents and child, the socialization process might look something like this: Parents provide appropriate food, clothing, and other protective devices by which the child can live in a culture with the maximum hope of surviving. As the child grows, the parents continue to provide a physical environment. The control of that environment is partially taken over by the child as he learns certain skills connected with the family as an economic unit. In the more primitive peasant family of which the modern European and American families are a derivative, the whole family constituted a productive enterprise, managed by the father as the head of the unit. In this enterprise, which was necessary for sheer physical survival, the child assumed responsibilities as his age and capabilities allowed. In the process of participating in the family economic pattern, he acquired what today is known as a set of vocational skills and, incidentally, a set of social standards which were acceptable to the group in which he grew.

As the child grew into the family culture, by the process of interaction with members of the family and near relatives or community members, he learned the difference between right and wrong, appropriate religious ceremonials, and correct behavior toward others. When he was ready for marriage, his mate would be negotiated for by his parents, most probably by his father. After marriage he might continue to live either with his own parents or with his wife's parents.

[14] Functions of the family adapted from M. F. Nimkoff, *The Family*, Houghton Mifflin Company, Boston, 1934, pp. 67–77.

In the peasant origin of the modern family, there was another important facet of this youth's socialization. This was the presence of models for his satisfaction and emulation. In a culture which changed little, the ten-year-old might see his baby brother as what he had been. He could see his fifteen-year-old brother, his father, and his grandfather as what he would be. He was always growing out of or into roles plainly played before him. Thus, this peasant ancestor lived all his life in an environment where the adults of the community took responsibility for reinforcing the appropriate behavior and stamping out the disapproved behavior. In the process of shaping behavior, the peasant adult family members also served as a buffer for the child against the shock of change; in this function, they differed markedly from the modern urban-dwelling family. Although the peasant community changed little, the point to be seen is that rural adult community members—unlike modern parents—were able to control the amount of change and, in the process, control the child's environment by passing on to him only the approved changes.[15]

Through this control, adult group members accomplished several tasks. They stabilized their society by allowing for addition only of elements which would enhance the functioning of the culture, and they smoothed the way for the easy introduction of these elements into the system. More important, they retained authority over their children because they were the only medium by which the child could take advantage of the past and anticipate a future. Through this process, adults assured the young that they would be children with a society. Furthermore, they fixed the continuity of their own culture, for the maturity of the young was acknowledged only when members of the new generation were themselves child rearers and transmitters of the cultural heritage.[16]

For the hundreds of years of human existence preceding the rise of nationalism in the eighteenth century, the family, bulwarked by the local community, was the only behavior-shaping agency with which the great masses of children had contact. If there were local loyalties to be developed, this primary agency developed them. Whatever behavior was judged good for survival purposes was patiently taught by parents and adult community members. The kind of survival behavior indicated by allegiance to a state, a flag, a constitution, a form of government —this would have been largely ignored because there would have been little or no need for it prior to the development of modern nations.

Though there were no nations in the modern sense in ancient and

[15] W. Lloyd Warner and Leo Srole, *The Social Systems of American Ethnic Groups*, Yale University Press, New Haven, Conn., 1945, pp. 143–144.

[16] *Ibid.*, p. 144.

medieval days, there were civilizations and there was a need for specially trained personnel. Thus schools arose in most early civilizations.

*Historical Tasks of the School*

That a school exists in a society indicates that some enculturative job has already been usurped from the family or added to the tasks done by a family. Usually a school emerges when a society learns to write its language in more abstract forms than in the simplest pictures. It is language in written form that is the first of many culture items which can be transmitted only by a specialist group. Schools had existed in the European civilization before the peopling of America—and in the Egyptian and Chinese societies before the European. And so, institutionalized enculturation, apart from that provided by the family, was imported to America.

The existence of a school and written language points up other characteristics of a society. It is, or will be, highly developed technologically; and there are specialized personnel who, through the tool of written language, will control important functions such as the preservation and interpretation of the religious beliefs and other accumulated wisdom. Thus in ancient Egypt, those who used the written language and partly maintained the schools were the priests. Pupils in these schools were destined to be rulers, officers of the army, and engineers who directed the control of the Nile. Only a very limited number of youngsters were affected by the enculturative task of the school. The vast majority of laborers or slaves—who dragged the blocks of stones for the tombs and sphinxes and tilled the wheat fields bordering on the Nile, or manned the armies which protected the society—had been untouched in their youth by any agency except the immediate adult community.

A similar situation existed fairly generally in the medieval European society which immediately preceded the emergence of nation-states in Europe. From the fifth to the fifteenth centuries those who came under the influence of the schools were destined to be lords of the manors, priests, physicians, teachers. The professional and liberal arts schools of the twelfth-century university imply schooled personnel. Those who graduated from the curriculum of the seven liberal arts and who eventually became masters were to be the teachers. The professional schools of theology, medicine, and law turned out the professional people for the society. A limited number of persons of other than college grade (medieval style) were accorded the privilege of learning to read, write, and figure, and some were given religious training. A few were educated through an apprentice system. In response to economic and social needs, guild, chantry, monastery, and court schools were established. But the great masses of peasant youngsters, children of the serfs, would have had no use for written language and their enculturating agent would have been largely or solely the family and the limited group of adults on a feudal manor.

From the time of the crusades, certain forces began to push against the European mold. Two of these forces had eventual consequence for the development of schools: they were the increase of trade and exploration and the finally successful Protestant Reformation. As the European traders went out across the land masses of Europe and into the lands of the Middle and Far East, they gathered ideas and practices of societies unlike their own and brought them back to their home communities. The sharp expansion of knowledge brought expansion in numbers and kinds of specialized personnel, with consequent increase of kinds of schools and numbers of students.

The Reformation began from a somewhat different base, but had a similar effect. Regardless of the rigidity and authoritarianism of early Protestantism, the rallying cry of "Every man his own priest!" emphasized the necessity for everyone's reading the Bible in the vernacular. This had the effect of stimulating the drive for universal schooling. Thus the movement for a mass education began at least two centuries before industrialization and nationalism required it for other purposes. The abortive reformation of the eleventh and twelfth centuries had partially failed. The sixteenth-century Reformation, stimulated by a business and trading group for status and economic as well as religious reasons, was the one which gave impetus to schools.

Although this chapter is devoted to a general discussion of schooling prior to the development of modern nations, the course of educational history in America up to 1776 will partially suffice to illustrate this historical development. It was the Reformation system of schools which came to America, most particularly with the Puritans. The black cloth of the Commonwealth had no notion, of course, of allowing every man to be his own priest. The drive for a compulsory and mass school system was designed to keep the feet of the wavering in the paths of the righteous. Grammar schools and Harvard College were to function as training grounds for spiritual and civil leaders.

Schools and colleges in the other thirteen colonies would have had much the same function as those in the Massachusetts Bay colony. The charity or church school for some of the masses would have been established to reinforce religious and moral behavior; the colleges, to train the ministers and, to a lesser extent, lay leaders. The primary school would hardly have been conceived of either as replacing an enculturative task of the family or as adding a new socializing task. Parents in practically all of the colonies were charged by law with the moral and religious training of their young.   Providing reading skills as a tool for understanding the Bible or the catechism was merely enforcing a task of the parents.   Even the apprentice system, which required that the apprentice be taught to read and write, was a kind of family system of schooling.   The master, like the modern teacher, stood in place of parent to his pupil.   Only the grammar schools and colleges were charged with a socializing task the parents could not carry out.

The colonial college may inadvertently have played one other role, one not intended for it by its founders.   By serving as a meeting place for young men from several of the colonies, it may have become the medium for the development of a group of revolutionary leaders who could function across colonial and religious lines.

The emergence of the new national state in 1776 gave a new role to schools in America.   This role had already been assumed in some European countries, for leaders in a monarchy must ready their people for a shift in loyalty from king or master to an impersonal national state. As the nation-states gathered power in the nineteenth century, their education systems became more firmly fixed as necessary adjuncts to development of political power.   By the twentieth century, it was tacitly acknowledged that—whether the nations were democratic or totalitarian —the mass school system of Europe or the Western Hemisphere must somehow reflect the values and the symbol systems of their respective nationalisms.

## Modern Education and Nationalism

What and why is there this relationship between education and nationalism?   In itself nationalism means that a political form has been developed—a form to which there is a new relationship and a different kind of loyalty.   The emotional basis for patriotism has been shifted from church or king or feudal lord to an impersonal state which is recognized as sovereign.   The state may be viewed (as in most democracies) as an agency through which the people at large can regulate their common life; or it may be looked at (as in totalitarian systems) as a monolith which is more than the sum of the people who make it up.

Whatever the nature of this half-mystic state, the people who are at its base must be educated either to participate effectively in its development or to accept the fact of being manipulated by leaders in its behalf. Again, whatever the nature of the education, all citizens must come under its influence if the state is to survive.   No longer is it conceivable that schooling be limited to scholars or leaders or specialized personnel. The modern state, unlike the earlier kingdoms or feudal manors, is kept alive either by an actively participant people or by an acquiescent people.

Thus mass education, ushered in by Protestantism for religious reasons, is made imperative by nationalism because of a new kind of political—some would say religious—faith.

A child's education in loyalty to his nation begins before he attends school. When he is very young he learns to salute the flag and recognize his national anthem. He early comes to know national heroes and some of the legends of his people. During his elementary schooling, and it is the elementary school which carries the burden of education for nationalism, he learns national history and geography; he participates in patriotic exercises; he celebrates Flag Day or Constitution Day, or Bastille Day or Guy Fawkes's Day. As an adjunct to secondary schooling, he and his sister join the Boy Scouts and the Girl Scouts. During high school days he becomes politically conscious of the necessity of participation in his government, whether this participation is for the purpose of free or manipulated choice of representatives. He begins his young adulthood with universal military service and his patriotic gesture is rewarded by girls who have been taught to admire the soldier. By the time he achieves full economic, political, and social participation in his society, it is hoped that he has developed a "loyalty and devotion to that half-real, half-mystical entity which is the nation-state."[17]

A series of agencies are used in training the nationalist citizen. The government services such as the navy, the schools, patriotic organizations, political parties, the press, and the mass media—all at some time are found to be enforcing nationalism. These agencies employ such tools as a common language, symbols, traditions, literature, rituals, and an emphasis on a preferred locality.[18] But the school, which employs most of the agencies and all of the tools available for the development of the proper emotional set, is often central to the process of citizen making.

The importance of the schools in the nationalizing process can be ascertained from prevailing regulations about schools and teachers. In Afghanistan, for instance, teachers are civil servants; in certain schools in Belgium they must be of Belgian origin.[19] In several states, teacher oaths are in force. Nation-states can and do censor texts, set qualifications for teachers, and inspect as well as censor private and religious schools. How any of these tasks is carried out and whether specific

[17] Frederick L. Schuman, *International Politics: The Western State System in Mid-century*, 5th ed., McGraw-Hill Book Company, Inc., New York, 1953, pp. 280–281.

[18] Charles Edward Merriam, *The Making of Citizens: A Comparative Study of Methods of Civic Training*, University of Chicago Press, Chicago, 1931, pp. 88–174.

[19] *World Survey of Education*, vol. II, *Primary Education*, UNESCO, Paris, 1958, pp. 66, 132. See whole volume for aims of schooling in various countries.

ones are present in any society depend on the life style of the nation-state.

Charles Merriam says that every state has a political article of faith (*credendum*). For the United States it is liberty; for Switzerland, federalism. France puts great store by centralization, while Germany exalts expert administration. These preferences are judged the highest good not through a process of reasoning, but through emotional responses.[20] These articles of faith plus the individual value structures, of which the articles are a part, determine the ways in which the schools reinforce nationalism.

A cursory introduction to the interrelationship of value structure and education can be had from a look at stated aims of education and particularly primary education. The Soviet bloc provides a clear-cut example of commitment in schooling to a secular ideology. Communist education, so says a statement on the Union of Soviet Socialist Republics, is provided at all levels of schooling, only being "modified according to the age of pupils." Likewise, Bulgaria calls for "training according to the principles of Communist education." The new China insists on "ideological education along the lines of Marxist-Leninist principles," in a system which shall be "national, scientific and popular."[21]

The small country of Ceylon is an example of a society which, like England, puts stress on freedom and nonintervention in professional matters. Education in Ceylon is for the development and enrichment of personality; in this educational system, man is an end in himself. Nationalism is broadly interpreted in such permissive democracies as England and Switzerland. Other societies forthrightly state a narrow nationalism as an aim of schooling, as well as a particular religious direction. In Afghanistan the task of primary schools is to develop the young into "true Moslems, staunch Afghans, and valuable members of society." Among the subjects presumably expected to develop this religious nationalism are history and geography, the mother tongue (Persian or Pushtu) and a second national language, and the Holy Koran.[22]

A more restrictive ideological education is that of Christian-national education in South Africa. It rests on three principles. The first of these is the religious, which is described as "Calvinism" and based on "Holy Scripture and the articles of Confession of the three Dutch Afrikaans Churches." The second principle is nationalism, which is to be Dutch South African in character, and achieved through study of such subjects as the national culture, geography, language, and history.

---

[20] Merriam, *op. cit.*, pp. 24–25.
[21] *Primary Education*, pp. 178, 253, 1016.
[22] *Ibid.*, pp. 62–64.

The third principle is politico-educational and defines the place of the state, the church, and the home in the education of the child. This principle requires control of schools and selection of teachers by Christian-nationalist parents in a state-aided, rather than a state-controlled, system.[23] Thus the anticipated life style of a people determines the aims for schooling.

A somewhat more detailed analysis of a limited number of systems will reveal further interrelationships of life style and education. In this analysis, perhaps it would be helpful to move between two polar positions as described by Isaac L. Kandel. Dr. Kandel says that nationalism may be supported in schools in two ways: (1) by helping youngsters to understand the environment in which they live and to develop a certain pride in that milieu; or (2) by direct indoctrination.[24]

Education systems in England and Switzerland aptly illustrate the first. A statement by the London County Council Education Committee indicates the lack of concern of Englishmen with aggressive nationalism. The committee noted that in countries where nationalist teachings had been strongest, such teachings had not prevented disruptions in the sociopolitical development and so concluded that "real patriotism cannot be made to order." The committee both disavowed the need for and the wisdom of communicating "a strained interpretation of historical truth."[25] In the same vein, the president of the board of education in 1927 staunchly upheld the right of the teacher to teach what he judged best, and not according to national prescription, as had been suggested by the patriotic Royal Society of St. George. If the government should so prescribe, said the president, the English would "run the risk of all those evils" to be "seen in various forms, both in the Prussia of the past and in the Russia of to-day."[26] So the schools in England have—in the past, at least—been used little or not at all to enforce a prescribed nationalism, making a bow to the need only in providing for a nonprescriptive teaching of English literature, history, and geography. Instead, cohesive factors in Great Britain appear to be the Crown, the peerage, the Commons, the courts, and the Church of England.[27]

In maintaining national unity, the Swiss have the problems of three

[23] Johannes Chr. Coetzee, "Christian-national Education in South Africa," in George Z. F. Bereday and Joseph A. Lauwerys (eds.), *Education and Philosophy,* The 1957 Year Book of Education, Harcourt, Brace & World, Inc., New York, 1957?), pp. 143–150.

[24] I. L. Kandel, "Nationalism," in *ibid.,* p. 139.

[25] John Merriman Gaus, *Great Britain: A Study of Civic Loyalty,* University of Chicago Press, Chicago, 1929, p. 158.

[26] Kandel, *op. cit.,* p. 138.

[27] Gaus, *op. cit.,* pp. 11–14, 154–155.

language groups and a dichotomy between Catholics and Protestants. The answer to these problems has not, however, been an aggressive and prescriptive national program but decentralization, with large autonomy given to cantons to control and develop the schooling process. At the heart of the process is a profound belief in democracy, which is above question as a preferred form of government. The mechanism of government can be criticized, and its faulty working is ordinarily attributed to the need for a new device or a change in people, which means a change in public education.[28] The Swiss appear to have a penchant for self-criticism and, like Americans, are inclined to attribute their shortcomings to the imperfect working of their school system. In the past they have been appalled at the gulf between the Teutonic and Romance populations. They have been likewise alarmed at the low marks of their young men in civics—yet an extended discussion among teachers and laymen alike, over a period of years, failed to result in any kind of national prescription. Instead the Swiss rely on politically conscious teachers, who are encouraged to participate in politics, and also on a kind of general pattern for inducting their young into Swiss life.

The civic training pattern begins with attention to folk songs and legends. It utilizes political problems in arithmetic exercises. It is pursued as well through local geography, history, and natural history. All of these subjects are fused in the lower grades into homeland lore. Fatherland lore is the theme of the upper grades, and at all levels the inquiry into the environment is enriched by trips and excursions which are planned in minutest detail to yield the richest returns. This never bellicose local and national patriotism is finally connected with internationalism by a study of the international agencies based in Geneva. Thus a deep commitment to federalism (meaning decentralization), democracy, and such practical matters as quality workmanship results in an education for nonchauvinist pride in a Switzerland which is part of a world community.[29]

A democracy of another kind, France, can be taken as illustrative of a society which has moved toward the aggressive-nationalism pole as described by Kandel. France's nationalism is based on a series of traditions. These include a central government and Catholic Christianity, military courage with *élan*, a missionary zeal and a colonial mission, and an economic concept that France sets the style in manners, apparel, and food. This peculiar democracy supports a highly centralized and autocratic education system in which the state supervises the schools, prescribes the qualifications of teachers, censors texts, imposes a uniform

[28] Robert Clarkson Brooks, *Civic Training in Switzerland: A Study of Democratic Life,* University of Chicago Press, Chicago, 1930, p. 10.

[29] *Ibid.,* pp. 172–204.

program regardless of local variation in culture, and regulates the catechism taught in Catholic schools.[30]

Under such a regime, the French child is treated to a liberal dose of what Carlton J. H. Hayes calls "national subjects": French morals and citizenship; reading, writing; and study of the French language; French songs; and military and other physical exercises related to patriotism. When the child is six to seven years old, over twenty of thirty school hours are devoted to the national curriculum. So heavily nationalist is the prescribed curriculum that in the elementary grades no translations of literatures other than the French are allowed, and historic heroes such as Charlemagne, Ferdinand de Lesseps, and King Philip Augustus abound. In church schools, patriotism is reinforced by emphasis on the Christian mission of France.[31]

Nationalist teachings are not confined to the common or elementary school. In the *lycée* are to be found two years of ancient history and five years of European history, in which emphasis is placed on French development. Geography of France and her colonies is studied not only in every year of the seven primary years, but also in the *lycée* or *collège*.[32]

Through an analysis of French texts, Dr. Hayes found illuminating trends. First, there was a similarity within grade among all texts. Authors praised the French Revolution as well as exalted the Republic, but gave little attention to the Church. French genius and civilization appeared to be uniformly praised, as were the "preëminent services of France to the world and the paramount duties of Frenchmen to France." Most texts gave a great deal of space to war and preparedness, with appropriately colored adjectives used to describe the enemy and France. Germany was "barbarous," "warlike," and "brutal." It was emphasized that Germany was responsible for World War I as well as for all atrocities. France emerged unscathed as "great," "pacific," "just," "generous," and "heroic." Hayes's concluding remark was to the effect that he was impressed alike by what the texts did not say, that is, they gave the French child so few conflicting points of view or unreconciled facts that he could not exercise his critical faculties.[33] France has rightly been described as a nation of patriots and, one might add, a country in which patriotism carries the banner of aggressive nationalism.

So much publicity has been given to the making of Communists, Nazis, and Fascists that perhaps the totalitarian aspects of aggressive nationalism might be better explored through reference to one aspect of

[30] Carlton J. H. Hayes, *France: A Nation of Patriots*, Columbia University Press, New York, 1930, pp. 7–9, 36–38.

[31] *Ibid.*, pp. 39–44.

[32] *Ibid.*, p. 47.

[33] *Ibid.*, pp. 52–55.

a less well-known education system—that of prewar Japan.  This discussion will also serve as background for the Japanese language schools
which have flourished in the United States and which are described
later in Part III.

The Imperial Rescript on Education, which will be found to have
been read and recited in these American Japanese schools, provides the
clue to the philosophy of Japanese nationalism, according to Robert
King Hall.  The rescript was issued by Emperor Meiji on October 30,
1890, and thereafter was read in Japanese schools and committed to
memory by Japanese children at least through World War II.  To a
Western reader, the document appears innocent enough.  It is only
when connections between phrases in it and other national symbols are
given interpretation that the extreme nationalism of its intent makes
understandable the fact that Japanese school children have been known
to mutilate themselves or commit suicide on hearing it.[34]

Know ye, Our Subjects:
Our Imperial Ancestors have founded Our Empire on a basis broad and ever-
lasting and have deeply and firmly implanted virtue; Our subjects ever united
in loyalty and filial piety have from generation to generation illustrated the
beauty thereof.   This is the glory of the fundamental character of Our Empire,
and herein also lies the source of Our education.   Ye, Our subjects, be filial
to your parents, affectionate to your brothers and sisters; as husbands and
wives be harmonious, as friends true; bear yourselves in modesty and moderation; extend your benevolence to all; pursue learning and cultivate arts, and
thereby develop intellectual faculties and perfect moral powers; furthermore,
advance public good and promote common interests; always respect the Constitution and observe the laws; should emergency arise, offer yourselves
courageously to the State; and thus guard and maintain the prosperity of
Our Imperial Throne coeval with heaven and earth.   So shall ye not only be
Our good and faithful subjects, but render illustrious the best traditions of
your forefathers.

The Way here set forth is indeed the teaching bequeathed by Our Imperial
Ancestors, to be observed alike by Their Descendants and the subjects, infal-
lible for all ages and true in all places.   It is Our wish to lay it to heart in all
reverence, in common with you, Our subjects, that We may all thus attain to
the same virtue.   [*Complete official English translation.*]

The opening line of the rescript referring to the founding of the Empire by imperial ancestors is taken from *Fukko Shintō*, the expression of
the national religion.  It shows consent to the belief that Japan was
"created by the deities of ancient mythology," which conditions the
government to be unchanging and succession to the throne continuous.
The reference to the people's being united in loyalty and filial piety is

---

[34] Robert King Hall, *Education for a New Japan*, Yale University Press, New
Haven, Conn., 1949, pp. 162–163.  Quoted by permission of the publisher.

Confucian in origin, indicating the divine leadership of Japan and the subordination of the citizen to the state. Japan's uniqueness and fundamental character, which inflame the emotions, are symbolized in the reference to the fundamental character of the empire, which is again from *Fukko Shintō*. Some of the virtues extolled in the rescript are of Confucian or Buddhist origin and some from *Bushidō*, the code of chivalry. "Extending benevolence to all" can be read to justify force in imposing virtue. The final admonition to the Japanese child to offer himself to his state to preserve the throne which is one with heaven and earth was inspired by national *Shintō*. This is the innocent document which sets the pattern for the nationalism taught in the schools and which has caused teachers to commit suicide for stumbling over the words.[35]

This philosophy of nationalism was partly enforced by a tool almost unique to Japan. This was the written language, a corrupted version of Chinese ideographs overlaid with Japanese adaptations. Japanese as well as foreign observers have long since called attention to the retarding influence of this complex written language on schooling. It is said that few can read or write it without at least twenty years of language study. Yet written Japanese can be quickly and adequately learned by school children through Romaji, which is based on a Roman alphabet. Why the resistance to change, even after Japanese scholars as well as American mission members have advocated it?

Dr. Hall lists a variety of reasons for such resistance, such as emotion, indifference, pedantry, and others. One such reason is ultranationalism. A rationale of nationalists and militarists has been that the nation and the language make progress only through the Way of the Gods or the Divine Will. That the people should make changes is unthinkable. With this seemingly irrefutable argument, under militarist rule, texts have in the past often been written in the most difficult language forms so that the people will be denied access to political writings. Coupled with this negative enforcement of nationalism has been an aggressive campaign carried on by militarists and nationalists via articles designed to delineate the devastating consequences of language reform.[36] Such is the unexpected turn which education for nationalism has taken in the past.

## SUMMARY

A fact of modern life to which little attention has been given is the consequences of the development of the nation-state to education. De-

[35] *Ibid.,* pp. 164–166.
[36] *Ibid.,* pp. 345–348.

velopments and changes in political forms required that education systems be sharply remodeled.   To shift the loyalty of subjects of the king to that of citizens of a state, mass education has been a *sine qua non*. With due regard to the character of the nationalism, various aims and practices and curricular innovations have been introduced into the new compulsory elementary, and occasionally secondary, schools.   Traditions; preferred subjects, such as history and geography; a common language; a presumed and occasionally mythical ancestry; and occasionally a common religion—all have been used by various nations in making citizens.

How the schools should be used has been determined by the value structures of the several nation-states.   Extremes of these patterns can be characterized on the one hand as the humanitarian nationalism of the eighteenth-century intellectual who saw the gracious development of the nation-state as the key to domestic justice and international amity. On the other hand would be found the integral nationalism of the nineteenth century, which put emphasis on power and might, a nationalism symbolized in communist, fascist, and Nazi dictatorships of the twentieth century.   These extremes might in turn be supported by an education for a decent induction into a particular cultural environment, or an education designed to propagandize for unquestioning obedience to a fatherland.   Whatever the character of education and nationalism to be found in the twentieth century, it seems reasonably certain that the creation of the nation-state has also created a schooling sharply different from that of previous periods.

Of so much importance is this new kind of schooling that it seems worthwhile to explore the relationship of education and nationalism in the United States.   To this task the remainder of this book is dedicated.

# 2

## Building an American Nation

> Four score and seven years ago our fathers brought forth
> upon this continent a new nation . . .
>
> ABRAHAM LINCOLN, PRESIDENT OF THE
> UNITED STATES, NOVEMBER 19, 1863

What is the relationship of nationalism and education in the United States? This is the question to be answered in the remainder of this book and for which Chapter 1 has provided a general background. The answer lies partly in the concept and nature of nationalism as it developed in America, but more particularly in the nature of the American population. The concept of nationalism (Kohn's "state of mind") and the character of the people conditioned in part the unique education system which has developed.

Before discussing the problems of nation making, certain introductory statements need to be made respecting schooling, United States style.

In the United States some 43 million children and youth and some 40 million adults are active participants in education. The activities and students are as diverse as youngsters in a primary class pondering over the words "cat" and "rat" on a blackboard and men and women in a community discussion group arguing over foreign policy. They include a role-playing session for foremen in industry and a laboratory hour on nuclear fission in a technical college. The students may be thirteen-year-olds in a student council, judging the fate of an erring peer, or seventy-year-olds at an informal round table planning an old-sters' talent show. The agencies of education are public and private in control, formal and informal in structure. Schooling is compulsory for children and youth and voluntary for adults.

The 83 million students herald the fact that in America practically everyone either goes to school or, through some lay organization such as a board or a parent-teacher organization, is concerned in some way with schooling. In the United States going to school is as much a way of life as drinking wine in France or kneeling for prayer in Iraq.  The idea of studying, inquiring into, or discussing *the problem,* whatever it may be, has invaded business as well as civic, service, and labor organizations, the Armed Forces, and the inner sanctums of beauticians. The League of Women Voters began as a suffrage organization.  It has turned into a formidable organization for study, discussion, and action concerning local, state, national, and international matters.  American industry spends thousands of dollars a year on educational enterprises for improving and upgrading employees.  The International Ladies' Garment Workers' Union employs an educational director.  As early as 1950, it was estimated that 1 million persons were enrolled in private correspondence schools.[1]  Mass media have been pressed into educational service.

About 30 per cent of youth, ages eighteen through twenty-one, are already in some kind of higher-education institution.  Yet the President's Commission on Higher Education has said that at least 49 per cent of Americans have the capacity to complete fourteen years of school, and, at a minimum, 32 per cent could complete "an advanced liberal or specialized professional education."[2]

The efforts put forth to get youngsters to school make an impressive story.  In a bay community, a boat is a necessary adjunct to the schoolhouse.  In many a consolidated or suburban school district, a fleet of buses is a commonplace part of education equipment.  A shuttle airplane is called into service for the educational enterprise in a Southwestern state.  On Western ranches, a good riding horse must be available for the school boy or girl.  When transportation cannot bring youth and schools into juxtaposition, correspondence courses are called into service.  Getting to school is a sufficiently important activity to employ any of the inventions of the machine age.

Americans carry the idea of schooling and of schools wherever they go.  For children of United States citizens and those in the host countries, North American business and industrial companies, private citizens, and religious denominations have developed over 250 schools in the twenty Latin-American countries and the Netherlands West Indies.[3] In far and near corners of the earth, American soldiers, airmen, sailors, and marines are putting to good use their leisure time in furthering their own education.  In 1958, some 573,000 members of the armed services were participating in 858,878 correspondence courses, group study

[1] Paul H. Sheats, Clarence D. Jayne, and Ralph B. Spence, *Adult Education: The Community Approach,* The Dryden Press, Inc., New York, 1953, p. 3.

[2] President's Commission on Higher Education, *Higher Education for American Democracy,* vol. I, *Establishing the Goals,* 1947, p. 41.

[3] *List of Schools Founded by United States Citizens and Organizations in Latin America,* American Council on Education, Inter-American Schools Service, Washington, November, 1954.

classes, and civilian school classes.   Schools for dependents have followed the service families abroad.   Americans are as careful about schooling for people under their care as they are of their own education.   When the United States took over the Philippines in 1898, one of the first official acts was to open schools staffed by American soldiers.   In the same tradition, schools for natives have been opened by Armed Forces personnel on obscure Pacific islands and by Federal employees on Indian reservations.

The schooling habit is as pervasive among American citizens in the United States boundaries.   A county agent follows a farmer into his wheat fields to teach the latest in disease control, and a home demonstration agent chats in the farm wife's kitchen about best ways of canning tomatoes.   At any given hour of the day an American of any age may be studying something in a meeting house in Connecticut, a Quonset hut in Thule, Greenland, a rough board schoolhouse in the Kentucky hills, a Mies van der Rohe building in Chicago, a temporary structure in Tokyo, the parlor of a Dakota farmstead.   The place and the means are incidental; the subject is specific to the student and the situation.   The imperative is the right and the necessity to study or be schooled.

The continuous criticism to which education is subjected in the United States is a function not so much of its failings as of the esteem in which it is held.   Education is a way of life, and whenever the society is put out of joint, schooling is put under the microscope.   Nothing can be wrong with government, social institutions, or individual personality which was not first wrong with the process by which public servants, the society, or the individuals were educated.

That the idea of being schooled has permeated American society is no happy accident.   Education has been built into the life style of Americans since the writing of the Declaration of Independence.   It has been a necessary concomitant to an experimental government and an imported citizenry.   It is the product of a nation of dreamers for whom the real is often out of harmony with the ideal.   It is the moral standard-bearer of a people who have been reared in the traditions of many lands.   It is the social cement of the American nation.   So it is to the nature of the American nation that one must turn for an introduction to American education.

## THE PROBLEMS PECULIAR TO
## THE UNITED STATES

In 1776 some 3 million people began the creation of a new nation. Lincoln's words belie the magnitude of this feat of forging a nation, and particularly a new and different nation, out of a patchwork of peoples and remnants of foreign loyalties. Lincoln's next words, "testing whether that nation . . . can long endure," strike the proper note of extended and extensive experimentation which is the key to understanding the development of the United States and the role of the schools in that development. These words hail the several momentous ways in which this nation was and is a new venture, and it is in the character of the venture that the characteristics of the schools must be explained.

The development of a nation means in the first instance the creation of a new political form. Here three kinds of differences distinguish American from European problems. Whether for good or ill, Americans were the first people in the Western civilization to say that they proposed to devise a republican nation-state. Note that this statement can be made despite the example of Switzerland, which would hardly have been classed with the powerful countries of Europe. The statement respecting primacy of their government conditioned Americans, so they and European observers felt, to pioneer in establishing a somewhat new and different set of political values.

The second difference lay in the nature of the leadership. Making a modern democratic nation may presuppose a ready-made group of political leaders who can shift the gears of the political machine from the old forms to the new nation-state. The younger sons of the nobility or an elite group of university professors and graduates have stood some European countries in good stead in this respect. Some such people were available in the American society. But as the latter defined itself, no designated leadership group emerged. Though the founding fathers had hoped to keep the steering of the ship of state in the hands of a relatively select, sober, and propertied group by removing the appointment of the President and senators from the tempers of the mob, it was clear by Jackson's day to some particularly sour commentators that the Presidency was open to anyone. Power was shifted rapidly to the general electorate. By the late 1840s there was white male suffrage, irrespective of economic qualifications, in most states. Although concerned commentators have, for the 180 years of national existence, talked of the possibilities of a groomed leadership, the latter has never really materialized and provisions have always had to be made for leaders coming from a wide-open society.

Some observers would insist that making a nation requires orderly movement toward a central government, despite the striking exception of Switzerland. Leaders in the new twentieth-century nations are deeply concerned for the power and authority of the central governing body. The United States, however, began with thirteen states lately separated by colonial jealousies and dedicated to federation rather than amalgamation. The government by committee and consent of the states under the eight years of the Articles of Confederation proved to be ineffective for operating in European power politics. Yet the relatively strong Constitution which replaced the inept Articles of Confederation did not thereby banish the concept of federalism.

Although the development of a political form is basic to nation making, this development is often based on a set of conditions which can evoke properly patriotic emotions. Commitment to a piece of land which can be envisioned as an integral part of the geographical confines of a nation is one of these conditions, so it is said. But the character of the farming and the vast expanse (or so it seemed until 1900) of the land discouraged attachment to a particular piece of soil. The farmer who was one month in Wisconsin and the next in Oregon could hardly be expected to develop geographical loyalties. A loyalty of place did, of course, develop, but it was for an abstraction—the greatness, the beauty, the expanse became the subject of patriotic orations. But, unlike the role of soil in Europe, this abstraction became a vehicle through which could be developed a doctrine of manifest destiny which fed an institutional form of loyalty.

A far more important and a commonly accepted condition for nation making is a tradition based on people or items in a revered past. It may be born of the feeling of a people for a family line stretching back in time ("my father before me and his father before him") or often an occupational line established firmly in a local society which can be enveloped in a larger society. It may have roots in a sacred literature such as the *Veda* of India or in a record of heroic achievements such as the Norse sagas. It may rest on proximity to ancestral burial grounds or lineal descent from some divine ancestor.

None of these characteristics of a common tradition was to be found in the new nation. As early as 1800 it was clear that there was to be no common sacred literature, except as the Bible served in part for some Americans, and a common secular literature had to be invented as the new nation celebrated its patriotic events and its never-ending rocks and rills. But more crucial was the absence of any basis for tracing common descent or developing a common tradition. A striking characteristic of the new society has been that it is largely imported. Except for the original settlers who had been here for some 25,000 years and who were systematically decimated or isolated, Americans have arrived by boat fairly recently. Before the so-called original settlers were used to being Americans and had fairly established a few common customs, the shores of America were assaulted by new groups speaking tongues other than English.

These diverse origins, in turn, presented problems in welding one people out of many. The first is the nature of the migrations. No group that came was ever a nice rounded sampling of an Old World society, one which might be expected to form the contours of a complete society. Each was a splintered section of the old nation and many were composed of minority dissenters. The first migrants constituted small knots of people who refused to conform to the rules of the established churches, but they were followed throughout the nineteenth century by other religious dissenters. Some, such as the Germans who came after 1848, were political refugees from the revolutions of Europe. Some were fleeing the economic rigors of subsistence farms or of the ghettos of large cities. A few were debtors. The relatively select group of scholars and professional people who have come in recent decades should not blind Americans to the origins of most of the population. Aside from the substantial first settlers of Massachusetts, many of whom were college graduates, Americans were mostly peasants and dissenters from the practices of their home countries. They had a common cause in their penchant for thinking otherwise. A land of imported minorities seemed admirably designed for the full exercise of that tendency.

The second problem in this migrant American population has been its increasing heterogeneity. The first settlers were English, then came Scots, next a sprinkling of Swedes and Dutch, and here and there a few from other nationality groups. Very soon the slave ships from Africa began to arrive. In the nineteenth century the Irish fleeing from the potato famines crowded the cities of the Eastern seaboard and changed metropolitan religious patterns. Germans and Scandinavians came before the Civil War and in increasing numbers thereafter. In 1848 a long-established Spanish-speaking population was acquired in the Southwest. There were always the Indians, of course, and some of them early began to fuse with white traders and settlers. After the Civil War, there began a steady trickle from practically all the countries of Europe—not only Anglo-Saxons, so-called, but Slavs and people from the Mediterranean countries. As the West Coast areas and later the Hawaiian Islands began to open up to modern agriculture, the United States drew on populations from around the Pacific rim. A miniature United Nations is what somehow had to be fused into some semblance of one people.

## THE NATURE OF THE NEW SOCIETY

Against the background of these peculiar circumstances of government, tradition, and people, what was the nature of the American society which began to emerge in the national period? In every society, a unique garb of nationalism has had to be tried on for size, occasionally discarded via revolution, and altered with changing circumstances. There have been few societies, however, which have been so permeated as has the American with the idea that the process of nation making or society making is experimental. Thus an examination of the society from the beginning of the national period leaves one with the impression of a nation that has not arrived, but is in the fluid, dynamic first stages of becoming. Far from a commitment to a core of values, earnest men and women were engaged in sorting out, selecting, and creating values for a new society. Appropriate symbols had to be devised. Thus thirteen stripes and a field of stars had to come to take the place of the Union Jack, and a man in a white wig had to replace George III.

Concurrently, through the national period to the present time, there has gone on a vigorous definition in ideas and actions of what the proportions of this citizen of a new society should be. Freedom based on the concept of individual worth has been the keynote. Defining the meaning and boundaries of individual freedom has been the steadily recurring crucial problem in this fluid society which is ever being renewed from people across the seas. To what extent may an individual go in seeking economic opportunity for himself before he must be restrained from interfering with the rights of others to achieve material prosperity? And what are the appropriate restraining measures for a republican society to use? As the society moved rapidly from an agricultural economy to industrialism and from toleration of slavery to its condemnation, these questions were fought out in a war, in labor-management strife, and in congressional debates and court decisions.

What does freedom of religion mean? Does it give the individual the right to refuse to go to war or to salute the flag, symbol of national unity? Does it mean worshipping as a Jew or Roman Catholic worships? Does it mean the right to be an atheist? Answers to these questions have been proposed by restrictive political parties and vigilante movements, and also in interfaith councils by the acceptance of diversity in pursuit of common purposes.

In the acculturation of the young and of adults, any society has two hard questions to answer: How wide is the allowable range of individual differences? How narrow are the limits of prescribed conformity? The democratic society bears down hard on the first question, the monolithic society, on the second. Americans from the first had less difficulty in reconciling their answers to these questions than did most of the older societies of Europe. They could feel that in the fact of the process itself there was identity with the experience of the race, and that in the particulars of the process there were sharp differences. In Europe a man who talked like a gentleman dressed like one. As emissary of the thirteen colonies abroad, Benjamin Franklin could dress in homespun while delighting the French court with his wit. In Britain and even in France, a man's idiosyncrasies could be estimated from conformities more readily than in the United States. George Washington's hair was powdered and he wore lace at his throat and wrists but his men, as well as those in the forces against him, could never be sure when he would employ daring un-European frontier tactics. In this experimental society it became very difficult to pigeonhole individuals by class or caste; as a consequence, the question of the individual versus the society had to be fought through on each new issue.

The new American society was developed on the concept of law and order. But this concept had rough going in the face of an emergent dual tradition.[4] It is to the Puritans that Americans owe the concept that all aspects of behavior "are amenable to control by law" and that the people will be better off if behavior is so controlled. This concept calls for "legislating on matters usually left to private conscience."

The second part of this emergent tradition puts a premium on individualism. It stems from the moving frontier, where there were areas in which only rudiments of the law could exist. In these areas Americans "became accustomed to doing things for themselves," and this custom was coupled with a belief in a higher law, God's law, which took precedence over man-made laws. This tradition is responsible for the voluntary associations which still flourish in this over-organized society. They are means by which individuals—individuals who resent government interference and who show scant respect for unwanted and inconvenient laws—will still do much in humanitarian terms both for themselves and for their society. This concept of free and voluntary association puts emphasis on a particular kind of individualism—not the individual's independence of other individuals, but his and their freedom from government restraint. This tradition has said that the government which is too weak to interfere with individual purposes is best and, having no fixed classes, this government has necessitated free association.[5]

Then where was the new nation to find a common denominator? On what could its early leaders and textbook writers pin their hopes for

[4] The discussion on the dual tradition is taken largely from Morroe Berger, "Racial Equality and the Law: The Role of Law in the United States," in *Race and Society*, UNESCO, Paris, 1954.

[5] For a discussion of the role of voluntary organizations in the United States, see Arthur M. Schlesinger, "Biography of a Nation of Joiners," *American Historical Review*, vol. 50, pp. 1–25, October, 1944.

developing a common sentiment among a people whose government was experimental and lacked a groomed leadership, whose geographical loyalties were diffuse, whose origins defied a unified tradition, and whose concept of the law was ambivalent?

Whether they have judged well or not, legislators and schoolteachers have put part of their faith in a common language.[6]   Although English in the early decades had minor skirmishes with German and has had to fight for place among the babble of tongues in large American cities and isolated rural areas, it has been pervasive enough to link together the American peoples and provide a bridge to a British homeland.   This insistence on a language as a key to nationalism is reminiscent of the Filipinos who have established Tagalog as the national tongue and the people of India who are turning to Hindi.   It is to be hoped that the latter will look for other props as did Americans.

The people of the United States invented a new kind of base for loyalty, which in turn became the firmest foundation the nation had. A particularly observant, sensitive, and sympathetic Scotsman, Alexander Mackay, put his finger on the key to loyalty in his book *The Western World, or Travels in the United States in 1846–47.*   His argument was that an American cares little for a piece of land but much for his institutions. Mackay said that republicanism was inevitable in 1776, and had remained so.   In the ensuing period (to 1846) the American had taken to his heart the essential value of his political institutions, their experimental nature, and their importance to other peoples in the world.   This loyalty to a form of government, furthermore, prevailed among merchants and manufacturers, artisans and farmers.   Mackay had been able to find only one frightened old lady and one simple-minded lieutenant who showed disaffection for democracy.   Unlike a European who took his government for granted and made the best accommodation to it he could, the American passionately embraced his political institutions and made them the rallying point for a society.[7] This loyalty to institutions, furthermore, was governed by varied interpretations of the meaning of the institutions.   As illustration, to the individual in the Puritan tradition, the Constitution was a divine mandate which prescribed the conditions for an orderly, lawful, and carefully circumscribed society.   To the staunch and unquenchable individualist, the fundamental law of the land was the Bill of Rights, which guaranteed his individual liberties and gave force to the proposition that he could govern himself.

[6] For an extended discussion of loyalty, see Merle Eugene Curti, *The Roots of American Loyalty,* Columbia University Press, New York, 1946.

[7] Alexander Mackay, "Every American Is an Apostle of the Democratic Creed," *America in Perspective,* Random House, Inc., New York, 1947, pp. 107–122.

A sentiment favoring republicanism merged readily with a belief in progress and the infinite perfectibility of man. In fact, the latter two aspects of the emerging democratic creed could not have found expression except under a republican government, many Americans would have said. Along with these sentiments went a fervent belief in equality which, like the Constitution, meant all things to all men but nevertheless provided a necessary rallying ground for a new people.

In 1776 "our fathers brought forth on this continent a new nation." By continuous discussion and change in practice, they created a creed to form a basis for nationalism. But as few others, this particular kind of creed required wholesale change and adaptation of behavior to fit it. It presupposed the forging of an American, a free and equal citizen, whose traditions had to be invented as the nation emerged. It rested on no easy acceptance by the people of lawful processes by which to achieve the goal, but on a fluid process through which freely associating individuals could set up unofficial and irregular governments known as clubs, societies, and associations.[8] It was developed around the idea that anyone in a wide-open society could be a leader, and required the constant assimilation into the society of newly imported citizens and of natives of long duration but of other cultures. The making of the American nation was a task for which an old institution, formal education, had to be refurbished to play a role perhaps more important than it has assumed in other democratic countries in modern times.

## THE RISE OF THE AMERICAN DREAM

Though the American people, including some of the educators, rail at the school (all levels) for its inadequacies, they have consistently allowed school people to carry the burden of culture transmission. Why? The answer to why the schools play a central role lies embedded in the emotional overtones and undertones of the people themselves.

The history books have long taught that America was, is, and will be the land of opportunity. The poor boy who became great has colored many reveries and lightened the gloom of lonely farms and crowded slums. This is the land where a young dairy hand can stump the experts and the son of an immigrant Italian musician can become the Reform mayor of the country's largest city. This is the republic of the Dream.[9]

The facts of life in America have, of course, often belied the Dream. What might Indians, wetbacks, Negro slaves, poor whites, and victims

[8] Schlesinger, *op. cit.*

[9] Credit for introducing the author to the Dream should be given to Prof. Verne E. Chatelain, Department of History, University of Maryland.

of religious persecution have to say to the Dream? Even they in some instances might have believed it was real, regardless of personal circumstances. The important issue is not whether the Dream is true, but rather the fact of its persistence in the lore of the people. In the way it enters into drives for social and economic reform and into the daily verbal patterns of Americans lies its importance. The facts of life for some people may belie their aspirations, but there is no doubt that, since the founding of this nation, men and women have held high hopes for riches to be showered on the individual in this culture. The springboard for these aspirations is the school, which is the tool by which "my children if not I" will come into the opportunity which is America.

The Dream has persisted in spite of a peculiar dichotomy in the American creed. In its beginnings our country was beset by two warring doctrines. Hamiltonianism called for government by men of property, a Federal bank with hard money and high tariffs, and a strong Federal government with checks and balances. Jeffersonianism insisted on government by the masses, a state bank with easy money and low tariffs, and a weak Federal government with autonomy left to local units. The issues since the first days of the nation have changed, but the dichotomy has remained in spirit. Curiously enough, the facts of national life have frequently clustered around Hamiltonianism, but the Dream has persisted around Jeffersonianism.

Quite apart from these central facts of our life, however, certain behaviors and attitudes early isolated themselves as necessary hallmarks in a land which held opportunity for all. In the last of the eighteenth century and through a part of the nineteenth century, curious travelers to this country were able to agree on definable national characteristics. Because of the numbers of visitors, this agreement was in itself significant. It has been estimated that this peculiar country, beholden to the masses and without benefit of royalty, has been the most-visited spot of the earth. What were these characteristics on which visitors agreed?[10]

Some of these characteristics appeared to center around a set of goals which could be assumed either from statements of the people or from the ways in which they behaved. For instance, most Americans appeared to give lip service to the concept of democracy, though there appeared to be no universally accepted definition of the term. Meanings were being expressed, however, in other desires and in the ways in which people lived. For instance, there seemed to be a drive toward achievement of higher standards of comfort for the average man. Food, even in frontier areas, was plentiful. Houses appeared to be more com-

---

[10] Again credit must go to Professor Chatelain for some of the facts on American characteristics.

fortable than those of lower-class people in Europe. That democracy was being interpreted partly in terms of material comfort was supported by further generalizations of visitors that there was more or less national neglect of abstract thinking and of aesthetic things of life. If one should turn to twentieth-century terminology, he could say that democracy is neither a tightly woven philosophical argument nor the opportunity to view Rembrandts. It is rocking chairs, ice water, the privilege of living in overheated houses, and efficient and preferably colored plumbing arrangements.

The goal of a greater order of material comfort for the common man was supported by another aim, which could only be described as the American Dream. There appeared to the visitors to be a general prevalence of a belief that life was going forward, that there was tangible progress in the American society, that things were going to be better tomorrow than today. The aspirations of Americans were always in a future which was not, after all, so far away.

These goals were actively supported by both verbal expressions and behaviors of Americans. One of the most important of these was a profound belief in and devotion in practice to manual work. Work was inevitable and desirable. There was a universality of belief that everybody works because there is an obligation to work. Happily enough, work was seen as a leveling process, as a bulwark against the development of a European caste system. The dreams of Americans were rosy. They anticipated an almost impossibly inflated standard for the masses, but this comfort was not to be won without labor on the part of everyone. So important was work to the building of a future that it became a measure by which to judge the so-called wellborn as well as the peasants. It was the poor boy who rose early and labored long who would some day become rich and famous. Teachers, scholars, professional people had to prove their merit by reference to their humble origins and their capacity for putting in a good day's work in the field or in the factory. In 1829 a backwoodsman and in 1861 a railsplitter became President of the United States.

Along with the instrumentality of work went restlessness and fidgetiness, said the visitors. Americans were in almost perpetual motion, and they were in incessant pursuit of material gain. But how was America to yield up its riches to the newly possessed masses if not through constant movement in the direction of limited as well as long-term goals?

There were implied, also, other means to ends, particularly in the role of women in American society. Foreign visitors were inclined to believe that there was undue deference paid to women and to the ideal of woman. If this attitude were prevalent, then probably it was partly a function of a frontier society in which there was a scarcity of women. But a frontier environment was not the whole explanation. Women were needed to exploit the Dream. To be sure, they were honored but only if they, too, subscribed to the doctrine of hard work. They hoed corn outside the stockade while the men watched the nearest thicket for the telltale scalp locks and, when the attack came, they loaded rifles and sometimes fired them. They were early thought capable of running businesses. Colonial Philadelphia, just before the Revolutionary War, boasted female proprietors of a chocolate works and a beefsteak house. In the early 1800s women could travel, by stagecoach and unescorted, up and down the East Coast. Nor were they so tender-minded and frail of intellect as a minority of men had believed them to be. Coeducational primary schools were a familiar sight in the early 1800s. Evening schools in late colonial days were open to women in business positions. In 1833 Oberlin College was opened as a coeducational institution, and from then on state universities and private institutions of higher education followed, either with coeducation or with separate colleges for women. Again, according to foreign visitors, women were more aggressive and freer in their behavior than females in Europe, but they were winning their right to their behavior because their labor was needed if the American Dream was to become a reality.

The American Dream has been responsible for the success of many otherwise suspect appeals. If this is the land of opportunity, then it must be God's will that it grow not only in people and wealth, but in size. If it is the most favored environment for the average man, then why should its benefits not be extended to others? Conversely, if it is the Promised Land, should not its borders be secured against the influx of those not able to understand its value? If this is the final outpost of a society dedicated to the welfare of the individual and of the masses, why should this country not go it alone?

Out of these arguments, and a host of others equally logical or illogical, has come support for many kinds of political movements. Americans in many times and places said that it was their manifest destiny to expand their territories from ocean to ocean and across the whole continent. "Florida is rightly ours," said Southern frontiersmen in the early 1800s. "Canada must also reap the benefits of this great democracy," said negotiators during the Revolutionary War and instigators of the War of 1812. "Americans are destined to spread their influence through the whole of Central America," said those whose eyes were on Mexico in the War of 1848.

Aggressive as were the claims of the doctrine of manifest destiny and harsh as were the measures taken to achieve ends, Americans demonstrated up to 1860, at least, that they meant what they said about spreading the benefits of democracy to others. They developed a unique plan for the incorporation of new territories into the union on an equal footing with the older states. Beginning with the acquiring of Alaska in 1867, however, they reverted to a mild form of European colonialism until post-World War II when Puerto Rico was given commonwealth status; the Philippines, their independence; and Alaska and Hawaii, statehood.

The unfolding of the doctrine of manifest destiny was accompanied by alternating cordiality to and rejection of new peoples and new ways. George Washington warned his countrymen in his Farewell Address against foreign entanglements. He was not talking about new immigrants, of course, but rather about new political alliances. The American spirit of political isolationism by 1823 was developed to the point where Monroe could proclaim his doctrine that Old World nations should forbear all meddling in the affairs of the Western Hemisphere.

Isolationism was by action defined as confined to the governmental sphere until the 1850s, when the nativist movement broke out against the Catholic immigrants. The post-Civil War American world had little need for exclusiveness, however. The West was continuing to open not only to farmers, but to ranchers, to lumbering, to the railroads. New people were needed to exploit the new land and to share, in turn, in its benefits. By 1910, however, the Federal government had become concerned about immigration. In a series of volumes a Federal commission reported on the fate of these newest Americans. World War I intervened but, following that holocaust, self-styled patriots charged that the country had to be saved from subversive elements and from foreign perverters of the faith. In 1924 immigration was severely restricted and restrictions have been lifted only briefly since that time.

Caught in the web of the entanglements of an interdependent world, the results of which they see in their material possessions, some Americans are still bedazzled by the Dream. Their comments are inconsistent with the facts of the modern world. The United States is the last stronghold of the Dream, so they say. Americans are the chosen people. The United Nations? Take its teaching out of the schools before children become corrupted. Americans are going to go it alone. Stop this foolish spending abroad. Democracy is going to be lost or won on American soil. The material and spiritual rewards of the Dream are for the people of this country alone, and only by holding fast to them can they secure the vision. This is a restrictive reading of the Dream.

Whatever the outcome of the Dream, that outcome—as well as its realization in the past—is partly a function of the American education system. Confronted with an experimental government, a diverse people, and a unique set of conditions for nation making, early leaders chose the schools as the agency for nationalism.

## THE EDUCATIONAL IMPLICATIONS OF
## THE AMERICAN NATION

Who is an American? This is the question which has been posed to the schools since the founding of this nation. What should this American know and what should be his behavior? These were the queries when the national enterprise got under way. How may he be a good American citizen? This is the question posed in the twentieth century. Both questions have often been phrased in declarative statements linking content and behavior: "morality, and knowledge, being necessary to good government"; the good citizen cooperates with his fellows. Both questions have necessitated describing the proportions of the good American, developing the role of the school in the making of the American, and charting the curricular processes by which the desired behaviors under the guidance of the school might emerge. This continuous making of choices respecting the direction in which behavior should be guided to develop the ideal American has made schools into a gigantic moral enterprise.

This venture in schooling a nation, furthermore, is unique. It is probable that in no other civilized country has a single social agency been charged with so much of the responsibility for providing the social cement. Denis W. Brogan, professor at the University of Cambridge, infers this expanded role when he says that a United States school must be understood in its Greek sense. It is a comprehensive institution which educates for leisure as well as for work, and in each succeeding decade becomes more compatible with its society. As the school is a socially sensitive instrument, the teachers and professors embark on more enterprises than they can complete and complete more than could be anticipated. Both of these characteristics, according to Brogan, are very American.[11]

Professor Brogan goes on to say that if the American school is viewed purely as a system of formal instruction, the observer will overlook its mission as a social and political instrument.[12] Some Americans are prone to overlook Brogan's caution; hence the recurring waves of criticism of American schools leave teachers bewildered and the public confused. Schools ought to teach the school subjects, so goes the European

[11] Denis W. Brogan, "A Cambridge Professor Celebrates the American Public School," *America in Perspective,* Random House, Inc., New York, 1947, p. 358.
[12] *Ibid.*

tradition, and the tag ends of this tradition are to be found in articles, the press, the minds of critics. But other portions of the public have been urging the teacher to "teach the child," which means preparing him to participate as family man, breadwinner, voter, scholar, or what have you—helping him to find his niche in an American society without disrupting the harmonious development of the whole. When the private interests of two kinds of critics find widespread acclaim without clarification of the role of the school, the public is treated to two totally different universes of discourse.

"We must all hang together or we shall all hang separately." This was a piece of sage and prophetic advice given to Americans on their initiation as a self-determining people. Hanging together was recognized by political leaders and educators alike as important for the new society. It early became clear that if the people of the United States were to develop behaviors, attitudes, and values which could be called common, some agency was going to have to take the initiative in promoting a set of universal mores and folkways. For this task political leaders and educators selected the school and, in early national history, the common school.

Selection and promotion of common interests and behaviors was only part of the task, however. In a democratic society the individual cherishes those rights which reassure him that in some matters he can be different. The increasing diversity in religion and national backgrounds of the American people meant that the struggle between individual and society would be intensified. The battle was fought on many fronts, but the sting was often taken out of the fight because education rather than force was used as a means of reconciling differences. In carrying out the function of chief adjudicator for the society, the school has had more than enough cut out for it.

## The Role of the Education System Emerges

The expanded role of the education system becomes more meaningful when attention is given to the limitations of other social agencies in the American society. In most societies, a host of social institutions hold tight to the old ways until the new are established and help to shape and to define the new behaviors. But could American social institutions be trusted, and were they available?

The family takes primary responsibility for shaping the behavior of the young. But what of the member of an immigrant family? Obviously—so many American leaders believed—he can know little of equality between rich and poor, the classes and the masses, because he has not experienced it. His family patterns will not fit the emerging democratic family pattern. His language is not one which is used in the new society, and he must slough it off or allow his children at least to be instructed in a language foreign to him. He may receive his religious instruction in a church not only of foreign ways, but of a foreign tongue. It is best that his children be not wholly inducted into the American culture by the family.

The church in most societies is responsible for setting the pattern of moral as well as spiritual behavior. But in the early national period, Americans took the only feasible step in respect to religious diversity by disestablishing the church or churches. They thereby cut themselves free not only from a common set of practices and beliefs in respect to the supernatural, but from commonly accepted views respecting family relationships and many kinds of personal behavior.

The family was not a family but families, often foreign families, and parents were frequently Poles or Italians or Japanese who had recently held allegiance to another government. The church was not an established church, but a host of competing churches often, too, with the flavor of foreign ways. What then was an acceptable agency for pointing the direction for the development of an American value pattern, and what was an agency which could be trusted with the task of culture transmission for the new society?

Though they did not put it in quite that way, early national leaders recognized as an appropriate Americanization agency a school which should be under public control and direction. The school which began with the common branches now embraces the college and university, but the school, in whatever extension, has been and still is the chief cultural transmission agency for the ever-emerging society.

What this central role of the school has meant to the teaching force can be illustrated by some hypothetical examples. It probably is unnecessary for the "public" schools of England to do more than reinforce patterns of social and personal behavior already well established in families before youngsters have enrolled in school. How to dress, how to eat, how to act in company, what is "cricket," how to act toward inferiors, superiors, and elders—all these are matters of general accord in church and family as well as in the schools. The two primary agencies necessarily take responsibility for pointing the direction of acceptable behavior long before the child has become a concern of the school. The school, therefore, can relegate to a relatively minor place a whole complex of ways of behaving, and concentrate on the learning functions which are peculiarly its own.

What of the American high school teacher? He can take nothing for granted. He must wrestle with eating habits, manners of dress, codes of etiquette, relationships of peoples to one another, toleration for or lack of tolerance of religious beliefs, and, most of all, the teaching of a foreign language. His troubles are not over, however, when he sees his job as dealing with larger slices of behavior than the schoolteacher in the ordinary Western culture must deal with. He has, in addition, a creative role to perform in respect to his culture. For the American schoolteacher has nothing so comforting as a commonly accepted set of values which he can implement. Although some may give lip service to such concepts as *democracy, equality, Americanism,* there is less agreement about how a democratic individual or an equal man or a good American should behave. How should one act toward elders, inferiors, superiors if one is striving to be equal to them? Indeed, are there either inferiors or superiors? How should one talk and eat and play and work? More intimately, what should be habits of personal hygiene, sex practices, modes of dress? How is one to know what is "cricket" in American society?

The American schoolteacher would have had enough cut out for him if his job had been addressed only to inducting the children of immigrants into the American culture. But he had still another group to deal with and in a slightly different way. This is a vertically mobile society where a poor boy may eventually be the manager of a great corporation, or so the schoolbooks say. Anyone, furthermore, can be President or senator or representative or governor. The teacher then conceived of his job as remaking not only second-generation young people but also those who had come from generations of American stock but who were so unfortunate as to be stigmatized by poverty, an un-American trait. Shaping the young into Americans acceptable enough to hold any position in a fluid society was his mammoth task.

What were the proportions of this American which might serve as a model for the job of the American schoolteacher? The schoolteacher would make these new Americans into members of the middle class, a happy neutral ground in the class system. (His judgment in this choice is amply supported by that great middle-class figure Benjamin Franklin, who is frequently referred to as the "first American." Recently it came as a shock to American educators that they had been discriminating against lower-class children through judgments arrived at via standardized intelligence tests. If the foregoing assumptions are correct, then the findings should be neither as sinister nor as blind in implication as they have appeared. If teachers have been forging a middle-class culture, how else should they judge the products of their instruction?) Feeling secure in the rightness of forging a middle-class society made the task no easier for the American teacher. Could he be sure of the proportions of the traits he was to emphasize? Could he count on the wisdom of his judgment when no traits were forthcoming to emphasize, and he had to invent them?  Where could he get an acceptable measuring instrument which would both define the traits and measure their pervasiveness?

Although psychologists must be credited with some of the initiative in the so-called scientific movement in education, their efforts probably have been directed by the whole American teaching body.  From its inception, the scientific movement has been beset by a passion for standardization.  A corollary of this has been a hysterical concern with minimum essentials in arithmetic, handwriting, spelling, reading, and an elaboration of the essentials in a series of basic-vocabulary studies.[13]  In the absence of any tradition-defined measuring stick for behavior, what a boon it has been to the American schoolteacher to have at least limited ways of behaving defined infallibly through a magic test instrument.

Another phenomenon of American education which is explainable in terms of the task of the teacher is the inordinate concern with "English." The graduates of sixteen-year education programs have had fourteen years of something called "English."  Yet according to their taskmasters, many of them cannot spell, read, or write properly.  Employers are in the habit of making such charges also.  Why after so many years of English should there be such deficiencies?  Largely because our standards are conservative middle-class standards.  Many youngsters whom teachers have been consistently trying to move into an American middle class speak a lower-class English or a second-generation English. Neither is appropriate for the emergent American.

Another concept which seems to be little understood in European educational circles is the American notion of "general education" or "education for citizenship."  Why indeed should an English or German or Swedish or French youth learn how to be an Englishman, a German, a Swede, or a Frenchman?  Does he not already know the customs and traditions of his culture?

Let us get on to the business of scholarship.  American high school and college teachers are not at all sure that an American youngster knows how to be an American in proper style.  College teachers, who have no mandate for teaching English or American history or the forms of government, are illustrative of the preoccupation with general education.  Like their public school colleagues, they are unsure of who is an American and what hyphenated Americans should know.  Consequently they spend hours defining a general education and more hours fitting it

---

[13] For a discussion of the scientific movement in education, see *The Scientific Movement in Education,* Thirty-seventh Yearbook of the National Society for the Study of Education, Public School Publishing Company, Bloomington, Ill., 1938, part II.

into crowded college schedules. The happy persistence of American parents in putting into college more youngsters than have ever gone in any other society has made this preoccupation with general education particularly crucial. After all, Tom Jones, who can do mathematics and aspires to be an engineer, comes from a family in which there have never been any college graduates. Tom has to learn more than mathematics: he has to learn how to be a good, middle-class professional man, American style. So American college professors spend time not only in defining general education, but in chaperoning dances, acting as sponsors of student clubs, advising officers of the student government, counseling on personal problems, and correcting the English in term papers.

When the American schoolteacher finally caught up with the proportions of his task of creating Americans, he found himself in a psychologically insupportable position. What is more, following on his willingness to be both an educator and a creator of culture, he found himself attacked for doing what he thought was his job. He had to turn to sanctions other than tests for the traits he was developing. Hence there has been a recent upsurge in the movement of involving parents and other adults in the concerns of the schools. The rationale for such involvement is, of course, democracy. The psychological explanation is very different. The educator needs the support of the adult community in the standards he is maintaining, and he needs to be told it is proper to do the whole job.

That the American teacher still feels it is necessary to do the whole job is eminently clear through the way in which he works with parents. He willingly spends afternoon and evening hours visiting round, or leading parent study groups. That he may have to give deference to other roles is evident in the questions he raises with himself when he leads these groups: Should a teacher be a reflector of values so that he may gain insight into how people want their youngsters brought up? Should he be a placid transmitter of research on children? Or should he tell these people how to be good middle-class parents? His secret commitment to the last concept is clearly evident in his charge that the parents who really need it (instruction in proper behavior) will not come to school. It is evident also in his way of working with the parent-teacher associations so that members may communicate about the school program. Furthermore, this program includes not only the three R's, but education in cooperation and competition, in getting along with peers, in self-government, and in all the other practices and values which ought to characterize the good American.

The emphasis on individual differences has necessitated the cult of "permissiveness"; in turn, this has introduced some interesting and crucial problems for the American teacher who is standardizing the population. He must accept this motley crowd as they are. Be they dirty or clean, foreign- or native-born, quiet or noisy, the teacher is dedicated to accepting them. A crucial problem arises, however, when he asks, "What then?" Tom shall not be "scored" for a dirty face—we shall find out why he thinks it is important to have a dirty face. Then, gently, by working with the home and with Tom, we shall change him into a clean-faced youngster. For is it not unthinkable in the American culture that Tom shall go through life with a dirty face?

What shall be done with Maria who is never on time? The teacher shall allow her more time to learn the meaning of time. For again, it would be—would it not?—unthinkable to allow her to progress through school without recognizing the importance of time. One day she will be a mother who must get her youngsters to school on time. One day she will be a wife who will have to get her husband to the commuters' train on time. One day she will be an employee who will have to arrive at work on time. The concept of permissiveness has been just another emotional aggravation to the schoolteacher who, chosen as he is, will reconcile it with his strategic role, maker of the American culture.

*Educational Outcomes of the Dream*

Though the American education system is faulty, it would have been more so if there had been no American Dream. The Dream provided the emotional bedrock on which a common school could be built, then a common high school, and now a common college. It was the motivating power behind the drive for an equal opportunity for all children. It built log-cabin colleges, spread a system of compulsory taxation for schools, and committed the educational institutions once and for all to continuous lay participation in educational business.

The attitudes and behaviors characteristic of people possessed of the Dream are mirrored in the educational enterprise. The manual-labor colleges which flourished in the middle of the nineteenth century and still are found in some private school systems were dedicated to character building. An exaltation of work was partly responsible for the spread of agricultural and mechanical colleges as well as technical institutes. Everybody and especially the leaders, was to be educated for work. The thought that it took only hard work to build an educational institution was behind the drive to establish log colleges with a house raising and loads of turnips and provision of tallow by the students. Good work habits are still among the most genuinely admired of the outcomes of elementary schooling.

The value of work has been the motive power for the Dream. A uniquely structured educational system has been one of the Dream's outcomes. The open ladder, peculiar first to the United States of all the nations of the Western culture, has been invented in response to the Dream. In the open ladder system, there are no bars to keep a young person from traveling as far as he will in search of opportunity. The open ladder says that a social, economic, or intellectual elite shall not have a monopoly on educational favors. The open ladder says that the son of a farmer or an industrial worker shall have opporunity.[14] Only in the South has a dual system lingered on to remind one that an anachronistic caste system still blots the vision.

In response to the Dream, a unique school enterprise, the junior high school, has been developed. At first, it was often misunderstood by both Americans and Europeans. Educators in the early twentieth century had looked at the extraordinary dropout rates in the eighth grade and proposed a break to a new institution before youngsters had reached the age limit for compulsory schooling. Teachers thought that if the young ones could be shifted into a secondary institution before they reached the age of fourteen or sixteen, then perhaps they would follow through with one more year of schooling than they would ordinarily have. The few whose parents were unenlightened could secure their right to educational opportunity. But laboring people misread the intent of educators. They suspected that their children were to be denied a regular secondary education and that they were to be given only a second-class educational opportunity. Consequently, they would have none of the new institution. Only when educators were able to communicate to parents that they had no intention of denying the Dream could they institute the junior high school on a wide scale.

The junior college, like the junior high school, was designed to continue the expansion of educational opportunity. It resulted in part from the desire of parents to afford some portion of a higher education to their youngsters when they had neither the means nor the wish to send them to four-year institutions. A common practice of educational administrators in the twentieth century has been to survey community opinion before instituting a community junior college. Almost inevitably the administrator secures an affirmative response from his community, for the junior college has followed the high school in being the people's college.

Curricula for petroleum engineers and foremen, institutes for dairy-

[14] For a most illuminating discussion, see Cornelis W. de Kiewiet, "The Dual Mandate of American Higher Education," *The Journal of Teacher Education,* vol. 6, pp. 251–257, December, 1955. See also Cornelis W. de Kiewiet, "How Different Types of Institutions Are Planning for the Future," *Action Underway to Meet the Rising Tide of College and University Enrollments,* American Council on Education, Washington, 1955.

men and beauty-shop operators—as developed by institutions of higher education—symbolize that proliferation of professional and vocational curricula which is an outgrowth of the Dream and the butt of jokes by European university graduates. But this miscellaneous collection of courses, curricula, and careers looks logical to most Americans. Every individual shall be developed to his fullest potential and in an institution of higher education, if necessary. He shall be fitted for his work in the world, and training for his work shall be given status equal to that of training ordinarily encompassed by a European university.

American higher-education institutions have responded to these policies by producing vast numbers of college and university graduates. Some foreign educators are quick to question the quality of a higher education given to so many. They also inquire petulantly, "What do you do with all those people? You haven't enough high-level positions for the supposedly high-level people." To this, Americans could well reply, "These people are the product and the reinforcement of the Dream." In more materialistic terms Americans could add, "We have 6 per cent of the world's population and no more than 6 per cent of the world's material resources. Of many important resources, we do not have 6 or even 1 per cent. But these men and women, with their college degrees and secondary school diplomas, can and sometimes do produce more than all the other 94 per cent of the world's people put together. What power does it take? It takes the power of the Dream."

An absence not of classes, but of permanent class barriers was the nineteenth-century observation on American society. The number of young people who have gone to college has enforced the fluid nature of the society. Delaying decision on a career so that a young person may make his own decision about college-going and providing an open ladder of opportunity to young persons of all classes have militated against the development of labor parties led by disgruntled, dispossessed, and intelligent members of the lower classes. Equal opportunity breeds a feeling of equal status. Providing a reasonably literate group of public servants has made for generally intelligent government, despite occasional outbreaks of corruption.[15]

Public tampering in higher education, providing career training for every youth, and an emphasis on vocational or professional preparation have paid high dividends for the Dream, but they may, in the new age of science, destroy it. For basic research is poorly comprehended by those who control and sometimes chart the destinies of higher education. The Dream says that anything can be conquered by hard work and frugal living—the only important activities are those which are practical in terms of immediate progress toward a vocational goal. He who sits

[15] *Ibid.*

still to think or he who uncovers a fact of no practical value is a shirker fit only for a European society that can afford scholars. As the institutions of higher education burgeon in the years to come, laboratories may give way to dormitories, research professors to freshman instructors, libraries and equipment to student unions and playing fields. If the many are to be given opportunity, can the few be tolerated and supported? If these few are given short shrift by upward-striving Americans, then the capital of the American's technological world may well disappear, and the Dream may destroy the Dream.

## SUMMARY

In the United States, as in other countries, the education system has responded to a unique kind of nationalism. Its building has been complicated by the absence of commitment to a particular soil and of a groomed leadership. It has had to be built with an experimental government, a fluid society, an imported citizenry, and an ambivalent concept of the law.

The fact that the nation was to be built on such foundations and that there was no state church meant that the education system had to be charged with more responsibility than would ordinarily have been the case. The school has educated for work and leisure, for personable behavior and social responsibility. In this process, the teacher has been both a transmitter and a creator of culture.

The schools have been both assisted and complicated by the American Dream, which is the emotional bedrock of the society. It is the Dream which has reinforced the concept of the school as the way to economic achievement and social acceptance in the American society. This role is one more way in which education for nationalism is unique in the United States.

# 3

# Political Influences on American Education

A popular Government, without popular information, or the means of acquiring it, is but a prologue to a farce or a tragedy; or, perhaps, both.[1]

JAMES MADISON, FOURTH PRESIDENT OF THE UNITED STATES, AUGUST 4, 1822

Education for nationalism begins with a discussion of the relationship between education and a particular kind of government. The United States enjoyed a *popular* government. This government rested on such ideals as equality, inalienable rights, the general welfare, and universal suffrage. Unless the people were informed, this kind of government would be but a prologue to a farce or a tragedy. For many people of rich and poor estate, such a political system called for emphasis on the education of the whole people through a common school system.[2]

Some early national leaders who were dedicated to the ideals of the American form of government still believed that those ideals could best be achieved through institutions of higher education for a groomed leadership. Many would insist that even though the masses were educated, there must be special provision for the leaders, preferably through a national university.

[1] *Letters and Other Writings of James Madison, Fourth President of the United States,* vol. III, *1816–1828,* published by order of Congress, R. Worthington, New York: 1884, p. 276.

[2] Materials for this chapter have been drawn largely from collections of readings and documents. Essays in these volumes, of relatively contemporary authors, will for the most part be individually cited in the bibliography and in footnotes. Statements of early national leaders and documents will be cited by reference to editors of collections or to contemporary authors who cite them.

From the founding of this nation to 1860, leaders in public life were defining, describing, and clarifying the relationship between the enlightenment of the whole people and the success of an experimental nation. This phase was initiated by the founding fathers at the national level and sustained by state and local officials, as well as citizens at large, to the time of the Civil War.

The antebellum period opened with the remnants of scattered private and public schools. During the period, propaganda went forward for a universal system from elementary school through university. The volume and strength of this propaganda is in a small way indicated by the statement that education was mentioned frequently in economics texts in the first half of the nineteenth century, but not so frequently in the last half.[3] Public figures used voluntary organizations, speeches, campaigns, and journals to persuade the people to support a compulsory free school system. Unknown Americans made scores of small donations to open several hundred private seminaries and colleges. Dedication on the part of the many secured firm education planks in new state constitutions. This was the era which opened with a few scattered schools and meager colleges and closed with state systems from elementary school through university and land-grant colleges. This first phase, then, absorbed the efforts of national and local figures and established the close relationship between government and education.

## THE FUNCTION OF THE COMMON SCHOOL

In the period from 1800 to 1860, primary attention was addressed to the function of the common school. Such a school system was a necessity if a government of, by, and for the people was to function effectively as an experimental instrument and an example to all the world. What the people were to be educated for, however, changed as the decades of the first half of the nineteenth century went by and varied according to how political and educational leaders viewed the people. Nevertheless, the arguments appeared to revolve around two central themes. The first had to do with the necessity for educating the rulers (the people); and the second, with reinforcing inalienable rights, equality, and the general welfare.

### Education for the Rulers

In 1812 a special committee reported to the New York Legislature on that most important of topics, a common school system. In the course

---

[3] John E. Waldron, "The Historical Development of American Secondary School Economics Textbooks to 1900," unpublished doctoral dissertation, University of Pittsburgh, Pittsburgh, Pa., 1955, p. 149. (Microfilm.)

of the report, committee members took occasion to point out that in a monarchical government there was no necessary relationship between education and government because the latter rested on authority and not on intelligence. But in this country, where the people were sovereign, citizens must be intelligent enough to know the right and virtuous enough to do it. Hence, they must be educated.[4]

The arguments of that prince of political manipulators, Machiavelli, were used in 1825 to give weight to the plea for a common school system. The safety of the state, so Machiavelli had contended, rested on the proper education of the Prince, on public teachers, and on schoolmasters. The prime object of interest in government was the education of the sovereign. In the United States government, where the people are sovereign, the education of all must become of prime interest to all.[5] Commentators in 1825, 1826, and 1832 repeated the sentiment that where people were guardians and protectors of rights and must not only obey but be a party to law, they must be educated. The destiny of the country depended on the children who were to be the legislators, political economists, and defenders. Elementary education for all was indeed one of the most important considerations for a free people.[6] Distances and state, regional, and local loyalties might grow to such proportions among the ignorant that jealousies and civil war would tear the society apart. So in the 1820s Charles S. Moorehead, member of the Committee on Education of the Kentucky Legislature, addressed himself to common schooling as the remedy. The government in the United States, more than in any other country, depended on an enlightened public opinion. If the society was to hang together, men and women must be educated to look with sympathy on all members of the commonwealth, and so to conduct themselves as to protect their rights.[7]

[4] Ellwood P. Cubberley, *Readings in Public Education in the United States: A Collection of Sources and Readings to Illustrate the History of Educational Practice and Progress in the United States,* Houghton Mifflin Company, Boston, 1934, pp. 148–149.

[5] Joseph L. Blau (ed.), *Social Theories of Jacksonian Democracy: Representative Writings of the Period 1825–1850,* Hafner Publishing Company, New York, 1947, p. 47.

[6] Edgar W. Knight (ed.), *A Documentary History of Education in the South before 1860,* vol. V, *Educational Theories and Practices,* The University of North Carolina Press, Chapel Hill, N.C., 1953, p. 24; *ibid.,* vol. IV, *Private and Denominational Efforts,* p. 153. Serena Jane Lake, "The American Institute of Instruction: A Study in Educational Propaganda," unpublished master's thesis, University of Maryland, College Park, Md., 1956, p. 75.

[7] Moses Edward Ligon, "A History of Public Education in Kentucky: A Study of the Development and Control of Public Education Based upon the Constitutional Provisions and the Legislative Acts of the General Assembly," *Bulletin of the*

A singular turn to education for citizenship was given by Capt. Alden Partridge in his argument in 1825 for military education. Captain Partridge had first opened a military school in Norwich, Vermont, in 1819, and had developed another one at Portsmouth, Virginia. Captain Partridge had six criticisms of the prevailing education, including the charge that it was not sufficiently practical or destined to prepare Americans for duties they would be called on to perform. One corrective of the latter deficiency was the inclusion of military science as a compulsory part of the program. The good captain argued that military defense in a republican government resided with all males aged eighteen to forty-five. If Americans wished to avoid a standing army, that bugaboo of a republic and "engine of oppression in the hands of despots," then through education they must improve the militia.[8]

Members of both the executive and legislative branches of government in Pennsylvania were, through the 1830s, concerned about the education of the rulers. A house committee in the 1832–1833 session of the Legislature pointed out that the people were the source of all power and that any hope for the continuance of free institutions rested on the education of all. Committee members extended this argument in a curious way. They noted that in South Carolina, tariff acts had been nullified in 1828 and again in 1832. These actions were the springboard for a declaration that it was far cheaper to educate people to support law than it was to leave people in ignorance and thereby have to deal with nullification.[9]

In 1833 Governor Wolf of Pennsylvania pointed out the peril of allowing children to grow up uneducated. In a few years they would be the rulers and lawmakers, defenders of the country and pillars of the state upon whom would depend the fate of republican liberties.[10] Thaddeus Stevens pointed out to the Pennsylvania Legislature in 1834 that, if a republic was to endure, the electors must have information. This was necessary not only for the individual's personal economic welfare, but so that he might give wise direction to his legislators, ambassadors, and executive officers. This argument, according to Stevens, ought to be sufficient for those who would question whether they should be taxed for the education of other people's children.[11] In something

---

*Bureau of School Service, College of Education,* vol. 14, no. 4, p. 70, University of Kentucky, Lexington, Ky., June, 1942.

[8] Knight, *op. cit.,* vol. IV, pp. 153–162.

[9] John A. Dwyer, "Some Factors Influencing Public Opinion on Free Schools in Pennsylvania, 1800–1835," unpublished doctoral dissertation, Temple University, Philadelphia, 1956, p. 90. (Microfilm.)

[10] Cubberley, *op. cit.,* p. 177.

[11] *Ibid.,* p. 180.

of the same vein, Walter R. Johnson, also of Pennsylvania, in 1834 advocated state support of education as a sign both of patriotism and of progress.[12]

The Right Rev. George W. Doane of the Protestant Episcopal Church drafted an address for a New Jersey convention in 1838. In his paper he stated that knowledge was a universal right of man. Whoever failed to help individuals to exploit their talents thwarted the Creator's design and neglected the gifts of God. Ignorance thus allowed to flourish would dissolve all institutions. Reverend Doane saw an even closer relationship between government and education, however. The people at large were the governors. The blessings and advantages they enjoyed also brought responsibilities and duties. The Constitution was in the safe keeping of all, but if the people were uneducated, they could not uphold their duties and responsibilities, including support of the Constitution. Education, therefore, was not a private matter but was indispensable for the preservation of free institutions. The common school should consequently be common not in the sense of serving the poor, but as the light and air are common.[13]

In 1838 also, Thomas H. Palmer, at a meeting of the American Institute of Instruction, reminded his audience that in other countries government was in the hands of the few, whereas in the United States it was in the trust of the whole people. Consequently, the eyes of the world were upon Americans, and the hopes of mankind would be dashed if the latter did not succeed. What better argument for a common school system! In 1840, Robert Rantoul, Jr., repeated much the same argument before the institute. Self-government was on trial in the United States for the "whole world and for all time." Such an opportunity had never before been afforded any other people, and whether Americans would seize and capitalize on it depended on the development of universal education.[14]

Magazines in the year 1840–1841 carried the basic argument that public support for education was a necessity for the training of an electorate. Democracy could function properly only if the voters were intelligent.[15] Such sentiments were attributed as late as 1858 to the Hon. C. G. Memmiger, who said that education must be provided for all if all were entrusted the power to serve on juries in judgment on life and property, to vote, to confer political power, to hold office, and to defend

[12] Arthur Alphonse Ekirch, *The Idea of Progress in America, 1815–1860,* Columbia University Press, New York, 1944, p. 203.

[13] Cubberley, *op. cit.,* pp. 182–184.

[14] Lake, *op. cit.,* pp. 75, 79.

[15] Eleanor Wolf Thompson, *Education for Ladies 1830–1860: Ideas on Education in Magazines for Women,* King's Crown Press, New York, 1947, p. 75.

the country as soldiers.[16]    In 1841, A. B. Muzzey pointed out that what the country would be depended on all the children.  If the people of the United States could isolate—as those in other countries could—the few who were to rule, educational efforts could be directed to the select. But in America public servants might come from any part of the population.  It was more important to educate the nine-tenths who should be in common schools than the one-tenth who were in colleges and academies.  It was the genius of American institutions that anyone might be in a position to affect the general welfare.[17]    In 1843 Muzzey expanded on his argument.  As all offices were open to everyone, the schools must teach the science of government.  Included in the latter was civil history of the United States, a study of the Constitution and how it is enforced, and the nature, duties, and responsibilities of and qualifications for public office.  Every child must be prepared to be legislator, justice, juror, or witness.[18]    In 1844, R. B. Hubbard returned to Muzzey's argument in favor of the common school as against the college or academy.  The latter would dry up, said Hubbard, unless the source, the common school, were purified.[19]    About the same time, Robert Rantoul, member of the Massachusetts Board of Education, pleaded for universal education as a means by which the United States might spread democracy.  Providence had endowed human beings with the instinct for progress, but this instinct must be improved by education.[20]

In 1846 Caleb Mills and Robert Dale Owen returned to the theme already familiar to many.  Before the Indiana Legislature, Mills testified that education would benefit everyone.  It would give permanence to civil and religious institutions, increase the social and literary capacities of the citizens, and add to everyone's happiness.[21]    Owen, an American congressman and son of the English socialist, contended that those who governed should be both wise and enlightened.  Therefore, schools, teachers, and a school system should be cherished.[22]

George Bancroft, the historian, reminded his audience in 1855 that intellectual and moral power was spread throughout the population, and that this universality of potential called for a national right to culture. As a matter of fact, revolutions had been fomented and reforms effected not by individual excellence, but by infusing the "common mind" with

[16] Knight, *op. cit.*, vol. V, p. 197.
[17] Lake, *op. cit.*, pp. 77–78.
[18] *Ibid.*, pp. 81–82.
[19] *Ibid.*, pp. 85–86.
[20] Ekirch, *op. cit.*, pp. 203–204.
[21] Cubberley, *op. cit.*, p. 172.
[22] Ekirch, *op. cit.*, pp. 195–196.

great principles. The people at large were the agents of progress.[23] Hence, an education for all was a logical necessity. Bancroft's argument had been supported in another way in 1853 by J. H. Stearns. As prosperity was necessary to good government, it was felt meet to point out that workingmen who were intelligent could support business better than could those who were ignorant.[24]

By the time of the Civil War, then, most commentators took for granted or tried to persuade the populace to take for granted that, as the people were the source of power and active participants in republican government, they should all be educated.

## THE DOCTRINE
## OF UNALIENABLE RIGHTS

The theme of the education of the rulers was interwoven with that of an education to preserve the principles underlying the government. One of these, the doctrine of unalienable rights, had its roots in a movement which had gained impetus in seventeenth-century Europe.

In 1687 Sir Isaac Newton had dealt a formidable blow to miracles and irrationality. He had reduced the universe to a formula and God to a machine tender.[25] Sir Isaac in the physical world was complemented by John Locke in the human; Locke described the mind as a blank tablet on which an impersonal world wrote its impressions. Human being and physical universe were one in some kind of order foretold by Cotton Mather in his characterization of God as the "Great Architect." Locke and Newton were symbols rather than chief instigators of the new order. They were but two in a long succession of philosopher-scientists who were gradually recovering in modern terms the rational world and rational human being of the ancient Athenians. They were also harbingers of the "heavenly city" of America's eighteenth-century deists.

In the particular city of George Washington and Thomas Jefferson, Benjamin Franklin and John Adams, as well as others of the Revolutionary and early national periods, there was projected both a perfect form of government and an education system to go with it. The Declaration of Independence was the manifesto of this new order. It capitalized on the *common sense*, meaning the consensus of Revolutionary leaders respecting both the nature and function of government. The

---

[23] Blau, *op. cit.*, pp. 271–272.

[24] Ekirch, *op. cit.*, p. 197.

[25] For historical development of a modern world view, see Edwin Arthur Burtt, *The Metaphysical Foundations of Modern Physical Science*, rev. ed., Doubleday & Company, Inc., New York, 1954.

authors "employed ideas from whatever source bore authoritative weight" in their society. Both the authors and the signers were revolutionary not in their ideas, but in the fact that they were the first makers of a new nation who had "declared the purpose of the state, enumerated some of man's natural rights, and affirmed the right of revolution."[26]

This universe, composite of the liberal philosophers' thought through the ages, was governed by "the Laws of Nature and of Nature's God."[27] In this orderly world, man found his rightful place as a part of Nature, in consequence of which he was endowed by his Creator with certain unalienable rights which became the trust of man's government. In the twentieth century, promoting the general welfare has compelled governments to take on a whole range of functions; it is well to remember that governments in 1776 had as their primary function "securing the blessings of *liberty*," which was a component of man in his natural state, and that governments were instituted among men for the primary function of securing man's natural rights.

It is probable that education has never before or since had such a clearly logical set of functions as it did when it was directed to participate in the process of educating people to participate in a government which was guardian of rights. There were two necessary functions of education: One was the education of the whole people to cherish their rights and to select as their agents in government those who would be proper guardians. The other was to prepare for high calling, the eighteenth-century version of Plato's philosopher-kings.

Although the leaders for the new nation were a concern of the fathers of our country, there was a parallel commitment to the masses. What use for a whole people to have fought a war for a government based on natural rights when the ignorance of the people might blind them to the machinations of charlatans and tyrants to usurp those rights? Instruction for the masses would serve as an impassable obstacle to the growth of despotism. For even though rights are inalienably man's own through his position in the natural order, they can be usurped by the unscrupulous or given away by the ignorant. "Education is more indispensable, and must be more general, under a free government than any other," said John Adams, second President of the United States.[28]

When political leaders got beyond the generalities of their statements

---

[26] Julian P. Boyd, "The Declaration of Independence," in Edward N. Saveth (ed. and author), *Understanding the American Past*, Little, Brown & Company, Boston, 1954, p. 98.

[27] The version of the Declaration of Independence being used is that cited in Henry Steele Commager (ed.), *Documents of American History*, 3d ed., Appleton-Century-Crofts, Inc., New York, 1945, vol. I, p. 100.

[28] *Expressions on Education by American Statesmen and Publicists*, U.S. Office of Education Bulletin 1913, no. 28, whole no. 538, 1913, p. 13.

on the relationship of education and government, how did they look at the aims of education and the processes by which the aims should be reached? In the early national period the ways in which leaders talked about the common schools were much the same as the ways in which they talked about the colleges, according to most commentators. "Intelligence" and "virtue" were the key words. "Religion, morality, and knowledge, being necessary to good government and the happiness of mankind, schools and the means of education shall forever be encouraged." So ran the Northwest Ordinance of 1787.[29]

According to most interpreters of pre-Civil War education and the directives for it, the concepts about schooling were rooted in the Baconian doctrine that knowledge is power. As early as 1790, Thomas Mifflin, Governor of Pennsylvania, asked the Legislature to turn its attention to education because knowledge made the individual aware of his rights and helped him to meet his duties as a member of society.[30]

If observers wished to go back before Bacon, they might pick up this particular conceptual thread with the ancient Athenians. But the Baconian doctrine had long since been coupled with Christian doctrine and dogma. The schools were responsible for the moral tone of the republican society, as well. A linkage could be made between government, morality, and education, as was done by Governor Snyder of Pennsylvania in 1811, when he declared that liberty would degenerate into licentiousness unless Americans were educated.[31] Intelligence and virtue, according to most commentators, were to be secured for the republican society by piping information and moral aphorisms into young heads, in the hope that what would emerge would be the intelligent and moral behavior befitting a citizen of a republic. "Virtue and intelligence are the true basis on which every republican government must rest," said David Buel, a moderate Democrat in the 1821 New York constitutional convention. Buel also called attention to the fact that "the universal diffusion of information" would forever distinguish the American from the European peoples.[32] This point of view was again echoed in a speech in 1822 by De Witt Clinton, Governor of New York, who said that, among the duties of the state, foremost was that of prop-

---

[29] Commager, op. cit., vol. I, p. 131. For a discussion of intelligence and virtue in the common schools, see Rush E. Welter, "Democracy and Education: The Role of Education in American Political Thought, from 1828 to the Present," unpublished doctoral dissertation, Harvard University, Cambridge, Mass., 1951; and in the colleges, see Richard Hofstadter and C. DeWitt Hardy, The Development and Scope of Higher Education in the United States, Columbia University Press, New York, 1952.

[30] Dwyer, op. cit., p. 21.

[31] Ibid., p. 39.

[32] Welter, op. cit., p. 37.

erly educating its citizens. To Clinton this meant developing their virtue through moral discipline, general enlightenment, purification of motives, and instruction in rights and obligations.[33]

Not all of the statements were in anticipation of an ideal future, however. The rosy-eyed already saw the ideal processes in operation in an infant school described in a Hartford newspaper in 1829. Under God's guidance and with His approbation were being developed "the intellectual and moral powers of those little beings" into whose hands would be put the future of the country. According to the reporter, this educational scene filled one with the "highest degree of moral sublimity."[34]

## The Doctrine of Equality

Although the Declaration of Independence had said that all men were created equal, some of the early national leaders never quite believed this honorific statement. Others took it literally. At least, they worried about such matters as whether a republican society could support a class system. They were concerned about whether an autocratic government could be staved off if there came to be too wide a gulf between the classes and the masses. They were afraid of such a formidable combination as wealth and knowledge if both were concentrated in the hands of a few. Most of these amateur political philosophers called on a system of common schools to promote that equalitarianism which would save this crucial experiment in government.

Charles Porter, Pennsylvania legislator, was a responsible citizen who worried about class distinctions. In 1805 Porter insisted that all the children of all the people must be educated at public expense so that no "invidious distinctions of rich and poor" would be apparent in the republican society. A committee of the Pennsylvania House, chaired by Nicholas Biddle, had more to say in somewhat the same vein in 1810. Political equality would not continue, according to committee members, in the face of educational inequalities.[35] As another instance, in 1822 a committee of administrators and legislators reported to the Kentucky House of Representatives on the virtues of a system of common schools. The latter was a system "of practical equality, in which the children of the rich and poor, meet upon a perfect level." The committee went on to note that the wealthy plantation owner would

[33] Edward Augustus Fitzpatrick, *The Educational Views and Influence of De Witt Clinton,* Bureau of Publications, Teachers College, Columbia University, New York, 1911, p. 65.

[34] Vera M. Butler, *Education as Revealed by New England Newspapers prior to 1850,* Majestic Press, Inc., Philadelphia, 1935, p. 262.

[35] Dwyer, *op. cit.,* pp. 30, 36.

undoubtedly resist any attempt to educate his children with those of the lowliest farmer. But in South Carolina, where extremes of wealth were greater than in Kentucky, a school system had been developed, and so it ought not to be impossible for their own state.[36]

Walter R. Johnson of Pennsylvania was undoubtedly as impressed as were the Kentucky legislators with the ideal mission of schools. But the practical reality was another matter. In the early 1800s, he accused the colleges and academies particularly of widening the distance between the different classes of society. He called on Pennsylvanians to express their strong disapproval of such snobbish practices.[37]

A fascinating turn was given to the argument over schooling by Frances Wright, English socialist and reformer. When she had reached her majority, Miss Wright, reasonably wealthy and living in England, had decided in favor of a visit to the United States rather than to Italy. She declared that she would rather travel through a free country than through one left in shambles by slavery (the latter in her eyes, curiously enough, was Italy). In the United States she visited such experimental communities as Brook Farm, built a rehabilitation center in the South for Negro slaves, lectured at New Harmony, and finally interested herself in the problems of the American laborer.[38]

In 1829 Miss Wright prepared a fiery condemnation of present evils and proposed a remedy. The reform so nobly begun in 1776, she said, had come to little. National policy had changed, but not social economy. The foreign church was still uncontrolled in America, Americans were still bound by English law, and the system of education was still English in flavor. Parish schools were under the control of priests, and colleges were reserved for the upper classes. Americans had more distinctions of class and sect than all the European nations put together. Men could not be made free and equal by words, she charged. The signing of the Declaration of Independence did not secure rights to the people; for one could not speak of liberty when the mind was in chains. The opening words of the Declaration were "insulting." The word is hers. Nor could equality be assured by the mere provision of a system of education. Children who worked ten hours a day and were often hungry could not take advantage of the educational equalizer. There was no equality when there was demoralizing poverty. Miss Wright's answer was boarding schools under public auspices; these could in truth be "nurseries of a free nation."[39]

---

[36] Ligon, *op. cit.*, pp. 60–61.

[37] Dwyer, *op. cit.*, pp. 186–187.

[38] Alice Felt Tyler, *Freedom's Ferment: Phases of American Social History to 1860*, University of Minnesota Press, Minneapolis, 1944, pp. 64, 201, 206 ff.

[39] Blau, *op. cit.*, pp. 283–286.

Two other writers must have had some of the same criticisms in mind. Theodore Parker, a Unitarian clergyman, charged, like Miss Wright, that there was too much of Continental education in America. As a consequence, the besetting sin of wealthy Americans was that they despised work with their hands. Beriah Green had an answer for this unfortunate circumstance. In 1835 he advocated a fusion of manual and intellectual training as a way of bringing scholars and workingmen together.[40]   Green was expressing approval of a kind of education which was already in effect in the manual-labor colleges of the Old Northwest.

The lawyer Charles Stewart Daveis had stated in 1825 that diffusion of knowledge was the process by which power could be distributed throughout the nation.[41]   Organized workingmen were also taking note of the same process in the 1830s.   In the United States minor political parties are often the portent of reforms which will one day be the common property and the achievement of major parties.   The United States had its share of such parties prior to, as well as after, the Civil War. Surprisingly enough, their pronouncements on education were meager and often couched in terms which aped the prevailing political language respecting the role of schools.

Some of the earliest of these minority groups were the workingmen's parties which developed in the 1820s in the cities and most vigorously in New York and Philadelphia. They stemmed from the Mechanics' Union of Trade Associations. A first demand of these parties was for labor unity. But this unity was a desired good not because of the economic advantages it would bring, but rather for its stimulus to the formation of "labor morale." From subsequent statements of members of the parties and those to be found in party planks, the *esprit de corps* of the working class was intimately interwoven with the development of a public school system free of the taint of a pauper institution. Workingmen had the right to refuse to patronize public schools which were charity institutions inimical to free institutions and the national character. The core of the argument stemmed from the immortal words of the Declaration of Independence, "liberty" and "equality," and from opinions of its immortal author, Thomas Jefferson. Liberty and equality would have no meaning, so ran the argument, unless knowledge were the "common property of all classes." Free government rested on the will of the whole people; monopoly, on power. The latter, in turn, was the product of knowledge, which must be equally distributed if the people were indeed to share power equally. As one man expressed it in a newspaper of a workingmen's party, "Next to life and liberty, we consider education the greatest blessing bestowed on mankind." One

[40] Lake, *op. cit.*, pp. 102–103.
[41] Blau, *op. cit.*, p. 46.

of the committees, following on this statement of how the Declaration of Independence was to be implemented, agreed with "the people's advocate," Thomas Jefferson, that the money which would be spent for the education of all children was but a small part of that which would "be paid to kings, nobles, and priests" who would soon be parasites among the people if they were not educated.[42] Meager as were the pronouncements of the workingmen's parties, they were in a sense prophetic of the peculiarly irrational flavor of educational thinking in the twentieth century. Frankly endorsing the doctrine of individual difference, educators and the lay public alike were inclined to believe that if the doses of education were large enough, the classes and the masses would somehow be equalized.

By the 1830s the battle over education was being waged with fury, and a common school system was in the news and in the speeches of politicians. According to a report of 1831, attention had been given to it in messages of the governors of Maine, New York, Pennsylvania, Delaware, South Carolina, Ohio, and Illinois.[43] Schools were becoming increasingly available, but not all were taking advantage of them. So, in 1832, James Walker addressed himself to the question of the influence of common schools on youngsters from the right side of the tracks. These children, according to Walker, were too sheltered. They were being kept from evil by being kept from knowledge of it, and this was wrong. The children should mingle with a cross section of youth and learn to resist evil. It was the mind, not the circumstances, which should be altered. Gardner B. Perry was, in 1834, more optimistic in his outlook. There were all kinds of youngsters in common schools, and this was good, for it would fit all for life.[44] The child was being prepared for the world as it is, and not as it was or would be in fiction, according to Theodore Edson in 1838. To the parent who worried about the corruption of his child, Edson replied that as the boy or girl began the study of books at a tender age, so also should the child begin early the study of mankind. David P. Page in 1844 countered that because some people would not put their youngsters in public school, they had withdrawn some of the most favorable influences from the school.[45] The sense of social obligation on the part of the wealthy was apparent in Page's words.

---

[42] Jack West Sutherland, "The Educational Ideas of Minor Political Parties," unpublished doctoral dissertation, Stanford University, Stanford, Calif., September, 1956, p. 45. (Microfilm.) For statements by workingmen's parties on education, see *ibid.*, pp. 39–45, and Cubberley, *op. cit.*, pp. 159–161

[43] Cubberley, *op. cit.*, p. 162.

[44] Lake, *op. cit.*, pp. 87–88.

[45] *Ibid.*, pp. 87–89.

In his report of 1838–1839 the superintendent of schools in Kentucky returned to the problem of the rich and the poor as it was manifested in a now committed slave state. Both the scarcity of population and slavery were working against the common schools, he reported. Slavery fostered in slaveholders a spirit of pride which made them unwilling to have their children associate with those of the poor. Such an attitude portended aristocratic government and was a deterrent of republicanism. If such be the case, it were better that slavery be abolished than that the common schools be abandoned.[46]   This was a strong statement for a Kentuckian in a period when the tides were running strong in defense of slavery.

In an 1840 issue of Hertford's *Connecticut Courant*, a reporter turned to a glowing example of equality in action. He had apparently visited a girls' high school in Middleton. He observed with satisfaction that the casual visitor could not tell the poor or orphaned from the wealthy girls. He affirmed that this was a "practical [sic] republican equality" which could be brought about by one means only: good schools.[47]

A commentator turned to a variety of reflections on equality in the pages of the Florida *Commercial Advertiser* in 1845. He insisted that equality did not mean reducing all to a low level of ignorance, but building all to a high level of intelligence. Furthermore, if through education every man was made a freeholder, each would have such a stake in the nation that there need be no worry about either freedom or republican institutions.[48]

Horace Mann, champion of the common school and believer in infinite perfectibility, returned to the relation between education, prosperity, and government in a report of 1848. He charged that, in Massachusetts, capital was domineering and labor was servile. If the upper class had both wealth and education and the lower were poor and ignorant, the latter would be "subjects of the former." The remedy for this imbalance between the classes was education, for intelligent men and women would not long be poor.[49]

Although the charity school gradually disappeared in the older Middle Atlantic and New England states, it continued to haunt the dreams of the dedicated in other areas. As late as 1846 a commentator in the Florida *Commercial Advertiser* condemned those who did not care to have their youngsters educated with charity scholars. He pointed out

[46] Ligon, *op. cit.*, p. 82.
[47] Butler, *op. cit.*, p. 391.
[48] Nita Katherine Pyburn, *Documentary History of Education in Florida, 1822–1860*, The Florida State University Press, Tallahassee, Fla., 1951, p. 23.
[49] Edgar W. Knight and Clifton L. Hall (eds.), *Readings in American Educational History*, Appleton-Century-Crofts, Inc., New York, 1951, pp. 165–166.

again, as had been done many times before, that one of the advantages of systems in other states was that children of the rich and poor were educated together. In defense of educating all youth together, he uttered the prophetic words that the son of the "wood sawyer" might one day "become the chief magistrate of our nation."[50]    In 1850, Mrs. Jane Swisshelm repeated again what had become, by now, gospel. In an editorial on the common schools, she asserted that education was the only means by which to approximate that state of equality desired by reformers and philanthropists. In other words, it was the only means for elevating the masses.[51]    Mrs. Swisshelm's words were uttered in the vein of the unquestioned assumption.

By the Civil War, then, it had been reasonably well established as an ideal that there could be no substantial differences between persons in a republican government. A society of sharply defined classes would defeat the grand plan of the founding fathers. A few voices in the wilderness still cried out for the selected few who would protect and inspire the many. By and large, most were agreed that the society should move toward reconciling one group to another and, in so doing, enforce equalitarianism. The fundamental differences between persons was seen as wealth before the Civil War. In the period from 1865 to the present, this difference would continue to be of concern but other kinds of differences, such as race and religion, would also be discussed with some heat. Whatever the specific, the argument would continue to be addressed to the problem of how to make people equal when they were obviously different. Somewhere embedded in the school system would be the answer.

### The Doctrine of the General Welfare

The period from 1820 to 1860 was an age of reform. Education of females, care of criminals and the insane, juvenile delinquency, and slavery were all the objects of concern of people with a mission. All of these problems had exercised the city fathers since colonial days, and Dr. Benjamin Rush, in 1786, had insisted that "fewer pillories and whipping posts" would be needed if young people were universally educated.[52]    But social problems in the first half of the nineteenth century had become aggravated with increasing immigration and urbanization. In their discussion in the antebellum period, they were linked to the health of a republican government which should be Christian and moral. Inevitably they were also linked to education,

---

[50] Pyburn, op. cit., pp. 24–25.
[51] Thompson, op. cit., p. 27.
[52] Dwyer, op. cit., p. 17.

which was the cure-all for evils of any kind in the government of the people.

Into this sociopolitical educational hopper, Daniel Webster threw a few choice bits in 1822. Webster, the conservative, was interested in any expedient which would preserve the society from violence either against persons or property. Therefore this defender of the substantial argued for taxing all in the interests of educating any. Education, he argued, was an effective police system which worked to protect life, property, and the general peace of society. It improved the moral sentiment and gave proper direction to the public will. By these means it acted to reduce crime and to secure the political fabric against violence, revolution, and licentiousness.[53] A more humanitarian note was struck by Pennsylvania legislators in the early 1800s. A joint committee of the House and Senate declared that to educate human beings so that they would not commit crimes was more humane than to punish ignorant convicts.[54] In Webster's view, the taxes paid by the wealthy for schools were but an assurance of security in property; to others, they were an act of mercy.

The New England-born president (1824–1836) of Charleston College, South Carolina, raised some questions respecting the directions the new nation was taking. Jaspar Adams admitted that the United States was making substantial scientific and material progress, but was this the only desired end? President Adams noted that the best-educated nations were those which were most moral and religious, and in which the energies of the people were "guided by virtue and knowledge." These nations were also the most powerful. In view of such evidence, Adams was alarmed that moral education had gone begging in educational institutions. Somewhat later Mark Hopkins, president of Williams College, was to remark that progress was a function of individual and religious improvement. It was not purely material, but was coming to understand "the true end of man as a social being." Improvement must be in conformity with God's plan.[55]

The New England Brahmins rarely left fundamental matters to chance. As will be remembered, they had an inordinate sense of security about the observance of preferred behavior if only it appeared in some form in the law. In 1827 the Massachusetts legislators revised and codified the school laws and, in the process, laid the burden of developing the New Englander's list of virtues directly at the school's door. In section 3 they declared that it was the duty of the officers and

[53] Cubberley, op. cit., p. 150.
[54] Dwyer, op. cit., p. 102.
[55] Ekirch, op. cit., pp. 212–214.

teachers at Cambridge and other colleges and academies to teach principles of piety and justice, a sacred regard for truth, and love of country. As if this were not enough, they were to develop in the young the traits of universal benevolence, industry, frugality, chastity, moderation, temperance, and all other virtues which might be basic to the perpetuation of a republican constitution.[56]

In the 1830s Joseph Story and Governor Wolf called attention to different aspects of the relationship of social welfare, government, and education. Story in 1835 insisted that the United States had no guard against disaster and ruin "except the intelligence and virtue of the people." If they were to succeed in running a successful government, Americans must be better people than those in other societies.[57] Governor Wolf in his message of 1833 noted that universal education would be a check on vice and crime.[58]

Poverty, crime, revolution, and the public welfare were of concern to others in the 1830s. An advocate for workingmen urged them in 1836 to mitigate their lot through reading and self-education rather than through political parties. An educated people would ensure a better society. In 1837 a contributor to *Godey's Lady's Book* wrote that through education the oppressed would be rescued and the dangers of revolution by the ignorant, who would undo all authority, would be averted.[59] Education made patriots and Christians and so controlled persons and brought order out of chaos, said the Rev. Elipha White in 1838. Education "is the secret of self-control."[60] In 1838 a speaker at the American Institute of Instruction called for Federal aid to education on the ground that a comprehensive school system "would advance the public welfare" and allay the evils attendant on increasing population. Throughout world history, whenever there had been an educated population, there had also been progress.[61]

There was no better and cheaper means of combating crime than education, said Daniel Webster in 1838. If the American government were ever destroyed, it would be the work not of a foreign enemy, but of the people who, for neglect of their government, had become the dupes of corrupt public servants. Intelligence as secured through education was the only salvation of republican government.[62] Another aspect of this sentiment was echoed in the *Southern Literary Messenger*

[56] Butler, *op. cit.*, p. 293.
[57] Lake, *op. cit.*, pp. 80–81.
[58] Cubberley, *op. cit.*, p. 177.
[59] Ekirch, *op. cit.*, pp. 196, 199, 202.
[60] Lake, *op. cit.*, pp. 74–75.
[61] Ekirch, *op. cit.*, p. 205.
[62] Cubberley, *op. cit.*, pp. 150–151.

in 1841, in an argument that schools were cheaper and more effective than militia systems.  Furthermore, they were just as good as the courts in defending life and property.[63]

The *Elements of Moral Science* was published in 1835.  It was written by Francis Wayland, Baptist minister and president of Brown University.  Wayland's argument was that the Creator had endowed man with intellectual and moral powers which, if used properly (educated adequately), would lead to general improvement.  It was the will of God that when man had improved, he should have the fruits of his labor or else he would have no incentive for continuing his progress.  On much the same theme, Wayland remarked in 1850 that progress depended on a knowledge of the laws of nature.  Therefore the schools must spread a knowledge of the useful arts.[64]

In raising the moral tone which would secure the republican society, females came in for somewhat more attention than males.  The connection of women with morals was, of course, not unusual.  In most societies the mother is revered as the font of the moral life.  What was unusual was that woman's special contribution should be ensured through education.  This interesting linkage between morality and the formal schooling of girls was probably the achievement of the New Englanders who since colonial days had persistently educated their daughters and put on the school doorstep the answer to any social problem.  In the 1830s and 1840s the argument for educating females took two different turns.  The one was in the direction of describing the maternal influence on society.  The woman, as the mother of statesmen, was a moral force of such proportions that she directly influenced the "destiny of our rising nation."  The other turn was in the direction of insisting that women be the teachers of young children.  Only thus could the morality of the masses as well as the classes be assured.  Many believed that reform in any direction would be achieved only through education of girls.[65]

These two positions are illustrated by speeches of Solomon Adams and Catherine Beecher.  In 1844 Adams called attention to President John Adams's contention that he had never known a good man who did not have a good mother.  Good men were but the instruments which good women developed.  There could be no argument against the schooling of future mothers.[66]  Mrs. Beecher took another tack in an essay in 1845, in which she called on American women to save their country.

[63] Thompson, *op. cit.*, p. 78.

[64] Ekirch, *op. cit.*, pp. 214–215.

[65] Thompson, *op. cit.*, p. 37; Thomas Woody, *A History of Women's Education in the United States*, The Science Press, New York, 1929, p. 401.

[66] Lake, *op. cit.*, p. 107.

Such disasters as social decay and revolution could be prevented only by literate, intelligent citizens.  If women wished to do their duty by their country they could not do better than to prepare for teaching in the common schools.[67]

In the 1840s a series of writers and speakers continued to argue for moral adequacy as underpinning government, to be secured only through education.  A writer whose work appeared in the Florida *Commercial Advertiser* argued that people with moral and religious restraint were the best guard against enemies from without and from within.  Therefore, practically all the purposes of legislation could be secured if the lawmaking bodies would but first develop schools.[68]  In 1846 Joel Hawes claimed that a Christian education was the only kind which ought to be supported in a democracy.[69]  Samuel G. Goodrich (Peter Parley), in discussing the course of civilization, was inclined to believe that Protestant countries made the most progress.[70]

The belief that morality can stem only from Protestantism has had a profound effect on schooling in America and has had repercussions of one kind or another too varied to relate here.  However, the main issues may be clarified by reference to a dramatic incident in New York in the 1840s.  The background was laid in the firm belief of Protestants of the early 1800s that Catholicism was inimical to free government.  The power of the clergy and the severely limited authority of the congregations in Catholic churches were considered to be deterrents to the development of free civil institutions.  A series of incidents in Baltimore and Philadelphia, where a Catholic congregation had lost control over its church, only served to enforce the belief about the essentially autocratic character of Catholicism.  In consequence, a Protestant parent who sent his child to a select and sheltered convent school was charged with risking both his "daughter's virtue" and his "country's future."[71]

Stimulated by the threat of a miseducated population, the members of the American Bible Society vowed in 1838 to continue their missionary work until the Protestant Bible was read in every classroom in the entire country.  In New York, Bible reading was a prominent part of the program provided by the Public School Society and partially financed by the public school funds.  Such practices brought strong protests from Roman Catholics.  Governor William H. Seward of New York, who was in sympathy with Catholic immigrants, recommended that

[67] Woody, *op. cit.*, pp. 327–328.
[68] Pyburn, *op. cit.*, p. 23.
[69] Lake, *op. cit.*, p. 111.
[70] Ekirch, *op. cit.*, pp. 209–210.
[71] Roy Allen Billington, *The Protestant Crusade 1800–1860: A Study of the Origins of American Nativism*, The Macmillan Company, New York, 1938, pp. 37–40, 68.

schools be established for immigrant children who should be instructed in their native language by teachers of their parents' faith. In the meantime, however, Catholics muddied the waters of the school issue by clamoring for money for their own parochial schools. The difficulty over religion, morality, and the character of instruction in public schools was finally settled by abolishing the Public School Society and replacing it with school commissioners elected by wards. The compromise became law in 1842.[72]

Horace Mann, to whom education was the "balance wheel of social machinery," related the argument on compulsory taxation for schools to the general social welfare. He began his argument by saying that no one had the right to deny a natural life to children. If a child were not educated, he was doomed to a life not worth living. The property of the commonwealth must be pledged to youth. The schooling so provided would prevent poverty and vice and would prepare youth for proper performance of their social and civic duties.[73]

The happy results of educating a community were dramatized by Daniel P. Thompson in a novel called *Locke Amsden, or the Schoolmaster: A Tale*, published in Boston in 1847. Locke's influence on the community in which he taught was electric. The town became a reading and thinking community which now magically produced scholars where none had been before. Industry, general competence, and rational happiness all were on the increase, while vice and crime were on the wane. The "whole tone of society" had altered.[74]

Nevertheless, the battle for compulsory taxation had not yet been won. So Henry Barnard returned to the fray in 1848 by contending that Dorr's Rebellion had cost more than education for all the people.[75] Professor (later President) Noah Porter of Yale vowed in a reprint in 1850 that it was better to pay a schoolhouse than a poorhouse tax.[76] Public education was very cheap when one recalled that it contributed to virtue and so diminished expenditures for crimes. Furthermore, it was not manual labor but intelligence which "creates new values." Publicly supported education was an investment which returned substantial interest to the state.[77]

Articles in magazines, books, and newspapers in the later 1840s and the 1850s continued to emphasize the wide-scale benefits to be secured

---

[72] *Ibid.*, pp. 143–154.

[73] Cubberley, *op. cit.*, p. 171; Ekirch, *op. cit.*, p. 196.

[74] Ekirch, *op. cit.*, p. 208.

[75] Thompson, *op. cit.*, p. 77.

[76] Cubberley, *op. cit.*, pp. 166–167.

[77] Knight, *A Documentary History of Education in the South before 1860*, vol. V, p. 150.

through a system of common schools.   In women's magazines the sentiment was frequently voiced that education helped to prevent delinquency.   For was it not a well-known fact that there were more illiterate
criminals than there were criminals who could read and write?   And as
for slavery, Indiana, it was claimed in 1856, was more strongly proslavery than any other Northern state because it had more illiterates
than any other state North or South, except Virginia and South Carolina.
However, the proslavery sentiment would be bound to disappear because the percentage of youngsters in school in Indiana was decidedly
on the increase.[78]

The editors of *Godey's Lady's Book* argued in 1854 for equal educational opportunity for men and women, for the ignorance of one-half of
the population would impede the progress of the other half.   Female
education was the surest sign of progress.   But as Rufus Dawes, the
poet, said, progress was not inborn; it was the result of education.[79]

The character of the equal education for women had to be clarified.
As Mrs. Paulina Wright Davis said in 1854, women were not asking for
education identical with that of men, but rather for a development of
their abilities which would assure them of equal dignity and of being
considered necessary and useful to their society.   As the unique function of women, Mrs. Davis saw controlling the home, the ministry, and
social relations.   To men should be relegated those affairs having to do
with muscles and logical reasoning.[80]   To most commentators, however, women were to be educated for more limited functions: serving
as helpmates to men and teaching school.[81]   It was to women, after all,
that the moral customs of society had been entrusted by their Creator.[82]
Education was to perfect woman in those jobs in which she would have
the greatest moral influence.   After all, education was, in effect, life,
according to the editor of *Godey's Lady's Book* in 1858.   Life, in turn,
was a school designed to prepare for the afterworld.[83]

Another kind of social good was attributed to education in 1854 by
George Fitzhugh, ardent supporter of white supremacy.   Antagonism
between Negroes and poor whites would vanish if the latter were raised
in socioeconomic status.   They must be educated as freemen and for
substantial occupations.   Negroes would be left in jobs unbecoming

---

[78] Thompson, *op. cit.*, pp. 27, 75–76.
[79] Ekirch, *op. cit.*, p. 210.
[80] Thompson, *op. cit.*, pp. 41–42.
[81] Ekirch, *op. cit.*, p. 211.
[82] Knight, *A Documentary History of Education in the South before 1860*, vol. V,
pp. 197–198.
[83] Thompson, *op. cit.*, pp. 24–25.

whites. With the two groups no longer in active competition, their disagreements would lose their meaning. "The path of safety is the path of duty!"[84]

Another charge which would be brought into sharp focus only in the last of the nineteenth century was inadvertently made to the public schools by the notorious American or Know-Nothing party which came into prominence in the middle of the 1850s. This nativist movement, which first was expressed in a secret society, revolved around the threat from the influx of ideas presumed to be alien and influences of immigrants having cultural backgrounds different from those of the original settlers. Hysterically groping for a basic and defined Americanism, members hit upon the Bible (King James Version, undoubtedly), the Sabbath, and the common schools as the underpinnings of national freedom and prosperity. Foremost among the agents for maintenance of national strength were the schools, which were responsible for molding an American character impervious to the subversive influence of the Papacy, French infidelity, German skepticism, and secularism in general. Reacting to the heavy immigration of Roman Catholics between 1830 and 1850, the members of the American party called for a "purely American school system," by which they meant a public school system which was "the true basis of democracy."[85] However critical one may be of the tenor of the Know-Nothing movement, one needs to look with some degree of objectivity on the emergence of a new role for schools: an enculturative agency designed to assimilate the increasing numbers of first- and second-generation youngsters in such a fashion that the American society would somehow hold together without bursting its seams.

## THE FUNCTION OF THE COLLEGES AND THE UNIVERSITIES

Arguments for education of the rulers as well as for education to enforce rights, equality, and the general welfare usually centered on the common school. A good number of fearsome souls, however, were not willing to concede that a republican government would be safe in the hands of the whole people, even if the people were educated. Others contended that there ought to be educational institutions for leaders as well as for the people. These commentators addressed their remarks to colleges in general and to a proposed national university.

[84] Knight, *A Documentary History of Education in the South before 1860*, vol. V, pp. 161–163.

[85] Sutherland, *op. cit.*, pp. 76–83.

## Education of the Few

The chief argument for the education of the few, as opposed to, or in addition to, that of the many, had its foundation in government as guardian of rights and in the development of a groomed leadership to preserve the rights. Hanging together in the first years after the Revolution was also a desideratum. In 1788, an article in the Philadelphia *Independent Gazetteer* called attention to the glories of a Federal university. When young men who, after finishing their education in such an institution, went back to their home communities, they would be "so many *capital links of the Federal union*" and also "centripetal forces to give eternal stability."[86]

The demands of progress proved to be an even more potent argument for education for an elite. America believed in progress and if the latter could be somehow showed to depend on the able, the cause of college and university education would be won. In the 1830s, Caleb Sprague Henry, professor of philosophy at New York University, denounced materialism as inimical to the country's welfare, and called for "an intellectual High Priesthood."[87] Brownson and Tefft tried to stem the tides of equalitarianism as well as plead for a privileged group by calling attention to the essential inequality among men. Benjamin F. Tefft, professor at Indiana Asbury University and a Methodist minister, insisted in 1845 that the inevitable inequality among men must not be tampered with. At Dartmouth College in 1843, Orestes A. Brownson pointed out that education would not overcome inequality; it would only level down, not up. He insisted that scholars must promote progress and redeem the poor from their wretched lot.[88]

Educators and professional people alike were afraid of the explosive effects of a people-centered government. William Kent, lawyer, in 1841 saw the big New York estates being threatened and thought that the popular will must be guided. He believed in progress, to be sure, but a progress in which hereditary property was protected by a softened public opinion. Joseph Story was frankly afraid of forces unleashed in the Jacksonian era. He cautioned Harvard alumni in 1842 not to take too rosy a view of the past and future.[89] In Rhode Island, where rights in property had been threatened by Dorr's Rebellion, Judge Job Durfee in 1843 insisted that popular opinion had never been effective in promoting progress. It was rather the best minds which had discovered the key to progress in the natural laws of the universe and in scientific

[86] Cubberley, *op. cit.*, p. 242.
[87] Ekirch, *op. cit.*, pp. 215–216.
[88] *Ibid.*, pp. 216–218.
[89] *Ibid.*, pp. 221–222.

advance. David H. Riddle, president of Jefferson College in Pennsylvania, summed up one argument for the elite by insisting that in scholarship was to be found *"the true conservative principle of our age and country!"*[90]

A denunciation of materialism became a favorite theme with pre-Civil War commentators. Concomitantly, there was a plea for moral progress. This could be accomplished only by scholars, according to John M. Krebs, Presbyterian clergyman and educator, in 1847. Scholars must denounce materialism and radicalism and promote moral progress. Still others, in a more delicate vein, asked that scholars guide moral progress.[91]

Daniel Dewey Barnard, lawyer and Whig congressman from New York, believed that there was a prominent place for the man who was both patriot and scholar. American political institutions, which were the best so far known, would be preserved and extended to all by the intellectual force of the scholar. Barnard called on the educated classes to temper the more unfortunate results of majority rule by seeking public office. Presumably in these positions scholars would be instructors to the people, who must learn to submit to established law and regularly constituted authority if they were to be the inheritors of progress.[92] In 1853 one Southern educator went so far as to assert that if there were a choice between establishing common schools or founding colleges, the latter must have priority. Abstract thinkers keep society in motion, for it was people in colleges who created a demand for culture. The schools could not do without the colleges.[93] Furthermore, according to a kind of elaboration of this argument in 1856, a state college was useful because it would educate an elite group who would develop a common school.[94]

The argument, as finally resolved after the Civil War, was a compromise. Both a common school and colleges were to become prominent parts of the American education system. But in the meantime, thoughtful men were turning their attention to the idea of a national university as a bulwark of democracy.

## The National University

Apart from his role as executive, President Washington contributed directly to the possibility of education of the elite of a free government

[90] *Ibid.*, pp. 217, 222–223.

[91] *Ibid.*, pp. 217, 219.

[92] *Ibid.*, pp. 219–221.

[93] Knight, *A Documentary History of Education in the South before 1860*, vol. V, pp. 145–146.

[94] Thompson, *op. cit.*, p. 88.

in two ways. The first was through example. He exemplified in his person and in his conduct the proper guardian for a free people. He kept the reins of government firmly in his own hands; he never swerved in his purpose of carrying through a decision merely because it was unpopular or resisted; and, above all, he maintained an air of aloofness proper to the public servant who will not be swayed by private and special interests. Whatever the estimate of Washington's intellect or the stands he took on particular issues, none could ever doubt "the grandeur of his character."[95]

He was the ideal executive or legislator as conceived by those who held to the political doctrine of a state based on natural law. He properly kept an ear to the public voice at the same time that he took firm responsibility for decision making. He listened to and was advised by Cabinet officers and other functionaries, but such advice was his to seek, not theirs to give, and his final decisions rested on his own conscience and with himself as final authority for their being. He coupled with these characteristics a thoroughgoing disregard of political parties and he warned the people against them in his Farewell Address.[96] There could be no parties in a state in which public officials were enjoined by their high duty to uphold the natural rights of their constituents. Parties only brought factions and disaffection of peoples one from another. Public officials must be above such enmities and free from the persuasions of special interest.

President Washington in a second way contributed to the education of republican leaders. Throughout his official political career he promoted the cause of a national university. Samuel Blodget claimed to have suggested the idea of a "noble national university" to the General at his quarters in October, 1775. The suggestion had followed on a complaint of Maj. William Blodget that the colleges were in a ruinous state because they had been used as militia quarters.[97] Whether or not Samuel Blodget was indeed the originator of the idea, when General Washington became President Washington, he continued to argue for a Federal institution of learning. Apparently he never raised the question of the right of the Federal government so to proceed because of what had occurred in the constitutional convention, of which he had also been president.

A striking characteristic of this convention, so far as reported evi-

[95] See discussion of Washington as administrator in Leonard White, "George Washington: Administrator," in Edward N. Saveth (ed. and author), *Understanding the American Past*, Little, Brown & Company, Boston, 1954.

[96] Commager, *op. cit.*, vol. I, pp. 169–175.

[97] Knight, *A Documentary History of Education in the South before 1860*, vol. II, *Toward Educational Independence*, 1950, pp. 8–9.

dence is concerned, is the absence of any extensive discussion of education except for a single institution. The diaries report no talk of common schools, nor even seminaries (secondary schools) or academies. Neither do they report any conversation on the topic which was to be on every leader's lips in the early national period, the necessary relationship between education and a republican government.

In the constitutional convention were a number of men like Washington, Madison, and Adams who, regardless of political views, were later, as Presidents of the United States or as leaders of other kinds, to make strong private and public statements about the development of intelligence in the public interest. Why did not a national system of education come up for discussion?

The education of the guardians of the state did, however, come up for consideration, and thereby hangs an interesting tale. On May 29, 1787, Charles Pinckney laid before the convention a draft of a Federal government. In August, 1787, James Madison submitted, for consideration of the committee of the whole, the proposition that authority to establish a university be added to the powers of the General Legislature. In September, Madison and Pinckney moved to insert amongst the powers vested in Congress one which gave authority "to establish an University, in which no preferences or distinctions should be allowed on account of Religion." The motion was supported by Wilson but it was voted down because Gouverneur Morris pointed out that as Congress had exclusive power at the "Seat of Government" (later the District of Columbia), it also had power to establish a national university therein.[98] Thus was extinguished the only mention that might have been made in the Constitution of an educational institution.

In the early national period, George Washington kept alive the memory of a national university. Taking for granted the authority of Congress to establish such an institution, the first President made it a charge to the legislators in his first message on January 8, 1790. He first argued for knowledge as "the surest basis of public happiness," contributing as it did in various ways to a free constitution. It acted favorably on those in the public trust, and it taught "the people themselves to know and to value their own rights to discern and provide against invasions" of their rights, "uniting a speedy but temperate vigilance against encroachments, with an inviolable respect to the laws." The Congress needed to take under consideration whether the object of promoting knowledge would be best served through "aids to seminaries of learning already established, by the institution of a national university, or by any other expedients."[99]

[98] *Ibid.*, pp. 13–14.
[99] *Ibid.*, p. 14.

It was quite obvious that the first President conceived of his university as something other than a popular institution—popular, that is, in the sense of enrolling all the children of all the people. It was quite clear that those who were to be admitted were not to be selected on the basis of creed, but obviously some selective principle was at work. It seems reasonable to assume, from Washington's insistence on qualifying "our citizens for the exigencies of public as well as private life," that he contemplated the education of a group of public servants. In this plea to the Commissioner of the Federal District for these youth who were to serve the nation, he would hope for an education which would contribute to "their intercourse and interchange of information" which would have the effect of removing "prejudices which might perhaps sometimes arise from local circumstances."[100]

The First Citizen knew well the corroding effects of prejudice. He had had to battle the Continental Congresses to pay his troops. He had known the delays in times of crisis and the cost of those delays in battle. He hoped that the new ship of state would not founder on the animosities of regions one to another or on the competing interests of the several sections. He hoped to guard against the divisive elements in the states and regions by educating a leadership free from such animosities. The first place in this education must go to a study of principles underlying republican governments. Students should not be educated in foreign countries, lest they contract ideas unfavorable to the new government. Brought together, however, from all parts of the nation to a central institution, they might "by the freedom of intercourse and collision of sentiment, give to their minds the direction of truth, philanthropy, and mutual conciliation." As an underscoring of the importance of this institution, President Washington reiterated in a letter to Governor Brooke of Virginia his resolve to give to the proposed university the fifty shares in the Potomac Company which the General Assembly of Virginia had given him for his service to the nation.[101]

George Washington was ably abetted in his designs for the education of public servants by other early leaders. Thomas Jefferson anticipated that the highest rung in his educational ladder should be occupied by philosopher-kings. The difference between this concept and that already in operation in Europe was that intellect alone would be the selective factor for college or university attendance.

Washington and Jefferson are only two among many who, in the early national period, addressed themselves to the education of leaders. Another story has it that, in his address to the people of the United States, Dr. Benjamin Rush rather than President Washington was the

[100] *Ibid.*, p. 17.
[101] *Ibid.*, pp. 18–19.

first to propose a national education institution.   One of the agencies he sketched was quite obviously a graduate institution to which students repaired after college in their respective states.   It was envisioned as a research center for the study of government, law, history, economics, military science, agriculture, and "all useful subjects."   By Rush's own statements, it was designed to prepare citizens (obviously leading citizens in the political sense) for the responsibility of government.   To establish such an institution was more important, according to Rush, than to build a capital city.[102]

In 1806 Joel Barlow developed a prospectus for the reconstruction of the American education system along the lines of the University of Paris. Barlow's proposal called for two kinds of bodies: an association of learned scholars dedicated to research, and a professoriate having instructional responsibilities.[103]

Up to 1829, the national university continued to have proponents. Washington corresponded on the subject with Adams, Jefferson, Hamilton, Edmund Randolph, Governor Brooke of Virginia, and the commissioners of the District of Columbia.   President Madison made three requests to Congress to establish such an institution and Samuel Blodget presented memoranda on its merits to the national legislative body. John Quincy Adams reinforced its claims in his message to Congress. Finally, in 1819, in the hope that Congress would adopt their college, a group of scholars led by Josiah Meigs, a college meteorologist, founded the Columbian Institute for the Promotion of the Arts and Sciences. Congress incorporated the institute in 1821, and loaned it rooms in the Capitol.   The institute died and the college was finally sponsored by a church.[104]

Although no president advocated the establishment of a national university nor did any congressman introduce a bill in its behalf in the period from 1829 to 1869, it became clear within that period that the function, as conceived by sporadic advocates, was changing.   It was no longer a training ground for political leaders, but a leading research and graduate institution dedicated to stimulating inquiry in many fields.

The plan for a national university was kept alive until at least 1936. But its function and proportions changed along with the changing concepts of the nature of the nation and the instruments needed for its fulfillment.[105]

---

[102] Edgar Bruce Wesley, *Proposed: The University of the United States,* University of Minnesota Press, Minneapolis, 1936, p. 4.

[103] *Ibid.,* p. 9.

[104] *Ibid.,* pp. 5–12.

[105] For a history of the idea of the national university to 1936, see Wesley, *op. cit.,* and publications of the National Education Association.

## SUMMARY

The early national period had opened with decided attention to the education of the leaders who would steer the new ship of state. These "leaders," though they continued to be of concern, never quite materialized. In succeeding generations, they were thought of as scholars on whom the hopes of the nation must be pinned, according to the thinking of a minority group.

The change in sentiment about leaders was influenced by the Jacksonian revolution, which had brought into prominence a fluid and wide-open society in which anyone might be president. Consequently, attention came to be focused on the intimate relationship of a publicly supported school system to a republican government, a republican equality, inalienable rights, and the general welfare.[106]

The school was charged with an assortment of tasks which were succinctly described by reformers demanding the ideal school. They asked that education prepare young Americans for everyday living, for moral progress, and for citizenship. When conservatives and liberals addressed themselves to the specific behaviors required for republican citizens, they were correspondingly grandiose in their visions. The schools must see to it that society was protected, by the high level of its citizens, against "demagogues and aristocrats" and "mischances and personal misbehavior." Body and soul must forever be united. The schools must be the corrective of a host of social and political diseases; education must preserve the positive values of the republican society and "inhibit the dangers of freedom." The republican experiment had such "intrinsic value" that political education was indispensable.[107] By 1861, according to Welter, the belief of conservatives and liberals alike in education was so deeply felt that it was like the commitment to law and the word of God, and was equally unquestioned.

[106] For a review of the development of the common school, see Lawrence A. Cremin, *The American Common School: An Historic Conception*, Bureau of Publications, Teachers College, Columbia University, New York, 1951.

[107] Welter, *op. cit.*, pp. 46–48.

[108] *Ibid.*, p. 1.

# 4

# Social and Economic Influences
# on Education

> From the ethical point of view, therefore, it is not too much
> to say that the democratic ideal poses, rather than solves, the
> great problem: How to harmonize the development of each
> individual with the maintenance of a social state in which the
> activities of one will contribute to the good of all the others.[1]

JOHN DEWEY AND JAMES H. TUFTS,
ETHICS

In the period from 1800 to 1860 the school had already been conceived
of as having social aims related to the development of a strong American
national state, but the aims were limited in number and relatively vague
in statement. In the period from 1865 to 1900, these aims were modified
very little, but the details of the arguments respecting the role of schools
became more profuse and kinds of schooling began to change in response
to socioeconomic changes.

The philosophical argument respecting schoools in the period from
1865 to 1900 had a social-political referent. The growth of cities had
spawned corruption in politics and a variety of social evils. In this
setting proceeded what Welter calls "the great middle-class debate."
The "well-meaning elite" would have been inclined to address themselves to the social problems of the slum dwellers and the educational
means by which these problems could be met. Politicians successfully
diverted attention to political evils, to which they attributed all the
failings of republican government. In this setting, as in pre-Civil War
days, schools were again charged with developing an intelligent citizenry
and assuring obedience to law. In dealing with these last tasks, school

[1] John Dewey and James H. Tufts, *Ethics*, Henry Holt and Company, Inc., New
York, 1932, pp. 388–389. Quoted by permission of the publisher.

75

people were expected to alleviate the problems arising from the new immigration and to mitigate the evils arising from newly aroused laboring men.[2]

These arguments about the role of common schools were paralleled by a revival of the concept of philosopher-kings. The colleges were charged by reformers with developing a group of dedicated leaders who would be above the persuasion of special interests. When labor and farm organizations got into the debate, even they tended to repeat current middle-class views about the role of the educational enterprise.[3]

### EDUCATIONAL ADJUSTMENT TO THE ECONOMY (1860–1890)

While the debate was going on in the last of the nineteenth century, educational institutions were accelerating their adjustments to the changing society. These adjustments meant that there was a continuous shift in the responsibility for enculturation of children and youth from the home to the school.

The first shifts in the period from 1860 to 1890 were the fruit of a growing awareness that the basis of prosperity lay in industrialization and scientific agriculture rather than in small-scale trade and extensive farming. The change in the economy in turn signaled a need for re-balancing social institutions. Until the advent of wide-scale urbanization, industrialization, and machine agriculture, it had been quite possible for the home, as a production unit, to provide education for work. When youngsters should seek jobs different from those of their parents, whether the latter were native- or foreign-born, it became apparent that some agency other than the home must get the child ready for the "race of life,"[4] as Babson would later put it.

The leaven of upward striving was at work, rapidly transforming the society—and thus its education—for production. The Americans who were emerging from this economic process had certain definable characteristics which were worthy of note by an English critic in 1866. They were active, restless, many-sided in their interests and skills. They were deeply interested in politics and ambitious. The American scene was alive with the unending flow of commerce and speculation run wild. In this setting, the American's chief lesson to be learned was

[2] Rush E. Welter, "Democracy and Education: The Role of Education in American Political Thought, from 1828 to the Present," unpublished doctoral dissertation, Harvard University, Cambridge, Mass., 1951, pp. 100–143.

[3] *Ibid.*

[4] "What Is Americanism?" *The American Journal of Sociology,* vol. 20, no. 4, p. 446, January, 1915.

dissatisfaction with his lot.[5] Seething humanity was pushing into the unfamiliar environment of factories as well as to the West, looking for opportunity and often unprepared by any prior home training to seize that opportunity.

The new education got formally under way through the incorporation of industrial education into the schools. According to Stombaugh, it was stimulated by several movements and ideas. Basic to its success were the economic effects of a receding frontier and the consequent expansion of American industry. The resultant specialization was already being felt in the immediate post-Civil War period, so that there was a call for training youths for industry, or at least acquainting them with industrial processes. It was reiterated that it was no longer possible for youth to learn these processes under home and parental guidance and the public school was *ipso facto* the natural agency to fill the need for this kind of training.[6]

It was also believed that it was no longer possible to revive the apprentice system, which was decidedly on the wane. Versatility rather than specialized-skill training was what the worker needed to survive in a society where any day a machine might take his place. For this and other reasons, an education in all subjects and with a practical turn was to be a must.[7]

Intimately bound up as was the republican government with material prosperity and competition as well as with education, it was natural that educators should be sensitive to intersectional as well as international rivalries. New England would survive as an industrial center only if her children were trained in the use of tools. American industries would fall into the hands of foreigners, so said one alarmist, unless manual training were introduced into the schools. Fed by these fears, Americans may have taken more than casual notice of developments abroad as these were manifested in the international expositions in 1850 (London), 1867 (Paris), and 1876 (Philadelphia). The manual-labor movement, general criticism of schools for their abstract and theoretical teachings, and equalitarianism, which insisted that the most neglected individual (the manual laborer) be given a place in the sun—all these combined to affect the introduction of manual training.[8]

The harbinger of change came at the Federal level, however, in the

[5] Edgar B. Wesley, *NEA: The First Hundred Years, The Building of the Teaching Profession*, Harper & Brothers, New York, 1957, p. 144.

[6] Ray M. Stombaugh, *A Survey of the Movements Culminating in Industrial Arts Education in Secondary Schools*, Bureau of Publications, Teachers College, Columbia University, New York, 1936, p. 11.

[7] *Ibid.*, p. 12.

[8] *Ibid.*, pp. 13–18.

form of the land-grant-college act. It properly was so because of the relationship of material prosperity and republican government. However, the course of events in securing land-grant colleges implied no one-to-one relationship between agricultural and mechanical education and the public welfare.

How the land-grant college came into being is a commentary on American society. It illustrates the increasing variability of motives and economic interrelationships which would have to be taken into account in charting educational innovations. Some congressional proponents emphasized the public welfare aspects of the proposed colleges; some opponents were concerned about land speculation which might occur as a function of the land grants. Yet an increasingly heterogeneous public had also to be reckoned with.

According to Richard G. Axt, it was not, in the first instance, either the working man or the small farmer who pressed for the college. The farmers were primarily interested in measures which appeared to have a direct connection with their immediate interests. Both Southern agriculturists and Western farmers combined to force President Buchanan's veto when the bill was first passed in 1859. The Southern group acted on the grounds of states' rights. Western farmers wanted the public lands which were to be given to the colleges for homesteading. If the lands became the property of the states, so the argument ran, they would be opened to land speculators. The strongest supporters of the land-grant bill were Easteners who wished to establish a principle in the use of the public domain: that it should be used wherever it was for the general welfare and probably for land speculation. It was only after Southern representatives were canceled out by secession and the Homestead Act was in the offing that the bill was favorably reported and signed into law.[9]

Agricultural and educational reformers did raise their voices for the land-grant college. Some of these stimulated the agrarian societies "whose desire for agricultural colleges was greater than their fear of land speculation." The societies were in turn assisted by farm journal editors, occasionally by organized labor leaders, and by vocational educators.[10] Although their ideas were vague concerning what they wanted, vaguest was the desire in respect to mechanic arts. The need of industry had not yet made its impact on the American public. Support for engineering came largely from engineers and scientists whose ideas of higher education were more highly developed than those of

---

[9] Richard G. Axt, *The Federal Government and Financing Higher Education,* Columbia University Press, New York, 1952, chap. II. Published for the Commission on Financing Higher Education.

[10] *Ibid.,* p. 41.

farmers and laborers. It can be inferred, furthermore, that their impact was initially greater, for early enrollments in engineering and mechanic arts far exceeded those in agriculture.[11]  Many agricultural colleges had been well under way before 1862, but in that same period there had been only six colleges having any offerings in engineering and only one (in Michigan) had a school of engineering. By 1872 there were 70 engineering departments and by 1880, 85. By 1875 there were 74 schools of science of which 41 were land-grant colleges. Paul W. Gates has suggested that the act has been overvalued in respect to the stimulation of agricultural higher education. Its real impact has been on applied science.[12]

With this background of positive stimulation of vocational higher education for industry, the vocational educators went ahead to introduce manual training into the elementary and secondary schools in the period beginning with 1870. But by the early 1900s, social workers and educators alike were jarred by the inadequacy of unadorned manual training in substituting for the task of the home in inducting the young into work.

## SOCIOECONOMIC PROBLEMS AFFECTING SCHOOLS (1890–1918)

A discussion of the problems affecting schools—problems which could not be solved by piecemeal innovations such as manual training—must be prefaced by two explanations. The first is historical. A social phenomenon never springs full-blown; it is always long in development and dilatory in resolution. The dates which are given are therefore arbitrary and mean only an acceleration of concern and educational adjustment.

Second, the emphasis in pages to follow on the immigrant or his children signals not exclusive concern for him and his progeny, but their importance in calling attention to prevailing problems and the necessity for adjustment of schools to those problems. It appears to be true that the attention of social workers and educators focused on social ills because there were immigrants and second-generation youngsters who would be a menace to the American nation unless they were Americanized or standardized. These professional people operated in large city institutions which had more facilities for the alleviation of social ills and where the new arrivals would have been most noticeable. The same disabilities as beset the new arrivals would have been characteristic of many native city dwellers and small-town or rural native populations.

---

[11] *Ibid.*, pp. 49–50.
[12] *Ibid.*, pp. 59–60.

The literature reflects, therefore, not the pervasiveness of the problems or the educational adjustments, but the focus of professional workers. The realization of the inadequacy of educational tinkering was forced on school people in the period from 1890 to 1918 by a host of socio-economic maladjustments. Among them, three appeared to receive special attention. The first was the miserable conditions provided by industry for the youth who were going forth from the schools. A second concerned the widespread evidences of malnutrition among the child and youth population. Still a third was the inadequacy of parents to deal with problems with which their children needed help.

*The Problem of Industry*

Ellen H. Richards, who had been prominent in the founding of the American Home Economics Association, said in 1911 that the economic function of the home had long since been taken over by the factories. Along with this movement, restaurants, hotels, and places of amusement in an urban center had encroached on other functions of the home, such as providing work and play opportunities and caring for physical well-being of its members. So families no longer led a "common life" or pursued "common interests."[13]   Of immediate, though not primary, concern in Ellen Richards's period was the fact that some agency had to take over from the economically defunct home the function of providing efficient workers for the emergent industrial society. This need, along with others, stimulated the organization of the Vocational Guidance Association in Grand Rapids, Michigan, in 1913.

Inherent in the arguments used as a basis for the establishment of systematic vocational guidance was the operation of value systems. It was the business of education to support industry, which was central to republican government; but it was the business of industry and schools together to offer opportunity to youth. If the latter objective were to be achieved, then youngsters could not go out to work at age fourteen. There was no place for such a youngster in industry, said Owen R. Lovejoy.[14]  If he went out to work so early, he would be in a dead-end occupation.[15]  For centuries human beings had been kept by manual labor at a bare subsistence level from which there was no possibility

[13] Ellen H. Richards, "The Social Significance of the Home Economics Movement," *Journal of Home Economics,* vol. 3, no. 2, p. 118, April, 1911.

[14] Owen R. Lovejoy, "Vocational Guidance and Child Labor," *Vocational Guidance Papers,* U.S. Office of Education Bulletin 1914, no. 14, whole no. 587, 1914, p. 12.

[15] Sophonisba Breckenridge, "Guidance by the Development of Placement and Follow-up Work," *Vocational Guidance Papers,* U.S. Office of Education Bulletin 1914, no. 14, whole no. 587, 1914, p. 61.

of rising.[16]    This same level had unfortunately been manifest in America.    As a consequence, guidance work had begun with settlement-house misfits (adults) who had been sidetracked into the wrong vocations. The "niche theory" had it that adults and jobs might be reshuffled so they would properly harmonize.    But this theory had been invalidated. There were not enough right niches and when people had worked in the wrong job for a while, they were inevitably ruined.    The role of the school, then, was to ascertain how not to ruin ("spoil" was the word used) human beings.[17]

European countries had already developed machinery to aid in transition from school to work.    But the European solution could not be accepted for America because it encompassed labor exchanges which obscured the problems of children under eighteen, contended Meyer Bloomfield.    Medical and factory inspection in England and Germany missed fire at the point of the child.    Instead of raising the compulsory school age, the people overseas had developed night schools.    Americans knew that the only time for children to be in school was in the daytime. Bloomfield hoped that in the United States doctors would be developed into vocational specialists who would become guidance workers.[18]

The problem of the school, adjusting people to jobs and jobs to people, was put in the context of a special social situation by these educators of 1913.    Poor parents were the problem.    They had never had a standard of seven years of school, hence it was natural for them to want to send their youngsters to work at too early an age.    This was the point at which the school, with the duty of enforcing the compulsory school age, stepped in to protect the children against the parents.    The latter were "forced by the compulsory education law to a higher level of child care."[19]    Thus the child through the school became a "ward of the state."    The child's labor must not be used to maintain himself or his family.    A child was not fit to choose an occupation at age fourteen. A poll of thirty-five prominent educators showed that only two of them had selected their occupations before the age of twenty.    If the school took over the guardianship of the child, it could break down class distinctions and help industrial leaders and statesmen to rise from the ranks.[20]

In accepting this guardianship, what must the school do?    The first

---

[16] Lovejoy, *op. cit.*, p. 9.

[17] Helen T. Woolley, "The Present Trend of Vocational Guidance in the United States," *Vocational Guidance Papers*, U.S. Office of Education Bulletin 1914, no. 14, whole no. 587, 1914, p. 43.

[18] Meyer Bloomfield, "Lessons Europe Has for Us," *Vocational Guidance Papers*, U.S. Office of Education Bulletin 1914, no. 14, whole no. 587, 1914, pp. 31–33.

[19] Breckenridge, *op. cit.*, p. 61.

[20] Lovejoy, *op. cit.*, pp. 14–16.

task was obviously the assumption of the family duty of orienting the child to the world of work. The school must develop courses of instruction in the nature of and personal qualifications for jobs.[21] Psychological testing, which aided in the selection of people for jobs and jobs for people, must continue to go forward. When work and workmen could be matched, both could contribute to the commonwealth and the common good; for tasks would be better done with more happiness in their doing. Though vocational tests were already being expanded in America, there had been no general work in this area in Europe, according to Leonard Ayres.[22] The identification of the American with work as a good and a way to prosperity were clearly evident in this technical report on testing.

The school would fail in its guidance task, according to George H. Mead, if it did not abandon its medieval position of assuming that its doctrines and techniques were justified. They could be justified only in the nature of the child's conduct at home, in neighborhoods, and in vocations. The school must be organically related to the parents, social workers, members of employment agencies, employers, and persons in other educational institutions. The school was the "rational, intentional" agency in the training of the child, and however important other institutions were in this task, the school must assume the role of "central and organizing agency." For its important function, it must utilize vocational guidance, through which it consciously assumed its central role.[23]

In the year 1913–1914, schools were apparently already relating organically to their communities. Teachers had already been sent into the field to make industrial surveys.[24] There was a demand—the origin of the demand was not clear—that schools enlarge their function to encompass not only vocational guidance and vocational education, but also placement in jobs.[25] Furthermore, supervision on the job was contemplated. People in industry were human. If a Polish boy could not work next to a Bohemian boy, the school placement officer could reason

---

[21] F. M. Giles, "Guidance by Systematic Courses of Instruction in Vocational Opportunities and Personal Characteristics," *Vocational Guidance Papers,* U.S. Office of Education Bulletin 1914, no. 14, whole no. 587, 1914, pp. 52–59.

[22] Leonard Ayres, "Psychological Tests in Vocational Guidance," *Vocational Guidance Papers,* U.S. Office of Education Bulletin 1914, no. 14, whole no. 587, 1914, pp. 33–37.

[23] George Herbert Mead, "The Larger Educational Bearings of Vocational Guidance," *Vocational Guidance Papers,* U.S. Office of Education Bulletin 1914, no. 14, whole no. 587, 1914, pp. 16–26.

[24] Giles, *op. cit.,* pp. 52–59.

[25] *Vocational Guidance Papers,* U.S. Office of Education Bulletin 1914, no. 14, whole no. 587, 1914, pp. 5–6.

with the foreman to bring about a situation temporarily congenial to the youngsters. The school must follow the child into the job and hold the job for him.[26] If industry needed to be reformed in order to be a fit place for a youngster, then educators should undertake that reformation. When industrial leaders asked, "What kind of children have you to offer?" the school people must counter with "What kind of industry have you to offer?"[27]

The beginnings of the vocational guidance movement were more portentous than the initiation of a new service. They reveal the ideological step the educators took when they proposed to take over from home and society a child's job training, induction, and follow-up. They had relieved "ignorant" parents from a burden they could not assume and, in the process, proposed to reform the industrial society, if necessary. They were now the guardians of the children *in loco parentis,* in whose behalf they would build a new economic order if they had to.

### The Problem of Nutrition

Providing a physical environment in which children may grow, including the food they eat, the clothes they wear, and housing for rest and leisure is a time-honored function of the family. One by one, these functions basic to physical care began to slip away from some homes to the school.

The conditions under which feeding youngsters became a school function were similar in some respects to those in European industrialized countries, but in other respects peculiar to the American environment. As educators, welfare workers, and medical men began to discuss the efficacy of school or settlement lunches for children and to provide for them, they frequently referred to practices in Germany, England, Scotland, France. Government provision for feeding of school children had begun in those countries (not necessarily under the auspices of the schools) in the last of the nineteenth century. The practices appeared to have a forthright rationale: Here are some hungry children; let us feed them.[28]

The American solution of the feeding problem was not so simple as the European. The home of rugged individualism could hardly harbor the bedfellow of a welfare state. An American rationale had to be developed for doing what needed to be done. Furthermore, American social workers and educators were convinced that they faced a difficulty not to be found in the European environment. Theirs was not the

---

[26] Breckenridge, *op. cit.,* p. 62.

[27] Lovejoy, *op. cit.,* p. 13.

[28] See early issues of the *Journal of Home Economics.*

simple task of persuading nationals that a school lunch program was needed. It was rather the job of teaching good health practices to parents who were of alien or unapproved cultures and superstitious ways ("ignorant," according to the missionaries).

The school feeding program had been originally stimulated by a series of studies done in large cities in the 1890s. From 1892 to 1897, the staff of Hull House, Chicago, gathered information through house-to-house canvasses. Two findings were forthcoming: Workers were too tired at night to go far for proper food; and national food habits were diverse. In response to the second finding, Ellen Richards remarked that public kitchens, a European expedient, were not suited to the American environment.[29]

School systems themselves undertook individual studies, as Baltimore did in 1907, for instance. Of the children in the selected school, 65 per cent were Jews (Russian, Polish, Austrian, German, Finnish), 20 per cent were Italians and Lithuanians, and only 15 per cent were "Americans." A poorer school could have been found, so said the reporter, but in terms of lack of an American standard of living, unsanitary conditions, "absence of ideals and ideas, in short, in real wretchedness," the situation in this school was probably at lowest ebb. Some American children might be found to be suffering from malnutrition if their mothers worked in factories and did not understand good food practices. But the reporter was inclined to believe malnutrition was to be found largely among children of the foreign-born.[30]

Another study of a similar character was done by Dr. E. Mather Sill in New York City, circa 1909. The results of this study of East Side youngsters, largely the children of foreign tenement-dwelling parents, were appalling, according to the tone of the report. Among the 210 families in Dr. Sill's studies, 62 per cent kept their windows closed, 50 per cent of the children ate between meals, and 82 per cent of the children went to bed from 8 P.M. to 12 midnight when they should have been in bed by 7 P.M. A previous study of the whole school population showed that 23 per cent of the 12,800 school children came to school with no breakfast or a poor one.[31] Note that in these studies, the assumption is unconsciously made that the situation is worse because the homes are foreign-oriented.

It was but a step from an examination of home and food problems to the acquisition by the school of a feeding task. This apparently was

[29] Richards, op. cit., p. 120.

[30] M. L. White, "A Study of the Under-nourished School Children of Baltimore," Journal of Home Economics, vol. 2, no. 2, pp. 170–173, April, 1910.

[31] "Malnutrition in School Children in New York City," Journal of the American Medical Association, vol. 52, pp. 1981–1985, June 19, 1909. Reported in Journal of Home Economics, vol. 1, no. 4, pp. 369–374, October, 1909.

first assumed in large cities.  New York, Buffalo, Boston, Chicago were the cities in the school lunch news.

Social settlement workers who had begun the social center, which it was hoped the schools would take over, maintained the school lunch program in New York until 1919, according to Morris Berger.[32]  Under the auspices of the New York School Lunch Committee, lunches were first served on November 23, 1908, in schools attended by the Irish and Italians, as well as "special anaemic" children.  With the opening of a school lunch program in two nationality areas, and as the program expanded into schools attended by other ethnic groups, problems mounted.  Members of the lunch committee found themselves adapting food practices to the several ethnic groups.  In the school of Italian youngsters, the committee had to have an Italian cook and serve macaroni, dried lima beans, and Italian oil.  For the Irish, there was stew and potatoes.  In the Jewish schools, only kosher dishes approved by the rabbi were served.[33]  Thus inadvertently, the committee and the school people promoted a cultural pluralism, as Berger says, in the period from 1914 to 1924.[34]

The traditional feeding agency, the home, posed other problems to the school lunch committee of the early 1900s.  Italian families, for instance, wanted to have children at home for lunch.  This prejudice was very strong among the less educated, who did not see the happy effect on the child of the hot midday meal at school.  An investigator visited the homes of eighty-three undernourished children from an Irish school.  Mothers were indifferent to children's welfare, said the reporter.  Mothers who drank were equally unenlightened and in some cases parents were "shiftless."  Occasionally children took matters into their own hands.  They insisted on having money for lunch which parents charged they used for cigarettes.[35]

The social workers and educators persisted, however.  In 1910, Alice Boughton, superintendent of schools in Philadelphia, reported that lunches were being served in five elementary schools: one was a school of Italian youngsters, another enrolled mainly Jewish children, another was for Negro children, and two schools were for incorrigibles.[36]  In

[32] Morris Isaiah Berger, "The Settlement, the Immigrant and the Public Schools. A Study of the Settlement Movement and the New Migration upon Public Education: 1890–1924," unpublished doctoral dissertation, Columbia University, New York, 1956, p. 85–86.  (Microfilm.)

[33] Mabel Hyde Kittredge, "Report of the New York School Lunch Committee," *Journal of Home Economics*, vol. 4, no. 5, pp. 482–486, December, 1912.

[34] Berger, *op. cit.*, p. 30.

[35] Kittredge, *op. cit.*, pp. 486–489.

[36] Alice C. Boughton, "Report of the Penny Lunches Served by the Starr Centre Association, Philadelphia," *Journal of Home Economics*, vol. 2, no. 2, p. 178, April, 1910.

1911, Miss Boughton reported that a home-and-school visitor was going to the homes of youngsters who were being fed in school. These youngsters were also getting physical examinations. There was an endless field for investigation because of wretched working conditions, which increased the poverty and ignorance of foreign parents and their neglect of children.[37]

In May of 1911, penny lunches were made a part of the domestic science department program in Buffalo, New York. Criticisms of the lunch program when it had been under other auspices were being met in this new school program, according to the reporter. To the charge that feeding youngsters relaxed maternal control, the lunch personnel answered by serving only those whose mothers worked. To the statement that the child was given false money values by being given more food than he paid for, the domestic science teacher answered that teachers were teaching the value of money. To overcome the difficulty of insufficient food, personnel were using a dietary standard. Under this plan they were daily serving 353 Polish youngsters at one school, and 221 Italian youngsters at two other schools. Syrians, Irish, and others in distressing social conditions were being served at another school. Two other schools having lunch programs served mixed nationalities in favorable conditions.[38]

These statements are illustrative of what occcured in city after city over the country. It may be said that roughly from 1912 the school lunch program, staffed often by social workers, took over from the home, or selected homes, the feeding of the child. The assumptions were made that the child would not be fed at home or that he would have the wrong food, and that a well-nourished child was essential if learning was to go forward in the school.

Moral or humanitarian outrage which prompted the initial feeding was often obscured by an elaborate educational rationale for school lunches. In an article of 1913, for instance, it was proposed that the effects of school lunches were these: They increased the mental efficiency of children; promoted friendship between teachers and students; and provided a basis for the study of hygiene and physiology. All three were conditions necessary for effective learning.[39] In this connection, Caroline L. Hunt had said in 1909 that it was expensive to educate a

[37] Alice C. Boughton, "School Luncheons," *Journal of Home Economics*, vol. 3, no. 1, pp. 79–80, February, 1911.

[38] Mary E. L. Small, "Elementary School Lunches under School Department Direction, Buffalo, N.Y.," *Journal of Home Economics*, vol. 4, no. 5, pp. 490–492, December, 1912.

[39] "Lunches in Elementary Schools," *Journal of Home Economics*, vol. 5, no. 3, p. 249, June, 1913.

child, and money was wasted if it was spent on an undernourished child.[40] In 1911, Mrs. Mary Moran enforced the educational argument by pointing out that a high school lunch program involved children and teachers in teacher-pupil planning.[41] School lunches did more, however, than reinforce the learning situation. They also made for good dietary habits and increased interest of parents in the school.[42]

*The Problem of the Home*

The persistent home visiting which went along with feeding or with other school or welfare activities called attention to other ills which could not go unchallenged. The divorce rate was up.[43] The birth rate and marriage rate were going down. Women were deserting the home. Homes were unsanitary and women did not know how to use modern appliances.[44] Children were leaving the grammar school before they were ready for marriage.[45] Making a home was almost impossible for families in congested urban areas, and one of the "most difficult problems in modern social life."[46] With such comments as these in current usage, it was not difficult to see that the school would try to stem the tide of evil emanating from the home, as it had in the case of industry.

One of the first formal moves to support the home was taken when the American Home Economics Association was organized in January, 1909, at George Washington University. The expressed purpose for organizing was to give strength to the movement of providing through the school the kind of worth-while environment the majority of youngsters did not enjoy at home.[47] The home had had ethical as well as economic meaning, according to Ellen H. Richards, first president of the American Home Economics Association. The home must be saved. There was a close relationship between the fundamental necessity to save the

[40] Caroline L. Hunt, *The Daily Meals of School Children*, U.S. Office of Education Bulletin 1909, no. 3, whole no. 403, 1909, p. 7.

[41] Mary H. Moran, "Boston High School Lunches," *Journal of Home Economics*, vol. 2, no. 2, p. 184, April, 1910.

[42] "Lunches in Elementary Schools," *Journal of Home Economics, op. cit.*

[43] J. Lebowitz, "The Home and the Machine," *Journal of Home Economics*, vol. 3, no. 2, p. 142, April, 1911. Gwendolyn Stewart, "The Economics of the Family," *Journal of Home Economics*, vol. 2, no. 2, p. 209, April, 1910.

[44] Lebowitz, *op. cit.*, pp. 141–142.

[45] "Second Annual Meeting of the American Association for the Study and Prevention of Infant Mortality," *Journal of Home Economics*, vol. 3, p. 501, December, 1911.

[46] Euphemia Clark, "A Campaign for Home Making," *Journal of Home Economics*, vol. 1, no. 2, p. 167, April, 1909.

[47] "Organization and First Meeting of the American Home Economics Association," *Journal of Home Economics*, vol. 1, p. 25, February, 1909.

home and the introduction of home economics and manual training into the schools. The latter would stem the tide of domestic disintegration and preserve the social fabric. The home economics movement in particular was designed to keep home and the general well-being of youngsters "from slipping away over the cliff."[48] Life in the United States demanded that there be increasing efficiency, according to Eva W. White in 1913. Yet the American people were confronted by problems of labor, government, immigration, and the effect of these on American standards of living. If it were conceded that efficiency is a product of home training, then domestic training should be the core of education and be directly related to the experience of the child.[49]

Educators used their ingenuity in subverting school subjects and activities to the purpose of bolstering the home. The traditional domestic science classes were put to good use. If the present generation of parents were lost, at least the next generation could be prepared in school, according to several public figures in the period.[50] The school was the agent of the larger society. If the home were inadequate to the task of preparing youngsters to be the parents and adults of the future, then the school must provide the education which the home should have given.[51] Since mothers could not often be lured into schools, youngsters were instructed about diet, proper preparation of meals, table service. Private philanthropies and social workers, according to Ellen Richards in 1911, had come to realize the importance of the family table to the development of the moral society.[52]

Social workers and home visitors had already done some spadework. They had called attention to the limitations—serious in their eyes—of the homes, particularly foreign homes. Although the next generation of mothers needed saving, the present one did also, or at least efforts must go forward on this front. Ignorance, superstition, lack of knowledge of modern conveniences were all to be combated with the pure light of reason emanating from school and settlement. Mrs. Hansen in 1913 reported a conversation she had had with an Italian in Buffalo. This father and husband insisted that some people were born clean, others dirty; his wife had been born dirty. "She's happy, so why

---

[48] Richards, op. cit., pp. 118–123. For historical interest, see A. D. Mayo, "The Demands of the Coming Century on the American Common School," The Addresses and Journal of Proceedings National Educational Association, Baltimore, Md., 1876.

[49] Eva W. White, "The Home and Social Efficiency," Journal of Home Economics, vol. 5, no. 2, pp. 122–127, April, 1913.

[50] Sarah Louise Arnold, "President's Address," Journal of Home Economics, vol. 5, no. 4, p. 323, October, 1913. Richards, op. cit., p. 124. Ira S. Wile, "School Lunches," Journal of Home Economics, vol. 2, no. 2, pp. 160–169, April, 1910.

[51] Arnold, op. cit.

[52] Richards, op. cit., p. 119.

bother her?" Mrs. Hansen well understood the depths of such ignorance, however. She and her cohorts did bother the dirty but happy woman until the unfortunate lady cleaned up. Mrs. Hansen says nothing of the effect on the husband or the lady's temperament. But she could report that for twelve months the woman had continued in her changed ways without "backsliding."[53]

Whatever one may think of this invasion of family privacy, it is illustrative of the drives and peculiar conditions which spearheaded the invasion of the enculturative tasks of the home. The effect of applied science had been greater in America than in Europe. One of the outcomes of this movement had been raising cleanliness to the level of godliness. At the same time, America was being assaulted by European peasants who, if they were to capitalize on what America could offer, would have to bridge a gap of several centuries from the rural, unmechanized society of the European farm to the modern, urbanized, and mechanized society which was America. To American educators and social workers in Chicago, Buffalo, Boston, New York, this population must have obscured all others. These humanitarians must have participated in an ethical argument. If they left the peasants to their own devices, they doomed them to ignorance of modern plumbing, sanitation, mechanical devices, the mastery of which was necessary for urban living. If they refused to bring these people the latest information on child care, then for ignorance of mothers, children were doomed to die. One can almost hear these educators and social workers asking, "How much can we honor the customs and traditions of these people and to what extent will their customs and traditions prevent them from seeking opportunity, American style?"

In 1913 Sarah Louise Arnold, president of the American Home Economics Association, expressed both sympathy and determination in respect to the Americanization task of the schools. The "poor bewildered mothers" had to be helped, as did their children, the parents of tomorrow. Educators could not be satisfied until foreign-born mothers appreciated the health aspects of sanitation and the control of disease and understood that sewing youngsters into clothes was dangerous.[54] In the same year, Mrs. Mabel Hyde Kittredge pointed out that peasants who had been wont to sweep dirt out of their homes could hardly be expected to know how to cope with drains, garbage pails, and dustpans. Yet if they did not attend to these elementary health devices, they would be continuously harassed by city inspectors of one kind or another. Superstitions also got in the way of effective adjustment. Ruth-

[53] Anne L. Hansen, "Two Years as a Domestic Educator in Buffalo, New York," *Journal of Home Economics*, vol. 5, no. 5, p. 435, December, 1913.

[54] Arnold, *op. cit.*, pp. 323–324.

enians, for instance, believed that pregnant mothers must not bathe and that a child's head must not be washed before his second birthday. It was not enough to put in bathtubs in homes where such superstitions flourished. Mrs. Kittredge had been in an Italian home where the clothes wringer and sleds were kept in the bathtub, and this was not a poor home. It was the job of the educators to help these people to appreciate the virtue of bathing and the vice of dirt.[55]

The same Italian home gave Mrs. Kittredge a chance for other kinds of observations. There had been a "cheap elaborateness" about it. Paper drapes were hung on shelves, there were ruffles on the bathtub, pictures were pasted on the walls. Windows were shut tight and the father, who worked at night, was often asleep in the bed, which was in plain view. These people did not understand their responsibility to the owner of the building to maintain this flat in a well-kept fashion. This home, like others, was over-furnished and unhealthy, a place where children were growing up with the "wrong ideals"—a place which was incidentally serving as a wretched model for the even newer immigrant across the hall.[56]

The question was: What could educators and social workers do about these dispossessed peasants? In 1911, Lebowitz detailed the social changes needed if rural people were to be urban Americans. One suggestion was very mild: Home economists must teach the use of mechanical appliances. Another was far-reaching. Lebowitz called attention to "oriental vestigia" surviving in the American urban society, the economic dependence of the wife, the parent who owned his child, and the double standard of morality—all these had to go.[57] Educators and social workers were more modest but as penetrating in their statements. Furthermore, they had achievements to their credit. For example, the Society for Italian Immigrants was looking forward to the time when schools would assume their burden, and had already begun labor camps in New York.

In Pennsylvania, responsibility for education of the foreign-born had already been assumed by the state. In 1907 Pennsylvania legislators authorized local schools to open evening classes on petition of at least twenty adults, including foreigners. Evening classes had already proved their usefulness and would be even more useful when they were to be found in school systems all over the country. Conditions would change when teachers were available to instruct mothers not to feed beer and

[55] Mabel Hyde Kittredge, "The Need of the Immigrant," *Journal of Home Economics*, vol. 5, no. 4, pp. 308–309, October, 1913.

[56] *Ibid.*, pp. 309–310.

[57] Lebowitz, *op. cit.*, p. 145.

whiskey to their infants. These new Americans must be treated with justice and friendliness when they arrived. The key agency to induct them into the new society was the schools. It was crucial to the larger society that this "great mass of inert and helpless ignorance which threatens to obstruct all intelligent self-government" not be allowed to destroy the American society through corrupting "organized political life," according to Sarah Wool Moore.[58]

When the connection had been made between ignorance and the welfare of the republican government, it followed logically in Mrs. Moore's argument that the induction of peasants into political life ought to be taken over by the state. Many other institutions important to the general welfare, as kindergartens and trade schools, had been begun by private enterprise, she argued, and eventually incorporated into the welter of publicly supported enterprises.[59]

The assault of the school (representing the state) and the social work agencies on the home was even more direct than Mrs. Moore's night classes would lead one to believe. It took the form of classes in child and infant care. In 1908 household science was already being taught in secondary schools in New York, Cleveland, California, Springfield and Boston, Massachusetts, and in a few other places, according to a summary at the first home economics convention.[60] The expansion in subjects and locales must have been explosive.

In 1910 Mary E. Williams reported on adaptations made in domestic science classes of the New York City schools to the preferences of Jewish and Italian students. Italians were being taught how to prepare macaroni and spaghetti properly, and kosher practices were being observed with Jewish youngsters. The school "respects all religions but favors none." Tucked in among these ethnic adaptations were instructions on American cooking and habits of living which were filtering back into the homes. After children had been in public school for a time, they came to look on themselves as Americans rather than as foreign nationals. Italians particularly were anxious to become Americanized, said the reporter.[61]

In 1913 Anne L. Hansen described a social work center in a Polish district in Buffalo. Center personnel enrolled those girls who could not go to public schools. These youngsters were apparently attending

[58] Sarah Wool Moore, "The Teaching of Foreigners," *The Survey*, vol. 24, pp. 386–392, June 4, 1910.

[59] *Ibid.*

[60] *Journal of Home Economics*, vol. 1, no. 1, p. 16, February, 1909.

[61] Mary E. Williams, "Teaching Domestic Science to Different Nationals," *Journal of Home Economics*, vol. 2, no. 3, pp. 271–273, June, 1910.

parochial schools where sewing or domestic science was not taught, hence the settlement work. Polish mothers were pleased at the attention shown their youngsters and probably were thereby influenced in their practices.[62]

In 1911 Mary Wright reported on experiments in teaching child care in public elementary schools. Teachers had attempted to instruct mothers, but some of the latter were of low mentality and others of Russian, Polish, or Italian birth could not understand English. With the consent of the superintendent, child care was being taught to elementary school youngsters who could influence home practice because they often cared for young children. The instruction had finally been limited to grammar grades enrolling girls aged ten to sixteen. Instruction was given by five school medical inspectors and five school nurses who were assisted by the director of household economy. Classes of from fifteen to twenty girls had been organized in most foreign districts. "Practice babies" were brothers and sisters of the girls. Good results in homes were being reported by visiting nurses, physicians, and other social workers, according to Miss Wright.[63]

These school efforts had not been enough, however. Baby refuge or nursery centers had been established on two city piers in New York. These centers were equipped by the director of physical education and the superintendent of playgrounds. Two nurses were assigned to each center to give lessons to mothers and older girls. Mary Wright said that one could not estimate the effect of the spreading of information to young girls in the simplest duties of motherhood and spreading knowledge among "the simple, the helpless, and the ignorant." So deeply did the health problem penetrate the "general school problem" that, in addition to the above facilities, school gardens, playgrounds, doctors and nurses, special classes, and school lunches were now necessary adjuncts to the school program.[64]

In 1911 Ella Henry described instruction in high schools in the care of infants and children. In bacteriology and hygiene, girls were receiving instruction in home care of the sick and general hygiene. In addition, they were securing information on bodily care of the infant, including instruction in clothing, bathing, and diet. Miss Henry delicately suggested what has been the bane of the schools ever since—sex education. Girls should be taught, so she said, "some of the fundamental laws which govern human relations" by a person of tact who was well equipped with scientific knowledge and who would leave only

---

[62] Hansen, *op. cit.*, p. 436.

[63] Mary Wright, "Experiments in Teaching Child Care in the Public Elementary Schools," *Journal of Home Economics,* vol. 3, no. 2, pp. 153–157, April, 1911.

[64] *Ibid.*

agreeable impressions with the neophytes. The goal of this home-oriented instruction was helping girls to become efficient mothers.[65]

Meal planning in domestic science classes had already taken on an Americanization purpose. In 1910 it was noted that such activity could be used to teach foreign pupils what Americans eat and what they could find available in their stores. These people could not find their native foods in America. When they substituted American foods without instruction in selection and use of such foods, they were often subjected to poor dietary combinations. Meal planning in school had applied a necessary corrective.[66]

Programs in elementary and secondary schools were already under way. But how were they to be staffed? Euphemia Clark, of New York City, in 1909 addressed herself to this question in her advocacy of a campaign for homemaking. The teacher, whom she was equating with a social worker, must have thorough technical training, a pleasing personality, a knowledge of neighborhood life and problems, and wide acquaintance with "betterment" agencies. She must have helpers if she were to set styles in housekeeping and child training. These housewife-helpers could be secured in each block. Findings of this teacher–social worker should be reported in records which could be passed on to other social workers. These records could contain such information as why people lived where they did, what was the nature of unsatisfactory living arrangements, how a rise in rents was affecting homes, whether there was a health committee. The social settlement was the place to begin.[67]

The place of the elementary and secondary schools and the social settlements in reforming home life was being spelled out in some detail. What of the college and university departments of home economics? William Hurd contended in 1910 that such departments ought to find in New England a fertile field in which to spread the gospel of "better homes, better schools, better government, and a higher social order." As President Lowell of Harvard had said, a university must grow out of the community in which it operated. "All persons in the commonwealth are properly students of a state educational institution," Prof. Bailey remarked.

The institutions to which Hurd referred were possibly land-grant colleges, for he put stress on rural concerns which had not heretofore come into prominence. Rural life or native life, as well as that of

---

[65] Ella Henry, "Instruction in the High School in Regard to the Care of Infants and Children," *Journal of Home Economics*, vol. 3, no. 2, pp. 160–161, April, 1911.

[66] Florence Willard, "How to Teach the Preparation of Meals," *Journal of Home Economics*, vol. 2, no. 6, p. 612, December, 1910.

[67] Clark, *op. cit.*, pp. 167–169.

urban immigrants, needed bolstering. There was particular call for instruction in home nursing and the control of disease, as well as in a preventive for the drudgery of farm life. More important, moral conditions ought to be looked into. Country girls were furnishing the recruits for the white slave traffic, said Hurd.[68] The college, if not the school, must reach out to reform the rural as well as the urban home.

## EDUCATIONAL ADJUSTMENT TO SOCIOECONOMIC PROBLEMS (1880–1910)

If the school were going to adjust to the problems of industry, nutrition, the home, and many others, it would have to undergo extensive reorganization and be identified as a more comprehensive institution than it had been up to the last of the nineteenth century. The most symbolic change would come when the school was designated a social center in the period from about 1910 to 1918. In the years between 1880 and 1910 the school took on a set of new functions, and voluntary organizations propagandized for opening up the school to community functions. These were the preparatory years.

Horace E. Scudder was a harbinger of things to come when he wrote in the *Atlantic Monthly* in 1896 of the schoolhouse as a center. He said that in a recent political convention, the symbols of party principles had been the little red schoolhouse, for the school was a "sign of national order and progress," and "accepted by men of every race and tongue and creed." It was "the most obvious centre of national unity" and was likely "to stand for a long time to come as the most conspicuous mark of a common American life."[69]

In view of the school's central role, the school building needed to be beautified, said Scudder. The school had begun to take on the functions of domestic life and therefore should be like a well-ordered home. In consonance with the function of being a home, the school had returned to a duty it had had before the Civil War. There was "a communistic duty of leveling which the school can perform better than any other institution." The school was the natural medium for unlimited development and the key to problems of American civilization.[70]

Scudder's 1896 report had been a harbinger, but there were others in addition to school lunches and home visiting.

---

[68] William D. Hurd, "The Relation between College and University Departments of Home Economics and the Outside Community," *Journal of Home Economics*, vol. 2, no. 3, pp. 257–267, June, 1910.

[69] Horace E. Scudder, "The Schoolhouse as a Centre," *Atlantic Monthly*, vol. 77, p. 103, January, 1896.

[70] *Ibid.*, pp. 108–109.

*Social Activities of the Schools*

School people were already caring for children's leisure by providing vacation or summer sessions. Vacation schools were opened in Boston, for example, about 1901.[71] By 1901 the Manhattan school board had already established both vacation schools and playgrounds, and had increased the staff correspondingly. Youngsters often went to school mornings and to their school playgrounds in the afternoons.[72] The first vacation or summer schools in the United States, according to Randall D. Warden, were opened in Newark, New Jersey, in 1885 and at approximately the same time in Providence. The Newark Educational Association opened summer playgrounds in 1899 and by 1902 had prevailed upon the school board to take them over. The opening of the playgrounds was followed by development of kitchen gardens, folk dancing, industrial training, and quiet game rooms. Playgrounds were open from November to April for after-school recreation for girls. Additional personnel, such as nurses, were used on the playgrounds.[73]

School gardens began to crop up in the schools all over the United States. Gardens were an education for work and a way of stressing good diet as well as being a motivating force in all kinds of school learnings, according to those who advocated them. Through efforts of The Home Gardening Association of Cleveland, school gardens were a feature of schools there by 1901.[74] School fairs, another way of putting youngsters' leisure to constructive use and interesting patrons in the schools, had first got started in Virginia in 1907, under the auspices of the Federation of Women's Clubs. After another beginning in Campbell County, Virginia, in 1908, they had spread throughout the United States.[75]

Parents had lost another training function when the first school savings bank was opened in 1885, at School No. 4, Long Island City, New York. As of January 1, 1912, twenty-five states had school savings banks. The extent of the movement was shown by statistics for Pennsylvania. The latter state had 44,443 school depositors who had deposited $1,778,738.13.[76]

---

[71] *Charities*, vol. 8, no. 20, p. 475, May 17, 1902.

[72] "Vacation Schools and Playgrounds," *Charities*, vol. 6, pp. 449–450, May 25, 1901.

[73] Randall D. Warden, "Vacation Playgrounds," *The City School as a Community Center*, Tenth Yearbook of the National Society for the Study of Education, Public School Publishing Company, Bloomington, Ill., 1911, part I.

[74] *Charities*, vol. 8, p. 232, 1902.

[75] U.S. Office of Education, *Report of the Commissioner of Education for the Year Ended June 30, 1913*, 1914, vol. I, p. 192.

[76] U.S. Office of Education, *Report of the Commissioner of Education for the Year Ended June 30, 1912*, 1913, vol. I, pp. 172–173.

In 1901 a plea for the education of defective children was made to the National Education Association,[77] and about the same time, special classes were established in Boston for the feeble-minded.[78]   When the New York State Hospital for Crippled Children was opened prior to 1901, it was hoped that the Legislature would take under consideration a system of education for patients, a task undoubtedly to be delegated to the schools.   In 1904, a New Jersey institution offered a course for teachers of atypical children.   This was an improvement on the arrangement heretofore in operation, in which public school teachers had to seek this training individually, according to one comment.[79] The first class for handicapped children was opened in New York in 1900.   Along with this last development, it should be noted that in New York schools, medical supervision was introduced in 1897 and school-nurse supervision in 1902,[80] two movements which were soon to get under way in other schools.

By 1909 it was stated with some authority that schools over the country were promoting these activities: (1) school health programs; (2) medical care programs, though few schools had moved in this direction; (3) physical education, though the "corrective and therapeutic aspects" had as yet been little exploited; (4) bathing (in school); (5) disease prevention; (6) feeding; (7) recreation programs through public school playgrounds (schools could not afford to wait for city or civic organizations to act); and (8) education for home life.   The authors of this summary indicated that twenty years earlier (circa 1889) there would have been no school which would have undertaken the last activity; whereas in 1909, the school which did not have such a program was outdated.[81]

By 1913 Henry S. Curtis was pleading for a school community center which would have a playground, swimming pools, a theater, a library. Each school should also have a camp in the country, for social betterment ought to center in the school.   At camp youngsters would be on a common footing with their teachers, and this air of camaraderie would be carried back to the school, which would be improved in tone.[82]

[77] "The Education of Defective Children," *Charities*, vol. 7, p. 64, July 20, 1901.

[78] "Dependent and Neglected Children," *Charities*, vol. 8, p. 313, Apr. 5, 1902.

[79] "Professional Schools in Philanthropy," *Charities*, vol. 12, no. 9, p. 229, Mar. 5, 1904.

[80] Berger, *op. cit.*, p. 84.

[81] Samuel Train Dutton and David Snedden, *The Administration of Public Education in the United States*, The Macmillan Company, New York, 1909, pp. 562–570.

[82] Henry S. Curtis, "The School Center," *The Survey*, vol. 30, pp. 89–91, Apr. 19, 1913.

*Preparing the School for a*
*Comprehensive Role*

Certain tasks had to be undertaken before the school as social center could perform all of the kinds of activities Dutton and Snedden listed as their province in 1909. The legal stamp of approval had to be put on the expanded role of the school, and school people had to be persuaded by the larger society of which they were the servants that it was proper for them to be regenerative agents.

Public pressure was such that school boards and legislatures acted promptly and within a short space of time to authorize expanded use of school property and additional activities for schools. Clarence A. Perry, a staff member of the Russell Sage Foundation, listed some of the actions of boards and legislative bodies in a report of 1912 on the social center movement. The Massachusetts Legislature had authorized the use of Boston schoolhouses for social, civic, and other purposes. A bill had been introduced in the United States Senate, permitting community use of school buildings in Washington, D.C. The Wisconsin Legislature passed a law authorizing school boards to grant the use of the schoolhouse to "any responsible inhabitant of the district . . . for such public meetings as will . . . aid in disseminating intelligence and promoting good morals." The Oregon Legislature authorized full use of school buildings for any and all purposes except "that all religious and political bodies be given equal rights and privileges." By Kentucky law, schoolhouses could even be used as places of public worship.[83] Even though these states and possibly others had acted early, others did not. Berger says that by 1924, however, thirty-two states and the District of Columbia had enacted legislation for extended use of public schools.[84]

The public opinion that school people needed to turn their institutions into social centers came from many directions. It emanated from the voluntary association which is the peculiarly American vehicle for getting things done. Charitable organizations were credited with much of the pressure; but "charitable" has to be given a peculiarly American twist. It apparently referred to organizations of settlement house workers (today they would be known as social workers) and to organizations that included physicians who were giving their time to the unfortunate of the cities. Teachers and principals were also a part of these organizations.

The Playground and Recreation Association, founded in 1906, made

[83] Clarence A. Perry, "A Survey of the Social-center Movement," *Elementary School Teacher*, vol. 13, pp. 125–129, November, 1912.

[84] Berger, *op. cit.*, pp. 122, 154.

the first nationwide effort to provide for and organize the leisure time of adults, and was instrumental in opening up schools for social activities. The National Education Association passed a resolution in July, 1911, approving the community use of school buildings for recreation, cultural, civic, and cooperative purposes.[35] In Columbus, Ohio, pressure for use of schools in foreign districts came from the United Brotherhoods of Churches and the board of trade, which appointed a committee of twenty-five to guide the movement to open up schools.[86] The Newark Educational Association (made up of women) opened the first summer playgrounds at school sites, and continued to operate them until 1902, when they prevailed on the school board to take them over.[87] The New York Public Education Association was active in promoting social center work in New York.[88] The first school fair in Virginia was organized by the Federation of Women's Clubs.[89] In Philadelphia, the recreation program was promoted by the Home and School League. In Boston, the Women's Municipal League established a first center at the East Boston High School. In St. Louis, the neighborhood association rented a school from the board. The school was used as a meeting place for clubs and recreation and social groups. In Springfield, Massachusetts, a men's church group agitated for the use of schools for neighborhood center work. The Women's College Club in Paterson, New Jersey, put on a campaign to get the schools opened to the community.[90]

Social workers must have exerted pressure at many points and rather continuously. A 1910 report of the National Conference of Charities and Correction meeting in St. Louis indicated that there was a standing committee on school and community. Speakers at the conference were arguing for expanded domestic arts education for girls who were lured by industry, and manual training for both boys and girls after the age of fourteen. Agricultural and trade education must become a part of the regular curriculum and not be shunted off into separate schools. The latter led to separation of classes, the former to a "genuine democracy of people." One-half of the country's intelligence was in the working class. Only the school, so the argument ran, could exploit this intelligence.[91]

[85] *Ibid.*, pp. 151–152.
[86] "Social Centers in Columbus Schools," *The Survey*, vol. 23, pp. 696–697, Feb. 12, 1910.
[87] Warden, *op. cit.*, p. 22.
[88] "A Successful Experiment," *The Survey*, vol. 27, no. 25, p. 1963, Mar. 23, 1912.
[89] *Report of the Commissioner of Education, 1913*, p. 192.
[90] Perry, *op. cit.*, pp. 124–126.
[91] Thomas J. Riley, "School and Community," *The Survey*, vol. 24, p. 459, June 11, 1910.

At this same conference, a professor of education pointed out the demands of the community on education. The school would change under the impact of social forces. These forces were inventions and developments in industry, accumulation of wealth, increase of leisure, crowded housing, lack of creative opportunities in the home, and school attendance and truancy. One of the reports at this conference closed on a note which indicated the attitude of social workers toward cooperation with schools and shifting of the social work burden to schools. If only, said this report, all agencies of the community "combined" with the schools, within ten years a good two years could be added to the period of youth.[92]

Extension divisions of universities were active. The off-campus division of the University of Wisconsin was a leader. Other propagandists for the social center were the state universities of Virginia, California, Kansas, Missouri, Texas, and Oklahoma. The National Municipal League was active, as was the Social Service Committee of the New York Federation of Churches and Christian Organizations, and the Men and Religion Forward Movement. Certainly, the Russell Sage Foundation was active, if not other educational and charitable foundations.[93]

One group of associations must have been particularly active, though their function was broader than urging the wider use of school buildings. These were reported by the U.S. Commissioner of Education as the community-and-school-improvement associations. They were both local and state in scope. State and city school-improvement associations flourished in many parts of the nation. Six state associations, in Mississippi, Louisiana, Kentucky, Tennessee, Arkansas, and Virginia, had state organizers. Illustrative of these associations is the Bennington County (Vermont) Improvement Association, organized in March, 1912, by over 100 prominent businessmen. The association members sought to improve agriculture, roads, schools, homes, sanitation, hygiene, and play and recreational facilities. They aimed for a "more evenly distributed social life," and had plans for general civic betterment and beautification. They had the active cooperation of many agencies, including the agricultural extension service and the schools.[94]

Another improvement association organized in 1911, the Montgomery County (Maryland) Life Commission, surveyed all economic, social, moral, and educational conditions in the county. It was assisted in this work by the Presbyterian Board of Home Missions, which published the survey report. The Prescott (Wisconsin) People's Club, which enrolled men, women, and children, held its meetings in the schools. Its

---

[92] *Ibid.*, p. 460.
[93] Perry, *op. cit.*, pp. 130–133.
[94] *Report of the Commissioner of Education, 1913*, pp. 195, 201.

function was to bring community members together in social, religious, and educational affairs. In the interest of doing something about these affairs, it kept in regular touch with the state legislators on social and educational concerns.[95]

A whole bevy, then, of educational, improvement, social welfare, social, and political organizations combined to convince the schools they should take over the job of regeneration of a society.

## DEVELOPMENTAL OF THE SOCIAL CENTER (1910–1918)

Berger's timetable for the changes in organization of the New York City schools is useful in charting roughly the course of educational transformation around the country. From about 1898 to 1904, so he said, schools were play centers. From 1905 to 1911, they were recreation centers. From 1912 to 1918, they assumed the role of social centers, and from 1919 to the present they may be described as community centers.[96] Of these several transformations, it is the transformation to the social center which is crucial in the shift of socialization responsibility from the home to the school, and in the assumption by the school of the role of guardian of the child in home, community, and industry.

That Berger's timetable has meaning for schools around the nation as they changed to social centers can be supported by the listings in the *Reader's Guide to Periodical Literature* as noted in Table 4-1. The heading "Schools as Social Centers" appeared for the first time in the 1905–1909 volume. Thereafter a separate heading of "Social Center" appeared along with another heading designating the school specifically as social center. Numbers of articles (by date) showed an upsurge in the period 1910 to 1916, with the high point in 1912. A few articles appeared throughout the 1925–1928 volume. By the time of this last volume, the separate heading "Social Center" had been dropped out, leaving only "Schoolhouses as Social Centers." A heading, "Community Center," appeared first in the 1915–1918 volume and continued through the 1928 period. This heading, however, appeared to subsume indiscriminately articles on both social work and school centers.

This development of a role for the school opens the way for the full-blown social-center movement which must have developed within the short span of five or six years, a commentary on the reactive capacity of America's basic institution.

Berger makes it plain that the school as a social center was, in the eyes of the public in the early 1900s, necessary for character building

[95] *Ibid.*, pp. 198–200.
[96] Berger, *op. cit.*, p. 141.

because of the presumed failure of the home and the church. The home had lost its influence in an urban setting; the church had lost its influence because it insisted on saving souls instead of teaching conduct.[97]    Samuel Dutton and David Snedden admitted in 1909 that the church, which was bound by ancient forms, was slow in allying itself with the state. But the church was reforming. It was going forward with the school in moral reform and, in the process, imitating the school and becoming pedagogic in method.[98]

Table 4-1. Numbers of Articles Classified under Social Center,* Readers' Guide to Periodical Literature (1900–1928)

| Date of articles | Number | Date of articles | Number |
|---|---|---|---|
| 1900 | 0 | 1915 | 9 |
| 1901 | 0 | 1916 | 15 |
| 1902 | 2 | 1917 | 9 |
| 1903 | 1 | 1918 | 2 |
| 1904 | 4 | 1919 | 9 |
| 1905 | 4 | 1920 | 1 |
| 1906 | 4 | 1921 | 1 |
| 1907 | 2 | 1922 | 3 |
| 1908 | 2 | 1923 | 1 |
| 1909 | 5 | 1924 | 4 |
| 1910 | 13 | 1925 | 1 |
| 1911 | 15 | 1926 | 8 |
| 1912 | 23 | 1927 | 2 |
| 1913 | 16 | 1928 | 3 |
| 1914 | 21 | | |

* Three headings were used: "Social Center," "Schools as Social Centers," and "Schoolhouses as Social Centers."

Whether the church was a useful ally of the school—note the reversal of roles from the time when the church was the educational agency—the school assumed the role of social center. It has inherited the role from the social workers who had first begun the settlement house which in turn had originated in England. In the work and atmosphere of the settlement house, emphasis had shifted from reconciliation of classes in England to promotion of a series of social causes in the United States. The American center concentrated on improving race relations, helping the foreign-born to adjust to the American culture, promoting community ventures. The American version incorporated the idea of "share the race life" and was in effect a "renaissance of Christianity." The social workers had viewed the settlement only as a temporary ex-

[97] Berger, op. cit., p. 129.
[98] Dutton and Snedden, op. cit., p. 585.

pedient designed to demonstrate its effectiveness and fully anticipated the institution's being taken over by the public school.[99]    Although this did not in all cases occur, the public school did reform into a social center with settlement-house aspects, and it could well do so because of the democratic flavor of the settlement house, so harmonious with the premises of the common school.

A stamp of approval was put on the social-center movement by members of the first social-center conference meeting October 25 to 28, 1911, at Madison, Wisconsin.    The conference had been organized by the Social Center Association of America (with headquarters in New York) and the Extension Division of the University of Wisconsin.    Two hundred delegates of all interests, races, creeds, and localities participated in this event, which was animated by a spirit "akin to the fervor of a great religious revival."[100]

The origins of the Social Center Association, one of the sponsoring groups, was in itself a commentary on how the schools would eventually be asked "to do the whole job."    Mrs. Frances G. Vandergrift of Pittsburgh, who was interested in social welfare work, had wanted to do something worthwhile for her society.    She asked Mrs. David Kirk to help her.    Mrs. Kirk either visited or moved to New York, where she became interested in improving the moral and educational aspects of the motion-picture business.    Mrs. Kirk's resolve eventuated in that valued American institution, a committee, the members of which saw that they would have to deal with other forms of entertainment than the motion picture if they were to succeed in their uplift job.    Out of the committee's work came the People's Recreation Company, experimenting with directing commercial amusements of the "better sort," and the Social Center Association of America.[101]

Members of the new Social Center Association soon found that the social center was well established in such widely separated places as Rochester, New York, and Texas and Oklahoma.    Their organization would have to be more widely representative than its largely New York constituency would allow.    Furthermore, members of the association had discovered that sending out "missionaries" (Ford's word) to start social centers was impractical.    A social center was a success only when it was the outgrowth of spontaneous interest in the local community. Hence, the national convention with its 200 delegates from over the nation had been called.[102]

---

[99] Berger, *op. cit.*, pp. 1–7.

[100] George B. Ford, "Madison Conference on Social Centers," *The Survey*, vol. 27, p. 1229, Nov. 18, 1911.

[101] *Ibid.*, pp. 1229–1230.

[102] *Ibid.*, p. 1230.

The purpose of the association was broad in intent, yet simple in statement. It was to develop an intelligent public spirit through using public schools and other public places for discussion of public questions and for wholesome civic, educational, and recreational activities. The intent of the school, according to the first plank in the association's platform, was parental; but the social center should also be fraternal, which meant the wider use of the school buildings in accord with the "Lincoln spirit."[103] John Collier, who attended and spoke at the conference, had more grandiose ideas for the social center which was to be stimulated by the association.

In order to make his meanings clear, Collier asked and answered several leading questions. His first query concerned the school as a nonpartisan and secular institution. Must it, in view of its foundations, sacrifice ethical teaching and civic influence? If one accepted the tacit assumption of a wider scope for the school, then how could it meet the ever-expanding demands on it? A third question took note of the fact that church and home were losing their influence over the child. American life was making serious inroads on the unity of the family and the school was partially responsible for this assault. In view of the resultant change in the child's phenomenal field, should the school "continue to perfect itself as a *substitute* for the family?"

To Collier, the means by which the school might answer his questions affirmatively was clear. The school could do a technical job during school hours and promote a many-sided education after school. Such an approach would have an inevitable effect, of course, on the curriculum pursued during school hours. The concept of the school as social center was not simple. The social-center conference members were, according to Collier, working toward some kind of synthesis of the forces in American life and American institutions. Inherent in the social-center idea was a melding of scholarship, science, and the school on the one hand; and community, the family, and emotional life on the other. The social center might yet be destined to be "the keystone in the completed arch of American life."[104]

Collier had a grand plan for the social center, but delegates were not always in agreement with him. Some of them, according to Ford, looked on the social center as a place where citizens of a local community would gather for the open discussion of public questions. Others said it was a social medium through which families might be brought together for mutual cooperation. Still others thought of it as a center for the education of parents, who were usually neglected in the modern

[103] *Ibid.*
[104] John Collier, "The Keystone of the Arch," *The Survey*, vol. 27, p. 1200, Nov. 18, 1911.

educational system. A few delegates saw the institution as a center of community life, with social, civic, and educational purposes.[105]

Delegates to the social-center conference were undoubtedly reflecting what they had already seen for, by about 1912 to 1915, different patterns had developed in various parts of the country and in accord with what the missionaries for the social-center movement might have judged the needs of the local community to be.

## Social Center as Civic Center

Since their origin, the schools had always been responsible for bulwarking republican government. But their function had been largely described in terms of the education of youngsters in intelligence and virtue. Now they were asked to attend to the whole community. Cities, European peasants, unsophisticated farm families, and political machines had resulted in a corrupted democratic government. The local control of public affairs was in danger of slipping out of the hands of the naïve and uninformed. Shady politicians and special-interest groups were assaulting the provinces of the people and manipulating political opinion for their own purposes. Scandal and corruption were legion. The society would be saved only if the people got back the control of their own affairs at the local level. So ran the argument, and central to the back-to-the-people movement was the school.

In helping to return government to the people, the school was often considered largely as a facilitating agency. Schoolhouses should be opened for civic purposes of all kinds. They should serve as meeting places of improvement groups, as polling places, as arenas for discussion of public questions. Occasionally some public figures would ask that school people as well as buildings be actively used in improving civic life. Educators must be active agents in promoting an aroused community. By the years 1912 to 1914, both school buildings and school people had been involved in civic improvement movements.

The Rochester social-center movement, credited with being one of the first, exemplified the facilitating function of the school. The president of the board of education reported on the movement to the Social Center Conference in 1911. The movement had encompassed the development of civic clubs, which were independent of any control by the schools, but which met in public school buildings. Encouraging such clubs was part of an effort to give back to the people the control of civic and community affairs. The movement, according to George M. Forbes, only confirmed a faith in the common man who, if properly educated, would allow his ethical spirit to predominate. More interest in civic

[105] Ford, *op. cit.*, p. 1229.

affairs had been shown in the poorest wards than in the wealthiest ones.[106] The social-center movement in Rochester, however, had run afoul of the political machines, the members of which did not appreciate the open discussion of public questions. There was evidence, nevertheless, that the Rochester civic groups would win the fight to use the school buildings; for the school was the place to right political wrongs.[107]

Schoolhouse as symbol and schoolhouse as facilitating agent were both mirrored in the drive to establish the educational building as the nation's polling place. Schoolhouses throughout the nation were being used for voting, according to Clarence Perry in 1912 and Carl Beck in 1914. By that date, Chicago was using seventy of its schools for this purpose.[108] In Long Beach, California, political parties were allowed to hold their caucuses and other meetings in school buildings.[109]

Beck's reference to the Chicago situation was by way of example and for purposes of persuasion, for he was quite put out by the New York Legislature, which had refused to make it possible for New York citizens to cast their votes in schoolhouses. "Where shall the citizens of New York vote?" he inquired, oratorically. The only way to cure political corruption in New York was to transfer the voting activity to the schoolhouse, that symbol of honest education and nonpartisan politics. Such a move would save money, some $125,000 per election. Beyond that, it would eliminate political patronage by encouraging untrammeled voting and the sanctity of the ballot. It would prove to be an education in practical civics for the children. With immigrant citizens and parents particularly, it would encourage a sense of ownership of the schools, with which they had no familiarity. To Beck, the New York Legislature was indeed obtuse.[110]

The schools as rallying places for the community had served other civic purposes. In Ohio, schoolhouses had been used in the campaign for changes in the state constitution. Meetings in advocacy of the initiative and referendum were sponsored in the Cleveland schools by the Federation of Labor. Conservative members of the school board attempted to restrict these meetings. So much interest had been aroused that the board was forced to rule that schools could be opened for civic use on petition of twelve voters of the school district and on payment of $3 to the caretaker. Hearings on highways and public properties, for purpose of getting opinion on playgrounds, had been held in the Chelsea,

---

[106] George M. Forbes, "Buttressing the Foundations of Democracy," *The Survey*, vol. 27, pp. 1231–1235, Nov. 18, 1911.

[107] Ford, *op. cit.*, p. 1231.

[108] Carl Beck, "Where Shall the Citizens of New York Vote?" *The Survey*, vol. 32, p. 53, Apr. 11, 1914.

[109] Perry, *op. cit.*, p. 127.

[110] Beck, *op. cit.*, pp. 53–54.

Massachusetts, schools.  In Brooklyn, the Evergreen board of trade had called citizens together in the school to discuss questions of sewage and water.[111]  The belief was current that the school would purify public purposes merely by its use.

Symbolic of the central place the school was coming to hold in community life is the story told in 1914 of the civic center built around a tricity high school.  The story shows how school as civic center merges into school as social center.  In its very building as a civic center, it anticipated that goal of social centers, community cooperation; for it was the culmination of a long campaign by a public-spirited citizen of German descent.  This civic visionary wished to unite the people of the Illinois townships of LaSalle, Peru, and Oglesby by providing jointly a facility they could not provide separately.

The campaign issued in the building of LaSalle-Peru Township High School in 1898.  The second step in securing a central place for this school was taken by a Mrs. F. W. Matthiessen who in 1903 gave money for a manual training and domestic science building to be attached to the high school.  It was but a short step to a social center provided by private funds of $75,000 and deeded to the high school trustees.  The center had been planned for the families of workers in the plants of the donor.  It was attached to the main building by a passageway.  It housed pools, a library, a bowling alley, and class, club, and billiards rooms, as well as space for music and art activities.  A full-time director was secured for the center.

Stimulated by this joint community effort, the mayor of one of the towns called attention to the need for promoting public health among the immigrant and shifting population.  Each of the towns, he noted, had some health service, but each was inadequately equipped and staffed.  Alongside the high school, the mayor established a hygienic institute equipped with a bacteriological laboratory.  Encouraged by the necessity for using this fine facility, the people of the three towns finally developed a single department of health with school nurses, and a milk- and food-testing service.  The development of the civic center around the school had led to closer ties between school and community.  Industries in the area each year invited teachers and youngsters to tour their plants.[112]

What was most illuminating about this 1914 account by Graham Taylor was the way in which the development of the civic center tied the school in with support of American value patterns.  In calling attention to the generosity of a private donor, Taylor talked of the "democracy of wealth," another way of commending the stewardship of wealth, an

---

[111] Perry, *op. cit.*, p. 128.

[112] Graham Taylor, "Building a Civic Center around a Tri-city High School," *The Survey*, vol. 33, pp. 65–66, Oct. 17, 1914.

old New England idea which has persisted in strength throughout the industrial and business community of America. The individual holds his wealth in trust for the community, to which he yields ownership when the time and cause are right.

Still other values, such as orientation to the present and future and the necessary overcoming of obstacles, could be inferred from Taylor's account. Taylor stated, in reference to the tasks which had to be undertaken to bring the center to completion, that it was not the way of democracy to look backward in time at the monastery, but to face one's problems and solve them. The tricity high school as social-civic center symbolized the American value pattern in operation.

### Social Center as "Social" Center

The tricity civic center merged into a social center with emphasis on the social, as did many another school throughout the country. The vacation school, summer school, and summer playground movements had already pointed the way to some of the activities of a social center. It might be said to have been for general uplift, both by luring children and youth from the wrong avocations and by improving the taste of youth and adults alike. The necessity for such a center had probably been apparent first and most crucially in the areas where there was the greatest number of foreign parents whose children would get into trouble if not under the shepherdship of the schools, but there were undoubtedly other forces at work. The American culture had in it the elements of upward striving for all persons, regardless of origins. It was as important that native rural people be uplifted as that first-generation young people be saved from the dens of iniquity.

It is not strange, therefore, to find in an article of 1912 a report on a social-center movement in Oklahoma, where so-called native Americans would have abounded. Oklahoma, so said A. Grant Evans, was moving in the direction of improved organization of social and civic activities, and was "coming to look upon the public school organization as the nucleus about which such work must develop." A state social-center association had already been formed to get help for rural schools, and many activities were already a part of school business. Schools were sponsoring parent meetings, local conferences of charity groups, entertainments, lyceum courses, and summer chautauquas. Eric L. Castle, a teacher in a country school, had taken it upon himself to see that there was "at least one lecture or entertainment in every rural school in the [his] county." Oklahoma, said Evans, was awake to the community-organization need.[113]

[113] A. Grant Evans, "Social Center Movement in Oklahoma," *The Survey*, vol. 28, p. 297, May 18, 1912.

Part II of the *Tenth Yearbook of the National Society for the Study of Education* (1911) was devoted to a description of the rural school as community center. The school in this setting was conceived of as a general uplift agency. It should be a general-education and social center. It must foster an extension program in agricultural education and in housekeeping. It ought to be an agency through which the hard-working farm wife, who found so little time for learning new skills, could be reached. It should maintain a community library and be a center for art and organized recreation activities.[114]  Improvement was in the air, and country as well as town needed a good overhauling.

In 1912, Edward J. Ward sang the saga of schoolhouse or saloon. His leading characters were a school principal in Minnesota and a saloon keeper. The principal had come to the conclusion that working-men frequented saloons not because they cared for "booze" (Ward's word), but because they wanted sociability. The principal, thereupon, went on a campaign to raise money for a motion-picture machine, an item for a social center he hoped to develop for the sociable working-men. One day when he was walking down the street, he met the saloon keeper from whom he solicited a donation. The saloon keeper gave it and not reluctantly. But he reminded the principal that the latter might put him out of business.[115]

Drink and vice in general were social ills which prompted some of the social-center work. The terrible facts revealed by the Chicago Vice Commission had given impetus to the movement for providing substitutes for vicious dance halls, said Perry in 1912. Social dancing was being actively discussed in school circles. The Social Service Council of Portland, Oregon, was attempting to open up school buildings as substitutes for dance halls.[116]  A member of the Board of Education of New York City commented in 1912 that, while the social workers lamented the dangerous influence of the dance hall, the board of education had gone ahead to deprive these evil places of many prospective customers "by conducting, at fifteen centers, mixed dancing under proper chaperonage." Martin concluded that it was no effort at all in these halls to ban the "grizzly bear," the turkey trot, "and the other indecencies which have invaded high society."[117]

Not all was vice, however. Sometimes it was only poor taste which

[114] *The Rural School as Community Center*, Tenth Yearbook of the National Society for the Study of Education, Public School Publishing Company, Bloomington, Ill., 1911, part II.

[115] Edward J. Ward, "The School-house or the Saloon," *The Outlook*, vol. 102, pp. 487–488, Nov. 2, 1912.

[116] Perry, *op. cit.*, pp. 125, 127.

[117] John Martin, "Social Work of New York Schools," *The Survey*, vol. 28, p. 296, May 18, 1912.

needed to be improved.   John Franklin Bobbitt was proud of the record of a school in the town of Richmond, Illinois, a small manufacturing city of less than 25,000 persons and no different from many others.   The work of the people of the community should be an inspiration to others. The city had an elementary school, a junior high school of the seventh and eighth grades, and a high school which had been built with a view to its being a social center.   By 1911, the high school had become the musical center of the city.   It was used for and actively sponsored the people's symphony orchestra, the people's chorus, the high school chorus, and the high school orchestra, which was fed by the junior high school group.   The director of music employed by the school board was the most highly paid teacher in the system.   His salary was almost as large as that of the superintendent.   He had charge both of the community and the high school groups.   With this fine record of musical leadership, the school people had agreed that music should enjoy the same status in the high school curriculum as did the time-honored subjects.   Not only was music on the upgrade in Richmond, but so was art.   Three rooms on the top floor of the high school were set aside for the city's art museum.   The new leisure of workingmen, according to Bobbitt, had made such school innovations necessary.   There must be education for free time which, in turn, was bound up with moral education.[118]

*Social Center as Educational Center*

The social center merged easily and readily into the educational center.   Yet in accounts of the years 1910 to 1915, no one quite seemed to explain the meaning of the center as educational.   By implication from stories about particular centers, it must have encompassed the education both of youth and adults.   For youth, it was education in after-school hours; for adults, in the evenings or through day classes for mothers.   It was an educational accommodation to adults, yet it was also a way of bringing parents into schools.   As example, in 1909 the superintendent of schools in Walla Walla County, Washington, divided the county into twelve districts with a school at the center of each.   He began a campaign of interesting patrons in the school through promoting spelling and declamation contests for youngsters.   The contests were expanded in kind by including sewing and cooking in the competition. From this point on, having aroused interest in the work of the school, the superintendent promoted lecture courses, discussions, and school fairs.   An incidental outcome of the educational program was the consolidation of one-room schools.[119]

[118] John Franklin Bobbitt, "A City School as a Community Art and Musical Center," *The Elementary School Teacher*, vol. 12, pp. 119–126, November, 1911.
[119] *Report of the Commissioner of Education, 1913*, p. 191.

Lectures were in the program of many social-center schools throughout the country. On January 1, 1907, the Board of Education of Cleveland created the Free Lecture and Social Center Committee. The committee promoted lectures, concerts, glee clubs, and quartets. The lectures were varied in nature, running all the way from topics in art to some of a patriotic character. At the latter, school children were asked to sing patriotic songs. Both principals and teachers were on hand to greet the guests—a practice which had led to greater cooperation between teachers and parents, according to Sarah Hyre.[120]

Besides mothers' meetings, evening lectures, and other events, libraries were often a part of this educational-center movement. The literature abounds with references to public libraries being opened and housed in public school buildings. The library movement in schools appeared to be particularly strong in rural areas where the only public buildings would have been the local schools. Librarians tried to enhance their own institutions by talking of the library as social center. But the school managed to win the naming race, partly, perhaps, because it often did promote a library as one of its many facilities.

In a commentary of 1912, two writers asked that the domestic science department be considered as the social center. This plea introduced a somewhat broader and vaguer meaning of "social" in social center. Through quotations from several authors, the writers made it clear that the school was the social unit in the community, and the trend in education was social. The primary aim of the school was not to give academic training, but to give students practice in real life. The school was an institution in which people of all classes could meet together as equals. Youth should be socialized and sent into the community to give their best service. As social training must go on during school hours, the domestic science department should be the logical center for this training.[121]

## Scope of the Social Center

School as social center attempted to uplift the community and reform the homes, young parents, and youth in school. It did this through the medium of social events, educational activities, and providing facilities for civic improvement. No one set of practices characterized all of

[120] Sarah E. Hyre, "Public Lectures, the Cleveland Plan," *The City School as a Community Center*, Tenth Yearbook of the National Society for the Study of Education, Public School Publishing Company, Bloomington, Ill., 1911, part I.

[121] Bertha M. Miller and Viola M. Bell, "The Domestic Science Department as a Social Center of the School," *Journal of Home Economics*, vol. 4, pp. 162–163, April, 1912.

the school social centers, but those in New York City probably came as close to being comprehensive in scope as did any in the country.

Spurred on by the "peasant families" whose youth loomed large in the juvenile courts and whose members apparently degraded even the slums, the New York City schools went forward to be educator to a total population. In 1912 a member of the board of education talked of the schools as social work institutions. In all modesty he declared that his city led the United States "and probably the world, in the social use of the buildings, grounds, and staff of the school system."[122]

In the winter of 1911–1912, recreation centers in the schools were attended six times a week, from October to May, by over 17,500 people. Six hundred and fifty athletic, literary, social, musical, civic, dramatic, dancing, and parent clubs had met in the schools. Teachers were on hand as instructors for boys and girls and as advisers for adult clubs. In forty-one centers, there had been vocal and instrumental music. In each center, some forty or fifty youths and maidens under the guidance again of a teacher, had sung old and new songs such as "Down upon the Swannee River" and "The Star-spangled Banner." Mixed dancing had also been promoted in some fifteen centers. To the school board, said Martin, no plan for the uplift of parents or youngsters would appear to be inappropriate for an educational agency to undertake. The schools had even challenged the motion pictures; in cooperation with the People's Institute, they were showing educational moving pictures.[123]

On the educational side, Sunday evening concerts and lectures had been promoted for nonchurchgoers, who were allowed to pay a small admission fee so they would not feel like paupers.[124] Public lectures during the week were being sponsored in 118 school buildings. There were groups in literature, history, sociology, and art; general and applied science; descriptive geography; and special topics. The last category was intriguing, for it was not a subject-matter classification, but a set of lectures in Italian, Yiddish, and German, planned for the foreign-born, and covering such areas as preparation for citizenship, first aid, and tuberculosis prevention.[125]

A second group of lectures had the word "studies" attached. These lectures were accompanied by examinations. They covered such topics as fiction, history, economics, electricity and magnetism, first aid to the

---

[122] Martin, op. cit., p. 295.

[123] Ibid., pp. 295–296.

[124] Ibid., p. 296.

[125] Henry M. Leipziger and Clarence A. Perry, "Adult Education and the New York Plan of Public Lectures," The City School as a Community Center, Tenth Yearbook of the National Society for the Study of Education, Public School Publishing Company, Bloomington, Ill., 1911, part I, pp. 10–13.

injured.  A last group of lectures was put in the "Miscellaneous" category.  They ranged from "Goethe: Man, the Mirror of the World," to
"The Man That Is Down and Out."  Approximately 1,575 different topics
were the subjects of these three kinds of lecture system.[126]

A report of 1912 on lectures expanded on the activities of the New
York Public Education Association, as these activities affected the
foreign-born.  Gatherings were held in schools, with the clients being
90 per cent Russian and Hungarian Jews and 10 per cent German Jews.
Names of students had been secured from settlement houses which promoted kindergartens.  The schools and the centers cooperated in distribution of clothes as well as in programs of movies and lectures.
Among the latter were found topics on boys and how to deal with them,
the vote for women, improvement of comic supplements, what the
kindergarten does for the child, school lunches, and aspects of city
government.  For this clientele of new Americans, such familiar tunes
as "Annie Laurie" were adapted to newly written songs such as "School
House on Our Street."  According to the author, the spirit of the American forefathers lived on through "all the disturbing changes."[127]

During the 1911 season, there had been in attendance at New York
public lectures some 959,982 persons.  This was an average of 135 per
lecture.  Each lecture (with equipment) cost the board of education
$26.05, though lecturers (among whom there were very notable ones)
received a standard fee of $10 per evening.  Teachers often were super-
intendents of these affairs because they appeared to be especially well
suited to the task.[128]


SUMMARY

The school activities of New York City, in the period from 1910 to
1915, are both illustrative and symbolic of the shift in responsibility
from the home to the school as primary socializing agency.  Throughout
the country the schools had moved through the stages of play centers,
recreation centers, and, finally, social centers.  When the last stage had
been reached, the roles of the school and the home were reversed.  The
modest changes to come about in school business up to the middle of
the twentieth century would make little difference in the direction and
intensity of school activities.  Beyond the change to community centers
(largely a naming process), schools would merely improve, formalize,

[126] *Ibid.*
[127] "A Successful Experiment," *The Survey*, vol. 27, no. 2, pp. 1963–1964, Mar. 23, 1912.
[128] Leipziger and Perry, *op. cit.*, pp. 13–16.

and systematize those activities by which they reached out to control the whole development of the whole child.

The shift of responsibility from home to school had begun in a limited way when schools first were begun and later when they took over vocational training. Urbanization, industrialization, and heavy peasant immigrations in the last of the nineteenth century accelerated the pace at which school people expanded ideas of their function. Educational personnel were not wholly responsible for this redefinition of the role of the school. They were urged and abetted by social workers and professional and civic leaders, who turned naturally to the school as the single agency under public control which was charged with keeping the society going. The definition of the role of the school as Americanization agency changed, not in intent, but in terms of social change. As the nature of American society changed, so also did the tasks of the school. Whereas in pre-Civil War days, simple literacy tools plus patriotic observances served to develop a nation, the schooling tasks in the post-Civil War period burgeoned in response to the same need to develop Americans. In the face of new social forces, educators felt they must prepare peasants and rural folk for urban living, root out the disinterest and destroy the corruption in public and industrial life, and remake the home to fit the child. All of these tasks were to be done in the name of developing a strong and united nation in the face of overwhelmingly divisive forces. These tasks the school people confronted through the social center of 1910 to 1915. In the 1960s they have still not been relieved of their extraordinary burdens.

PART II

# Evolution of the
# American Educational Pattern

# 5

# The Search Abroad
# for Educational Patterns

> On reflection, it seems to me that it would be most strange,
> if, from all this variety of system and of no system, of
> sound instruction and of babbling, of the discipline of
> violence and of moral means, many beneficial hints, for our
> warning or our imitation, could not be derived.[1]
>
> HORACE MANN (on foreign school systems),
> SEVENTH ANNUAL REPORT, 1844

The American education system has been charged with being the basic social institution for an experimental nation. In the period from 1776 to 1865, it was to produce enlightened and moral citizens and to stem the tide of social disease. Since the Civil War, it has been asked to take the place of the home and church in inducting the young into the American culture and, occasionally, to reform the home, industry, and any other institution which might have a degenerative effect on youth or adults. For this extensive job, a faculty and the structure and organization of a school system had to be developed. But where could a pattern for educational development be found?

Part II on the evolution of the American education pattern explores the question of developing a system for a country based on the political ideals and social problems as outlined in Chapters 3 and 4. In the five chapters in Part II it will be noted that the base of operations shifts in respect to individuals who are defining the system and practices judged desirable for schooling. Some general agreement upon a method of making American citizens has been urgently needed. In place of a

---

[1] Horace Mann, *Report of an Educational Tour in Germany, France, Holland and Parts of Great Britain and Ireland,* being part of the Seventh Annual Report of Horace Mann, Esq., Secretary of the Board of Education, Mass., U.S., 1844; with preface and notes by W. B. Hodgson, 4th ed., Simpkin, Marshall, and Co., London, 1857, p. 3.

ministry of education, however, the United States has had a series of state and often weak state boards, many of which have been largely advisory to a host of local boards which have autonomy in adapting education to local populations.

In the face of state and local autonomy and of the participation of large numbers of persons in the development of the American educational system, the evolution of the pattern has gone forward in a series of movements in which voluntary participation by educators, legislators, and the public has been the only guarantee of some uniformity in education for nation making. In this chapter, educators will be found to be searching abroad for an elementary and a secondary system in the period from about 1800 to 1860, and for a university system in the last of the nineteenth century.

One phase of educational borrowing which will not be considered in this chapter has to do with the presumed influence of particular Europeans on philosophical and psychological aspects of American education. Johann Heinrich Pestalozzi, the Swiss educator, is an example of these Europeans. He is said to have "psychologized" education and to have given strong impetus to the idea of designing schooling to be in harmony with the laws of organic development. Friedrich Froebel also put emphasis on natural evolution, the importance of inner activity, and constructive activities and play as essential to the kindergarten child. Johann Frederich Herbart contributed the five formal methodological steps and associationism to the American normal schools of the last of the nineteenth century, and gave his name to the organization which later became the National Society for the Study of Education. Through William T. Harris of St. Louis and John Dewey, George William Frederick Hegel contributed elements of his absolute idealism to the philosophies underlying American education. The list of these contributors to American education could be multiplied several times and their influences followed with profit through several chapters.

The intent of this chapter, however, is not to trace the influences of European educators on the American educational pattern, but to follow the search for a *system* of education which would be appropriate to the new American nation, for it was a system which was desperately needed. This search, which extended from the beginnings of the nation through the last of the nineteenth century, falls roughly into three phases.

PHASE 1: SEARCHING FOR BRITISH AND
FRENCH INSTITUTIONAL PATTERNS

The first phase of the search is difficult to describe, for it has been very inadequately examined and concerns several kinds of attempted borrowing. It had to do with the importing of ideas not for an institution like the normal school in the general sense, but for particular associations and institutions. Chronologically, it covered the period roughly from 1750 to the early part of the nineteenth century. In an era when educational planning was still being done by a group of public men rather than persons identified with educational institutions, it showed a groping for architectural models for scholarly and institutional endeavors.

Americans had been Americans before the Revolutionary War, but until the war was under way, British institutions served to set the pace for scholarly innovation. The drive to make the colonies a center of culture in the folk sense began in the seventeenth century. Boyle, Bishop Wilkins, and other learned men who were friends of Governor Winthrop of Massachusetts wanted to leave England for the colonies to establish a society for promoting knowledge. Charles II was well aware of the intended move and also of the value of the proposed organization. Before the learned party had got under way, Charles took it under his wing and chartered The Royal Society of London.[2]

For approximately one hundred years (1675–1775) The Royal Society was also an American society. To it belonged such eminent colonial leaders as Cotton Mather and the Winthrops of New England; Franklin, Rittenhouse, and Morgan of Pennsylvania; Bannister, Clayton, Mitchell, and Byrd of Virginia; and several men from the Carolinas. Between the members in America and those in England, there went on a brisk exchange of views on topics natural and philosophical. Colonial research was published in The Royal Society's *Philosophical Transactions.*[3]

About 1743, Benjamin Franklin, to whom the society was known, issued a circular titled *A Proposal for Promoting Useful Knowledge among the British Plantations in America.* Franklin's petition was addressed to "virtuosi" and "ingenious men." Out of the interest aroused by the circular came the first American Philosophical Society, which soon languished and died.

The surviving members of the American society revived the organization in the 1760s by proposing a plan to observe the transit of Venus. Dr. Franklin secured a telescope for them abroad. In 1769 the society combined with another begun by Franklin in Philadelphia, and out of the combination came The American Philosophical Society Held at Philadelphia for Promoting Useful Knowledge. This society, which survived, began to publish *The American Philosophical Transactions* in 1771 in Philadelphia, metropolis of American science and literature.[4] Despite the imminence of war between the colonists and England, the

---

[2] G. Brown Goode, *The Origin of the National, Scientific and Educational Institutions of the United States,* Knickerbocker Press, New York, 1890, p. 5. Reprinted from the Papers of the American Historical Association.

[3] *Ibid.*

[4] *Ibid.,* pp. 6–7.

latter was still the mother country, and the first surviving learned society thus partially reflected—through the name of its publications and in its general organization—the influence of The Royal Society of London.

When the war was finally on, the pendulum swung toward that firm friend, imperial France. Americans in the late eighteenth century and indeed, in any age, could hardly be Francophiles. The French, according to the early national textbook writers, were gay, fickle, and infidel.[5] The religious scepticism of the French intellectual would have sat ill with a middle-class American who, despite his disaffection from Calvinism, would have retained a strong leaning toward a religiomoral commitment. The excesses of the French Revolution would have disgusted and alarmed American leaders, who were concerned about the potential of mobocracy in democracy. Airs and graces, satins and white wigs, idle conversation and suspect personal conduct would have been abhorrent to a sober Boston merchant or divine.

In a somewhat less passionate vein, American leaders schooled in the individual democracy of British philosophers would have questioned the penchant for centralization of power in the French government. Nevertheless, France did indeed contribute money and arms for the American Revolution in its first few years, and French officers gave substantial service to the Revolutionary Army. During the period of the Articles of Confederation, Thomas Jefferson represented the United States government in France. In 1778 and 1779, John Adams, along with the good Dr. Franklin and Arthur Lee represented the Continental Congress at the court of the king of France. Other American leaders had contacts in person or by correspondence with French scholars. It was thus quite natural, for a brief period, largely in the last of the eighteenth century, that French institutions should serve as models for Americans.

John Adams, soberest of New England Brahmins, surprisingly enough was the one to introduce to America the idea for a society whose founders intended to give it "the air of France rather than of England, and to follow the Royal Academy, rather than the Royal Society."[6] Even more surprising, this specification of intent appeared in a 1785 letter of the New England divine, the Rev. Manassah Cutler. John Adams's interest in a learned society began mildly with a visit to view the French king's collection of birds, insects, and other specimens. The inspection was made during Adams's 1778–1779 mission to France.

---

[5] Ruth Virginia Miller, "Nationalism in Elementary Schoolbooks Used in the United States from 1776 to 1865," unpublished doctoral dissertation, Columbia University, 1952, p. 283. (Microfilm.)

[6] Quoted in Goode, op. cit., p. 11.

Adams's interest was also stimulated by favorable comment from French academicians on the Philadelphia society.[7] It is not unlikely, therefore, that the so-called French influence in the society which Adams was to found was inspired by the desire that Boston not be outdone by the English-oriented Philadelphia.

Whatever the motives, John Adams was supported in his intent by being in the company of the Chevalier de la Luzerne and M. Marbois on the return journey to this country in 1779 aboard the French frigate *La Sensible*. At the conclusion of the trip, the Harvard corporation gave a dinner in honor of Ambassador Luzerne and his party. Adams was also invited to the affair. His dinner partner was the Rev. Samuel Cooper, long pastor of the Brattle Street Church in Boston. Adams entertained Cooper with what he had seen in Europe and how he had heard Philadelphia praised. This should have been enough for Cooper, for the congregation of the Brattle Street Church was noted for the intellectual leadership it had supplied to the colonists. It should have been almost superfluous for Adams to have added that a "future legislature of Massachusetts should institute an Academy of Arts and Sciences."[8]

Dr. Cooper did give thought to the pride of Massachusetts, Harvard. Would not the proposed organization rival the college? No, indeed, said Adams, it would do honor to the institution. The president and principal professors might be members of the academy, and meetings of the society might be held at the college.

Reverend Cooper was won over and thereafter spread the gospel of a learned society. While he was so engaged, Adams, as a member of the first constitutional convention of Massachusetts, had a chance to insert into the constitution some materials on the encouragement of literature. It was the duty of the magistrates and the legislators to cherish literature and science as well as to protect temporal interests and political rights. Thus was born the Academy of Arts and Sciences with a French air and memoirs in place of transactions.

An abortive attempt to get the American colonists on their intellectual feet was initiated, in 1788, by the Chevalier Quesnay de Beaurepaire, grandson of the founder of the French physiocrats. His plan, so it was said, had been endorsed by the king of France, the Royal Academy of Sciences, the Royal Academy of Painting and Sculpture, and by such prominent men as Antoine Lavoisier, founder of modern chemistry, and Antoine Condorcet, philosopher and mathematician. The scheme was simply to found an Academy of Arts and Sciences of the United States of America in Richmond, Virginia.

The plan got so far that large sums were subscribed by Virginia

[7] *Ibid.*, p. 9.
[8] Account of Academy of Arts and Sciences taken from *ibid.*, pp. 8–11.

planters and citizens of Richmond. A building was erected, and Dr. Jean Rouelle, mineralogist-in-chief in France, was commissioned to make collections in America and Europe. The plan was instituted, however, just one year before the French Revolution. There was no time to get the organization under way. It ended as only a French dream of what a bit of French culture might have been in America.[9]

There is still in operation a University of the State of New York. It is governed by a Board of Regents, and yet is not a university in the sense in which the term is ordinarily used in the United States. It has been in the past largely a way of governing a large collection of schools, colleges, and universities, and of protecting admissions to institutions of higher education through the Regents' examinations given to secondary school students in New York. The original act establishing the university was passed in the 1780s, but it was inspired by events occurring two centuries earlier.[10]

The germ of the idea of the New York university was to be found, according to Sidney Sherwood, in the Edict of Blois in 1579. In that directive there was proposed an organization which would incorporate all the universities of France into one system. The idea of this general governing of institutions of higher education was revived in a report of 1768, by Rolland d'Erceville, president of the Parliament which had expelled the Jesuits in 1762. D'Erceville proposed a plan for a national education system which would be supervised by a bureau of correspondence, an arm of the civil government, rather than by the bishops and clergy. The plan called for visitation by the bureau of all teaching bodies and colleges. Its system of civil control was generally a revolt against arbitrary power and allowed for the development of the natural sciences and positive knowledge as against dogma. It was D'Erceville's attempt to reinforce freedom and equality, religious tolerance, and sense impressions as a source of knowledge. It was anticlerical, and pro reason in the sense of the eighteenth-century deists.

In 1775, Turgot addressed a memorial to the king of France. This able French minister proposed a council of national instruction which would have control of academies, universities, colleges, and primary schools. Even though Turgot was dismissed by the misled king, his ideas were of common knowledge in intellectual circles.

[9] *Ibid.*, pp. 11–12. B. A. Hinsdale, "Notes on the History of Foreign Influence upon Education in the United States," *Report of Commissioner of Education for the Year 1897–1898*, 1899, vol. I, p. 597.
[10] Account of University of the State of New York adapted from Sidney Sherwood, *University of the State of New York: Origin, History and Present Organization*, University of the State of New York Regents' Bulletin, no. 11, University of the State of New York, Albany, N.Y., January, 1893.

From the backwash of several decades of French plans for education, the New York leaders took, according to Sherwood, ideas relating to secular education, state control, and centralized administration. As the organization finally emerged in the nineteenth century, the governing of the state university was vested in nineteen elective regents, the Governor, the lieutenant governor, the secretary of state, and the superintendent of public instruction. The governing of the colleges was imperial, not Federal, in that members of the colleges could not sit on the Board of Regents. The office of "Regent," which originated at the University of Paris and was a name for a person qualified to teach and to govern, became in the New York organization a governor divorced from the teaching body.

The organization period of The University of the State of New York took place from 1784 to 1787, when the plan took form in law. The French flavor of the plan might well have been enforced by Ezra l'Hommedieu, descendant of a French Huguenot family. L'Hommedieu had traveled in France and was a member of the Board of Regents from the begininng of the state university to 1811. As the University of New York began to emerge, it was faintly like an English system in which education is a corporation, but it was more particularly the first realization of the plans of the French parliamentarians and encyclopedists for a system of education under state control.

Some of the first attempts at education in Michigan had been made by French priests. The French, though not in complete control when Michigan became a territory, were nevertheless prominent in the affairs of the region. It was not strange, therefore, that the outlines of the first complete system of education in Michigan territory should bear the mark of French origins.

A University of France, an organization for the general governing of education through a centralized system, had come into being in the period 1806 to 1808 under Napoleon. This organization may have been the inspiration for the Catholepistemiad authorized by the Governor and judges who constituted the first territorial Legislature in Michigan in 1817. Much in the French manner, the Catholepistemiad or University of Michigan provided for a complete school system. The faculty of the university was to control the teachers of all levels in the state. The Catholic priest and the Presbyterian minister who became the first faculty set up a classical academy and a primary school. The first teacher of the latter put the intent of this French system in perspective by his comments on the University of Michigan. He said that when he arrived in Detroit to begin his teaching, the Catholepistemiad was nothing more than a corporation designed for the control of monies appropriated for education and for the supervision of educational institutions in the Michigan territory.[11] A law of 1821 changed the control of the Catholepistemiad, and subsequent laws altered the educational system of Michigan; but in the state's educational memories is a colorful interlude when the system was a replica of the University of France.

What influence directly bore on Jefferson's plans for education is obscure. Speculation has been free in respect to this influence. Jefferson's knowledge of French liberal thought and the close correspondence of his plans to those of French writers on education form inevitable links between the Virginia sage and Europe.

Characteristics of Jefferson's educational plans have been compared to those of eighteenth-century education as outlined by Compayré. These were described as nationalistic, equalitarian, secular, and philosophically grounded.[12] To three of these characteristics, Jefferson subscribed in his plans for a Virginia education system and the University of Virginia. The equalitarianism of the French he translated into universal education, for though he did not and would not have advocated elementary-through-college education for all, he stressed the necessity for a common school education for all. Furthermore, Jefferson insisted that the talented youth who were to be screened for secondary schools and colleges were to be selected on intellectual rather than socioeconomic grounds.

That the schools should be secular was a point with which he most heartily agreed. This attitude could have been inferred from his authorship of a bill on religious freedom. It is also apparent in the absence of any mention of religion as a subject of study in primary schools as described in the famous 1817 bill. Central to the idea of a secular school system was its incorporation as an arm of government.

Jefferson's educational ideas were firmly grounded in the philosophy of the eighteenth-century Enlightenment. His philosophical premises which were bulwarked by "rights" and "reason" would have sounded much like those of a Parisian intellectual. However, it was precisely this emphasis on a rationale for schools that pointed up the difference in his ideas from those of the French writers.

Jefferson's plea was for an education through which the people might secure their rights. This kind of education must be managed by the people at the local level. In an 1816 letter to Cabell, he stressed the

---

[11] Claude Eggertsen, "The Primary School of the University of Michigania," *Michigan Alumnus Quarterly Review*, vol. 55, no. 10, p. 39, Dec. 4, 1948. For mention of the Catholepistemiad, see Hinsdale, *op. cit.*, p. 600. Also see Daniel Putnam, *The Development of Primary and Secondary Public Education in Michigan: A Historical Sketch*, George Wahr Publishing Co., Ann Arbor, Mich., 1904, p. 4.

[12] Charles Flinn Arrowood (ed.), *Thomas Jefferson and Education in a Republic*, McGraw-Hill Book Company, Inc., New York, 1930, p. 49.

necessity for local control of schools. He was frankly sceptical of the wisdom of any scheme to put the management of educational institutions in the hands of any central authority, whatever its nature. He implied, instead, that schools would be best off if under the general control of parents.[13] This strong bias for local management of schools stemmed from two sources. When he had been President of the United States, he had been much impressed with the strength of the New England town meeting, which rested on community consensus. He was, in addition, faithful to the Enlightenment theory which said that the province of government was limited to promoting the happiness and protecting the rights of the people.

The only part of Jefferson's educational plan which came to fruition in his lifetime was that relating to the University of Virginia. In various university plans leading to the emergence of the state university, European influences were readily discernible. The governing of the institution as originally proposed provided not for a president, typical American administrative head, but for a rector, a European official, who was a member of the board of visitors and who became, in effect, an administrative head. Hinsdale is also inclined to think that the distinct school of arts and sciences at the University of Virginia was due to French influence.[14]

Other adaptations were made from the College of William and Mary which was, in turn, heavily British in orientation. Jefferson himself acknowledged that Americans should select from European institutions of all kinds "the materials which are *good for us*," and with them to develop institutions suited to American social conditions.[15]

One last European slant on the University of Virginia, on a matter in which Jefferson must have participated, anticipates a late nineteenth-century American practice. This was the importing of professors. After distinguished American instructors had been asked to come to the University of Virginia to no avail, the visitors decided that to secure high-level science professors they must go abroad. Consequently, Francis Walker Gilmer, in the midst of a violent reaction to his mission, was sent in 1824 to Oxford, Cambridge, and to Edinburgh to secure staff. He obtained five men who, with three Americans, made up the first faculty.[16]

This description of a few early national attempts to import British and French organizational and administrative patterns is probably incomplete. As has been said, these attempts have not as yet been adequately

---

[13] *Ibid.*, pp. 66–67.
[14] Hinsdale, *op. cit.*, p. 598.
[15] From letter to Peter Carr in Arrowood, *op. cit.*, p. 75.
[16] *Ibid.*, p. 47.

explored. The description may serve to introduce succeeding and more comprehensive searches abroad.

## PHASE 2: REPORTING ON FOREIGN EDUCATION SYSTEMS AND PRACTICES

A second phase of the search abroad was the reporting of and general interest in foreign school systems. This movement got under way in force when men and women who were interested in promoting the cause of public education began to print educational journals, distribute handbills about education, and petition legislatures in the interests of a publicly supported system of schools. In general, these journals and writings for the most part had their inception in the late 1820s and continued in permanent form when state teachers' associations began to come in. Accounts similar to those found in education journals began to be a regular part of the annual reports of the U.S. Commissioner of Education when that office was created in 1867, and were numerous during the administration of William T. Harris.

In the early nineteenth century, men whose experience had been in the professions or in public life were deeply concerned about an appropriate institutional setting, classroom practices, and learning processes for the new society without tradition. With few guide lines from a still underdeveloped social science, they began to grope around among the educational institutions of many foreign states. Their gropings were recorded to a limited extent in the regular press, which carried accounts of their findings, but more fully in the newly begun journals of education.

In 1826, William Russell of Massachusetts began to edit a journal variously titled the *American Journal of Education,* the *American Annals of Education,* and other titles. This journal, one of the first in the new nation, will suffice to indicate the editorial beginnings of this interesting movement. In Volume I, appearing in 1826, there were these varied accounts. Institutional descriptions were provided for the English infant schools, the French Academy, the University of London, the European monitorial schools, the primary schools in Holland, the University of Edinburgh, the mechanics' institutes in England and France. Accounts of the education systems in Mexico, Buenos Aires, and Scotland were also included in detail. There was also an account of the classical literature and public examinations in English universities. Most astonishing, there was an article on the progress of education among the Hottentots. This was Volume I, but it was little different from the volumes to follow and would have been quite like issues of subsequent education journals in the period before the Civil War. When the

U.S. Office of Education was opened in 1867, accounts of foreign school systems continued to appear in the annual reports.

The movement to describe foreign school systems and practices was strengthened by many public men who deliberately undertook trips abroad for the purpose of reporting back to legislators and school boards on fruitful educational innovations. Some observations of Horace Mann, who is often acknowledged as the father of state educational organization, may serve to introduce a sample of these searches abroad.

After a few years in office as secretary of the Massachusetts Board of Education, Horace Mann turned "to some new quarter of the horizon" to see whether he could spy out "a brighter beam of light." The horizon was in Europe and the brighter beam was assumed to be striking off from the elementary schools of England, Prussia, or Italy. Mann was typical of a bevy of American educators who turned the searchlight on the Continent for an education system. His predecessors could trace their journeys in search of a school system to the beginnings of the 1800s.

*John Griscom*

One of the earliest ventures abroad to observe European ways was made by John Griscom, Quaker, in the years 1818 and 1819. The trip was wholly unofficial, but it seems to have been purposeful. This Quaker schoolmaster and lecturer systematically visited prisons, hospitals, manufactories, charitable institutions, and schools in England, France, Switzerland, Italy, Belgium, Scotland, and Ireland. The story of his trip subsequently went through two editions, and the profits from it were sufficient to pay the expenses of the trip. That its intent was for social service was assumed by a writer in *The North American Review*, January, 1824: "Professor Griscom seems to have gone to Europe in order to be able more effectually to do good, after his return home."[17]

Griscom's account is a delightful record of a charming person's journey into new lands. As such, it will hardly bear summary. However, there are at least two kinds of descriptions which are full and systematic enough to report; at the same time, they will introduce two Europeans who were to make a deep impression on the school men of the nineteenth century.

In Hofwyl, two leagues from Berne, Griscom visited Phillip Emmanuel von Fellenberg and the Hofwyl institutions. He found the famous Swiss educator to be a mild and polite gentleman of middle age who was attempting to institutionalize his own set of educational prin-

---

[17] Account of John Griscom's travels adapted from Edgar W. Knight (ed.), *Reports on European Education* (by John Griscom, Victor Cousin, and Calvin E. Stowe), McGraw-Hill Book Company, Inc., New York, 1930. For quotation, see p. 15.

ciples. Fellenberg's ideas, as described by Griscom, are most illuminating, pointing up a rationale which Americans did not accept and the shell of educational practice which they adopted.

Fellenberg began the account of his institutions with a frank acknowledgment of three classes of society which "would always prevail, in every civilized country." Youngsters in each class should be educated for their station in life, but in accordance with their abilities. At the same time, there should be encouraged a feeling of mutual respect among the several classes.

In accordance with this view of society, the Swiss educator had begun several institutions. One was for the sons of nobles and government officials. The "class of the rich" contained about eighty youngsters, twenty of whom were under ten and were cared for in a separate house, by a couple. The twenty had a teacher or two. The other sixty privileged youngsters were instructed by twenty or more professors. They, likewise, had what was apparently an elaborate plant. The building in which they were accommodated was large, yet two more were under construction. One of the new buildings was to house (besides dormitories) a chapel and a wine cellar; the other, facilities for a riding school, dancing, and exercise. For these youngsters, among whom were princes and sons of ministers of states, there were provided all the accommodations for the education of gentlemen.

Youngsters from the very poorest class were clothed and boarded in the simplest style and instructed largely in the useful arts. They dined on hasty pudding, whey, and boiled potatoes, and breakfasted on bread and apples. Two hours of their summer days and a few more in the winter were given to letters and music. The rest of the time was spent in shop and field, learning the trades of blacksmith, carpenter, shoemaker, and farmer, and raising produce which paid for a part of their maintenance and instruction. They would always occupy the humbler stations in life, so they must be conditioned to simplicity, frugality, and industry and a regard for religion, which was inculcated through hymns. Their instruction was not confined to the schoolroom. Their teacher would seize on every occasion, while they were in shop or field, to question them on natural history, geography, religion, and morals, in order that their minds be expanded and their "best affections" be cultivated. The germ of the manual-labor college was apparent in the Hofwyl institution for the poor.

This picture of the Fellenberg institutions, if reasonably accurate, provides a nice backdrop for assessing what may have been borrowed from the Swiss educator. When the New Englanders got busy in the Old Northwest particularly, they put into practice the manual-labor idea, but with a difference. No one in America need be poor, nor need there be necessarily such a sharp division of classes as was accepted in the manual-labor school of Fellenberg. In America, manual labor became a tool of moral education for any and all youngsters rather than an occupational training for a lower class. The upper-class education as described for Fellenberg's princes never really got started in the United States, except as some mild semblance of it was perpetuated in the Latin grammar schools and certain select private colleges. Even here, however, it was apt to be a humanist education strained through New England puritanism rather than an education for nobles, European style. The much-vaunted effect of Emmanuel von Fellenberg on American education may bear reassessment. For this reexamination, the Quaker Griscom's own comment might provide a starting point: "But the greatest recommendation of the Pestalozzian and Fellenberg plan of education is the moral charm which is diffused throughout all its operations." To American educators, education for work was fast to become not an instrument of class education, but a tool for the development of industrious, intelligent, and responsible citizens.

*Alexander Dallas Bache*

In September, 1836, Alexander Dallas Bache, great-grandson of Benjamin Franklin, set sail with his wife, Ency, and her young sister Maria for Europe. Bache's foreign mission had been commissioned by the board of Girard College, still not established, of which Bache had been chosen president. The board was sending Bache abroad to look at schools and to bring back certain specified information about them. For each school, the emissary was to provide data on history, administration, source and amount of funds, and organization of faculty. He was to inquire into such details as admission requirements, occupational and educational placement, the disciplinary system, recreation, diet and clothing, schedules, and health rules. As far as purely educational matters were concerned, he was to study the curriculum and, in particular, character and religious education and "mechanical instruction."[18]

By the time of his return in October, 1838, Bache had seen "more than 278 schools in the British Isles, France, Switzerland, Belgium, Holland, Italy, and the several German states, including Austria."[19] In addition to his recollections of his studies, he had with him journals and several varieties of notes for his report and much of the educational material, including books and documents, textbooks, scientific apparatus and instruments, and models of machines. Bache, scientist and educa-

---

[18] Account of intent of Alexander Bache's journey and facts of his life adapted from Merle M. Odgers, *Alexander Dallas Bache: Scientist and Educator, 1806–1867,* University of Pennsylvania Press, Philadelphia, 1947.

[19] *Ibid.,* p. 79.

tor, was ready to begin his *Report on Education in Europe* and to enter on his duties as president of Girard College.

Bache entered upon his foreign labors with a judicious, penetrating, and scientific turn of mind. He had recently come from a professorship of natural philosophy and chemistry at the University of Pennsylvania. Before his life was done, he would make notable original contributions in several scientific fields and would play a part in the establishment of the Smithsonian Institution and the founding of the National Academy of Sciences. With his turn of mind, he had not been hurried in his observations of European education, nor would he be pushed into premature conclusions, even though a letter from Nicholas Biddle of his board had expressed impatience with his extended stay. In Hamburg in November, 1837, Bache had recorded in his journal that, after all, his trip had been undertaken for purpose of inquiry. If he were to tell the results of his investigation before he had made it properly, he would be acknowledging that he was blessed with the gift of prophecy. He added that if he could immediately set up Girard College, he would be more than delighted to save his time and proceed to America at once.[20]

Bache did take his time, and he did return home with as comprehensive a survey of foreign schools as has been done by any one man in American education. His volume of over 600 pages is also one of the most orderly accounts of foreign schools.[21] It covered in systematic fashion (1) institutions for the education of orphans and other destitute children; (2) institutions for education in general (largely infant, primary, and elementary schools); (3) schools of the elementary class intended to prepare for some particular occupation in life; (4) seminaries for the preparation of teachers of primary schools; (5) superior schools (universities and special higher schools). The description of schools which prepared for life, including schools of agriculture and industry, as well as the account of institutions for orphans, were probably particularly for his clients, the board of the orphans' college. But Dr. Bache, educator, needed to take a look at the whole sweep of education in order to put his work in context, hence the exhaustiveness of his survey.

Scientist Bache was objective in his reporting, so much so that it is difficult to ascertain what was making an impression on him. In order to discover in what direction his observations may have influenced his future course of action, it is well to take a look at an instance in which he put his tour to use.

[20] *Ibid.*, p. 35.
[21] See Alexander Dallas Bache, *Report on Education in Europe to the Trustees of the Girard College for Orphans*, Lydia R. Bailey, Philadelphia, 1839.

Dr. Bache had impressed the High School Committee of the Board of Public Education of Philadelphia with his plans for reorganization of Central High School. In about 1839 or 1840, he committed these plans to writing.[22] They are now happily bound with a report of the first year's operation of the reorganized school. This latter report was also by Bache, who became principal of the high school. The plans for the reorganization of the school began with some general observations on education. To be complete, said Bache, a system must combine moral, intellectual, and physical education. The moral and the bodily training must be adapted to the age of the student or his constitution of mind and body. Intellectual education, both as to kind and degree, depended on the mental growth of the pupil and his destination in life.

In illustration of the complete education and as a backdrop for his reorganization plans, Bache then sketched and charted secondary schools in Leipzig and Potsdam, the City Trade School in Berlin, and the Industrial School of Berne, Switzerland. He wished his audience to know, however, that even the Prussian system of schools, which was the best known and which did indeed supply a complete education, was disjointed. He wished to guard against the possibility that this disjointedness might become a part of American education. His care in respect to this matter was one of the earlier considerations of articulation, which has plagued American educators ever since.

Bache used the foreign backdrop to good effect in emphasizing the necessity for a complete education. He pointed out the desirability of subjects which were found in foreign schools but not in American institutions. Drawing, which was used to admirable purpose in the Prussian schools, could improve handwriting and contribute to the correctness of eye and hand so valuable for future manufacturers or mechanics. Equally praiseworthy was the efficient teaching of music, particularly in the canton of Berne where school songs had replaced popular songs. "A good voice is said to expose the possessor to many dangers from temptations to conviviality," mused Dr. Bache, "but these are by no means increased by cultivation of music, which rather tends to lead from, than towards what is low."[23]

It is not surprising that Dr. Bache should include drawing in the courses that he projected for the reorganized Central High School. It is also noteworthy that music was not among the required courses, even though the educational planner had paid it high praise.

When Dr. Bache came to set up the courses for the high school, he

[22] See A. D. Bache, *Report to the Controllers of the Public Schools on the Reorganization of the Central High-school of Philadelphia*, High School Committee, Philadelphia Board of Public Education, Philadelphia, 1840?.

[23] *Ibid.*, p. 23.

paid due attention to three programs roughly corresponding to those in three separate types of schools abroad. These were (1) the principal course of four years, which corresponded roughly to the *Realschule* of Prussia; (2) the elementary course of two years, which was perhaps patterned after the higher burgher schools and is known in Europe today as the advanced elementary school; and (3) a classical course of four years, which was designed to prepare for university and was roughly comparable to the program of the *Gymnasium*.

There appear to be few striking differences between these three courses as projected by Dr. Bache, except that there were apparently several levels of work, even though names of subjects might be similar. Foreign languages (French and Spanish) as opposed to the classical languages (Latin and Greek) appeared to be the sole difference between the principal and the classical courses. There was an absence of foreign language in the elementary course. Youngsters in all courses were to have moral lessons, writing, drawing, geography and history, elements of mechanics and natural philosophy, and elements of natural history. All were to be instructed in mathematics, though young people in the elementary course were to be confined to lower mathematics.

What is far more striking than Dr. Bache's European orientation was his typically American modifications of the foreign secondary patterns. This is to be seen when Dr. Bache said, in preface to the course outlines, that he understood the high school to have as its objectives (1) higher elementary education; (2) education preparatory to commerce, manufactures, and useful arts; and (3) a classical course as entrance to college. Dr. Bache was accepting a comprehensive high school in place of the separate institutions he had seen in Europe. Perhaps it was his answer to the "disjointedness" he had noted in the Prussian school system.

Just as striking were his modifications of European admission requirements. To be sure, Bache recommended an admission examination which, in his incumbency at least, was used to screen applicants. But socioeconomic considerations apparently played no part in the entrance requirements, as they would in foreign secondary schools of that day, and a great point was made that the classical course must be offered to accommodate those parents who wished their children to go to the university. Parental choice was to play some part in selection of program, and this choice was to be made not necessarily by privileged parents but by those of any socioeconomic level. The occupations of parents, as listed in the principal's first report, showed that there were among the parents three laborers, a portrait painter, a clerk, a baker, several cordwainers, a merchant, a military storekeeper, and a variety of others. This high school was partly a cosmopolitan American institution.

Dr. Bache, educator and scientist, had observed European schools carefully. From them, he had adapted patterns of education suitable to the American scene. In his adaptations, he showed what he had thought of the practices he had seen. He approved of the way in which individual abilities were taken into account through variation in curricula, but he disapproved thoroughly of the class system which was reflected in school organization. He had borrowed the idea of adaptation to differences and to it he had added additional ideas for broadening school programs by inclusion of new subjects. These ideas he expressed through development not of several class-structured schools, but in a comprehensive high school.

### Calvin E. Stowe

Calvin E. Stowe, professor of Biblical literature at the Lane Theological Seminary and husband of Harriet Beecher Stowe, set out in 1836 for Europe to purchase a library for his seminary. This New Englander, now a resident of Cleveland, was requested by the Legislature of Ohio to collect while in Europe "such facts and information as he may deem useful to the state, in relation to the various systems of public instruction and education" and to "make report thereof . . . to the next General Assembly."[24] In December, 1837, he presented to the Governor and the Legislature of Ohio a *Report on Elementary Public Instruction in Europe*. This very readable report was ordered by the Legislature to be printed in 10,000 copies, which were sent to every school district in the state. Reprints of it were eventually ordered by the legislatures of five states in the East. It mildly rivaled in interest the sensational *Uncle Tom's Cabin* which would appear a dozen years later.

Stowe found that "monarchies have actually stolen a march upon republics in the promotion of popular intelligence." To forestall what had happened in France, enlightened monarchs in Russia, Prussia, and Bavaria, to take only three examples, were energetically instituting wide-scale systems of public education. These systems, well ordered and economical, were addressed among other things to securing the loyalties of subjects to their countries, through "a strong moral power over the understanding and affections of the people." Despite the intent, Stowe found little but good in this evidence of a widespread interest in public education, this educational renaissance which was sweeping not only the old and traditional monarchies, but states in the United States and such places as Arabia, Turkey, Greece, and Egypt. These manifestations appeared to him to indicate that the states of the United

---

[24] Quoted in Knight, *op. cit.*, p. 248. Account of Calvin Stowe's journey is adapted.

States must redouble their efforts so that they be not "exposed to double danger from vice, and neglect of education."

Stowe made some general observations preliminary to his detailed discussion of the schools of Prussia. The first of these had to do with the economy with which the schools were run and the good internal management of the schools. In this latter connection, he noted with pleasure the habits of industry, care, and order which were developed in the youngsters in the boarding schools. He pointed out that the frugality which the system promoted should be made a part of female education.

The inheritor of New England traditions could not but make some general comments on moral instruction and the Bible, and the skill with which the arts of drawing, designing, and music were taught to all youngsters. He inquired of all classes of teachers and of educators of every religious faith and he could find none who would forego moral instruction.

Stowe was interested in teacher education and particularly in an institution for the free education of needy teachers of the poor. He remarked in this connection that people of the United States did not need institutions of this class, for American communities did not "*need* to be poor."

Institutions for reform came in for Professor Stowe's attention and observation also. He noted that these schools were set up often for the most despairing of juvenile delinquents, and he found institutional practices working their wonders. Manual labor, prayer, the Bible and singing, severe punishment, and affectionate conversation worked a reformation among them. Stowe made especial note of such tender interludes as the effect of Christ's love as an incentive to reformation.

It would be assumed that the real purpose of the Legislature's enjoinder to Stowe was to receive information on the management of schools and learning. To meet this requirement, Professor Stowe described in detail the course of instruction in the common schools of Prussia and Württemberg. These had relatively good equipment, most of them having a bathing place, a garden, and a mechanics' shop. With this kind of facilities, a great amount of instruction could go on in the eight years of the elementary course.

In Stowe's simple description, the eight-year program (in four parts of two years each) would have looked much like any other curriculum then or now. Oral teaching, reading, writing, and arithmetic were to be found in the first two years. The three R's were retained in the second two years, and added to them were religious and moral instruction, language or grammar, doctrine of space and form or geometry, and singing by note. The new studies in the fifth and sixth years were real instruction or knowledge of nature and the external world, and ornamental writing preparatory to drawing.  In the fourth part (seventh and eighth years) there was, in addition to subjects retained from earlier years, the application of arithmetic and mathematics to the business of life, including surveying and civil engineering; an extension of the knowledge about the world and mankind, including civil society, elements of law, agriculture, mechanic arts and manufactures; and the science of music.  This curriculum was put into effect by keeping the younger pupils at school but four hours a day; the older pupils, six hours a day.  Each hour of the day was broken with a recess for the younger ones and as often as necessary for the older ones.

The vast amount of instruction in these eight years could be accomplished, according to Professor Stowe, because the teachers were professional people who had been educated for their jobs.  The expertness of the teachers was to be seen in modes of teaching, methodology used, care in concluding each unit before another was begun, and the fine attendance record of the youngsters.  No one who had not seen what could be accomplished by skillful teaching could quite believe it.

When Stowe described the way in which the curriculum operated at the classroom level, he emphasized some of the practices to be pointed out by Horace Mann some six years later.  He spent considerable time in detailing the opening conversations between teachers and pupils, a way of developing vocabulary for later reading and of sharpening youngsters' observations of the world around them.  From these beginning lessons, the youngsters went on to the part-whole method of learning their letters and of writing.  In the former, such devices as flash cards were common; in the latter, posture and form in holding a pen were the subjects of drill.  In arithmetic, Stowe saw no practices not already in use in the United States, and so he did not dwell on methodology in this area.

As the children proceeded through the grades, other kinds of methodologies came into play.  It was not long before children were practicing their writing, including spelling and punctuation, by recording what the teacher dictated to them.  One of the objects of writing in the third and fourth grades was to develop "a neat, swift, business hand."  Religious instruction was given by each teacher in his own way.  Sometimes it consisted of having one or more children read from the Bible, followed by friendly interchanges between the children and the teacher.  Often the teaching would lead to the development of some moral for daily living such as this: "Diligence, scrupulous fidelity and conscientious self-control, are the surest guarantees" in life.  According to Professor Stowe, it was hardly necessary to note that if the teacher who dealt with moral issues were professional, he would avoid sectarian bias and belittling reference to any particular creeds.

Professor Stowe spent some time explaining the teaching of grammar. He likewise outlined what appeared to be a modern social studies program. Stowe called this "real instruction" in the proportions of nature and of the external world. It included work in geography, history, elementary natural science, and the arts of life. The instruction was designed to answer the following questions: What is man both corporeally and intellectually? What does man need for body and mind for preservation and for satisfactory living? Where and how do men find the means to supply their wants and make themselves comfortable and happy in this life? These questions allowed scope for study of the vegetable, mineral, and animal kingdoms, as well as anatomy and physiology, and the Bible, in which the child learned that the Lord God formed man of the dust of the ground.

Stowe closed his description of the system with some comments on its character. He said that the striking features were obvious. The casual observer would note its completeness, both as to the scope of the curriculum and the ease with which it could develop human potential and give it direction. Then he said that the practical nature of the system was also obvious. Every subject was treated with a view to its useful ends. The abstract concepts in the several studies were not presented first, but the teacher proceeded according to nature "from practice to theory, from parts to demonstration." This system educated for participation in daily living activities. A final outstanding feature of the system was the moral and religious instruction. The professor of theology again emphasized that in order to lead a good life, a human being needed a proper moral code. For Calvin Stowe, this was to be found in the New Testament, which was sustained by the authority of God.

After this closing summary, Professor Stowe did battle with hypothetical foes who would say that this was an ideal plan but not practicable. He reiterated that he saw it in operation, and if Prussia could institute it, certainly so could the people of Ohio. The latter had but to say the word, for the voice of the people was stronger in the United States than was the voice of the monarch in Europe.

How would the people get at their task of establishing such a system? Professor Stowe had several recommendations. The first three related to teachers. First, the teacher must be educated for his task if he were to wean himself from textbook and recitation teaching, and learn how to use the developmental methods seen abroad. Dull routine might be satisfactory in Turkey, where the function of the school was to assist the youngsters to pronounce the words of the Koran in meaningless fashion, or in China, where men were bound by stultifying tradition, but it would never do in the United States, where education was dedicated to using the talent of each individual.

If teachers were to be trained, there must be some means of doing so. New institutions need not be opened in view of the fact that institutions already established were not adequately supported. Teacher training departments might be added to all the academies and high schools. In the large towns there might be demonstration schools manned by the most experienced and ablest teachers. Candidates for the teaching profession could act as assistant teachers in such schools.

If teachers were adequately educated for their jobs, then they must be adequately paid. In many district schools, it was not possible to employ men, for there was other and more profitable employment. People of the United States might take a leaf from the notebooks of Russia, Prussia and other European nations where support was given to families of teachers, and the latter were cared for when they were no longer able to teach. Nevertheless, to be practical, in America young women must be persuaded to care for the younger children in elementary school. There was no country in which women were held in such high esteem as in the United States, and for this regard, they should repay their country with service. "Our fair countrywomen," it was fervently to be hoped, would never wish to enter legislative halls; but they could well distinguish themselves by helping young minds open to that which was good and great.

Professor Stowe went on to three more recommendations, two of which had to do with the children. First, they must be made more comfortable, otherwise the poor plant would cancel out all the work of the teacher. Second, children must come completely under the supervision of the school. The teacher must have control of the students. The parent must not deny his child the advantages of a comfortable schoolhouse and a competent teacher.

Last, Professor Stowe comforted his readers by saying that all the reforms could not be carried through at once. They must be introduced gradually. The government should not by fiat institute a school system. Government was most effective when it was used to stimulate citizens to help themselves. The Legislature had already taken a forward step by choosing a state superintendent. His job should be made more profitable to the community by making the appointment like those of the judges of the United States Supreme Court. Foreign-speaking children should be taught in schools in which teachers had facility in English and in the children's native language. Thus the exercises could go forward profitably in two languages. With a few additional polite remarks, Professor Stowe ended his description of European education and its application to American education.

*Horace Mann*

When Mann started for Europe in 1844 to refresh his educational thinking by taking a look at foreign systems, it was obvious that he intended to be selective in what he would recommend to the Massachusetts Board of Education. He needed to be cautious if his previous educational endeavors were not to have been undertaken in vain. There had been criticism from the Legislature on a proposal for teacher training schools on the ground that the latter were Prussian institutions. Educators assumed that the charge was a red herring designed to divert attention from the legislators' dilatory behavior in respect to taxing for such schools. Nevertheless, the secretary of the Massachusetts Board of Education tried to forestall criticism of foreign borrowing by admitting the limitations as well as the advantages of European school systems.[25]

Mann began the account of his 1844 journey with a statement about what he had seen. He said it would be strange if, out of all of the "sound instruction" as well as babbling, there could not be found some hints for American educators. He then elaborated on his argument by saying that some of the evils of American school systems could be seen in even baser form abroad, whereas there were some practices which might well be imitated. An instance of the latter was the Prussian system of reading instruction, which seemed to be superior. Could not Americans adopt this system without adopting the Prussian's blind obedience to government and his equally "blind adherence to the articles of the church"? With this bow to local prejudice, Mann proceeded to give his estimate of the foreign school systems.

One would have thought there might have been a lingering sentimentalism over English education, which had been a first inspiration for American colonial practices. Not so. The energetic and systematic secretary deplored the system of England, which he found to be partial or lacking, and both inadequate and expensive. This educational pattern, which put a premium on local and private effort, enforced class differences. As a consequence, contrasts between the classes were appalling. On the one hand, the visitor found in the upper classes people of wealth and refinement, products of the best of the English schools. On the other hand, here was the vast mass of the people in ignorance and poverty and spawning all manner of crime. Mann found that there were available for education about £500,000, but the distribution of the funds was so poor that 1½ million youngsters were left in total ignorance.

Mann was moving in his own thinking toward what today is called

[25] Account of The Journey adapted from Mann, *op. cit.*

"equal opportunity for all." He rejected in general the whole of the English education system. Not only were very different amounts of money available for the education of children in different schools, areas, and classes, but there were the same inequalities in teachers' salaries. The only group of children who appeared to be faring better than those in the United States were the ones in the wealthy private schools of England, and even they had inferior fittings in their school buildings.

Although Mann visited many countries on the Continent as well as Scotland, he reserved most of his praise, as did other American educators, for the Prussian system. He duly took note of the criticisms which had been leveled at the importation of items from that aristocratic and authoritarian culture and saved until the last of his report a counterargument to the prevailing one, for he had seen many practices worthy of emulation.

Most surprising of all these praiseworthy practices was one which a visitor would hardly have expected to find in Prussia. This was the relatively mild discipline. There was little or no corporal punishment. It was possible to control youngsters by kindness and good lesson planning rather than by the ferule.

The first element of superiority in Prussian schools, however, was in the classification of pupils. It was clear to see, from Mann's enthusiasm, the direct line of ancestry of the American graded system. Such superiority in educational practice was followed by an almost equal superiority in the teaching of reading and grammar.

The schools of Prussia were using the developmental method. Teachers began their reading lessons with conversations about familiar things. They did this without having books in their hands and they continued to hear lessons without any visible props for their own security. Only after small youngsters had developed a vocabulary and an awareness of their environment did they have their attention turned to the printed word, which was taught to them through phonics. Accompanying this superior method of teaching reading through concentrating on familiar things were texts which dealt with real things. Prussian reading books avoided the oratorical, sentimental, and poetic material to be found in American books and concentrated instead on science and useful subjects. All in all, American educators could well take a look at Prussian school practices.

The Massachusetts secretary took a look at institutions other than regular elementary schools. He visited many orphanages, tolls of the long line of European wars, as well as the prison schools, with which he was much impressed. His fancy was taken with education for the deaf and mute. In the United States the latter would have been taught the sign language, which would have handicapped the users in communicating with any except their own kind. The Prussian institutions, on the other hand, were teaching youngsters to lip-read, a very superior practice.

Only one German practice struck Mann as distressing. This was the use of feather beds, particularly in boarding schools. If German rulers wished to depress their subjects utterly so that they would never yearn for liberty, they should continue to promote poor ventilation and sleeping between feather beds. All in all, however, the secretary had much wisdom to relay to his board.

*Other Reporters*

Although the reporters of foreign education were, in the period from 1820 to 1860, numerous and varied, they for the most part described in attenuated fashion the same systems as those comprehensively reported by Stowe, Mann, and Bache. Two more reports, however, deserve mention.

In 1854 Henry Barnard published a thick volume on national education in Europe. It purported to be an account of the organization, administration, instruction, and statistics of public schools of different grades in the principal states.[26] This volume, which had been published in part in 1851, was not of the same character as the other reports. Like the others it was based in part on observations made by the author while on a tour of Europe in the year 1835–1836. But it had been supplemented, according to Barnard himself, from materials in reports such as those already summarized. The completed volume appeared at a time when foreign education systems were not quite as burning an issue with legislators as they had been. Whatever use Barnard expected to put his personal observations to, they probably would have been done more adequately piecemeal and in educational journals. His volume does serve, however, as a token of the continuing interest in foreign education.

Although an account of the next work probably does not belong in this section because it is not the work of an American, the impact of Victor Cousin's volume on American educators and legislators demands inclusion here.[27] It was Sarah Austin's translation of the Frenchman's work for an English audience that found its way into a New York edition in 1835. Subsequently, it was said to have impressed John D. Pierce, first head of the Michigan public school system, and Isaac E. Crary, chairman of the committee on education in the Michigan con-

---

[26] Henry Barnard, *National Education in Europe: Being an Account of the Organization, Administration, Instruction, and Statistics of Public Schools of Different Grades in the Principal States*, 2d ed., published for the author by Case, Tiffany, & Co., Hartford, Conn., 1854.

[27] Account of Victor Cousin's report adapted from Knight, *op. cit.*

stitutional convention. Cousin's report is said also to have impressed Charles Brooks, James G. Carter, and Horace Mann in Massachusetts. Victor Cousin, who had been born in Paris in 1792, was serving as lecturer at the University of Paris when he made a trip to Germany in 1831 to study the public school system. His report was subsequently made to the Count de Montalivet, peer of France, Minister of Public Instruction and Ecclesiastical Affairs. In 1832 he was subsequently appointed a member of the Royal Council of Public Instruction in Francois Pierre Guillaume Guizot's ministry. Cousin became Minister of Public Instruction in 1840 and continued at the same time as director of the Normal School.

Cousin carried with him official letters of introduction. In consequence of this and partly also through the aid of one of the Prussian minister's confidential councilors, he had all doors open to him. Both printed sources and manuscripts were available to him, and he could verify official accounts through his own observations. His account, according to Knight, is very convincing.

Cousin's report dealt with the general organization of public instruction, primary instruction, secondary instruction, and higher education. He dwelt especially on elementary education, teacher training, and the organization and administration of public education, these being the items of chief concern in the reorganization of French education. The report led to the French law of 1833, and came to have importance for English education, also.

Edgar W. Knight, historian of education, was inclined to believe that Cousin's report was one of the most important published in the second quarter of the nineteenth century.

PHASE 3:
IMPORTING GRADUATE EDUCATION

A third phase of the search abroad for an educational pattern was largely confined to the colleges. It involved the importing of foreign scholars in hope of building the graduate and the professional schools. This phase included sending young Americans to Europe for graduate training in order that they might come back to man the graduate departments.

"The American graduate school was a nobly conceived institution; it is now a mere post-graduate catch-all,"[28] said Henry Suzzallo in 1931. Whether it is indeed a catchall or a very useful and largely American

[28] Henry Suzzallo, "The Enquiring Mind" in *Trends in Graduate Work; A Program Commemorating The Thirtieth Anniversary of the Founding of the Graduate College of The State University of Iowa*, John W. Ashton (ed.), University of Iowa Studies, new series no. 194 and series on aims and progress of research, no. 33, p. 65, January 1, 1931.

institution, the graduate school does have noble origins in a kingdom, and in the same system which gave Stowe, Mann, and others so much educational stimulation. The conceptual pattern and many of the first teachers of the American graduate school were German. They were supplemented by both ideas and men from Scotland and England and occasionally, France. The graduate school can be counted as an import if the reader notes that it bears little resemblance to present-day graduate schools.

The beginnings of the German influence in higher education can be traced to American students who studied in the German universities in the period from about 1780 to 1850. It must be remembered that American college graduates who would be eligible for study abroad would be small in percentage terms, and that they would in the antebellum period be forced to take many parts—as scholars, educators, government leaders, and professional people, including clergymen. Whatever might happen to turn the direction of their thought would eventually come to have some bearing on the direction of social and political events in this country.

That the numbers of such students was considerable, considering the poverty and practical bent of Americans, is attested to by the names of American students listed by Hinsdale as studying in German universities.[29] He described among these students George Ticknor, later to be professor of modern languages at Harvard—and he was only one of many studying at Göttingen in the pre-Civil War period. There were students at Leipzig, the Royal Friedrich Wilhelm University, and the University of Halle. Ticknor is, in a sense, a symbol of these students. He was later to take a stand with Jefferson for the elective system in colleges. Like many of those who went abroad, he was convinced of the necessity of specialization as a prerequisite to scholarship.

Despite these early students abroad, it is considered that foreign influence in the development of higher education was at its peak when presidents of so-called universities were ready to make their institutions in fact universities, by inaugurating graduate study.

There had been graduate work in a scattering of institutions before the Civil War. Henry P. Tappan had developed both the elective system and graduate study in the University of Michigan. To inaugurate the latter, he had brought to the campus Francis Brunnow, the German astronomer, and several other American scholars who were to become presidents of American universities.[30] Tappan's work was anticipatory

[29] See Hinsdale, op. cit., p. 603 ff.
[30] Richard Hofstadter and C. DeWitt Hardy, The Development and Scope of Higher Education in the United States, Columbia University Press, New York, 1952, p. 62. Published for the Commission on Financing Higher Education.

rather than a firm beginning, however. Graduate study would begin in earnest only in the late 1860s and in the last quarter of the nineteenth century when Harvard, Cornell, Johns Hopkins, and others of the present-day great universities would have begun their programs. The age of the university, the last thirty years of the nineteenth century, was ushered in by a succession of great university presidents who turned to the development of research, scholarly and specialized study, and professional schoools and colleges. Where were they to find teachers for their new enterprises, and how were they to set them up? Answers to these questions were found in a special kind of exchange, and in methodological and institutional borrowing.

Professors were crucial to the success of the new enterprises. Consequently, there began a long succession of transoceanic journeys. Young and promising instructors were sent abroad to Halle, Leipzig, Oxford, Cambridge, and many of the other honored institutions. Presidents of American institutions made trips abroad to raid the same universities. When David Starr Jordan was still president of Indiana University, he made it known that it was important to secure faculty who had lived in and understood the Middle West, but he also required his provincials to take advanced training in Eastern or European universities. Henry Tappan was of the opinion that "as the republic of letters overlaps national boundaries," American universities might well augment their staffs with foreign scholars. Harper of Chicago reached out to Freiburg for a historian; Eliot of Harvard, to Göttingen for a professor of philosophy and to Königsberg for an entomologist. The sentiments of the great presidents might be summed up in a statement of Andrew D. White, president of Cornell University. He reported that he secured a professor of history, Goldwin Smith, at Oxford, and a veterinary scientist, Dr. James Law, from Scotland. As a consequence, much fun was made at his expense, to the effect that he had employed "an Oxford professor and a Scotch horse-doctor." White insisted that the selections had been most propitious.[31]

A somewhat more nebulous movement was going on while professors were changing institutions. Professors and presidents, as well as interested friends, were searching for libraries, documents, and equipment, and those interested in graduate study were borrowing the methodologies of advanced study. Charles William Eliot on his trip to Europe from 1863 to 1865, before he had become president of Harvard, "displayed an insatiable curiosity about organization and methods employed in educational institutions, including how floors were laid and how the *lycées*

---

[31] Gladys A. Wiggin, "Selecting and Appraising Personnel," in Harold Benjamin (ed.), *Democracy in the Administration of Higher Education*, Harper & Brothers, New York, 1950, pp. 136–138.

kept their systems of accounts." He secured for the department of literature a large order of books and periodicals from Germany.[32] He was typical of those who were importing instruments, plans for laboratories, and techniques. Among the latter, the three presently identified with advanced study—the lecture, the seminar, and independent research— were said to have had much favor with Americans abroad.

Toward the end of the nineteenth century, a movement stimulated by the great university presidents would eventually give way to a typical American institution, the junior college, but even that had roots in Europe. Two kinds of phenomena impinged on the thinking of the university men. First, they were interested in the fact that on the Continent much of the liberal arts education they found in American colleges was actually a part of the elite secondary school, which European young people were wont to attend until they were nineteen. The European university could then dispense with baby-sitting activities in favor of working with mature students in specialized research. At the same time, it was borne in upon the university presidents and people in the school system that somewhere along the educational ladder there was a wasted year or two.

With these two kinds of facts in mind, the university presidents began to argue for a junior college with a largely prescriptive curriculum roughly comparable to that in operation in the liberal arts colleges, but they asked that this lower division be attached to the high school. They hoped on the one hand that the wasted year would be squeezed out of the public school system; on the other hand, they hoped that the universities could be freed for elective programs of specialized research or professional work.

The great university presidents ordinarily saw farther than their own institutions. Most of them had broader plans for the junior college than preparation for advanced work at a university. Nevertheless, part of their argument for the separation of the lower-division school revolved around improvement of their own institutions. President Harper of Chicago discussed in 1903 the reorganization of elementary and secondary work, with the latter to include the first two years of college. Some of his arguments for this reorganization were that it was already being done in foreign countries; it would lift standards for professional schools; and it would save time, allowing the abler students (for whom the time in secondary school might be reduced) to get to work earlier.[33]

In 1852 Henry Tappan had pointed out that two years of general college training would be offered in the larger municipalities of the state. In 1883, the University of Michigan adopted an instructional plan

---

[32] *Ibid.*, p. 135.
[33] William Rainey Harper, "The High School of the Future," *The School Review,* vol. II, no. 1, pp. 1–3, February, 1903.

which recognized a separate function for the first two years of college. The latter were to be organized around general requirements for all. For the last two college years, the student would be assigned to a committee which would plan an individual and specialized program for him. The plan was abandoned when the committee work got too heavy. The university did go on to encourage, and eventually to recognize as acceptable, work in separate junior colleges providing the latter were approved by the university.[34]   As late as 1915, James R. Angell explored, via a questionnaire, the feelings of colleges and universities about junior colleges.   University people were more enthusiastic than four-year college people about the institution.   Junior colleges deprived the four-year colleges of students, but relieved pressure on universities, allowing them to carry on their function.[35]   In 1916, H. R. Brush reported the results of a questionnaire which indicated again that university people were of the opinion that junior colleges reduced overcrowding in the freshman and sophomore years; helped to free the universities for advanced work; stimulated conservative university faculties to do better teaching; and generally raised standards.[36]   By this time, of course, the junior college was changing so that it would soon bear little resemblance to the European elite secondary school; but it was, nevertheless, still considered in much the same way as the secondary school by the university faculties, and the latter had inadvertently helped, through their European commitments, to reinforce an American institution.

## AN EVALUATION OF THE SEARCH ABROAD
## FOR EDUCATIONAL PATTERNS

The effects of European philosophical and psychological ideas on American education are recounted in many a text on education. Whether the search for institutional and organizational patterns as described here has had an effect on United States schools and colleges is highly speculative.   Some evidence will be presented respecting the school system at large and the colleges and universities.

### European Influences on the Organization and Administration of the School System

The first question which arises is whether there was any impact at all from the numerous trips abroad and the accounts in education journals

[34] Arthur Andrews, "Development of Junior Colleges in Michigan," *The Junior College Journal*, vol. 2, no. 9, pp. 513–522, June, 1932.
[35] James R. Angell, "The Junior-college Movement in High Schools," *The School Review*, vol. 23, no. 5, pp. 289–302, May, 1915.
[36] H. R. Brush, "The Junior College and the Universities," *School and Society*, vol. 4, pp. 357–365, Sept. 2, 1916.

in the antebellum period. The opinions of distinguished American educators have been sharply divided, for instance, on the single point of grading as a heritage from Prussia. F. F. Bunker and Charles H. Judd inclined to an affirmative answer; but Paul Monroe, I. L. Kandel, and E. P. Cubberly tended to discount any such influence. In pursuit of an answer to this question, Frederick Dean McCluskey turned out a first-class mystery story.[37]

The first clue in McCluskey's story comes in connection with the Western Literary Institute which had been organized in Ohio, a center of reforms. Samuel Lewis, first superintendent of Ohio schools, was a member of this institute and helped to get attention for Calvin E. Stowe's report on European education. Presumably at the urging of Lewis, Stowe reported directly to the institute on the subject of Prussian education at its seventh annual meeting in 1838. Following this report, the Cincinnati city school reports for 1838 and 1839 carried a discussion of grading and graded schools. As an addendum to this movement, it is recalled that Horace Mann visited Cincinnati in 1840 and four years prior to his own trip abroad.

McCluskey finds the second clue in the Common School Convention held in Hartford, Connecticut, in August, 1839. To this convention came Stowe of Ohio; Everett, Cushing, and George B. Emerson of Boston; and Henry Barnard of Connecticut. Stowe talked on the Cincinnati schools. Following this meeting, Barnard discussed in the *Common School Journal* for November, 1839, the matter of improving schools by grading. He followed this discussion with a report to his board in May, 1840, on grading. He remarked that several systems at home and abroad had adopted the grading system.

From Ohio and Connecticut, the story now shifts to Massachusetts, where some of the most far-reaching changes were made in the 1830s and 1840s. To introduce the nature of these changes, it is necessary to know something of the district system in effect prior to 1830. That system operated almost wholly under local authority. Without much attempt at classification of pupils, district schools enrolled people from the ages of four to twenty-one years.

One of the first attempts to change the system was made in 1830 by Charles Brooks of the distinguished American Institute of Instruction. Along with another member, W. C. Woodbridge, Brooks had been a recent visitor abroad, and now lectured to the institute on Prussian

---

[37] The answer to the divided opinion has been provided by Frederick Dean Mc-Cluskey from whose work the account of grading has been adapted. Frederick Dean McCluskey, "Introduction of Grading into the Public Schools of New England," *The Elementary School Journal*, part I, vol. 21, no. 1, pp. 34–46, September, 1920; and part II, vol. 21, no. 2, pp. 132–145, October, 1920.

normal schools. He followed up this speech in 1835 by securing the publication of the Cousin report. With Brooks's help and that of Woodbridge, and on behalf of the institute, George B. Emerson in 1836 wrote two memorials to the Massachusetts Legislature. The memorials referred to Prussian and French education, and the separate departments of education. Following these memorials, the Legislature established state normal schools (European institutions) in 1836, and decreed a state superintendency (mark of European centralization of school authority) in 1837. These acts prepared the way for establishing the board of education and the first normal school in 1837 and 1838.

In this drive to change the schools of Massachusetts and particularly of Boston, Edmund Dwight, businessman, was prominent. His decision to work for the changes in schools came after he had read Cousin's report, according to his own story. With his help, plus that of all others who had worked on changes, the first union schools with graded classes were established in Massachusetts in 1838.

Following on the establishment of the union schools inspired by European examples, the fight was on in Massachusetts. The legislators made the charge that the new board established in 1837 was trying to Prussianize the public schools. By order of the House, its committee on education was directed in 1840 to consider abolishing the Massachusetts Board of Education and the normal schools. In accordance with the directive, the committee found that it was the aim of the board to remodel the schools on the French and Prussian systems. These latter systems, said the committee, had central boards and promoted uniformity and discipline, whereas Americans had clung to local administration of schools and confidence in their employees. The committee saw in the establishment of a board of education the beginnings of a centralized control of education, which was a source of danger to democratic institutions.

When committee members came to the normal schools, however, they admitted that they must approach them with some delicacy, inasmuch as one-half of the support for the schools came from private funds. All this was the majority report. Significantly, the minority report of the committee did not deny any of the majority's charges but instead pointed out that, during the Revolutionary War, Americans borrowed a system of military tactics. Why not also borrow school practices?

The minority report finally prevailed and brought on the wrath of the Boston schoolmasters. Running parallel to the investigations of the committee was a continuous movement of Massachusetts school men dedicated to carrying on after the committee's work was done. At the Hartford convention in 1839, George B. Emerson described first the old Boston graded system in which the first grade was the primary schools, the second grade was the grammar and writing (double-headed) schools, and the third grade was the Latin grammar and the English high schools. Then he described a grading system which was very different in plan and intent, ostensibly the European graded system. This latter scheme required thoroughness in study and promoted emulation and competition. It was obviously superior.

Following Emerson's report, the Haverhill School was opened as an experiment in the graded school, with the proviso that there would no longer be a place for the age span from five to twenty-one. Then came Mann's *Seventh Annual Report*, after which grading was introduced into the Boston grammar schools. Finally, there was the Quincy Grammar School, which the board decided to make a single-headed school in 1847. By this it meant a school with a single room to a teacher and youngsters classified roughly according to age and ability. This new kind of class carried the stamp of approval of William T. Harris, who talked of it as requiring an architectural innovation in the design of school buildings and as a way to reduce corporal punishment. In connection with the latter subject, he said that for 700 pupils, the ordinary number of cases of corporal punishment averaged 500 per week under the old ungraded system; under the new, it had been reduced to 3 cases per week. Grading was here to stay.

McCluskey has made a case for the influence of foreign systems on antebellum educational leaders in New England and the states of the Old Northwest. The depth of that influence is still in question. School leaders were looking for ways to build up state school systems. Did they adopt French and Prussian systems, or did they take elements which appeared to them to be meritorious and adapt them to the American scene? Did they merely receive support for their own predilections? The force of the foreign influence will probably never be fully known. In the meantime, it can be said that, barring other evidence, a knowledge of French and German school practices may have reinforced the establishment of certain organizational and institutional patterns in American education.

First, there may have been some reinforcement of the final authority in school affairs—the state as against the local district. Concurrently, a knowledge of foreign practices may have strengthened the claims for state boards of education and state superintendents of public instruction. Note that the more centralized systems of education are apt to flourish in older states which would have felt the initial impact of investigation of foreign systems in the antebellum period. Note, also, that local American school districts have ordinarily retained more authority than have local units in foreign school systems, except for those in England.

To French normal schools and Prussian teacher training institutions, Americans may owe their separate system of teachers' colleges. They began in much the same way as similar institutions were developed abroad. They were originally set up for elementary schoolteachers, for whom foreign countries also established separate institutions. They began as departments in academies; progressed to two-year normal schools in the second quarter—particularly in the last half—of the nineteenth century; and eventually became four-year colleges for both elementary and secondary teacher education in the twentieth century.

That the normal schools were originally planned for elementary teachers only is a mark of the class system of Europe, which made a distinction in teacher institutions because they also made a distinction in school systems for the lower classes. Because the class system of a poor boys' elementary school supported by a poor boys' normal school did not fit the American scene, the American normal school changed in organization and status. Finally, such education became incorporated in separate colleges in universities, a pattern which is typically American and not yet to be found very widely dispersed in European countries. A graduate-school education for educators was added in the twentieth century—again an American innovation not to be found in many European systems of education.

A final generalization respecting possible influence of foreign systems on American education relates to the effect of classification on youngsters and schoolroom practices. American educators were indeed moving toward more efficient systems of education. Grading, which called for the one-room-to-a-teacher plan, appeared to them to have advantages over the monitorial system, which they also imported from Europe and found wanting, and over their own system of grading, with undifferentiated age and ability groupings. The early nineteenth-century study hall, surrounded by small classrooms for recitation with the teacher who manned the study hall, gradually gave way to the Prussian system of a single age or ability group for each teacher. Some stimulation to improved techniques, particularly in respect to the teaching of reading, probably came to American education. Methods for disciplining youngsters without resort to corporal punishment may have been a foreign importation. When these practices were subjected to research—as they would be in the last of the nineteenth century—they would be influenced indirectly by philosophical and psychological considerations which, though European in origin, were more heavily exploited in the United States. The American school system seems indeed to have imported, but the origins of the imports are hardly recognizable in the twentieth century.

*European Influences on the Organization and*
*Administration of Higher Education*

Conclusions respecting the foreign impact on higher education are in much the same state of confirmation as those in elementary and secondary education. Certainly university presidents looked abroad when they were building their graduate schools. That they liked what they saw can be attested to by the persistence with which American professors studied and received degrees abroad. In his study of American scientists, Visher found that, of those considered outstanding in 1903, 127 had received doctorates in universities abroad, notably Berlin, Göttingen, Heidelberg, Leipzig, Munich, and Würzburg. Of the 1903 group, the number receiving degrees from six German universities was almost as great as the number receiving degrees at all American universities. Harvard and Johns Hopkins were excepted from the list. Of the 758 scientists named as outstanding in the period 1932 to 1943, 124 received their doctorates in foreign universities, attesting to the persistence of foreign training for scholars in American universities.[38] Of the 53 professors and lecturers on the Johns Hopkins staff in 1884, nearly all had studied at German universities, and 13 had their doctoral degrees from such institutions.[39]

The study abroad and the importing of foreign scholars are straws in the wind. In what directions did the straws blow? Toward the general outline of the graduate school and the development of the junior college may be the answer. In connection with the graduate school, it is said that Americans imported the idea of the university as a place for mature scholars to pursue specialization and research; this led, in turn, to the establishment of the junior college to take care of the prescribed liberal arts training of the first two college years. John W. Burgess, Columbia University political scientist, argued in 1884 that the American college was an educational deviate: it was incapable of becoming a university and its personnel were opposed to its becoming a *Gymnasium.* Burgess believed that the college ought to go out of existence.[40] The college did not die, nor did the universities wholly follow the European mold. They changed first the rationale under which foreign graduate study operated, and then the institution itself.

[38] Stephen Sargent Visher, *Scientists Starred, 1903–1943, in American Men of Science: A Study of Collegiate and Doctoral Training, Birthplace, Distribution, Backgrounds, and Developmental Influences,* Johns Hopkins Press, Baltimore, Md., 1947, pp. 277–278.
[39] Richard Hofstadter and Walter P. Metzger, *The Development of Academic Freedom in the United States,* Columbia University Press, New York, 1955, p. 377.
[40] *Ibid.,* p. 379.

Freedom to teach and freedom to learn were the watchwords of the nineteenth-century German university. The former was peculiarly restricted, however. It was an "inner freedom," that is, confined to university halls, in which it was all-embracing. It encompassed the right to pursue whatever problems were deemed advisable to inquire into and embraced the right of professors to persuade students to their points of view. "Outer freedom," the right of the professor to say what he thought in public life, was discreetly foregone by German scholars, who believed it the better part of wisdom to refrain from comment about the course of social and political events in a monarchy.

Students likewise had a kind of freedom. As they were mature individuals and not seventeen-year-old freshmen, they had the right to seek out the institutions in which they would like to study and to pursue such specialties as they were fitted for. Their freedoms, of course, were circumscribed by the limitations set on university entrance.

Some flavor of these freedoms probably filtered over to the United States. Of the leaders and victims in academic-freedom cases up to the time of World War I, a goodly number had studied in Germany.[41] Nevertheless, it was the spirit rather than the substance of the German freedoms and practices which came to the United States.

The American professor, like his fellow citizens in all walks of life, was an American first and as such he needed to speak his mind in meetinghouse and hall on all manner of subjects. Furthermore, he operated in a typically American institution, one controlled by a lay board. The focus of attention of American educators became not educational, but institutional. Did the American professor have the right to declare himself in public? And how, as a research man, could he operate effectively in an institution controlled by persons who knew nothing of research?[42] These became pressing problems in American institutions of higher education. The freedom of the student was given short shrift, because American professors found that they had to deal with the immature as well as the mature students.

That the American student was dispossessed is a clue to what happened to American universities. Instead of relegating junior college work to the European-type secondary school, university administrators found they had to keep what lower-division work they had and add more. American universities developed into collections of colleges in which undergraduate instruction was of first moment; graduate instruc-

[41] *Ibid.*, p. 396.
[42] Much of the above discussion is influenced by the writing of Visher, *ibid.*, chap. VIII. For German freedoms, see also Lyle Vernon Mayer, "A Study of German Universities in the American Zone of Occupation, 1945 to 1953," unpublished doctoral dissertation, University of Maryland, College Park, Md., 1954.

tion became an appendage to an undergraduate and professional institution, and in consequence became oriented in the direction of advanced subject-matter preparation rather than research, though the latter was retained in the university proper.

The student lost his freedom, in one sense, but he gained it in another. The American professor, guided by his memory of the Bill of Rights, refused to perform the function of persuading the student, either undergraduate or graduate. He could demand conformity of the student only where incontrovertible facts were concerned and in connection with program planning, though election remained a practice in American education. The intellectual orientation of the American professor in respect to his student was one of neutrality rather than authority. The graduate school did indeed become a catchall for programs having many purposes; the German scholarly student, with freedom to learn but under strict control of the professor, became in the American adaptation both a charge and a peer of professors who were under obligation to protect his right to freedom of intellectual choice.

## SUMMARY

In the search for an appropriate educational pattern for the new nation, Americans looked abroad in the period from the beginning of the United States to the last of the nineteenth century. This quest had three phases, beginning with a hunt for institutional patterns in England and France, continuing with a reporting of organizational and administrative arrangements in several European countries, and ending with a search for European university practices. It is possible that American educators used many elements of the patterns they found abroad; but as educators increased in numbers and professionalization, they turned to the development of a unique American system for the unique American nation. To this development the next four chapters are devoted.

# 6

# Professionals Chart a Course:
# The Age of Committees (1890–1918)

> While seeking to evoke the distinctive excellencies of individuals and groups of individuals, the secondary school must be equally zealous to develop those common ideas, common ideals, and common modes of thought, feeling, and action, whereby America, through a rich, unified, common life, may render her truest service to a world seeking for democracy among men and nations.[1]
>
> COMMISSION ON THE REORGANIZATION
> OF SECONDARY EDUCATION, 1918

Educators and laymen alike had attempted to find bits and pieces of a school system in Europe. These were at some times systematically and at others haphazardly woven into the fabric of the American educational enterprise. By the time of the Civil War, patchwork educational systems stretching from elementary school to meager normal schools and universities were in operation in states above the Mason-Dixon Line. In these states, parents and educators had managed to shepherd most of the youngsters of elementary school age into the common school. But academies and high schools together were enrolling only a limited number of youth, and colleges and universities, very few indeed. The outlines of state systems, however, were clearly apparent.

In most Southern states, with such notable exceptions as North Carolina, systematic development would have to await both reconstruction and recovery. Patterns, however, were available and would begin to be established more firmly in the period from the Civil War to 1900.

[1] U.S. Office of Education, *Cardinal Principles of Secondary Education: A Report of the Commission on the Reorganization of Secondary Education,* Bulletin 1918, no. 35, 1918, p. 32. Commission appointed by the National Education Association.

The chief problem, then, in schooling a nation from about 1890 on was not so much to organize systems as to develop a curriculum for Americans.

Foreign imports had been sufficient to the day, but the late nineteenth and the twentieth centuries were a new era in which educators would see their problems as uniquely American in origin and needing unique American solutions. The society was becoming more complex at an astonishing rate.

The population was changing radically also. In 1860, in sheer numbers, it was 31,443,321; by 1900, it was 75,994,575, an increase of 140 per cent. More difficult for educators was the fact that the percentage of urban as against rural dwellers had changed from 19.8 in 1860 to 39.7 in 1900; and numbers of youngsters in the eligible school ages were increasing rapidly. In 1880, children five to fourteen years old numbered 12,194,846 and by 1900, they had jumped to 16,954,357, an increase of 39 per cent in the short span of twenty years.[2]  These changes in population were but portents of far-reaching social and economic changes which called for reassessment of a schooling for Americans and forging a curriculum which would fit increasingly diverse youngsters and an increasingly complex society. Educators addressed themselves to this problem at the national level in the period from 1890 to 1918.

BACKGROUNDS OF
CURRICULUM REFORM (1860–1900)

In 1902, John Dewey described the process of curriculum revision which had obtained to the year of his writing. Processes rather than a process characterized the events which had transpired and anticipated the multiple forces found to be at work. On the one hand, according to Dewey, were the educators, both liberal and conservative. On the other hand was the public, handily divided into liberal and conservative factions. Liberals on the professional and lay sides of the fence would achieve a minor victory by sneaking in the curricular back door some of the newer subjects (art, music, industrial arts) calculated to contribute to the development of that mysteriously proportioned "whole" child. Liberals would have their day, if a brief one, until conservative parents and educators alike worked up enough concern for the fundamentals (the three R's and the disciplines) so that they could swing the curricular pendulum in the direction of the older emphases. The latter, however, never quite disturbed the new education, which was still to be found tucked in among reading, declamation, and mental

<hr>

[2] Population figures taken from U.S. Bureau of the Census, *Census of Population: 1950*, vol. II, *Population 1952*.

arithmetic. Thus the curriculum (a set of subjects) had developed by alternating pressures, each of which left untouched any new additions which had accrued in the meantime.

"New wine in old bottles," according to Dewey, had had the inevitable effect of bursting out the seams of the curriculum without actually achieving any fundamental changes in the conditions under which the educative process went forward.[3] Dewey saw a new day dawning, however, and so also did educators who had already inaugurated the era of national committees.

## Socioeconomic Backgrounds of Reform

The new day, if it indeed were one, had desperately needed in-auguration since the Civil War, for that event, in addition to its devastating effects on the American people, had signaled also the closing of the agrarian hand-tool age, and the opening of the industrial power-tool era. Slums and machines, monopoly and competitive capitalism, agrarian revolution and human evolution were some of the keys to the new American scene. Following in their wake were floods of new immigrants whose children would swell the schools with both students and problems.

Aside from the reshaping of these schools by youth from new sub-cultures and by an urban-technological society, their nature would change in less obvious ways. The heyday of the frontiersman's log-cabin college was almost over. The educational enterprise needed to support an industrial society would henceforth be big enterprise, sup-ported by increasing public monies and by substantial private gifts and foundations. The intrepid souls with big ideas and small pocketbooks who had begun the schools in the Old Northwest would give way to legislators and millionaires. Ministers and local idealists of modest means who had served on boards of schools and colleges would yield their places to those calculated to do the schools the most good—businessmen and lawyers and other men of substance in their com-munities.

The school enterprise had in one sense been readied for the change in its nature and control. Above the Mason-Dixon Line, public support of elementary schools through the university had been reasonably well established. Brushes with the law experienced by advocates of public secondary education in the 1870s would only reinforce more firmly the principle of tax support. Men of large fortune would soon get in the habit of giving substantial endowments to open such new universities as

---

[3] John Dewey, The Educational Situation, Contributions to Education, no. 3. University of Chicago Press, Chicago, 1902.

Stanford, Chicago, Cornell, and Johns Hopkins, and legislators would extend their largess to state-controlled colleges and universities.

In another sense, however, the school men were unprepared for both expansion in student populations and change in the objectives of school programs. They had spent their energies in getting the plant under way, staffing the increasing institutions, and professionalizing their membership. They were dealing, too, with a public which had long accustomed itself to a finger in the pie, so that there would never come a day when professionals would be quite free to build a school system. It was in this setting of sharp change in socioeconomic forces and continuous public intervention in school business that the curriculum got out of hand in the period from 1860 to 1900.

### The Elementary School Curriculum
(1860–1900)

The early reports of the United States Commissioner of Education are replete with statistics and brief descriptions of particular school systems, but singularly lacking in surveys of country-wide practices in education at any level. Perhaps, in view of the local control of education, a comprehensive statement can never be made.

The closest approximation to such a statement about the elementary school program in the late nineteenth century was made in connection with a survey of selected city systems in about the year 1888–1889 by a specialist in the U.S. Office of Education.[4] However, caution must be used in generalizing for all elementary schools, particularly in view of the fact that the typical one-room school is not included. Despite its limitations, this study must serve to give some kind of picture of the elementary curriculum in the years from 1860 to 1890.

In this survey, J. C. Boykin considered twenty-nine subjects being taught in eighty-two leading cities ranging from San Francisco to New York and Mobile to St. Paul. He ascertained the number of hours devoted to these subjects in the several systems, investigated a limited group in detail, and included brief references to particular courses of study. He had something to say not only about the current status of elementary school programs, but also about their antecedents. Furthermore, he placed his remarks in the context of the presumed role of the elementary school in American society.

At the heart of the changes was the disproportionate growth of the "lower stratum of our educational system." Formerly the elementary school, like the high school, had been a preparatory institution for

---

[4] Report to follow based on J. C. Boykin, "Course of Study in Public Elementary Schools of Cities," *Report of the Commissioner of Education for the Year 1888–1889*, 1891, vol. I, pp. 373–410.

college; now it was a common school attended by children in general. Because only a limited number would ever go on to secondary school, elementary schooling constituted the only formal instruction for 84 per cent of the youngsters.

In response to the new role, educators had tampered freely with the program. They had stuffed the course of study with subjects considered of most worth, which would ordinarily have been included in secondary school. They had added subjects assumed to be of immediate value to living. They had changed the content of many of the traditional subjects. These changes had apparently been made within the framework of an expeditious reinterpretation of how behavior is controlled and directed. There was no doubt that "mind grows by proper exercise of the faculties." There was also no doubt that the place of the elementary school in training of the mind was that "in it is given that instruction which precedes the assumptions of the studies proper for the stage of reasoning" which would be reached at puberty and in secondary school.

Nevertheless, here were the 84 per cent who would never see the inside of a secondary school. They, too, were prospective American citizens who needed to be equipped with facts "useful for the present and profitable for the future." For their practical education, to the elementary course of study had been added civics, bookkeeping, and manual training. In deference to the children's short stay in school and out of respect for mental training, both algebra and geometry had been retained in some courses of study.

Still, there was an apparent concern about formal subjects undertaken too soon, practical subjects substituted for the disciplines, and striking changes in the teaching of the three R's. Referring to the necessary training of the mind, Boykin addressed himself to the subtle change in rationale for the 1888 programs. He said that there had probably been a trend away from the commitment to study for the sake of the power it brings. School people had instead embraced the Spencerian doctrine "that the acquirement of those classes of fact which are most useful for regulating conduct involves a mental exercise best fitted for strengthening the faculties."[5]

Educators' interpretation of Spencer could be most clearly seen in the new emphases in the traditional school subjects. Reading, one of those subjects, was no longer to be combined with practice in oratorical skills. Comprehension of what was read had become the key to an ability to be acquired by pupils whom the school was soon to lose. In order that it might be useful as well as a guide for conduct when youngsters would no longer be in school, emphasis was being placed on what to read and

[5] Quoted in *ibid.*, p. 374.

how to use reading as a tool. The Chicago course of study, for instance, allowed 30.9 per cent of school time for it. Some of the reading instruction and practice would remain unrecorded, for it would be a part of activities in geography, history, and the natural sciences.

A basic part of reading and of writing had always been technical grammar, that is, analysis, declension, and conjugation. This honorific member of the original seven liberal arts had usually been introduced after two or three years of elementary schooling. An 1888 survey, however, of grade levels for beginning grammar in sixty-nine cities showed the following:

2 cities.........third grade
2 cities.........fourth grade
14 cities.........fifth grade
27 cities.........sixth grade
20 cities.........seventh grade
6 cities.........eighth grade

Boykin also recorded, with some show of feeling, the fact that one city did not begin grammar study until the ninth grade. Exclusive attention to technical grammar in grammar classes had, furthermore, given way to what was called "conversation and language" lessons. The art of good speech, rather than the science of grammar, was already in vogue.

Arithmetic, another of the basic three R's which had long been considered an ideal disciplinary subject, was likewise undergoing radical change. Course-of-study makers were eliminating all that did not interest or concern pupils in their daily lives. They were deleting all the parts "which no child or man but a specialist will ever use."

In addition to these basic subjects, Boykin generalized about a number of others in which he claimed there had been little if any fundamental change. The aims for spelling, writing, music, and drawing remained much the same. So did those for geography and history, which had always been taught as informational subjects, though the latter two had shown material improvement in the way they were taught. It might be said as an afterthought that of the eighty-two cities under survey, only two, Cincinnati and Memphis, did not offer United States history in the grades.

New subjects were also to be found. How new they were is purely speculative, for Boykin did not have a chronology of newness. It can be assumed from what is generally known about the history of education that these new subjects dated from about the late 1860s. Of these newcomers, Boykin found the natural sciences and civil government to be most generally taught. He could say this even though the total hours for the sciences appeared to be very few in his charts. He remarked that the amount of time was obscured because time for natural science instruction was often given in reading lessons. Of the cities under survey, Washington, D.C., seemed to have the most elaborate and extensive program in the sciences in elementary school. In the lower grades, children observed plants and animals and studied some physiology. Science instruction continued throughout the grades with something of a culminating activity in physics in the seventh grade.

The influence of the Civil War was undoubtedly being reflected in the increased attention given to civil government. It was being taught as a separate course in twenty-two of the eighty-two cities, and, through history, geography, or reading, its principles were being taught in nearly all of the systems. The object was better preparation for citizenship—in support of this, attention was being given to the nature and forms of government and facts about the United States and state constitutions. Whether the aims of the subject were being achieved was a matter for discussion so heated that Boykin referred at some length to the opinions of R. W. Stephenson, superintendent of schools in Columbus, Ohio. Stephenson had apparently raised the question as to whether facts alone would influence conduct—he stated that more important than knowledge were virtue, obedience to rightful authority, integrity, industry, and patriotism. These traits were a part of the moral man. As such, they were inculcated in most courses and obviated the necessity for any special attention to political morality. The moral man would be moral in all situations.

In addition to these new subjects, there were a good number of other subjects which were not yet extensively introduced. Besides algebra and geometry, these included general history and manual training. According to the charts, the last-named subject appeared to be confined to woodworking. In some places there was instruction in German, French, or Spanish. Boykin said that language study was based on local and administrative rather than on general and pedagogical grounds—what he meant was that foreign languages were offered whenever a sufficient number of parents spoke the language and demanded its inclusion in the school curriculum. An extreme example was found in Cleveland, Ohio, where 1,360 hours per school year were given to German instruction in the regular course of events and where children of German parentage received 289 hours more.

This survey of eighty-two city elementary programs concluded with an elaborate chart showing by cities the amount of time devoted to some twenty-nine subjects. What can be concluded from this chart is that when course-of-study makers got beyond certain basics in the curriculum, they were obviously going in divergent ways in respect to new subjects or grade placement of old ones. The chart indicated that there was no general agreement about what ought to be taught, nor was there any general agreement in respect to the amount of time to be devoted to the time-honored subjects, such as arithmetic. Diversity characterized the programs of these elementary schools.

The conclusions of the national committees soon to be inaugurated were already beginning to be practiced. Local pressures had already brought about the criterion of community adaptation. An assumed practicality of content, meaning facts and skills for immediate use, and selection of such skills and facts by reference to majority standards were characterizing instruction in basic subjects. In a few instances the committees, which would be elected to bring order out of chaos, would try to stem the tide of diversity and practicality. But for the most part, they would provide in the early twentieth century only a somewhat more elaborate and statistically respectable rationale for practices already under way.

## The Secondary School Curriculum
(1860–1900)

Preparation for college and preparation for life already characterized the public high school in the period from 1860 to 1900. As a matter of fact, the latter aim was probably a heritage from the academy; through courses in everything from Greek and moral philosophy to surveying and pedagogy, the academy had attempted to be the people's college in the middle decades of the nineteenth century. By the later decades, the curves showing decrease in numbers of academies and increase in high schools would cross. Some institution would have to pick up the tasks of the academy, and the high school and later the junior college were destined for this.

The high schools, however, did not at once begin where the academy left off. The curricula of the 1850 academies would have appeared wide ranging in the extreme beside the limited programs of the 1860 public high schools. A sample of high school programs in the North Central area in 1860 to 1865 showed that twelve of them offered only one course, most likely a classical or Latin course, and that the largest number of courses offered by any one institution was three.[6] (See Table 6-1.) The high school of 1860 was, in effect, a preparatory institution, while the academy was still "preparing for life."

By 1900, however, the high school had taken over the academy's job, and in so doing had allowed for the rapid multiplication of courses

---

[6] Report to follow based on John Elbert Stout, *The Development of High-school Curricula in the North Central States from 1860 to 1918*, Supplementary Educational Monographs, vol. 3, no. 3, whole no. 15, University of Chicago Press, Chicago, June, 1921.

(curricula) and of subjects. Where no public high school of the North Central states had offered more than three curricula in 1860, one school in 1896 to 1900 was offering seven, and eight were prepared to give four. If a diagonal can be assumed to be superimposed on Table 6-1, running from the 3 column in 1860 to 1865 to the 7 column in 1896 to 1900, the trend of the high school program will be clearly indicated. It will be seen to have got out of hand in very short order.

The burgeoning of courses suggests a first very obvious conclusion: Subjects had multiplied in number and kind. The subjects added can

Table 6-1. Number of Courses Offered by Secondary Schools in the North Central States (1860–1900)

| Years | Number of courses offered | | | | | | |
|---|---|---|---|---|---|---|---|
| | 1 | 2 | 3 | 4 | 5 | 6 | 7 |
| 1860–1865 | 12* | 6 | 2 | | | | |
| 1866–1870 | 10 | 9 | | 1 | | | |
| 1871–1875 | 9 | 9 | 1 | | 1 | | |
| 1876–1880 | 17 | 4 | 3 | 1 | | | |
| 1881–1885 | | 5 | 18 | 2 | | | |
| 1886–1890 | 20 | 7 | 5 | 1 | 2 | | |
| 1891–1895 | 28 | 13 | 9 | 5 | 3 | 2 | |
| 1896–1900 | 25 | 12 | 12 | 8 | | 2 | 1 |

* Number of schools offering one course, i.e., the Latin course.

souRCE: Adapted from John Elbert Stout, *The Development of High-school Curricula in the North Central States from 1860 to 1918*, Supplementary Educational Monographs, III, no. 3, whole no. 15, June, 1921, University of Chicago Press, Chicago, 1921, pp. 46–50. Adapted by permission of the publisher. Copyright 1921 by the University of Chicago.

first be inferred from the kinds of courses (curricula) appended in the period under survey. By 1860 to 1865, there were already courses known as "general and normal." To these, plus the classical, one called "English and German" was added in 1866 to 1870. In the period from 1871 to 1875 a commercial English course was added. The five-year period 1876 to 1880 saw the recognition of the new industrial age with the introduction of scientific, scientific engineering, and technological courses. By 1886 to 1890, a general science course had come in. Probably as a defensive emphasis on an earlier purpose of the high school, a course clearly designated "college preparatory" was introduced in the period 1896 to 1900. With the addition of these new courses, plus those already a part of the high school program, there were in the period from 1860 to 1865 but seven ways of titling courses, while from 1896 to 1900 there were thirty-six ways in North Central schools alone.

In these same states, subjects in courses had shifted in emphasis and changed in nature, and substitutions were being made in traditional curricula. An illustration of the last was found in the introduction of the English course, which retained all the subjects of the classical curriculum except Latin and Greek. For the last two, science and mathematics had been substituted. Other course changes, however, can best be described by reverting to changes in subjects and shifts in emphasis on subjects.

The handwriting on the wall was clear from two significant shifts in subject patterns. By 1900, mental and moral philosophy as well as logic had pretty well dropped out of the list of high school subjects. Commercial offerings, on the other hand, had shown a sharp increase. By the 1906 to 1911 period, 90 per cent of the secondary schools in the North Central states were offering commercial subjects, and 70 per cent of them were offering the fine and practical arts. Terminal as well as college preparatory courses were now included in high school offerings.

Certain subjects maintained relatively the same places in at least one course throughout the forty-year period. All schools offered something in mathematics, English, and science in each five-year period from 1860 to 1900. Beginning in 1870, social science was also to be found in all schools.

A change in content and also in emphasis was to be found in two subjects, and significantly so. United States history, the *sine qua non* for developing citizens, was sharply on the increase. It was offered in 1860 to 1865 in but 15 per cent of the schools, while in 1896 to 1900, it was given in 45 per cent of them. By the latter date, English was offered in the freshman year in nearly 50 per cent of the schools. This percentage dropped by high school grades, but 15 per cent of the schools gave English in the senior year. The move to four years of high school English was clearly to be seen by 1900.

There were three ways in which the character of and emphasis on English had changed. First, increased time was obviously given to its study. Second, there was an indication of its growing importance, as evidenced in the tendency toward uniformity in the curricula. Third, there was a change in the nature of the subject matter. There had been a relative decrease in emphasis on grammar and rhetoric, and an increase in emphasis on literature. The latter had two purposes: training in oral reading, and introducing students to "good" literature. Table 6-2 indicates the highest-ranking pieces of literature (those found in more than 25 per cent of North Central states school lists). As the anticlimax to this story of the growing importance of English, it can be added that English was the only field which at the turn of the century was to emerge with subject areas universally required.

Certainly no definitive explanation can be made of the growth of the importance of English in the period 1860 to 1900. One might speculate, however, against a background of socioeconomic developments. It was in this period that Americans became self-conscious about the foreigners flooding their shores. It was in this period that schools were beginning to dip more persistently into first- and second-generation Americans for their ever-increasing numbers of teachers. It was in this period that Americans were recovering from a civil war in which their nation had

Table 6-2. Pieces of Literature Found in North Central States High School Lists (1860–1900)

| Rank | Pieces of literature found in 25 per cent or more of school lists |
|------|------------------------------------------------------------------|
| 1 | Merchant of Venice |
| 2 | Julius Caesar |
| 3 | Bunker Hill Oration |
| 4 | The Sketch Book |
| 4 | Evangeline |
| 4 | Vision of Sir Launfal |
| 5 | Snowbound |
| 6 | Macbeth |
| 7 | Lady of the Lake |
| 8 | Hamlet |
| 9 | Deserted Village |
| 10 | Gray's Elegy |
| 10 | Thanatopsis |
| 10 | As You Like It |

SOURCE: John Elbert Stout, *The Development of High-school Curricula in the North Central States from 1860 to 1918*, Supplementary Educational Monographs, III, no. 3, whole no. 15, June, 1921, University of Chicago Press, Chicago, 1921, p. 137. Adapted by permission of the publisher. Copyright 1921 by the University of Chicago.

almost gone under. Could it be that first- and second-generation teachers, required to be self-consciously American, and a lay public, urged to a growing nationalism as defense against foreign tongues and dissension, unconsciously combined to strengthen a symbol of Americanism?

In the period 1860 to 1900, school people had coped as best they could with curricula to fit the increasing diversity of youngsters in elementary schools and, to a lesser extent, in secondary schools. The magnitude of the behavioral problem was brought into focus in the closing decade of the nineteenth century when professional educators emerged on the national scene simultaneously with technology, urbanization, and slums. Once the problem was analyzed, its proportions became apparent: What curriculum to provide for the emergent average American citizen?

What course of study to propose for each of the kinds of specialists needed in the expanding industries and in technological agriculture? What sequence of experiences to propose for that elite group that some hoped vainly to produce which would be dedicated to steering the ship of state? Educators must order school conditions not for a handful of philosopher-kings, but for a whole society of would-be citizens and vocational specialists.

Educators operated at the local and state levels, of course. But large groups of them attempted to forge something approximating a national curriculum. The remainder of this chapter will be concerned with this urge toward a framework that was generally agreed to and the contributions thereto made by national committees.

## RECOMMENDATIONS FOR REFORM OF THE
## ELEMENTARY SCHOOL CURRICULUM (1890–1918)

As has been seen in the discussion of the city school systems, sporadic attempts to reform the elementary curriculum had been going on through the nineteenth century. These attempts, though largely unheralded, pointed the way that committees would eventually go. The latter would, in a sense, merely discover a rationale and develop a set of techniques for doing what superintendents and teachers would be inclined to do anyway. But it was probably the work of the widely publicized committees that hastened the transition to "life adjustment" education. In the transition of the elementary curriculum, the Committee of Fifteen and the Committee on Economy of Time in Education were of the greatest moment.

### Committee of Fifteen

At its Boston meeting in February, 1893, the Department of Superintendence appointed a Committee of Fifteen to (1) investigate the organization of the school system, (2) inquire into correlation of studies in primary and grammar schools, and (3) make recommendations on the training of teachers. The report which the group finally issued is labeled as conservative in modern texts, meaning in the preparation-for-higher-studies tradition. If it were, it can hardly be charged to the ivory-tower college professors. All members of the committee were state or local superintendents of schools except for Andrew S. Draper, president of the University of Illinois, and the U.S. Commissioner of Education, Dr. William T. Harris, who had been superintendent of schools in St. Louis, Missouri.

Under Dr. Harris's guidance, the final report on the inquiry into correlation was issued as a beautiful example of nineteenth-century philosophical idealism.[7]    The unfolding of the natural powers of the child and identification of the "wholes" in which the child unfolded were central to the planning of the curriculum.    Whether this kind of thinking was pervasive is purely speculative.    Opinions of persons over the country were sought, and items of the final report were voted on, so that only majority-agreed-upon materials were included.    Extreme care was taken to record dissenting opinions, which were ordinarily on items of methodology or minor content matters rather than on main outlines.    The same care was taken to print, with the report, answers to questions asked of consultants around the country.    In an age when empiricism and social evolution were in the ascendancy, the stronghold of idealism in a school administrative population is an interesting commentary—unless this was a packed committee which represented Harris's point of view.

What were these wholes which were central to the proposed curriculum?    One quite obviously was the child, whose proportions are apparently rediscovered every generation.    The whole-child enthusiasts of the second half of the twentieth century, however, would hardly recognize Dr. Harris's whole-minded human being, whose curriculum must exhibit a psychological symmetry that would afford his mental faculties the best exercise and unfolding in their natural order.

To produce this symmetry, there would be a proper balancing of the branches of study, and a "whole" of studies in the world of human learning.    Logical order of topics and branches must pervade the curriculum.    For varying reasons, this symmetry of studies was to be struck first through a kind of core of the branches: language, arithmetic, geography, and history.    To balance the studies, there must be a judicious and not overenthusiastic emphasis on arithmetic.    If there continued to be an overemphasis (one hour to mental, one hour to written arithmetic), then the child would be distorted, a creature given to thinking quantitatively rather than qualitatively.    There would be neglect of the powers of observation and of reflection upon causal relations.    Arithmetic in grades 2 to 6 was enough, with some attention to a transition (to secondary school mathematics) algebra in the seventh and eighth grades.

The symmetrical child and the whole essence of human learning were not the only or the most important wholes.    "Man has two selves, they say, the individual self, and the collective self of the organized state or nation."[8]    To the end of recognizing this higher self, there must be

---

[7] Report to follow based on National Education Association, *Report of the Committee of Fifteen on Elementary Education with the Reports of the Sub-Committees: on the Training of Teachers; on the Correlation of Studies in Elementary Education; on the Organization of City School Systems,* American Book Company, New York, 1895.

[8] *Ibid.,* p. 30.

correlation of the pupil's course of study with the spiritual and natural environment. This whole, in which his being was submerged, was civilization, and the requirements of civilization determined school studies, the extent to which they were studied, and what the child learned before he came to school. It was to meet the demands of this all-embracing whole that the child must be fitted to perform his duties in the family, civil society, the state, and church.

With the most important whole identified as the correlating agent of the child's study, the curricular task became one of selecting content situations which would allow him to unfold and find his place in the transcending whole. Language, of course, was primary, for it was what made human social organization possible.

Language study had three phases. The first, which occupied the first three years of the child's schooling, was obviously the mastering of the new form, written language, by which the door to the larger world would be opened. The second phase was that by which the child was led out of and beyond himself through the great literature, which was a spiritual guide to the most practical of all knowledge, human nature. The latter was revealed through the human struggle, which had aesthetic and ethical content and ended with the vindication of ethical and rational interests. Thus, free of moral maxims which might only offend the child, the great classics would communicate the moral by emphasizing the aesthetic.

The third phase of language study was formal grammar, which revealed the essential nature of thought itself. That this study should meet the demands of its task, there must be a decreased interest in memory. For the latter was often cultivated at the expense of insight into the organizing principle of the whole.

With language study as the essential base of the curriculum, it logically followed that the whole elementary program was nothing more than an extension of the process of learning the art of reading. First came mastery of the printed word. This was followed by excursions into five special vocational languages: literature, grammar, and arithmetic (the virtues of which have been already described), followed by geography and history.

In the Middle Ages in Pliny's work, according to the committee, geography was included in geometry, one of the seven liberal arts. It was proposed in the new curriculum to separate them. Arithmetic contained the abstract or general conditions of material existence, while geography was a study of the material habitat as it related to man.

History, the final extension of the art of reading, was of less importance in the early grades and of more importance in the later grades than geography. History related to that more important extension of the individual human personality, for it was "then, the study of this larger, corporate, social, and civil self." It was a special branch for instruction in the duties of citizenship; properly taught, it could dispel false individualism by showing the freedom which comes from true obedience to just laws enforced by strong government. "History gives a sense of belonging to a higher social unity which possesses the right of absolute control over person and property in the interest of the safety of the whole."[9] Because of this special function of communicating the nature of the corporate self, there must be intensive study of United States history in the seventh and eighth grades, with general history one hour a week in the second half of the eighth year.

In summary, the staple branches of study in the elementary school were grammar, literature, arithmetic, geography, and history, and the disciplinary work of the school must be concentrated on these. But there were other supplementary branches of study. The latter included such mechanical exercises as drawing, which trained the hand and eye; penmanship; calisthenics; and natural science, which afforded a training in observation. To these could be added woodwork and metalwork, sewing and cooking, and music. Moral training should come through discipline rather than through instruction in ethical theory. The child should be trained to be regular and punctual, truthful and sincere through every exercise in which he participated. Stress should be put on accuracy of statement.

Withal, the studies must be correlated through a proper understanding of the meaning of correlation. This referred to the logical order of topics and branches, the symmetrical whole of studies in the world of human learning, psychological symmetry, and the correlation of the pupil's course of study with the world in which he lived. An artificial center for such correlation, such as the story *Robinson Crusoe*, must be rejected. This was "a temporary scaffolding made for school purposes." It would only "stand in the way of the true objective correlation."

When all the reports, including that prepared by Dr. Harris's subcommittee, were in, the committee of the whole adopted some propositions unanimously. These included the following:

1. The environment into which the child was born should determine the objects of his study.
2. Psychology should determine the topics.
3. Language had a relation to the induction of the child into his civilization, and was the basis for the correlation of studies.
4. The elements of physics and chemistry should be given in all grades in connection with topics in physiology and physical geography.
5. Elementary geography should be incorporated into nature study.

[9] *Ibid.*, p. 31.

6, 7, 8. The study of English grammar should be made subordinate and auxiliary to the study of English literature, and writing as a course should be taught only through the sixth grade; but children should be encouraged to use good English in all courses.

9. Manual training in woods and metals should be offered for boys in the seventh and eighth grades. For girls, sewing should be offered in the fourth, fifth, and sixth grades, and cooking in the seventh and eighth.

10. Music should be offered throughout the elementary grades.

Despite the use of the language of a Hegelian, or perhaps because of it, the report paved the way for the overhauling of the curriculum to be undertaken by those interested in economy of time. Formal as the curriculum still remained, the whole child and the whole civilization were fast acquiring primary importance. It would be but one short step from the symmetry of these somewhat idealized wholes to the everyday concerns and practices of Americans as the measure for elementary curriculum planning.

## Committee on
## Economy of Time in Education

One of the more significant attempts at the national level to initiate wide-scale reform and investigation was begun in 1903, with the appointment of the Committee on Economy of Time in Education, under the guidance of James H. Baker, president emeritus of the National Council of Education. The tasks of the committee eventually engaged the attention and services of college and public school people, of superintendents and teachers, of educational psychologists and professors of education. The youngsters and lay people eventually brought under study must have numbered well in the thousands. The chief reports of the committee were impressive enough to appear as independent yearbooks of the National Society for the Study of Education from 1915 to 1919.

The emergence of the committee rested on the premise that somewhere in a school system which had grown like Topsy both time and energy had been wasted in progress toward whatever were the goals of universal education. The period given over to elementary and secondary education must be shortened through selection and elimination of subject matter, vitalizing of methods, relating education to modern life. "A great secret of education is to accomplish a maximum of training with a minimum of material."[10]

[10] National Education Association, Committee on Economy of Time in Education, *Minimum Essentials in Elementary-school Subjects—Standards and Current Practices,* Fourteenth Yearbook of the National Society for the Study of Education, Public School Publishing Company, Bloomington, Ill., 1916, part I, p. 12.

The chief target of the committee was the curriculum of the elementary school because society was "still depending primarily upon the elementary schools to furnish not only the tools of knowledge but also those facts, concepts, and principles essential in a democracy to common discussion and to the collective consideration of common problems."[11] The chief method was the determination, through survey and analysis of various kinds, of that minimum of subject content or that technique for teaching and reinforcing content which would constitute the minimum desired equipment for an American citizen. Minimum essentials in the school subjects, which in turn became general education for citizenship, were the common referents.

Edward L. Thorndike's famous phrase, "Whatever exists at all exists in some amount," had already taken hold among educational leaders. Though they gave lip service to such generalities as desirable attitudes and mutual understandings, the chief investigators of the minimum essentials confined their efforts to analyzing relatively simple aspects of verbal behavior which would yield to their measuring instruments. In addition, they spent an astonishing amount of time developing what might be termed a list of criteria by which suitability of a content for emergent citizens might be judged.

The problem of criteria was by nature philosophical, but this never appeared to be recognized by investigators or committeemen. They did realize, however, the difficulty of determining the nature of minimum essentials in the face of the absence of criteria. There were as yet no acceptable achievement levels for students of varying abilities, nor was there any measure of performance needed in a democratic society.[12]

Whatever the difficulties, the committee launched a full-scale study designed to answer two questions: What subjects are essential? What is essential content? In answering both of these, they made those unacknowledged assumptions so engagingly described by Alfred North Whitehead as the most important any group makes. They assumed that the standards of inclusion and exclusion in the school subjects should come out of the new society, without ever raising the question as to whether they might be secured in any other way. The predominant practices of adults or children, the prevailing practices in school systems, the pervasive problems in society, and the prominent content in most-used texts became criteria for the selection of school subjects and subject content. What could be more American than school practices based on majority practices?

Devising a method by which a standard distribution of time and subjects could emerge from practice must have confounded superin-

[11] *Ibid.*
[12] *Ibid.*, whole report.

tendents when the first report was issued. An opening study of distribution of time for subjects and distribution of subjects to grades in fifty American cities showed little agreement as to either the grade or the allotment of time for beginning accepted subjects except reading; and recess was shown to take more time than any subject except reading and arithmetic. One can almost see the worried frown of the efficiency expert as he looked at this majority standard for recess and sympathize with him in his groping for a rationale for its inclusion; for he added, ominously, that it brought to mind a series of problems in hygiene and management of organized play. If recess there would be, he must make it pay its way in the curriculum.

Consolingly, though, in fifty cities the school arts (reading, language, spelling, penmanship, and arithmetic) did absorb 70 per cent of the class time. Of the remaining 30 per cent, more time was allotted to music and drawing than to science or manual or physical training. The *status quo* of the curriculum and the nature of ongoing experimentation having been ascertained, committee members were ready for investigation of the separate subjects.

From the beginning, a favorite topic of discussion had been the minimum-knowledge equipment which would allow citizens to "discuss and confer on a sufficiently high level to insure the progressive evolution of our democratic society." This statement of purpose resulted in the inevitable proposition that the same items of information ought to be included in all curricula throughout the country. To this end, various techniques were devised for assessing "commonness." One of these was a comparison of school texts for their common content. The committee members were certain that because democratic government was based on discussion of common problems, a common stock of concepts and facts ought to be available. One investigator determined the vocabulary of ten grade 2 readers in common use in elementary schools and endeavored to find a base for the quality of reader.

A variation of the text technique was used in securing a suggested minimal spelling list. On the assumption that the list should first contain words which children used in their elementary school written work and would use most frequently when they left, Hugh Clark Pryor tried combining spelling tests and word lists. He secured the most widely used lists or scales and extracted all words which occurred in at least six of the twelve. These extractions added up to 1,309 words. To these he added additional words from the Ayres scale.[13] Thus a standard

[13] National Education Association, *Second Report of the Committee on Minimal Essentials in Elementary-school Subjects,* Sixteenth Yearbook of the National Society for the Study of Education, Public School Publishing Company, Bloomington, Ill., 1917, part I, chap. V.

commonness of words in readers and spelling lists was to be a measure of common learnings.

Often the verbal behavior or activities of either children or members of the adult community were used as criteria for establishing accepted items in courses of study. Thus W. W. Charters devised a method for developing a grammar curriculum based on errors of school children. The value of such a study, so he said, was in obtaining genuine facts about children's errors. The first such study, according to the author, had been done in about 1908 by Guy M. Wilson in Connersville, Indiana, and up to the time of the author's proposal, there had been about nine such studies.[14]

This majority standard, however, was given really full play when some of the investigators got at the larger scholarly or lay community. A study of social and business arithmetic by Guy M. Wilson brought with it the conclusion that criticisms of business people and educators had been substantiated. It was indeed true that selected arithmetical processes which were time-consuming could well be stricken from courses. This statement reinforced a habit of thinking about curricular items in terms of their "needs" value, that is, their assumed usefulness for solving the everyday problems of daily life. As a preface to this conclusion, the investigator had had youngsters keeping case records on their parents to discover the kinds of arithmetical problems their parents solved day by day.[15]

H. Edwin Mitchell carried on the social-demands concept for the development of arithmetic skills by gathering data from a standard cookbook, payrolls of a number of factories, marked-down sales adver-tisements, and a hardware catalogue from which he proposed to build curricula for the elementary school. Alice Camerer mailed question-naires to fifty bank employees and to parents at the University of Iowa elementary school asking for the kinds of information she hoped would yield to the new "life-needs" concept in the area of banking.[16]

It was in the area of the social studies that life needs could be pur-sued with the greatest energy. When B. B. Basset was beginning his study of the proposed civics content, he posed to himself the question as to what were the problems to which Americans sought answers through their government. To answer the question, he examined (1) national platforms of all political parties since 1832; (2) state platforms

---

[14] *Ibid.*, chap. VI.

[15] *Ibid.*, chap. VIII.

[16] National Education Association, *Third Report of the Committee on Economy of Time in Education*, Seventeenth Yearbook of the National Society for the Study of Education, Public School Publishing Company, Bloomington, Ill., 1919, part I, pp. v–vi.

in nonpresidential years since 1889, in so far as they dealt with national issues; (3) all state platforms of major parties in 1910; (4) platforms of major parties in California, Indiana, and New York since 1850; (5) all platforms of parties of Iowa since 1889; and for harmony's sake (6) all platforms of one Southern state. From these he proposed to secure a list of issues suitable for the new students being prepared for life.[17]

The only group unsure of themselves were the historians, whose consciences were nagged on the one hand by the patriotic mission of history, on the other, by the demand for adherence to scholarly writing. They salved their consciences by many means. They appealed to the American Historical Association for help. They investigated problems in civics to ascertain the amount of historical information needed to understand political science questions and came out with inconclusive results. Finally, they carried on a debate through essays by several contributors on what American history ought to be in the schools.

Although, as has been said, a curriculum tells little of what a youngster learns, the proposed curricula of the history professors tells much about them and their concept of the schools. W. H. Mace from Syracuse asked for the study of great characters in grades 4 and 5. He saw in this study a chance for children to sense the moral or ethical issues in the hero's struggles against obstacles. Prof. Charles A. Ellwood of Missouri stated that the child should be taught not patriotism, but loyalty to ideals. American history must be seen as a movement to realize an ideal society founded upon liberty and justice, and the child must be made aware of how tragic would be the loss to humanity if America failed to realize itself.[18] The cumulative fervency of disciples of a new society, of which the school was an agency, had transformed the ultimate of the philosophical idealists.

## RECOMMENDATIONS FOR REFORM OF THE SECONDARY SCHOOL CURRICULUM (1890–1918)

### Committee of Ten, 1892

The survey of courses (1860–1900) in secondary schools of the North Central Association points out by implication some of the concerns of the Committee of Ten, first influential and impressive professional group to address itself to secondary school curricula. The North Central survey had pointed up the multiplication in subjects and courses and might by inference have suggested the corresponding lack of uniformity in grade placement and in time given to each subject. These, in turn,

[17] *Ibid.*, p. vii.
[18] *Ibid.*, whole report.

might have suggested that college admissions requirements were in a state of confusion. The course multiplication which was uncovered by the North Central survey, together with its inferred results, became in a sense the focus of the Committee of Ten, appointed by the National Council of Education president in 1892. This focus might, in turn, be thought of as the first professional step in the march to the Carnegie unit.[19]

The Committee of Ten would ask its conferees in nine selected subject areas to address themselves to eleven questions. These can be shortened to the following topics:

1. To what age pupil should each subject area be introduced, and how many hours a week and weeks in a year should the latter subsequently be pursued?

2. How might the area be included in college entrance requirements and what might be the mode of testing for college entrance and the limits which should be set for the period between preliminary and final entrance examinations?

3. What topics were to be covered, including a designation of those reserved for the last four years and recommendations for differentiated curricula, providing they were thought desirable for college-bound, scientific school–bound, and terminal pupils? In other words, what might be a formula for a minimum conformity which, if approved by secondary school people, would bring secondary schooling to some kind of order?

In the form of eleven questions, these topics were put to a series of nine conferences, the participants of which had been selected by the Committee of Ten. The ninety conferees, representing the ten selected areas in Table 6-3, consisted of forty-seven who were from colleges or universities, forty-two in the service of schools, and one who was a government official with university experience. "A considerable number of the college men, however," according to the committee, "had also had experience in schools." The topics, then, though they were to be treated by experts in the several subject fields, were also to be looked at by practicing or practiced secondary school personnel.

Both the topics as well as the areas selected probably developed in part out of questions raised in the National Council of Education meetings. The subject of uniformity in school programs and in college admission requirements had come up for discussion earlier. James H. Baker, then principal of the Denver High School, had reported on the deliberations of a special committee at a meeting of the National Council of Education in 1891. Out of subsequent work of this same com-

[19] Report to follow based on National Education Association, *Report of the Committee of Ten on Secondary School Studies with the Reports of the Conferences Arranged by the Committee,* The American Book Company, New York, 1894.

mittee came the recommendation for a series of conferences on the principal secondary subjects. These conferences were to be called by the eventual Committee of Ten chaired by Charles W. Eliot, president of Harvard University. This committee, in turn, designated which subjects were crucial to secondary schools, though a guess may be hazarded that these, too, might have been suggested in part by the concerns of Baker and his original committee.

The nature of the rationale for designating the subjects in Table 6-3 as "principal" was never made clear by the committee. However, discussion of the conferees respecting the functions of their several subjects

Table 6-3. Subject Representation of the Nine Conference Groups of the Committee of Ten

---

1. Latin
2. Greek
3. English
4. Other modern languages
5. Mathematics
6. Physics, Astronomy, and Chemistry
7. Natural History (Biology, including Botany, Zoology, and Physiology)
8. History, Civil Government, and Political Economy
9. Geography (Physical Geography, Geology, and Meteorology)

---

SOURCE: National Education Association, *Report of the Committee of Ten on Secondary School Studies with the Reports of the Conferences Arranged by the Committee,* American Book Company, New York, 1894, p. 5.

and remarks by the committee in its introduction to the nine reports provide clues to the subject selections. For instance, the committee noted that conferees in the sciences (including natural history) and in what we would now call the social sciences or social studies made the most elaborate reports; they were dealing with subjects "imperfectly dealt with in primary and secondary schools," and they "ardently desired to have their respective subjects made equal to Latin, Greek, and Mathematics in weight and influence in the schools; but they knew that . . . many teachers and directors of education felt no confidence in these subjects as disciplinary material." Mental discipline, then, would be one of the clues to inclusion and exclusion.

According to the committee, English was to be described by such means as would indicate its "disciplinary or developing power." Its study was to be "as serious and informing as the study of Latin." But English had burdens other than disciplinary efficacy to bear. It was, after all, the mother tongue. Through the study of words, which it demanded, it could be used as a medium for illustrating the development of the English race. Whatever the implications of the report, the English conferees laid stress on just two objectives in the teaching of English: (1) to help the student develop the kind of language by which he could make himself understood and could understand others; and (2) to cultivate such a taste for reading that the pupil would continue to expand his understanding of good literature. To these two ends the conferees, running in the face of mental discipline, so to speak, depreciated the study of formal grammar, even though it was valuable for training in thinking. Because they were determined to hew to their two objectives, they pointed out that pupils could learn to speak and write good English (a principal objective) without instruction in formal grammar, and that if it were to be dealt with, it should be done only incidentally. It will be remembered from the North Central survey, English as a secondary school subject had reached a place of universal prominence by 1900; consequently, perhaps, English professors and school people no longer felt called upon to rationalize it in honorific terms.

Beyond this rather radical departure in objectives for English, apparently no other explanations—except that of mental discipline—were to be offered for the central positions of the selected subjects. Those which were not central were dealt with in cursory fashion by the committee and not by special conferees. The committee made it plain, of course, that programs containing recommended groupings of the selected subjects should not thereby imply that other courses recently added to secondary school offerings should necessarily be omitted. Rather, they should be left to local choice and should be given consideration as incidental offerings in the standard proposed programs. For instance, drawing might well be introduced in the sciences, for the most useful drawing is "that which is applied to recording, describing, and discussing observations." The commercial subjects might be considered as substitutes for mathematics, the useful arts, for some of the sciences. Thus was dismissed much of what appears now in the some 700 separate subjects presently offered in secondary schools.

When the report was finally concluded, it contained a chart of the duration and character of the subjects through the grades and secondary school, and another chart giving standard times through the four years, both based on the conferees' reports.

Two other charts were constructed by the committee after they had reworked the reports. The first of these was a modification of the periods-per-week recommendation of the individual conferences. It used the standard of four periods—as opposed to the varying amounts of time recommended by the conferees—and it contained some minor adjustments in grade placement as well as in emphasis on the natural sciences.

The committee's standardization in four-period weeks was significant, for it was this recommendation which would pave the way for the Carnegie unit. It was reasonable, observed the committee, that if each of the principal subjects was to be extensively and thoroughly taught, each should be allotted adequate time. Time in class was an indirect measure of learning. A pupil who had spent twice as much time in Latin as in mathematics would be expected to know Latin twice as well as mathematics. There was, furthermore, a greater profit to be gained from extensive study of one subject than from cursory immersion in several. Hence there was to be thoroughness in instruction and equal time in each subject. But just as telling was the attitude in respect to electives. Some choice by students was apparently considered desirable; that in itself was a portent of the 700 courses to come. These electives were to have the stamp of approval put on them by making them "approximately equivalent to each other in seriousness, dignity and efficacy." The groundwork had been firmly laid for the twentieth-century standard unit.

A second tampering of the committee with the conferees' recommendations foreshadowed another typically American-school feature: provisions for delayed occupational choice which, to the present time, have successively been built into the single-ladder system. This tampering was referred to as an argument which might arise to the effect that Greek was introduced too late and physics, too early. The readjustments had been made, according to the committee, with an eye to allowing a boy to taste both languages and science before taking the serious step of choosing between the classical and the Latin-scientific courses, for this step would probably determine his future college and vocational choices.

Beyond the modifications which it made, Dr. Eliot's original Committee of Ten summarized the common patterns of thinking which characterized the nine groups. It was notable that there were common patterns even when groups worked in isolation. Some of these recommendations were common to the several conferences in an area. For instance, all three language groups (Latin, Greek, and modern languages) agreed that it was inexpedient to begin the study of two foreign languages in the same year. All the science groups were convinced of the necessity for laboratory work.

More important were the recommendations on which all agreed. First, as might be expected, all wished the study of their subjects to begin earlier than it did—in the elementary school, for the most part. But in case the reader of the report might think that these educators were calling for an overburdening of young minds, be it noted that all groups called for some kind of correlating or associating of the several disciplines, especially at the earlier levels.

After the subcommittees had laid out their plans for changes in the curricula of the several disciplines, most of them became concerned about whether there were teachers available to teach as they had planned. Most of them called for a higher-caliber teacher in the lower grades.

Most engaging was the unanimous agreement of ninety-eight teachers, so said the Committee of Ten, that there should be no differentiation in materials taught to the three kinds of youngsters in the secondary schools. Individual differences which seemed to be tied to the demands of the college preparatory, scientific preparatory, and terminal programs were to be met through the programs themselves or through limited election. Every subject—whether elected or required, and in whatever program—must be taught in the same way and to the same extent so long as a pupil pursued it. The logic of the subject rather than the psychology of the child was to rule the tenets of inclusion and exclusion in a field, even though adaptations to grade and maturity levels had been made within the structure of topics in each field.

The opening guns of the professionals in the secondary field had thus paved the way for that false equivalency which has prevailed through the middle of the twentieth century. The Committee of Ten provided a wedge for the elective system already adopted in higher-education institutions such as Harvard. It opened the door on multiplication of courses, even if only a few inches, by approving four standard programs. It reinforced the pattern of delayed choice in subsequent career, a sharp departure from the European practice which required a child to take the decisive step as early as his eleventh year. It paid homage to the citizenship tasks of the secondary school, particularly by its report on English. It subtly reinforced the idea of equality among Americans by insisting on their equal immersion in the several disciplines, regardless of ability. Often scored as conservative, the ninety-eight committee members and conference participants were nevertheless developing, for good or evil, a thoroughly American pattern for secondary education.

*Committee on College Entrance*
*Requirements, July, 1896*

The work of the Committee of Ten might be characterized by the phrase "developing the outlines of the open-ladder system." George H. Martin put it more aptly and in the language of the day when he said that school people "must devise some way by which all grades of schools, from the kindergarten to the college, shall be so correlated that there shall be a straight and open pathway from the lowest to the highest . . . along which free-acting children may be led by teachers acting freely within the necessary limits of relativity."[20] Though this sentiment was originally expressed in a work which had no connection with the Committee of Ten, it is a clear statement of a kind of framework for operation which characterized not only the 1892 committee, but its implementing body, the Committee on College Entrance Requirements. He who would be misled by the Latin, Greek, mathematics, and history with which both committees dealt would be missing the direction of secondary education which was being reinforced by both committees.

That the work of the Committee of Ten would not be lost, the Department of Secondary Education of the National Education Association passed a motion in 1895 for a committee to develop a plan of action for the previous report. The new committee of ten, consisting of five from the Department of Secondary Education and an invited five from the Department of Higher Education, came into being and presented an unofficial report in 1896. The new committee was called the Committee on College Entrance Requirements. Its chairman, Dr. A. F. Nightingale, superintendent of Chicago schools, presented its report on July 13, 1899.[21]

The pervasiveness of the commitment to a peculiarly American direction for secondary education can be judged from the character of the organizations which Dr. Nightingale and his committee invited to help with the report. The methodological must was the development of equivalent units of study which could be used over the country. For the development of these units, Dr. Nightingale invited the cooperation of the American Philological Association, the Modern Language Association, the American Historical Association, the American Mathematical Society, and committees of the Science Department of the National Education Association. Whether or not all the participants saw clearly the direction in which they were heading, a good part of America's scholarly community was raising no obstacles to the development of an American secondary education pattern.

This pattern can be seen best in the resolutions of the parent committee, which based its conclusions on the reports of its distinguished special committees and subcommittees. In turn, these resolutions can be best looked at if they are seen from the standpoint of an implicit—rather than an explicit—structuring of a secondary education for all.

The problem of preparing (in the narrow sense) citizens who could tackle problems in a democracy was of lesser importance, perhaps, in the thinking of committee members. At least, only one resolution im-

[20] "Report of the Committee on College Entrance Requirements," *Journal of Proceedings and Addresses, Thirty-eighth Annual Meeting of The National Education Association,* University of Chicago Press, Chicago, 1899, p. 639, footnote.
[21] Report to follow based on *ibid.,* whole report.

plied such an aim. This came in a plea to the colleges to accept a year's work in economics as a unit for admission. Economics was conceived of as incorporating elementary political economy, commercial geography, and industrial history. Of these elements, it appeared to the committee that political economy had as much disciplinary and cultural value as other recognized subjects and furthermore, was already being taught in secondary schools. More important, the three areas of economics could be linked by appropriate teaching of the practical subjects. Such reasoning inevitably led to the conclusion that citizens, as they must constantly be involved in economic decision making, should be prepared for their task through systematic instruction in economics.

The remaining twelve resolutions of the committee reinforced the citizenship function of the secondary schools, but in a larger context. The aim for all American schools could be expressed as getting as many youngsters as possible through high school and as many as feasible through college on the assumption that schooling was the open road to opportunity for the individual.

This aim could be achieved first by eliminating barriers to progress through the grades 1 to 16. Thus in Resolution 5 it was acknowledged that not all secondary schools could offer all of the proposed courses, nor was it so intended by the committee. Small schools might have to content themselves with few subjects, while the large ones could have them all. It was thus important that colleges be explicit not only about constants, but also about electives and equivalents. As a matter of fact, in order that choice should not be unlimited, the committee offered in Resolution 6 its suggested constants: 4 units in foreign languages, with no language accepted in less than 2 units; 2 units each in mathematics and English; and 1 each in history and science.

In both Resolution 6 and Resolution 12 the committee returned to electives. Secondary schools must be permitted to adjust their programs to the "local environment, the demands of their constituency, and the tastes of their pupils," and the barrier of personal preference must be overcome. If work in subjects so selected were well done, it ought to be accepted for admission by higher-education institutions. Resolution 1 had stated flatly that the principle of election must be recognized. To ensure that there be at least a limited election, Resolution 12 called for recognition (for admission credit) of any of the studies in its report, provided the study covered at least one year of four periods a week in a good secondary school where competent instruction was available. Eliminating the barrier of a restricted and fixed group of subjects for college entrance allowed for indulging personal tastes, adjusting to individual differences, and straightening out the ladder which ran from kindergarten to college.

Adaptation to the individual differences of the brighter youngsters was recognized through three resolutions. One approved the practice of encouraging "gifted students to complete the preparatory course in less time than is required by most students." Another asked that colleges give credit for secondary school work which went beyond the requirements for that level of the school system. Still another pleaded for advanced work in the sciences in college for those who had already had considerable science in high school. A fourth, in a related vein, asked colleges to recognize at least one-half year of intensive study of some period of history (particularly United States history) in addition to the year of United States history and civil government already allowed or recommended. This proviso was not so much aimed at instilling patriotism as allowing a pupil to pursue a favorite subject—again an adaptation to individual difference.

Adaptation to other kinds of individual differences in deference to the aim of extended schooling for all was recognized indirectly in other resolutions. The six-year high school (grades 7 to 12) was commended —not because some of the experts in the disciplines would like to start their subjects earlier—but to ensure that more youngsters would achieve high school graduation. "The seventh grade, rather than the ninth, is the natural turning-point in the pupil's life," said the committee, recognizing the necessity for change in methods with adolescents. Furthermore, the committee had discovered that the number of students dropping out of school at the end of the sixth grade was small in comparison to the number dropping out at the end of the eighth. Better to make the transition to the new school before the leaving age in the hope that, once begun on a new course of schooling, more might be induced to remain to the end. An indirect benefit to the student would be to increase with number of grades the number of high schools and enable the people's college to be more accessible and less expensive for many pupils.

Another kind of adaptation was implicit in the resolution respecting lengthening the school day. Such an extension would permit more supervised study in school. Discussion pointed out that homes in cities and large towns and the homes of some of the new pupils were inappropriate for study. Many youngsters did not know how to study. They needed the suitable surroundings provided by a school and the direction of a sympathetic teacher. In this resolution, but with no fanfare, the committee recognized the variation in backgrounds of the new secondary population; at the same time, the committee bulwarked the position of the school as an agency which must take the place of other social agencies in all cases of need.

Before the committee members were done, they needed to pay homage to that equality for which the schools educated, and about which concepts had never been clarified. They said in Resolution 2 that "the requirements for admission to technical schools should be as extended and thoro as the requirements for admission to college." If admission requirements were lowered, students would enter on technical studies at an earlier age; they would have less general culture than would the high school graduates; and they would leave high school before the completion of their high school work. Requiring the same kind of training for the technical-school-bound as for the college-bound would complicate the matter of admissions and high school programming. Complication was preferable to the present practice of preparing technical-school people in special manual training schools. Such differentiation was "not in accord with the fundamental principles and ideals of the American education system." It reduced the opportunity of the individual who would like to go to a technical school because special preparatory institutions were not nearly so accessible as regular high schools. Regular high schools should include enough different programs to prepare the pupil, whether his eventual choice were to be literary or technical.

Any summary of this committee's work should acknowledge that it was first enforcing the recommendations of the Committee of Ten. Practically all that could be said of the latter would apply to the Committee on College Entrance Requirements. Could it be said to have advanced the reorganizing of secondary education? Probably not, except through reinforcement. What it did do, however, was to show the good grace with which some in the scholarly community were accepting a pattern of secondary education radically different from that known in Europe in the present and the past.

## Committee of Nine on the Articulation of High School and College, 1910

Those interested in secondary education again attacked the entrance requirements of the colleges on July 6, 1910, when the Secondary Department of the National Education Association requested the colleges to discontinue the entrance requirement of two foreign languages and to recognize as electives all subjects well taught in the high school. Until such modifications were made, the faculties of public high schools would be greatly hampered in their attempts to serve the best interests of pupils. Having so summarily requested the colleges to modify their practices, the department people thought it meet to "prepare a rational statement of the work that the high school should do." Therefore, the

Committee on Articulation of High School and College was established.[22] What was specifically meant by "articulation" was never made clear by the committee. It is possible that there could be no "rational" definition. The word was perhaps coined to cover this proposition: How far can we go in getting the colleges to accept our choice of subject pattern for college entrance credits? The nature of the reports, the subsequent activities of the committee, and the composition of the articulating and articulate nine would suggest the validity of this definition.

In itself, the committee was a kind of handwriting on the wall. Of the nine, only two were college people. Of those two, one was a professor of education from Chicago, Charles H. Judd, who showed himself to be even more liberal in his concept of a high school curriculum than other members of the committee. Of the remaining seven, one was a superintendent of schools and another a deputy state commissioner of education, while the other five were from high schools. The chairman, Clarence D. Kingsley, was a high school mathematics teacher and, more significantly, from the Manual Training High School, which was not necessarily to be looked on as a college preparatory institution.

Committee members were amply aware that the high school had increased fourfold during the preceding twenty years (1890–1910), and that the task of the high school was no longer catering to a "literary class." The education for an elite had been defined in terms of Latin, Greek, and mathematics. But as more people sought higher education, the colleges had relaxed their requirements in the preferred subjects and had occasionally allowed substitutions of modern languages for part or all of the classical languages. Now it was time to consider other young people who were denied college education because of the remaining insistence on modern languages and mathematics. Preliminary to any reorganization of the high school curriculum must be a consideration of the function of that education.

According to the committee, secondary education had a carefully defined field and a comprehensive role. First, following on the recommendations of Dr. Henry S. Pritchett of the Carnegie Foundation, it must include new curricula for different types of students, not merely add subjects to the old requirements. Second, there should be a

---

[22] Report to follow based on National Education Association reports: "Report of the Committee of Nine on the Articulation of High School and College," *Journal of Proceedings and Addresses, Forty-ninth Annual Meeting,* 1911, pp. 559–566; "Report of the Committee on the Articulation of High School and College," *Journal of Proceedings and Addresses, Fiftieth Annual Meeting,* 1912, pp. 667–673; "Third Report of the Committee on the Articulation of High Schools and Colleges," *Journal of Proceedings and Addresses, Fifty-first Annual Meeting,* 1913, pp. 489–491. All reports published by the University of Chicago Press, Chicago.

minimum core of citizenship education for all students. Third, the high school should be a tryout period; as such, it should allow for changes. Fourth, the high school should make a contribution to the general efficiency of the individual. Fifth, "mechanic arts, agriculture, or household science should be recognized as rational elements in the education of all boys and girls." Unfortunately, according to the committee, tens of thousands of boys and girls held false ideals of culture as being exclusively bookish. "A chasm is created between the producers of material wealth and the distributors and consumers thereof." The high school should reflect the major industries of the community which supported it, and should cater to such fundamental needs as that for proper management and conduct of a home.

In view of the foregoing considerations, these committee recommendations followed:

1. Quality being preferable to quantity, 15 rather than 16 should be the required number of units. The extra unit would take care of possible failure without costing the student an extra year. However, students poor in ability should be encouraged to complete the high school course in five rather than four years.

2. In every high school course, there should be at least 3 units of English, 1 unit of social science including history, and 1 unit of natural science. Systematic physical training should also be given and required of all, but this work should not count toward the 15 units.

3. Every high school course should require the completion of two majors of 3 units each, and one minor of 2 units. One of the majors should be English.

4. The requirement in mathematics and in foreign language should be held to 2 units each. In place of either of these two requirements, there should be allowed to be substituted a second unit of social science and a second unit of natural science. There might be one plan which would omit mathematics entirely, and another which would leave out foreign languages. Following on recommendations of these latter plans, it was suggested that the colleges make provision for teaching beginning languages or mathematics when college officials discovered that the lack of these was a handicap to fulfilling a particular student's educational plans.

5. Of the total of 15 units, not less than 11 should be devoted to English, foreign languages, mathematics, social science, natural science, "or other work conducted by recitations and home study." The remaining 4 units might be used in further academic work or in mechanic arts, household science, commercial work, and other subjects adapted to the potential of the students.

The above set of recommendations would eventually open the curriculum to the several hundred subjects now found on the high school books, though the committee members could hardly have anticipated such an eventuality. There was one member, however, who might have done so.   Dr. Judd recommended that no subject specifications be made for high school curricula.   Rather, he favored two majors of 3 units each, and one minor of 2 units, a plan already adopted by the University of Chicago, requiring only that a certain amount of the high school work be "coherent." Thus ended the first report of the Committee of Nine on Articulation.

Despite the radical suggestions for change in college entrance requirements, the committee's work had not ended.   Two reports were to follow before members were ready to suggest the organization of an entirely new commission of inquiry.   These two reports were addressed largely to consolidation of gains and implementation of recommendations.

A grant from the National Education Association had been used to print 30,000 copies of the 1911 report for distribution.   As a consequence, the report had been discussed and endorsed by faculties and associations and was receiving favorable notice from the colleges.   Progress in implementing the report would be slow unless information on all current reorganization were made widely available.   The articulation committee therefore recommended that twelve subject-matter subcommittees survey work going on in large and small high schools, and that their reports be published by the U.S. Office of Education.[23]

Articulation-committee members knew precisely the kind of information the subject-matter committees should be gathering.   Detailed information on the course of each subject in each high school was wanted. Its place in the curriculum, the nature of the content, the purpose for which it was being taught, persons for whom the course was believed to be valuable, methods, equipment, and examinations—all were matters to be studied.   The most important questions to be asked were those relating to purpose and clientele.   In the former could be seen the outlines of recommendations of the still-to-be-established Commission on the Reorganization of Secondary Education.   The articulation committee had noted that a subject might make contributions to (1) specific efficiency (civic, vocational, domestic); (2) general efficiency (intellectual power); (3) ideals (civic, vocational, domestic, personal character); and (4) appreciation (aesthetic, literary, scientific, social).   The subcommittees were also charged to show how the overriding aims in a subject would change and condition methods.   Fast disappearing was the day when the scope of a course might be justified in terms of the development of concepts in a discipline.

That the internal logic of a subject or the authority of its discipline was to be replaced was amply evident also in the questions to be asked

[23] Report to follow based on National Education Association, "Report of the Committee on the Articulation of High School and College," *Journal of Proceedings and Addresses, Fiftieth Annual Meeting,* 1912, pp. 667–673.

about the persons taking the course. "For whom valuable?" was the sixth question in the proposed subject-matter questionnaire. It was obvious that "valuable" was to be interpreted in the context of students of varying backgrounds. The interviewee was asked to ignore prevailing college entrance requirements and to consider whether the course was of value to a future enrollee in a college of liberal arts, of engineering, of agriculture. Also: Might the course be of value to a student undecided as to his vocation or further education? To one who had made up his mind to stop his schooling with high school graduation? The development of the student, not the demands of discipline, was to be the criterion by which the value of a particular segment of subject matter was to be measured.

After this introduction of the new subcommittees and the proposed questionnaire, the second report of the articulation committee closed with encouraging notes, including commendations from prominent school people on the 1911 report and reports of changes in college and university entrance requirements. The committee concluded that increasing numbers of institutions of higher education were relegating to high school faculties the tasks of selecting subjects and choosing methods of instruction.

The report's surprising success with college people emboldened the committee; members anticipated a general reorganization of all secondary education rather than tampering with the curriculum of the college-going group. Consequently, the third report asked for the appointment of a Commission on the Reorganization of Secondary Education with the old subcommittees raised to the status of committees of the commission. This suggestion was made so that the committees would not be bound by the traditional conception of secondary education as preparation for college.[24]

The newly suggested commission, besides incorporating the ten subject-matter committees already appointed, was to include a committee on mathematics (earlier suggested but never appointed), a committee on art (instead of on pedagogy and psychology as previously suggested), the extant Committee on the Articulation of High Schools and Colleges, and a reviewing committee, consisting of chairmen of committees plus ten members-at-large. The last were apparently to guard against the tendency of the specialist to think of subject matter rather than the development of boys and girls.

Members of the old articulation committee had gone so far in anticipating changes in the secondary field that they had written the score

[24] Report to follow based on "Third Report of the Committee on the Articulation of High Schools and Colleges," *Journal of Proceedings and Addresses, Fifty-first Annual Meeting of The National Education Association*, 1913, pp. 489–491.

for the work of the more famous commission to be. The latter would only need to add the words.

## Commission on the Reorganization of Secondary Education (1913–1918)

Between 1913 and 1918 the several subject-matter committees of the new commission were busy meeting with representatives from organizations of their allied disciplines. Out of joint deliberations came a series of statements which paved the way for the commission's final report of 1918. These statements, published as bulletins of the U.S. Office of Education, included a set of preliminary statements by the chairmen of committees in 1913, followed by separate bulletins on community civics, the social studies, English, music, physical education, moral values, and vocational guidance.[25] Although the 1913 preliminary statements contained reports from committees such as that on ancient languages, detailed committee reports in subsequent bulletins reflected the socially oriented life-purpose curriculum to emerge as the recommendation of the commission.

What appeared to be emerging from committee deliberations were reinterpretations of democracy and how to maintain it, and of learning and how to promote it. Both reinterpretations were undoubtedly sparked by the changing nature of the secondary school. The latter was now being frankly recognized as a people's college or a more expansive instrument for mass education. According to most committeemen, it was quite clear that in the foreseeable future the American

[25] The commission appointed by the National Education Association reported in the following bulletins issued by the U.S. Office of Education: *Cardinal Principles of Secondary Education;* Henry Neumann, *Moral Values in Secondary Education,* Bulletin 1917, no. 51, 1918; Will Earhart and Osbourne McConathy, *Music in Secondary Schools,* Bulletin 1917, no. 49, 1918; *Physical Education in Secondary Schools,* Bulletin 1917, no. 50, 1918; James Fleming Hosic (comp.), *Reorganization of English in Secondary Schools; Report by the National Joint Committee on English Representing the Commission on the Reorganization of Secondary Education of the National Education Association and the National Council of Teachers of English,* Bulletin 1917, no. 2, 1917; *The Reorganization of Secondary Education: Preliminary Statements by Chairmen of Committees of the Commission,* Bulletin 1913, no. 41, whole no. 551, 1913; Arthur William Dunn (comp.), *The Social Studies in Secondary Education, a Six-year Program Adapted Both to the 6-3-3 and the 8-4 Plans of Organization: Report of the Committee on Social Studies, Commission on the Reorganization of Secondary Education,* Bulletin 1916, no. 28, 1916; Committee of the Commission on the Reorganization of Secondary Education, *The Teaching of Community Civics,* Bulletin 1915, no. 23, whole no. 650, 1915; *Vocational Guidance in Secondary Education,* Bulletin 1918, no. 19, 1918. The account to follow is based on these bulletins.

people proposed to put all or most of their youngsters through high school. The new role of the secondary school as an institution for all demanded the subordination of college preparation to the provision of enriched education for all. No longer was the problem of articulation one of the relationships between the secondary and the college curricula; rather it was between the elementary and the high school aims and courses of study. Several of the committees recognized this changed articulative process by reviewing elementary as well as secondary subject-matter aims as contributing to a continuous and expanding educative process.

Members of practically all of the committees were interested in the pupil as a citizen, in the appropriate behavior for a citizen, and in the nature of a democratic society. Social efficiency was the keynote to the demands on its members of the American body politic and body social.

The needs of the newly perceived society were most vigorously put forth. The Committee on the Social Studies related the shaping of youth to the kind of citizens needed in America. Because the United States was growing increasingly complex, young people must be anchored by a steadfast faith in human beings and by awareness of the agencies through which civilization had been advanced. Implicit in the educational job of the social studies was the nature of social democracy. "The social studies are understood to be those whose subject matter relates directly to the organization and development of human society, and to man as a member of social groups." In this respect they differed only in their content, not their aim, from the other high school studies, for the governing principle of the educative process was social efficiency, and all instruction should make contribution to the end of the socially efficient citizen.

It was not enough for the citizen to be aware of his privileges. He must develop a feeling for the laws which governed social life and an awareness of his obligations to his social groups. Along with these feelings and understandings, he must develop the intelligence and acquire the motivation to take part in furthering social health. The student was a social animal, dependent for his welfare on the cooperative work of all people to whom his welfare was related, and equally responsible to them for assisting in improving group life.

The social studies would help the young citizen to acquire the "social spirit." So would music, for the group feeling would be enhanced through group singing and performance. English could contribute to the development of noble ideals and high character, and help the young to improve "relations with and service to others in the community and nation." A study of music of other times and peoples, when accompanied by an inquiry into related political and social development, would contribute to the same end. Science could be changed from a series of knowledge systems to a series of inquiries into how scientific knowledge had contributed to the improvement of health and the development of the industrial system. Almost any subject in the curriculum had its part to play in the primary aim ascribed by the committee to American history. Through history the student should acquire a brilliant picture of American nationality; a deep, abiding, and informed patriotism; and a clear understanding of the obligation of every citizen to promote the general efficiency of the United States. Only a citizen so equipped could perform his functions as a member of one of the family of nations.

The youth who was to be developed into the group-minded American citizen was a different kind of youth from the one who had pored over Greek and mathematics in the nineteenth century. The new student was not susceptible to mental discipline for which there was now only a fine scorn, nor was he to emerge after having gone through a particular pattern of course experiences. Even the college-bound youth would not be served by the old rigid subject-matter prescription—according to no less an authority than Clarence D. Kingsley, chairman of the commission, the best way to prepare for college was to forget college entrance requirements and to develop motives.

Something approximating another "whole child" had been rediscovered. This one was full of needs and life purposes and immersed in the process of growing. Some committee members thought they were getting next to this new youth when they quoted Prof. John Dewey. He had said that if educators were committed to the idea that giving attention to ongoing growth needs would be the best provision for future learning, then necessary changes in educational ideals would soon be made; other desired changes would come about automatically. This student was not getting ready to live, he was living. He needed not grammar, facts, and analytic geometry, but good health, a sense of community, and vocational guidance. To suit his newly discovered propensities and the social role he was to serve, there had to be a thorough overhauling of the several disciplines and the addition of new units of study.

The most aggressive group had been the English teachers. Theirs had been the almost universally required subject by 1900, and they were strong in numbers and in grievances. The children of foreign tongues and lower-class status had been offending their ears; the colleges had been bedeviling them with longer lists of books from which college entrance examinations might be taken; and the work of none of the prior committees had quite seemed a solution to their almost-overwhelming problems. The members of the Committee on English, along with representatives of the National Council of Teachers of English, were ready for a thorough renovation of the English curriculum.

The English bulletin was long and detailed. Sufficient to this account, perhaps, is a statement of the ends to which it was addressed. English did not consist of subject matter; this was very clear. It was rather a set of activities through which there might be developed ideals, attitudes, skills, and habits. It was an art, not a science; thus it was to be acquired through practice rather than through generalization. Its immediate aims must be concerned with a command of the art of expression in speech and writing, and with helping the student to read thoughtfully and with appreciation so that he might develop a taste for good reading and the skill to find worthwhile books. If these skills were properly taught, they would help the student to newer and better forms of pleasure (culture), assist him in reaching the highest success in his vocation, and help him to form that social character so necessary to the good community.

In contrast to the tenor of the English committee was that of the Committee on Ancient Languages which timidly proposed some preliminary statements in 1913. The committee had not got very far, being tied up in such questions as whether Latin was losing or gaining ground, who ought to be taking it, and whether it was practical. The last question had been partially settled; it was justified provided it contributed to the development of good English. Most of the aims of its teaching were discovered to cluster around the mother tongue. Wanted was a Latin instruction which enriched the English vocabulary and promoted clearness of English expression. Through it could be developed an appreciation of word, phrase, and clause relationships. It was obviously a foundation for the study of English and modern languages. It enabled one to become an intelligent critic of one's own speech. It had some aims in its own right, however. Through it one could come to know the masterpieces and to gain a wider view of life. In view of its timidly defended vitality, it might well substitute for formal English grammar. The committee members closed their preliminary deliberations with the faint hope that they might have an eye to the child rather than to college entrance requirements.

The Committee on Modern Languages started out with the flat assumption that the aims of instruction must be determined by service to pupils. Aims and curricula of modern language teachers would be charted in terms of those who left language class early and those who continued through the four years. In their teaching, they would strive to assist students to phonetic accuracy and precision in the use of words, along with developing a corollary understanding of grammatical relations and common terms and an interest in foreign nations. To these general aims might be added for a fourth year that of preparing students, through special work, for scientific or commercial subjects required by particular schools.

The Committee on Natural Science, reporting in 1913, lamented the fact that too small a percentage of high school students elected science. The explanation of this failure was that science teachers did not adapt their materials to students' needs. As laboratory equipment had increased and multiplied, and as more time was given to quantitative methods, science instruction became increasingly remote from daily concerns. Students were urged to secure good marks in physics, chemistry, and biology, but they did not thereby come to understand the applications of these sciences to everyday life. The science curriculum must be weaned from the aim of knowledge for its own sake and reoriented toward life experiences and life needs.

The Committee on the Social Studies and the Special Committee on Community Civics really came into their own in the reorganization of the high school subjects. Social studies teachers had a golden opportunity to guide the 1⅓ million high school youngsters (the largest group of its kind in the world) toward serious effort "to acquire the *social spirit.*" Neither a civics which was an exclusive study of government, nor a history which was to be studied for its own sake would do. Anything not contributing rather directly to human betterment had no claim in the curriculum.

The social studies proper (economics, geography, history, political science) should be reorganized in cycles. In the elementary grades, instruction would touch on all the areas of the social studies, but not as separate subjects. The aim in certain elementary schools was to promote an enriched living and growing during which the interconnections of life's processes (civic, geographic, vocational) would be naturally uncovered. In this spirit, there should be developed for grades 7 to 9 a junior cycle on geography, European history, and American history. A senior cycle for grades 10 to 12 should include European history, American history, and problems of democracy—social, economic, and political. Thus, the cycles would follow the ways in which young people completed their schooling, and each cycle would provide a nice whole in each period.

For this social man who was to emerge, subject matter should be organized around problems. Such propositions as these might be proposed in sixth grade geography, for instance: Egypt was once a leading world power. Why is it now of little influence and under the sway of England? What are the conditions under which the United States has risen to industrial power? History topics must be selected not in terms of the periods with which they dealt nor with their importance, but rather in terms of whether they could be reconciled with the interests of the student or utilized by him in his growth processes. To meet these criteria and that of social efficiency, recent history was more important than that of ancient times, and history of the United States was more significant than that of foreign countries. The labors and plans of the multitudes were of greater import than the pleasures and dreams of the few. A subhistory was demanded before a subhistory had been written.

The committee members cautioned against excessive differentiation of courses. By this they meant adaptation to regional or local differences in interest. However, they did admit that immigrant children might be given slightly larger doses of American than European history, and that topics for study and discussion might reflect, within limits, industrial or other specific needs.

Their new contribution to the development of the social man was the course Problems of Democracy; for this, everybody in the community must be drafted into the service of the youth who were trying to become effective citizens and helpful group members. For these youth it was not so important to know how the President was elected as how the health officer worked. Acceptable topics for them to explore were community health, crime and reform, family income, human rights versus property rights, and, as a vague bow in the direction of rampant individualism, the selfish conservatism of traditions. It was not the purpose, of course, to give the student an exhaustive account of these matters, but to help him to see the significance of the issues to him and his community—in other words, to help him to think and live "civically."

The interest in Problems of Democracy was so high that a special committee was appointed to develop a community civics. The latter group began deliberations by marking out the four stages in training for good citizenship. The first was the period before formal schooling began. Here the family was the chief educative agent and social habits were the chief outcome. The second stage carried on from six to twelve years of age, encompassed learning right social relations in school and developing ideals of loyalty, personal honor, and integrity. With the twelve- to fifteen-year-olds in the third stage, the outside community had to come into prominence; these youngsters might well be introduced to elementary history, community civics, and a survey of typical vocations. Now was the time, also, to channel the gang loyalties of boys and the sentimentality of girls into social feeling, social thought, and social action. The fifteen- to eighteen-year-old youths were getting onto firmer emotional ground, apparently, for in the fourth stage they could study history, elementary economics, and an advanced course in civics—all designed for the preparation of good citizens.

Community civics was aimed at dislosing the importance and significance of community welfare, at promoting a knowledge of government and voluntary agencies, and at helping youth to recognize their civic obligations, to which they should respond by appropriate action. In the past, civics teaching had been largely ineffective, according to the committee, because the student had had to work out the applications of its general principles for himself. Community civics must cultivate a motive which was to be found in common interests. In this identification with the community, the student could come to link his obvious self-interest in health, education, and character, as well as industriousness, efficiency, and thrift, with the welfare of the cooperating agencies and with obligations to fill places in government. The virtues of the good American, which were as old as the founding of the nation, were preserved and enshrined as the necessary attributes for promoting social efficiency. Even the ideally rugged and independent man was given a place in the new cooperative social order through a final admonition against oversentimentalized charity. Students must be made aware of the bad effects of unthinking almsgiving. Such could only be degenerative to the receiver.

The social man, of course, did work. So the Committee on Manual Arts was safe in stating that the major purpose of its field was to contribute to vocational efficiency. To this end, more and shorter courses with vocational purposes were needed, and earlier opportunity for differentiation in purposes, courses, and methods. Manual arts was an uneasy newcomer to the field of the secondary school disciplines, and the committee members had some bad moments. Academic teachers were a drawback to the progress of their subject. Manual arts teachers must avoid the impression that some courses should be held in less esteem than others. Nonetheless, could the manual arts contribute anything of value to the college-going group, the criterion group for testing the worth of any high school subject? Tentatively, the answer of the committee members was "Yes," the manual arts could be taught so that they would contribute to "intellectual power and social outlook," and thus they were good for all.

The preliminary statement on manual arts was followed by a bulletin devoted to vocational guidance. The latter, according to the committee, was a continuous process designed to help the individual choose, plan his preparation for, enter upon, and make progress in an occupation. The school had long since taken over many of the functions of the home, including inducting the young into vocations. An elaborate program was necessary to carry out the task of vocational preparation. Youngsters must first survey the world's work; then they must be studied and tested for their potentials. They must have guidance in choice and re-choice of vocation and course preparation for that vocation. Next there must be provided a placement service along with supervision on the job. Finally, to carry out this elaborate program, there must be progressive modification of school practices and, most astonishing of all, progressive modification of economic conditions.

Women work, too, if not in industry, at least in the home. They must be taught to be better homemakers, according to the Committee on the Household Arts. More than that, they must become intelligent about the occupations formerly a part of the home and must come to have an appreciation of the municipal environment and its influence on the home. The immediate aim of developing in girls a concept of the responsibility and function of homemakers was not to be carried out through an inspired new program. Rather it was to be met through a knowledge of elementary principles of biology, chemistry, physics, and bacteriology as applied to food preservation and preparation and to conservation of the health of the family. Action was the order of the day, however, and this subject was ideally suited to activity. Laboratory work was to be promoted in cooking, making clothes, planning houses, and in purchasing household supplies and equipment.

Committees on business and on music had brief but uninspired preliminary statements. The former addressed itself forthrightly to enabling the student to fill a place in the commercial world. The latter considered the contributions of its field to the subjective life, the appeal to the ear, the mind, and the soul. The physical educators concentrated on the health needs of the pupil, including the health examination, the healthful environment, instruction in health, physical activity, and listed school credit for physical education as one of the "needs" of the pupil.

Provisions had now been made for making this high school youth healthy, wealthy, and wise. But had his character been given enough attention? Some members of the commission must have thought not, for the reviewing committee called for a special statement on moral values. How this might be made and what it could contain must have given some real concern to heritors of the several Protestant traditions which said that morals were inevitably linked with religion. What was needed was a secular morality (to some, a contradiction in terms) which would nevertheless be not too offensive to those who had to do some soul searching to separate moral from religious guidance in character building. For the task of stating the issues, the reviewing committee called on one of its members, Dr. Henry Neumann, teacher in the Ethical Culture School of New York City. Before its issuance in 1917, Dr. Neumann's statement was reviewed and discussed by the committee. But it was carefully stated that the committee's approval did not commit any member of the committee to agreement with the argument put forth.

Dr. Neumann hewed close to the line of a democratic ethic. Intelligence, proper habits, and ideals were all required for making the moral man. That time which could be best capitalized on for developing the moral virtues was the high school age when students craved freedom, self-reliance, and a chance to show what they could do as independent human beings. They were at this time fully conscious of their new personal worth, they had a quickened sense of justice, and they were filled with the desire to help their fellow human beings. All these impulses of high school youth could be used to advantage in helping the young to become better persons.

First in importance as a moral agency, according to Dr. Neumann, was action. Character was a matter of activity, of the habitual performance of preferred deeds. To make full use of this agency, high school students must first be enabled to live democracy in the classroom. To achieve this goal, old-fashioned classrooms must go. The one desk to a child, the concentration on individual effort called attention to the importance of the "I" rather than the "we." Members of a democracy must be animated by the spirit of cooperation. Student self-government must be stressed so that pupils might learn how to behave under group authority. They must be helped and urged to assist in community ventures. Learning the habit of cooperation was apparently a key to morality.

Teachers must, of course, take an active part in interpreting experience and suggesting new ideals. Ethical interpretation might be regarded as a necessary link between two sets of experiences: behavior already performed and the preferred sort which was yet to take place. This ethical interpretation could go on not in a class called "Moral Values," but within any of the subject-matter classes. In science sessions, students might learn how physical order improved health, industry, homemaking, and communication with one's fellows in peace or war. In the social studies classrooms, students could be helped to understand right and wrong and social progress. These were the places where due attention could be given to the meaning of liberty and equality, to the end that there could be a de-emphasis on the enjoyment of privileges and a corresponding emphasis on equality as a concept of each one trying to do his best for the common good. In like manner, any subject area would yield rich opportunities for the discussion of ethical issues and the development of right habits. Thus did Dr. Neumann provide a morality for a secular institution, the public school, and skirt the dangerous waters of religious orthodoxy.

With much attendance at committee meetings and national meetings, and with undoubtedly more paper work than has been reported above, the Commission on the Reorganization of Secondary Education, Na-

tional Education Association, was ready for its final report. In a famous
bulletin of the U.S. Office of Education, there was issued in 1918 the
*Cardinal Principles of Secondary Education.*

## Report of the Commission on the Reorganization of Secondary Education

High school youth, full of needs, abilities, and aptitudes, and the
democratic society demanding particular kinds of citizens—both received a royal send-off in proper educational pathways in the commission's culminating report. The goals and the objectives were firmly
charted, the enlarged role of the school was outlined, and the needs
for reorganizing thus could be succinctly pointed out. The larger
society had changed in such measure that industrial life had become
more complex, with a consequent increase in leisure which might be
misused, while agencies other than the schools diminished in importance
in the life of the adolescent. Yet youngsters were dropping out of
school at an alarming rate; only one-third of the pupils who had been
in first grade remained to enter high school. How were they to be
saved for society by the one agency that ought to be equipped to
save them?

A new educational theory might point the way. Educational psychologists had emphasized the fact of individual differences, the continuity in the development of the child, the faulty premises of mental
discipline. Subject values and teaching methods had only to be tested
by the laws of learning and the application of knowledge to life rather
than "in terms of the demands of any subject as a logically organized
science." Then secondary education might stand firmly on Clarence D.
Kingsley's platform. Kingsley held that a framework for secondary education should take into account the demands of the society in which it
operated, the nature of the individuals to be educated, and the
knowledge available on educational theory and practice.

The psychologists, according to the commission, were not out of line
with the goal of education in a democracy or with the nature of that
society. The purpose of the latter was to allow full play to the personality development of each member in such a fashion that each,
through appropriate activities, might contribute to the well-being of
others and of the society as a whole. It would follow quite logically
from this personalized definition that education in such a society,
whether pursued within or without the school, should be devoted to
assisting the student to acquire such interests, ideals, habits, and powers
as would stand him in good stead in finding his niche in society and
shaping both himself and the society "toward ever nobler ends."

It would follow that objectives for the properly educated person ought to come out of the society of which he was a part. The latter's membership in family, vocational, and civic groups would lead naturally to such objectives of education as worthy home membership, vocational efficiency, and citizenship. Furthermore, it was clear that, in deference to the sanctity of his person, he ought to have time for personal and social interests; thus, both worthy use of leisure and maintaining optimum health could well become additional objectives. To attain these, however, he needed tools (the three R's) and most of all, ethical character or conduct founded upon right principles "clearly perceived and loyally adhered to." But having listed the objectives separately, it did not follow that they could be neatly separated in educational practice, for the student was an organized whole.

The objectives which finally emerged from the needs of society and those of the individual applied quite naturally to all education, so said commission members. But they could be redefined to apply particularly to the twelve-to-eighteen-year group.

1. *Health.* Many subjects and much equipment contributed to this area. Physical education and sanitary and healthful buildings would be ignored to the danger of the larger society.

2. *Command of Fundamental Processes.* The elementary schools would have concentrated on this objective. New rather than review materials were needed in the seventh and eighth grades. Democratic citizenship demanded ever-higher levels of competency in this area.

3. *Worthy Home Membership.* Literature, music, and art all contributed to this objective in the education of both boys and girls. In addition, all girls ought to have homemaking and boys ought to know something of food values, sanitation, and household budgets.

4. *Vocation.* Each youngster ought to be equipped to earn a livelihood so that he might give good service to society and maintain right relationships. To this end, youngsters ought to be able to survey occupations and have for their assistance adequate vocational guidance and an appreciation of the significance of vocations. The extent to which any high school offered preparation for a specific job must be determined by the job and the facilities available. If there were such preparation, schools ought to employ teachers who were proficient in the job so that they might provide *real* experiences.

5. *Civic Education.* Each young person ought to be able to function well as a member of the neighborhood, town, city, state, or nation, and he ought to have the basis for understanding international problems. It was essential, if he were to emerge as such a citizen, that he have many-sided interests, loyalty to ideals of righteousness, a practical knowledge of social agencies and institutions, good judgment, and habits of coopera-

tion in social undertakings. Social studies, civics, and English could contribute to the development of these attributes and to "training in collective thinking."

6. *Worthy Use of Leisure.* Literature, art, and music were seldom taught with the objective in mind of providing for leisure; but they ought to be attuned to such an end. They could be well seconded by work in science which aroused a genuine interest in nature.

7. *Ethical Character.* In a democracy, ethical character was paramount. The principles of true democracy should permeate the school.

Members of the commission went on to treat of many things which were important in carrying out objectives, including the organization of the high school, interrelation of the objectives, need for explicit values, differentiated curricula, and many others. They were emphatic in their denunciation of the college's determining the high school curriculum, among other things, and pleaded for the over-age child to be taken care of in the high school.

Most interesting of the discussions of commission members was that on the unifying and the specializing functions of the schools. It was quite obvious, so they said, that the school was the one agency of the American democracy which might be used to unify the people. Unification was fundamentally necessary in this society. Unlike many other countries, Americans had no common heredity, established religion, or strongly centralized government which might operate as agent in promoting social solidarity. Quite the reverse, people of the United States came from many stocks, adhered to a variety of religious beliefs, and were rapidly developing into a nation of vocational specialists. For this society, the school must operate as an agency for promoting an understanding of common interests. As such, it must provide for instruction in the social studies, literature, and the mother tongue for social mingling and for participation in common activities.

Yet individuals were different and they were destined for a great number of special functions in society. To this end, they needed special curricula and unique preparation. How could the functions of unification and specialization be cared for satisfactorily in secondary education?

The answers were those which have since been written into policy by educators and school boards alike. The first was curricular juggling. There must be a set of constants taken by all or nearly all the pupils and determined by the objectives of secondary education. Then there must be curriculum variables determined by vocational needs and supported by such devices as continuation schooling and guidance, and tryout periods in the seventh year. Last, there must be free electives chosen in terms of aptitudes and interests and generally nonvocational in nature.

The second answer to the dual function of the secondary school was the comprehensive high school. This kind of school was "the prototype of a democracy"; in it, various groups had a degree of self-consciousness while yet being federated into the nation-school through pursuance of common interests and ideals. "Life in such a school" was "a natural and valuable preparation for life in a democracy." With much more attention to the needs of boys and girls and the insistence on schooling until eighteen years of age, as well as comments on the organization of an appropriate democratic school, the commission closed its report on the stirring statement appearing at the head of this chapter.

## SUMMARY

Professional educators in the period from 1890 to 1918 had, so they thought, successfully reorganized elementary and secondary school curricula in response to individual differences in the burgeoning school population and the demands of the larger society for socially efficient citizens. They had bridged the gap between optimum development of the individual and optimum unification of a diverse population. In the process, they had loosened the hold of the colleges on the secondary schools through insisting on standardization of units of all kinds of subject matters which were to be accepted for college entrance. They had upheld through their deliberations the tried and true American virtues of industry, morality, and knowledge by modifying their meanings for twentieth-century society. They were set to give the perfect American citizen to the enriched American society. The bright tomorrow of the 1890 educators was dawning.

# 7

# General Education as a Curriculum for Americans (1930 to the Present)

> What is wanted, then, is a general education capable at once of taking on many different forms and yet of representing in all its forms the common knowledge and the common values on which a free society depends.[1]
>
> HARVARD REPORT ON
> GENERAL EDUCATION, 1945

In the period 1890 to 1918, educators at the national level had been trying to devise curricula and principles which could be accepted by state and local school people as guides for schooling for Americans. From the time of the report on the reorganization of the secondary school in 1918, professional committees continued activity at the national, state, and local levels. But in the period from 1918 to the 1930s, school people were overwhelmed by socioeconomic crises. This complicated their task of dealing with the increasing end products of compulsory school acts and the restlessness of Americans who equated schooling with opportunity.

Social crises have always had more effect on American education than they have had on schools in other societies. One of these crises opened the period from 1918 to the 1930s. In World War I, democracy had been threatened and had triumphed. But for how long? Communism had become an international threat. Subversion from within must be stemmed. In response to war and foreign ideologies, the foreign-born

---

[1] Harvard University, Committee on the Objectives of a General Education in a Free Society, *General Education in a Free Society: Report of the Harvard Committee,* Harvard University Press, Cambridge, Mass., 1945, p. 58. Quoted by permission of the publisher.

were enrolled in citizenship classes; the German language and German ideas were purged from the schools; a new set of loyalty oaths demanding conformity in thought and action from teachers was put into effect. The fundamentalists took legal issue with the teaching of evolution. In the resulting hysteria, school and college people struggled to maintain their own academic equilibrium and tried to keep their institutions out of legislative halls and investigating committees.

Hardly had the America-for-Americans movement subsided when the crash in Wall Street reverberated around the forty-eight states and three territories, and the debtor and creditor nations as well. With the ensuing panic came a surge of popular protest movements from agriculture and labor, followed by popular panaceas and national action to save the youth. During the decade of radical ideologies and the WPA, NYA, and CCC, and the ten years preceding them, educators began to take stock once more.

What had happened to the American society of the 1930s? Nothing more nor less than that its economic foundations had appeared to crumble. This was a depression either to end all depressions or to end the society. Free enterprise had come on evil days and so had the society. The farmers were embattled, labor leaders demanded drastic revisions of the economy, the unemployed lined the streets. Among the unemployed were adolescents whose schooling had set their sights on conquering the bright world outside the school, and whose monetary anticipations were stipends from the Federal government.

Youth was the business of the schools. And the schools took to heart the unlikely thought that somehow they had failed both their charges and the American society. The concept was abroad in the 1930s that if the educators had gone about their proper business, the Depression would not have occurred. Instead, they had kept their eyes on facts and disciplines and on academic bead telling, which was treason to the youth and adults they were meant to serve.

It was not difficult for educators to be aware of youth. They had more boys and girls than they knew what to do with. In 1928 the high school population was 3,911,279. By 1936, it had jumped to 5,974,537.[2] The population had expanded sharply not only in numbers, but also in characteristics. Increasing heterogeneity was an inevitable concomitant of a population now drawn from groups which in other times would have been at work rather than in school. Numbers, however, were no guarantee of funds with which to cope with population increases. It was the Depression. School budgets were cut on every hand, teachers

[2] Alfred Ehrhardt, "A History of the Problem of General Education in the United States on the Secondary Level," unpublished doctoral dissertation, University of Southern California, Los Angeles, Calif., June, 1950, p. 123.

were often paid in script. The years from 1930 to 1935 were educational chaos, according to some commentators.[3]

## CURRICULAR DEVELOPMENTS
## (1930 THROUGH WORLD WAR II)

The chain of socioeconomic events from World War I through the Depression of the 1930s, coupled with the increasing percentage of youth in high schools and colleges, set educators to assessing current practices and devising new curricula. Two phases of the new curriculum movement are identifiable. The first phase, with which this section will deal, began in the late 1930s, particularly in the junior high school, and continued in the 1930s and 1940s through high schools and colleges. This phase was devoted largely to self-criticism but was combined with groping toward more acceptable school practices. The term *general education* began to come into professional literature in anticipation of the movement toward identifying this concept as an acceptable American curriculum. This first phase closed roughly during the early 1940s.

### High School Developments

Ehrhardt is not so sure that the high schools had made a start on general education by the thirties. At the end of the 1900 to 1930 period, the high school was still highly selective, subject-centered, and departmentalized, according to him. It did have constants and variables, but extracurricular activities rather than the curriculum carried the burden of socialization. The 1918 cardinal principles still underpinned the curriculum. There was emphasis on the development of the individual who was to be prepared either for college or for "industrial efficiency." The courses, as always, had proliferated, so that in 1931 there were some 306 as opposed to some 52 a quarter of a century earlier. General education was to be found only in a core of constants; but a new general education would emerge from the ruins of the old.[4]

The junior high school had been developed to extend the school life of adolescents who would ordinarily have finished their schooling in the eighth grade. Consequently, junior high school faculties had had to design programs addressed to other learnings than subject-matter mastery. In 1927, Leonard V. Koos reported on a canvass he had made of school documents and statements of educational leaders to determine the agreed-upon functions of the junior high school. First on the list

[3] *Ibid.*
[4] *Ibid.*, pp. 77, 80–81.

was realizing a democratic school system through retention of pupils, economy of time, recognition of individual differences, and exploration and guidance. Low on the list was securing better scholarship.[5] Rejection of the last function and realizing a democratic school system through exploration and guidance was bringing the concepts of the curriculum closer to general education. The study anticipated also the nature of the popular pressure for the new curriculum. Interest in general education would be partly a function of increasing heterogeneity in the school-going population.

Although advocates of general education would often in the 1940s and 1950s reject the idea that "generally educated" youth could emerge from mere tampering with subject matter, a necessary first step in the development of a new curriculum appeared to be generalizing the school subjects. Under sponsorship of the Progressive Education Association, volumes were published in the thirties on general English, general mathematics, general science, and general social science. Such areas as these continued to be developed from the 1930s to the 1950s. They were the product of college faculty members, as well as high school teachers and professors of education.

One kind of generalizing is that which uses several disciplines within a single broad area. A product of this process is general science, which was described by Koos in 1927. About this subject, given predominantly in the eighth grade, there was no ready consensus. One investigator whom Koos quoted had, however, secured general agreement from eighty teachers on certain of its components and behavioral outcomes. It promoted understandings and appreciations of the control of "one's everyday environment" and of the "applications of science in industrial and social life." In the course of acquiring these understandings, the student secured valuable information about the sciences and about nature itself. He also secured training in scientific problem solving and preparation which would stand him in good stead for later study of any of the specialized disciplines.[6] Since that writing (1927), there has been a proliferation of high school and college conferences on general science and statements about what it is or will do.

Still another of these curricular innovations is *general language*, about which there were firm statements in the 1930s. By 1932, it had found its way into the junior high school as a semester's or a year's work. Somewhat later in the 1930s, an inquiry to 100 schools offering general language yielded a return of 55 questionnaires from twenty-three states. This gave some encouragement; so did the multiplication of texts

[5] Leonard V. Koos, *The Junior High School*, Ginn & Company, Boston, 1927, pp. 15–18.

[6] *Ibid.*, p. 253.

for its teaching.  In 1932 there were but four general language texts available; by 1935 there were ten.[7]

While the generalizing of the school subjects was going on, educators concerned with the secondary schools were criticizing secondary school patterns and practices.  The New York Regents' Inquiry of the late 1930s provided a groundwork for secondary general education by being a medium for emphatic statement of the limitations of the prevailing high school program.  It could be argued that the state-supported schools were established not for the sake of teaching particular curricula, but for preparing youth to take part in the life ahead of them, Francis T. Spaulding said.  This rationale would support such educational outcomes as preparation for vocations and social competence.[8] But New York schools had not been carrying out their civic duty to everyone.

A study of typical secondary school graduates in New York showed that they were deficient in citizenship preparation.  They were likewise deficient in knowledge of social issues and fundamentally conservative in their approach to change.  They gave verbal assent to principles of democratic living and government but were not able to recognize democratic practices.  They showed reluctance to assume responsibility for civic cooperation, an activity which by other names had been approved by educators for at least a hundred years.[9]

More serious than scant achievement of graduates was the fact that the high school was obviously not doing the job the state wanted it to do for all matriculants.  A study of students who left school early (in modern parlance, *dropouts*) showed that they came from homes which offered few educational advantages, had fewer desirable traits, and were often failing when they dropped out.  The schools were distinguishing between good and poor academic accomplishment, and penalizing the latter.[10]

How could such schools serve youth in the way the state desired? The deficiencies in the preparation of those who graduated could be eliminated.  Schools could be made to serve the dropouts more adequately.  In the case of girls who were found to be passive in their interest, the school might try to counteract the outside influences. Above all, the schools must aim to do that which they were not now

---

[7] William Mark Taylor and James B. Tharp, "An Analysis and Evaluation of General Language: The Language Arts Survey Course," *The Modern Language Journal*, vol. 22, pp. 83–91, 1937.

[8] Francis T. Spaulding, *High School and Life: The Regents' Inquiry*, McGraw-Hill Book Company, Inc., New York, 1938, pp. 3, 15–93.

[9] *Ibid.*

[10] *Ibid.*, pp. 76, 92.

doing: develop a social conscience.[11]   Was this *social efficiency* (1905–1918) or *intelligence and virtue* (1820–1860) in another guise?

A 1934 text provided both a framework for approved secondary education and a criticism of prevailing practices.  Thomas H. Briggs's account had in it a mixture of terms.  Some, like *social progress* and *differentiation,* harked back to the social center; others, like *integration* and *needs,* looked forward to the new era to come.  Among the school's functions could be found the whole child, whose needs were to be satisfied; whose interests, aptitudes, and capacities were to be explored; whose guidance was to be effected; and whose interests were to be directed.  Systematization and appreciation of knowledge, as well as revelation of the cultural heritage and integration, were other functions of this high school of an educational realist.  Like Spaulding, Briggs put emphasis on retention of pupils, but also on differentiation.[12]

The crux of Briggs's statement lay, like Spaulding's, in a commentary on the role of the school as an instrument for Americanization.  It was an agency whereby democratic society might perpetuate itself; it therefore devoted itself to improvement of life practices.  The home, the press, the platform were agencies also responsible for general socialization, but they could not be trusted to perform an adequate job.  Hit-or-miss efforts and conflicting philosophies of many of these agencies prevented them from operating satisfactorily to adjust the young to the mores and folkways—or to readjust them—so as to ensure a better state.  Under these circumstances, so important did the role of the public school become that it appeared unreasonable of public officers to allow children to attend private schools uncommitted to (though not subversive of) the ends of the democratic society.  Only the public school could ensure social progress.[13]   Briggs was still in the era of the forth-right social-center educator.

In 1940, a special secondary school curriculum committee of the American Council on Education was ready to propose agreed-upon curricular changes based on social changes.  Fields of knowledge had been expanding, the school clientele had been enlarging, and youth unemployment had been increasing over a long period of time.  Hence the central question: Is it possible to develop programs of general education for all and yet make provisions for special education for groups of youngsters?[14]   This committee was not prepared to be single-minded about general education, but another group was.

[11] *Ibid.,* pp. 106, 119.

[12] Thomas H. Briggs, *Secondary Education,* The Macmillan Company, New York, 1934, pp. 252–288.

[13] *Ibid.,* pp. 210–241.

[14] *What the High Schools Ought to Teach: The Report of a Special Committee*

In 1939, members of a commission of the North Central Association of Colleges and Secondary Schools appointed a general education committee. The preface to their 1942 report contained a firm explanation of the meaning of "general" in "general education." General education was for everyone, took account of the total personality of the individual, and subsumed the individual's nonspecialized activities. As such, it was amply supported by the American value system, which put an emphasis on the individual and his freedoms, his moral worth, and his ability to master his own destiny, as well as on the majority, who were sovereign (not instruments of the state) and whose will should prevail.[15]

With general education and the democratic value system in harmony, it followed logically that the foundation for general education should be found in the society (the majority) and in the youth (the individual). The out-of-kilter social and economic organization came in for analysis. Increasing leisure, ineffective home training, specialization of labor, waste of natural resources, the break-out of derivative (not face-to-face) groups, and other limitations were detailed. More time needed to be given to teaching the meaning of government by consent before the citizenship task of general education could be considered completed. Then followed the developmental tasks of adolescents (individuals) whom the new program purported to serve.[16] That general education was indeed embedded in the American society was evidenced by the readiness with which the authors accepted the proposition that all American youth needed education to orient themselves to agemates and establish independence from family.

There was one dissonant note in an otherwise harmonious whole. Someone had to take account of individual differences and aspirations, and Robert J. Havighurst chose to do so. The secondary school had four tasks, said he. It must make distinctions among students of differing abilities. It must help the able to rise in the social scale, assist some of the upward strivers to find satisfaction with activities other than climbing to the top, and enable the slowest to raise their standards of living.[17]

While educators had been criticizing current programs and suggesting

---

on the Secondary School Curriculum, American Council on Education, The American Youth Commission, Washington, 1940, pp. 6–11.

[15] North Central Association of Colleges and Secondary Schools, Commission on Curricula of Secondary Schools and Institutions of Higher Education, General Education Committee, General Education in the American High School, Scott, Foresman and Company, Chicago, 1942, pp. v–xii, 4–6.

[16] Ibid., pp. 10–13, 37, 40, 106 f.

[17] Ibid., pp. 165–167.

new ones, experiments had been tried in some public and private secondary schools and were ready for evaluation. The most elaborate job of appraisal was done by various committees of the Progressive Education Association and under the general supervision of the Commission on the Relation of School and College, which in 1932 undertook the eight-year study. The core of the problem had to do with encouraging experimentation in some thirty high schools. Carrying out the objectives of the study required colleges and universities over the country to accept the graduates of the experimental programs largely on the basis of recommendations from principals and headmasters.

In consonance with the general aims of the study, two broad kinds of evaluation were carried on. The first was concerned with appraising and recording student progress as high school students moved through the experimental programs. The evaluative procedures were in part an answer to the vagueness which characterized answers as to whether these programs were actually achieving the aims of assisting students to develop character, think clearly, acquire social responsibility, develop good health habits, prepare for earning a living, and acquire skills. The most pressing reason for the appraisal was to be able to supply data to colleges that had agreed to accept the guinea-pig graduates. Evaluation—in preference to measurement, test, or examination—was used to describe this study because evaluation implied "a process by which the values of an enterprise are ascertained."[18]

With the help of school faculties in describing objectives and carrying out the study, the evaluation staff developed or adapted instruments for evaluative aspects of thinking, social sensitivity, appreciations, interests, and personal and social adjustment. The appraisal was made with a clear recognition that it involved the process of analysis as well as synthesis. The evaluation accepted the assumption of the organic unity of behavior, which was expressed in the range of aspects of human growth that were studied and in the structure and plan for the instruments to assess behavior.[19] Planning and administering the evaluative program and recording for guidance and transfer were also part of the report on appraisal.

The evaluation of the educational processes which were closely related to general education was striking; even more striking was the evaluation of achievement to be inferred from the progress of the experimental high school graduates in colleges and universities. Some 2,108 graduates of the thirty experimental schools were brought under

[18] Eugene R. Smith, Ralph W. Tyler, and the Evaluation Staff, *Appraising and Recording Student Progress*, Harper & Brothers, New York, 1942, foreword, preface, p. 5.

[19] *Ibid.*, chap. 7.

study. An exhaustive investigation was made of 1,475 graduates, who were matched on a student-for-student basis with graduates of so-called conventional schools. The matching was done in terms of scholastic aptitude, interests, and socioeconomic background. The sample included four entering-college classes, and students were followed up for four, three, two, and one years. The students were studied in thirty-eight institutions of higher education, including men's, women's, and coeducational colleges, and private and public universities. Instruments included marks, professorial judgments, student questionnaires, and interviews.

Findings indicated that the experimental group came out somewhat better than the comparison group in most areas evaluated. These areas included total grade average, grades in all subjects except foreign languages, academic honors, judgment of intellectual ability, judgment of precision, systematization, objectivity in thinking, and quality of ideas. The experimental group was also superior in such social behaviors as resourcefulness in meeting new situations, solving problems of adjustment, participation in student activities (except religious and service) and in the arts, and nonacademic honors. Furthermore, the graduates of the thirty schools were found to be somewhat better off than conventional high school graduates whether they were judged by professors, contemporaries, or individual students. The only area in which the control group appeared to show superiority was in foreign languages, and there were some social areas in which they were at least equal to the experimental group.

A special study of the graduates of the two most progressive schools and the control students showed differences greater than those reported for the total group.[20] If it was general education which the thirty schools were promoting, then something was to be said for whatever it was. But the programs of the schools showed the difficulties inherent in general education in that they differed rather markedly from one another.

## College and University Developments

The first phase of reaction to the socioeconomic crises from World War I to the 1930s was to be found among college and university educators as well as among the high school people. World War I, as all modern wars, had put a premium on applied science and technology. This emphasis had begun to reflect on liberal education, which was the predecessor of general education at the college level. The reaction of the 1930s began with a defense of liberal education.

[20] For results of the study, see Dean Chamberlain et al., *Adventure in American Education*, Harper & Brothers, New York, 1942, chap. 10.

The inevitable relationship between education and society was the starting point for John B. Johnston in a liberal arts college in a university, when he replied to criticisms of liberal education in a 1930 publication.[21] The charge, according to him, was that democracy was breaking down. If it were, then the question was whether the educational institutions within the democracy could adjust and reorganize—for schools and the means of education were charged with keeping the democratic society intact.

Dean Johnston was committed firmly to the doctrine of individual differences and corresponding differentiation of programs to fit human differences. The most academically capable group of students should, in their beginning years, take work to prepare them for their major endeavors because the college developed the personality and trained the powers of students by helping each to master the part of human knowledge which interested him. By developing students, the college carried out its function of making learning available to the society at large.[22]

It was proposed that the liberal arts college adjust itself to the democratic society by making equal but different adaptations to persons of lesser ability. For students who were not necessarily mediocre, but who were uncommitted, there would be general education. For some of the less able, there would be programs designed to help them function in ordinary occupations, local government, community health, and social and industrial relations.

In the course of his discussion, Dean Johnston raised some interesting questions. One had to do with whether the college of liberal arts could function for the student under the business spell. He came with his program mapped out. He was satisfied with society as it was and was interested only in forging ahead in the occupational field. It was the function of a university which served society, however, to question society and the direction in which it was going. How could the goals of the university and the student be reconciled?[23]

For some time, the focus had been on the liberal arts colleges and their function—particularly on the small college, which was in danger of being lost in the shuffle of university vocational colleges or in the competitive struggle in higher education. As an act of preservation, liberal arts faculties had instituted new practices not on any systematic or planned basis, but rather as they saw gaps in educative processes and could convince themselves to fill the gaps.

These intermittent changes needed examination and publicity so that

[21] John B. Johnston, *The Liberal College in Changing Society*, Century Company, New York, 1930.

[22] *Ibid.*, pp. 3, 21, 234–235.

[23] *Ibid.*, pp. 18–19.

their strengths might be called to the attention of other educators. The American Association of University Women embarked on such an examination in 1930, and the results were published in a yearbook of the National Society for the Study of Education.[24] The expressed purposes of this study were (1) to give facts regarding the status of liberal arts colleges in changing education, and (2) to gather and tabulate data for forming judgments as to the worth of the changes.

To develop a procedure to meet these purposes, the country was first divided into nine regions, with representatives from colleges in each region holding meetings. Representatives from 315 liberal arts colleges contributed in some fashion to the final report. Findings from regional discussion meetings were further sifted by a national committee composed of regional chairmen and a director.

The Greek tradition of a liberal education for elite free men had largely disappeared except for selectivity in respect to student body. Liberal arts colleges were found to be raising admission requirements and instituting such practices as honors courses, tutoring for a select group, and deviating for the best-prepared from the standard four-year unit to a shortened one. This select group, however, was not to operate apart from any obligations shared with the citizenry at large. Professors were moving toward helping the students develop a "total view of life problems." To this end, colleges had tried out orientation courses, a department of American citizenship, a department of euthenics, a department of biography, and one devoted to human relations in industry.

In harmony with a broadly defined citizenship purpose, fitting a student for life, most colleges had moved away from the specialization to be found in a European institution toward a pattern of breadth of educational experiences in the first two years and specialization in the last two. In some institutions, content had been so reorganized as to emphasize fields of learning.

Within the framework of general-special education, student personnel services encompassing vocational guidance and mental and physical health assistance had been developed; these were both to deal with admission and to guide the student through his first two tryout years. The University of Minnesota had tried adjusting the curriculum to the individual student, and Antioch and Whittier had tried helping students to learn through practical work experiences. Many values stressed by elementary and secondary educators—emphasizing American consideration of the worth of the individual and honoring good work habits—had

[24] Kathryn McHale, *Changes and Experiments in Liberal-arts Education*, Thirty-first Yearbook of the National Society for the Study of Education, Public School Publishing Company, Bloomington, Ill., 1932, part II.

been translated into college practices.  Along with these was a general education for citizenship.[25]

More influential because of their sponsorship were the statements on general education published in 1934 as the *Proceedings of the Institute for Administrative Officers of Higher Institutions*. Officialdom had taken enough note of general education to devote a program to its nature, scope, and elements; to its relationship to the several broad liberal fields; and to experimental programs.

In his definition of general education, the president of Lawrence College came fairly close to elements which would commend themselves as essential to educators of the forties and fifties.  President Wriston said that "general" had a double meaning: It applied to students, on the one hand, because it referred to all students as potential candidates for the program.  On the other hand, it applied to a quality in content. This quality was "universal validity" which connoted an education useful to all who had it—in all times and under all circumstances.  It was universal in the sense of being permanent not in respect to facts or indoctrination, but in respect to discipline.[26]

Wriston's disciplines were *precision, appreciation, hypothesis*, and *reflective synthesis*.  Of the third, hypothesis, which he preferred to call "opinionation," he remarked that its chief quality was tentativeness.  It involved developing "coherent patterns of thought from available data" and coming to understand that different conclusions might be reached from the same data.  Such exercises ought to deliver the student from dogma, particularly in the settling of social questions.  The final discipline of *synthesis* demanded a criticism of the intellectual experience itself, for it asked for the establishment of the validity of the latter.[27]

Although Wriston's presentation set the tone of the discussions to follow, it did not indicate the mode of details.  Most of the other commentators concentrated on intellectual processes inherent in general education, but expressed them differently.  One called for clear thinking, clear expression, the development of imagination, and the acquisition of knowledge of the past and present as general-education outcomes. The last outcome appeared as purpose in the discussion of the humanities in general education.  This purpose was seen as tracing the human story as it had evolved.[28]

Wriston's discipline could be seen in another form through a discus-

[25] *Ibid.*

[26] William S. Gray (ed.), *General Education, Its Nature, Scope, and Essential Elements: Proceedings of the Institute for Administrative Officers of Higher Institutions*, University of Chicago Press, Chicago, 1934, p. 1.

[27] *Ibid.*, pp. 9–14.

[28] *Ibid.*, pp. 21, 49.

sion of the contributions of the natural sciences to general education. The sciences might be used first of all to help the learner seek the truth, even if he did not find it. In this endeavor, the sciences, like the humanities, had the virtue of being removed from the context of any immediate situation and thus free from the biases which beset the social sciences. The natural sciences also promoted a healthy scepticism, trained in accuracy, required the use of a philosophical background, and could make use of concrete material.[29]

Despite the flavor of the eternal verities (universal validity) in these 1934 accounts, the changing world was an assumption inherent in most of the arguments. Continuous readjustment, not adjustment, of the individual and the social order symbolized change. So also did the comment that, when the findings of physics and chemistry were applied to human affairs, there was an almost inevitable upheaval in the human environment—an axiom which must be driven home to students.[30]

That general education was a standard around which diverse groups might rally was abundantly clear in a Latin professor's remark that its advent might prophesy a new era—an era in which school men and university teachers, bound by their commitment to a new faith, could bury their differences in friendly discussion. Not so optimistic were other commentators. The college of liberal arts, which symbolized general education, was in the anomalous position of the House of Lords, which did nothing in particular and did it very well.[31] Louis Wirth, in commenting on the unprecedented growth of knowledge, asked whether, through educational devices, educators could hope to integrate that which scientists and scholars had not yet integrated, and whether examinations could integrate that which had not yet been integrated in the literature and in the classroom.[32] Also, an attempt was made in this 1934 report to defend the university as an institution. One educator implied that possibly there had been an unnecessary contrast drawn between *life* and the *university,* as if the latter were death.[33]

By the 1930s the colleges and universities had already taken account of Americanization by putting foundation symbols into general education. They had experimented with new programs as reported by the American Association of University Women and the administrative officers. They had accepted general education as education for all, for life, for universal validity. They had even offered to look at their traditional offerings through the eyes of the more varied Americans now

[29] *Ibid.,* p. 64.
[30] *Ibid.,* pp. 3, 35, 63.
[31] *Ibid.,* pp. 45–46.
[32] *Ibid.,* p. 27.
[33] *Ibid.,* p. 21.

flooding the institutions of higher education. They embraced general education while maintaining their individual points of view. College educators were ready for evaluation activities.

General education in institutions of higher education was put under scrutiny by an encouraging study undertaken from January, 1939, to September, 1944, by the American Council on Education. This study grew out of the interest of a number of college representatives in improving the programs to which their Americanizing function so deeply committed them: general education.

The institutions from which there was heaviest faculty and student participation were in the Middle West, but they were also scattered from Pennsylvania to California, from Minnesota to Alabama. They included land-grant colleges, municipal institutions, state teachers' colleges, liberal arts colleges. By control and student population they included, in addition to coeducational and secular institutions, a Catholic college, a Protestant institution, a Negro college, and four-year and junior colleges for women. Content-wise, the study covered the humanities and social studies, student personnel services, and cooperation in general education. Only the social studies report is reviewed here.[34]

In this study, the concept of citizenship had matured. It had moved from identification with simple items of symbolic behavior, such as saluting the flag and repeating facts of American history, to a level of understandings which could be described critically through cross-checking verbal behavior.

The purposes of social studies were still couched in generalities: to provide a genuine understanding of the American society, to exhibit conflicts in values, to provide social information prerequisite to citizenship policy making, and other expansive and traditional aims. Such terms as *intelligent action, policy-making knowledge,* and *values* still were awaiting definition in measurement terms. These last, however, were partially forthcoming through indirection.

The investigators started out much the way their predecessors had done, with a definition: "General education is the education which is suited to, and needed by youth for life in American society."[35] The study group continued with generalizations and finally admitted their commitment to a series of beliefs, of which very few, if any, could be foreseen as yielding to any kind of measurement. They were standard statements made in elaboration of the so-called democratic way of life. They were not automatically susceptible to translation into behavior

[34] Albert William Levi, *General Education in the Social Studies; The Cooperative Study in General Education,* American Council on Education, Washington, 1948.
[35] *Ibid.,* p. 6.

patterns which could be described statistically. The committee members, nevertheless, must have been committed to behavioral measurement, for the director concluded one of his discussions with the insistence that the purpose of the social studies is "to provide knowledge of fact and value to the end of intelligent action."[36]

The concerns of the study group were further elaborated by a research associate who set the tone for subsequent investigations by insisting that the needs of students must be seen in the context of the social order, for the needs of the social order and of students were practically identical.[37] One problem of general education was to identify the needs of the culture.

On such assumptions the group went forward to develop an inventory of social understanding. The inventory included 150 items which competent social scientists had scored prior to testing students. Students were instructed to mark items "true" or "false," "preferred" or "not preferred," or as falling in none of these four classifications. The inventory was administered to various student populations, usually beginning college students, both in 1941–1942 and again between March and June, 1943.[38]

One outcome of the study was a revealing descriptive analysis of socioeconomic beliefs of a young college population. This is the kind of analysis which is rarely ever forthcoming from ordinary classroom measures. By cross-checking items, it was seen that American youth tended to identify the ideal with the actual on some issues. Holding the traditional American values in esteem, they believed in the realization of those values in American life. Educators from McGuffey to the group who had developed the *Cardinal Principles* had taught well, so well that the American Dream was accepted as fact.

This population which had just emerged from secondary schools could be described as "American" in the sense that they held highly inaccurate and romantic ideas about socioeconomic equality; that they distrusted government (and probably preferred voluntary association); that they distrusted organized labor even more strongly (a man should be able to stand on his own two feet); and that they showed a strong bent for religious institutions and their moral effects on character (knowledge and morality are power).

Equally revealing were the differences between subcultures discovered through item analysis. Even though forty females at Michigan State showed 58 per cent agreement on the proposition that everyone had an

[36] *Ibid.*, pp. 3, 5–6.
[37] *Ibid.*, pp. 27–28.
[38] *Ibid.*, pp. 32–33.

equal chance in America, forty males at Talladega, a Negro college, showed only 17 per cent agreement with the same statement.

The group of social scientists—whose agreement with American values was supported by their direct affirmation of them—were nevertheless interested in some goal for general education other than merely reinforcing beliefs. They were interested in the degree to which action in the direction of their attainment might be stimulated by development of an ability to distinguish between belief and reality. Their analysis dug deeper than beliefs. Out of their study came such generalizations as that *"logical thinking is an ability closely associated with other abilities such as knowledge of fact and ability to discriminate between fact and preference."* It was also discovered that the great deficiency in social knowledge appeared to be in the field of economics.[39]

The real impact of this study of general education in the social studies was forthcoming at a later date, when professors would use the inventory for diagnostic purposes and would base their teaching on defects discovered in student concepts. One such study by a professor at Antioch was of more than passing interest as a commentary on the social inventory. With that at hand, he proceeded with diagnosis and remedial work in a course in the economics of peace and war, and concluded with a study of the effect of his work. He was able to state that education might not be so hopeless a task after all, for it apparently was possible to educate for democracy by selection of appropriate classroom procedures. His conclusion was premised on a set of specific findings such as these: Students were educable in their social beliefs; furthermore, they knew whether a course had had an impact on them and whether the changes in them did or did not disappear. He found that liberality in religion (whether Protestant, Catholic, or Jewish) portended high scores on inventories; and orthodoxy, the opposite. The nature of the religious background of the student appeared to be the most significant factor in his educability.[40]

Although a social movement rarely has a beginning or an ending which can be identified accurately, it can be said that the first phase of curricular development following on World War I closed with World War II. High school and college educators had criticized prevailing programs of the 1930s, had suggested new programs, and had experimented with and occasionally evaluated others. During the period from 1930 to World War II they had gradually come to agree that a new curriculum for Americans should be called "general education."

[39] *Ibid.*, pp. 12–15, 53.
[40] *Ibid.*, pp. 183–216.

## CURRICULAR DEVELOPMENTS
## (WORLD WAR II TO THE PRESENT)

The second phase of curricular development began with the end of World War II or around 1948, the earliest date by which educators could have recovered from the war effort and returned to the normal pursuit of changing schooling practices. During this period came severe criticism of American schooling in the sciences and mathematics, following on publicity given to Soviet Russia's technological achievements. Adjustments to meet such criticisms were made, but the chief theme of the period from 1945 to the early 1960s was general education, a curriculum for Americans. It is with this theme that the balance of this chapter is concerned.

### Elementary School Developments

Since the period 1820 to 1860, the elementary school has been the "common" school. As such it might be said to have been for some 150 years a general-education school. For purpose of identifying the elementary school more firmly with general education, it may be well to review a 1953 statement of the Mid-century Committee on Outcomes in Elementary Education.

The study of the committee was sponsored in large part to provide a basis for further work in measurement and evaluation of elementary education. Evaluation is the appropriate activity; in it one takes account of values with which American education and a democratic society are filled. So the committee was readying elementary education not only for measurement, but also for evaluation. To carry out this purpose, committee members proposed to define goals and to search for new and better instruments to reach them.

The committee made a bow to the original three R's by talking of communication and quantitative relationships as two of nine broad areas of elementary school learning. Included in the goals also was the whole child—his physical development, health, and body care, as well as individual, social, and emotional development, and the achievement of ethical behavior, standards and values, and aesthetic development. So as not to ignore any elements unintentionally omitted, goals for social relationships were mentioned, including world involvement, as well as interest in the physical world. To assure the commonness of this common or general-education school, emphasis was to be put on achievement norms, not standards, for *average* children.[41] Thereby

---

[41] Nolan C. Kearney, *Elementary School Objectives: A Report Prepared for the Mid-century Committee on Outcomes in Elementary Education,* Russell Sage Foundation, New York, 1953.

practically everybody could be subsumed under the common goals of the total curriculum of the elementary school.

## High School Developments

It would be impossible to describe in a chapter of this length the program variations of general education in the secondary schools. The relationship between general education and a schooling for American youth will instead be established by calling attention to definitions of and rationale for general education, variation in terms for the same content, and the movement to attach special subject areas to general education.

A series of statements in articles and books published from 1945 have turned up few completely new definitions, practices, or issues. The American Secondary School Administrators, who have addressed themselves to citizenship, and a host of individual authors occasionally change the social issues or invent new terms. But the problem is essentially the same: How to immerse everybody in common experiences or learning tasks while taking due account of the American value pattern and the developing self, at the same time recognizing individual differences which are a product of biological heredity and cultural conditioning?

To carry out this mammoth task, educators have reached out to engulf everyone (general education is for all and the "all" keeps expanding) from the nursery school through old age.[42] They have studied the life situations of Americans, and from them have drawn curricula.[43] They have called attention not only to the technological revolution, but also to the demographic and the democratic revolutions, the latter being moral commitment to a system of values.[44]

Clearly apparent in most arguments is the dedication to the Americanization task of the schools, which includes defining the American. Thus conformity is always warring with uniqueness, and citizenship is always undergoing redefinition. "Adjustment" is frequently found in common parlance. Every youth should be helped to have experiences by which he may adjust to his society.[45] This goal allows for enough conformity for the child to be clearly identified as an American. General education is charged with developing traits and understandings

[42] *The Expanding Role of Education,* Twenty-sixth Yearbook of the American Association of School Administrators, Washington, 1948, pp. 5–6.

[43] William B. Featherstone, *A Functional Curriculum for Youth,* American Book Company, New York, 1950, pp. 145–146.

[44] *Educating for American Citizenship,* Thirty-second Yearbook of the American Association of School Administrators, Washington, 1954, pp. 26–42.

[45] Harl R. Douglass (ed.), *The High School Curriculum,* 2d ed., The Ronald Press Company, New York, 1956, p. 202.

that men must have in common in order to sustain democracy.[46]  Closely allied to the adjusted child is the public school, unifying agent and coordinator of the work of all other social agencies, including the church.[47]  The heavy burden of the school as the primary institution, which was assumed by social-center educators, has become firmly fixed in the symbol pattern of American educators.

Americans always did have a sense of mission.  It has been their duty to spread the gospel abroad among the uninitiated, as well as to uphold democracy at home as a necessary condition of its being sustained elsewhere.  Following on two world wars, America's ascent to world power has allowed American educators to expand on the mission concept as it was not possible for earlier educators to do.  This expansion has taken the form of education for world citizenship.  Citizenship education needs to be meshed with dynamic national and world movements.[48]  World citizenship is one of four critical issues involved in the expanding role of the school.[49]  For on the continuously rising level of citizenship activities of Americans depends the welfare not only of the United States, but of the world, says a statement in a 1954 publication.[50]

Since the introduction of general education into the junior high schools in the twenties and into the high schools in the thirties, one other kind of movement has caught fire—inventing terms for the part of the curriculum which carries the general-education burden.  These terms include *fusion, correlation, broad fields, core, general studies,* and probably a host of others.[51]  Of these, most time and attention has been given to core.  This concept is beset by the problem of definition, as is *general education,* of which "core" is a curricular expression.

Some characteristics of core include the use of problem solving and evaluation as applied to common needs, and problems and interests which are its scope or content.  Teacher-pupil planning, a decent block of time, a wide variety of human and nonhuman resources, and any and all subject matters are brought into play for these activities.  They may be planned around many areas—school living, self-understanding, use of leisure, family living, world peace, democratic government, and others.  Through this curriculum organization, the child or youth should grow in self-understanding and participation as a group member.  It is

[46] J. Paul Leonard, *Developing the Secondary School Curriculum,* rev. ed., Rinehart & Company, Inc., New York, 1953, p. 377.

[47] Description of Chicago public schools in Stephen A. Romine, *Building the High School Curriculum,* The Ronald Press Company, New York, 1954, p. 180.

[48] *Educating for American Citizenship,* p. 9.

[49] *The Expanding Role of Education,* pp. 5–6.

[50] *Educating for American Citizenship,* p. 8.

[51] Douglass, *op. cit.,* pp. 204–209.

axiomatic that this growth will extend to his understanding of democratic principles and social and moral principles underlying his adjustment to self and others.[52]   The content and possibly the activities of core can be organized as unified studies, culture-epoch, contemporary problems, or adolescent needs.[53]

Of the curricular responses to general education, general studies is by far one of the more fascinating, as defined by one author.   It is not a new name for homeroom programs or activities, according to Featherstone.[54]   Furthermore, it is only a part, not the whole, of general education.   It is a matrix of general guidance and the center for coordination, evaluation, and exploration.   It is drawn from life situations of youth, and is centered in sociocivic, personal development and home- and family-life studies.   It is so firmly life-study centered that there must be massive resistance to building into it anything which looks like a traditional academic pattern.   Rather than to pursue the unrewarding task of trying to name or define the general studies, it is best to look on it as "an incommensurable quantity, indivisible into real parts."[55]

In the meantime, the "real" world has impinged on general education.   Rather, general education, along with the project on all American youth, may have generated an educational prairie fire.[56]   By the very words, "life adjustment," educators may be brought back to the reality of America.   The citizenship aims of general education were all well and good and in the best tradition, but because of their emphasis on nonspecialized education, they ignored one aspect of the good American: the worker.

Life adjustment education has the singular advantage, according to its advocates, of subsuming the whole child in his myriad relationships as home member, worker, and citizen.   Its origin was found, like most curricular practices, in the larger society.   A group of vocational educators had asked for some nationwide attention to certain facts respecting the American economy.   At a national conference in May, 1947, Dr. Prosser called attention to the fact that 60 per cent of the employed had received no specialized training for their jobs.[57]   Were schools once again failing their society?

Following the national conference, nine national organizations sub-

---

[52] Lucile L. Lurry and Elsie J. Alberty, *Developing a High School Core Program,* The Macmillan Company, New York, 1957, pp. 28–42, 60. For core, see also Romine, *op. cit.*

[53] Romine, *op. cit.*, p. 332.

[54] Featherstone, *op. cit.*, p. 144.

[55] *Ibid.*, pp. 144–146.

[56] Harl R. Douglass, *Education for Life Adjustment: Its Meaning and Implementation,* The Ronald Press Company, New York, 1950, p. vi.

[57] *Ibid.*, p. 6.

mitted nominees for the Commission on Life Adjustment. Out of the commission's work came a suggestion for a life-centered program. It stressed life needs, time-for-life areas, all activities of the school, work experience, and expanded guidance. The whole child, including all of his attitudes, ideas, interests, habits, skills, information—in short, his social, mental, physical, and emotional development—were taken into consideration. The new curriculum was designed to help the youth to adjust not only to all areas of life in the present, but also in the future.[58]

Life adjustment then subsumed the general and the specific, the curricular and the extracurricular, the physical and the spiritual, the present and the future. It provided a synthesis of a multiplicity of theses and antitheses. This was one reading of general education in the secondary school.

It has been easy enough to identify the content of the time-honored academic subjects as being useful (after suitable rearrangement) for use in general education. The special subjects have had to fight their way in the curriculum even when traditional subject-matter arrangements were in vogue. The undervalued subjects of study had to be established as being as good as Latin or Greek or algebra in order to be assigned units in the high school program. With the swing to general education, there is now a movement to identify the special areas with general education.

As late as 1957, business education has been firmly defended as general education. Accepting the premise that the latter is designed for effective living and is based on common experiences, it follows that the content of sociobusiness or basic business or nonvocational business contributes to the aims of general education. It seems reasonable that experiences common to all ought to include such topics and activities of general business as financial planning, wise buying, credit, insurance, taxes, everyday legal problems, labor relations, and collective bargaining. The subjects in sociobusiness, such as economic geography, business law, consumer problems, economics (but not economic theory), and others, are designed to incorporate just such topics and activities as were common to all.[59]

Home economics (domestic science) has had an equally difficult time in becoming accepted as a subject of study for all. Teachers have complained that they are sent only youngsters who cannot get along in academic courses. Home economics is now being proposed as general

[58] *Ibid.*, pp. 7–8, 42–43.
[59] Ray G. Price, "Business Education as General Education," *Bulletin of the National Association of Secondary-school Principals,* vol. 41, no. 225, pp. 18–22, January, 1957.

education, however, because of its recent incorporation of family-life education, which can be seen to be a necessary part of the education of all. The secondary school principals put their stamp of approval on this aspect of home economics education by devoting a 1955 bulletin to a framework for family-life education, including sex education.[60] Now that home economists are joining with social studies experts and general business teachers in family-finance workshops, the claims of these areas to favored niches in the general-education system seem assured.

Physical education has likewise been an undervalued subject. In the 1950s it was an important phase of general education with necessarily consonant aims. It puts strong emphasis on the total development of the child, including his social and emotional development as well as his health and recreation needs.[61]

Even the unique task of physical education makes it not a specialty, but a part of general education, according to its advocates. Its job is to educate for the acceptance of the body "as a symbol of the self," which included knowing how to make one's body a responsible instrument "for living democratically both with oneself and with others."[62] With this as a general aim and with appropriate adaptation of activities to all age groups from childhood to later maturity, physical education might well "hold the key to life."[63]

Although manual work as a value has fared better in American than in European society, it nevertheless has often been given short shrift by traditionalists in the secondary schools. Although industrial education (in its manual training phases) was hailed in the last of the nineteenth century as the "new education"[64] and as completing the circle of schooling, it nevertheless has had to bear some of the onus showered on home economics and physical education. It, too, has had to seek status.

As of 1948, industrial arts had the mission of inducting all youth into experiences common to all: recreation, consumption, and production. If general education fits youth for life, how could industrial education be other than general education when it centers attention on the American industrial democracy?[65]

[60] "Framework for Family Life Education," *Bulletin of the National Association of Secondary-school Principals*, vol. 39, no. 215, December, 1955.

[61] Leslie W. Irwin, *The Curriculum in Health and Physical Education*, 2d ed., The C. V. Mosby Company, St. Louis, Mo., 1951, pp. 30–40.

[62] Rosalind Cassidy, *Curriculum Development in Physical Education*, Harper & Brothers, New York, 1954, pp. 131–132.

[63] Jay B. Nash, *Physical Education, Interpretations and Objectives*, A. S. Barnes and Company, New York, 1948, p. 60.

[64] For reference to the "new education" see nineteenth-century issues of the annual meetings of the National Education Association.

[65] Gordon O. Wilber, *Industrial Arts in General Education*, International Textbook Company, Scranton, Pa., 1948, pp. vii, 17.

For industrial arts to be worthy of its role, teachers must take account of the ways in which general educators must look at the child if they are to help him to live. Industrial arts teachers are especially well situated to help children to be accepted in peer groups and to feel a sense of achievement. On the basis of the latter alone, industrial arts might find a defense. Industrial arts teachers have more to offer, however. They can help youth explore the American industrial civilization and, in the exploring, develop skill in industrial processes and secure an orientation to vocations. This exploration also can help youth increase their consumer information.[66]

Another area of development is opened up through activities which are an inevitable concomitant to industrial arts. Creative expression, as well as an appreciation for crafts past and present, can be encouraged. Desirable social relationships can be stimulated. Most of all, industrial arts can help to develop critical thinking, without which there could be little social progress.[67] Industrial art bears a necessary relationship to general education. It assists in transmitting a way of life and clarifying it through adherence to the basic precepts of democracy. It is a medium for improving the culture by assisting youth to think critically through practice. It can help to meet the needs of the individual as a biological and social being through stress on personal development, personal-social, social-civic, and economic relationships.[68]

Business education, home economics, physical education, and industrial art have been outside the pale of traditional schooling. Their struggle to establish themselves was therefore to be anticipated. Not so, however, with foreign languages. They were a heritage from European secondary education, which, it would be assumed, would go unquestioned. But Americans have the habit of equating foreign language study with commitments to foreign ideologies, and second-generation youth have the habit of rejecting foreign language as a mark of a foreign culture. Consequently, the modern foreign languages fell on evil days. In 1951, therefore, Harold B. Dunkel called on the new movement for support by addressing himself to the question of determining the place of foreign languages in general education.

Dunkel justifiably asked why foreign languages, which had been studied for some two thousand years, should have to fight their way in general education. Unlike the advocates of the less-preferred subjects, Dunkel did not allow his argument to rest on equating aims of foreign language teaching with those of general education. He answered his question by stating that teachers of foreign languages, like those in many other areas, had not bothered to isolate the conditions under

[66] *Ibid.*, pp. 25–27, 42–43.
[67] *Ibid.*, pp. 22, 42–43.
[68] *Ibid.*, p. 3 f.

which the values and objectives of their discipline could be met. The foreign languages might regain their ancient status in the curriculum through pressure and propaganda of their advocates. He hoped that the same end might be obtained by more appropriate means: demonstrating their contribution.[69]

Educators had attempted to evaluate general education in secondary schools through the eight-year study. But these efforts were some years back. So personnel from the Russell Sage Foundation and the Educational Testing Service (two groups involved in an earlier evaluation of elementary education), along with representatives of the National Association of Secondary-school Principals, described behavioral goals of general education in high school.[70]

These groups were firmly committed to the new curriculum. The question at issue was not whether there should be general education in the high school, but rather what were the procedures for developing the most effective general program? This major question led to four basic questions on purposes, desired outcomes, evidences of effectiveness, and the scope of the curriculum.

In the views of these investigators, the individual and the group are reconciled. The purpose of general education is to assist people to live rich and satisfactory lives and to participate responsibly in a democratic society. The purpose is really two coordinated purposes: self-realization, and growth toward responsible citizenship. So emphatic are these investigators on the latter point that they emphasize that no program in a public or private institution should be allowed to continue if it does not contribute to society's welfare. This position does not represent a seeming rejection of the coordinate purpose of self-realization, for in a democracy the ends of the society for its preservation and the concerns of the individual for his own development "tend to coincide."[71]

Answers to the other three basic questions have a familiar ring. Outcomes of general education are exhibited in the practical application of morality, ethics, and spiritual values by young persons of American standards. Evidences of the success of programs are to be found not in skills, abilities, and knowledges, but in kinds of behavior. The scope of general education encompasses meeting the common needs of youth as individual human beings and as citizens of a democracy.[72]

---

[69] Harold B. Dunkel, "Determining the Place of Foreign Languages in General Education," *The Journal of General Education*, vol. 6, no. 1, pp. 59–63, October, 1951.

[70] Will French and Associates, *Behavioral Goals of General Education in High School*, Russell Sage Foundation, New York, 1957.

[71] *Ibid.*, pp. 11–31.

[72] *Ibid.*, pp. 31–39.

The common needs and common standards and uncommon human beings and uncommon backgrounds required from these investigators the same kind of reconciliation which confronts other general educators. There is a quality of unselectedness about present-day secondary youth. They display wide differences in home backgrounds and training, economic status, growth levels. These all affected general education, which is a function of all schooling and of life itself. Nevertheless, educators must look at each goal and ask: What important behaviors characterize growth toward self-realization and citizenship? As members of a responsible social agency, educators must discover whether they are helping youth to develop "common kinds and levels of behaviors in all aspects of living." The common behaviors are necessary for effective living after high school or in college, and are fundamental to citizenship. If educators cannot help students become effective citizens, they undersell both America and the world.[73] Note here again the sense of mission which has characterized educators and laymen who have commented on their country since 1776.

The remainder of this study was devoted to an elaboration of general-education goals, with corresponding statements about behavior for the use of curriculum planners, test makers, and citizens interested in constructing and evaluating their own general-education programs.[74] The broad objectives which are elaborated are those of the Educational Policies Commission: self-realization, human relationships, economic efficiency, and civic responsibility. These goals and their behavioral outcomes are too lengthy for reproduction here. Interestingly, these outcomes (listed only if 75 per cent of consultants agreed to them—the American majority standard again) reflect values and practices about which there has been general agreement in the American society for some one hundred years or more. There is high priority on health and health practices. The student is developing properly if he avoids drinking, use of narcotics, sex play, fast driving, loafing on street corners. The good American youth rejects supervision and accepts independence, change, and science. He takes proper care of equipment, clothing, food, and he recognizes the free enterprise system as a dominating factor in American life. He is prepared to help meet community health and safety emergencies, and he joins organizations designed to promote community welfare.

This same youth maintains excellent relationships with family members through sharing and self-discipline. But he recognizes that he must win independence from family as a part of growing up, and at the same time he pays due consideration to his parents. Above all, he

[73] *Ibid.*, pp. 39–44.
[74] The account to follow is based on *ibid.*, pp. 58 f.

takes pride in all that is America because he understands her achievements.  This study is a description of a curriculum fit for an American and based on an American value pattern which has been developing since the beginning of the nation-state.

Since World War II, secondary school educators have accepted the necessity for providing general education for all American youth.  They have been chiefly concerned with defining their terms, refining curricular content, and inventing variations of the earlier general-education concept.  While these developments have been taking place, the special subjects, such as home economics and industrial arts, have also found a place in the structure of general education.  During the period, a secondary school curriculum for American youth has crystallized.

## College and University Developments

The elementary school and the secondary school have successively been incorporated into the concept of the common school.  After World War II it began to look as though the junior college might in the very near future become a part of this same common school.  It was quite natural, then, that educators in the junior college should seek to discover the proportions of an education for all late adolescents.

In 1948–1949 a comprehensive study of general education in the junior college was originated in California.  In 1950, junior college faculty members met for a six-week summer workshop, and continued in regional conferences throughout the 1950–1951 academic year.  They ended their deliberations with a general-education workshop at the Los Angeles branch of the University of California in the summer of 1951.  Out of their deliberations came definitions, principles, and approved practices.[75]

A common assumption was that all youth needed general education.  One unnamed doubter did inquire as to why there should be so much energy expended on the "nebulous whimsey of general education."  Answers from a questionnaire sent to a large group of educators put the doubter in his place.  How could anyone be so stupid as to raise such questions, said scornful defenders, when workers lose jobs because personal relationships are out of kilter, broken homes and mental disorders are increasing, and between 1900 and 1930 we killed in war one-third more people than had been killed in all wars in the previous eight hundred years?[76]

---

[75] B. Lamar Johnson (dir.), *General Education in Action: A Report of the California Study of General Education in the Junior College*, American Council on Education, Washington, 1952, pp. vii–x, 3 f.

[76] *Ibid.*, pp. 3–6.

The junior college workshop group put the worker of the life adjustment educators into their definition of general education. General education was built out of common knowledge and common skills and attitudes which were fundamental to the individual who hoped to function effectively not only as a person, family member, and a citizen, but also as a worker. In view of these principles, it seemed reasonable to accept a set of assumptions much like those which underlay the deliberations of the secondary school advocates. The youth must grow and develop in accordance with his needs, interests, abilities, and experiences, which were necessarily different from those of every other student. It must be clearly recognized that agencies other than the schools affected his growth, and that he would not be well served if his general education did not extend into his out-of-school future. General education must reach for roots, American fashion, in the characteristics of students and of American society; the test of its effectiveness would lie in producing behavior based on the student's desire to improve both himself and the society.[77]

The tug of war between the uncommon youth and common needs had one outcome in favor of the latter when the California study group suggested that there might be greater uniformity in course patterns. Common skills; American history and institutions; psychology of personal adjustment, including vocational orientation, family-life education; health education, including science, the creative arts, and physical education—all these were considered largely mandatory. There was further defense for some of these because they were required by the state. To remove the onus of conformity or uniformity, there were several suggestions for individualizing the program, including making guidance central to it. Guidance was the only medium through which both a mass and an individual job could be done.[78]

Junior college educators, like their colleagues of the social center, aspired to strengthen the home. Industrialism, so they said, as did their earlier colleagues, had made inroads on the family and it behooved the school to understand the forces beating on the family. To this end their proposed family-life education was designed to help parents and prospective parents to understand the effect of home training on personality, to help young people develop goals and understanding for courtship and marriage, to assist family members to share home responsibilities, and to enable prospective parents to develop appropriate attitudes and skill for guiding children.[79]

Educators were amply supported in their attention to family-life

[77] Ibid., pp. 20–21.
[78] Ibid., pp. 51, 54.
[79] Ibid., p. 137.

education by the responses of students to questionnaires. Studies of the problems of both men and women showed that sex instruction was of greatest concern to them. Several hundred women listed causes of mental illness as first in their concerns. A group of 1,339 students from thirty junior colleges, members of a student government conference, ranked exercising the privileges and responsibilities of democratic citizenship as of first concern. Developing a balanced personality, social adjustment, sharing in home and family life, developing a set of sound moral and spiritual values, and other aims corresponding roughly to those of educators followed closely. None of these aims were ranked so low but that junior college teachers could take comfort in their general-education goals.[80] The junior college, via general education, was now prepared to be the common school in the all-embracing sense of enrolling all, taking account of the whole of each one, and preparing for the entirety of the life span.

Educators in four-year institutions and universities have been concerned with general education since the thirties. The seriousness with which their faculties endorse their Americanization function through general education is indicated by the readiness with which educators in the professions point out the general-education aspects of their programs. In 1955 the U.S. Office of Education published a manual on professional education. It contained statements from experts in thirty-two professional fields on the content, aims, and programs established for professional training. Engineering, medical, architectural, and other professional educators called attention to the general education for each of their programs.[81]

One of the motivating factors for this interest in the new curriculum appears to be the emphasis in recent years on human relations. Doctors, for instance, must often advise on family problems and they must at all times understand human behavior. Furthermore, they are often an influence in the civic affairs in their communities and need to know how to use their influence for the best interests of the community. The colleges of arts and sciences which prepare students for medical schools should take stock of their programs, according to one medical educator, to ensure that human relationships as well as professional competence are being served. In connection with the former, he would suggest English and psychology, with the possible additions of sociology and anthropology. He would advise dropping geometry and advanced algebra in favor of the mathematics of probability and statistical theory. These subjects are needed for measurement of biological phenomena

[80] *Ibid.*, pp. 30–31, 103.
[81] Lloyd E. Blauch (ed.), *Education for the Professions*, U.S. Office of Education, 1955.

and for increasing precision in the formulation of questions.   Most of all, premedical students need great teachers.[82]

This was only one doctor's prescription for one kind of general education for one profession; as such, it is illustrative but not representative. A committee of the National Society for the Study of Education tried to develop statements which would serve the higher-education community more widely.   These covered, among other topics, the philosophy, psychology, and social foundations of general education, as well as the place of the sciences, the humanities, and the social sciences in the new curriculum.   In order to provide the well-rounded picture for the faculty member or college officer, the report also dealt with instruction, organization and administration, preparation for college teachers, personnel work, evaluation, the participation of the faculty in the evaluative process, and the student.[83]

The whole child is the referent of curricular plans.   The human being acts, thinks, and feels in a single inseparable process.   He is goal-motivated and unique, according to Dr. Stephen M. Corey.[84]   Although the plans or programs for this college student differ in detail, there is agreement that general education should develop critical intelligence as well as assist in creating intellectual unity.   It should develop and improve moral character as well as citizenship and provide equal opportunity for all.[85]

The college also makes its appearance as primary socializing institution.   The single most important fact about general education is that it signals the state's taking over certain functions from the church and the family.   The advocacy of general education should not, however, trouble those who fear the power of the state; general education does not mean aggrandizement of the state but controlling and demolishing its power.   General education also has an effect on world order.[86]   So also had the program of the secondary school educators.

The same knotty problems of the secondary school educators turn up to confound college general educators.   Difference versus uniformity—which should it be?   The task of the social sciences professor in general education is to define behavioral norms and execute and develop tasks to secure the behavior.   Yet indoctrination should be no part of social sciences general education.   Its goals are rather to develop an aware-

[82] Alan Gregg, "General Education in Preparation for Medicine," *The Journal of General Education*, vol. 2, no. 2, pp. 91–95, January, 1948.

[83] T. R. McConnell (chairman of the committee), *General Education*, Fifty-first Yearbook of the National Society for the Study of Education, University of Chicago Press, Chicago, 1952, part I, pp. 1–19.

[84] *Ibid.*, pp. 46–70.

[85] *Ibid.*, p. 73.

[86] *Ibid.*, pp. 89–90, 93.

ness of social phenomena while developing critical intelligence, and to communicate the fact of a spectrum of values. There should be complete intellectual freedom, said Arthur Naftalin. Thus, social science education recognizes the existence of two forces at war with one another: community cooperation and harmonious group life on the one hand, and the individual seeking to maximize his own rewards on the other.[87]

Another universal problem of all general educators came to light in a discussion of junior-division dropouts. If general education is for everyone, then everyone ought to be enrolled. In the thirties, one educator had been worried about the unserved high school dropouts. In the fifties a college educator, Dr. Robert J. Havighurst, notes that in one program, that of the Minnesota General College, less than half of the youths in the 100–110 IQ bracket complete a program of general education. Conversely, out of three young people of high-average or superior ability who do not go to college, one is the victim of economic difficulties, and two lack motivation. Practically all college students who come from the lower and lower-middle classes regard general education as a means of personal social mobility.[88] How could more youth be enrolled in the general education program designed for all, and how could they be kept in college?

College educators, no doubt by reason of their professional careers and educational backgrounds, have done more probing than their secondary school colleagues into the commitments, assumptions, and philosophical underpinnings of general education. This does not mean that their statements are any more sound, merely that college professors have a somewhat different universe of discourse than secondary school educators.

This universe of discourse is different partly because the college inherits a different tradition. It was once liberal in a somewhat different, or more committed, way than the high school. The Educational Policies Commission recognized this tradition by referring to both "liberal and general" and "liberal or general" education, as though the word with the Greek derivation and that with the American meaning were one and the same.[89]

Llewellyn Gross, however, devoted an article to describing the differences between the liberal arts (special education) and general education proper. The liberal arts program begins with facts and relationships and is concerned with problems only to the extent that they

[87] Ibid., pp. 119–135.
[88] Ibid., pp. 84–87.
[89] Higher Education in a Decade of Decision, National Education Association, Educational Policies Commission, Washington, 1957, pp. 46–48, 51–61.

are generated by facts; general educators use student problems as their beginning point. With this problem-solving approach, students gain insights derived from their efforts to apply general principles. They are ready for the arts only when they have matured. To the liberal arts professor, the most relevant knowledge is not insights, but knowledge which corresponds to reality or functions in a descriptive capacity. With the student-centered-problems approach, general educators give first place to ideas and concepts which extend beyond partisan learning and have meaning for modes of understanding. The arts teacher must rely on empirical generalizations for synthesis. He helps the student to enlarge his store of facts and generalizations in a special field; the general educator aids the student in unifying his knowledge.

This contrast in points of view and processes leads to a more generalized contrast between the two approaches: the liberal arts are particularized; general education, through general studies, makes use of several disciplines. A contrast in attitude toward student learning results. The liberal arts professor does not care how a student learns, nor is he interested in students' values. He is either suspicious of or neutral about values. The general educator is interested in the learning process and in how the student might become self-directed and develop appropriate life values. He is interested in permissive teaching and in encouraging diversity in the learning process.[90]

The universe of discourse is also different in higher education and secondary education because college educators are more acutely aware of private education than their high school colleagues. The private colleges, in turn, are occasionally church-related or parochial. It is in terms of the Roman Catholic liberal college that William F. Cunningham introduced some metaphysical postulates into general education. Cunningham, along with his secular colleagues, recognizes the appropriateness of a general education for a democratic society. It is general in that all citizens receive it and in that it takes account of ordinary knowledge and culture. Cunningham's liberal education is concerned with ideas, too, rather than with facts,[91] a rough equating with Gross's general education. The Catholic colleges have proximate and ultimate purposes, however. The proximate goal, which is to prepare students to be contributing citizens in a democracy, must be well served; high morals cannot be substituted for low intelligence. Liberal education is designed to assist the student in attaining truth, appreciating beauty, and choosing the good, in maintaining bodily physical and mental

[90] Llewellyn Gross, "Specialized and General Education Programs," *The Journal of General Education*, vol. 7, no. 3, pp. 197–200, April, 1953.

[91] William F. Cunningham, *General Education and the Liberal College*, B. Herder Book Company, St. Louis, Mo., 1953, pp. 6, 9.

health, and in assuring himself of "temporal well-being" by becoming prepared economically.[92] Perhaps this is where general education or liberal education stopped in Cunningham's view, and thus there was little conflict with the views of secular educators. But the inevitable stress on the ultimate purpose of the Catholic college would suggest otherwise. In this one view, it was to "bring souls closer to God with the aid of His grace, and to assist them in fulfilling the purpose of their creation."[93] Of necessity, the ultimate purpose has implications for character development as well as means, ends, and emphases. If ultimate purpose thus controls proximate purpose, then general education in a public secondary school or nonsectarian college might well have a fundamentally different meaning from that in a church-related college.

Other attempts to state principles have been made in a lighter and more folksy vein. One such attempt was made in an article by John W. Kidd, "General Education: A Nontweedy View." Translating general education into practice comes not through design, but through coincidence, said this author, with a resulting conflict between general and liberal education and the deveolpment of a concept which means all things to all men. This author proposes to put some order into chaos by contrasting the main current of general education (the "Nontweedy" view of which he was a proponent) and the "Tweedy" view, which smells of unpressed woolens, old pipes, and ivy walls.

To professors in the Tweedy group, curricular planning is based on traditional values and grounded in knowledge, the mark of the scholar; preponderant emphasis is put on the past. The main-current educator bases his curriculum on evidences of usefulness of the content, tries for understanding and critical thinking rather than knowledge, and emphasizes the present and the future. The Tweedy program is subject-centered, for its content comes from authoritatively selected phases of the cultural heritage, and its teacher practices are often based on outmoded faculty psychology, automatic transfer, and such concepts as "absolutistic idealistic standards." More important, its program is planned for the able. The main-current educators plan for all whose individual needs are to be taken into account.[94]

Malcolm M. Marsden chose as subjects for his essay on a philosophical dichotomy a spokesman for transcendentalism, Charles Eliot Norton, a Harvard professor in the last three decades of the nineteenth century, and John Dewey. It was Marsden's task to show that there was some correspondence between their points of view on four of five common

[92] Ibid., pp. 12, 22, 28.
[93] Ibid., pp. 21–22.
[94] John W. Kidd, "General Education: A Nontweedy View," The Journal of General Education, vol. 8, no. 2, pp. 100–102, January, 1955.

assumptions underlying general education. First, both Norton (a possible representative of the liberal arts) and Dewey (a possible representative of general education) are opposed to vocationalism and specialization, even though Norton drew his subject matter from the classics and Dewey from life situations. Second, both wished more required courses: the liberal arts professor so that all might be exposed to the unique virtues of the humanities; the progressive educator so that all sharing common interests might serve democracy better. Third, both agreed that a course ought to cut across departmental lines: Norton, because he believed that underlying art forms there was a moral and physical unity which was determined by political, moral, and social conditions; and Dewey, because he believed that all facts focused on man's living. Fourth, the liberal arts professor and the general educator were also in agreement on the teaching of moral and aesthetic values, though Dewey was inclined to believe there were no moral meanings apart from a social context, whereas Norton would have argued for the eternal verities. So far, so good.

When it came to the proposition of general education, that its content should be immediate life problems, there would have been almost no agreement between Norton and Dewey. It is on this point, said Marsden, that the liberal educators (or transcendentalists) and the general educators (pragmatists) part company. In the search for content in the disciplines which the former carries on, and in the search for content in experience which the pragmatist pursues, lies the answer to why the two groups often advocate the same thing (see points one to four above) yet carry out different plans in the classroom.[95]

President Harold Taylor of Sarah Lawrence College, in the *Fifty-first Yearbook of the National Society for the Study of Education,* attempted to bring order out of chaos by setting forth three positions under which liberal and general education programs might be subsumed. These philosophical postulates he described as a set of ideas about the ends of human life and the principles of nature to which people give assent.[96]

Taylor's first philosophical position is that of rationalism, represented in practice by the Roman Catholic clergy and the advocates of the Great-books Programs. The former look to principles in the nature of man as he is related to God and in a hierarchy of being; the latter, to classical texts, which represent the unity of the medieval university.

[95] Malcolm M. Marsden, "General Education: Compromise between Transcendentalism and Pragmatism," *The Journal of General Education,* vol. 7, no. 4, pp. 228–239, July, 1953.

[96] Harold Taylor, "The Philosophical Foundations of General Education," in *General Education,* Fifty-first Yearbook, part I, National Society for the Study of Education, University of Chicago Press, Chicago, 1952, p. 21.

The classical disciplines—in the eyes of both groups—produce rational truth valid for all students everywhere. The values of both groups are ethnocentric, being grounded in a small portion of the society: the educational elite, the clergy, the owners and rulers, and the scholars.[97] Presumably the lower-division courses in the great books and the Catholic colleges would be representative of this position.

Eclecticism and neohumanism, said Taylor, is another position which emphasizes training of the mind, but this one has no special philosophical system. Its advocates separate mind from body, reason from emotion, and thought from experience. A representative writing which illustrates this position is the Harvard report on general education.[98]

Advocates of naturalism and instrumentalism, Taylor's third group put emphasis on areas of knowledge. Truth in this system emerges from individual experiences which are transformed into concepts and facts which are continuously denied or affirmed. In seeking for content and methodology, the instructor asks: What are the uses to which knowledge is to be put? What are the needs of individuals? What are the general needs of society? Out of answers to these questions emerge aims and principles based on a process of assisting students to grow in maturity and in personal qualities. Professors recognize no eternal laws of nature but rather patterns of behavior worked out in practice. The development of moral behavior emerges from a situation in which free, spontaneous growth is encouraged. Emphasis is placed on the individual student and the quality of his experience. In the process of participating in his growth, the student learns how to cooperate in the achievement of ends which he helps to determine. The instrumentalist position is firmly embedded in the context of democracy. Two writings, according to Taylor, throw particular light on this position: Sidney Hook's *Education for Modern Man* and the report of the President's Commission on Higher Education. The programs at Sarah Lawrence, Bennington, and Antioch and the General College in the University of Minnesota are in the naturalist or instrumentalist vein.[99]

Other articles, such as the one by Charles Leonard Stone, have been written on assumptions underlying general education.[100] For the most part, they cover ground already covered in reports above. In general, writers attempt to distinguish between liberal and general education, or to reconcile liberal education with general. They accept the whole child

[97] *Ibid.,* pp. 26–29.
[98] *Ibid.,* pp. 30–33. See also *General Education in a Free Society: Report of the Harvard Committee.*
[99] *Ibid.,* pp. 26, 36–41.
[100] Charles Leonard Stone, "Some Postulates of General Education," *The Journal of General Education,* vol. 2, no. 1, pp. 24–26, October, 1947.

(but perceive him differently), attune themselves to the needs of society (but assess those needs in many ways), cut across subject-matter lines (but in a search for content which will be put to different uses). The general educator has come in for his share of attention because in the skills and the qualifications of the guide of the learning process lies the key to the health of the general-education movement. At one and the same time, the teacher must be cognizant of the nature of man, loyal to science, which, however, is ethically neutral, and willing and able to examine "alternative moral directions."[101] As these statements lie within the broad context of general education, they show the same variety of conclusion which is characteristic of the movement itself.

As general education is a citizenship movement, it follows that the teacher must, first of all, have qualities found in any cultured citizen. Professors in some institutions prepare that generalist, the physical-education or recreation teacher, by spending too much time on specialization.[102] One graduate school in an Eastern university makes its contribution by being first to offer a generalist's rather than a specialist's doctoral degree in the social sciences. This is, according to William Pearson Tolley, the first important departure from research training (although a project is required) since the establishment of Johns Hopkins University. This new program was planned by the Maxwell Graduate School of Citizenship and Public Affairs at Syracuse University and put under the direction of a doctor of education, not a doctor of philosophy.[103] The candidate must acquire some research techniques (excluding languages), but does not concentrate on special or research training, said the writer, who looked forward to the need for some 50,000 generalists.

Robert Redfield has a rather different idea of the qualifications of the general educator. He asks how general education in social science can continually reflect the influence of research upon the change in and expansion of knowledge. Redfield's answer is that an understanding of how research is done should be a part of general education, and professors of general education, in order to meet the challenge of the central question, must themselves be research workers.[104]

[101] Nathaniel Cantor, "The Teacher in a General Education Program," *The Journal of General Education*, vol. 6, no. 3, pp. 209–213, April, 1952.

[102] Raymond Albert Snyder and Harry Alexander Scott, *Professional Preparation in Health, Physical Education, and Recreation*, McGraw-Hill Book Company, Inc., New York, 1954, pp. 49–50.

[103] William Pearson Tolley, "The Doctor of Social Science Program at Syracuse University," *The Journal of General Education*, vol. 3, no. 1, pp. 16–19, October, 1948.

[104] Robert Redfield, "Social Science Research in General Education," *The Journal of General Education*, vol. 6, no. 2, pp. 81–91, January, 1952.

## SUMMARY

Socioeconomic crises from 1918 to the 1930s conditioned secondary and college educators to seek an adjustment of their programs to the increasing heterogeneity of youth and the needs of society. From self-criticism and some experimentation in the 1930s and 1940s, they progressed to defining and clarifying general education as an acceptable curriculum for American youth in the era after World War II.

There has been no easy consensus on the meaning of the new curriculum. It has had to be reconciled with or distinguished from liberal education. It has had its philosophical foundations examined and pinpointed. Its major premises have occasionally been doubted, but by and large it has found acceptance in some form among most secondary and college educators. Though its behavioral outcomes are difficult to evaluate, its acceptance is almost assured so long as it rests (as it does now) on an honored and long-developing American value pattern.

# 8

# Legislative Influence
## on the American Educational Pattern

> The plaintiff in error was a teacher in the public schools. . . .
> He was under contract with the state to work in an institution
> of the state. He had no right or privilege to serve the state
> except upon such terms as the state prescribed.[1]
>
> FROM THE SCOPES TRIAL, 1927

Educators and laymen had searched for a school system abroad. When
this kind of activity no longer proved to be effective, professional people set up, at the national level, guide lines which would serve the state
and local school systems in shaping the schools to an American curricular pattern. These guide lines were issued in a series of committee
reports dating from the 1890s to 1918. Finally, the secondary and
college educators devised a curriculum for Americans: general education.

The people, however, are organized officially and formally for action
on matters of the general welfare. The national government, and the
interlocking web of state and local governments provides means by
which Americans can ensure some kind of united assault on social, economic, and international problems.

Since that first great crisis of the new republican government, the
Civil War, state legislators have taken decisive action to make certain
that the basic Americanization instrument, the school system, should
carry out its function. With a surprising degree of agreement, legislators in the several states have moved to put teeth into the schooling
process by requiring the teaching of subjects designed to produce the

---

[1] Madaline Kinter Remmlein, *School Law*, McGraw-Hill Book Company, Inc.,
New York, 1950, p. 288. (Quotation.)

235

acceptable American, and prohibiting practices that would interfere with the fundamental principles of republicanism. State legislators, according to their own lights, have guarded American nationalism. This activity has run parallel, time-wise, to the activity of professional people who were working in national committees and developing general education.

The results of legislative activity for schools have been to enmesh school people in a tangle of regulations and to usurp what otherwise might be called professional prerogatives. The story of a mythical superintendent in California will serve to introduce curriculum by law.

The year is 1923; the locale, a district in California; the actors, a superintendent and teachers; the plot, the development of a school system in a new area which has not previously been incorporated as a school district. This setting for an educational drama brings with it a sense of anticipation—here is high adventure in charting new educational pathways. Here is a chance to start fresh, to develop a school system from the ground up, to experiment with new ideas, different programs, unique techniques. Yet if such a drama had been unfolded in a new district in 1923 in California, the plot would have unfolded on old, rather than new, pathways and on prescription rather than experimentation. High adventure would have been carefully circumscribed by the law.[2]

Teacher selection would have been the first order of business in which the new superintendent would have to take note of prescription. In addition to the well-known requirements of specified teacher education and good character, he would have had to make sure his new employees were citizens of the United States, had declared their intention to become citizens, or were native-born wives of foreigners.

With his staff selected, the superintendent's concern with the law would be only beginning. His first big problem would be deciding whether his community was such that it required separate schools for Indian, Mongolian, Japanese, or Chinese children, as had been authorized by the Legislature since before 1900. If the superintendent in a community survey discovered numbers of youngsters from these populations, and whether he decided for or against separate schools, he would need to caution his teachers against the easy expedient of instructing any of the children in their native tongue. Since World War I, it had been compulsory to have all instruction in English.

[2] Legal requirements in story on California taken largely from J. K. Flanders, *Legislative Control of the Elementary Curriculum*, Teachers College Contributions to Education, no. 195, Bureau of Publications, Teachers College, Columbia University, New York, 1925; and Bessie Louise Pierce, *Public Opinion and the Teaching of History in the United States*, Alfred A. Knopf, Inc., New York, 1926.

When the crucial decision of number and kinds of schools had been made, and as they got down to the hard business of building a curriculum, the superintendent and his staff would find themselves in a veritable tangle and maze of prescriptions. They would not have to spend much time, it is true, on the elementary course of study, for the mandatory regulations had taken care of it in thorough fashion. In the several grades in which they might be required, instruction was to be given in reading, writing, spelling, arithmetic, geography, language and grammar, with special reference to composition, the history of California, and history of the United States, including the history of the Constitution. In respect to the last document, reference was to be made to the reasons for the adoption of each of its provisions, with instructions in the duties of citizenship, together with instruction in local civil government. The health and welfare of the children had not been forgotten by the lawmakers, either. Included in the required courses were elements of physiology and hygiene, with special reference to the injurious effects on the human system of tobacco, alcohol, and narcotics. Morals and manners were also to be subjects of required instruction.

There need be little arguing about the time to be allotted to these mandatory subjects, for in the first six grades, so the law read, at least two-thirds of the pupil's time during each week was to be devoted to study of and recitation in these subjects; and in the seventh and eighth grades, at least 12½ hours of each week would be given to them. "In the time remaining, physical training, nature study, music, drawing, elementary bookkeeping, humane education, and thrift must be taught."[3] The prescription ended, however, with the mystifying statement that boards of education might authorize other studies, but these must be in lieu of, not in addition to, the above.

If there were any time left over after the required subjects were done with, it might well be taken up with another prescribed set of activities. According to law, March 7, which was the anniversary of the birth of Luther Burbank, was to be given special attention as conservation, bird, and Arbor Day.[4] Officials in public schools and other educational institutions were directed to observe this special day, not as a holiday, but with appropriate exercises which would call attention to the economic uses of the items designated and would promote a desire to protect them.

Protection of another kind would be a subject of a reasonable amount of time each month if the local board should so prescribe, for a course in fire prevention to bring about an undersanding of fires and their danger and promote an interest in their prevention was mandatory.

[3] Quoted in Flanders, *op. cit.*, p. 146.
[4] *Ibid.*, p. 110.

A final blow to the freedom that the superintendent might have thought he had when he started in 1923 was the fact that he could not even have selected his textbooks, for since the year 1883–1884, that duty had been the prerogative of the state board of education.[5]

The sense of adventure in beginning a school system in 1923 would have been absent in California. It would have been equally lacking in practically any of the other forty-eight states. Since the early national period, prescription by state constitution or by state law had been a trend which had intensified after each war and in response to population changes. By the middle of the twentieth century, school men were probably so immune to prescription that they no longer gave it much thought, but if they had cared to recount the ways in which educational institutions were prescribed, they would have found a network of regulations which stretched into many areas of the teaching-learning process.

J. K. Flanders put these mandatory teaching prescriptions into the following categories: nationalism, health and prohibition, conservation, practical and cultural subjects, humaneness, the "fundamental" subjects, religious and ethical subjects, and a miscellany of others.[6] All of these categories called for subjects or time in the curriculum, except the prescription on religion, which was often phrased in prohibitive terms.

If Flanders had ventured into the national field he would have found another set of categories which overlapped those for the state, and which took into account Federal monies and prescriptions for their spending in the form of curriculum and faculty imperatives. Reimbursements would be forthcoming to local school systems and state universities if certain conditions were met, these being related to curriculum content in homemaking, vocational or industrial education, distributive education, and agricultural education; and to qualifications not only of secondary school teachers, but of "teacher trainers" in state universities. Because by law the Federal government has no jurisdiction over educational systems, however, there would have been a difference between Federal and state educational lawmaking. State and local provisions for schools could be and usually were mandatory; the Federal government's finger in the educational pie would not have been so obvious. Federal lawmakers would say, in effect, "You are not required to chart your educational course as we see fit, but only if you do so will you be reimbursed for your efforts." Another story is the increasing entry of the United States Supreme Court into the educational enterprise. This new phase of education by law is one which will be left for further consideration.

[5] Pierce, op. cit., p. 38.
[6] Flanders, loc. cit.

## A RATIONALE FOR CURRICULUM BY LAW

That state and Federal governments have entered into the educational enterprise in respect to curriculum, faculty, and institutions raises two kinds of questions. The first has to do with right; the second, with reason.

### The Question of Right

The question of right raises two subsidiary questions. The first of these might be stated thus: Who has the right to prescribe educational enterprises? The second is more obscure: How far can authorized agencies go in their prescription?

The answers to both of these questions of right have been changed through the generations in response to reinterpretations of the age-old quandary of the rights of the individual as against the rights of society. This ancient problem implies an antagonism between the welfare of the individual and that of society—an antagonism which needs to be clarified by raising a series of questions around which discussion could be centered. A basic but confusingly phrased query is the following: Where do the rights of the individual leave off and where do the rights of society begin? Emerging from this question is a counterinquiry: Are the rights of the individual and society antagonistic? Through a century and a half of national life, local and state governments have been interpreting this first question in terms of curricular and behavioral conformity in schools, only to have their restrictions called into question by such bodies as the Supreme Court and frequently by the public at large. Federal lawmaking bodies have imposed restrictions on the rights of local governments to educate their children in ways termed best by making monies available only for curricular purposes judged to be in the interest of the general welfare. In the seeming contradictions by which the educational process proceeds, programs enriched by the Federal government have probably opened opportunities which would have been long delayed if left to financing by the individual states. Thus the claims of the individual and society, often obscured in the instant of governmental intervention, have undergone continuous interpretation, clarification, and adjudication in educational terms.

In educational history, certain issues raising questions of rights have received more attention than others. Such an issue was fought out immediately before and after the Civil War, when some of the state governments instituted compulsory schooling. What right had the government (society) to intervene in the child-rearing practices of the parent (the individual) by mandating that the child should spend a specified number of years in school? Did not the child (the individual) have the right in an expanding agricultural-industrial society to be educated to participate fully in that society, even over the negligence of his parents? The forty-eighth state finally disposed of the issue of compulsory education in 1918. But a subsidiary issue was raised subsequent to the Oregon Act of 1922, which required that all children between the ages of eight and sixteen attend public schools. As the law was first challenged by a Roman Catholic order, it might be presumed that the state government was being held accountable for interfering with the religious liberty of individuals. Curiously enough, the case was decided on the basis of the Fourteenth Amendment. "No question is raised concerning the power of the state reasonably to regulate all schools." So said the Court, but the necessary outcome of enforcing the act would be the forcible closing of the Catholic primary schools as well as other private schools in Oregon. Statements were made to the effect that "the child is not the mere creature of the state" and that his parents or guardians had the right to nurture him and direct his destiny, but the "decision was based upon the due-process clause of the Constitution." The private schools, including a military school, were upheld by the Court on the grounds that the state had interfered unlawfully with school patrons and in such a way as would lead to "destruction of their business and property."[7]

Recent developments are the abolition of compulsory schooling in some Southern states and the indirect financing by states of private schools. Issues which will undoubtedly be decided by the courts in the near future will be whether the state has the right to neglect its children by failing to enforce schooling, and whether it has the right to support schools not under public control. These issues are related to the general welfare which the Constitution was designed to promote.

Other familiar institutional issues are a part of the story of the development of both secondary and higher education. Whether a taxpayer could be deprived of his property by being forced to finance secondary schools was fought out not only in the well-known Kalamazoo case in Michigan but in cases in other states. The status of a privately owned and operated college (the property of a private corporation) was settled in the Dartmouth case of 1819. These and other institutional cases have decided for the general welfare and against the individual taxpayer, and for the private corporation and against society at large.

### The Question of Reason

Interwoven with the questions of right, not separate from them, are questions of why the society, in the form of the governments, should

---

[7] Remmlein, op. cit., pp. 224–226.

direct the educational enterprise. "Reason" must be interpreted here not only in its logical sense as the premise of an argument, but also in its folk sense as ground or cause. The grounds for a prescription, and particularly a curricular one, cannot easily be analyzed except through case study of particular instances in which the logic is applied.

In 1923 there were 926 legislative prescriptions respecting curriculum of the public elementary schools of the United States. These did not represent all that had ever been devised. Some past ones had been repealed, and some had been made inoperative through court decision. The 926 represented only those in effect in 1923, and only those which had to do with curriculum or "things to be taught." Furthermore, curricular prescription appeared to be on the increase. A similar poll of prescriptions in 1903 showed 564. A figure for 1913 showed 720, or an increase of 28 per cent. The figure for 1923 was an increase of 64 per cent over that for 1903.[8]

Douglas Lehman, who studied controls on the secondary curriculum as of 1941, 1947, and 1953, found a decided increase in prescriptions in the forty-eight states. In 1941, there were 1,079; in 1947, there were 1,134; and in 1953, there were 1,166. During the period 1941 to 1953, there were a total of "133 curricular prescriptions, either mandatory or prohibitive," enacted by thirty-eight legislatures.[9] Developing curriculum by law appeared to be a well-established habit if not a well-thought-out device.

As important for seeing the outlines of a logic as numbers of prescriptions, is their nature. The area of health and prohibition is as good as any for illustration, for it is this area which, next to nationalism, showed the greatest increase in prescription from 1903 to 1923.[10] Here was found that mandatory subject which represents our most important American branch of learning: stimulants and narcotics. J. K. Flanders asserted that this was so universal as to be a "national subject of instruction" and the "one minimum essential."[11]

For purpose of analysis of prescription, particularly in the area of health and prohibition, it might be useful to look at curriculum not as *things to be taught* but as *conditions under which behavior takes place.* With this latter orientation, emphasis can be put on ends in behavior and prescriptions can be looked at as means to ends.

Presumably, the countless legislators who framed the laws on health —particularly on stimulants and narcotics—were primarily interested in

[8] Numbers of prescriptions from Flanders, *op. cit.*, p. 175.
[9] Douglas A. Lehman, "Legislative Control of the Secondary School Curriculum from 1941 to 1953," unpublished doctoral dissertation, University of Pittsburgh, Pittsburgh, Pa., 1955, pp. 164, 189. (Microfilm.)
[10] Flanders, *op. cit.*, p. 64.
[11] *Ibid.*, p. 68.

prevention. The study of alcohol and narcotics, proper training for teachers in this area, and special days of observance were all calculated to prevent the occurrence of alcohol-imbibing and drug-taking in the young. It appears only remotely possible that legislators were interested in changing the behavior of young recalcitrants who were already drunks or drug addicts.

If prescription is analyzed in terms of prevention of particular kinds of behavior, then the sheer number of prescriptions indicates something of the orientation of legislators to how behavior is prevented. There was no let-well-enough-alone attitude in this area. Attention needed to be called to the undesirable behavior in order that it be exorcised, according to lawmakers in practically all of the forty-eight states. Note that this technique for prevention is in marked contrast to that suggested for exorcising communism, which in many states and school districts is treated by ignoring it.

Analysis of individual prescriptions indicates some range of ideas regarding what kind of calling attention to would be calculated to prevent undesirable behavior. A central assumption appeared to be that if a growing human being understands what will harm him, he will stay away from it for, in nearly every instance, the language of the law indicated that emphasis was to be put on the effect of these substances on the human system.[12] The emotional tone in which the instruction was to be given was by implication different in the minds of different sets of legislators. Several of the laws merely called for mandatory teaching about the effects of tobacco, alcohol, and narcotics on the human system. However, California legislators, at one end of a continuum, asked that the nature of the effects of alcohol and narcotics be determined by science. At the other end of the scale were statutes in states such as North Carolina, where lawmakers asked for an education which pointed out "the evil effects of alcohol and narcotics."[13] The latter wording is faintly reminiscent of the attitude toward sin as expressed in the old hornbook.

Behavior was not to be prevented, however, by simple mandatory *teaching about* the subjects, whatever the emotional or scientific overtones of the teaching. Guarantees that such teaching was to go forward were set up in some states by fines and forfeitures for neglect of the law and by requiring that normal schools give teacher candidates special training in the prescribed subjects. Some laws were quite specific about the text or reading requirements necessary for appropriate treatment of the subjects. Michigan required that textbooks for such instruction contain at least twenty pages of matter relating to alcoholic

[12] *Ibid.*, p. 65.
[13] Illustrations are from laws quoted in *ibid.*, chap. III.

drinks and narcotics. New York required that for students below high school grade, texts must give at least one-fifth of their space, and those for high school students, not less than twenty pages to the nature and effects of alcoholic drinks and other narcotics. Knowledgeable teachers, approved texts, and fines were calculated to prevent undesirable behavioral occurrences.

Mandatory teaching requirements have been reinforced by the buckshot approach to learning. If one kind of sensory stimulus or activity did not work, perhaps another would. Some states required that preventive measures be communicated through reading except in case of those who could not read—in this case instruction was to be oral. Reading and talking about stimulants and narcotics was reinforced in fifteen states[14] by a ceremonial occasion which might be designated a temperance day, though the specific name would vary. There were a Temperance and Good Citizenship Day, a Frances E. Willard Day, and a Temperance, or Law and Order, Day. According to Lehman, Kentucky had the most novel specifications on alcohol and narcotics. Injurious effects were to be taught in every grade from the fourth to the tenth. In addition, the superintendent and principal of every school were to hold assemblies at least twice each term or semester; at these gatherings, there was to be a thirty-minute program on the effects of narcotics and alcohol.[15] Beliefs about how behavior is suppressed apparently varies from that which says that behavior is changed through knowledge (the scientific approach) to that which holds that behavior is changed through exorcising the devil.

The question next in order is whether any generalizations can be made about the logic of legislators who drew up curricular prescriptions on prohibition, narcotics, and tobacco. Tentatively, it can be said that ideas about learning had not changed radically from those of colonial or early national leaders. Supposed facts and moral judgments were to be piped into the young and out would come the appropriate behavior. Knowledge and morality were to be reinforced by appropriate ceremonials. Schools were to be responsible for both the piping and the obeisance processes.

AN INTERPRETATION OF
CURRICULUM BY LAW

It has been said that naming studies in a curriculum will tell a reader very little of what youths learn, but it will reveal the nature of the

---

[14] See *ibid.*, p. 79, for states in which there were temperance teaching laws.
[15] Lehman, *op. cit.*, p. 85.

knowledge the educated community considers of most worth.[16]   In a similar vein, an investigation of legal prescriptions for education will reveal little of resultant behavior, but will reflect indirectly the consensus of the adult community, and directly that of the responsible legal community, respecting the pattern of behavior deemed appropriate for socially acceptable youth.

Reference has already been made to the national minimum essential, the *teaching about* stimulants and narcotics.   It can be asked what this reveals of legal or community consensus.   The same procedure could be followed with all the other areas in which there has been prescription.   A chart of these prescriptions might be a good place to start. (See Table 8-1.)

Table 8-1. General Summary of Curricular Prescriptions for the Public Elementary Schools of the United States, 1903, 1913, 1923

| Topic | Number of prescriptions | | | Increase | | |
|---|---|---|---|---|---|---|
| | 1903 | 1913 | 1923 | 1903– 1913 | 1913– 1923 | 1903– 1923 |
| Nationalism.................. | 147 | 196 | 304 | 49 | 108 | 157 |
| Health and "prohibition"........ | 102 | 131 | 171 | 29 | 40 | 69 |
| Conservation of life and property | 1 | 20 | 43 | 19 | 23 | 42 |
| Practical and cultural subjects... | 24 | 44 | 59 | 20 | 15 | 35 |
| Humaneness.................. | 12 | 28 | 36 | 16 | 8 | 24 |
| Fundamental subjects.......... | 197 | 216 | 216 | 19 | ... | 19 |
| Religious and ethical subjects.... | 74 | 76 | 84 | 2 | 8 | 10 |
| Miscellaneous subjects......... | 7 | 9 | 13 | 2 | 4 | 6 |
| Total...................... | 564 | 720 | 926 | 156 | 206 | 362 |

SOURCE: J. K. Flanders, *Legislative Control of the Elementary Curriculum*, Teachers College Contributions to Education, no. 195, Bureau of Publications, Teachers College, Columbia University, New York, 1925.   Reproduced by permission of the publisher.

One way of looking at this curriculum by prescription is as an expression of the meaning of the good American broadly defined.   The good American must read, write, spell, and figure, because on his wisdom depends the fate of a nation.   That fate likewise rests on an informed American, who realizes the crucial importance to this country and to the world of the Declaration of Independence, the United States Constitution, and the stirring struggle for liberty as revealed in American

[16] Richard Hofstadter and C. DeWitt Hardy, *The Development and Scope of Higher Education in the United States*, Columbia University Press, New York, 1952, p. 11.   Published for the Commission on Financing Higher Education.

history. The good American is not reluctant to work with his hands (symbolized by the practical subjects) for it is by hard work rather than by accident of birth that the door to opportunity is opened in this hospitable land. Most important, the fingers of the good American must not be stained by nicotine nor his breath fouled by alcohol.

The good American believes in the separation of church and state and is properly suspicious of threat to his political and religious liberties, against which the separation guards him. He is nonetheless interested in the welfare of his church and the necessity for moral training, which should properly belong with the school as well as church and home. Nor, in a country where status is based on property openly acquired rather than on class or lineage, does he destroy property so hardly won and so respected. These are some of the qualities of the good American as revealed in the educational concerns of legislators. As a matter of fact, Lehman found legislative prescriptions for secondary schools designed to enforce truthfulness, temperance, a public spirit, health and morality, and a respect for honest labor. Added to these virtues were purity, virtue, kindness, patriotism, and avoidance of profanity and falsehood.[17] Even more revealing, however, is speculation on why the characteristics of most worth—as reflected in the curriculum—should have been what they were. Exploring a few of them might provide links between schooling and previously disconnected aspects of American experience.

*Health and Prohibition*

Nearly 60 per cent of the health and prohibition prescriptions in force in 1923 had been law since before 1903. Of the 102 prescriptions which constituted the 60 per cent, 47 related to teaching about stimulants and narcotics. Thus, by 1903, forty-seven states had mandatory provisions respecting temperance and drug-addiction instruction.[18] Considering secondary schools alone, 42 states in 1953 provided for such instruction, 40 states demanded health education, 37 states asked for physical examinations, and 34 required physical education. Only 1 state, Oregon, required mental health education.[19]

Women who had been "called of God for a specific purpose," the promotion of total abstinence, are frequently credited with national prohibition and with having pressured into law the acts relating to stimulants and narcotics.[20] Besides their efforts to influence legislators

[17] Lehman, *op. cit.*, p. 90.
[18] See table in Flanders, *op. cit.*, pp. 66–67.
[19] Lehman, *op. cit.*, p. 80.
[20] Bessie Louise Pierce, *Citizens' Organizations and the Civic Training of Youth,* Charles Scribner's Sons, New York, 1933, chap. 26.

directly in the enactment and enforcement of prohibition legislation, they had made attempts to influence the young through literature and contests for schools and outside activities such as vacation schools, the Sunday school, and their own youth organizations. During 1929 alone, they "crushed 4,642,316 cigarette stubs" as well as sent out 490,000 pieces of literature, were involved in 1,700 public meetings, and among other things, made 2,092 scrapbooks.[21] As Bessie Pierce says, it is difficult to assess the nature of influence; furthermore, it is more rewarding to look behind whatever influence the Women's Christian Temperance Union and its ally, the Anti-saloon League, might have had.

The *looking behind* the façade of organizations which operated in the United States can produce only speculation as to their origins and influence, but nevertheless it does give a feeling of the consistency and relative continuity of cultures through time.

In the last half of the eighteenth and the first half of the nineteenth centuries, the Great Awakening swept across America. Frontiersmen and the lesser folk in towns joined the evangelical Protestant churches. Methodists, Baptists, and more than ordinarily emotional Congregationalists and Presbyterians built their churches, testified in meetings to their moral transformation, and expressed themselves volubly against the sins of this world as evidenced in drinking, smoking, card playing, and other indulgences. Concurrently, in the first half of the nineteenth century this country's people became alternately hospitable to and hostile to a whole series of immigrating reform groups, most of which had their origins in minority religious movements.[22] Out of the fervency and reforming zeal of all these groups came the "gel" which formed a substantial part of the American character on into the twentieth century.

This character, more than is ordinarily assumed, was formed by the memories of a European lower-class past. Whatever the religious rationale, the peasants who migrated to these shores and the frontiersmen who mastered the forests were unconsciously rejecting the excesses of a largely imagined upper class. Silks and satins, and wine, women, and song, crude symbols of their oppressors, became the targets of their exorcising zeal, even though their emergence on the American scene was an expression of a newly won—not an inherited—privilege.

Whatever the validity of the assessment of the American scene, out of the zeal of these nineteenth-century evangelical Protestants rather than out of the tepid arguments of the eighteenth-century deists came the drive for small colleges, primary schools, and, toward the last of the

[21] *Ibid.*, p. 301.
[22] Alice Felt Tyler, *Freedom's Ferment: Phases of American Social History to 1860*, University of Minnesota Press, Minneapolis, Minn., 1944. This book provides a survey of minority religious movements.

nineteenth century, the use of schools to assure a moral population. Out of the way in which they approached behavior came the methodological interpretation of most of the prescriptions written into law.

*Nationalism*

By 1923, there were 304 kinds of prescriptions for elementary schools which could be subsumed under the general term *nationalism* (see Table 8-1). These were multiform. They still include such elements as the oath of allegiance and respect for the flag, teaching of state and national constitutions as well as the Bill of Rights and occasionally the Declaration of Independence, and singing of the national anthem.[23]  In 1953, there were 434 legislative provisions on nationalism for secondary schools. Of the 434, some 410 were mandatory, 19 were prohibitive in nature, and 5 were permissive. From 1941 to 1953, 9 new occasions designed to celebrate America were set aside by legislators. These included National Anthem Day, Sir Walter Raleigh Day, Good Government Day, Loyalty Day, and Civil Rights Week.[24]  This complex of mandatory teachings about which legislators have been so emphatic might well be called the special American symbol system.

Like the items in the series on health and prohibition, the mandates in the American-symbol system are often described as being there in part because of the efforts of various voluntary groups. Cited as the most active agencies are the American Bar Association, the National Security League, the American Legion, the two national labor organizations, the two Revolutionary War associations, the National Association of Manufacturers, professional education groups, and such organizations as the Constitution Anniversary Association and the America First Committee.[25]

These organizations plus many others, some of which appeared briefly in history for a particular purpose, have played their part in the pressures exerted on legislatures.[26]  Efforts of these organizations have gone beyond the aspiration for legislative mandates to the schools. They have encompassed special contests of all kinds, utilization of mass media, organization of unofficial investigating committees, and, occasionally, terror. In their efforts to define the American, they have encompassed all manner of unlike stuff.

*An American,* as defined by a great range of voluntary organizations

---

[23] Clarence E. Swingley, "The Legal Basis of Civic Education in the United States from 1900 to 1949," unpublished doctoral dissertation, University of Chicago, Chicago, 1951. (Microfilm.)

[24] Lehman, *op. cit.,* pp. 39, 43.

[25] Swingley, *op. cit.,* p. 19.

[26] Pierce, *Citizens' Organizations and the Civic Training of Youth.*

stretching back at least a hundred years, would have embraced anti-Semites and anti-Catholics, as well as believers in a world brotherhood both of peoples and of nations. Members of the Ku Klux Klan, for instance, said that only "good true hundred per cent Americans" must be allowed to be administrative or teaching personnel in American schools. The definition of a good American excluded "papists or anti-Christian Jews." Teachers, particularly Jewish teachers, were charged with teaching socialism under "the guise of social betterment," and during 1924, approximately 2,250 high school boys and girls alone were interested in socialism. Such doctrines must be extirpated from the schools, and the best way to see that they did not intrude in the curriculum was to select the teaching force with care, according to the Klan.[27]

In contrast to the Klan, which carefully defined the boundaries between the American and the un-American citizens, many peace societies have worked for universal brotherhood of man primarily by asking for the study of other peoples and, occasionally, by the improved study of American history. Many of these organizations have not had programs specifically designed for youth, but expect their organizational impact to be through the adult teacher, though they also recognize the crucial importance of the public school in the process of developing attitudes toward other people.[28]

Of a somewhat different order from either of the above kinds of organizations is the American Bar Association. As early as 1922, this group became worried about the indifference of the American people to the Constitution. Members of its Committee on American Citizenship were inclined to believe that if it were put to a vote, a large number of citizens would act to abolish the Constitution. The national group then formed local committees. Members were to inquire into the teaching of the Constitution, including the qualifications of teachers, texts used, and other matters. The association's slogan became "The schools of America must save America." By 1927 it was judged by the citizenship committee that the Constitution was fundamental enough to the United States to justify being studied as a separate subject. In 1943, the association began promoting "I Am an American Day," but by 1943 decided to leave citizenship education to the educators, who were already earnestly wrestling with the problem of civic education.[29]

Defining the American and deciding on what he should know as well as stamping in the appropriate behaviors has taken the civic organizations far and wide in their methods and in their convictions. Legislation alone has been only one of their instruments. But whether a group has investigated how red is the little red schoolhouse, or co-

[27] *Ibid.*, chap. 11.
[28] *Ibid.*, part 3.
[29] Swingley, *op. cit.*, pp. 11–15.

operated with teachers in the development of improved work in the social studies, one and all have judged the "school"—kindergarten to college—to be the agency on which hangs the fate of the nation. Is the United States strong militarily? The school will make the nation strong by incorporating physical education and military training in the curriculum. Can Americans resist the several "isms"? The character of the teachers and the nature of school programs will determine the depth of resistance. Is the United States to be a central force in developing world unity? The schools will determine the attitudes by which the character of other peoples is judged. This concern for what the school does as central to any minority concern of the citizens' group is so pervasive that another explanation other than that of sheer pressure may be in order for the mandatory curricular provisions of legislators.

After all, lawmakers are themselves members of many of these organizations. What the organization stands for in respect to schools is also what the legislator stands for. He, too—whatever his ideological leanings—is as convinced as members of citizen groups that democracy will stand or fall on how school keeps. What any group of legislators may do in respect to schools in any legislative session may depend less on specific pressures and more on who has been elected to the legislature. It also may reflect the prevailing opinion among a majority of the groups throughout the United States at the time of enactment. Such an interpretation of the whys of legislative mandates is borne out in part by a study of when particular kinds of laws have been enacted.

*The Crisis Thesis.* A study of dating of legislation introduces the crisis thesis. Although there is no one-to-one correspondence between crisis periods in American history and dates of legislative enactments, it might be said that curricular enactments are crisis responses. The American society is threatened by war or by migration. Legislators—either on their own volition or stimulated by patriotic or special-interest groups—move to dam the largely imagined tide of disaffection by insisting on the compulsory teaching of certain content, which is calculated to change behavior in desirable directions. At the same time, they ensure the employment of personnel that will conform with the direction change.

Such legislative moves are often accompanied by enactment of teacher oaths and investigation of textbooks. Book burning, charging teachers and professors with subversion, restriction of immigration, and renewed emphasis on symbolic behavior, such as saluting the flag—all these may follow in the wake of defensive hysteria. In recent decades, the ostrich technique has been implemented in such places as the District of Columbia, where a teacher could not get his check if he mentioned in class the name of a certain power prominent on the wrong side of the cold war.

The crisis thesis is largely a phenomenon of the ninety years since the Civil War. Although the War of 1812 deepened the patriotic distrust of England, it brought in its aftermath little impact on the patriotic role of the schools. The year 1827 marked the beginning of the compulsory teaching of United States history, one of that complex of subjects which constitutes the hard core that Americans should know. In 1827, Massachusetts and Vermont passed legislation respecting the compulsory teaching of American history—in the elementary school in one case, and in the secondary school in the other.

Up to 1860, only six states had passed laws respecting compulsory social studies: Massachusetts, Vermont, New Hampshire, Rhode Island, Virginia, and California.[30] California's prescription of the teaching of the Federal and state constitutions in the grammar schools and political economy in the high schools had come in 1851, the year following her admission to the Union and three years after the treaty by which her territories were incorporated into the Union. The pressure of new populations and of internal or external threats to the government had not yet been keenly felt.

The period directly following the Civil War was one of strong national sentiment. The nation had been saved, and it must be preserved. Localism and regionalism were in abeyance. The country was being knit together by improved transportation, increased mobility of the population, nationalizing of industry, and urbanization. The country had, however, felt the wrenches of disunity, and in the four or five decades after the war it was to feel the wrenches of the immigrants which were flooding the Eastern cities. New efforts must be asked of the schools.

In the forty years following 1860, twenty-three states adopted laws respecting the teaching of history in the public schools.[31] Several states took action in respect to the teaching of American history or the Constitution or otherwise promoted patriotic endeavors in the decades immediately after the war. Such actions were found in the 1860s in Vermont, West Virginia, Missouri, Maryland, Arkansas, and Minnesota; and in the 1870s in South Carolina, Tennessee, Kentucky, Wisconsin, and Montana. Specific stipulations related to Americanism rarely are a part of state constitutions; but in those for New Mexico and Arizona, admitted in 1912, there was firmly embedded a requirement that instruction should be in English,[32] an acknowledgment of the threat of Spanish-speaking Americans.

[30] Pierce, *Public Opinion and the Teaching of History in the United States*, pp. 6, 9.

[31] *Ibid.*, p. 14.

[32] Swingley, *op. cit.*, pp. 22–23.

If a Civil War and immigration had brought concern to Americans, World War I touched off alternating waves of genuine concern and hysteria. Bessie Pierce has made a summary of the laws which were promulgated during and immediately following the war. They related to oaths of loyalty by teachers, instruction in patriotism through courses on United States history and government, denial to aliens of the right to teach in the public schools, special directives on observances of the flag and patriotic occasions, specifications about textbooks, and directives on Americanization of the foreign-born.[33] By 1949, some forty-five states had laws respecting the compulsory teaching of the Constitution. Of the six states that passed laws prior to the 1920s, three had done so in the 1890s and 1901, and California had passed such a law in 1917, presumably in response to World War I. Of the remaining thirty-nine states, thirty-seven passed such laws during the 1921 to 1929 period of hysteria following the war,[34] such actions being partly occasioned by the emergence of the Soviet Union in 1917.

The teaching of the Federal as well as the state constitutions was accompanied by two other kinds of legislative enactments immediately after World War I. The one having to do with languages caused an unprecedented furor which ended in court decisions.

It will be remembered that Arizona and New Mexico, when they were brought into the Union, had in their state constitutions a stipulation that instruction be given in the English language. Before 1912, only one other state, Louisiana, had such a mandate, presumably to counteract the influence of the large French-speaking population. In 1920, when the state of Nebraska undertook to revise her constitution, a similar provision was inserted. General provisions for instruction being in the English language had been made by seventeen states prior to World War I. In the ten years from 1913 to 1923 the number of states having such a provision jumped from seventeen to thirty-four.[35] The loose wording of some of the laws thereupon occasioned controversy and court cases. Some acts were so worded, for instance, that instruction in foreign languages, ordinarily considered a necessary part of secondary programs, was prohibited.

One set of acts which occasioned a final decision by the Supreme Court was passed in the state of Nebraska.[36] The first of these contained two provisions: the one that persons in public, denominational,

---

[33] Pierce, *Public Opinion and the Teaching of History in the United States*, p. 72.

[34] Swingley, *op. cit.*, pp. 30–39, gives a listing of states in which teaching of the Constitution is required.

[35] Flanders, *op. cit.*, p. 19.

[36] Facts in the language case and quotations from court decisions taken from Otto Templar Hamilton, *The Courts and the Curriculum*, Bureau of Publications, Teachers College, Columbia University, New York, 1927, pp. 38–45.

and parochial schools were prohibited from teaching any subject in a language other than English, and the other that languages other than English might be taught only to students who had successfully passed the eighth grade. In the same year, 1919, the Nebraska District of the Evangelical Lutheran Synod of Missouri, Ohio and Other States, asked for an injunction to restrain the state from enforcing the law; but the latter was upheld by the state supreme court.

The Nebraska Legislature followed its 1919 action by another act intended to strengthen the earlier law. This act declared the English language to be the official language of the state and, among other provisions, called for all "school branches to be taught in said language in public, private, denominational and parochial schools." Following on this second act, the actions of the Legislature were tested in the supreme court again and upheld, and finally reached the United States Supreme Court, where the decisions of the lower court were reversed.

The decision of the Supreme Court is significant both in respect to the basis on which the decision was made, and to some of the side issues raised by dissenting opinion. The decision as written by Justice McReynolds did not question the right of the state to compel attendance at some school and to make reasonable regulations for all schools "including a requirement that they shall give instructions in English." The question at issue was the matter of whether the liberty of the plaintiff, a teacher, had been infringed as prohibited by the due-process clause of the Fourteenth Amendment to the United States Constitution. On this basis, the Court found that state authorities were prohibiting language teachers from pursuing their vocations, and were interfering with the rights of students to acquire knowledge and of parents to control the education of their own offspring. Then what was to become of the power of the state to foster American ideals through promoting instruction in the English language? The Court recognized that the state might go far in improving its citizens morally as well as physically and mentally, and that it might be desirable if all citizens had an adequate understanding of the common language. "The desire of the legislature to foster a homogeneous people with American ideals prepared readily to understand current discussions of civic matters is easy to appreciate." But understanding of the common language could not be coerced. "A desirable end cannot be promoted by prohibited means." In time of peace the state could not tamper with the rights of the teacher to instruct in a foreign language.

The Supreme Court of the United States dismissed four other cases similar to the Nebraska one. The concern of the Court, however, over the development of the homogeneous people is quite apparent, and is even more keenly evident in the dissenting opinion of Justice Holmes. That Justice Holmes should be the dissenter is striking. The New England philosopher of the law is held up as a liberal whose primary concern has been for the liberties of all the people, even those with whom he might violently disagree.    Yet Justice Holmes was exercised enough over the process of developing a people that would hang together to disagree with a reversal of the requirement of English as a medium of instruction in the grades.    Holmes pointed out that the concern of the law was with children and that childhood is the period when language habits are fixed.    He went on to say that "if there are sections in the state where a child would hear only Polish or French or German spoken at home, I am not prepared to say that it is unreasonable to provide that in his early years he shall hear and speak only English at school."    Justice Holmes followed this statement with an explanation of his reasoning, which took due account of the liberties of teachers, but he insisted there was room for difference of opinion and he was "unable to say that the constitution of the United States prevents the experiment [presumably instruction in English] being tried."    Whatever the reasonable doubts, the states which had passed laws respecting instruction in English and which thereby interfered with the teaching of foreign languages amended their laws to exempt foreign languages from the legislative restrictions.[37]

A good number of the language laws were undoubtedly in part a response to the reaction against the Germans occasioned by World War I.    There was, however, a language characteristic of the American population which probably stimulated concern for the teaching of English.    With the initiation of the draft, it was revealed that 700,000 out of 10 million registrants could not read, write, or sign their names. Most of these illiterates were immigrants.[38]    The problem of the immigrants had been recently aggravated; in the four years preceding World War I, 5,174,701 immigrants had come to the United States, and out of this number 22.1 per cent were not able to read or write any language. In 1920, immediately preceding the opening of the campaign for instruction in English, it was discovered that nearly 1½ million (11 per cent) of the foreign-born white people in the United States could not speak English.[39]    During the war, preceding it, and immediately following it, the illiterates and the non-English-speaking people were a matter of concern both for the 100 per cent Americans and those committed to a more broadly oriented societal fabric.

The special character of the immigration in the decades following 1875 had stimulated prewar activities designed to hasten the process of assimilation of the foreign-born.    The groups which had begun to come

---

[37] Swingley, *op. cit.*, pp. 87–88.
[38] Edward George Hartmann, *The Movement to Americanize the Immigrant,* Columbia University Press, New York, 1948, p. 187.
[39] Pierce, *Public Opinion and the Teaching of History in the United States*, p. 110.

from the Slavic countries and Italy were largely Roman Catholic, Eastern Orthodox, or Hebrew in religious persuasion, had little if any formal education, and little experience in self-government. The reaction of labor and management, of state and Federal agencies, as well as patriotic societies, was the more intense because the populations contrasted so sharply with the hitherto Protestant, largely Anglo-Saxon, and public school–oriented group which had come in earlier migrations.

The treatment of immigrants was often far from honorable. On the other hand, some local communities had begun educational efforts, some states were active in what might be called desirable directions, and in the U.S. Office of Education there had been instituted a Division of Immigrant Education. The war did not provide the original stimulus for the Americanization movement, but was rather its catalyst.

World War I demanded—as the Revolutionary War long ago had demanded—that the American people, immigrants included, hang together. The hanging together involved full and often extraordinary participation in military service, in industry, in home and community activities. The foreign-born ill understood the war or its meaning, might have had a hankering for enemy causes, were ill equipped for full participation in the war effort even though they might be willing—how could they be knit rapidly into the American fabric? Immediately after the war the question was to be raised as to how they might be kept from disaffection to the Red Goliath.

Legislative efforts at the state level to Americanize the immigrant revolved largely around making monies available for local communities for their education. Between 1917 and 1926 "more than one-third of the states . . . enacted legislation for the purpose of developing a love for this country in the foreign born." Unlike the legislation for the curriculum of the common schools and the colleges, the acts for education of immigrants were largely permissive and facilitatory. However, the New York Legislature in 1918 passed a law mandating attendance at English and civics classes for young non-English-speaking and illiterate minors, ages sixteen to twenty-one.[40]

State acts passed in the interests of Americanization ordinarily gave authority to the local school districts to conduct classes for the foreign-born and provided money along with indications of the nature of the instruction. In compliance with state acts, educators in local districts set up night classes typically in schools but occasionally in industrial plants and homes. Though the language of the acts varied, the courses of study most often included English and civics, with attention to the Constitution and the American form of government and accompanied by some American history. In some states, permission to organize classes in homes permitted the instruction of adults and children together in

[40] *Ibid.*, pp. 105–106.

many aspects of American family living. The entrance of public schools into Americanization in most local communities where there was any concentration of the foreign-born had two effects. The first related to the immigrant who, despite the American-colored glasses of most Americanization teachers, could expect to receive reasonably humane treatment. This had not always been the case when other national organizations had been at work. The immigrant might now find himself wearied after a hard day's work communicating in another language and memorizing facts for his Americanization papers, but he carried on these tasks in perhaps as uniformly congenial an atmosphere as would have been devised by even the most accommodating of the national organizations. The necessity for his education finally gave rise to publicly supported adult education for any or all who would wish it, another aspect in a broader perspective of the Americanization of all Americans.

The mandatory teaching of American history and the Constitution as well as the education of the foreign-born were not the only measures to which state legislators addressed themselves during and immediately after World War I. One set of laws was addressed to the citizenship of teachers and oaths of loyalty for instructional staffs. Few states prior to World War I had such laws, though in 1915 three states had enacted statutes calling for teachers to be citizens of the United States. During and following World War I, state after state enacted legislation calling for citizenship and loyalty requirements. An example of the close relationship of such laws to states of crisis is the series on citizenship in New York State. As of April 4, 1918, a teacher who was not a citizen could retain his position only if within a year he should make application for citizenship. By a subsequent law he was excused from such requirement, providing he were a citizen of an allied nation. A good number of other states followed with citizenship laws, or with laws expressly prohibiting criticism of the United States form of government, or disrespect for the flag or the Holy Bible, or actively inculcating disloyalty. Interestingly enough, two states, Massachusetts and Pennsylvania, continued to retain on the books laws "emphasizing a faith in the integrity and patriotism of their teachers." These laws stated that neither religious nor political test was to be required of applicants for school positions.[41]

Symbolic ways of reinforcing patriotism also were the subject of legislative action in the period during and following World War I. The statute of the state of Maryland possibly reflected best the sentiments of many a legislator in this wording: "The love of liberty and democracy, signified in the devotion of all true and patriotic Americans to their flag and to their country, shall be instilled in the hearts and

[41] *Ibid.*, pp. 85–93.

minds of the youth of America."[42]　Display of the flag became a common occurrence and along with this came statutes requiring the singing of patriotic songs and, as in Nevada, setting aside a specified amount of time each school week "for the purpose of holding patriotic exercises." The force of the war can be felt in the fact that in 1913 there was only one state requiring that patriotism be taught in the schools, whereas in 1923 there were twelve.[43]

Other kinds of legislation also characterized the period. Textbooks came in for examination and for lawmaking. By and large the course of other kinds of legislating merely strengthened the general intent of legislators to bulwark the societal fabric by as many means as possible for inducing the desired behaviors in the young.

World War II brought with it some additions to the legislative symbol system. But so many of the states had already moved in the direction of bulwarking behavior by law that nothing much was left to be done. A study of a random sample of high schools in the years 1933–1934 and 1946–1947 showed a marked increase in percentage of pupil semesters for United States history in grades 7 and 8 as well as in grades 9 to 12.[44] However, this may have been due to the patriotic fervor of the teaching personnel rather than to any additional legislative decrees. Teachers' oaths came in for some legislating as well as rather considerable condemnation after World War II. For the most part, official and unofficial inquiries into the patriotic endeavors of the schools were for the purpose of enforcing a narrow conformity rather than for the purpose of legislating. The defensive character of the movements across the country are not unlike the waves of legislation after the Civil War and World War I. The crisis thesis can be supported by varied evidence.

*The Courts and the Schools.* The importance of the schools in preserving the social fabric is underscored by the actions of the courts in respect to legislative decrees. That the courts should concern themselves with some of the issues of school legislation is in itself significant. Professor Brogan from Cambridge relates the story of the children of Jehovah's Witnesses who, upon refusing to salute the flag, had been excluded from school. The case came before the United States Supreme Court, the highest court in the land, which, after reversing itself, finally upheld the religious rights of the children.[45]　In an earlier decision the

[42] *Ibid.*, p. 94.

[43] Flanders, *op. cit.*, p. 15.

[44] Howard R. Anderson, *Teaching of United States History in Public High Schools: An Inquiry into Offerings and Registrations, 1946–47,* U.S. Office of Education Bulletin 1949, no. 7, 1949, p. 12.

[45] Denis W. Brogan, "A Cambridge Professor Celebrates the American Public School," in Henry Steele Commager (ed.), *America in Perspective: The United States through Foreign Eyes,* Random House, Inc., New York, 1947, p. 360.

flag salute had been upheld under the assumption that "national unity demanded certain sacrifices of individual freedoms, including possibly religious freedom."[46] What was significant, according to Professor Brogan, was not the maneuvers of the Court. Rather it was that the Court should have dealt so seriously with the issue. In Brogan's eyes, the refusal of the children to salute the flag was as unreasoning to members of the Court and the American people as the refusal of Christians to make sacrifice to the Emperor had been to Trajan and Pliny.[47]

Despite such reverses, the lawmakers have generally been upheld in taking a part in school business. The trend has been in the direction of recognizing the right of either the legislatures or the school boards to prescribe courses of instruction for schools and to add subjects considered desirable.[48] A Tennessee law prohibiting the employment of alien teachers has been held to be constitutional.[49] However, certain recent actions of the Court may be interpreted to secure for the school a place so central to the national welfare that even the legislatures may be overruled in their traditional control by law. Swingley says, "The Supreme Court, also, has been taking a more liberal view towards its right and responsibility to review problems related to education."[50] Both this statement and the expanded concept of the school's function are amply born out by the desegregation issue of recent years. Neither the prejudices of sizable minorities nor the presumed rights of legislators shall stand in the way of the enculturation role of the school.

## SUMMARY

To secure the general welfare of the republican society, official political bodies have prescribed and clarified the schooling process. Legislatures have mandated the *teaching about* certain preferred subjects with numbers of prescriptions—the highest number in subjects and activities related to health and prohibition and nationalism. These prescriptions have been accompanied by others, such as those related to teacher loyalty and textbooks. The number of legislative mandates bears a relationship to crisis periods in American history.

Both state and Federal courts have passed on the legislative prescriptions and have generally upheld the lawmakers. The interest of both lawmakers and members of courts in issues affecting schools attests to the central position of educational institutions in the preservation of the nation.

[46] Remmlein, *op. cit.*, p. 253.
[47] Brogan, *op. cit.*, p. 360.
[48] Hamilton, *op. cit.*, p. 23; Swingley, *op. cit.*, p. 29.
[49] Swingley, *op. cit.*, p. 110.
[50] *Ibid.*, p. 112.

# 9

## Textbook Influences
## on the American Educational Ideal

A FRENCHMAN was travelling in one of the lower counties, not long since.—He met one of our men with a musket and furniture going to attend muster.—"Pray, young man," says Monsieur, "be you one ARISTOCRAT or one DEMOCRAT?" "Why," replied the youth, "I am SUPERIOR TO EITHER, I am an AMERICAN."[1]

PITTSBURGH GAZETTE, 1798

In the antebellum period, dedicated people searched abroad for a school system; in the postbellum period, equally dedicated people described a national curriculum that included general education, and legislators mandated curriculum items. In the meanwhile, a group of largely unsung heroes were building up an image of America—an image designed to engage the attention of the young, the heritors of all that was America. It was so constructed that the young American could find a description of himself in the proportions of the good American. This image was developed by the textbook writers who began their work in the post-Revolutionary period and have continued it to the present.

"Teacher to America" might well characterize the textbook. Both as educator of other educators and educator of youth, the textbook has occupied an exalted place in this country, which is the world's leading producer of literature for children and adolescents. In the nineteenth and the early twentieth centuries, the text was an instrument for training teachers even as it is today in a more limited way. The teacher education institutions and the supervisory staffs have never quite caught up with the numbers of inexperienced or untrained teachers which the continually expanding school systems have had to employ. Hence the

[1] William F. Keller, *The Nation's Advocate,* University of Pittsburgh Press, Pittsburgh, Pa., 1956, p. ix. Quoted by permission of publisher.

258

good text of the nineteenth century had its methods sections for teachers. The good text of the twentieth century has its teacher's manual, and occasionally accompanying films, filmstrips, and other props. In addition, of course, textbooks have been needed for the continuously burgeoning school population. In this wealthiest of all countries, where the young are indulged in material goods, youngsters have never been without books of some sort and in many cases a surfeit of them. Hence the important place of the text in American education.

Books imply reading and the latter would suggest some little influence on behavior. But what effect the printed word has had on child or teacher attitudes or actions has been inadequately explored. The few studies on the effect of good or bad literature on what the child does have been inconclusive. Going a step further—and by inference from our present knowledge of behavior—it would seem naïve to assume that a child enjoined by a text to be honest would therefore exhibit behavior designated as honest by a majority of adult Americans. Such an assumption would call for intensive study of the nature of learning, which is not the province of this book.

An inquiry, however, into what American children and youth have read and what teachers have by inference taught can be fruitful in another way. If there are any patterns to be seen in these texts over a relatively sustained period of time, they may disclose the nature of the ideal America and the ideal American. That the authors may have meant them to do so is given credence through an analysis of the aims of writers of junior high school history texts published from 1886 to 1954. According to the prefaces in these eighty-eight texts, the chief aims of authors were to (1) develop an interest in American history; (2) help in making good citizens; (3) stimulate patriotism; and (4) present the history of our country.[2] As the authors of a 1926 text said, they had "to fire the youthful imagination with a vivid sense of the abounding life and glowing idealism that have made America the lodestar of the freedom of the world."[3]

This inquiry into America's self-image is not as pretentious as that which meets the criteria for a study of national character. The latter purports to isolate regularities in the behavior of all members of a society so that a culturally regular character can with confidence be delineated.[4] Such a study might well come after an identification of

[2] Frank R. Caputo, "Development of Junior High School United States History Textbooks from 1886 to 1954," unpublished doctoral dissertation, University of Pittsburgh, Pittsburgh, Pa., 1956, pp. 13–31. (Microfilm.)

[3] Quoted in *ibid.*, p. 19.

[4] Margaret Mead, "National Character," *Anthropology Today: An Encyclopedic Inventory*, prepared under the chairmanship of A. L. Kroeber, The University of Chicago Press, Chicago, 1953, p. 642.

images and ask to what extent behavior is in accord with the ideal selves.

This chapter will be addressed to the ways in which textbooks handle items of national history and character so as to describe America and Americans. The descriptions will be based only on analyses designed to uncover prevailing attitudes communicated by children's reading matter. Relatively little attempt will be made to affirm or deny the historical accuracy of statements. This is a task which has been and is being undertaken by scores of historians, occasionally with scant success. For the purposes of this inquiry, the repetition of an assertion is more important than its truth. What young Americans are expected to believe and their teachers to teach is the theme of this account. Hopefully, in the telling of this story of America's growth and development, what ought to be the religious, economic, nationality, and character background of the good American—as conceived by text writers—will be clear.

As reflected in colonial and early national textbooks, two rather unlike movements affecting children took place. The one was in the larger society outside of the school and had to do with the attitudes toward children. During most of the colonial period, youngsters had lived in the shadows of the harsh Calvinism of the Puritans. They were reminded daily of their innate depravity and of their more than likely chances of landing in hell. Even for the gay and healthy, death might be just around the corner. It was well to contemplate one's Creator and one's duty to Him, and take every opportunity to improve the chances of one's salvation. Morbidness and an unremitting awe were steadfastly communicated to youth through their books and in daily observances.[5]

The child of colonial days was sternly taught. His duty was to God, to his parents, and to his neighbors, and he did not confine this duty to isolated occasions. To God he paid special homage on the Sabbath by going to church even if it lay miles from his home, and by thinking of God for the rest of the week. To his parents he owed always the respect of being seen but not heard. Toward his neighbors he must display at all times that charity characteristic of Christians. This stern role for the child was accompanied by even sterner punishment for his transgressions. Some believed there should even be resort to the law to restrain undisciplined children. In 1641 it was actually proposed in Massachusetts that children who persisted in their erring ways after

[5] Most of the account to follow on the transformation in children has been adapted from Monica Mary Kiefer, *American Children through Their Books, 1700–1835*, University of Pennsylvania Press, Philadelphia, 1948.

correction from parents be put to death.[6]   The child's fate and welfare were largely bound up in a stern and doctrinal reading of religious prescriptions.   His status was apt to be a reflection of adult status rather than of his inherent worth, and he was more than apt to have to bear adult responsibility for his behavior.

Certain aspects of colonial life tended to foster this harsh disciplinary regime for children.   The exigencies of a frontier life coupled with a lack of medical information made for high mortality rates among the young.   Deep and abiding commitments to the doctrinal rather than the broadly moral phases of religion suggested that the only comfort— either for parents who had lost their young or for the young themselves —was in early conversion and in supplication to a harsh but just God.

Attitudes toward children and their training were reflected in another colonial phenomenon which directly affected the school.   Reading matter for children was chosen in light of the stern measures needed for their salvation.   The Bible was ever present and read in home as well as in school.   Coupled with this basic text were such morbid readers as the old *New England Primer, Xerxes the Great did die/And so must you and I.*   These, supplemented by catechisms and some few other equally gloomy tomes, constituted the children's academic fare.

Both of these movements, the treatment of the child and provision for his reading matter, began to change about the time of the Revolution. Many forces were at work.   Reconciliation of doctrinal differences had gone forward as a necessity for keeping a society together, hence there was decreasing emphasis on peculiarities in the several sects and increasing stress on the broad moral implications of religious belief, whatever its character.   Among the middle and upper classes there flourished in the eighteenth century an increasing belief in a perfect and naturalistic universe designed by God, the Great Architect, who wished nothing but good for His children.   This belief among intellectuals opened the way for a more humane outlook on all human beings as well as on children, and promoted the development of science, which was an approved way of discovering the proportions of God's perfect universe. The resulting development of medical science, coupled with a prosperity which allowed for indulging children and a deepening feeling of equalitarianism, reflected favorably on the health and status of youth. Gradually they began to acquire worth in themselves as immature beings and the right to be children rather than defective adults.

In response to this new judgment about children, there began to appear in the early national period texts which confined their admoni-

[6] R. Freeman Butts and Lawrence A. Cremin, *A History of Education in American Culture,* Henry Holt and Company, Inc., New York, 1953, p. 67.

tions to mild moral tales. More authors began to write with an eye to children and the secular interests of the larger society, rather than to religious prejudices of parents. Fairy tales and stories about youngsters for youngsters found their way into bookstores and schools. The stage has been set since first the United States became a nation for an examination of what the literature designed for children and youth has attempted to communicate to them.

The picture of America and Americans from 1776 to the present is, of course, not complete. Not every piece of reading matter has been put under a magnifying glass. But analysts of texts have been careful to choose for study both a wide range of materials and those most used by schools. Thus the story is reasonably well sketched by studies already done. The story to follow, which is largely based on these studies, can be judged a reasonably sound account of the emergence of America and Americans in elementary and secondary texts.

## AN EMERGENT AMERICA

What does any country need to be a nation—what particularly do people in the United States need to be a nation? Every nation needs a set of symbols around which people can rally and which can be relied upon to invoke the hoped-for emotional overtones. Some countries have kings and queens or create a mystic fatherland or all-embracing mother. Most of them have glorious heroes either of war or of peace. Americans had these latter heroes, but they had no authority figures to stand for unity, so in their place textbook writers put such inanimate objects as the flag and various honorific documents. Some say that as a result the United States developed an ideology.

Every nation needs an image of itself which holds up well against the images of other peoples. This image may be of a freedom-loving people, or a folk destined to rule the world, or a subtle purveyor of culture to less enlightened people, or a people living in grand isolation from a peripheral barbarian populace. The American image was ambivalent—glorious in wars, all of which were forced upon the people, yet peace loving and an asylum for the oppressed.

Every people needs a set of comparative characteristics. A favorable set of terms will be used to delineate themselves and those neighbors who are so enlightened as to be like them. An unfavorable set of terms is a necessary concomitant to describing those who unfortunately are not in their circle. By likenesses and contrasts they can build the preferred image. These terms are often coupled with a comparative analysis of political systems with the desired terms being an outcome of or inevitably coupled with a particular form of government. The range in terms is wide, yet not so extended as one might think, for the same term used in different contexts can mean various things to various peoples. Both Russians and Americans are "democratic" in their own eyes, and both put stress on equality. Americans have had and now do have words for describing themselves—"just" and "liberty loving," for instance. Americans have and are taking a set of positions about other nationals as well as those who came to the United States as immigrants. Americans, too, have built an image of themselves by comparison.

Inevitably—out of the symbols developed, the images built, and the terms adopted about themselves and others—Americans have built an ideal people. This other peoples have done and this Americans do. So there is a list of virtues which ought to characterize any good American child or adult, and a contrasting list of vices which are a negation of the emergent American. Americans are abstaining, kind, loving, industrious, saving. They abhor intemperance, gambling, selfishness, and niggardliness. They strive to achieve and to save for another day; they frown on him who idles away his time and lives only for the moment. Thus is built the ideal emergent American.

## Setting Up a Symbol System

Standing for the nation in the modern day are the flag and an eagle. In early national texts, the last was a most popular bird. The United States and the eagle were equated. Both had lofty aims and strength, and happily the bird was one of rare courage. The flag, however, was not popular until the 1840s.[7] Through the McGuffey readers, the latter continued to be one of the three watchwords of the nation, and better still, one of "the rocks on which the lusty patriots of the nineteenth century built their arguments."[8] By the 1920s the flag was a symbol of unity of the American people in history books and other social studies texts. An elaborate flag etiquette had been built up, and a set of concepts respecting the flag were current. The flag was a symbol of unity which a child loved to salute and would be bound to respect even if all he could say was that it was his flag. But he knew more than this about it. If it were suddenly to speak out and to ask of passersby "Who goes?" the answer would be a "single, myriad-tongued word 'American.'"[9] With this heavy burden to carry, the flag must be celebrated in

[7] Ruth Virginia Miller, "Nationalism in Elementary Schoolbooks Used in the United States from 1776 to 1865," unpublished doctoral dissertation, Columbia University, New York, 1952, pp. 340–341. (Microfilm.)

[8] Richard D. Mosier, *Making the American Mind: Social and Moral Ideas in the McGuffey Readers*, King's Crown Press, New York, 1947, p. 41.

[9] Quoted in Bessie Louise Pierce, *Civic Attitudes in American School Textbooks*, University of Chicago Press, Chicago, 1930, p. 116.

song and story, and in appropriate ceremonials. It was flown from every schoolhouse and addressed each morning by thousands of youngsters over the land. It appeared in elementary school readers of all grades, even the first. "Your Flag and My Flag," "The Flag Goes By," and "Flag o' My Land" as well as "The Star-spangled Banner" appeared in readers and music books. It has never known defeat and wherever it goes it carries with it liberty and justice for all.[10]

If junior high school texts in history had appendixes, the items appearing in them in twentieth-century editions were most apt to be the Declaration of Independence and the Constitution of the United States.[11] For these were the items which, along with the flag, could well serve as substitutes for titled authority figures. This was a land, so it was said, in which loyalty was built on institutions rather than on geography or people; and in this land, the documents basic to those institutions were ones which stated that all men were created equal and that Americans had ordained a fundamental law designed to ensure the blessings of liberty to themselves and their posterity.

In texts of the 1920s, the Mayflower Compact and papers of the Revolution were important in developing American political concepts. The Declaration of Independence, according to these texts, may even in its emphasis on equality have had its roots in the Magna Charta, the Bill of Rights, and the Petition of Right. Whatever its origins, it was still an "immortal" document in history texts.[12] Although in early national texts it was not to be examined, its birthday, July 4, 1776, was estimated by one investigator to be "second in importance only to the birth of Christ." It was "a nation's natal day" and "Freedom's jubilee," sang an 1824 speller and so Americans "with thankful hearts due homage pay/The homage of the free."[13]

But to conservative folk, the Declaration of Independence might well smack of French Jacobinism. So, for the descendants of the staunch New Englanders who wrote the McGuffey readers, the document was tolerated largely as a propaganda device, one calculated to enhance American interests abroad, to exchange civil for national war, and to urge on troops in their endeavor. The great Webster reinforced this view, for he found that power followed property, and the latter must have been at the core of the American Revolution, and a document which extolled other purposes in nation making must have been forged to please more sentimental folk.[14]

[10] Ibid., pp. 114–116, 170–171, 207, 208.
[11] Caputo, op. cit.
[12] Pierce, op. cit., pp. 104, 143.
[13] Miller, op. cit., p. 342.
[14] Mosier, op. cit., pp. 13, 155.

This reinterpretation proved not to be a setback to the Declaration, however. In texts of the 1920s youngsters were treated to the "Supposed Speech of John Adams on the Declaration of Independence" by Daniel Webster, and in their histories, they were told it was "a great human document" and "the most famous document known in the history" of their country. From the Declaration of Independence, as well as from colonial charters and a knowledge of mankind, the founders of the United States drew their ideas for the making of the Constitution.[15]

As to the Constitution, Jefferson's queer notions about its being rewritten every generation have rarely, if ever, intruded themselves into a discussion of that great document. The vague and ill-defined liberty of the early texts, which Americans had for good and which it was their mission to spread, was theirs because of the Constitution.[16] It was framed, according to the McGuffey readers, by men who "for stolidity of reasoning, force of sagacity, and wisdom of conclusion were superior of all groups of assembled legislators throughout the whole course of history." So long as Americans had this great document, they could bear all misfortune. Only if it were destroyed would they be in peril, for who would put together the pieces of a dismembered government, build again those constitutional liberties, and unite the national sovereignty "with state-rights, individual security, and public prosperity"?[17]

The young reader of the texts of the 1920s should have been still aware that in Gladstone's words, his Constitution was "the most wonderful work ever struck off at a given time by the brain and purpose of man." It might not be perfect, to be sure, but it was the best work of those ablest of Americans who framed it, and it had stood the test of time. Its principles were unchanging, even though it wisely made provision for alteration with succeeding generations. It was "the oldest written constitution or complete instrument of government in actual use."[18] The rights elaborated therein were the ideals on which the American government was founded. It has preserved for Americans those rights and liberties. It epitomizes that long struggle of mankind for liberty and equality, and acts as a "beaconlight to all the world."[19]

*Creating Ancestors and Heroes*

Ancestors or honorific authority figures Americans have too, even though their country is still young. As befitting a nation in which loyalty is rooted in institutions, these human symbols have been, for the

[15] Pierce, *op. cit.*, pp. 104–105.
[16] Miller, *op. cit.*, pp. 146–149.
[17] Mosier, *op. cit.*, pp. 51, 53–54.
[18] Pierce, *op. cit.*, pp. 104, 142.
[19] *Ibid.*, pp. 104, 143, 168.

most part, political figures, many of whom were connected with the writing of the great documents or served in times when the institutions have been judged to be in greatest danger. At first these heroes were few in number, but as the history lengthened, there were others to add to the list, though the first ones never quite disappeared from view. A space-allotment analysis of a 1923 text showed that 4,387 out of a total of 6,722 lines on men in American history were devoted to men connected with political and military concerns.[20]

One would expect Americans to have acquired some heroes when their continent was discovered, and one is not disappointed. In the early days of the nation, when texts were more frankly religious in tone, God guided Christopher Columbus to these shores. Columbus himself was pure of motive, being activated wholly by scientific concerns. His personal qualifications for the voyage must also have been divinely inspired, for he was grave, courteous, moral, and persevering, had complete control over himself, and most fortunately had a perfect knowledge of mankind.[21] He did not lose stature in the McGuffey readers. There he was found to be a godly man of inventive mind who had sanctified the shores of America by landing there.[22] He held up well in the twentieth century also. In the books of the 1920s he was still a man with faith and courage enough to cross a broad ocean and show the way to this bright new world.[23] In some elementary history texts dated up to the 1940s, he was still "one of the most glorious figures in history."[24]

Other explorers have been mentioned, of course, but the people who have received the highest accolades are "our forefathers," meaning late colonial and early national leaders as well as forgers of the documentary symbol system. In earlier histories, William Penn was simple, peace loving, and tolerant in religion, and maintained friendly relations with the Indians.[25] In the McGuffey readers, it was discovered that there had been steady progress from the frail but worthy beginnings of the Pilgrim Fathers.[26] In the twentieth century they were still sung for their achievements in making the Mayflower Compact.

But the Pilgrims are only vaguely and not specifically "our forefathers." The latter are really the heroes of the American Revolution who, in early American texts, were next to the top of the select list of

[20] Ibid., p. 117.
[21] Miller, op. cit., pp. 366–368.
[22] Mosier, op. cit., p. 39.
[23] Pierce, op. cit., p. 117.
[24] Latin America in School and College Training Material, American Council on Education, Committee on the Study of Teaching Materials on Inter-American Subjects, Washington, 1944, p. 103.
[25] Miller, op. cit., pp. 365–366.
[26] Mosier, op. cit., p. 39.

the praised.[27] Marshall, Franklin, Patrick Henry, and Hamilton found their way into this list, though Hamilton was driven into a duel, a barbarous custom which deprived Americans of one of their great men.[28] In the texts of the 1920s, these first heroes all remained and were joined by others of the early national period. As the later books moved along into other national periods, others not in earlier lists were included. Jackson was accorded much space, as were Lincoln, Grant, and Lee. In later history, Admiral Dewey and General Pershing were leading military figures, and Theodore Roosevelt, Woodrow Wilson, Grover Cleveland, and William McKinley were outstanding Presidents.[29]

The highest praises, however, were reserved for George Washington whom, in early texts, God raised up to command the Revolutionary armies and protected for the duration of the war. In these accounts, said one investigator, Washington bore more resemblance to Christ than did any other early leader. By 1830 Mount Vernon had become a shrine and Virginia was described largely as Washington's home. Whatever other illustrations texts might carry, they would include a picture of the first President.[30] To the writers of the McGuffeys, Washington was a means of building a patriotic sentiment—particularly would he be so in the West, that large, well-meaning, but barbarian and uncultured giant, where patriotism could thrive best, but where it might be diluted by foreign influences. Washington was amply suited for the job, moreover, for where could be found another like him? He had not a fault, not a mean spot; if American institutions had done nothing else for the world, they had given it George Washington.[31] In the twentieth century, Washington still maintained his preeminence as the greatest man in early American history. With his compatriots, he had fought the Tories. In his role as general, he exemplified that greatest of all virtues, military service to one's country. He influenced the history of other lands and he charted a wise course, even for an unknown future, in that he warned Americans against entangling themselves in the quarrels of the European countries.[32] He was the only irreplaceable leader.

Against a backdrop of solid documentary bases for government and an appropriate set of unimpeachable heroes, the American society emerged. The flavor of it was probably very different from that of other ideal societies in that it was rooted in written agreements and

[27] Miller, *op. cit.*, p. 364.
[28] Mosier, *op. cit.*, p. 55.
[29] Pierce, *op. cit.*, pp. 117–120, 188.
[30] Miller, *op. cit.*, pp. 88, 344, 375–380.
[31] Mosier, *op. cit.*, pp. 36–38.
[32] Pierce, *op. cit.*, pp. 23, 69, 100, 111, 118, 120, 165.

contracts rather than long-developing traditions and persons. What persons there were had been, in a sense, derived from the documents; in turn, the documents were developed not from an imposing philosophical system as in nineteenth-century Germany, but from particular bits and pieces of an economic and political rationale largely Anglo-Saxon in origin.

### Locale for a Society

Geographic expanse and the richness of it have always apparently been impressed in some measure on the youthful reader. In the earlier national texts, geography became a symbol and vastness was extolled. Natural wonders were held up for acclaim and they became larger as the decades passed. By the 1820s Niagara Falls had supplanted the Natural Bridge of Virginia as the great emotion-producing natural phenomenon.[33] In earlier modern texts natural wealth in field, forest, and mines served an even more important purpose than backdrop for a society; it was a reinforcement of the worth of that society. This was a promised land in which "a Divine Purpose" was "working out some mighty aim for America," and this aim was not to be fulfilled until a special group of people learned how to conserve and govern it. This group was, of course, Americans. Even in geography texts this wealthiest of all countries, partly a product of an ingenious people, was coupled in descriptions of its affluence with comments on its being a democracy. The two factors together—wealth to be had for hard work, and the efficacy of the government—explained why so many had sought these shores.[34]

### The Mission of America

The government which emerged against the larger working forces of the universe was, of course, superior to all others, and ideas of republican government were tailored to fit the United States government. Very early it was accepted as axiomatic that "the law of history is one of steady and inevitable progress toward greater material wealth and comfort as well as toward greater virtue and freedom." Symbols which came into favor in the 1820s were used to stress the fact that America was the "home of simplicity, strength, liberty and economic plenty for all."[35] Thus the urge toward economic gain in this wealthiest of all countries was rationalized as being a part of the law of progress under which the United States government operated.

Out of an economic and political orientation, there emerged an Amer-

[33] Miller, op. cit., pp. 349–350.
[34] Pierce, op. cit., pp. 113–114, 189.
[35] Miller, op. cit., pp. 110, 141–146, 346.

ica with a mission. July 4, 1776, was the birth date not only of America, but of freedom for the world, so said early national readers. For were not Americans the chosen people of God? As Americans moved west, they were always justified in taking over new geographical expanses, for they always brought with them the bulwarks of the good society, including truth, safety, and liberty. Thus Americans were justified in their demands that the Indians be conquered, for though the red men had some superior traits, nevertheless they were cruel—an un-American trait and one which could be readily replaced if only good Americans would take over Indian territories.[36]

As the nation expanded abroad as well as at home, later readers could extend their arguments to both domestic and foreign implications of the mission. The McGuffey readers were quite clear about America's glorious destiny and its mission which "had been ordained by divine Providence." America's destiny to spread beneficence around the world was evidence of the working out of the "moral government of the world." If Americans should be opposed in their efforts to spread the benefits of their great society to foreign lands, they must remember that it was God who had ordained that they shed light on the dark places of Europe and the empires of Asia.[37] The readers published before 1865, yet subsequent to the Mexican War, could dwell on this episode as a "triumphant American pageant"; the relatively unfavorable characteristics of the Mexicans, who were after all Spanish, could be thrown against the desirable traits of the Texans, who were after all thoroughly American.[38]

The mission had two parts or possibly three. America was destined to be an asylum for the oppressed. It was also destined to expand geographically and thus to spread enlightenment wherever it went. Furthermore, it was destined to serve as the great example to the world. The idea of America—if a single all-encompassing idea of this country can be said to have existed in early national texts—was that of a haven. Its obvious advantages for this purpose were its humanitarian zeal, its natural resources lying ready to the hand of the poor but industrious, and the general opportunities it offered to the immigrant. Even for the Jews, who were often unpleasantly sketched in New England texts, the United States could yet serve as an asylum.[39]

The McGuffey readers likewise sang the praises of expansionism and the enlightenment which it brought, but still displayed a conscience about war as a vehicle for such enterprise.[40]

---

[36] *Ibid.,* pp. 56–57, 84, 229–230, 342.
[37] Mosier, *op. cit.,* pp. 41–42.
[38] Miller, *op. cit.,* p. 213.
[39] *Ibid.,* pp. 218–226.
[40] Mosier, *op. cit.,* pp. 44–47.

Twentieth-century texts had more history with which to deal in developing the three-pronged character of America's mission. Wars had been fought; territory on both the Continent and in the oceans had been acquired; the nation had been involved in conflagrations and crises which had been international in scope.

Against this broad background, the United States continued to retain the ideal form of government in modern texts. That was a truth accepted by people everywhere, according to books of the 1920s. Americans, furthermore, had been most generous with their political riches. They had spread their ideals to people everywhere. They had done this even though they had to go to war to do it. In World War I, for instance, Americans were "battling for the cause of humanity." In the Battle of the Argonne the brave heroes of the United States had a magnificent share in democracy's victory.[41]

Though occasionally a writer would raise some questions about American conduct, most will report that wherever we have gone, we have ordinarily brought nothing but good. The peoples in the island possessions have developed both economically and spiritually through the wise guidance of the United States, according to histories and geographies. To be sure, Cuba was but a short distance from American shores, and her possession by Spain might subsequently present the United States with a dangerous enemy, and Americans did have investments there. Nevertheless, the first consideration in entering the Spanish-American War was a concern for the brave liberty-loving Cubans. The inhuman cruelties inflicted on them by their mother country had led Americans to send them aid during the years preceding the war, and had goaded them into putting an end to this awful suffering.[42] Even in relatively recent elementary history texts, it has been suggested that the people of the United States called for war because Cubans were oppressed by their mother country, and the war which resulted was glorious.[43] It has been only since 1940 that a note of discord has been sounded in junior high school history texts. Writers have been noting the unfavorable direction in which the press influenced public opinion, and have reflected on the fact that Spain wished to avoid war, the United States to court it.[44]

George Washington's policy has been credited with keeping America out of foreign quarrels, and the Monroe Doctrine has done likewise. But the latter had an even more commendable purpose. Not only was it beneficial to the United States, but also it protected the weaker blos-

[41] Pierce, op. cit., pp. 66, 103, 130.
[42] Ibid., pp. 6–7, 184.
[43] Latin America in School and College Training Material, p. 58.
[44] Caputo, op. cit., p. 75.

soms of liberty which it was designed to assist. It was the preserver of liberty through offering protection to Spanish-American patriots fighting for their own independence. How curious then, that Latin Americans should often resent America! Perhaps it was because of America's greater strength and older democracy. The spirit promoted through the Pan-American Union should overcome the difficulties and lead to growing trade and good will.[45]

The United States has been the benefactor of many countries other than those in her immediate peripheral area. She has acquired Samoa, the Philippines, and islands of the Pacific. These acquisitions came largely by accident; nevertheless, "fortunate indeed were the native populations which came under our sway." By taking over Samoa, "the United States fortunately prevented the islands from falling into the hands of the imperialistic Germany."[46]

Even though writers pay them little attention in their texts, they insist that Americans have also shed a bright light on Far Eastern societies. One analyst of modern texts says that there was little attention paid to them even in world history texts, except as they came into contact with the West. He noted in this connection that an analysis of eight secondary world histories published in the 1940s showed only 5.4 per cent of the space devoted to this better than one-half of the world's people.[47] A study of 108 elementary and secondary school geography and social studies books of several kinds and in use in the same period showed a corresponding lack of material on the Far East. Furthermore, inadequate as was the material, an undue amount of it was devoted to China, with a consequent neglect of Southeast Asia and India. There was also indulgence in broad generalizations which obscured wide variations in Asiatic cultures. Certain investigators of geographies of the same period noted that one-half of the very limited space given to Asia was devoted to the journeys of Marco Polo, a European. In these same texts, Asia was rarely treated as Asia but only in connection with the stories of European countries. The Netherlands East Indies were included in the story of Holland; India was a part of Britain's story; and the Philippines were ordinarily described only as a dependency of the United States. The story of Asia was the tale of its westernization and of the white man's burden. It was replete with natives, native ways, barbarians, and uncivilized peoples.[48]

[45] Pierce, *op. cit.*, pp. 74–76.

[46] *Treatment of Asia in American Textbooks*, American Council on Education, Committee on Asiatic Studies, and Institute of Pacific Relations, Inc., New York, April, 1946, p. 67.

[47] Herbert J. Wood, "The Far East in World History," *Social Education*, vol. 15, pp. 155–159, 162, 195, April, 1951.

[48] *Treatment of Asia in American Textbooks*, pp. 5–8, 30–31, 41.

Despite the meager treatment of the Asiatic countries, much can be made of little. China, so said the geographies of the 1920s, developed a great civilization long before the United States and the European nations. The Chinese had learned how to live in houses and pursued the art of printing. In addition, having invented gunpowder (a sign of superiority), they were so wise as to settle disputes by arbitration rather than war. Something happened to them, however—they ceased to make progress. One of their difficulties was obviously that they had no national patriotism.[49] In general histories on ancient peoples, published from 1896 to 1916, it was occasionally noted that China had made no contribution to America, that its ancient history was of little value, and that it had done little in advancing civilization.[50] A book of the 1940s tried another kind of analysis: "most Orientals have little or no conception of the art of government." In another context, a textbook writer construed the philosophy of Confucius to mean that the average citizen of China must not inquire into right and wrong, but react only to the dictates of laws promulgated by those in authority.[51] Thus pre-Communist China, whether ancient or modern, was replete with unrewarding un-Western ways.

Yet in relatively modern times, China has had contact with the West. So the texts of the 1920s addressed themselves to the consequences of this meeting. Fortunately, she began to change for the better. America was justified in putting up a vigorous fight for China's preserving her lands and her independence. Although, because of their low standards of living, the Chinese have been undesirable as American citizens, nevertheless they must be protected as a weaker people; one of the brighter pages in United States history was the admirable conduct toward China following the Boxer Rebellion.[52] This beneficence has apparently had a halo effect, for in the elementary and secondary texts of the 1940s, the writers continued to pay her the homage of the greatest amount of space devoted to a Far Eastern society.[53]

Stories of American contacts with Japan and of the Japanese people themselves often provided opportunity for more reinforcement of the concept of mission than could be attained in accounts of China. After all, the United States opened up Japan, she negotiated the peace following on the Russo-Japanese War, and she had occupied Japan at the end of World War II. Japan, if not a dependency, was at least an ideo-

[49] Pierce, op. cit., p. 182.
[50] Timothy T. Lew, China in American School Textbooks, The Chinese Social and Political Science Association, Peking, China, 1923, pp. 17–19.
[51] Treatment of Asia in American Textbooks, pp. 43, 47.
[52] Pierce, op. cit., pp. 81–82, 182–183.
[53] Treatment of Asia in American Textbooks, p. 14.

logical protectorate. Consequently, she could participate in an extension of the American image rather than as a reflection of it, as was the case with England and her dependencies.

In social studies texts, including American histories published from 1895 to 1950, Japanese immigration to this country was apt to be looked upon sceptically.[54] The "menace of Oriental immigration" was noted and was underscored by reference to the influx of laborers, with little or no mention of the large body of Japanese students who had come to these shores.[55] Exclusion was ordinarily approved. After all, the Japanese by their skin, traditions, language, government, and religion were so far removed from the American self-image that it was difficult to stroke them into the painting without blurring the portrait. But for those Japanese who were so fortunate as to become American citizens, there has been in recent texts a stout defense. A few authors are willing to point out that Americans of Japanese descent were treated unfairly during World War II and were not accorded the respect ordinarily given to loyal citizens of this country.[56]

Whatever the verdict on immigration or citizenship, Japan and the Japanese had their uses in the texts. By the late 1920s, Japan was judged to have made steady progress, until it had become the foremost nation of Asia, a judgment enhanced by the fact that Admiral Perry had opened up Japan and America had since kept it under her protective wing.[57] In consequence thereof, Japanese history prior to 1853 has been ordinarily dismissed as the record of a culturally backward people. Some texts paid no attention to the flourishing trade promoted by Japan in the sixteenth and seventeenth centuries. Most mysteriously, little attention was given to the constructive relations between the United States and Japan, or to the upsurge in Japanese history of liberal and democratic relations. But there has been increasing attention in more modern history texts to the modernization of Japan. This gives occasion to describe the Japanese in terms honorific to Americans; they are "keen, ambitious, courteous, exceedingly industrious and intensely patriotic." It allows also for mention of the favorable effect of American inventions and American education on Japanese progress. In some texts, modernization can be used to reinforce the fact that Japan did not amount to anything until it was opened up.[58]

---

[54] Pierce, *op. cit.*, pp. 82–83; and Tori Takaki, "The Treatment of Japan and Peoples of Japanese Descent in Senior High School American History Textbooks," unpublished doctoral dissertation, University of Michigan, Ann Arbor, Mich., 1953. (Microfilm.)

[55] Takaki, *op. cit.*, pp. 139–140, 156.

[56] *Ibid.*, pp. 155–156; and Pierce, *op. cit.*, pp. 82–83.

[57] Pierce, *op. cit.*, pp. 82–83.

[58] Takaki, *op. cit.*, pp. 38–42.

Unlike the descriptions of other Far Eastern peoples in geographies of the 1940s, little attention was given to the poverty of the Japanese masses.[59] Possibly this was an inverse reinforcement of the idea that a people industrialized in the American image could not have the misery which plagued the other Asian nations.

In histories published from 1913 to 1944, the Russo-Japanese War provided an opportunity to emphasize America's mission to spread peace and good will. Of seventeen texts published from 1914 to 1930 which dealt with the war, all emphasized the mediation effort of President Theodore Roosevelt and the prestige accruing to the United States from his good offices. Texts from 1931 to 1944 continued to emphasize the American President and to underscore his constructive attitude—that Japan could not "be robbed of her victory a second time." Later texts still mentioned the war and the mission, but they were not so sure of Roosevelt's attitude. Did he have a sympathy for the underdog, or did he suspect that Japan coveted the Philippines and so proposed to keep her at a distance by making her a debtor?[60]

Japan's relationship to World War I is interesting. That holocaust was a fight for democracy in which only democratic nations could participate, and it was well known that Japan was not a democracy. Had she not an emperor and an aristocratic government? Her intervention in the war was mentioned in an increasing number of texts of later publication dates. But her contributions to the Allied cause in the form of munitions and ships and her ensuing economic prosperity, which resulted in her becoming for the first time a creditor nation, were not mentioned in American history texts up to 1950.[61]

Japan and her involvement in World War II were mentioned in twenty-one American history texts published from 1945 to 1950 and in general, according to one investigator, she was given remarkably fair treatment. But moderates in Japan were given no credit for having fought for an earlier peace. Following on the war discussion, in 90 per cent of these texts there was some statement of the occupation of Japan. General MacArthur was the leading figure, and both native and other American leaders were given scant attention.[62]

In general, then, Japan's position in the texts is ambivalent. She serves as a reinforcing agent for the American value system as she mirrors the West and as her progress can be related to our good auspices. Some of her story is ignored because it does not properly reflect credit on the United States or reflects too much credit on a backward nation.

[59] *Treatment of Asia in American Textbooks,* p. 21.
[60] Takaki, *op. cit.,* pp. 69–74.
[61] *Ibid.,* p. 92.
[62] *Ibid.,* pp. 230, 256, 261–263.

Yet texts are beginning again to treat her as a nation of importance in her own right, and even though exclusionism is condoned, they are beginning to condemn the treatment of American citizens of Japanese descent.

If Japan serves well as an extension of the American image, the Philippines are even more effective. Their story allows the writers not only to emphasize the general humanity and benevolence of Americans, but to do so at the expense of a European nation, Spain. Elementary and secondary school students reading the social studies texts available in 1932 would have found very little on the Islands, but that little would have been highly selective. They would have found that the most frequently discussed topics were the discovery of the Islands and their acquisition by the United States. The intrepid Magellan had found the Islands and then had been attacked by the natives, who were savages. When Admiral Dewey finally sailed into Manila Bay, he was able to take over the Islands easily: no American man or ship was lost, but all the Spanish ships were sunk and many Spaniards were killed. Perhaps this was but the just deserts of the former conquerors, for they had done little for the Filipino peoples except to Christianize them.[63]

When the Spaniards were bested, all was not smooth sailing in the 1932 texts. The Filipinos revolted and in a particularly savage way. Americans retaliated in kind, but only because they had learned cruelty from the natives. The motives of the Americans were wholly altruistic. The Spanish-American War was, after all, fought for the sake of humanity, though an occasional textbook author would suggest that perhaps the United States wanted a naval base. The successful conclusion of the war might have meant that the United States could have taken the Philippines, but it did not do so. The Islands were sold to this country, and they have cost more in modernization than will ever be repaid by their resources.[64]

When the war was successfully concluded and the Islands purchased, the United States, according to the texts, had to set up a government for the Filipinos, who were not fit for self-government. The progress of the people under American rule was remarkable, so much so that texts emphasized the "before" and "after" aspects of the Islands and their people. As of the twenties and the thirties, the Philippine people were found to be intelligent and eager to learn, and one-half of them could already speak English.[65]

For some authors the Philippines were an attraction because of their

[63] Jesus E. Perpinan, "The Philippine Islands in American School Textbooks," *Journal of Experimental Education*, vol. 2, pp. 369–372, June, 1934.
[64] *Ibid.*, pp. 372–374.
[65] *Ibid.*, pp. 373, 377–378.

raw materials, but only one book dwelt on the necessary development of friendly relations between the United States and the island peoples. In the meantime, the American image said that Americans believed in freedom and independence for all peoples. The textbook writers had to deal with the course of independence for the Philippines. Some Americans were pictured as always favoring independence when a stable government could be assured. But on this question there was some quibbling. Textbook authors were inclined toward the judgment that the people were not yet ready for self-government.[66]

Thus was the image extended in a humane war, and enhanced by taking education, medicine, and progress in general to a native people who had been ground under the heel by an unfavored European nation.

## SOCIETY MAKING

Emphasis and contrast are techniques of the great painters. So the artists of the American scene envelop their subject in striking hues enhanced by portraits of other like peoples and surrounded with contrasting colors of those who are so mean as to be unlike Americans.

### Origins

Our first peoples were the Indians and in a vague way they served their purpose in early texts, though it may not be quite clear that they were responsible for America's honorable beginnings. These origins were clothed with wondrous mystery. It was rather obvious that Americans were of more ancient and honorable lineage than their supposed European forebears. The mounds of Pennsylvania and Ohio were tantalizing evidence that the North American continent may have given birth to civilizations comparable to those of ancient Greece and Rome. According to a more fashionable rumor, the Indians may even have been the ten lost tribes of Israel.[67]

Having got the United States under way, Indian relations became a nuisance, particularly as settlers moved west over their lands. The aborigines had to be disposed of in such a fashion that their going would be justified. Even though they were more commendable fellows than most savages, they were on their way to extinction, said some pre-Civil War texts. The exigencies of developing an American nation required their elimination not only from the civilization, but also from the soil.[68]

A New England conscience plus a superiority complex was at work

[66] *Ibid.,* pp. 374–375, 382.
[67] Miller, *op. cit.,* pp. 353–355.
[68] *Ibid.,* p. 242.

in the McGuffey readers, which consistently deplored the treatment of the Indians as being unworthy of a great and humane people like the American. To promote a better feeling toward the red men, the McGuffey readers carried many a story of these unhappy people, "Murderer's Creek" and "The Grateful Indian" being two of the more striking. These people were rude savages and they were inevitably on their way to extinction, but the Christian spirit of good will and brotherhood demanded that they be pitied and protected. The speech put into the mouth of the Indian leader Chief Joseph, when he was confined to the reservation, carried with it a brooding sense of doom designed to induce sympathy. The Chief said that an Indian could not be expected to be happy or to prosper if he were confined to a very limited piece of ground. His heart was heavy, he said, when he thought on the plight of his people.[69]

Subsequent to the earlier McGuffey readers, the aggressive, westward-moving American met and tangled with successive groups of Indians whom he had to exterminate or contain if he were to satisfy his land hunger. In relatively modern texts Indians have often been described as uncivilized, cruel, savage, and barbarous, even though handsome and courageous. But there have been differences of opinion respecting the wisdom, justice, and honesty of American practices. Some writers will acknowledge wrongdoing on the part of some Americans; others by implication will take the same position through commending United States government policy since 1885, whereby the Indian can pay his taxes and become a good citizen.[70] As late as texts of the 1940s, there was apt to be one of two prevailing views of the first Americans. They were either bloodthirsty and savage or noble sons of nature.[71]

*The Western Complex*

Having attended to origins, textbook writers needed to put Americans in a somewhat broader context. As the United States was continuously assaulted by migrants from abroad, they must be screened for their desirability as eventual American citizens. Blood relations must be selected and described. Thus American immigrants have come in for attention in readers and social studies books, and other nations have been attended to both in respect to the characteristics of their peoples and American relations with them.

---

[69] Mosier, *op. cit.*, pp. 39–40, 44, 148–151.

[70] Caputo, *op. cit.*, p. 120; Pierce, *op. cit.*, pp. 91–92, 163.

[71] *Intergroup Relations in Teaching Material: A Survey and Appraisal*, American Council on Education, Committee on the Study of Teaching Materials in Intergroup Relations, Washington, 1949, pp. 113–114.

Early texts raised the question as to whether Indians, Negroes, or Europeans would be most readily assimilated into the American society. Even neater and more specific categories were proposed: Eskimo, Tartar, East Indian, Negro, American Indian, European. The focus provided by the captains of the New England sailing vessels will be noted in the specifics of the categories. Despite this interesting range of peoples, the answer to the question of their merits for assimilation was always clear. The broad grouping "European" always had preferment.[72]

In modern as in earlier texts the United States was the asylum for the oppressed. But authors pointed out that making these poor benighted folk into good Americans had been no mean task. Some were ignorant, and ignorance was equated with worthlessness and therefore dangerous. Many came from the less desirable parts of Europe. If immigrants came from Northern Europe, the movement into this country was commended. In texts being used as late as the 1940s, Northern Europeans made better Americans than did immigrants from other parts of the Continent. Those who came before 1880 (largely North Europeans) were identified with members of the "we" group, the founders of this country. Immigrants who came after 1880 were often described as "waves," "swarms," or "hordes." Anglo-Saxons (pre-1880 migrants) had stability of character—not so those who came after the crucial date. Italians, Hungarians, and Poles, according to one text, were slow to become Americans.[73]

In relatively recent anthologies, Scandinavians were overrepresented. But there was little attention paid to Italians, Greeks, and other non-Anglo-Saxons. Italian Americans were represented in these texts only by dialect stories. They were ignored in short stories and novels. To enforce the particular character of the American, only solidly "American" names were used to designate countrymen.[74]

However, Americans wished to share their good fortune with the unfortunates. To them the United States offered free land and the blessings of liberty. In turn, some of them made substantial contributions to the prosperity of this country. Such behavior was no more than right. It was the duty of these favored people to become faithful citizens of the country which gave them so much.[75] In school and college texts to the 1940s, the melting pot was still the ideal solution for building an American nation. Conformity of behavior to a presumed American pattern was preferred to diversity in unity.[76]

[72] Miller, *op. cit.*, pp. 28–31.
[73] *Intergroup Relations in Teaching Material: A Survey and Appraisal*, pp. 87–91.
[74] *Ibid.*, pp. 96–97.
[75] Pierce, *op. cit.*, pp. 86–88, 151.
[76] *Intergroup Relations in Teaching Material: A Survey and Appraisal*, p. 71.

## The Negroes

The emphasis on the European origins of good Americans has left the contributions of Negroes and their general treatment unexploited in American texts. In books published before 1830, there were few references to Negroes. In texts published from 1831 to 1835, Negroes were ignorant, inferior, and well suited to a hot climate. Little attention was given in this period to the abolition argument.[77]

Texts published after the Civil War and up to 1900 pointed out the bad effects of slavery, but for the most part still did not discuss the abolition movement, insurrections, or the constructive efforts of Negroes during Reconstruction. The Negro was docile, humble, faithful, black, and better able than the white to work in the fields.[78]

In the period from 1901 to 1920, Negroes and slavery still received little attention from textbook writers. The effects of slavery on American life did come in for some discussion, and a favorite whipping boy, England, could conveniently be blamed for the hold of slavery on America. When Negroes were mentioned, they were usually described either in the terms used for model servants who know their place, or through adjectives which put them outside the pale of the good American. On the one hand, they were contented, docile, faithful, and excellent field hands. On the other, they were ignorant, inferior, black, no good for anything except farming, and occasionally vicious and unwilling to work. Their origin as savages in Africa was occasionally referred to, and related matters such as the fact that they were not used to the cold would be noted.[79]

The texts of the decade 1921–1930 did not seem to change materially in their treatment of Negroes. Many of the unfavorable traits were retained, but Negroes were given credit for being musical and good workers in tobacco. In descriptions of the Reconstruction period, they were described as believing that they did not need to work, and as not being fitted for political responsibility.[80]

As late as the period 1931 to 1939, textbook writers were still dealing in stereotypes about Negroes. They were pictured during slave days as good servants but irresponsible children in behavior. They were occasionally indolent and would not work unless driven. They were quite capable of doing work that white men could not do, and were less

[77] Marie Elizabeth Carpenter, *The Treatment of the Negro in American History School Textbooks: A Comparison of Changing Textbook Content, 1826 to 1939, with Developing Scholarship in the History of the Negro in the United States,* George Banta Publishing Company, Menasha, Wis., 1941, pp. 66–69.

[78] *Ibid.,* pp. 71–74.

[79] *Ibid.,* pp. 78–85.

[80] *Ibid.,* pp. 90–91.

troublesome than bond servants. During the Reconstruction period, as described in these texts of the 1930s, they were still found to be ignorant of self-government, "puzzled children," bewildered, and poor farmers. Life and property of whites were not safe during this period. There were some writers, nevertheless, who pictured them as ambitious to own land and as being race conscious. They had learned that they must work, and they had made considerable progress.[81] Textbook writers have apparently been hard put to extend the image of the ideal America far enough to incorporate one-tenth of the nation. Their answer has been to describe Negroes as an alien growth in an otherwise harmonious whole.

## American Neighbors

It was when textbook authors came to describe other nations that they could really extend the American image through attention to characteristics and relationships. In early national texts, "European" was a first broad category of preferment. But Americans needed to be distinguished from and compared to the British as a whole, and each European people had to be tested for similarity to and difference from the ideal American.

The British were a problem. Americans were originally of them, yet they had not yet sloughed off their feeling of uneasiness about present and previous motives of the mother country. America's origins in respect to population was thus disposed of as being selective of persons. According to Miller's findings, the "wicked [British] either did not come or did not stay." However, in deference to a common lineage, the British—like the Americans—were always superior to the French. The latter, whose violent and thoroughly radical revolution had outraged conservative New Englanders, had traits the opposite of those which writers were attempting to emphasize as American virtues. The French were gay—soberness was admired; they were fickle—the developing American society needed stability; they were infidel—God had ordained the Constitution of the United States. Even their higher education led to loose morals.[82] Thus the outrageous nature of their conduct and motives in civil war was explained by their character. Their only virtue was in their aiding the Colonies during the American Revolution.

Likewise, most of the Latin peoples, whether in Europe or in South and Central America, were found in these early texts to possess traits which were an anathema to the ideal American. The poverty of the Spanish was quite explainable by their laziness. Like them, their Latin-American offspring had neither enterprise nor intelligence. The Portu-

[81] *Ibid.*, pp. 110–113.
[82] Miller, *op. cit.*, pp. 263–267, 283, 358.

guese were in decline and their story merged gradually into that of Spain. The Italians, another Latin people, were immoral, superstitious, effeminate, and worst of all, not interested in improvement.[83] These Mediterranean peoples with whom Anglo-Saxons were not likely to have dealings, served as the necessary contrast to Americans.

There were some Europeans who were quite capable of enhancing the picture of the ideal America and American in these early texts. The Germans had acceptable social values and, as immigrants, were much to be desired over the Irish. The Dutch likewise were clean, industrious, frugal, honest, and patient. But the people who were always discussed in a favorable light were the Scotch and the Swiss. By the end of this early period (1865), textbook writers had seen fit to fuse them all, desirable or undesirable, into the American nationality. Immigrants from other nations had merged into a glorious American past and had been purified by the spirituality of the American environment, thus adding stature, even through their vices, to the emergent national ideal.[84]

## TWENTIETH-CENTURY SOCIETY

By the time of the twentieth-century texts, many additional and significant events had transpired. The United States, in company of allies or friends, had weathered several devastating wars. She had become, in truth as well as in concept, a world power. Her contacts abroad through trade, war, and diplomacy had now touched nearly all the countries and peoples of the world. Her picture of herself must be thrown against a continuously expanding backdrop.

### European Complex

Europeans again emerged in geography books of the 1920s as the most highly civilized of peoples who fortunately inhabited the mother continent and were responsible for most of the art and the humanities in the world. Once barbarians, through energy and competence, they had developed into the most enlightened of human beings.[85]

As the century moved on and books in several fields in current use up to the 1950s were examined, the identification with Europe was clearly evident. This preferred background with these preferred friends and relations of Americans was emphasized in several ways. In high school literature books, 58 per cent of materials were essays, poems, and stories about and by Americans and Europeans. Only 18 per cent con-

---

[83] *Ibid.,* pp. 288, 290, 297.
[84] *Ibid.,* pp. 234, 261, 302, 308.
[85] Pierce, *op. cit.,* pp. 176–177.

cerned the Orient, peopled by two-thirds of the world's population.[86] Another technique for improving the status of the Europeans, who, after all, were closest kin, was through the previously described device of putting the peoples around the Pacific Ocean rim in the orbit of the European nations. As colonial dependencies, they become sources of raw material or trade outlets rather than important nations in their own right, as were England and the Continental countries.

Among the latter, there had been a readjustment of roles since authors first wrote for their young charges. England was now in the forefront of the colonizing nations. She had more and larger colonies than any other nation, she boasted the largest city in the world (in the 1920 texts), her foreign commerce was extensive. In carrying on this vast business and Empire, she managed to maintain better relations in her colonies than did other European nations.[87]

In the history books of the 1920s, preparation had to be made for the American Revolution. The antagonisms between France and England during the colonial period were treated with mixed feelings. England sometimes blundered, sometimes was protective. The Colonies were occasionally sacrificed to the interests of the mother country, yet the colonists, with the odds against them, ordinarily showed up in a favorable light in the skirmishes. Once in a while the British rather than the colonists were given credit for having resisted the French. Whatever the character of the relationships between England and the Colonies, some authors would point out that some of the American people were not English and hence had no affection for the parent country. Thus the way was paved for the Revolution.

In these same texts of the 1920s and as a background for revolt, much attention was given to the infamies of the British. The English passed sinister and selfish laws, they appointed worthless men to office, they grew richer while Americans grew poorer. New England merchants were found to be facing financial ruin. The policies of the mother country were, to say the least, "unjust, selfish, and ill-advised." There was serious misunderstanding respecting taxation without representation. The rotten borough system of England had never promoted the idea that a representative should represent a particular people, whereas Americans were used to representation on a proportional basis. The franchise was unlike in the two countries, being much more widely dispersed in America. The upper classes of England refused to sympa-

---

[86] Charles Stephen Lewis, "The Treatment of Foreign Peoples in American High-school Literature Books," unpublished doctoral dissertation, University of Michigan, Ann Arbor, Mich., 1956, abstract. (Microfilm.)

[87] Pierce, op. cit., pp. 176–177.

thize with the solid frontier folk of America. George III was narrow-minded, bigoted, stubborn, selfish, insane, and dishonest, as well as German. So much was he at fault that many Englishmen sympathized with the colonists' struggle for liberty. In these modern texts, the American Revolution became a part of the long struggle of the English-speaking peoples for political liberty, "with the most advanced part of that people" living on this side of the Atlantic.[88]

For the most part, the War of 1812 provided an occasion to demonstrate America's invincibility against the British. A few books pointed to the United States as the sufferer following on the war, and occasionally there was mention of how the Westerners forced the peace-loving Madison into war. But for the most part, it was a glorious victory won by hard-fighting frontier troops, against overwhelming odds.[89]

Following on the War of 1812, little mention was made of England until the Civil War. There was some evidence in the history books that the two great English-speaking countries were learning the ways of arbitration. The Civil War was a disruptive force in this relationship. Although credit was given some Englishmen for supporting the Northern side, England was scored as having acted contrary to "the laws of nations."[90]

Social studies books other than histories put a somewhat different light on England and thus on America. They were apt not to be as caustic about the Revolution. America was the child of English rights, and as one Englishman was made to say, "Englishmen now understand that in the American Revolution you were fighting our battles." In discussion of governments, both the United States and England were enhanced because they had similar governments. England, to be sure, had a king, but he had no power to harm the people. In some books there was pause for comment that both the House of Lords and the British foreign policy were remote from the control of the English common folk.[91]

All in all, the case for America was generally strengthened by pointing to the development of accord between the English-speaking peoples. It was further improved because Americans were closely identified with England, through basking in the reflected glory of her far-flung empire. England, thrown against her world dominions, emerged triumphant in literature books. In a mild way she took up the white man's burden via Wee Willie Winkie, "child of the dominant race."

[88] *Ibid.*, chap. II.
[89] *Ibid.*
[90] *Ibid.*
[91] *Ibid.*, pp. 155–156.

Rudyard Kipling was the only English writer preaching white superiority who was considered of enough importance to be placed in all high school English literature texts.[92]

Equally forceful was the argument developed by sketching England's relationship to and contrast with India, formerly one of her chief dependencies. In world histories and geographies published from 1921 to 1952, England emerged as benefactor to a backward people. This occurred even in texts published since India's independence. In texts from 1921 to 1940, British rule brought peace and order, the development of industry, transportation, communications, and foreign trade. Britain was also responsible for introducing Western education, improving sanitary and medical facilities, and prohibiting female infanticide and child marriage.[93] Geographies of the 1940s ordinarily credited British money and leadership with producing a modern transportation system which would overcome famine.[94] Without respect to the truth of these claims, one investigator asked why such blessings were not identified with enlightened self-interest, as Asian historians would claim, rather than with benevolence, as was implied in American secondary school texts.[95]

Britain's case and thus America's reflected self were supported in other ways. India was continuously described as diverse and disunited, both characteristics being anathema to Americans; and little or no attention was paid to factors which had made for disunity among the Indian peoples. If Britain had not been at hand, India would have fallen into anarchy. Her people were "illiterate, ignorant, and unprogressive" in editions of one text up to 1943, and much attention was given to Hindu fanaticism and little to Hindu tolerance. Her weaknesses were apparent and all revolved around education. She had consistently neglected mass and technical education, and her secondary schools were examination-ridden, with little hint that some of these weaknesses may have resulted from a colonial policy which concentrated on India as a market for raw materials.[96]

As Britain was the benefactor of a backward, caste-ridden people, there is little warrant for attention being given in world history texts to pre-British India or at least to that country before any contact with Europeans. Early India and China might well be ignored in light of the

[92] Lewis, op. cit., pp. 34–36.

[93] Shyama Deodhar, "The Treatment of India in American Social Studies Textbooks, 1921–1952," unpublished doctoral dissertation, University of Michigan, Ann Arbor, Mich., 1953, pp. 136–138, 171. (Microfilm.)

[94] Treatment of Asia in American Textbooks, p. 25.

[95] Deodhar, op. cit., pp. 136–138.

[96] Ibid., pp. 126, 141, 159, 173, 204.

fact that their influence had not extended very far. Hence there was little material on India and China until they met the Western peoples and beheld "the light of western civilization." Accordingly, space was given to Vasco da Gama, rivalry for Indian trade, and Alexander's invasion of northwest India. When the early Indo-Aryan invasions were mentioned, they were used to point up an easy conquest by white or light-skinned Aryans of "black-skinned and culturally inferior non-Aryans or Dravidians." When the British finally conquered India, the latter was beset by a union of native princes (Maratha Confederacy) who were warring among themselves and so keeping their people in constant danger. England decided in 1816 to 1818 to suppress the princes. In pursuance thereof, British colonial leaders were stressed, and there was little or no attention to native leaders. British sources were used almost exclusively.[97]

When independence came to India in American texts, it was necessary to deal with the growth in Indian nationalism. The latter movement was explained as having resulted from the exposure of native leaders to Western education which, in turn, steeped them in democratic and specifically Western democratic traditions.[98]

There is some indication that the textbook image and foreign relationships are changing. The United States is being forced by the exigencies of the cold war to reckon with neutrals as well as Allies, Orientals as well as Occidentals. Whether she remains the beacon light of liberty and progress (the most cherished self-portrait) may well depend on the skill with which bridges are built to the non-European world. Hence texts since 1948 are taking a somewhat different tack in respect to the 400 million inhabitants of India. They are no longer an outpost of empire, but a people worthy of study in their own right. Inaccuracies in accounts of them are being eliminated. It is now permissible to introduce criticisms of British policy. Hinduism, even though it is not Christianity, is being given more space and is more favorably described. On the whole, accounts of India in world histories of the period 1948 to 1952 can be said to be reasonably "comprehensive, balanced and accurate."[99] The image of America is enlarging and changing its form.

It is probable that the portrait of England will not change materially. The record may continue to read as it did in the texts of the 1920s. Together the two English-speaking peoples fought a successful war for democracy, throughout which England was a firm ally of the United States. Together they moved forward in accord with the highest ideals, which will make their leadership of the greatest benefit to the

[97] *Ibid.*, pp. 42–44, 47, 88, 94.
[98] *Ibid.*, pp. 144–145.
[99] *Ibid.*, pp. 37, 72–73.

world.    After World War I there continued to develop in readers of the 1920s an affectionate regard and sense of kinship for England.    So one American saluted Britain:[100]

> All Hail! thou noble land!
> Our fathers' native soil!

### Some Other European Peoples

Generally, in junior high school history texts, there is omission of facts supporting the enemy or questioning allies, and emphasis on facts which defame the enemy and favor allies.[101]    France as one of the Allies is apt to be in high favor in modern texts.    But her present status is the latest product of an interesting transformation.    In the early national texts, France was seen in an unfavorable light, it will be remembered.    In the McGuffey readers, strangely enough, tribute was paid to such unlike representatives as Napoleon, Louis XIV, and Lafayette, who would always be praised for his part in assisting the American Revolution.[102]    Thus, France's role had already begun to change.

In history and other social studies texts of the 1920s, France emerged as the traditional friend.    When the United States entered World War I, she went to the aid of this friend either to pay a debt to Lafayette or to repay the debt of the Revolution, or better still, and as enhancement of both France and the United States, to save the world for democracy.    In readers of the 1920s, France was described as an ally in the battle for freedom, brotherhood, and equal rights.    A touching story is told of Leon, age ten, and his baby brother Marcel.    The children were left orphans by the cruel Germans.    When once more the enemy was venting its anger on their little French town, Leon fell on his small brother to save him, and both were found by a soldier in khaki who swore vengeance on the beasts that burned villages and shot babies.[103]    Thus did a formerly frivolous people now adorn in tender fashion the American's picture of himself.

The Dutch, as in earlier readers, emerged in modern texts unscathed. They were still a fair and industrious people, thus making them kin of good Americans; as a probable result of these sterling qualities, they were rewarded by enterprise in trade, an always-to-be-honored virtue.[104] In relatively recent texts they remained hard-working and clean.[105] Little space was accorded to the Scotch Irish, but that little also left

[100] Pierce, op. cit., p. 178.    Quotation from p. 201.
[101] Caputo, op. cit., p. 76.
[102] Mosier, op. cit., p. 55.
[103] Pierce, op. cit., pp. 53, 195–196.
[104] Ibid., p. 84.
[105] Intergroup Relations in Teaching Material: A Survey and Appraisal, p. 75.

them unscarred. They were hardy people, distinguished by their loyalty to the American cause in the Revolution.[106]

With these leading European nations used to enhance the American virtues, some scapegoat was needed to provide contrast. Germany was ready at hand. Little space was accorded to her prior to World War I. There was, to be sure, the redoubtable Baron von Steuben, that skilled Prussian officer who created the Revolutionary Army. But the texts of the 1920s, in preparation for Germany's new role, began to devote attention to her prior to World War I. There was the story of how she tore Alsace and Lorraine from France, and of what a disappointment the empire was to the revolutionists of 1848. These comments were followed up by pointing out her jealousy of the United States in connection with the Samoan incident, and her general hostility during the Spanish-American War. One further incident showed her ill intent: while Great Britain gladly accepted arbitration in the Venezuelan dispute of 1901, Germany scorned it.[107]

With World War I, Germany emerged in the texts as crafty, cruel, designing, and militaristic. Hers was the guilt of war. Hers was the overweening lust for power over Britain and the latter's Empire, and then for peace-loving and defenseless America. The crimes attributed to her were many. She was a colossus bent on destroying free government, to which end she had been forty years overburdening her people in preparation for ignoble conquest. She had robbed Denmark, despoiled France, and made war and ambition her keystones. Her aggression against Belgium was perfidy, ending in a policy of "frightfulness." It was this rape of Belgium that brought America's ally, Britain, into the war. Along with the heroic French, England saved the West "from a towering despotism."[108]

With the war fairly under way, Germany was shown for what she was. Deliberately, so said the texts, she bombed hospitals and innocent villages, she devastated Belgium and France.[109] Her cruelty, according to a 1924 and a 1948 text, was monstrous.[110] Again said a text of the 1920s, "Never since the ancient blood-spattered Assyrian monarchs stood exaltingly on pyramids of mangled corpses had the world seen so huge a crime." How could the United States but go forth on this great American crusade? She must, in American histories, share in "democracy's victory."[111] Even here Germany's perfidy was in evidence, for she

---

[106] Pierce, *op. cit.*, p. 84.
[107] *Ibid.*, pp. 56–59.
[108] *Ibid.*, chap. IV.
[109] *Ibid.*, pp. 60–65.
[110] Caputo, *op. cit.*, p. 76.
[111] Pierce, *op. cit.*, pp. 60–67.

had spread propaganda in the United States to get America into the war on her side; not until recently do texts acknowledge that both sides made efforts to engage the United States with them. This minor change in the story of Germany's participation in World War I, along with increasing attempts to question the truth of the atrocity stories,[112] may again herald a change in the self-portrait. Since World War II, Germany has been identified with the United States through the Occupation, and it may be up to textbook authors to show that American influence has been wholly beneficial. It may be necessary to rattle the checkers on the European board and rewrite the history of Germany.

As Pierce says, few authors of texts of the 1920s found much in the Spaniards to commend, and they gave them little attention. The Spanish were entirely lacking in their colonial administration and in religious and political freedom. They broke the law of their country to inflict cruelties on the Indians. Menendez fought his way up the coast of Florida against the French fleet and settlements, slaughtered male prisoners and some of the women and children; for his perfidy, he was commended by his king for slaughtering heretics. The Spanish misgoverned their own people and threw away a continent in a vain search for gold. It was no wonder that when historians had reached the Spanish-American War, they were full of sympathy for the oppressed Cubans. What more American than that the United States should come to the rescue of a victim that was suffering and oppressed?[113]

Latin Americans, who would be closely akin to the Spanish, have fared better in recent texts. In texts and other teaching materials of the 1940s, they assumed a role of adequate importance. However, they still did not appear as authors in anthologies, nor was there much attention given to recent social developments. The "Black Legend," a body of propaganda directed against the Iberian peoples in the sixteenth century, still was to be found in these texts. The backwardness of the Latin-American nations was attributed to the inborn laziness and general worthlessness of the Creoles, and to the lack of steadfastness of mestizos, Negroes, and Indians. They were a "politically inferior people."[114]

*The Others*

Even into the 1920s, the writers of children's texts had not extended their horizons much beyond the immediate enemies or allies on the European scene. Early national texts had practically no references to other peoples except in inquiry as to their desirability for assimilation.

---

[112] Caputo, *op. cit.*, p. 78.

[113] Pierce, *op. cit.*, pp. 4–6.

[114] *Latin America in School and College Training Material*, pp. 27–31.

Mosier makes practically no mention of the intrusion of "alien" peoples into the McGuffey readers.

However, there were a few scattered references to fringe European or non-European peoples in the texts of the 1920s. Russia's fate prior to World War I was not too bad. True, Russia had been issued a warning through the Monroe Doctrine when she was attempting to extend her autonomy over the Pacific Coast. But relations with her were most pleasant and even commendable during the Civil War. It was post-revolutionary (1917) days that proved menacing. False leaders betrayed their country and inaugurated a reign of bloodshed and terror. They undermined other nations, refused to fight the Germans, and plundered their own countrymen.[115]

In social studies texts, the Turk emerged as fanatical, cruel, oppressive, and utterly unspeakable. It was a minor triumph that he was humbled in World War I.[116] The Oriental peoples have already been described as appendages to the European colonizers. Thus was the world filled out for the emergent American reader of twentieth-century textbooks.

## SUMMARY

While professional educators have been developing education for nationalism, textbook writers have been creating images of America and the good American. They have helped to enforce such national symbols as the flag, the Constitution, and heroes. They have painted the ideal America and American partly through contrast with and comparison to other countries and peoples. The deepest identification has been with selected European peoples; some of the Europeans plus the remainder of the world have remained outside the American pale. Thus have the textbook writers, along with the legislators, the courts, and the professional educators, created a United States and Americans to people it.

[115] Pierce, *op. cit.*, pp. 77–79, 134.
[116] *Ibid.*, p. 134.

# PART III

# Establishing American School Systems

# 10

## Population Diversity and American Education

> I'm just an Irish, Negro, Jewish, Italian,
> French and English, Spanish, Russian,
> Chinese, Polish, Scotch, Hungarian,
> Litvak, Swedish, Finnish, Canadian,
> Greek and Turk and Czech and double Czech American.[1]
>
> JOHN LATOUCHE

Parts I and II have been concerned in part, though not wholly, with what ought to be rather than what is. They have suggested the relationship which schooling should have to the demands of American nationalism, which is based on institutions and for which a symbol system has had to be invented. These two parts have also dealt largely with movements which were national in scope.

The first two parts have implied that there have always been laymen and educators who have known what ideal Americans ought to be and what they ought to know to be functioning and supportive members of a republican society. But human beings have a way of confounding the designs of the planners of the ideal society; and there have always been a host of subcultures in this country which have conditioned particular groups and people so that they have adopted unique ways of behaving. Part III, then, will be devoted to how schools were actually established by or for minority groups or particular populations. The present chapter contains descriptions of three processes by which the minority groups may be woven into the American fabric, even though they may never really lose their identity. Chapters 11 to 14 will be devoted to

---

[1] John Latouche, *Ballad for Americans*, music by Earl Robinson. Copyright 1940 Robbins Music Corporation. Used by special permission Copyright Proprietor.

case studies of the establishment of schools for or by special groups in four different geographic regions.

## THE POPULATION BACKDROP

American school and college educators, anxious to make Americans, have had to make continuous adaptations to local populations. These adaptations have been made to three kinds of groups. The first group is composed of the so-called lower-class children who are striving to be middle class in the vertically mobile American society. The second is the youngsters or adults from minority religious groups, many of whom are immediately native in origin. The third is the children and youth who are themselves foreign-born or who have foreign or mixed parentage. It is this last group which presents the most dramatic statistical picture.

National origins have been of some concern since the day of Thomas Jefferson; in 1800 he signed a memorial to Congress from the American Philosophical Society, asking that the census be so taken as to show numbers of native citizens, those of foreign birth, and aliens. A like memorial was signed by Timothy Dwight for the Connecticut Academy of Arts and Sciences.[2] National authorities, however, did not heed requests for nativity enumeration until 1850; but from that date on various kinds of data for charting the population course of the American people have been available.

If the assumption is that at least two or three generations must elapse for comfortable assimilation of new populations, then the task of the American schoolteacher as implied in Table 10-1 has been formidable. The number of foreign-born reached its high point in 1890, when 16.6 per cent of the American people were reported to have been born abroad. Quite as impressive is the report on foreign stock, the foreign-born plus the native-born of foreign or mixed parentage. Since 1870 there has not been a decade in which the foreign stock did not constitute at least one-fourth of the population, and in 1910, it constituted close to 40 per cent.

It may have been this saturation of the population with first- and second-generation Americans that stimulated a comprehensive inquiry by the United States Congress; and in an act of February 20, 1907, created the U.S. Immigration Commission. The charge of the Commission was to "make full inquiry, examination, and investigation . . . into the subject of immigration." The work of the Commission extended

[2] E. P. Hutchison, *Immigrants and Their Children, 1850–1950*, Census Monograph Series, John Wiley & Sons, Inc., New York, 1956, p. 1. Prepared for the Social Science Research Council in cooperation with the U.S. Bureau of the Census.

Table 10-1. Nativity and Parentage of the White Population of Continental United States (1870–1950)

| Year | Total | Foreign stock | Foreign-born | Native white, foreign or mixed parentage | | | Per cent of white population | | |
|---|---|---|---|---|---|---|---|---|---|
| | | | | Total | Foreign parentage | Mixed parentage | Foreign stock | Foreign-born | Foreign and mixed parentage |
| 1950 | 134,942,028 | 33,750,653 | 10,161,168 | 23,589,485 | 14,824,095 | 8,765,390 | 25.0 | 7.5 | 17.5 |
| 1940 | 118,701,558 | 34,576,718 | 11,419,138 | 23,157,580 | 15,183,740 | 7,973,840 | 29.1 | 9.6 | 19.5 |
| 1930 | 110,286,740 | 39,885,788 | 13,983,405 | 25,902,383 | 17,407,527 | 8,494,856 | 36.2 | 12.7 | 23.5 |
| 1920 | 94,820,915 | 36,398,958 | 13,712,754 | 22,686,204 | 15,694,539 | 6,991,665 | 38.4 | 14.5 | 23.9 |
| 1910 | 81,731,957 | 32,243,382 | 13,345,545 | 18,897,837 | 12,916,311 | 5,981,526 | 39.5 | 16.3 | 23.1 |
| 1900 | 66,809,196 | 25,859,834 | 10,213,817 | 15,646,017 | 10,632,280 | 5,013,737 | 38.7 | 15.3 | 23.4 |
| 1890 | 55,101,258 | 20,625,542 | 9,121,867 | 11,503,675 | 8,085,019 | 3,418,656 | 37.4 | 16.6 | 20.9 |
| 1880* | 43,402,970 | 14,834,546 | 6,559,679 | 8,274,867 | 6,363,769 | 1,911,098 | 34.2 | 15.1 | 19.1 |
| 1870* | 33,589,377 | 10,817,980 | 5,493,712 | 5,324,268 | 4,167,098 | 1,157,170 | 32.2 | 16.4 | 15.9 |

\* Parentage data partly estimated.

SOURCE: U.S. Bureau of the Census, *Census of Population: 1950*, vol. II, *Characteristics of the Population*, part 1, "U.S. Summary," table 35; vol. IV, *Special Reports*, part 3, chapter A, "Nativity and Parentage," table 1. Niles Carpenter, *Immigrants and Their Children, 1920*, Census Monographs, no. 7, p. 5. Cited by E. P. Hutchison, *Immigrants and Their Children, 1850–1950*, John Wiley & Sons, Inc., New York, 1956, p. 3. Prepared for the Social Science Research Council in cooperation with the U.S. Bureau of the Census. Quoted by permission of the Social Science Research Council.

over several years and was finally reported in some forty-two volumes. Those of significance to educators are Volumes 29 to 33, *The Children of Immigrants in Schools.*

The intent of the school investigation, one of the most extensive planned, "was to determine . . . to what extent children of the various races of immigrants are availing themselves of educational facilities and what progress they make in school work." The Commission made an extensive survey of all children in thirty-seven cities, including seventeen of the largest in the country, and an intensive investigation of a limited number of youngsters to determine the factors impeding school progress.

Table 10-2. Cities in Which More Than 60 Per Cent of Public School Children Have Foreign-born Fathers (1908–1909)

| City | Total number of pupils | Children of foreign-born fathers | |
|---|---|---|---|
| | | Number | Per cent |
| Chelsea, Mass............ | 3,903 | 2,893 | 74.1 |
| Duluth, Minn............ | 10,895 | 8,069 | 74.1 |
| New York, N.Y.......... | 569,163 | 406,803 | 71.5 |
| New Bedford, Mass........ | 8,435 | 5,802 | 68.8 |
| Chicago, Ill.............. | 235,452 | 158,565 | 67.3 |
| Fall River, Mass.......... | 13,926 | 9,358 | 67.2 |
| Shenandoah, Pa.......... | 3,519 | 2,361 | 67.1 |
| New Britain, Conn........ | 4,718 | 3,081 | 65.3 |
| Boston, Mass............ | 91,443 | 58,110 | 63.5 |

SOURCE: U.S. Immigration Commission, 1907–1910, *Abstracts of Reports of the Immigration Commission,* 1911, vol. 2, table 3 and inserts, p. 17.

These factors were assumed to be related to the home. Impediment was to be measured partly by retardation. Public and parochial schools, as well as institutions of higher education, were solicited for information, and teachers were asked to give information about themselves.[3]

During the winter of 1908–1909, extensive information was gathered from 1,815,217 youngsters, all who were present in the thirty-seven cities on the day the census was taken. Of the number questioned, over a million (57.8 per cent) were the children of foreign-born fathers. The incidence of foreign paternity ran as high as 74.1 per cent in Chelsea, Massachusetts, and in Duluth, Minnesota. (See Table 10-2.) The highest incidence of youngsters with foreign-born fathers appeared to be, for the most part, in cities close to the East coast, although some

[3] U.S. Immigration Commission, 1907–1910, *Abstracts of Reports of the Immigration Commission,* 1911, vol. 2.

Middle Western cities reported considerable numbers of such youngsters. In addition to the data found in Table 10-2, Minneapolis reported 57.1 per cent; Milwaukee, 53.4; Detroit, 53.4; and South Omaha, 47.5. Other cities in the Old Northwest, as well as some scattered in other parts of the country, reported percentages over 30.[4]

Chicago, Illinois, was one of the twelve cities in which, in 1908–1909, an intensive investigation respecting schooling went forward.[5] Chicago, it will be recalled from Table 10-2, had 158,565, or 67.3 per cent, of public school youngsters whose fathers were foreign-born. The facts turned up in connection with schooling in this city may serve as one backdrop for education and point up the Americanization task of the school.

National (the Commission called it "racial") diversity of backgrounds was impressive. The Commission saw fit to list separately in tables only those races represented by 200 or more children. Yet these "races" constituted some twenty-six, with those of German parentage predominant (16.2 per cent), followed by Swedish (7.5 per cent), Russian Hebrew (6.8), and Bohemian and Moravian (6.9). The twenty-six did not represent all the races, for some were represented by fewer than twenty children, including such widely scattered groups as Hindu, Serbian, Turkish, Egyptian, and Cuban.

In this city, teachers were almost as diverse in origins as pupils. Of the youngsters, 67.3 per cent had foreign-born fathers. Of the kindergarten and elementary teachers, 51.1 per cent were native-born but had foreign parentage, and 8.6 per cent were themselves foreign-born. Thus the 67.3 per cent of the children were roughly matched by 59.7 per cent of the teachers.

The racial origins of teachers were rather different from those of pupils. Whereas foreign-born fathers of youngsters were predominantly German, those of teachers were predominantly Irish (23.7 per cent). However, 8.9 per cent of the teachers did have fathers of German extraction. The number of races represented by foreign-born fathers was twenty-four. The teachers of foreign birth were not concentrated in any one racial group but had twenty-five different origins.

The inferences that can be drawn from the diversity of youngsters and the heterogeneity of teachers are illuminating. It can be confidently assumed that child-rearing practices would have differed among the families of youngsters and those of teachers. These practices would have had a bearing on the behaviors the youngsters brought to school and the behavior modifications individual teachers thought desirable.

[4] See footnote, Table 10-2.
[5] U.S. Immigration Commission, 1907–1910, *The Children of Immigrants in Schools*, 1911, vol. 2, pp. 32–35.

Imposed on this diversity of culturally conditioned ways of behaving was another set of behaviors deemed proper for the good American—one which had been isolated out over the decades by school people, legislators, and the majority. If there had been instruments by which psychologists could have observed a cross section of behavior on any one day in the Chicago schools around 1908, the report would have required several cinematographic screens.

The intensive investigation of a limited number of foreign-speaking youngsters in Chicago schools brought out still more facts about their diverse origins and school problems as indicated by retardation and school practice. In the special group under investigation, some 7,272, or 34.4 per cent, had been born elsewhere than Chicago and 48.3 per cent of this group had attended school elsewhere. The fact that they had been schooled in other systems—whether in other parts of the country or abroad—had to be taken into account in the Chicago school process.

One result of schooling elsewhere—or no schooling—was that some 75 per cent of all youngsters entering school in Chicago at age eight or up entered the first grade. A breakdown of this group showed that 56 per cent with native-born fathers and 78.4 per cent with foreign-born fathers were so entered. In addition, a large number of youngsters in the latter group had themselves been born abroad, so that probably they entered school as non-English-speaking youngsters. It appeared to be common practice to put all of this last group in first grade, regardless of age or previous schooling.

Intensive inquiry was made into retardation in the smaller Chicago sample. In the population of youngsters eight years of age or over, 33.5 per cent were retarded. This percentage was obviously affected by the large numbers of youngsters of non-English-speaking fathers. Retardation was only 19.5 per cent among those of native-born fathers, and 19.1 per cent among those of English-speaking foreign-born fathers, but 39 per cent of those of foreign-born, non-English-speaking fathers.

Retardation was also a phenomenon among the school population of other cities having heavy concentrations of youngsters of foreign-born fathers. A report on the selected sample from twelve cities of children eight years of age and over showed that there was 40.4 per cent retardation among youngsters of foreign-born fathers and 28.1 per cent among those of native-born white fathers.[6] An interesting additional diversity is revealed by the fact that 66.8 per cent of those of native-born Negro fathers were retarded.

The youngsters of the several races showed wide divergence in retardation. Among those born of Polish Hebrew fathers, retardation

[6] *Abstracts of Reports of the Immigration Commission.*

was 66.9 per cent; of South Italians, 63.6 per cent; but of Swedes, 15.5 per cent; of Dutch, 16.1 per cent. (Note that in the two last groups, retardation was less than that among youngsters of native-born white fathers.) Inferences can be made about these findings. The impact of the Protestant Reformation in Sweden and Holland had made literacy highly prized. There would have been a strong drive for schooling and school achievement among Swedish and Dutch families. Because fathers were literate and because they spoke a language very similar to English, there would have been a fairly easy transfer in the home to the new language. "Good" behaviors for these youngsters would have been similar to or identical with those of the Anglo-Puritan culture, which was regarded as the preferred American culture.

These sets of conditions among Swedish and Dutch families would have been reversed among Polish Jews and South Italians. Probably neither of the latter groups would have been affected by the Protestant Reformation. Both would have been of the "wrong" religions. Polish Jews would have known no written language except perhaps a little Hebrew written in symbols different from the Roman alphabet. South Italians would most probably have been illiterate. Although there may have been a high drive for schooling among Polish Jewish fathers because of the reverence for the rabbi (teacher), their other characteristics —so different from the "preferred" American—would have prevented their giving assistance to youngsters in school. Among South Italians, there might have been little value placed on schooling because fathers would have had none and would have considered early employment for their youngsters an economic necessity. Some of their other practices, behaviors, and values would have been at variance with those in the dominant culture.

It can be inferred that in the twelve cities and Chicago schooling would have been a continuous cultural battle, with teachers fighting foreign ways among youngsters as well as among themselves and painfully forging an acceptable American pattern of behavior while wrestling with how to ensure its widespread adoption.

## The Recurring Phenomena of Population Change

The population composition of Chicago's schools in 1908 was unlike that of some fifty years later. In 1958, diversity was introduced by the influx of Southern Negro agricultural workers who were no longer needed on mechanized farms and who were seeking industrial jobs in cities. Moreover, the particular population mixtures in Chicago in 1908 and 1958 were peculiar to Chicago. They would not have characterized San Francisco in 1908, when Chinese and Spanish-American youngsters made their appearance there. It would have been a very different population also from that in New York in 1958. There the problem of new populations has been highlighted by the influx of the most rural of Puerto Ricans into the most urban of American cities. The Chicago school population picture is a photograph which is taken at one minute in time in one area, and which is representative only of the area recorded; but it is illustrative of the general characteristic of variability of population from community to community throughout the course of American history.

The composition of the school population has varied from homogeneity to heterogeneity in accordance with isolation of particular communities, immigration, and internal migration. The latter two have been affected by changes in immigration policy, the course of events abroad, and economic or social conditions which have determined people's movement from one community to another. A last factor is the geographic position of any portion of the United States in respect to its availability to an incoming group.

A combination of these forces and factors can be seen at work when commonly known facts about immigrations and migrations are referred to. The Irish were among the early migrants to this country; they came in increasing numbers during and after the potato famines in 1845 and 1846, and again in the 1880s. From 1820 to 1910, they numbered some 4,212,169. If they had been distributed evenly throughout the forty-eight states, their impact might have been modest; but 58 per cent of them chose to live in Massachusetts, New York, Pennsylvania, and Illinois.[7] This largely, though not entirely, Roman Catholic population was augmented by a more recent and heavy Catholic migration from Italy in some of these states.[8] In Massachusetts, the colonial stronghold of publicly supported and controlled common schooling, well over 20 per cent of the youngsters attend private and parochial schools.[9]

The movement of Negroes in the United States may well be cited in this population discussion. This migratory movement, which has been noticeable since the 1880s, has been out of the South and the border states and into the North and West and particularly into Northern cities. During the period from 1910 to 1920, the Negro population in New

[7] Carl Wittke, The Irish in America, Louisiana State University Press, Baton Rouge, La., 1956, pp. 23–24.

[8] Francis J. Brown and Joseph S. Roucek (eds.), One America: The History, Contributions, and Present Problems of Our Racial and National Minorities, 3d ed., Prentice-Hall, Inc., Englewood Cliffs, N.J., 1952, p. 248.

[9] See U.S. Office of Education, Biennial Survey of Education in the United States, 1952–1954, chap. 2, "Statistics of State School Systems: Organization, Staff, Pupils, and Finances, 1953–1954," 1956.

York, Detroit, Philadelphia, and Chicago increased by approximately three-quarters of a million.[10]   The growth of the Negro population in one of these cities was extraordinary.   In 1950, Negroes in Chicago numbered 492,000; they constituted 10.7 per cent of the population of the metropolitan area, and 13.6 per cent of the population of the city of Chicago.   Yet some fifty years earlier, in 1900, they had numbered only 30,000; they were estimated to constitute only 1.6 per cent of the population of the metropolitan area and 1.8 per cent of the population of the city of Chicago.   Furthermore, the greatest change had come in the decade 1940–1950, when their percentage in the population jumped from 8.2 to 13.6 in the city proper.   Even this increase was sharpest in the limited period from 1946 to 1949.   It is claimed that of all United States cities only New York has a larger Negro population, and that one in every thirty Negroes in the United States lives in Chicago.[11]

To civic leaders, a large influx of predominantly rural folk into an urban area may signify problems.   These may relate to housing relationships between newcomers and old inhabitants, relief, and employment.   Less often are such migrants thought of as increasing school problems; even more rarely are they thought of as changing the cultural conditions under which learning goes forward in city schools.   Of all the areas of concern, the last is not only the least investigated but also, perhaps, the most important.   In the end, schooling will largely determine the conditions under which the new group will or will not be assimilated into urban life.

The question as to what happened in Chicago schools when several thousand Negro youngsters moved in during the period from 1946 to 1949 can be raised in respect to many other areas in the United States— equally well and equally fruitlessly, as far as fundamental research is concerned.   For some years, the fruit growers of California were building their large plantations.   To man them, they welcomed agricultural workers from Mexico, Japan, China, the Philippines, and other Oriental countries.   Some of these laborers came only for brief periods; many stayed and raised families.   What happened to schooling and school populations in California with each of these new sets of Americans?   Groups of agricultural workers and their families regularly move up through the Eastern seaboard states, harvesting the truck-garden crops.   What happens to schooling in the areas where they settle for the winter?   There was a period of several decades when the Hoosier State was a refuge for various religious minority groups.   Indiana was the place to

---

[10] For discussion of Negro migrations, see E. Franklin Frazier, *The Negro in the United States*, rev. ed., The Macmillan Company, New York, 1957, pp. 171–196.

[11] Otis Dudley Duncan and Beverly Duncan, *The Negro Population of Chicago*, University of Chicago Press, Chicago, 1957, pp. 21–25.

be different. What was the cultural composition of Indiana's schools in the heyday of dissent?

Most of the time, these urgent questions can receive only the most superficial answers. Regardless of the quality of the answers, continuous change of population composition in American schools—as reflected in previous brief descriptions of population change in the larger society—is one of the keys to diversity in American education. The continuous process of confronting new faces almost monthly and the historical charge to build a nation—both have combined to activate American educators to constant tampering with practices, materials, and techniques.

PROCESSES OF ENCULTURATION

For an issue of 1933, the editors of the *Harvard Teachers Record* asked a group of foreign educators to comment on American education. One of them, a Frenchman named A. Desclos, had by his own admission taken only a hurried look on two different occasions at United States educational institutions and therefore, according to his own estimate, was in no position to make a profound analysis.[12] He was far too modest, however, for his designation of characteristics of American education was surprisingly penetrating. The key words Desclos used to describe what he saw were "diversity" and "mutability."

Desclos's analysis was simple and perhaps not original. It was entertaining because a foreign visitor in two hasty trips had been able to see key characteristics so clearly. The observations and the explanations argue for their validity. Although Desclos, the orderly Frenchman, did see order in American education, he recognized that school systems varied in terms of local circumstances; that there was no school system, but a series of systems and locally adapted schools. The local adaptations he attributed to the original pioneer Protestant communities, each of which worked out its destiny in its own peculiar way. Hence the diversity.

Coupled with this variability, Desclos saw on his second visit a change even in systems he had lately observed. Educational ideas which on his first trip he had been led to believe were held by American educators to be final and authoritative had, on his return, been discarded for a new set of absolutes. To one accustomed to the relatively unchanging nature of the school system of an old European nation, this mutability was both bewildering and startling. Yet it has been indirectly confirmed by an American educator in his lecture on the school

---

[12] A. Desclos, "American Education as Seen, Hurriedly, by a Frenchman," *Harvard Teachers Record*, vol. 3, no. 1, pp. 36–41, February, 1933.

administrator's task, as traced through the life history of one teacher-administrator. In the period, roughly from 1910 to 1938, this conscientious rural teacher, then principal, then small-town superintendent, found himself deeply committed successively to several different concepts. First it was the fundamentals-discipline approach, then the Herbartian method, followed by subject matter for its own sake, and in the recent past (not finally) the whole child.[13] The same succession of changes could have been found in the history of curriculum or of other aspects of schooling in America. Mutability has indeed been a characteristic.

No single explanation will account for what are undoubtedly multiple forces producing diversity and mutability in American education. One explanation, however, will probably cover more ground than most others. This has to do with the nature of the American population for, in an all-embracing sense, any social institution is a product of the people. First, the United States is composed of people of many cultures and races. Second, because this country was founded on religious freedom, it has been a haven for minority sects which may be foreign or native in origin. Last, the population is mobile, so that rural people may be becoming urban, or Westerners may be becoming Easterners. These varied population characteristics suggest as an explanation of mutability and diversity a multicultural assimilative hypothesis. It manifests itself in American society and education in three social processes.

*Process* 1:
*Transplanting a Culture*

The first process which introduces diversity and mutability into American society and education is the attempt to transplant a bit of a "home" culture in a new region. Sometimes it is a part of an old society which has been temporarily rejected, as in the case of religious establishments which have had to find a more congenial home than the Old World afforded. Other times, it is that part of the Old World which is familiar—a language, a press, a social organization.

Thus the so-called first settlers—John Smith's Anglicans, John Winthrop's Puritans, and William Bradford's Pilgrims—established a civil government, a church, and usually a school—on their first landing. Also, regardless of the relationship of government to schools, the latter were ordinarily under the supervision of the clergy, as they had been in the country of origin. As the school patterns grew more complex, the outline of the Dissenters' academies of England was to be seen in

[13] Harold Benjamin, *Emergent Conceptions of the School Administrator's Task,* Cubberley lecture, Nov. 12, 1938, Stanford University Press, Stanford, Calif., 1942.

colonial secondary schools, and Harvard was founded as an anemic copy of Cambridge. Most other colonial groups, the English Quakers, the German Lutherans, the Dutch Reformed, had already in the early colonial period—or would in the eighteenth century—established churches and schools under the supervision of the clergy as they had known such practice abroad. So the middle of the eighteenth century was the high point of private school establishment in the United States.[14]

During the whole of the national period, transplanting a bit of the Old World in the New has continued to characterize the practice of sizable immigrating groups. The process begins with immigration from a single ethnic group, extending over one or more decades. Despite the rigors of living in the country of origin, members of the group wish to maintain a link or links with that old country. They establish a foreign-language press, churches having rituals and a language common to the country of origin, and full-time or part-time schools for their children. The social tools or institutions (press, church, school) are forged on the one hand to give cohesiveness to the adult group, particularly when a special religious creed is involved; on the other, to maintain a hold on the children, who are only too rapidly absorbed in the larger American culture. Sometimes the culture item is a native growth, as in the case of the social reformers who, from 1820 to 1860, dreamed about and tried out ideal communities.

*Process 2:*
*Accommodating a Culture*

Process 2 begins as forces from without and within the ethnic group begin to challenge its cohesiveness. Thus the challenge of building a nation which would hang together produced in colonial settlers of diverse origins the response of forming a nonsectarian, publicly supported school system in the early national period. The challenge from without had begun to crack the shell of insularity. By this time, young men of different faiths, having different ethnic origins, had learned how to work together in a war and in intercolonial groups. They could be said to have been forces working from within each group to break down the walls of isolation. Reconciliation of diverse groups through loyalty to common civic institutions and a common school system was an assimilative device which the new national Americans in a sense forced on themselves as an answer to the divisive influences in their subcultures.

Among migrants of the national period, Process 2 has been at work as among the older immigrants, but the particulars of the process are different. The first generation of youngsters—if they were young when

[14] R. Freeman Butts and Lawrence A. Cremin, *A History of Education in American Culture,* Henry Holt and Company, Inc., New York, 1953, chap. 3.

brought to this country—or the second generation begins attending public school and mixing with so-called native Americans. The youth become impatient with the commitments to a foreign culture which they feel is not theirs. They see themselves as Americans and wish to identify with other Americans. They become rebellious about attending a foreign-language-and-culture school. Something approximating Toynbee's internal proletariat begins to work on the ethnic group.

At the same time, outside the ethnic group, "native" Americans may become perturbed about the assimilation of the older generation and equally concerned about whether youngsters of foreign parentage are learning American ways. The character of the concern and the nature of actions taken vary from place to place and group to group.

In some communities, groups of individuals—often social workers and educators—look with sympathy on the hardships of the older generation and attempt to set up welfare organizations, social centers, and evening schools where the foreign-born may secure help in adjusting to a new culture. They may be aided and abetted by better-established second- or third-generation members of the same ethnic group. In the same communities self-designated patriots may address their efforts to straightforward propaganda for what is called "Americanism" and to hunting down and exposing those judged to be subversive; extremists may use terroristic methods to intimidate the ethnic-group members.

To accommodate the younger members of the ethnic group (either first or second generation) or their parents, public and private American schools begin to make adaptations in programs and offerings. These include special classes for foreign-speaking children, introduction of the parents' language into elementary or secondary schools, special kinds of programming so that youngsters may carry "American ways" from the school to the home, and establishment of evening schools and social centers. Thus, through emergency changes in programs and offerings, mutability comes to characterize American education.

*Process* 3:
*Diffusing a Culture*

In Process 3 many kinds of developments may be apparent. Members of an ethnic group, especially if strongly oriented in the direction of a particular religious ritual, may resist any kind of assimilation either for themselves or for their children. Illustrative are some of the early Puritans. When Oliver Cromwell came to power in England in 1649, there was considerable emigration of New Englanders who had only been waiting for a congenial environment in the home country for the practice of their religion. They had no desire to build a new society in a new, raw world; they had only wanted to find a niche where they could be secure in their commitments to one of the Old World patterns. The emigration back to England became so epidemic that leaders who were committed to a new life in the New World were sorely troubled.

The emigration of Puritans in colonial days has been paralleled by that of many foreign-born individuals in national days. The immigrant who comes to make his fortune in America but who never reconciles himself to culture change is well known in American history. Many an Italian, Japanese, Swede, or Pole—whether he found prosperity or not—has returned to the homelike village of his origin. In another vein, "native" minority religious groups may remove themselves to isolated regions in an effort to retain their religious practices, as witness the Mormons and the Amish.

At the other extreme are those who lose themselves in the larger American society. They usually are identified with a group which is small in numbers or which lacks cohesiveness. The Latvians are such a group; today they are only some 50,000 strong and they have fanned out over the United States. Although people of some prominence may occasionally be identified as Latvians, the ethnic group has appeared to leave little impression on the larger American society.[15]   Therefore it is difficult to study the accommodations or the antagonisms of the larger society and the group to one another.

Between these extremes—the unreconciled who return home and the completely merged who lose their identity—are those who belong to substantial and cohesive groups which make such an impact on the larger society that diversity is introduced into the American social scene. The character of the impact is conditioned by the cohesiveness of the group, the readiness of American society to receive and adapt elements of the culture from the group, and the time of impact.

As illustration of a group which contributed to the larger society, there are the Germans who immigrated in substantial numbers and in compact communities during the eighteenth, nineteenth, and twentieth centuries. They prospered and assimilated in part; they also left their mark on American social institutions, including schools. The introduction of German into elementary as well as secondary schools in the period from the Civil War to World War I is attributable to the influence of this ethnic group. Likewise, the introduction of physical education into institutions at all levels may be traced to German turners and like-minded Swedish gymnasts.

Another one of the more substantial groups includes people who in the twentieth century would never be identified as an ethnic group— although they, too, were once upon a time immigrants. The group consists of the descendants of the "original settlers"—presently called

[15] Brown and Roucek, *op. cit.*, pp. 185–190.

New Englanders. A part of their story is described in Chapter 11. They left an impact not on the Old Northwest alone, but on school enterprises throughout the United States. By the nineteenth century, their interest in education had gone through such transmutations that the impact was general rather than particular. It was expressed in a strong drive for schools and education rather than for a particular kind of education. Representatives of their group were to be found in many of the local and national voluntary organizations which were propagandizing for free compulsory education in the antebellum (pre-Civil War) period. It is said that their influence extends even to American enterprises overseas. Among businessmen who are most persistent in establishing schools for native employees abroad are often the descendants of the saints who planted the church, the meetinghouse, and the school in early New England.

America has been the temporary or permanent stopping place for foreign nationals. It has also been the haven for minority religious groups and social experimenters.[16] Christian communists, millennialists, and transcendentalists have tried their hand at "the new community." The period between 1800 and 1860 produced most of these groups. Some of them came from abroad; but many were native-born and of a relatively old stock, such as those who began Brook Farm in 1841 on the Ellis property some nine miles from Boston. Whatever the origins of these groups, it is quite likely that in their history may be seen the operations of Processes 1, 2, and 3. Certainly in the story of the Mormons, who owe their beginnings to a Vermonter, there are clearly discernible the same cycles of difference, partial assimilation, and impact as are to be found among the Germans, for instance. Thus a group native in origin but markedly different from the hypothetical majority in cultural orientation can contribute to diversity and mutability in American society and education.

It is rather clear that Process 3 would eventuate in local characteristics of education and in continuous changes in particular educational enterprises. Coupled with the effects of Process 3, however, are effects of occurrences in the larger American society. The society itself is not static. In response to the impact of minority groups and socioeconomics forces such as urbanization and industrialization, educational programs at all levels are constantly changing to make continuous and immediate adjustment to forces in the larger society. The three processes and the generally dynamic character of the American culture, coupled with the charge to the school of being the primary Americanization agency—all of these eventuate in an educational enterprise which is a kind of mael-

[16] See Alice Felt Tyler, *Freedom's Ferment: Phases of American Social History to 1880*, University of Minnesota Press, Minneapolis, Minn., 1944.

strom.    To a Frenchman, that enterprise could only appear to be diverse and mutable.

PROCESSES 1 AND 2:
TRANSPLANTING AND ACCOMMODATING
IMMIGRANT CULTURES

Americans are so continuously being "added to" from foreign lands that the phenomenon of culture transplantation and accommodation almost goes unnoticed.    Therefore, it might be well to turn to some of the immigrant rather than native minorities to note their effect, if any, on American education.

*The French*

The French have appeared in many areas of the United States and in different periods of history.    They were among the early settlers in Louisiana; along the Mississippi Valley, including Illinois; and in Rhode Island, where the Protestant Huguenots took refuge.    Another group came during the Napoleonic Wars; and a more recent group came in the last decades of the nineteenth century.    Only two of these groups will be treated briefly.

In Louisiana, which might be called "French United States," the first French language school was opened by Ursuline nuns in 1727.    This was a bilingual school in that pupils had to converse daily in both French and English.    By 1775 there were in the territory some eight schools for boys also.    In 1811 the College of Orleans was opened, but it was soon reduced to an academy, and discontinued in 1826 because it was "too French in spirit."[17]

Process 2 set in when public and parochial schools and new American colleges made adaptations to the French population.    The general government made provisions for parish academies which went into operation around 1811.    A rival to the College of Orleans, Louisiana College, was established in 1825 and opened in 1826 in Jackson, East Felician Parish, with both French and Spanish as languages in the curriculum.    The College of Jefferson, which supplanted Louisiana College in 1831, and the College of Baton Rouge continued French as a foreign language.[18]

That early urge to continue a link with the mother country was long ago transformed into a French-American culture in Louisiana; it continues unchanged among French Canadians residing in a beltlike area

---

[17] Charles Hart Handschin, *The Teaching of Modern Languages in the United States*, U.S. Office of Education Bulletin 1913, no. 3, whole no. 510, 1913, pp. 10–11.

[18] *Ibid.*, p. 11.

stretching from New York to Canada. To these Franco-American parents, loyalty is to the parish, the family, the Roman Catholic religion, and the French language and institutions. So they still send their boys and girls to colleges and convents in Quebec.[19]

The bastions of the common school and the Congregational Church were assaulted by the French Canadians in the last three decades of the nineteenth century.[20]  A group of notoriously poor farmers, bedeviled by poverty,[21] were possessed of the *mal des États-Unis* and *la fièvre aux États-Unis*. Whole parishes deserted the village and the land for urban and occasionally rural living in the New England states. At first the Roman Catholic church officials bitterly opposed the migration. As they were unable to stem the tide, they sent French-Canadian priests to open up new fields for French Catholicism among the descendants of the Puritans.[22]

The experience of the New Englanders with these dissimilar folk must have begun in a small way immediately after the Civil War. Bounties had been offered to French-Canadian youth to serve in the Northern armies and about 40,000 probably responded. The industrial development of New England which followed on the war provided a means by which Canadians could be absorbed into the economy.[23]  But their coming from simple agricultural communities into mills in urban areas and among people who put stress on compulsory schooling created problems for state governments.

In 1888, Flora Haines was employed by the Maine Bureau of Industrial and Labor Statistics to look into the conditions for women textile workers who were largely of French-Canadian origin. Miss Haines found that French girls were neat of dress (with whisk brooms to dust lint from their frocks) and also that French women took snuff and the children used tobacco. One can almost hear the clucking of tongues at this last shocking development. Miss Haines, good New Englander that she was, thought of schools and public schools in which, she recommended, texts for both French and English instruction be used.[24]

---

[19] Francis J. Brown and Joseph F. Roucek, *Our Racial and National Minorities: The History, Concentration, and Present Problems of Our Racial and National Minorities*, 3d ed., Prentice-Hall, Inc., Englewood Cliffs, N. J., 1952, pp. 340–342.

[20] A. R. M. Lower, "New France in New England," *The New England Quarterly*, vol. 2, no. 2, p. 284, April, 1929.

[21] Iris Saunders Podea, "Quebec to 'Little Canada': The Coming of the French Canadians to New England in the Nineteenth Century," *The New England Quarterly*, vol. 23, no. 3, p. 365, September, 1950.

[22] Lower, *op. cit.*, pp. 284–285.

[23] Podea, *op. cit.*, p. 367.

[24] *Ibid.*, p. 370.

To these simple rural folk, turned urban slum dwellers, schools were useless institutions. Members of the New England governments were convinced that French-Canadian parents frequently evaded school laws and falsified children's ages to evade them. In 1881 the Massachusetts Bureau of Labor Statistics reported that when French-Canadian parents were finally apprehended for disregarding compulsory school laws, they would move to communities where they were not known in order to keep their youngsters in mill work. In 1872 another New England investigator reported that if French-Canadian parents were told one day that children under ten could not be employed, the next day all youngsters were ten. In 1885, the Bureau of Labor Statistics in Connecticut reported that French Canadians looked on their children as adding to family income and anticipated full employment of all members of the family. Authorities in Rhode Island complained of both illiteracy and child labor among French Canadians. Mill owners and school authorities were often equally at fault. The former wanted the labor force and the latter did not wish schools overwhelmed with "undisciplined children." Even organized labor would not have been happy about these children of the fields, for they were often used as strikebreakers.[25]

When French Canadians finally came to grips with compulsory schooling, they met the problem with parochial rather than public schools. The New England church hierarchy had accommodated the new population in 1870 when it had ruled that the language of a majority of the Catholic congregation would determine the language of the priest. The parochial school, in turn, helped the population to retain its French-Catholic identification. The path was not always smooth in this close-knit community, however; the Irish, who had also moved into New England, did not see eye to eye with their French coreligionists.[26] In turn, the French and Irish, united in a single church, posed additional problems of health for state authorities. They did not understand why wakes, for instance, should be prohibited during epidemics. Process 2 was in effect when health officials began to give child-care instructions in French and English.[27]

By the end of the nineteenth century, French Canadians were moving out of their squalid and rat-ridden slums. Statistics show that they were eating better than Canadians in comparable social classes.[28] But well into the twentieth century the French Canadians were still in Process 2. In 1927, authorities in Lewiston, Maine, testified that French

[25] *Ibid.*, pp. 371–373.
[26] Lower, *op. cit.*, p. 290.
[27] Podea, *op. cit.*, p. 376.
[28] *Ibid.*, pp. 375–377.

pupils appeared to have a reading knowledge of English in upper grades, but none in the lower.[29]   An explanation of such a state of affairs might be found in reports of Mgr. Olivier Maurault.   In 1950, he said that there were 970 priests working among Franco-Americans in New England.   There were 178 "national" parishes, 107 mixed parishes with Franco-American pastors, and 142 parishes in which Franco-Americans were important.   These groups were served by 264 colleges, high schools, and primary schools which might be presumed to enforce the French language and culture.   He referred also to a congress of French Canadians held in Worcester, Massachusetts, in May, 1949. Here these "hyphenated Americans" had affirmed that spiritually they were Roman Catholics; temporally, American citizens; and by tradition, language, and spirit, they were French.[30]   Would Process 3 ever begin among the Franco-Americans of New England, or would it be desirable?

*The Germans*

What the Germans did and how they did it depended on their original religious commitments.   German Lutherans, deeply devout, had a tendency to cling to their ways and practices more than did the freethinkers who came after the Revolution of 1848.

Illustrative of the first group are the early settlers in Maryland. Their religious commitments were first apparent in a grievance which had resulted from an act of 1692.   This had established the Anglican or Episcopal Church as the state church, for which each inhabitant must pay an annual tax of 40 pounds of tobacco.   In 1758 the German Lutherans of Frederick, Maryland, voiced their grievance at paying a tax, none of which was remitted to their own church.   Here, where all were equal, so they said, it was difficult to find good ministers and stewards and to keep in hand a congregation of voluntary members. Yet they, the protesters, had no need for either the Anglican Church or English schools.   They wished to retain their language for, if it were lost, this would mean the loss of their religion.   In the interests of both language and religion, they desired to establish both churches and German-language schools.   They asked that either tax money be used to support a German minister or that the tax be eliminated.   With or without taxes, however, the founding of schools went forward.   All the old German churches—whether Lutheran, Reformed, or Catholic—built church schools.[31]

[29] Lower, *op. cit.*, p. 291.

[30] Msgr. Olivier Maurault, "The French of Canada and New England," a Newcomen address in Vermont, The Newcomen Society in North America, New York, 1950, pp. 17, 20–21.

[31] Dieter Cunz, *The Maryland Germans: A History*, Princeton University Press, Princeton, N.J., 1948, pp. 118–120, 222.

One of the most famous of these schools was owned by the Zion church in Baltimore. It opened about 1769 and was known later as Scheib's School. To Pastor Heinrich Scheib, who took over in 1835, it owed its status. When the pastor first visited it, he testified that he saw nothing but dirt and cobwebs and the catechism being beaten into the heads of seventeen miserable children. Scheib was already in what might be considered a transitional mood. He was against the sponsorship of a sectarian school. Education for citizenship should be the keynote of the institution, and he proposed that the school be conducted in German and English. Under Scheib's supervision, the school reopened with seventy-one pupils as the first German-English school in Baltimore. The school continued to be supported by the Zion church, with the pastor as principal and members of the church as board of directors. The policy on admission was most liberal; anyone could attend. Within a short while, Catholics, Jews, and Anglo-Americans outnumbered Zionists among the enrollees. Immediately prior to the Civil War, the school had seven grades, plus a kindergarten, and an enrollment of 418 pupils.[32]

Innovations other than a nonsectarian English-German school may be credited to Pastor Scheib. He had apparently been influenced by the teacher training movement of Germany. He held faculty meetings and gave lectures on pedagogical questions. The faculty meetings must have been unusual in tone for the period before the Civil War. Teachers discussed physical education, care of babies, sex education, and general questions of hygiene. Scheib advanced the German teaching seminar and the elimination of corporal punishment in schools.[33] He paid special attention to music, drawing, and laboratory work. To enhance the latter, the classrooms were well equipped with charts, instruments, and stuffed animals for natural science teaching.[34]

Another German school in Baltimore was founded by Friedrich Knapp, refugee from the 1848 revolution and former schoolteacher. Knapp first became principal of a parochial school of the German Reformed congregation. In 1853, he opened his own school with an initial enrollment of sixty pupils. Knapp rebelled against the influence which either church or government attempted to exert over schools. This influence, so he implied, led to the "memory-stuffing" procedures which had produced a sterile education. His was the outlook of Pestalozzi, who suited his educational techniques to the nature of

[32] *Ibid.*, pp. 224–227.
[33] *Ibid.*, pp. 225–228.
[34] Albert Bernhardt Faust, *The German Element in the United States: With Special Reference to Its Political, Moral, Social and Educational Influence*, The Steuben Society of America, New York, 1927, p. 243.

the child and his abilities. A child-centered school was Knapp's goal, and it must have been one which appealed to parents for by the Civil War, the school was enrolling 700 pupils from many different states.[35]

Scheib's and Knapp's schools were not the only ones to open in Baltimore or in Maryland. After 1840, German-sponsored schools became more numerous because there was an increase in the number and prosperity of German inhabitants. These schools were relatively short-lived. After the 1880s many declined and a good number closed their doors. Process 2 was taking over. The impact of the German element on public school practices was being felt.

In 1873 the Baltimore Board of School Commissioners was asked to consider the incorporation of German-English schools into the public school system. In response to the request, an experimental school was opened in 1874 under the direction of Valentin Scheer and Karl Hessler. In two years' time, the board opened five new German-English schools; in 1876, they had an enrollment of 3,000 pupils. By 1897, there were seven such schools with an enrollment of 6,780; in 1900, when the schools were most generally patronized, there were 7,600 in attendance. These institutions were planned for youngsters of both German and English backgrounds, and instruction was given in both languages each day.

Process 2 finally came to an end in Baltimore in respect to the German element. After 1904, the schools no longer were listed in school reports and, though they lingered until World War I, they finally went out of existence in 1917. However, these public schools adapted to a special population had lasted long enough to sound the death knell of the private schools. Scheib's institution had closed in 1895 and, though the German-Catholic congregation had five schools with 3,193 enrolled as late as 1887, there were no German parochial schools left in Baltimore by the twentieth century.[36]

The freethinkers who swelled the groups of the forty-eighters (refugees from the 1848 German revolution) operated rather differently from their orthodox brethren in other parts of the country. In a sense, Process 1 had hardly got under way when Process 2 was initiated. They appeared to assimilate faster and to make their impact felt on the public school establishment much more rapidly than the German Lutherans.

The freethinkers spread through the Middle West—Wisconsin, Minnesota, Iowa, and other prairie states. From the outset, they were interested in the education of youth on a nonsectarian and humanitarian basis. The constitution of the freethinkers' society of Milwaukee contained a statement to the effect that the education of youth was a

[35] Cunz, *op. cit.*, pp. 230–231.
[36] *Ibid.*, pp. 231–232, 334–337.

"special duty." The National Conference of Freethinkers in 1871 sponsored a Sunday-school textbook. The Milwaukee contingent thereupon commissioned such a text to be done by a Swiss, H. M. Kottinger, who was assisted by Peter Engelmann and a Unitarian minister. According to commentators, this was no ordinary recital of religious dogma but "a fascinating catechism of humanitarianism."[37]

Foundings of private high schools—apparently with liberal traditions—went on apace in such Wisconsin towns as Mayville and Manitowoc, as well as Milwaukee. In Davenport, Iowa, where forty-eighters controlled the social lives of Germans for at least a generation, a nonchurch private school was opened. In New Ulm, Minnesota, which had been founded to preserve the liberal principles of the German Turner society, nonsectarian schools were also founded.[38]

The freethinkers soon put their mark on the public school establishments. One of the forty-eighters in Watertown, Wisconsin, campaigned for free textbooks in the public schools, and his community became the first in the state to use them. The socialist society of New Ulm, which abandoned some of its properties when the group turned capitalist, transferred ownership of school property to the public school district; with monies from the sale of land, the group established an endowment fund for salaries of public school teachers and purchase of textbooks. The fund was endowed with the proviso that no religious instruction be offered in public schools. The impact of the freethinkers in New Ulm was both direct and indirect. The German language and gymnastics became a part of the public school curriculum. Public lectures, as well as a public library, became extensions of the educational enterprise. It became established custom, furthermore, that the six-member school board should always have on it two freethinkers, two Catholics, and two Protestants. This board was symbolic of a large tolerance which must have resulted from the freethinkers' impact on the community and which had existed from the first immigration of Catholic Germans into the freethinkers' community. As an example—when the Catholic church was destroyed by fire, a freethinking brewer offered the priest the use of one of his buildings. This tolerance must have spread to the operation of the public schools.[39]

Freethinkers in Michigan had been firm supporters of the Northern cause in the Civil War and participants in the Republican National Convention of 1864. To this group, German countrymen who clung to German ways were a matter of concern. They therefore initiated a

[37] A. E. Zucker (ed.), *The Forty-eighters: Political Refugees of the German Revolution of 1848*, Columbia University Press, New York, 1950, pp. 56–57.
[38] *Ibid.*, pp. 57–70.
[39] *Ibid.*, pp. 58, 73–75.

move to develop a national education institution for training teachers of German birth or descent. These students would be steeped in American history and principles of government and sent out to work among young German Americans. Although this Americanization institution, developed in imagination by a foreign-born group, never materialized as a national college, a local German-American Seminary was founded in Detroit in 1864.[40]

It will be remembered that the Germans have been the largest immigrating group. It is no wonder, then, that Process 2 has been in formidable operation in respect to that group. In addition to cases already cited, there are many more cases of accommodation to the language in public elementary schools. In 1854, when refugee teachers would become available, the New York public school board adopted the policy of the optional study of German in public schools. In 1870 it was ruled that whenever there was sufficient demand, in the judgment of school trustees, German might be introduced as a regular branch of study in all eight grades of elementary school. By 1873, German had been taught to 19,396 pupils; by the fall of 1874, of the 1,200 students at the Female Normal College, 1,180 were studying German.[41]

On December 16, 1874, Commissioner Brown of New York City noted with satisfaction that pupils were leaving German private schools to attend public schools. This would make the public schools more effective Americanization instruments by bringing foreign-born parents and children into contact with Anglo-American children. It would make German youngsters a "thoroughly homogeneous part of our nation." The more effective instruction could become, the more nearly would the schools approach the ideal of bringing all classes, nationalities, and creeds under its influence. The importance to Commissioner Brown of such a movement was obvious when it was noted that 11,000 German pupils were still in attendance at Catholic, Lutheran, and German parochial and private schools.[42]

When the successor to Commissioner Brown moved to eliminate German in New York elementary schools, a protest meeting was called. One of the chief arguments for the retention of German was that it drew into public schools the children of German-American parents, and so made easier the development of an American sentiment.[43]

[40] John Andrew Russell, *The Germanic Influence in the Making of Michigan*, University of Detroit, Detroit, Mich., 1927, pp. 192–194.
[41] L. Viereck, "German Instruction in American Schools," *Report of the Commissioner of Education for 1900–1901*, U.S. Government Printing Office, 1902, vol. I, p. 641.
[42] *Ibid.*
[43] *Ibid.*, p. 642.

In the last half of the nineteenth century, German was being introduced into elementary schools in other cities with heavy populations of German origin. In 1872–1873, some 38.9 per cent of youngsters in St. Louis were studying German. The St. Louis school board introduced German into many schools, and into all grades for children of German parentage. Anglo-American parents had then demanded language study for their youngsters, so that by 1871 it had been introduced into lower classes for all pupils. In the 1870s, well over 50 per cent of the elementary youngsters in Louisville were studying German.[44]

On the motion of Lorence Brentano, member of the school board, German instruction was introduced in one Chicago elementary school in 1865. It was such a success that in 1873, after repairs of ravages of the Chicago fire, Miss Regina Shauer was elected superintendent of German instruction. Miss Shauer was succeeded by Dr. G. A. Zimmerman, who aroused even more interest in German language teaching. By 1884, there were 10,696 pupils being instructed in German by 73 teachers. In 1885, the language was introduced in the third and fourth grades. The height of popularity was in 1892–1893 when 44,270 pupils and 242 teachers were involved in German language instruction. When a motion was finally made to abolish German instruction, the cause of German was supported even by the *Times Herald,* and so strong was the pressure from the German press and associations that the motion was never put into effect.[45]

On May 1, 1873, the Ohio Legislature enacted a law stating that it was the duty of school commissioners to provide German language instruction in districts where seventy-five residents asked for it in the interests of not less than forty pupils, and where there was a desire to learn German and English concurrently. After passage of the state law, the school committee of Cleveland decided that all pupils must study German if at least eighty residents requested such study. English and German instruction was given alternately on the same day, with eleven periods a week being devoted each to English and to German. Arithmetic was taught only in English and singing, only in German; but other subjects were handled in both languages. At a German-American *Sängerfest* held in Cleveland in 1874, some 1,500 youngsters of German, Irish, Scandinavian, Italian, French, and Negro origins sang *"Die Wacht am Rhein."*[46]

Wisconsin and Indiana, as well as Ohio, had laws respecting teaching of German in public schools. Results of these laws were not always as encouraging as those in Cleveland, however. Karl Knortz reported in

[44] *Ibid.,* p. 641.
[45] *Ibid.,* pp. 644–645.
[46] *Ibid.,* pp. 643–644.

1898 that he was disappointed in the record of Evansville, Indiana. He estimated that there must be at least 4,000 youngsters of German extraction in the public schools. Yet only 2,500 pupils were studying German, and, of these, 900 were of English origin. Furthermore, of all German-born pupils in public schools, only 11 per cent could speak German with their parents.[47] He was experiencing the bitter fruits of unsuccessful effort with youngsters who wanted to be American.

Knortz's disappointment at developments in public schools was probably the keener because he was inclined to be highly critical of private schools, which might show a greater tendency to perpetuate language study. Nearly one-half of the youngsters studying German were attending Catholic, Lutheran, or Evangelical parochial schools. According to the German Teachers Association, enrollments were 193,627, 85,934, and 19,880, respectively. Yet according to Knortz, these schools were of little value for dissemination of German literature and science. Their teachers were trained in seminaries and concentrated on Bible history and catechism. He felt that only Lutheran colleges were respectable educational institutions. In connection with Catholic institutions, Knortz reported an interesting development. In May of 1897, the Pope had issued an ordinance to the effect that American-born children whose parents spoke a language other than English were not bound, when they were grown, to be members of the same parish as their parents; and that all Catholics not born in the United States but understanding English had a right to attach themselves to English-speaking parishes. In June of 1897, German Catholics met in Detroit, Michigan, and protested the ordinance. The Union of Catholic Associations of Illinois passed strong resolutions about maintenance of language, for German methods were planted in human hearts by God Himself. One authority was inclined to believe that German Catholics would be the last to give up German instruction.[48]

One of the more interesting transition institutions begun by Germans in America was a teacher training establishment. It had its beginnings in Peter Engelmann's German-English Academy founded in Milwaukee in 1851. Engelmann, a refugee of 1848, was in the learning-by-doing tradition. He had introduced visual aids as well as vocational education into his academy.[49] So well did the academy prosper that by 1865 there were 450 pupils enrolled in eleven classes taught by sixteen teachers. There was now an elementary school of four grades, a *Realschule* of four classes, and a female seminary of three years.[50]

[47] *Ibid.*, p. 646.
[48] *Ibid.*, pp. 650–653.
[49] Zucker, *op. cit.*, p. 57.
[50] Faust, *op. cit.*, p. 241.

Engelmann's academy was of such high repute that in 1878 it was selected by the National German-American Teachers' League as a German-American teachers seminary and use was made of the lower grades for practice teaching. Concurrently, the North American Turner League transferred the normal school for teachers of physical training to Milwaukee.[51]

This all too brief introduction to the schooling processes of the German population suggests variations in the several subcultures. With German Lutherans, their own schools were often dearly held and reinforced long after they had been rejected by the new generations because the schools were a reinforcement, so they believed, of a religious pattern. To lure the children of these immigrants into public schools, school boards made widespread language adaptations. The freethinkers, on the other hand, though they did establish nonsectarian private schools, supported public schools and reinforced the nonsectarian nature of the public establishment—a practice which might be said to be an adaptation to a liberal immigrant group.

### The Dutch

The Dutch immigration to America came first in the seventeenth century to New Netherlands; then in the 1840s, 1850s, and subsequent decades, it came largely to Michigan, Iowa, Illinois, New York, New Jersey, and California. These migrations were held together not so much by the language of the people as by their common adherence to the Dutch Reformed Church of America—although there had been a schism in the church, and out of it arose the Christian Reformed Church.[52]

Church members in New Netherlands in the 1600s sponsored schools. But this was not always the practice of those who came in succeeding centuries. Often the children of immigrants grew up in ignorance of Dutch. Nevertheless, in 1854 the classis of Holland had stated as a principle that wherever disbelief and superstition flourished, there schools should be established. Church congregations, therefore, tried to develop schools not so much with a Dutch as with a religious emphasis. In fact, in one school in Michigan, the congregation refused to appoint a teacher whose English was defective.[53] The drive of the Dutch for their own schools was like that of the Scandinavians—relatively weak. Under the leadership of the devout and fervent Van

---

[51] Zucker, *loc. cit.*

[52] Brown and Roucek, *Our Racial and National Minorities*, pp. 84–86.

[53] Henry S. Lucas, *Netherlanders in America: Dutch Immigration to the United States and Canada, 1789–1950*, University of Michigan Press, Ann Arbor, Mich., 1955, pp. 589, 601.

Raalte, the people in Holland, Michigan, opened a parochial school in the 1850s. By 1862 the school had closed, and Hollanders were sending their youngsters to the newly established district school.[54] Poverty, combined with the fact that the Dutch had acquired the language habits of their new country, doomed the parochial elementary and secondary schools to failure.

In the meantime, public schools in heavily Dutch communities began to adapt to the ethnic group, and Process 2 was under way. In 1880, instruction in Dutch was given in district schools in Holland, Zeeland, Vriesland, Graafschop, Callendoor, Muskegon, and Grand Haven, Michigan. In some of these schools, English and Dutch were taught concurrently; in others, such as the East Street School in Grand Rapids, Michigan, Dutch was taught in summer schools. These public schools were often Reformed Church in emphasis. As a part of the regular curriculum there was Bible reading, singing of hymns and psalms, and prayers, and after school there was catechism.[55]

Much as Englishmen in the 1600s reached out to colonials across the seas, so the people of the Netherlands reached out to their countrymen in America. Around the turn of the nineteenth century, the Netherlands established the Queen Wilhelmina Lectureship in Dutch Literature at Columbia University. Stimulated by this move from home to reestablish links already broken, Hollanders in America established a Dutch History, Literature, and Art chair at the University of Chicago in 1911; but it was discontinued in 1914. Attempts to establish Dutch chairs at the University of Illinois and the University of Michigan failed also, as did efforts to establish fellowships for study in the Netherlands.[56] The Dutch had assimilated too well. They had retained their church schools as religious—not Dutch—institutions; they had asked public schools to adapt to their needs; and finally, they had been enculturated into the larger American society as Americans, not as Dutch Americans.

### The Scandinavians

The strength of the immigration and the depth of religious orthodoxy determined the tenacity with which Scandinavians clung to old-country ways and supported public educational institutions. But the language question probably was not as acrimoniously debated among Scandinavians as it was among other groups, although there was some excep-

---

[54] Marian M. Schoolland, *The Story of Van Raalte: A Man Strong and of Good Courage*, William B. Erdmans Publishing Co., Grand Rapids, Mich., 1951, p. 89.
[55] Lucas, *op. cit.*, pp. 590, 601.
[56] *Ibid.*, p. 596.

tion to this among Norwegians. The languages are closely akin to English and, as a consequence, this immigrant group could learn the language of America rapidly. Furthermore, there appeared to be little feeling for continuing to be Swedes or Norwegians. The emotional drive was to remain Lutherans in the ways which suited the several migrating groups.

*The Swedes.* Up to the period of the Civil War, the Swedish groups assimilated fast. They were small and scattered, and their clergymen-leaders were apparently eager for rapid Americanization. T. N. Hasselquist, a clergyman educated in Sweden, wished that his flock might become good Americans, though he also expressed the hope that they would not lose certain desirable national characteristics such as "honesty, industry, and ideals of democracy."[57] This advice was the more remarkable in that Hasselquist's experience would have been largely in parochial schools. Compulsory public schools had been established in Sweden only in 1842. Consequently, the early Swedish immigrants to this country would have known church-related rather than secular institutions. Furthermore, because there also existed a state church, the public schools of Sweden would have been religiously oriented—aiming to prepare Lutherans rather than Swedes.[58]

Swedish immigrants in the early period proved themselves to be strong supporters of the separation of church and state. They began to participate, almost on their arrival, in public school activities. Educational efforts in support of their church were directed largely at colleges for training ministers, and only incidentally at the establishment of academies. In 1851 the Lutheran Synod of Northern Illinois set up an academy and seminary at Springfield. It was to serve Germans and Scandinavians. But the latter outnumbered the others, and so they appealed to the king of Norway and Sweden to take up a collection in behalf of the new institution. The king refused the request, and the Crimean War prevented a personal solicitation from a Scandinavian American. In 1856 the Rev. Olof Christian Telemak Andren was sent to Sweden to make a collection. After his return, the new college was moved to Paxton. At first, instruction was in Swedish, but there were not enough Swedes to maintain the language. Since 1890 all instruction, except for classes in Swedish and special classes in the seminary, have been in English. Augustana College has since been moved to a site between Moline and Rock Island, and the college and seminary

[57] Fritiof Ander, "Some Factors in the Americanization of the Swedish Immigrant, 1850–1890," *Journal of the Illinois State Historical Society*, vol. 26, nos. 1 and 2, p. 139, April and July, 1933.

[58] Adolph B. Benson and Naboth Hedin, *Americans from Sweden*, J. B. Lippincott Company, Philadelphia, Pa., 1950, p. 229.

have been separated. Benson and Hedin declare that, for a denominational college, Augustana has given rather considerable attention to science. Anton J. Carlson, the physiologist, is numbered among her graduates.[59]

The early Swedes had moved into the larger American culture very rapidly. But church, press, and immigrants combined to turn the tide of sentiment toward Swedishness. Figures for church membership in the Augustana Synod, the largest Swedish-immigrant church in America, will indicate the significant change in the size of the Swedish population. In 1860, the year of the organization of the church, there were 3,000 members; by 1926, there were 311,000.[60]

The church placed no particular emphasis on Swedish. Services were occasionally in English and the Sunday school was always conducted in English. The ground swell of Swedes was such that by the 1880s the same Hasselquist who had pleaded for rapid Americanization was urging that children be taught Swedish.[61] The drive to retain the language, however, was never strong. Neither was the urge to develop parochial schools and colleges. Swedish Lutherans have established Gustavus Adolphus College in St. Peter, Minnesota, and Bethany College, in Lindsborg, Kansas; Luther College in Wahoo, Nebraska, and Upsala College in East Orange, New Jersey. Swedish Mission Friends founded the institution later known as North Park College in Chicago. An occasional academy has also owed its origin to Swedish Americans.[62] In 1950 the only educational institutions still actively supported by Americans of Swedish descent were four colleges, two junior colleges, two seminaries, and one academy.[63]

Although Swedish groups have been deeply devoted to their churches and Sunday schools, they have been sceptical of parochial schools which, they feel, smack of Catholicism and which they have also considered un-American. Furthermore, their children preferred the public schools.[64] Swedes quickly moved into Process 2, in which public rather than private schools made accommodations to them—though so closely were they identified with the traditions of the Anglo-American culture that accommodations were few and minor in importance. The Swedes as rapidly moved into Process 3, in which, through higher educational institutions and their commitment to gymnastics, they have made a modest impact on educational patterns in the United States.

[59] Ibid., pp. 233–238.
[60] Ander, op. cit., p. 138.
[61] Ibid., pp. 140–141.
[62] Benson and Hedin, op. cit., pp. 239, 244, 251, 255.
[63] Brown and Roucek, Our Racial and National Minorities, p. 76.
[64] Ander, op. cit., p. 142.

*The Norwegians.* One of the arguments liberal Norwegians used against parochial schools of a Norwegian-Lutheran cast was their parallel with Catholic practice. But this introduction only hints at the acrimonious debate which went on in the Norwegian-American settlements in the period roughly from 1860 to 1890.

It would perhaps be more precise to say that the debate went on between the most conservative clergy on the one hand, and the more liberal journalists and clergy on the other. Though the Norwegians at large were a churchgoing population, there is some evidence that they ignored their clergy's requests for parochial schools as a reinforcement of the church and, instead, patronized the public schools. Their record in supporting a private parochial school system would indicate only token support for church schools. "The Norwegians in America have at various times founded, maintained, and lost almost every kind of school."[65]

Among the migrants of the 1830s and 1840s, there appeared to be little feeling for a parochial establishment which would be both a religious and a civic enterprise.[66] Norwegians in Wisconsin sent their youngsters to the district schools on weekdays and to Lutheran schools on Sundays. During the 1840s, pastors from Norway visited the Wisconsin settlements and some expressed themselves as appalled at the spiritual and academic ignorance of Norwegian Americans. District schools were poorly supported, often having only three-month terms and meagerly educated teachers. Buildings were indifferently kept. These schools, so said the pastors, were in no condition to contribute to the development of Norwegian-American children. Furthermore, the second generation might be weaned from the Norwegian-American community and church if more were not done to train them in proper religious habits. Parochial schools which gave the common branches plus religious and language training were the answer. But the sound and fury of clergymen did not dictate the answer of parents, many of whom continued to send their children to rural and town public schools.

The battle was opened in earnest in the 1850s when the Norwegian synod members made contact with the German Missouri Synod, which was committed to a parochial school establishment. In 1858 in Rock Prairie and at the instigation of A. C. Preus, eleven ministers and seventeen parochial schoolteachers combined to endorse the development of a parochial school plant which would supplant the public school system. This innocent act was the one which precipitated the battle.

[65] Brown and Roucek, *Our Racial and National Minorities*, p. 69.

[66] Facts in the account to follow are taken largely from Theodore C. Blegen, *Norwegian Migration to America*, vol. II, *The American Transition*, The Norwegian-American Historical Association, Northfield, Minn., 1940. See particularly Chapter VIII.

The opening gun of the opposition was fired by a Danish-born and Danish-educated schoolmaster, Rasmus Sörensen, of Wisconsin. The core of Sörensen's argument was a strong America. If each religious and national group in the United States attempted to enforce its home language and isolate its children, the United States would be a battleground of national and religious wars. To prevent this disastrous occurrence, Norwegian Americans should send their children to the free public schools, which would teach them loyalty to their real fatherland. If the public schools were not adequate, Norwegian Americans should watch over and nurture them. Sörensen went so far as to say that in the churches, Norwegian services should be reserved for the elderly and the new immigrants, and that young congregations should have their sermons in the English language.

The onset of the Civil War softened the replies, but immediately thereafter the fight broke out into the open when a strong statement in support of parochial schools was presented in a synod meeting in 1866 at Manitowoc, Wisconsin. From 1866 until the early 1880s, the battle raged in Scandinavian-language newspapers, from the pulpit, in synod and congregational meetings, and probably throughout Minnesota and Wisconsin as well as other Middle Western states where there were large congregations of Norwegian Americans.

The sharpness and intensity of the arguments varied with the skill of the debaters. Leaders of the conservative factions, who were ordinarily clergymen, tended to support the following stands. They had no quarrel with civic education or education for American citizenship—with this they were in general agreement. Rather, they objected to the heathen, godless, or religion-less public schools. In American institutions of higher education, the characteristic of godlessness was even more ingrained, in that these establishments were currently promoting the teaching of science, the natural enemy of religion. By their very nature, these institutions could not educate Christians. Particularly could they not educate Lutherans, since they might be staffed by teachers who were Catholics, Methodists, or atheists. The general worthlessness of the public schools was well known. Their teachers were poorly trained and paid; buildings were inadequate, often being some farmer's house or loft; and school terms (three months) were too short. The answer must be a parochial school taught largely in Norwegian, the language of the heart, but with instruction also in English and incorporating the common school branches as well as religion. Similarly, there must be religious academies and colleges for the training of ministers and leaders in the Norwegian-American communities.

The liberal position was equally clear-cut. It was outlined largely by professors who were often from Scandinavian colleges, journalists, and liberal ministers. To these inspired leaders, the public school was the tool by which Norwegian Americans might be incorporated into the life and times of their country and generation; and by means of it they would learn to be not an isolated, superstitious, and ignorant ethnic group, but a vital part of a larger developing and dynamic free society. Parochial schools were doomed not only because they were narrowly provincial, but because they could never be adequately financed. It was the better part of wisdom for Norwegian Americans to use their energies to improve their public schools; and these leaders urged them to sit on school boards, often setting them an example by serving in that capacity. For the religious training of their young, Norwegians could support two-month schools.

Furthermore, these liberals charged, Norwegian-American youth should attend their own colleges to learn Norwegian, but American colleges and universities to learn English and American ways. Science, which had found its way into the latter establishments, was completely compatible with religion. So fervent did these defenders of American institutions become that they charged conservatives with being enemies of liberty and progress and equated opposition to American public education with treason.

In general, the population supported the liberal position by action. Though an occasional parochial elementary school or academy would gain support, the majority was strengthened by action of legislators and school officials. To be sure, H. B. Wilson, superintendent of schools in Minnesota in 1869, charged parochial schools with subverting children and winning them to a foreign language, a foreign sentiment, and to foreign institutions. But through the auspices of Knute Nelson, the Wisconsin Legislature passed a law that Norwegian might be taught for one hour a day in the common public schools. School authorities made it quite plain that they were happy to employ qualified Scandinavian-American teachers in the high schools. Norwegian and Swedish took their place alongside other modern languages as subjects in the high school curriculum in states such as Minnesota. The adaptations of the schools and the adaptability of the immigrant population combined to settle the school issue in large measure in terms of support for publicly supported educational establishments.

## The Czechs

It was reported in 1928 that there were 161 pupils in Illinois and 24 in Nebraska who were enrolled in Czech-language classes in public high schools. In the same year 135 students were enrolled in Czech classes in private high schools.[67] As of 1950, it was claimed that the

[67] Carleton A. Wheeler (comp. with others), *Enrollment in the Foreign Languages in Secondary Schools and Colleges of the United States,* The Macmillan Company,

Czech language was being taught increasingly in public high schools in Chicago and Cicero, Illinois, and in Texas.[68]  These figures may serve as introduction to an ethnic group which has been small in numbers yet persistent in maintaining ethnic links, and strong in educational drive. The links have been maintained in both private and public schools. Approximately 50 per cent of the Czech groups are Roman Catholic,[69] though not all Catholic Czech youngsters have attended or do attend Catholic schools.  It was probably largely a Catholic group, however, which opened the first Czech-language school in Milwaukee on June 22, 1862.  This is credited to the Slovánska Lípa Society.  The same school was reported as meeting on July 24, 1864, in rooms of the St. Joseph Church.  After hearing mass, youngsters received instruction in spelling, reading, and arithmetic.  In the fall of 1864, another school was organized in the Slovánska Lípa Hall in Chicago.  This was a language school designed to supplement public or parochial instruction; lessons in Czech were given for youngsters every Saturday from 10 A.M. to 2 P.M., and for adults, every Sunday at 1 P.M.[70]

In 1881 members of Slovan Americký began calling for a Czech college in the Middle West.  A society to found a college was incorporated in Johnson County, Iowa, and set out to raise funds.  The drive was unsuccessful, but the Benedictines of Lisle (Du Page County, Illinois) opened a Czech-Slavic higher-education institution in Chicago in 1887.  This institution, which was described in 1950 as being administered by the Czech Benedictines of Chicago,[71] moved to Lisle in 1901.  It is called St. Procopius College and is known as the only higher-education institution of Czech origin in the United States.[72]

While some movement was going on in the field of higher education, part-time language schools were being founded in communities with Czech populations.  In 1915 it was reported that in the period 1910 to 1915, Czechs had supported sixty-nine schools with an enrollment of 5,292 children.  These schools were supported by the liberal Czechs only as supplements to the public schools to which they sent their children.  Instruction, said they, must be confined to afterschool hours.  By 1920, 7,500 to 8,000 youngsters were enrolled in the "liberal" schools.

New York, 1928, pp. 363, 378.  Compiled for the Modern Foreign Language Study with the cooperation of the Bureau of Education and with introduction and analysis by Robert Herndon Fife.

[68] Brown and Roucek, *Our Racial and National Minorities*, p. 163.
[69] *Ibid.*
[70] Thomas Capek, *The Czechs (Bohemians) in America: A Study of Their National, Cultural, Political, Social, Economic and Religious Life*, Houghton Mifflin Company, Boston, 1920, p. 241.
[71] Brown and Roucek, *Our Racial and National Minorities, loc. cit.*
[72] Capek, *op. cit.*, pp. 242–243.

In Chicago and suburbs alone, there was an enrollment of 1,340. New York language schools enrolled 800, and those in Cleveland, 700.[73]

As of 1950, over 100 Catholic Czech parishes were supporting parochial schools located largely in Texas, Illinois, and Ohio. Some of these parishes had also two-year commercial schools of junior or senior high school grade. The Benedictine order which maintains St. Procopius was also staffing three academies located in Chicago, Illinois, Omaha, Nebraska, and Shiner, Texas.[74]

The efforts of Czechs to maintain a language-culture link with their past have not been confined to opening their own schools. They have successfully petitioned American institutions of higher education, in addition to high schools, to make culture adaptations. At the instigation of the American (Congregational) Home Missionary Society, Oberlin College in 1885 organized a theological seminary in connection with the Slavic department. A special fund, set up in 1905, provided for about ten scholarships for the education of Czech-speaking clergymen. The Rev. J. Prücha of Cleveland believed that Oberlin College was the first American higher-education institution to offer instruction in Czech.[75] The University of Houston, however, is reported as having opened a Czech and Slavic department in 1848[76] and the University of California was offering Czech instruction in 1901. Since that date, others have followed. Among the universities are Columbia, Wisconsin, Ohio State, Chicago, Texas, Nebraska, and briefly (1913–1915) the State University of Iowa; and among the colleges, Coe, Dubuque, and Seminary.[77]

Czechs are at the midway point. They support parochial schools making special accommodations, yet are also strong supporters of public schools. Accommodations to their language-culture interests are still in effect in public schools and in American institutions of higher education. Incidentally, radio stations in the Chicago area regularly broadcast announcements and programs in the Czech language. The link, perhaps, never really breaks, and possibly this one will remain firm and strong for some years to come.

*The Italians*

Italy has contributed more immigrants to America than any other country except Germany. From 1820 to 1950, 4,776,884 Italians came to this country. As the heavy influx in this group has been recent, one

---

[73] *Ibid.*, p. 243.
[74] Brown and Roucek, *Our Racial and National Minorities, loc. cit.*
[75] Capek, *op. cit.*, p. 242.
[76] Brown and Roucek, *Our Racial and National Minorities, loc. cit.*
[77] Capek, *op. cit.*, pp. 242–244.

person in eight of the total foreign-born population in 1950 was Italian. The social disorganization in this group can be inferred from the fact that 66 per cent were agricultural workers in their own country, whereas in 1940 in this country, 88.5 per cent were urban; 9.4 per cent, rural nonfarm; and only 2.6 per cent were farm people.[78]

Early migrants were scattered. Their efforts went into promoting the study and enjoyment of music and the incidental pursuit of their language. Just after 1800, Filippo Traetta founded the first conservatory of music. In 1833 an Italian opera house was opened in New York City and soon became much like other national institutions, with the unrevealing name of Academy of Music. In New Haven, Richard Mezzotero, a language instructor, was active in the campaign to get city grammar schools to offer the Italian language. Italian musicians and singers who came to the cities in the early 1800s gave lessons in Italian and French.[79]

These scattered efforts, mostly individual and incidental in nature, were succeeded in the late 1800s and the early 1900s by concerted efforts of the rapidly expanding peasant migration to resist assimilation. The response was strengthened by the inadequacy of public schools in urban centers. Before World War I, public schools could not take all new children of Italian origin, but parochial schools could and did. Officials of the church imported teachers who could speak both English and Italian from among the Jesuits, Franciscans, and Ursulines.[80] The problem of public school accommodation may well have been aggravated by the nature of the population. In the years from 1899 to 1910, the highest illiteracy rate among immigrants was to be found in the South Italian group, where it was 53.9 per cent; though among North Italians it was only 11.5 per cent. The assimilative process must also have been stalemated in that many Italian migrants never apparently intended to remain, for some 30 per cent returned to Italy.[81]

Italians have continued to fight for preservation of their language by sending children to parochial schools or asking that Italian be taught in public high schools. In the meantime, individuals in the ethnic group have worked for some kind of accommodation to the American culture. Private welfare agencies, such as the Society for Italian Immigrants, and occasionally labor unions have set up schools at labor camps to teach English. These efforts have been largely superseded by immi-

[78] Brown and Roucek, *Our Racial and National Minorities,* pp. 244, 248.

[79] Lawrence Frank Pisani, *The Italian in America: A Social Study and History,* Exposition Press, New York, 1957, pp. 36–37, 709.

[80] *Ibid.,* p. 170.

[81] John H. Mariano, *The Italian Contribution to American Democracy,* The Christopher Publishing House, Boston, 1921, p. 65.

grant education (Americanization) supported by local and state school systems.[82]   Italians, too, are at a halfway station, having already made some impact on American education while still preserving some of their own culture, largely in the parochial establishments.

## The Japanese

The impact of the Japanese on American educational patterns will be spelled out in some detail in Chapter 14, which deals with educational development in Hawaii.   It is enough to note here the appearance of the same language-school patterns on the mainland as in Hawaii.

Language as a core for schooling was a two-way process among the Japanese in the early 1900s.   In 1909 in San Francisco, there were fifteen schools in which Japanese were being taught English.   Of these, five were conducted by Christian missions, five by American women, and five by men and women of Japanese origin.   On a Saturday morning when an observer attended one of the schools, the discussion topic was the landing of Columbus.[83]   These were the schools which were established to bridge the gap for Japanese between their own culture and that of the United States.   But the link was also being made with Japan.

Japanese-language schools had early been established in California. An investigation of two of them was undertaken in Southern California in about 1932.   The report concluded with the statement that, though the schools were Japanese-oriented, they certainly were not fostering un-Americanism as charged.[84]   The purpose of these two schools was to teach the language as well as the traditions and history of Japan.   Each was meeting six hours a week after public school hours.   In accordance with state laws respecting teachers, one of the latter had a master of science degree from the University of Southern California and the other had studied in an American university.

Activities of youngsters in these schools included writing, reading, memorizing, taking dictation, and translating from Japanese to English and vice versa.   Report cards issued after each three-month period showed marks in honesty, truthfulness, morality, and progress, as well as in formal school activities such as singing, spelling, and history. Schools were under the supervision of the Japanese School Organization of Southern California, but were financially independent.   Tuition was

[82] Pisani, *op. cit.*, p. 94.

[83] Yamato Ichihashi, *Japanese in the United States: A Critical Study of the Problems of the Japanese Immigrants and Their Children,* Stanford University Press, Stanford, Calif., 1932, pp. 213–214.

[84] Marian Svensrud, "Attitudes of the Japanese towards Their Language Schools," *Sociology and Social Research,* vol. 17, no. 3, pp. 259–261, January–February, 1933.

supplemented by special gifts of community members when there was a death or birth in the family, or when parents returned to Japan.[85]

Japanese schools have not always been given such a clean bill of health. The first strong drive for Japanese-language schools was made when the Nisei (American-born of Japanese descent) came home from World War I speaking English. The Issei (Americans of Japanese birth) established Japanese-language schools (*Gakuen*) where instruction was given in language, religion, morality, and the general Japanese viewpoint. Youngsters were taught both loyalty to Japan and emperor worship, according to one author.[86] According to another, steps had been taken to restrict these schools to the teaching of language only. As early as 1913, according to Reginald Bell, the Japanese Education Association of America had described the goal of the schools as being in the spirit of public school instruction. Students were being brought up to live and die in America; they must not be alienated from their native country. The association again in 1918 stated that texts must be in the American spirit; the schools were to teach language only and to send youngsters to public schools for other teaching.[87]

The argument for the language schools had been sound, according to one commentator. Unless youngsters could speak the language of their parents, they would be alienated from mother and father, and the family unit would be dissolved. Kiichi Kauzaki, secretary of the Japanese Association of America, had testified that the schools were temporary institutions and only a social experiment.[88]

Schools multiplied rapidly. From a beginning of one school in California in 1911, the number jumped to 118 in 1928. They ranged from kindergarten through high school grades. The official report on them in 1933 showed 220.[89] By 1939 the schools in California were costing about $398,000 annually and were being subsidized by the Tokyo government and employing Buddhist teachers. By 1941 there were 248 of these schools in California alone. They enrolled some 18,000 children in hours after public-school closing. With the coming of World War II and the relocation of people of Japanese descent, the schools were closed and probably have not returned, at least in strength. As in Hawaii, one other move to retain links was made by Japanese-born parents. They sent their American-born children to Japan to be

[85] *Ibid.,* pp. 260–263.

[86] Brown and Roucek, *Our Racial and National Minorities,* p. 328.

[87] Reginald Bell, *Public School Education of Second-generation Japanese in California,* Stanford University Press, Stanford, Calif., 1935, pp. 21–24.

[88] *Ibid.,* pp. 21, 25; also Kiichi Kauzaki, "Is the Japanese Menace in America a Reality?" *The Annals of the American Academy of Political and Social Science,* vol. 93, pp. 88–97, January, 1921.

[89] Bell, *op. cit.,* p. 20.

educated. In 1942 it was estimated that 25,000 United States citizens (born in the United States) had been educated in Japan.[90]

Although the separation between the Japanese and the American cultures was undoubtedly a factor in the drive for language-tradition links, public school policy was probably also of influence in alienating the Japanese-born from the main American culture stream—thus inadvertently reinforcing Japanese interest in foreign institutions. Public school policy reflected a generalized anti-Oriental prejudice which stemmed back to the middle of the nineteenth century. In 1852, Governor John Gegler had addressed himself to the menace of Chinese labor to white workers. In 1871 there was violence and a massacre of Chinese in Los Angeles. An outgrowth of these difficulties was a new United States treaty which instituted some control over the importation of Chinese labor.[91]

Public school practices had reflected anti-Chinese agitation as early as 1859, when a school for Chinese only had opened. This had followed on the opening of one for colored children in 1854. The state superintendent in 1866 secured an amendment to school law, making separate schools legal. In 1885 the School Board of the City and County of San Francisco excluded Chinese youngsters from white schools. But through a court case, the board was compelled to admit one girl of Chinese origin.[92]

In 1885 the school law was again amended to allow for establishing separate schools for Mongolians or Chinese. A Chinese primary school was opened the same year in San Francisco. When it was reopened in 1906 after the earthquake and fire, it was called the Oriental School.

Antagonism focusing on Orientals now shifted from the Chinese to the Japanese.[93] In October, 1906, the board of education ordered that practically all youngsters of Japanese descent be transferred to the Oriental School, which was remote from the residental area of the Japanese colony.[94] In ordering the transfer, reference was made to the contamination suffered by white boys and girls from contact with children of "less moral race," a charge which would have been enhanced by the fact that the Oriental youngsters were somewhat older than white youngsters of the same school grade.[95]

[90] Brown and Roucek, *Our Racial and National Minorities,* loc. cit.
[91] Bell, *op. cit.,* pp. 8–9.
[92] *Ibid.,* pp. 8–11.
[93] *Ibid.,* p. 11.
[94] Brown and Roucek, *Our Racial and National Minorities,* p. 320; see also Bell, *op. cit.,* p. 12.
[95] Donald Young, *American Minority Peoples: A Study in Racial and Cultural Conflicts in the United States,* Harper & Brothers, New York, 1932, p. 474.

Acts of violence against the Japanese, stimulated and condoned by Mayor Eugene E. Schmitz, resulted in representation by Japan. President Theodore Roosevelt, who was apprehensive of the strained relations between Japan and the United States, called Mayor Schmitz and members of the school board to Washington. When the school board rescinded its action, representatives of the Federal government dropped suits to test the constitutionality of the California school law. At the same time, the Federal government agreed to prevent Japanese laborers from entering the United States through Hawaii, Mexico, and Canada.[96]

Schools for Orientals continued to be conducted in California as well as in Oregon and Washington. Some of them, of course, were not planned as segregated schools, but resulted in segregation because of the concentration of Orientals in particular areas of the states and the cities.[97] It must be asked, however, whether housing laws or real estate practice did not create the isolated neighborhoods. Thus social policy of several kinds may actually have retarded assimilation and helped to enforce an exaggerated and persistent foreign-oriented schooling.

Without World War II and the subsequent actions taken to stamp out the Japanese culture in America, the ties might have died of disuse. American-born youngsters of Japanese descent, like their counterparts in Hawaii, resisted the language schools.[98] Coupled with this resistance, which represented a drive to be American, was change in religious affiliation on the part of the American-born Japanese. The Issei are usually Buddhists; the Nisei, Christians.[99] These new Americans probably would have settled their own fate without the restrictive measures taken against them in World War II. They show every evidence of driving toward the norm of the upward-striving, Protestant, middle-class culture. One deep-seated inheritance, however, is still theirs. Despite the vicissitudes of the Japanese groups in the United States, ties of family, if not of country, have remained strong and firm. Oriental family sewing customs, for instance, are still a controlling factor in the clothing interests and practices of Hawaiian youth.[100] The juvenile delinquency rate among youngsters of Oriental background is still one of the lowest in the nation, a tribute to family influence.

---

[96] Brown and Roucek, *Our Racial and National Minorities*, p. 321.

[97] Young, *op. cit.*, p. 475.

[98] Svensrud, *op. cit.*, p. 259.

[99] Brown and Roucek, *Our Racial and National Minorities*, p. 325.

[100] For a discussion of the relationship of national origins to clothing practices, see Elizabeth Ann Snoddy, "Clothing Interests and Practices of 4-H Girls in Hawaii," unpublished master's thesis, University of Maryland, College Park, Md., 1959.

PROCESS 3:
DIFFUSING CULTURES

There is a possibility that each new ethnic or minority population has contributed to the diversity and mutability of American education. There has been too little research in culture diffusion, however, to make many definitive statements. The descriptions to follow of groups that have made an impact on schooling practices concern the more obvious cases.

*The Germans*

To the New England group which set the pattern of education in America up to about 1850, health would have assumed some importance. Leaders of the New England group who spread the public school concepts through the Middle West would have been educated men to whom innoculation, temperate habits of eating, and prudence in all things related to individual well-being would have been no mystery. However, the way the goal of bodily vigor—as one aspect of health— would be reached in school was through manual labor. To the prudent writers of textbooks and to pedagogues who fostered schools and colleges, the way to keep body and soul together was through honest labor vigorously pursued. The way to health, wealth, and godliness was kept open through provisions for moral instruction and manual labor in colleges and academies which flourished in the period roughly from 1820 to 1860. That one should take exercise without any useful purpose except maintenance of health and happiness would probably have appeared frivolous to many of the New England educational campaigners.

Toward the last of the nineteenth century and into the twentieth, however, American public schools and private and public colleges began introducing regular instruction in physical education, which has since become one of the required subjects at all levels of the school system. The nature of this instruction and of appropriate activities has undergone metamorphosis, but commitment to the idea of recreational or physical activities has remained strong. That physical education now claims an important role in American education is credited in part to German Americans assisted by their Swedish brethren.

A core institution which Germans brought with them to this country and which put emphasis on physical education was the Turnverein, which was founded in 1849, one year after the unsuccessful revolution in Germany.[101] Although it came to light as a liberal, political-social organization, the seeds of it were sown in the last of the eighteenth cen-

[101] Cunz, *op. cit.,* pp. 248–249.

tury by Johann Guts Muths, a German teacher who opened a gymnasium on the Greek model and described his practices in a manual issued in 1793. Muth's efforts were supported by those of Friedrich Jahn "who combined the practice of physical training with the inculcation of ideals of a free and self-respecting citizenship." Jahn, who began his teaching in 1811, put stress on the well-rounded human being whose education, to be complete, must include physical training.[102]

The original purpose of the Turnverein was the cultivation in the German society of the rational being who subscribed to the ideals of the Republic and protected human liberty as it had been enthroned by representative government. The political aims of the society were canceled out when Germans found themselves a part of the American Republic, and, in 1872, the American executive committee stated that their organization had nothing in common with its German counterpart except physical training. Whatever political, religious, or social struggles German-American turners might participate in, said the committee, were purely local (American) concerns and could not, as a matter of fact, be understood in Germany.[103]

Although the society remained for German Americans a center of social, musical, theatrical, and political activity, the physical education aspect finally moved into the American educational enterprise through individual Germans and their organizational influence. Before the Turnverein had become formalized in Germany, Carl Follen, political refugee, taught German literature at Harvard and, in 1826, organized a gymnasium on the model of Jahn's earlier institution. Dr. J. C. Warner, a German professor in the Harvard Medical School, opened Tremont Gymnasium in Boston which, for lack of funds, died aborning. Another German, Dr. Carl Beck, became a Latin teacher in the Round Hill School, where he introduced a gymnasium.[104]

It was after 1850, when the German turner societies had organized as the American Gymnastic Association, that the influence of the physical training advocates became powerful. In illustration, Louis Hoffmann, a German-American turner, was elected to the Baltimore City Council and was successful in 1895 in securing an ordinance "to introduce physical training as a regular course of study in the public schools of the city."[105]

From about 1880, turners over the country were influential in introducing physical training into city school systems and into colleges and universities. In a report of 1898, Dr. Edward M. Hartwell, reporting

[102] Zucker, *op. cit.*, p. 79.
[103] *Ibid.*, pp. 93, 99.
[104] *Ibid.*, pp. 91–92.
[105] Cunz, *op. cit.*, p. 337.

to the U.S. Commissioner of Education, formally acknowledged the debt of American education to the turners. Prior to the work of the turners, said Dr. Hartwell, members of colleges and athletic organizations had not known the proportions of good physical training in elementary and secondary schools. In consequence, the work of turners had been "the more or less successful introduction of school gymnastics" into schools all over the country. Such geographically separated school systems as those in Chicago, Cincinnati, Denver, San Francisco, and St. Paul, as well as others, had adopted the "German free and light gymnastics." In New England cities as well, Swedish gymnastics had been introduced into public schools. Furthermore, directors of newly instituted departments of physical education were typically graduates of the "Seminary or Normal School of the North American Turnerbund."[106]

Though the gymnastics of the turners have gone through many transformations, including both recreational activities and spectator sports, the impetus to the latter movements and the secure place of recreation and physical education in American schools may have some relation to the absorption of one ethnic group into American society.

*The Amish*

The Germans who introduced physical education into American schools and colleges might be said to be the Old World—but in and of the New World. The Amish, who have striven to remain isolated from the dominant culture, might be said to be the Old World—in but not of the New World. The Amish record of culture persistence is remarkable in that the group probably came to Pennsylvania and to Berks County as early as 1714, at the invitation of Penn.[107] By that time, they had already become a group apart from the Mennonites, with whom they had originally been identified. Their emergence as a separate subgroup had followed on a schism in 1697. Jacob Amman, a Swiss exile to Alsace, was responsible. He premised his disaffection from the main body of the church on the laxness with which church members applied *Meidung*, meaning avoidance of those expelled from the church. Today the Amish still adhere to all the doctrines of the main body of the Mennonites, but to these they add strict attention to *Meidung* and foot washing.

Schooling among the Amish is something rather different from school-

---

[106] Reported in Zucker, *op. cit.*, p. 109.

[107] There are many accounts of the Amish. However, because it summarizes materials pertinent to this discussion, a single source has been used for the facts in the account to follow: Sheldon Madeira, "A Study of the Education of the Old Order Amish Mennonites of Lancaster County, Penn.," unpublished doctoral dissertation, University of Pennsylvania, Philadelphia, 1955. (Microfilm.)

ing among other American groups. This may be a function both of the way in which the Amish view their children and their insistence on uniqueness. Children are not in any sense creatures of the state, but are entrusted to adults by God. It is the mission of the Amish to teach, and parents set aside time to instruct their youngsters, and do so informally at table as well. The role of the school in the educational process is to provide an occasion and a place for the young to learn to read, write, and cipher. That is all. Everything else is provided by the family and community.

The carefully patterned life in the Amish community must be an education in itself. The young are assigned chores when they are four years of age. At sixteen, a boy is given a horse, a harness, a wagon, and blankets, with which he is expected to go courting. The girl begins at age sixteen to fill her hope chest with linen, table cloths, and bed-spreads. She may marry a man many years her senior. At her marriage she is given a stove, utensils, and furnishings. Whenever there is question about the correctness of any practice, a decision is made by a member of the clergy "on the basis of what the practice has been for centuries."

Added to this carefully circumscribed and controlled community education system is the impact of the belief in uniqueness. The most often-quoted phrase in the Amish community is from Titus, according to Madeira: "and purify unto himself a peculiar people." Under stimulation of peculiarity as a *modus operandi*, pride and conformity become cardinal sins.

The urge to nonconformity has conditioned the way in which the Amish have reacted to formal schooling. They insist on sending their youngsters to one-room schools only. Their children must not be contaminated by contact with persons of another culture. When in July, 1937, 10 one-room schools in Amish areas were consolidated, the "peculiar people" opened parochial schools in five locations. County records show no Amish child as ever having been enrolled in high school, and Amish adults do not teach in public schools. County officials leave them much to themselves. They never visit schools enrolling Amish children and require only that English be used and that teachers be at least eighteen years of age. This group has been partly successful in resisting the inroads of the New World.

In case the reader has any doubts of the variability in American education, let him now take an imaginary journey via the persons of several school-age youngsters. Let him be first a boy in a flat hat with hooks and eyes on his clothes, droning out his numbers in a sleepy little room in Lancaster County, Pennsylvania. Then let him be a youth in sweater and sneakers, manipulating a complicated apparatus in a science high school in New York. Last, let him be a slant-eyed youth with a "butch" haircut, singing, "The Star-spangled Banner" in a schoolroom in Honolulu.

## The Mormons

It is difficult to say which or how many of the religio-economic experiments carried out in this country have contributed more than incidentally to the diversity and mutability of American education. Certainly, one of them did—the one which began with Joseph Smith, who was born in Vermont on December 23, 1805, and who saw visions which eventually would take his followers to the Mountain state they called Deseret, later to become Utah.

Utah, Joseph Smith's spiritual home, can boast of a unique place in American educational history. By its uniqueness, it has brought diversity to national uniformity in education. In each of the last several censuses, Utah has stood first among the states in level of schooling of those twenty-five years of age and over, its record being 12 grades in 1950 and that for the nation being 9.3. In a study of educational accomplishments completed in 1946, Utah's population was rated first in educational accomplishment, degree accomplished commensurate with ability, efficiency of effort, and interest in adult education.[108] A study of comparative enrollments in all institutions of higher learning as of 1949–1950 showed Utah highest, with 329 per 10,000 population; its nearest competitor was Colorado with 292; and the national average was 164. The enrollment of 329 per 10,000 is 9.6 per cent higher than the enrollment estimated for 1960 by the President's Commission on Higher Education. What is the occasion for this educational phenomenon in a state not heavily endowed with wealth and somewhat oversupplied with youngsters to be educated?

Some would claim that it results from the impact of the Latter-day Saints, whose founding father, Joseph Smith, was told by the Angel Moroni that he (Joseph) was to establish the true church based on the sacred record written on metal plates and hidden in the New York hills.

---

[108] The literature on Mormonism is legion. Because Ray L. DeBoer has addressed himself specifically to the question of influence on education, however, his study is used largely for facts for the account to follow including citations of other studies: "A Historical Study of Mormon Education and the Influence of Its Philosophy on Public Education in Utah," unpublished doctoral dissertation, University of Denver, Denver, Colo., 1951. For another account of education in Utah, see John Clifton Moffitt, *The History of Public Education in Utah*, Provo City Schools, Provo, Utah, 1946. For one account of Mormon beliefs, see LeGrand Richards, *A Marvelous Work and a Wonder*, Deseret Book Co., Salt Lake City, Utah, 1950. Note particularly portions of chap. 26 on education.

Following on the discovery of the records, the church was formally established in Fayette, New York, on Tuesday, April 6, 1830, with six members. Gathering followers as they went, the flock traveled first to Missouri and then to Nauvoo, Illinois, where they founded a city independent in educational, judicial, and military matters. They followed this founding with the establishment of the University of Nauvoo and the Nauvoo Legion. In 1844, they introduced polygamy, a practice which was to disrupt their fortunes until they gave it up in 1888.

The Saints fell on evil days. Joseph Smith and his brother Hyrum were shot by soldiers while they awaited trial. Brigham Young, just and harsh taskmaster, took over the leadership of the group. Forced on by unfavorable community opinion, the group finally made winter quarters in Omaha. In 1847 a few started off for Utah and, pushing handcarts, 4,000 crossed the plains between 1856 and 1860. By 1850 there were twenty-six towns with five valleys opened to settlement in their State of Deseret. In March of 1851 Deseret became officially the Territory of Utah; in 1896, it was incorporated as a state. In the 100-year period 1851 to 1951, the Saints increased from 20,000 to over 1 million. In 1900, 1 American in 300 was a Saint; in 1950, 1 in 135.

Of their four sacred books, the Mormons' *Doctrine and Covenants,* which was accepted by the General Assembly on August 17, 1835, has the most to say on education. This contains pieces of educational wisdom which parents are expected to teach their children. The keynote is: "The Glory of God is intelligence." The argument in explanation of this key phrase has many facets. It is a sin to be ignorant if a man can be knowledgeable. It is not enough to carry out church duties. God requires not only "obedience to His revealed will, but a searching after His purposes and plans." Whatever knowledge is obtained in this life will stand one in good stead in the next. A person will be badly off among the astute and evil beings of another world if he has not prepared himself to do battle with his wits. As a matter of fact, "it is impossible for a man to be saved in ignorance."

With this firm religious commitment to the ways of intelligence, the Mormons opened schools for adult members in Kirtland, Ohio, in 1832, and when Kirtland Temple was built in 1836, classrooms for adults were provided on the upper floors. On the way to Utah, Brigham Young issued an epistle calling for schools and a museum. The Mormons followed this epistle with the opening of a school only a few weeks after coming to Salt Lake Valley. By 1850, plans for schoolhouses in every ward were under way.

Laws of 1850 through 1854 provided for schools throughout the state. School trustees were to be elected by voters and were given power to assess and collect taxes. Mormon meetinghouses were turned into schools and the local members received taxes for schools. This situation ended in the courts with a ruling that Mormon school trustees could not collect taxes while buildings were church property. Many meetinghouses were then transferred to school trustees, with the latter maintaining schools heavily biased in favor of the religious teachings of the Latter-day Saints.

In 1887 Congress passed the Edmunds-Tucker Law "disincorporating" the church because of its stand on polygamy. By the same law, the Perpetual Emigrating Fund Company was dissolved, and the stipulation was made that proceeds from expropriated property be used for common schools. Members of the church felt that insult had been added to injury. Congress had refused aid for common schools and was now preempting church property for the purpose it had refused to honor. However, Mormons had no recourse. They renounced polygamy and in 1890, the Federal government returned church property.

The state constitution of 1896 included a plan for a complete system of schools, including kindergarten, common schools of primary and grammar grades, high schools, an agricultural college, and a university. In addition, it contained the phrase "and such other schools as the Legislature may establish," which made adequate provision for the addition of special institutions as need would dictate. Under this constitution has been developed the kind of school system which ensures the highest level of education in the United States.

Mormons supported the public school establishments but like many foreign groups in the first flush of immigration, they set up their own competing institutions (Process 1). They opened academies and some colleges. These were judged too expensive to run, however. By 1911, the church had turned over most of its academies to the state. As of 1950, it maintained only one secondary school, the Juarez Academy in a Mormon settlement in Mexico. The only elementary schools the church maintains are also in this same community. In the 1930s the church members gave three junior colleges having a book value of $824,278 to the Utah State Board of Education, with the proviso that the board operate educational institutions in the locations of the colleges. The Legislature thereupon created junior colleges to be run under the jurisdiction of the state board. These gifts with strings might be considered a concession to a minority group (Process 2) and an impact of a minority group on American education (Process 3).

In the meantime, Process 2 began to operate in Utah in a unique way. Although for some time after 1896 the teaching of religion continued to be an issue in Utah public education, it became increasingly clear that the schools were to be secular. Any accommodation made by public education to the Mormons had to be within a nonsectarian framework. This was a complicated problem unlike such a simple matter as teaching a foreign language. A simple accommodation had been made in early Mormon-controlled schools. The Deseret alphabet had been introduced in hopes of keeping gentiles out of the state. But this move had come to naught.

What kind of accommodation could be made to this minority group, which was a majority in Utah? With the closing of their own elementary and secondary institutions, Mormons set up religious institutions adjacent to but separate from public and private educational institutions. As of about 1948 or 1950, in six states and the province of Alberta, they were supporting 100 seminaries which were in the vicinity of secondary schools. Junior seminaries were begun in 1929. High school students either on released time or after school were attending these seminaries for religious instruction. On the same plan, fifteen institutes of religion had been established adjacent to college and university campuses in five states. As of 1948, the church was employing 450 teachers on full-time salary, and serving approximately 37,000 students.

Educational efforts of Mormons did not stop with religious institutions adjacent to non-Mormon establishments. Though they maintain no elementary or secondary institutions in the United States, they do maintain post secondary institutions, including Brigham Young University, Ricks College in Rexburg, Idaho, and the Latter-day Saints Business College in Salt Lake City.

What accommodations have been made to this minority-majority group, and what impact has it had on public or private education? With the help of DeBoer's summary, plus review of facts already put in evidence, Processes 2 and 3 can be described in brief.

First, Utah has the highest amount of released time for religious instruction of any public school system in the United States. The commissioner of the Latter-day Saints schools estimated in 1951 that 57.4 per cent of Utah high school students attend the seminaries. Private and public colleges and universities in Utah accept one-half unit of credit for each of two courses taught in these seminaries: Old Testament and New Testament. Religious teachers are required to hold high school teaching certificates so that higher education institutions may make this accommodation. Accommodations to a dominant religious group by schools and colleges may be said to illustrate Process 2 in action.

Secondarily, Mormons have made a concerted impact in many ways on the public school establishment. Besides the outright gift of school plants to the state school system, they have contributed as lay board members, interested citizens, and teachers. Through persistent campaigning by a prominent Mormon, a law was passed in 1919 requiring compulsory school attendance of a minor between the ages of eight and eighteen. All except one of the state superintendents of public instruction since statehood (1896) and up to 1950–1951 have been Mormons. There was one exception, but he held office for only four months. Under the guidance of these Mormon incumbents, a state equalization plan has been set up. This includes a classroom unit as a measuring stick by which the local base levy can be adjusted each year; the state can make up the difference between proceeds in a local district and the amount necessary to provide a minimum school program. This has resulted in a minimal difference between support for rural and urban classrooms and has moved Utah forward in providing equality of opportunity for all children and youth.

The high priority put on education has conditioned Mormons as individuals to give service as educators. The Department of Commerce reported that, as of 1950, 68.8 per cent of the people of Utah were church members. Yet a 1950 survey showed 603 non-Mormons and 3,887 Mormon teachers and administrators in elementary through senior high schools: Mormons comprise 86.6 per cent of all professional educators. In Process 3 the Latter-day Saints have made a considerable contribution to the diversity of the American educational enterprise. In a relatively poor state, they have raised up a formidable educational system. "The Glory of God is intelligence."

## Foreign Nationals and Language

In recent years there has been a revival of interest in the study of modern foreign languages. The revival has been manifest in the introduction of foreign-language teaching in elementary as well as secondary schools, and the introduction of additional languages for study at the secondary and college levels. Since American education supposedly has deep roots in Europe, where foreign-language study is preeminent, the question arises: Why does foreign-language study need to be revived in the United States?

One simple explanation lies in the nature of the nation's original political society, something new under the sun—a society which, together with George Washington rejected the tyrannical ways of the old society. Early Americans often took seriously and continued to take seriously the admonitions of their first President to stay out of the bickerings and entanglements of a caste-ridden and degenerate Europe. Since that time, after each unfortunate entanglement in foreign affairs, Americans have been anxious to turn their backs on trials and intrigues so foreign, they believed, to their method of operation.

This reluctance to become entangled has conditioned Americans to think of language study as a kind of commitment to alien ways and aspirations. This viewpoint, coupled with the assault by many nationals, each arguing for his own tongue, has given rise to a concept of language study which is peculiar to America and foreign to European scholars.

To European teachers, knowledge of a foreign language is control of a tool needed for trade and scholarly research. Nothing can more aptly illustrate this generalization than the contrasting attitudes of England and France, on the one hand, and the United States, on the other, in respect to the study of German in World War I. Among the Allies, German instruction proceeded as in prewar days, with hardly a thought given to its inclusion in the curriculum. Few questions were raised as to a mysterious entanglement of alien thought with the study of the language of an enemy.[109]

To Americans German was a symbol of an alien culture, a militarism which Americans needed to defeat to save the world for democracy. It was the language of a people threatening America and could well be a medium for the introduction of alien ways into American democracy, for the United States had many citizens who were of recent German origin. So German classes suffered a large drop in enrollments, German books were burned, teachers of German lost their jobs. German was a symbol of cultures which had for years been trying to overrun the American culture, and the response to teaching it was indicative of the precariousness of the Great Experiment as it attempted to work out its destiny in the face of a gigantic assimilative task.

The American's view of foreign-language study has always been conditioned by what he considers the general welfare of his republican government. In the early days of the newly independent Republic, for example, officials of Brown University (then Rhode Island College) asked help of Louis XVI of France in procuring a professor of French. They wished, so they said, to know more of a people whom they admired.[110] This was in 1784, the heyday of national admiration for the French—after all, the French had partially financed the first two years of the American Revolution and had contributed officers and supplies to the American Army.

Other former colonial colleges, including Yale and Columbia, followed the lead of Brown University. But the national commitment to the French soon died and the war was quickly forgotten. A few institutions, such as Vincennes and Indiana universities, indicated they would offer French as soon as funds allowed. Yale and Columbia, along with the University of North Carolina, discontinued French study. In the last institution, a state-wide reaction to French infidelity, resulting from

---

[109] Wallace Henry Moore, "The Conflict Concerning the German Language and German Propaganda in the Public Secondary Schools of the United States, 1917–1919," unpublished doctoral dissertation, Stanford University, Stanford, Calif., 1937.

[110] Handschin, *op. cit.*, p. 18.

"the teachings of Voltaire, Paine, and Volney," was charged. French instruction in colleges and universities returned only incidentally until it was stimulated by the founding in 1883 of Alliance Française, an organization dedicated to improving French relations with other countries.[111] The varied fortunes of French-language teaching have been a result partly of the national commitments as Americans have seen them, though some impetus to the tool concept has motivated the wide-scale teaching of French in the twentieth century.

A second illustration of national involvement, concerning teaching of German, has already been mentioned. The violent reaction against the study of German during and following World War I is shown in Table 10-3, which gives numbers and per cent of youngsters enrolled in three modern languages in selected years. Note the drop from 24.38 per cent to .65 per cent from 1915 to 1922, and note that the study of German had not come back substantially even by 1928. French and Spanish seem to have absorbed some of those formerly studying German, but in percentage terms, enrollments in the three basic modern languages dropped from 35.57 per cent in 1915 to 25.30 per cent in 1928. This was partly a reflection of the change in high school population; partly also, it was a generalized reaction against things foreign following World War I.

As intriguing as this violent reaction against the language of an enemy is the source of the reaction. It becomes increasingly clear that the reaction did not result from either evil or patriotic designs of educators, but from the mandates of lay bodies controlling schools and from the influence of citizens at large.

Educators were of several minds.[112] Such a distinguished person as U.S. Commissioner Claxton early reminded the people that there were two tasks to perform: to win the war for freedom and democracy, and to prepare children for life and citizenship. In this second task, German apparently had a role to play in promoting commercial, scientific, and intellectual endeavors. It was charged that school principals in California influenced the state board to mandate, in 1918, against the teaching of German, but there is evidence to support the contention that community members influenced principals to take the action they did. College professors and presidents as well as secondary school people urged caution in dismissing German from the schools, while others demanded its removal.

The main objection to teaching German appeared to be that the language was a medium for the dissemination of German propaganda.

[111] *Ibid.*, pp. 19–20.
[112] The account to follow is based on Moore, *op. cit.*, which provides a handy reference to the leading facts in the German language controversy.

Table 10-3. Public High School Students Studying Selected Foreign Languages (1890–1928)

| Language | 1890 | | 1910* | | 1915* | | 1922 | | 1928 | |
|---|---|---|---|---|---|---|---|---|---|---|
| | No. | Per cent | No. | Per cent | No. | Per cent | No. | Per cent | No. | Per cent |
| French.......... | 11,858 | 5.84 | 73,161 | 9.9 | 102,516 | 8.8 | 333,612 | 15.46 | 402,012 | 14.02 |
| German.......... | 21,338 | 10.51 | 175,083 | 23.69 | 284,294 | 24.39 | 13,918 | .65 | 53,250 | 1.84 |
| Spanish.......... | ...... | ...... | 4,920 | .67 | 31,743 | 2.39 | 242,715 | 11.26 | 273,564 | 9.44 |

* Figures for 1910 and 1915 based on number of students in schools reporting language study; those for 1890, on total number of students.

SOURCE: Wallace Henry Moore, "The Conflict Concerning the German Language and German Propaganda in the Public Secondary Schools of the United States, 1917–1919," unpublished doctoral dissertation, Stanford University, Stanford, Calif., 1937, p. 2. Some of figures, in turn, secured from reports of the U.S. Office of Education.

At the height of the war, 1918, the *Readers Guide* listed no fewer than twenty-two articles on the language and twenty-three on German propaganda. The general hysteria promoted investigation not only of German language texts, but of American and world history texts to see whether historians were slyly poisoning the minds of youth against the Allies and promoting the interests of the enemy.

In the course of this deeply emotional involvement with German, the language of a hated enemy, the reduction in enrollments came about in three ways. In some states, such as California, it was taken out of the schools by state school board action. In other states, German was removed in selected communities by local boards. In still other school districts, schools ceased to offer German because students refused to elect it. In connection with the last movement, the superintendent of schools in Portsmouth, Virginia, reported that from the beginning of the war in 1914 enrollments in German were continuously fewer, until in 1916–1917 there were none at all. Thus it will be seen that the issue of German was neither an educational issue nor one promoted by ignorant or intimidated school people. Instead, it was an issue about which the American people as a whole became agitated—partly because of the previous large immigration of Germans and partly because of their influence in the society—and about which Americans reacted accordingly.

Closely tied into the alignment of language and political fortune is the issue of foreign language as representing basic national groups in the United States. To be sure, Americans have always given lip service to the classical languages, as witness enrollments in Latin and limited enrollments in Greek. They have promoted French and occasionally German as scholarly languages. But large enrollments have come also in Spanish and, to a lesser extent, in Italian, for which there appear to be no excuse except general ties with large migrations or with substantial native groups.

Note in Table 10-4 the peculiar nature of enrollments in foreign languages in states sensitive to Spanish-speaking populations. Five of the states offered no German or Italian. New Mexico, the most Spanish of the states, had enrollments only in Latin in addition to Spanish. In California, which has a good educational reputation, enrollments in Spanish outnumbered those in French, four to one, and enrollments in German constituted only about 2.5 per cent of those in Spanish. And the Italian figure may be explained not in terms of a revived humanism, but by the fact that by 1940 there were some 100,910[113] Italians living in California.

Table 10-5 includes all states in which there was enrollment in Italian in public high schools. In each of these states, the foreign-born of

[113] Brown and Roucek, *Our Racial and National Minorities*, p. 248.

Table 10-4. Enrollments in Foreign Languages in Public Secondary Schools in States Sensitive* to Spanish, 1925

| State | Enrollments | | | | | |
|---|---|---|---|---|---|---|
| | French | German | Italian | Spanish | Latin | Other |
| Florida............. | 755 | 0 | 0 | 1,815 | 4,679 | 0 |
| Arizona............ | 49 | 0 | 0 | 3,572 | 1,000 | 0 |
| Colorado........... | 1,453 | 0 | 0 | 6,863 | 8,742 | 0 |
| Nevada............ | 146 | 0 | 0 | 666 | 182 | 0 |
| New Mexico........ | 0 | 0 | 0 | 3,167 | 622 | 0 |
| Texas.............. | 1,227 | 199 | 0 | 21,996 | 13,157 | 0 |
| California.......... | 11,649 | 1,101 | 580 | 43,188 | 16,934 | 39 |

* Populated by Spanish-speaking Americans. The Southwest.
SOURCE: Carleton A. Wheeler (comp. with others), *Enrollment in the Foreign Languages in Secondary Schools and Colleges of the United States*, The Macmillan Company, New York, 1928, pp. 171, 219–229, 249. Compiled for the Modern Foreign Language Study with the cooperation of the Bureau of Education and with introduction and analysis by Robert Herndon Fife. Copyright 1928 by the American Council on Education. Used by permission.

Table 10-5. Enrollments in Italian in Public Secondary Schools in the United States, 1925 and 1948–1949

| State | Enroll. in Ital. 1925 | Foreign-born of Ital. birth, 1930 | | Enroll. in Ital. 1948–49 | Foreign-born of Ital. birth, 1950 | |
|---|---|---|---|---|---|---|
| | | No. | Per cent of foreign-born | | No. | Per cent of foreign-born |
| Connecticut.......... | 141 | 87,123 | 22.8 | 1,106 | 74,270 | 24.9 |
| Massachusetts....... .. | 198 | 126,103 | 12.0 | 1,431 | 101,548 | 14.2 |
| Rhode Island......... | 120 | 32,493 | 19.0 | 739 | 24,380 | 21.5 |
| New Jersey........... | 283 | 190,858 | 22.6 | 2,597 | 150,680 | 23.9 |
| New York............ | 1,465 | 629,322 | 19.7 | 8,129 | 503,175 | 20.1 |
| Pennsylvania......... | 14 | 225,979 | 18.3 | 1,040 | 163,359 | 21.0 |
| Mississippi........... | 30 | 1,613 | 21.2 | 0 | 1,023 | 12.3 |
| California............ | 580 | 107,249 | 10.7 | 119 | 104,215 | 10.6 |
| Illinois............... | | 110,449 | 8.9 | 955 | 83,556 | 10.7 |

SOURCE: Carleton A. Wheeler (comp. with others), *Enrollment in the Foreign Languages in Secondary Schools and Colleges of the United States*, The Macmillan Company, New York, 1928, pp. 138–249. Compiled for the Modern Foreign Language Study with the cooperation of the Bureau of Education and with introduction and analysis by Robert Herndon Fife. U.S. Office of Education, "Offerings and Enrollments in High-school Subjects, 1948–49," *Biennial Survey of Education in the United States, 1948-1950*, 1951, p. 91. U.S. Bureau of the Census, *Census of Population: 1950.* Note that this table, unlike Table 10-4, includes *all* the states in which there is enrollment in public high schools in the selected language. Copyright 1928 by the American Council on Education. Used by permission.

Italian birth are impressive in numbers.   In all these states they constitute the largest bloc of the foreign-born.   That they have made no greater impact on the public schools than is evidenced by the enrollments in Italian may be due to several facts.   First, the immigration is recent and would not have had time to make much impact on schooling. Second, in the late immigrations many were illiterate and so would not have been interested in secondary schooling quite so early as 1925. Third, many of these people use the parochial schools, the enrollments of which are not included in the table.

There are other examples of the way in which language study reflects origins of the American population.   In a 1948–1949 analysis of language enrollments, only one state was listed as including public school offerings in Hebrew.   This was New York, which reported 3,129 enrolled.[114] As of 1937 one-half of the American Jews lived in New York City.[115]

Figures in Table 10-6 on two other languages reveal another interesting nationality story.   In 1925, study of Scandinavian languages was

Table 10-6. Enrollments in Scandinavian Languages in High Schools, 1925

| State | Swedish | | Norse | |
|---|---|---|---|---|
| | No. of schools | Enrollment | No. of schools | Enrollment |
| Public: | | | | |
| Illinois............. | 1 | 71 | ... | ... |
| Minnesota.......... | 5 | 321 | 9 | 391 |
| N. Dakota......... | 1 | 16 | 20 | 356 |
| Private............. | 5 | 148 | 9 | 253 |

SOURCE: Carleton A. Wheeler (comp. with others), *Enrollment in the Foreign Languages in Secondary Schools and Colleges of the United States*, The Macmillan Company, New York, 1928, pp. 363–378.   Compiled for the Modern Foreign Language Study with the cooperation of the Bureau of Education and with introduction and analysis by Robert Herndon Fife.   Copyright 1928 by the American Council on Education.   Used by permission.

confined to states with heavy populations of these groups.   Americanization took hold, however, and in later reports there were drops in enrollments in Illinois, Minnesota, and North Dakota.   In 1948–1949, a brief flutter can be noticed in a few other states as new immigrants came in (Massachusetts, New York) or as the original settlers dispersed (Washington).

[114] U.S. Office of Education, "Offerings and Enrollments in High-School Subjects, 1948–49," *Biennial Survey of Education in the United States 1948–1950*, 1951, chap. V, p. 91.
[115] Brown and Roucek, *Our Racial and National Minorities*, p. 273.

Languages not ordinarily assessed as in wide use or as scholarly in intent also make their appearance in national reports. Bohemian was reported in 1925 as enrolling 161 public secondary school students in Illinois, and 24 in Nebraska. It persisted in Illinois to 1948–1949, but only 54 were then enrolled. Polish appeared also in the later report, with 610 public school enrollments in Illinois, Massachusetts, New Jersey, Ohio, and Wisconsin. In 1948–1949, Portuguese was being taught in California, Massachusetts, and Rhode Island.

This foray into the wilderness of foreign-language study in America may well yield inferences respecting such study as a symbol of a foreign culture. As such, its fortunes as an academic discipline will vary. It may be tied to national welfare—in this case a sizable minority speaking the language makes Americans uneasy, and both the people and the language will be rejected—witness Germans and the German language in World War I. It may be introduced to promote national welfare—witness the sudden affinity for Russian in secondary schools as well as in institutions for higher education. It may represent a hemispheric and ethnic tie, as in the case of Spanish. It may stand for an ethnic group (Polish, Czech, Norse, Swedish, German, Italian). As such, it may survive in the public schools as long as there is a group to argue its value. When a second and third generation reject the culture of their ancestors, the language dies a natural death. Thus the experimental quality of America and, more particularly the foreign groups in her midst have had a unique effect on American education.

## SUMMARY

Since 1776, educators, legislators, and laymen have developed what they considered acceptable patterns for American education. Immigrating and minority religious groups have combined to confound the process of instituting acceptable American patterns. They have transplanted, accommodated, and diffused their cultures, and so added to the variability of American education and the difficulty of educating for nationalism.

The impact of the many subcultures on the larger American culture has been only superficially examined, and impact of these subcultures on American education is in part inferential. That school people who were trying to Americanize had to make adaptations to special groups is apparent from the course of language study in the schools and released time for religious instruction. That the practices of some subcultures must have worried school people can be inferred from the story of the Amish and the descriptions of the foreign-language schools. The subtler aspects of culture impact have a way of eluding one, however. It can be assumed that children from each of these subcultures brought to school unique ways of perceiving. How different to each of these groups has been the meaning of the American symbol system? In response to these presumed differences, what practices have teachers in local classrooms instituted in order to make Americans? These questions are still largely unanswered. But they can be speculated about fruitfully when one calls to mind the rich variations in the American cultural fabric. A few of the divergences in American schooling, outgrowths of culture differences, will be examined in the remaining chapters in Part III.

# 11

# Establishing Schools in the
# Old Northwest

> The powers not delegated to the United States by the Con-
> stitution, nor prohibited by it to the States, are reserved to
> the States respectively, or to the people.
>
> TENTH AMENDMENT, CONSTITUTION OF
> THE UNITED STATES

This is the first of four case studies on establishing schools in selected
areas. The question is begged as to the relationship of school establishment to the ideal American education as described in Parts I and II.
An education which supports nationalism has always been premised on
a comprehensive common school system. Yet since the Constitutional
Convention, education in the United States has been destined to be
controlled locally and by state.

Coupled with this diffused control has been the influence of subcultures on the development of schools. The four case studies are designed, therefore, to throw light on two questions: How have schools
been developed by or for selected subcultures? How have these systems
been adapted to the necessity for supporting American nationalism?

The first two case studies on education in the Old Northwest and
Negro education in Georgia are confined largely to answering the first
question. Little attention is given to whether these systems support
nationalism as outlined by educators and laymen. They are included
because they illustrate the establishment of schools by the dominant
culture group in the United States on the one hand; and for the most-
discussed minority on the other hand. Their inclusion may be further
defended by pointing out again that a school system must be established
before it can support nationalism, and that they illustrate the premise
that there has been no easy single highway to developing schools.

349

The third and fourth case studies on school development in New Mexico and Hawaii answer both questions for particular cultures. These studies show how schools have been established and how these systems have been adapted to their Americanizing function.

New England is credited both with spreading public school concepts from East to West above the Mason-Dixon Line and developing the dominant American culture. The present chapter shows New Englanders at work in the Old Northwest, setting up schools to enforce morality and knowledge. The way they go about their business may give some depth to accounts which deal only with accomplishments, not with process. Their story may illustrate one way of building a school system—through a ground-swell movement produced by the people at large.

In view of the ground-swell movements in education throughout the United States, the writers of the Tenth Amendment appear to have underestimated their public in respect to the development of education. They seem to have expressed an afterthought in the final phrase—preceded by a comma—"or to the people." Historians of education have ever since been misassessing the nature of the controls operating in some formal education systems and, as a matter of fact, the nature of the systems themselves.

The United States is a nation of state systems of education and of great men who built them. Therefore, the important story must be how Americans rounded out and strengthened those state systems—so runs the fable. But even in the present generation, there are some 65,000 local boards of education and a host of state boards of education, private boards of education, boards of higher education. The greatest number of these boards, either local or controlling a limited number of higher-education institutions, have a good deal of autonomy. At the same time, as representative bodies, they are instruments not of an impersonal state and its power, but of the people, some of whom built the schools in the first instance, and today are still trying to control them.

Formal education in the United States was partly people-instigated in its origins and has reflected and still reflects its original orientation. It was developed not alone by the Horace Manns and the James Carters, great as was their intent, but by hundreds of housewives and educated women, farmers, ministers, business and professional men, mechanics, legislators, private school teachers. Most of them—if they had ever read the Tenth Amendment—ignored the comma which preceded the final phrase, and the state, and went about the business of setting up schools for their children according to their own purposes and with their own means.

As a matter of fact, a good case could be made for the argument that

Horace Mann and his present-day counterparts who consolidate schools have gone and are going contrary to the drive of the people to control and individualize their educational institutions.

From the beginning of the national period the drive for educational opportunity was expressed in a hurly-burly of institutions, public and private, practical and classical, publicly and privately endowed. Long before any state systems emerged, there were ordinarily a multiplicity of educational endeavors which served to whet the appetites of those who eventually would build a public school system. The frontier which put a premium on individual initiative, the aspirations of people who were actively seeking various kinds of opportunity, and the value systems of people in subcultures such as New England—all of these played their part in educational development. Illustrative, though not typical, is the story of how people in the Old Northwest came to develop their public and private school and college establishments.

## EDUCATION IN THE OLD NORTHWEST

Religion, morality, and knowledge, being necessary to good government and the happiness of mankind, schools and the means of education shall forever be encouraged.                NORTHWEST ORDINANCE, 1787

It is more than chance that the beginnings of school systems in the Old Northwest should be coincidental with the development of a typically American colonizing policy. The policy was planned to ensure colonizers of their eventual equality with established citizens, and education was to ensure the development of behaviors appropriate to that equality.

### Land Policy

In 1785, while the United States were still operating under the Articles of Confederation, an ordinance was passed which made provisions for the orderly survey of lands ceded to the central government by the larger of the thirteen original colonies. These lands included the present Ohio, Indiana, and Illinois, and portions of Michigan and Wisconsin. Among the provisions was one which read that "there shall be reserved the lot No. 16, of every township, for the maintenance of public schools within the said township; also one-third part of all gold, silver, lead and copper mines, to be sold, or otherwise disposed of as Congress shall hereafter direct."

That education should be singled out for special concern was no happy accident. The ordinance of 1785, which set aside lands for schools, and the ordinance of 1787, which enforced the claims of religion, morality, and knowledge, were both partially the work of New

Englanders, whose twin pillars were church and school. Although in 1784 Thomas Jefferson had been responsible for introducing in Congress an ordinance for governing public lands, it was the Rev. Manassah Cutler and his friends from Massachusetts who lobbied both ordinances through Congress. Reverend Cutler represented a group of New Englanders who wished to take up lands in the Northwest. To New Englanders, whose watchwords were law and order, it seemed inevitable to ensure these goods through provision for enforcing morality and knowledge by schools.

The 1787 document was concerned primarily with the governing of the new territories. It provided orderly means for the settlers to achieve a position comparable to that of citizens in the older states. Three stages of government would bring the new lands to full statehood. Thus the ordinances inaugurated an American policy sharply at variance with that of the colonizing nations of Europe. Orderly survey followed by full self-government within the Federal framework was the territorial policy of the United States and was so to remain until the acquiring of Alaska in 1862. Education was its cornerstone and was to continue as such throughout the incorporation of the states in continental United States.

Using land to support schools was a well-known practice among New Englanders,[1] a practice brought, in part, from England by the earliest settlers. With Henry VIII's suppression of the monasteries in the 1500s, the educational institutions sponsored by the church had been inadvertently suppressed. Petitions to the king eventuated in bringing some of the sequestered church lands back to use for support of grammar schools, but since the restored properties proved inadequate, knights, esquires, clerks, and grocers endowed schools. Thus the practice of school endowment through land grants by private persons came about.

Along with the practice came the concept of free schools or free grammar schools, which was to spread particularly to Massachusetts, Connecticut, and New Hampshire. Typical of the practice and the concept was the case of Capt. John Mason's bequest. When Captain Mason, a proprietor of New Hampshire, died in 1636, he left provision for 1,000 acres of land to be given for "maintenance of a free grammar school for the education of youth."

Quite apart from private beneficences, town and colony officials began to give lands for schools early in the 1600s. In 1635, the General Court of Massachusetts Bay granted Thompson's Island to the town of Dorchester, and in 1639 the town appropriated the island for schools.

---

[1] Joseph Schafer, *The Origin of the System of Land Grants for Education*, University of Wisconsin Bulletin no. 63, Historical Series I, no. 1, University of Wisconsin, Madison, Wis., August, 1902, pp. 1–53.

Rent from the land was paid to the schoolmaster. In 1641, a body of wardens was appointed to look after the land in "all things that concern the schools [in ways] most conducible for the glory of God and the bringing up of the children of the town in religion, learning, and civilitie." The course of events was not smooth. In time, the court took back its island, and Dorchester attempted fruitlessly to retrieve it. Finally the town fathers set aside town lands in Dorchester for their schools.

Town officials apparently were never as conscientious as the court would have liked in supporting their schools through rate-bills, even though fines were imposed on dilatory town officials. Yet there was urgent need for an educated ministry to be supplied by the college, which must, in turn, draw students from grammar schools. The situation could not be allowed to deteriorate. In 1659 the General Court of Massachusetts Bay granted each town 1,000 acres of land for maintenance of a grammar school. If the town failed to carry out its school obligations, the benefits of the sale grant would go to the nearest town having a grammar school.

By the close of the seventeenth century, the officials of the Massachusetts and Connecticut colonial governments had committed themselves to a policy of supporting grammar schools through rent or sale of lands, particularly wild lands, belonging to the colonies.

In the late colonial period, there came into being what appears to be a typically American practice, granting school lands in conjunction with grants of land for colonizing. In miniature, this pattern was to obtain throughout the United States as long as there was a moving frontier. Large tracts of unsettled land in Massachusetts and Connecticut were ordinarily bought by companies of people. The colonial governments made various stipulations in the charters they granted, and these often included provisions for school lands.

By 1728, the town of Lunenburg was sufficiently settled so that its inhabitants asked for incorporation. The act incorporating the town stipulated "that the inhabitants of the said town do provide for the comfortable and honorable support of a learned and orthodox minister among them, and likewise provide a school master to instruct their youth in reading and writing."[2] On petition, the general court in 1735 granted to Boston three townships of Hampshire wild lands. Each was to consist of three shares, "one to be for the first settled minister, one for the ministry and one for the school."[3]

Even royal governors inadvertently enforced the new land policy. To keep certain lands out the hands of the hated Governor Andros,

[2] Quoted in *ibid.*, p. 26.
[3] Quoted in *ibid.*, pp. 26–27.

Connecticut granted lands to the towns of Hartford and Windsor, but after Andros had been bested, Connecticut asked that they be returned. Thereupon ensued a controversy between colony and towns which ended in a compromise and the beginnings of the Connecticut common school fund. Monies from sale of lands in new towns were to be distributed among the settled towns as educational funds. Furthermore, in each of the new towns, three shares were to be set aside, one for the minister, one for the ministry, and one for schools.

The practice of granting lands for schools spread to other New England colonies. In the years 1748 to 1768, the proprietors of New Hampshire granted forty charters to towns, and in each charter there was a provision for a grant to education. After 1760 all grants in Vermont contained reservations for schools, and in 1794 the lands reserved for the English Society for the Propagation of the Gospel were appropriated and distributed to the towns for schools.

Practices prescribed in the Northwest Ordinance were New England colonial policy enlarged. In place of the general court was the American Congress, which granted lands to companies of people in orderly packages; and in those packages were the traditional grants for education. New England cast its shadow over the Old Northwest and eventually over a goodly portion of the territories acquired by the United States government.

## State School Systems Emerge

Despite the urge of New Englanders for orderly processes, setting up public school and state university systems in the Old Northwest was a patchwork affair, but two movements are discernible. First, for the most part, state systems emerged only against a backdrop of private and locally supported institutions which had eventuated from the efforts of many individuals. Second, state officials, whose positions permitted them to develop schools, were guided by local pressures and only established state systems when local pressures warranted it. An indication of this is to be found in the actions of territorial and state legislatures and in provisions in early state constitutions.

A look at Ohio school legislation in the period from 1803 to 1850 indicates no far-reaching and settled policy for developing a state education system. Rather, successive legislators seem to have been beset by devils. Lands, county and district school systems, superintendents, boards of trustees, private schools—all received attention, but in no systematic way. A compulsory school tax would appear on the books—with no way of enforcing it. Township superintendents would be required by law to visit district schools—then it would be made optional, with township trustees permitted to excuse them from their duties. A law of 1838 established a guaranteed state common school fund of $200,000, but in 1842 the fund was reduced to $150,000, with monies from fines added to the school fund. The office of state superintendent was created in 1837 and abolished in 1840. Certainly the legislators gave attention to schools, but there appeared to be no sustained planning leading in the direction of a state-controlled and state-operated system. State legislators were operating not by plan, but as a result of local pressure. This can be inferred from the numbers of special acts they passed to handle the school lands, presumably the sixteenth section of each township granted by Congress (see Table 11-1). If a settled

Table 11-1. Acts of the State Legislature Pertaining to School Lands in Ohio (1803–1850)

| Dates | Number of special state acts |
|-------|------------------------------|
| 1803–1817 | 30 |
| 1817–1823 | 21 |
| 1823–1827 | 11 |
| 1827–1831 | 54 |
| 1831–1838 | 102 |
| 1838–1845 | 59 |
| 1845–1850 | 117 |
| Total...................... | 394 |

SOURCE: Edward A. Miller, "The History of Educational Legislation in Ohio from 1803 to 1850," *Ohio Archaeological and Historical Quarterly*, vol. 27, nos. 1 and 2, pp. 152–153, January and April, 1918.

policy had been the motivating force, it would hardly seem reasonable to suppose that 394 acts were needed.

In the period from 1822 to 1833, the numbers of local as against state-wide general school laws will indicate very little systematic concern with a state-wide system of schools (see Table 11-2). To pacify local communities, the Ohio Legislature passed 368 local school laws in eleven years; but thought meet to pass only 81 general school laws. It is probably safe to say that some of the 81 laws canceled each other.

Data available for Indiana are less complete, but lack of systematic state planning must also have obtained there. In the first constitution of 1816, the state was given responsibility for establishing a complete system of schools from township to state university.[4] However, as Cotton points out, nothing came of the constitutional provision because

[4] Fassett A. Cotton, *Education in Indiana, 1793 to 1934*, The Progress Publishing Co., Bluffton, Ind., 1934, p. 9; and James Albert Woodburn, *Higher Education in Indiana: Contributions to American Education History*, (ed.) Herbert B. Adams, U.S. Office of Education Circular of Information, no. 1, 1891, p. 74.

there was no public source of revenue. The first state law for support of schools came in 1849, when 10 cents was levied on every $100 of property.[5]

The picture in Michigan is somewhat different. Michigan came in as a state in 1837. In an article of the 1835 constitution, a system was set up which contained either explicitly or implicitly all the essential features of the system as it was to obtain at least until 1904.[6] Wisconsin

Table 11-2. General and Local School
Laws in Ohio (1822–1833)

| Session | Numbers of laws passed by the state legislature | |
|---|---|---|
| | General | Local |
| 1822 | 5 | 14 |
| 1823 | 4 | 3 |
| 1824 | 3 | 13 |
| 1825 | 7 | 18 |
| 1826 | 8 | 19 |
| 1827 | 7 | 22 |
| 1828 | 9 | 28 |
| 1829 | 9 | 50 |
| 1830 | 8 | 42 |
| 1831 | 12 | 55 |
| 1832 | 3 | 45 |
| 1833 | 6 | 59 |
| Total........... 81 | | 368 |

SOURCE: Edward A. Miller, "The History of Educational Legislation in Ohio from 1803 to 1850," *Ohio Archaeological and Historical Quarterly*, vol. 27, nos. 1 and 2, pp. 220–238, January and April, 1918.

came into the union in 1848, with full-blown provisions for schools; but Jorgenson says that the constitution extended and consolidated a movement which had been under way for many years, and which developed in spite of the territorial legislatures.[7]

Whatever the attitudes or actions of state legislators and governors, school kept in the Old Northwest in the antebellum period. Samuel

[5] Cotton, *op. cit.*, pp. 10, 11.
[6] Daniel Putnam, *The Development of Primary and Secondary Public Education in Michigan: A Historical Sketch*, George Wahr Publishing Company, Ann Arbor, Mich., 1904, pp. 23, 63.
[7] Lloyd P. Jorgenson, "The Origins of Public Education in Wisconsin," *The Wisconsin Magazine of History*, vol. 33, no. 1, pp. 20, 27, September, 1949. Jorgenson now has a book out on the same topic.

Lewis, first state superintendent of schools in Ohio, showed in his first report in 1837 that there were 7,748 organized school districts in the state, 1,129 townships in 71 of the 75 counties, which would give an average of nearly 7 school districts to the township. Some 38,740 district school officers were functioning in these districts—enough, according to Lewis, "to break down any system however otherwise good."[8] Whether or not Lewis was right in his condemnation of the unwieldy officialdom, his report on districts indicated that, despite ineffective enforcement measures, the people were going ahead with districting for schools.

The Governor of Indiana pointed out in his message of 1842 that only 47 per cent of the children of school age were actually enrolled in schools. The Governor indicated that this was a shameful condition[9]— in the absence of state-wide compulsory measures it might better be thought of as noteworthy. In Illinois in the 1840s, it was said that 100,000 children were out of school, and 28,780 adults were illiterate.[10] But in 1840, the population of Illinois was 476,183 and in 1850, it was 851,470. In 1845, the Illinois Legislature passed permissive legislation allowing communities to levy a property tax for schools. By 1849, 36 counties were levying such a tax, and by 1852, 43 out of 69 were levying voluntarily.[11]

Despite the fact that no territorial or state-wide school law had obtained in Wisconsin until the constitution of 1848, there were 32,000 pupils in public schools in 1849, the first year under the constitution.[12] Obviously, it would have been impossible to enroll so many within a year's time if there had not been the beginning of a system prior to the constitutional mandates.

*Education as a Folk Movement*

School kept in the Old Northwest not because state officials so planned, but because hundreds of housewives, farmers, clergymen and other professional men, businessmen, and mechanics willed that it keep. Individual democracy was on the rampage. One expression of that

[8] Edward A. Miller, "The History of Educational Legislation in Ohio from 1803 to 1850," *Ohio Archaeological and Historical Quarterly*, vol. 27, nos. 1 and 2, pp. 29–30, January and April, 1918.

[9] Richard G. Boone, *A History of Education in Indiana*, Appleton-Century-Crofts, Inc., New York, 1892, p. 41.

[10] Theodore Calvin Pease, *The Centennial History of Illinois*, vol. II, *The Frontier State, 1818–1848*, A. C. McClurg & Co., Chicago, 1922, p. 431.

[11] Paul E. Belting, "The Development of the Free Public High School in Illinois to 1860," *Journal of the Illinois State Historical Society*, vol. 11, nos. 3 and 4, pp. 511–512, October, 1918 and January, 1919.

[12] Jorgenson, *op. cit.*, p. 21.

democracy was concern for the development of education not by rule, but according to the dictates of individuals or small community groups. Education advanced as hundreds of spirits moved, and was expressed in a hurly-burly of institutions, private and public, for children and for adults. Only two concerns seemed to be common to all who promoted educational enterprises. One was a burning desire for morality and knowledge. Both words had varying interpretations and might be subsumed under the even vaguer word "improvement." The other common attitude seemed to be a fierce desire of individuals, singly and in groups, to resist all efforts to be told what to do. "I'll manage my own and my children's education in my own way." This might well have been the motto of the Old Northwest.

In order to understand what was happening in education in the antebellum Northwest, it is necessary to abandon twentieth-century patterns of thinking. It is common today to think of a giant, publicly supported school system enrolling close to 90 per cent of the school-age youth from the ages of six to seventeen and to think of improving and extending this system through petition made to corporate bodies, such as local or state school boards or to local or state legislative groups. Public and private, academic and vocational, elementary and secondary—the words have reasonably well-defined meanings to today's lay and professional publics alike.

The pioneers of the Old Northwest had no clearly defined curricular and institutional terms, nor did they have established legislative procedures for instituting and expanding educational facilities. A school might be begun through putting on a drive for property taxes. Or it might be started by several citizens constituting themselves a corporate body authorized to open a private school. Even if the school were publicly financed, the manner of financing might be unique to the pioneer situation. In an Indiana school law of 1824, each able-bodied male of twenty-one or up, being a freeholder or householder, was liable to work one day in each week on building the local schoolhouse, and he was to pay 37.5 cents for each day he failed to meet his obligation.[13] Furthermore, there was usually no neat classification of population by age groups. Indiana academies in the period from 1825 to 1875 enrolled persons from six to sixty.

The establishment of schools was far from being the only educational enterprise under way. Volunteer groups also established agricultural societies, literary institutes, library companies—and any or none of them might subsist through public funds—or efforts might go in the direction of supporting newspapers, almanacs, and bookshops. Quakers, Presbyterians, and Catholics were reaching out for ways in which to

[13] Cotton, op. cit., p. 33.

improve themselves and their communities and to make equality a living reality, and any instrument which came to hand was good so long as it served its purposes.

The instrument which people of the Old Northwest used freely for many purposes was their church, or rather, churches, even though occasionally there would be cooperation among the denominations. (Presbyterians and Methodists would have their disagreements with Baptists on the matter of baptism, but all three would unite in common cause against a Universalist. "Hell-fire and endless punishment were too essential a part of their revivalistic gospel for them to allow its disparagement on the part of the upstart Universalists."[14] The Great Awakening had come to pioneer America in the late eighteenth century, and evangelical Christianity was to ride the circuit from rude community to ruder log church and school on successive frontiers throughout a goodly portion of the nineteenth century.) That these pioneers should have used their church organizations as nuclei for establishing educational institutions was only reasonable in view of their circumstances and beliefs. They had a deep attachment to their churches, if for no other reason than that they gave lonely folk on lonely frontiers an outlet for their pent-up emotions. Probably, also, reward and punishment were ever imminent in households and communities where Indian raids and crop failures might mean the difference between life and death. Morality and good character had long been identified as adherence to a fairly rigid pattern of beliefs as prescribed by any one of the church creeds. What more natural, then, but that those who would ensure good character in their children or themselves would establish schools under the protecting wing of the churches?

A motivation other than improvement was probably at work. It has been ever characteristic of a Westerner that he is suspicious of an Easterner, and what influence could be more insidious than that of ministers trained at Yale and particularly Harvard, that "sewer of atheism"? If ministers there must be, then let them be local boys, for whom schools must be built by local folk.

With the tendency of the Great Awakening to manifest itself in diversity, the multiplication of sects meant a multiplication of colleges. The dynamism of the sects is amply illustrated by Tables 11-3 and 11-4, which indicate the origins of some of the private institutions of Ohio and Michigan as they still existed in 1891.

Though the Northwest had sloughed off the East, New England had not abandoned the West. "By the third decade of the nineteenth century, New England had come to regard the Northwest as a boundless

---

[14] William W. Sweet, "Religion and the Westward March," *The Ohio State Archaeological and Historical Quarterly*, vol. 50, p. 83, 1941.

meadow spiritually 'whitening for harvest.' " Aided by New England, denominations competed to found colleges which would provide the West with the "most efficacious and practicable discipline of the intellectual powers,"[15] and would incidentally stem the tide of Roman Catholicism. As early as 1815, the American Education Society, a New England organization, was, in the interests of poor students in both East and West, collecting money and "clothes suitable to be made up into coats and pantaloons." Monies were to be paid back, but the obligation might be canceled "in case of sickness, entrance into missionary service, or 'settlement with a people in depressed circumstances.' "[16]

Table 11-3. Nineteenth-century Colleges in Michigan

| College | Date of founding* | Founding organization |
|---|---|---|
| Hillsdale College | 1844 | Free Baptist |
| Kalamazoo College | 1829 | Baptist |
| Olivet College | 1844 | Families from Oberlin |
| Albion College | 1835 | Methodist Episcopal |
| Hope College | 1851 | Dutch Reformed |
| Adrian College | 1859 | Methodist Protestant |
| Alma College | 1886 | Presbyterian |
| Detroit College | 1877 | Roman Catholic |
| Battle Creek College | 1872 | Seventh Day Adventist |

* Founding dates do not always tell the whole story of the institution. Often colleges begin much earlier as academies. Founding dates are usually those which mark the beginnings of collegiate-level work or chartering by the state.

SOURCE: Andrew C. McLaughlin, *History of Higher Education in Michigan*, U.S. Office of Education Circular of Information, no. 4, 1891, pp. 124–171.

Teachers for their brethren's children were also a concern of these New Englanders, including Miss Catherine Beecher, eldest daughter of Rev. Lyman Beecher, who organized[17] the Ladies' Society for the Promotion of Education in the West. The good ladies were particularly interested in sending pious Congregational females among the heathen.

New England was so flooded with appeals, particularly after the Panic of 1837, that college representatives saw a real peril in competition and pooled denominational efforts in 1842 with the organization of the Society for the Promotion of Collegiate and Theological Education at

[15] E. Kidd Lochard, "The Influence of New England in Denominational Colleges in the Northwest, 1830–1860," *The Ohio State Archaeological and Historical Quarterly*, vol. 53, no. 1, pp. 1–3, January–March, 1944.

[16] *Ibid.*, pp. 3–4.

[17] Louise Phelps Kellogg, "The Origins of Milwaukee College," *The Wisconsin Magazine of History*, vol. 9, no. 4, p. 396, July, 1926.

Table 11-4. Nineteenth-century Colleges in Ohio

| College | Date of founding* | Founding organization |
|---|---|---|
| Oberlin College | 1833 | Two missionaries |
| Ohio Wesleyan University | 1841 | Methodist Episcopal Church |
| Kenyon College | 1824 | Protestant Episcopal Church |
| Marietta College | 1835 | Congregational |
| Western Reserve University | 1826 | Originally Presbyterian and Congregational |
| Antioch College | 1853 | Christian Church |
| Wittenberg College | 1845 | Lutheran |
| Otterbein College | 1847 | Church of the United Brethren |
| University of Wooster | 1866 | Presbyterian Church |
| Denison University | 1831 | Baptist |
| Buchtel College | 1870 | Universalist |
| Baldwin-Wallace College | 1845 | Methodist Episcopal |
| Hiram College | 1850 | Disciples of Christ |
| Heidelberg College | 1850 | Reformed Church |
| Ashland College | 1879 | Dunkard |
| Capital University | 1830? | Evangelical Lutheran |
| Muskingum College | 1837 | Presbyterian |
| Franklin College | 1825 | |
| Wilmington College | 1871 | Quaker |
| Mount Union College | 1846 | Methodist |
| Wilberforce University | 1856 | Methodist Episcopal |
| Urbana University | 1850 | Swedenborgian |
| Belmont College | 1833? | Private person |
| Calvin College | 1866 | Reformed |
| Findlay College | 1881 | Church of God |
| Rio Grande College | 1875 | Freewill Baptist |
| Twin Valley College | 1886 | |
| St. Xavier College | 1842 | Roman Catholic |
| St. Joseph's College | 1871 | Roman Catholic (Congregation of the Holy Cross) |

* Founding dates do not always tell the whole story of the institution. Often colleges begin much earlier as academies. Founding dates are usually those which mark the beginnings of collegiate level work, or chartering by the state.

SOURCE: George W. Knight and John R. Commons, *History of Higher Education in Ohio*, U.S. Office of Education Circular of Information, no. 5, 1891, pp. 55–242.

the West. By 1847, members of The Board of National Popular Education, with headquarters in Middlebury, Vermont, were in Indiana trying to help engage teachers for the academies. The purpose of the board was to obtain and prepare well-qualified female teachers and to send them where they were needed.

Despite denominational cooperation, foundings went on apace. By 1840, New England had begun some 32 institutions in the Northwest, and by 1860 they had created 102. Most of them did not survive, but at least 9 of those founded between 1844 and 1859 were still thriving institutions in the mid-twentieth century.[18]

## Academy Movement

Whether it was New England in the guise of an aroused church, or Westerners through their own churches, evangelical Christianity was inextricably interwoven with the development of educational institutions including both colleges and academies. These last, says Mock, were called academies, seminaries, high schools, colleges, normal schools, institutes, collegiate institutes, or normal colleges. In level, they were, roughly speaking, secondary. In intent, they were college preparatory or concerned with preparation for life. They ordinarily required of matriculants no denominational test, but they were more than apt to be denomination-sponsored, though private stock companies and individuals were frequently responsible for their founding. Mock lists several of them as surviving until after World War I in Indiana, with denominations and numbers as follows: Catholics, 24; Friends, 13; Methodists, 18; Presbyterians, 24; Baptists, 8; and a few each for the Disciples of Christ, United Brethren, Lutherans, Episcopalians, Congregationalists, Dunkards, Moravians, and Universalists.[19]

In respect to finance and control, there were two types of academy. One grew out of provisions comparable to one in the first constitution of Indiana which called for "a general system of education ascending in a regular graduation from township schools to a State University." The secondary division of this system was to be a county seminary paid for by monies collected from military-duty exemptions and from fines for breach of penal laws. The county seminary was also the recipient of benefits from the lands set aside for academies. In the *Western Sun* in 1816, there was a memorial asking for confirmation by Congress of a "grant of township No. 2, south of range 1, west of the second principal meridian," for the use of an academy in Indiana territory.[20]

Mock also records the opening of twenty-three county seminaries in Indiana from 1830 to 1840, and two in the period 1840 to 1850. Similar institutions must have flourished in Illinois for, by act of April 18, 1818, Congress gave the new state one township for a seminary of learning, plus one township to be designated by the President.[21]

---

[18] Lochard, *op. cit.,* pp. 1–3; and Albert Mock, *The Mid-western Academy Movement: A Composite Picture of 514 Indiana Academies,* published by the author, 5752 East Washington Street, Indianapolis, 1949, pp. 24–25.

[19] Mock, *op. cit.,* pp. 2, 28–38.

[20] *Ibid.,* pp. 8, 15.

[21] Belting, *op. cit.,* p. 275.

According to Miller, Ohio developed neither the public academy nor the denominational school, although there was denominational influence in the founding of some academies. This limited denominational influence was not due to any lack of religious interest—in fact, the very multiplicity of sects was a source of religious tolerance, reflected in the founding of schools by adherents of closely related creeds.[22]

Omnipresent were private-enterprise academies chartered by stock companies formed by local citizens who wished to provide education for their children, teachers for their schools, ministers for their churches, and enlightened citizens for their communities. The increasing tempo of the academy movement is indicated by comparative figures for two early statehood figures. From 1803 to 1830, some 25 secondary institutions were opened in Ohio, but in the period from 1831 to 1850 there were some 143. Together with three miscellaneous institutions, this made a total of 171 for the period. Of the 171, there were 92 academies, 32 seminaries, and only 30 high schools. In Indiana, the number of academies founded before 1830 was approximately 13 and in the period from 1830 to 1850, the number was 87.[23] Publicly supported high schools were to be serious competitors only in the last decades of the nineteenth century.

The importance of the academy is not only in its pervasiveness, but also in its reflection of the development of education as a folk movement having the rich flavor of individuality in respect to both founders and curricula. No people were too mean or poor to found an academy. The very lack of pattern among the founders indicates that such institutions originated in a spontaneous, voluntary movement. Before statehood in Illinois, for instance, itinerant teachers began academies by inserting flowery advertisements in newspapers. The trustees of Monroe Academy were library officials whose additional duty it was to circulate books.[24] Organizations like mechanics' unions received their share of public funds for schools which they chartered. Ira Miltimore, master mechanic, was instrumental in beginning the Mechanics Institute in Chicago in 1837.[25] In 1827, John Mason Peck, a missionary, opened a seminary at Rock Spring, Illinois, as a theological training school.[26] Isaac Kinley, Quaker educator and lawyer, organized the Union Seminary near Maple Valley, Indiana, in 1848. Later, as a delegate to the constitutional convention of 1851 he was instrumental in securing far-reaching

[22] Miller, op. cit., p. 103.
[23] Ibid.; and Mock, op. cit., pp. 8–9.
[24] Belting, op. cit., pp. 279–281, 290, 293.
[25] Bessie Louise Pierce, A History of Chicago, vol. I, The Beginning of a City, 1673–1848, Alfred A. Knopf, Inc., New York, 1937, p. 192.
[26] Pease, op. cit., p. 22.

provisions for public education. The Friends established academies in Indiana in the antebellum period. The Spiceland School, later Spiceland Academy, was for many years one of the strongest teacher training institutions in the state, and in the early 1840s was taught by Robert Harrison, an Englishman and pioneer schoolteacher.[27] Hanover College was opened as an academy in 1827 by the Rev. John Finley, Presbyterian minister.

As important as individuality in their founding was the unique quality of the educational programs of the academies. In a day when accrediting associations, state curricula, and the Committee of Ten were still in limbo, teachers and patrons could afford to have taught what they wanted to have taught, and in the fashion that suited them. Many curricula were "liberal" in the sense of the Latin grammar school, as befitted college preparatory or preministerial programs. Many were already American in their emphasis on the practical and their concern with matters pertinent to the frontier or the growing towns. Among the Latin and Greek and moral and intellectual philosophy were to be found bookkeeping, stenography, and surveying, as well as a sprinkling of the sciences and various branches of mathematics.[28]

Governor Reynolds of Illinois described an academy he attended in 1806–1807 where he learned land surveying and navigation, as well as reading, writing, spelling, and bookkeeping.[29] Surveying and navigation had a direct bearing on antebellum life. Acquiring land, knowing what one had, or laying out new lands demanded a knowledge of surveying. To reach new territories, one floated down the Ohio River from Pittsburgh, and thence overland or by boat up one of the many river systems.

Teaching methods and subject matter put the academy in the midst of community life, for debating was both a teaching technique and a public relations tool. Social and political questions were discussed with such enthusiasm that "many times it was found convenient to have officers of the law present to help keep order."[30]

Slavery was an issue from 1820 to 1860. Though not many in the Old Northwest were kindly disposed to slavery, there were enough to constitute a vigorous minority. The Old Northwest had drawn its population from the older states, including Virginia and the Carolinas. Some of the Southerners were Quakers who had voluntarily freed their slaves and were fleeing from consequent impoverishment, as well as the hated institution. Others were the poorest and most fiercely demo-

[27] Cotton, *op. cit.*, pp. 89–91.
[28] Mock, *op. cit.*, p. 91.
[29] Belting, *op. cit.*, p. 284.
[30] Mock, *op. cit.*, p. 151.

cratic yeomen, who had no liking for the peculiar institution. Nevertheless, the Democratic party had some strongholds, and the battle was bitter in several parts of the Old Northwest.

The ordinance of 1787 had provided that there should be neither slavery nor involuntary servitude—other than in the punishment of crimes—in the new territory. Agitation for slavery had continued from the first organization of the Ohio territory, however. In the territorial assembly of 1799, a bill permitting slavery under the guise of indenture was reported. The issue was debated and the bill finally rejected on the grounds that slavery was not only immoral but also destructive of the "simplicity and industry" so ardently desired.[31]

Illinois came in as a free state, even though both slaves and indentured servants were to be found there in territorial days. When the state was admitted, the right to retain Negroes as indentured servants was recognized and secured. After admittance, there was a movement to make it a slave state and a call for another constitutional convention. The agitators were foiled by preachers, Governor Coles, and such men as Morris Birkbeck, English farmer and author of articles against slavery. Such leaders saw that there must be education in order to prevent slavery and ignorance; hence, they secured the passage of the Free School Law of 1825. One of the provisions was for a general property tax, which was made optional in 1827. Although there might be many reasons for the 1827 reversal, it underscores the heat of a controversy which was reflected in academies and colleges.

Slavery and the Civil War entered into school concerns in many ways. Occasionally students or administrative heads were scored as being either antislavery or proslavery. School charters were withheld or given in terms of the issue of slavery. Debaters used it as a subject. More important, the issue of slavery was intimately related to academic freedom. In the period when colleges and academies were being founded, Southern leaders were making a drive to cut off all discussion of the issue in the press, the educational institutions, legislative halls, and public forums. Even the President of the United States had charged abolitionists, in 1835, with wishing to foment slave insurrections and had requested legislation prohibiting the circulation of antislavery literature through the mails,[32] with severe penalties for violations. Mobs had destroyed presses, burned schoolhouses and people, and broken up antislavery meetings. The stand which some Northwest academies and

[31] Beverley W. Bond, Jr., *The Foundations of Ohio*, vol. I in Carl Wittke (ed.), *The History of the State of Ohio*, Ohio State Archaeological and Historical Society, Columbus, Ohio, 1941, p. 445.

[32] Dwight L. Dumond, "The Mississippi: Valley of Decision," *The Mississippi Valley Historical Review*, vol. 36, no. 1, p. 12, June, 1949.

colleges took in insisting on free discussion of the slavery issue must be thrown against this background of violent deterrents to discussion. The courageous stands of some faculties and students loom large as memorials to man's struggle for freedom.

New England's antislavery intellectuals were the cause of some of the difficulty. The strength of sentiment in that area is evidenced by the fact that the New England Anti-slavery Society was organized in 1831, two years before the founding of the American Anti-slavery Society.[33] The Band from Yale Theological Seminary who hoped "to raise the west out of intellectual darkness" accepted an invitation to help with a college in Jacksonville, Illinois. The college opened in 1830, with Julian Sturtevant as teacher and the Rev. Edward Beecher as president. The two complicated the life of the school through their strong antislavery views, though Sturtevant stayed on and rounded out a long career in Jacksonville.[34]

In 1852, through a bequest by Josiah White of Philadelphia, White's Indiana Manual Labor Institute was opened near Wabash for the education of poor children—white, colored, and Indian. In 1846, the Union Literary Institute in Randolph County was opened by antislavery friends. It was intended for colored youth of both sexes, and its charter read that "no distinction shall be made on account of race, color, rank, or wealth." It was known as "Nigger College."[35]

That more than one academy was interested in slavery is indicated by these debate topics:[36]

What has more right to complain, the negro or the Indian?
What will be the effect on the coming generation of the Emancipation Proclamation?
Should slave owners have pay for the slaves?
Should differences in color separate people in government?

The role of Oberlin College in the slavery issue is particularly dramatic and illustrates in educational action the new school theology of the Rev. Charles G. Finney. "The central idea of this new movement was personal responsibility and immediate duty."[37]

Oberlin was founded by John J. Shipherd and Philo P. Stewart, two

[33] *Ibid.*, p. 8.
[34] Pease, *op. cit.*, pp. 437–439.
[35] Boone, *op. cit.*, pp. 72, 226–227.
[36] Mock, *op. cit.*, pp. 151–152.
[37] Account of Oberlin to follow based on George W. Knight and John R. Commons, *History of Higher Education in Ohio*, U.S. Office of Education Circular of Information, no. 5, 1891, pp. 55–64.

missionaries who, after consultation and prayer, concluded that the needs of the Ohio country—

. . . could best be met by establishing a community of Christian families with a Christian school which should be "a center of religious influence and power which should work mightily upon the surrounding country and the world— a sort of missionary institution for training laborers for the work abroad."

Colonists were secured from New England and, as they settled, they signed the Oberlin Covenant, which was to ensure a Christian community.

The school was opened as the Oberlin Collegiate Institute on the site of the present institution—a gift from Messrs. Street and Hughes of New Haven, Connecticut. On opening day, December 3, 1833, there were twenty-nine young men and fifteen young women as students.

The event which was to put Oberlin in the midst of the slavery controversy occurred in 1835. The students of Lane Seminary in Cincinnati had been prohibited from discussing slavery by a vote of the trustees. About four-fifths of them immediately left school. One of the professors, Rev. John Morgan, was dismissed, and Rev. Asa Mahan, pastor of the Sixth Presbyterian Church of Cincinnati, resigned his position as trustee of the seminary. John Shipherd of Oberlin happened to visit Cincinnati at this time and invited the students, together with Morgan and Mahan, to transfer to Oberlin. They would, on one condition— that the college accept Negro students. Shipherd immediately wrote to his flock from whom, however, he had no answer until he had written a second time to inform them that, upon passage of the resolution he had requested, they would receive eight new professorships, a gift of Arthur Tappan and other antislavery men. The flock then voted, the result being a tie broken only by vote of the president, John Keep, in favor of the Negro. Once decided, the decision was adhered to. Not only did Oberlin admit Negroes, but became an important depot in the Underground Railroad on the route to Canada. The Oberlin-Wellington rescue of 1858 became famous throughout the nation.

Even more dramatic than the story of Oberlin's conquest of intolerance is that of the Lane Seminary students' stand on principle. According to Dumond, in the winter of 1833–1834, the students conducted the first complete inquiry into the institution of slavery and at the same time developed arguments for and against colonization and emancipation. The inquiry took eighteen evening sessions. Eight of the eighteen speakers had been brought up in the slave states, and six others had lived in the South for various lengths of time up to six years. The speeches and discussions were attended by both students and faculty. At the conclusion of the inquiry, "a unanimous endorsement of immediate emancipation was recorded."

The trustees of Lane Seminary ordered the expulsion of two of the students, set up censorship of student discussions, and authorized the dismissal of any student without cause. The Rev. Asa Mahan was the only member of the governing board who protested against such action. He resigned from the board, and fifty-one members of the student body left the institution after composing a statement giving their reasons for withdrawing. The story of their transfer to Oberlin has already been told. Asa Mahan became president of Oberlin and Prof. John Morgan, one of the faculty members who had protested, became a professor at Oberlin, while the fifty-one became the nucleus of a dynamic student group at Oberlin.[38]

The antislavery fervency of the New England group did not go unchallenged in this individualistic West; antagonisms were expressed in opposition to the founding of colleges and academies. Several charges were brought against the Brahmins. They were trying to federalize the West; the Yale Band was composed of heretics; there would be a union of church and state. This last would establish an aristocratic clergy and destroy the liberties of the people. In Illinois, between 1830 and 1835, several colleges sponsored by New Englanders were denied charters. Thereupon there were so many petitions for the academies that the Committee on Petitions had to make a special report to the Legislature. But only after it was decided that colleges were needed to provide teachers for common schools, to serve as depositories of science, and to provide professors who could write textbooks was a change permitted. In 1835 the Legislature finally granted charters to Alton College, Illinois College, McKendrean College, Jonesborough College, and Jacksonville Female Academy. The charters were probably copied from Yale and indicate the origins of these colleges.[39]

Aside from their dynamic role in the issues important to the Northwest society, the academies and colleges played their part in methodological experimentation. They also reflected the needs, real or presumed, of various groups in society. For example, patrons of a school in one district of Johnson City made themselves felt very directly. Records show that schoolteacher John Pruner could teach reading, writing, and spelling, but not arithmetic. Along came Abram Aten, who, in addition to his skill in teaching spelling, reading, and writing, could also teach arithmetic. The patrons met and voted two to one for the teacher who could teach arithmetic to the older youth,[40] and Pruner, presumably, was dismissed.

[38] Dumond, op. cit., pp. 8–9.
[39] Belting, op. cit., pp. 312–315.
[40] Cotton, op. cit., p. 56.

Practicality was the keynote in many an academy. "As late as 1845 the trustees of Vevay in employing a teacher required in the written contract that he 'should not teach grammar.'" Grammar was considered a waste of time, especially for the boys. The celebrated Scotch teacher Alexander Kinmont encouraged noise in his school in Cincinnati because he said it was good training for business on a steamboat or wharf or in other enterprises. M. F. Rickoff, preacher and city superintendent in two Indiana communities, had some surprisingly modern techniques. He had students working in committees on topics not found in texts but related to their everyday work. He sponsored debates and stimulated interest in music and drama. According to students, their principal helped to develop one of the most substantial literary societies in the area.[41]

## Manual-labor Institutes

A unique phenomenon in American society has always been the relatively high regard for manual labor which has prevailed, most particularly in the North and West. It is noteworthy because it is a direct reversal of sentiment in the European nations from which the early populations for the United States were drawn.

A dichotomy between those who worked with their heads and those who worked with their hands prevailed in colonial America to a limited extent and flourished among the planters of the South prior to the Civil War. But the experience of the new land did not lend itself to the luxury of the European class systems. Americans soon discovered that the way to prosperity was to be found through cutting a swathe in a wilderness. Furthermore, aside from a limited number of Massachusetts colonists, the mass of immigrants were peasants whose concept of the good life was to be found in America, to be sure, but with industry and hard work. The experience of the people with the land; plus the Protestant revival, which dignified the individual person; plus, perhaps, the effects of the age of reason—all these combined to elevate manual work as basic and enduring in American society.

By the opening of the nineteenth century, it was not uncommon to find that the old alliance of formal education, social position, and preferred occupation had disappeared in the Northwest. About 1817, Morris Birkbeck and George Flower, both English landowners, came to America to settle in Edwards County, Illinois. In one of his letters home, Flower remarked of his American Eden, Albion, "Within the circle of a few miles, there is more good company (I mean well educated persons) than in the same circle in most parts of England." This he attributed in part to poor but literate folk, English emigrés who

[41] *Ibid.*, pp. 40, 60, 96.

had come to seek a better living in America. But his ploughman was a native, a colonel of militia, and a member of the legislature whose address and manner of speech were superior. "Where," asks Flower, "will you find persons of this Class in England with equal intelligence?"[42]

Even earlier than the Illinois venture, the new pattern was reflected among schoolteachers, particularly in the New England settlements of the Northwest. These settlers often engaged their teachers before they started for Ohio. One of these early teachers in the area around Muskingum, in approximately 1788, was Daniel Mayo, a graduate of Harvard. In the summer he worked at clearing land and in the winter he taught school. Jonathan Baldwin, another well-educated early teacher, kept school in Blockhouse No. 3 while the garrison was alerted against trouble from the Indians.[43] Thus was inaugurated the practice of combining a college education with a manual-labor occupation (farmer) and a professional occupation (teaching), with no seeming inconsistency. Indeed, teachers who did not work with their hands were often held in scant esteem. To counteract this reaction, teachers often turned to manual labor to show they could do it.[44]

It was but a short step from the feeling of compatibility between head- and handwork to the development of manual-labor academies and colleges. These institutions were organized to provide for academic work in whatever areas were judged best for the students, plus a farm or workshop which would make manual-labor training possible. The manual-labor facilities undoubtedly had several purposes, not all of which characterized every institution. These included providing a means whereby poor youth could earn part of their keep, providing an education in agricultural and/or mechanical pursuits, and providing an education in manual work, quite apart from any occupational value it might have later.

The first circular of Oberlin Collegiate Institute set forth a comprehensive statement of the aims of one manual-labor department. The purposes for which the department was established were to maintain the health of students, to promote "clear and strong thought" and a congenial, moral demeanor, to assist students in earning money for college, to aid in developing industry and economy in the youth, and to acquaint the young with everyday things. Manual labor, according to the cir-

---

[42] For first-hand accounts of impressions of and travels in the Old Northwest, see Reuben Gold Thwaites (ed.), *Early Western Travels, 1748–1846,* Arthur H. Clark Company, Glendale, Calif., 1904, vol. X.

[43] W. Ross Dunn, "Education in Territorial Ohio," *The Ohio Archaeological and Historical Society Publications,* vol. 35, pp. 334–336, 1926.

[44] Cotton, *op. cit.,* p. 53.

cular, was necessary to round out an education. "In a word it meets the wants of man as a compound being, and prevents the common and amazing waste of money, time, health, and life."[45]

The manual-labor idea was presumably introduced in the United States through the influence of Fellenberg, a Swiss disciple of Pestalozzi, and Joseph Neef, a Pestalozzian who came to this country in 1806. Neef was partly responsible for the "new school" experiment in Robert Owen's New Harmony settlement in Indiana. An official pledge of the New Harmony Manual Labor College was that as soon as the governing body could arrange for facilities, mechanical and agricultural, as well as scientific and literary studies, would be provided for the able-bodied young students.[46]

In view of how rapidly the manual-labor movement spread, however, it seems unlikely that it was due entirely to an influence from abroad. The Cumberland Presbyterian Synod, for instance, was introducing manual labor in its schools in 1825.[47] It seems more likely that the idea, once introduced, found fertile soil in which to thrive, and that if it had not come from abroad, it might have been invented by some dedicated American, probably an evangelical church member.

It is difficult to tell at this date how many of the institutions were manual labor in character. It is probable that a good majority started out that way, and changed within the course of a few years to regular schools. Trustees, however convinced of the efficacy of learning to work with the hands, soon found that student labor could not compete with commercial labor and that it was less expensive to provide scholarships for poor students than to provide "made work." Nevertheless, a few denominational schools have maintained the manual-labor characteristics; the Seventh Day Adventists are a notable example of a group that regularly provides work opportunities in colleges in both the United States and the missionary field.

## DEVELOPING PUBLICLY SUPPORTED SYSTEMS OF EDUCATION

The accounts so far given make understandable the slow rise of publicly supported institutions. Close ties of church and school in the interests of religiomoral education, and aggressive individualism which found expression in the founding of schools on a voluntary basis—both resulted in a wide and broad foundation of private educational institu-

---

[45] George W. Knight and John R. Commons, *History of Higher Education in Ohio*, U.S. Office of Education Circular of Information, no. 5, 1891, p. 59.

[46] Mock, *op. cit.*, pp. 51–52.

[47] Belting, *op. cit.*, chap. VI.

tions. Furthermore, while this country was building and was still largely agricultural, the private schools served their communities well. They provided classical or practical curricula; education for the ministry and other professions, or for vocations in business or agriculture; and teacher training programs for those who were to serve in the common schools. Mock says they increased educational opportunity, providing secondary and college education for girls, the beginnings of the junior college movement, and an adult education program. The academies fostered new methods of teaching and training for character and citizenship, as well as extracurricular activities. Mock implies that the academies failed because they succeeded so well; they finally promoted a general demand for even more widely available and free secondary education.

Since the Republic had been founded, however, there had always been men who had spoken out for the necessity of mass education to serve national purposes. "If this republican government is to survive" —so had the argument always begun, and so it began in the interests of public institutions in the nineteenth century.

Because there always appeared to be a dedicated few on the education committees and in constitutional conventions, the outline of a system stretching from elementary school through state universities was apt to be included in early constitutions. Because locally controlled schools had to await the crystallization of opinion in hundreds of communities, it was ordinarily the state college or university which got first attention from state officials. Bringing it into being, however, was often the work of an interested person or persons wholly outside the state government. Land grants entered into their development, as into the development of common schools. But so little did the state institutions profit from such grants that they seem to have been the excuse rather than the *raison d'être* for the institutions.

The way in which the complete state system was developed is another illustration of education as a folk movement, one which was characteristic of the "native" populations from the older states. The former residents of New England who established institutions in the Old Northwest were, in a sense, the makers of the dominant American culture. They were used to voluntary association as a means for getting community jobs done. They were familiar with tax-supported schools. They were dedicated to knowledge and morality, and to work as a means of securing the good in this life. The story of how they built schools from the ground up in the Old Northwest is the story of the impact of one single group on American education. Their story will be illustrated by three examples: the building of school systems in Ohio, Illinois, and Indiana.

## Ohio Develops a School System

By the 1850s, there were in Ohio the outlines of a state system, town and city school systems, property taxes for schools, and some publicly supported higher-education institutions. Because the order of their development is that of freedom and not of logic, the story is difficult to follow.[48]

The germ of free and universal education was contained in the first constitution of 1803, although it made no special provisions for education. Instead, it indicated that education should be encouraged by actions of the Legislature, and that educational institutions partially supported by grants from the United States ought to be open to all. It further provided for incorporation by the Legislature of groups wishing to secure money and properties for their institutions.

Although the 1803 constitution was in force until 1851, Ohio legislators made no move to institute any general school law until 1821. From this date until 1850, eight general school codes, with amendments and supplementary acts, and many pieces of special legislation were enacted. The general laws were permissive rather than mandatory, and were intended to indicate methods of organization and control rather than to compel standardization. The constitutional mandate to the legislators to encourage education was interpreted to mean facilitating the work of local or community groups or individuals in meeting their special educational needs or interests. The sentiment respecting educational legislation in the period from 1803 to 1850 can be inferred from Superintendent Samuel Lewis's comment on the law of 1838, the best piece of legislation during the period:[49]

It gives to the people the power to do their own business whether in townships or districts as the majority may think best. The widest possible latitude is given for popular action: the most that the law does is to prescribe certain general rules within which the people can act under the sanction of the law, and it gives to such popular action the aid of law to effect its purpose.

Even though the principle of taxing all property for schools appeared in a law of 1825 and continuously thereafter, there was no way to compel enforcement of tax laws other than to deny funds from state sources to communities not supporting schools. Nevertheless, local communities did go ahead with taxing themselves and districting for schools.

---

[48] The story to follow is pieced together largely from Miller, op. cit., and Nelson L. Bossing, "The History of Educational Legislation in Ohio from 1851 to 1925," The Ohio Archaeological and Historical Publications, vol. 39, 1930.

[49] Third Annual Report of the State Superintendent of Schools, as quoted in Miller, op. cit., p. 138.

In accordance with the principle of popular action, throughout the period, the district was the unit for organizing schools. It was so established in an 1806 act for incorporating townships.

In 1838 a state organization was developed, with county and township officers whose duties were attached to offices created for other purposes. County and township superintendencies were created in connection with the offices of auditor and clerk, respectively. In the best tradition of people minding school business voluntarily, township clerks did valiant service in supervising schools and in appointing district school officers when districts failed to provide for them. When it is known that the clerk received a maximum of $1 per year for supervision of any one school, his service is further enhanced and the concept of overseeing educational affairs as a community duty is further reinforced.

By a law of 1848, districts were created for schools for colored children, and revenues from taxation of colored citizens were used to support the schools. By a law of 1849, cities, villages, and townships were required to create one or more districts for colored children if the latter were not admitted to common schools.

*Town and City School Systems.* Up until fairly late in the antebellum period, city and town systems operated under the district school organization plan, which was adapted to a state largely rural in nature. A few places like Cincinnati secured special legislation. (Through a school charter of 1829, Cincinnati secured an organized tax-supported free system of common schools.) But it was on the basis of two state legislative acts (1837 and 1849) on behalf of schools in Akron that planning for town and city school systems emerged. It is the background of the latter act that is particularly noteworthy.

In 1846, in the incorporated limits of Akron, there were 690 children between four and sixteen years of age, but only about 375 youngsters were attending schools. School children were often housed in poor buildings, "uncouth" quarters loaned to the schools by private persons. It was in response to the generally poor school situation that the Rev. I. Jennings, pastor of the Congregational Church of Akron—"self-moved," according to the account—campaigned to reorganize the Akron schools.

On May 16, 1846, at a public meeting which Jennings and others had organized, the Congregational minister was elected chairman of a committee to consider the educational scene and measures for its improvement. The substance of this voluntary committee's work was incorporated in an act of 1847, which called for (1) an elected school board of six members; (2) the incorporation of the city into one school district; (3) provision for six or more primary schools and one central grammar school to teach "subjects requisite to a respectable English education"; (4) free admission to schools; (5) a system of examinations and classification of children; (6) taxation, and some other provisions. Through laws of 1848 and 1849, essentially these same provisions were extended to all incorporated cities, towns, or villages of 200 inhabitants or more, when provisions had been adopted by a majority vote.

Despite the difficulties of the people of Ohio in establishing a school system, statistics by the mid-nineteenth century were impressive. By 1850, there were some 484,153 pupils in 11,661 schools. Teachers numbered 12,886. In addition, there were 206 academies and private schools with 15,052 pupils.[50]

Materials for schooling were also generally available. By 1850 each pupil ordinarily had a slate with pencils, a speller, an arithmetic, and a reader. For writing, he possessed a copybook, a goose-quill pen, and a bottle of ink. The ink might well have been made at home, from oak-bark ooze and copperas mixed with weak gum solution. Lindley Murray's *English Readers*, McGuffey's *Eclectic Series*, and Nicholas Pike's *Arithmetic* were to be found among the schoolbooks.[51]

*Secondary Schools.* The state took little account of secondary education during the period from 1803 to 1850, except to issue acts of incorporation or see to it that monies given for secondary education were used properly. Nevertheless, during the period, 171 schools higher than common schools were incorporated, including 14 high schools, the first of which was in Elyria in 1830. The Western Reserve far outstripped other sections of the state in numbers of institutions, having more than three times as many secondary schools as any other area.

*Higher Education.* Higher education met much the same fate as secondary education. There was no legislative responsibility for it during the period 1803 to 1850, though there was a willingness to incorporate colleges and universities and to exercise some appointing power in connection with state institutions. Nevertheless, some forty-five institutions of higher education were founded during the antebellum period, including Ohio University, Western Reserve University, and Miami University.

*Teacher Training.* Like all aspects of educational endeavor, teacher training was a voluntary activity stimulated largely by teachers during the period from 1803 to 1850. An association of teachers and friends of education met in Cincinnati as early as 1829. Out of this association came the Western Academic Institute and Board of Education, which

[50] Francis P. Weisenburger, *The Passing of the Frontier, 1825–1850*, vol. III, in Carl Wittke (ed.), *The History of the State of Ohio*, Ohio State Archaeological and Historical Society, Columbus, Ohio, 1941, p. 166.

[51] *Ibid.*, p. 167.

was incorporated by the Legislature in 1832 to promote "harmony, co-operation and efficiency in the diffusion of elementary knowledge, and discussing such subjects as may be conducive to the advantage of educators generally."[52]   This association spanned several states.   In 1835, on request of leaders in the institute, the Legislature passed an act to incorporate The Teachers' Institute, to be devoted to the instruction of professional teachers, an institution "much wanted" within the state, according to the act.   The institute never materialized, but teachers and their families continued to awaken interest in education through their discussions.

In the meantime, groups—people engaged in establishing colleges and teachers working voluntarily—went ahead with the development of teacher training institutes such as that at Marietta College and with associations such as the American Lyceum of Education in Cincinnati.[53] The last institution planned a model common school in which "experiments might be made as to the best modes and means of instruction with a view to advancing the interests of common school education throughout the state."[54]

In 1847 and 1848 there were permissive acts allowing the county governments to use certain surplus funds for aiding the teacher institutes.   School examiners were charged with employing lecturers and purchasing common school libraries for the associations.   However, individual effort was again at a premium.   Before the examiners could underwrite an institute, the signatures of forty county schoolteachers, plus those of the board of examiners, must be affixed to a document indicating that teachers had already raised one-half of the money.

No more official notice of teacher education was taken by the state before 1850, except for a plan proposed by Governor Bartley in a message of 1844 for normal departments in two state universities.   His plan materialized fifty-seven years later.

Although the state did not act in the interests of a teacher training institution prior to 1850, the people did.   Citizens of Farmington, Trumbull County (Western Reserve), gave a site and raised by subscription $2,575 for the support of the Farmington Normal School.   In 1849 citizens asked for incorporation and formed a joint stock company selling shares at $25 each.   Objects of the school were "a thorough education of common or elementary teachers of both sexes, and to secure a course of intellectual and moral discipline for the youth of the country."[55]

[52] Quoted in Miller, op. cit., p. 130.
[53] See James B. Taylor, A Manual of the Ohio School System, H. W. Derby, Cincinnati, Ohio, 1857, for popular movements.
[54] Quoted in Miller, op. cit., p. 131.
[55] Quoted in ibid., p. 132.

*Supplemental Agencies.* In the self-help tradition of the evolving dominant American culture, a number of institutions other than schools were developed by the people for their general edification. One group of them had to do with agriculture, and their history would be repeated in state after state.

The first agricultural society was begun in Marietta by prominent citizens who wished to help members of the community through sharing their "knowledge and experience."[56] This one, like others established from 1818 to 1830, had no charm for the practical farmer, and all of them soon withered and died.

An act of 1833 gave encouragement to the organization of agricultural societies and allowed for appropriation of money for their support. There were a few fairs—at which prizes were small and judging probably unscientific. Farmers were still not much interested, and an attempt to begin a state organization in 1838 was unsuccessful.

In February, 1846, the Legislature created a State Board of Agriculture of fifty-two members, half of whom were to be elected each year. The board was given money for matching with local funds to assist in developing county societies. By 1860 there were eighty-four organized local groups. The new organizations were active in promoting fairs, which were often brought into disrepute by side shows. Nevertheless, they continued to have amusements such as bands, clowns, fireworks, horse shows, and equestriennes. By 1860, fairs were charging fees and bringing crowds. Another interesting activity of local agricultural societies was meeting in private homes for dinner, to relate improvements they had made in farm practices, read papers, and generally exchange information. The Civil War interfered with the development of these agricultural societies, but by 1865 nearly all of them were in operation again.

Still other kinds of educational institutions were begun by these transplanted New Englanders. One of them was libraries. During a meeting in 1802, a group of neighbors in Ames, near Marietta, described to one another their "intellectual wants." A library would satisfy these wants, but there was no money at hand to begin one. At this point in the conversation, Josiah True of Sunday Creek settlement suggested that money be raised by trapping coons and "sending their skins to Boston by Samuel Brown, Esq., who expected to go east in a wagon the next summer." From this beginning developed the Coonskin Library.[57] (The library had got under way in the tradition of Benjamin Franklin's more famous Philadelphia institution. Prior to this venture

---

[56] Account of agricultural societies adapted from Robert L. Jones, "A History of Local Agricultural Societies in Ohio to 1865," *The Ohio State Archaeological and Historical Quarterly*, vol. 52, pp. 120–140, 1943.

[57] Miller, *op. cit.*, pp. 134–135.

others had been tried, notably the Belpre Farmers' Library which was organized in 1796 as the Putnam Family Library.) The state finally took notice of the concerted drives of adults to educate themselves and chartered the Dayton Library Society on February 21, 1805. By 1850, 192 library societies had been incorporated. From 1824 on, the state library at Columbus received regular appropriations, and in 1846, district school libraries were authorized—providing local communities could raise the money by local taxation.

In the first thirty-five years of the nineteenth century in Ohio there were many additional reading opportunities of a quite informal nature. Miller reports Atwater as stating in an 1838 book that "most of the towns in Ohio had reading rooms." There the wayfarer could find the chief newspapers and periodicals.[58]

Before 1850, sixty-four lyceums, institutes, athenaeums, and literary societies devoted to the diffusion of useful knowledge had been incorporated also.

### Illinois Develops a School System

Although the material on Illinois is different in particulars and in reportorial method, much of the same effervescence is apparent there in the locally stimulated movement toward a state system.[59]

Northern Illinois was peopled by New Englanders and Easterners, who developed the free common school system. Southern Illinois, on the other hand, was settled by Virginians and other Southerners, who established academies and select schools.

Like other states of the Old Northwest, Illinois was heir to congressional largess in the form of school lands when the state was admitted in 1818. Besides Section No. 16, some salt springs and proceeds of other lands were given to the state in addition to one township, plus another designated by the President for a seminary of learning.

Before statehood, schools were ordinarily begun by itinerant teachers. Based on the reserved township, however, the territorial assembly on November 29, 1806, passed "an Act to incorporate a university in Indiana territory." According to the act, every republic depends upon the "wisdom, virtue, talents and energy of its citizens and rulers." Furthermore, "learning hath ever been found the ablest advocate of genuine liberty, the best supporter of rational religion and the source of the only solid and imperishable glory which nations can acquire."[60] It was

---

[58] Caleb Atwater, *A History of the State of Ohio, Natural and Civil*, 2d ed., Glezen & Shepard, Cincinnati, Ohio, 1838, as cited in Miller, *op. cit.*, p. 135.

[59] Account of the development of a school system in Illinois adapted largely from Belting, *op. cit.*

[60] Quoted in *ibid.*, p. 285.

noted that, since any citizen can be elected to highest office, it becomes particularly necessary to have knowledge widely diffused. For this strategic institution, a board of trustees was organized, with William Henry Harrison as president. The board took office on December 6, 1806.

The benefits from Section No. 16 were ordinarily to go to the academies, which were under semipublic control. Very early the Belleville, Madison, and Washington academies were chartered through pressure from communities, and town trustees became academy trustees. An unusual amount of local interest may have been involved, in that Illinois citizens were inclined to feel that the chief function of the academy was to turn out teachers for the common schools.

As befitted folk schools, other purposes were peculiar to individual academies. Occasionally a charter would indicate a desire that aborigines enroll their children. One charter pointed out the importance of an academy education for girls who would one day form the character of the young.

There were no uniform means of control or admission requirements for all academies, although generally anyone who paid tuition charges was admitted. After 1830, trustees of chartered academies were made corporate bodies politic. By the 1840s communities could levy taxes with the consent of two-thirds of the voters; and by a law of 1842, certain academy lands were exempted from taxation.

*Common Schools.* The pioneers of Illinois took the same rambling journey toward a free, compulsory system as did the people of Ohio. The Free School Law of 1825 (seven years after the admission of Illinois to statehood) provided that on petition of a majority of legal voters of the county, a free school district could be laid out and a tax levied for support of education in the district. This law was amended in 1827, so that an individual could be taxed only by his own consent.

In 1833, friends of public education organized the Illinois Institute of Education, designed to obtain information on schools and scholars and to put this information before the public. True to their background, these school advocates solicited help via a questionnaire which was to be returned to John Russell, Esq., Postmaster of Buffdale, Greene County, and to J. M. Peck, Postmaster at Rock Spring, St. Clair County. Among other items were queries as to whether the respondent could promote a meeting on education on court day or other convenient occasions, and whether he would "make public addresses or deliver lectures" on schools and education. In order to secure information on how best to reach the public, the respondent was also asked what proportion of the people took newspapers or other periodicals. Answers to the questionnaire were ammunition for a strategic meeting held at

Vandalia in 1834, at the same time and place as the meeting of the general assembly.

In the meantime, various voluntary groups and individuals were carrying on agitations which would feed the public school movement. In 1833, at Jacksonville, a Ladies' Association for the Education of Females, designed to assist in educating women for teaching, was organized. The Mechanics' Union of Springfield opened a free public school for the city. The interdenominational state Sunday-school movement had got under way, and an estimate of 1831 put the schools at 375 with 2,000 teachers, 17,000 pupils, and 2,000 volumes. In 1835, John S. Wright of Chicago built a common school at his own expense. He was the man who edited the *Prairie Farmer*, a weekly devoted to agriculture, mechanic arts, and common schools. The Illinois State Education Society was organized in 1840.

In 1845 communities were allowed to levy a property tax by a two-thirds majority vote; in 1848 this was changed to a simple majority vote. A report of 1849 showed thirty Northern and six Southern counties levying the permissive tax. By 1852, thirty Northern and seven Southern counties were levying voluntarily; twenty-six counties, eighteen Southern and eight Northern, were not levying.

The new constitution of 1847 did not mention free schools. But the legislature established a separate department of public instruction, and provided for a state superintendent who was required to prepare a bill for the reorganization of the school system. A free school bill of 1855 prescribed a state tax of 2 mills on $1 of property, the income to be added to the common school fund. It called for a local tax levy by trustees of township and districts for at least one free school in every district for six months in the year. The common school fund was to be so distributed that two-thirds was to be on the basis of white children between five and twenty-one, "and the remaining one-third on the basis of the number of townships or parts of townships in each county" in proportion to the number of days taught in each township.

*Secondary Schools.* Because of the prevalence of the academy, the public high school got started late. The first legal specification for a high school was made by a special charter for one township in 1857; a township high school plan was incorporated in general school law only in 1872. Free public high schools were established when the State Supreme Court, some time after 1870, affirmed that high schools could be thought of as part of a common school education and the constitution of 1870 had given the Legislature the right to provide for a system of schools "whereby all the children of this state may receive a good common school education."[61]

[61] Quoted in *ibid.,* p. 540.

The folk built a rambling school system slowly and not by logical design. The folk are still in evidence in the offices of the county superintendent who functions largely as inspector and clerk, and a state superintendent who is still elected.

### Indiana Develops
### a Public School System

In 1868, a paper issued by Quakers contained a statement noting that the diffusion of knowledge among all its members was "peculiarly in accordance with the principles" of their religious society. "We have no trained order of Preisthood, but we recognize each true believer as boath preist and King."[62] This sentiment is a fitting opening for the educational drive of the people of Indiana who, like others in the Old Northwest, established educational institutions because each citizen was both priest and king.

In the act of April 16, 1816, the year of the state constitution, the usual sixteenth Section was given for schools, and the state could neither sell the lands nor appropriate the proceeds.[63] Revenues from lands were to constitute the Congressional Township Fund.

The first constitution likewise had several provisions for schools, among them a complete system including township schools, county seminaries, and a state university. As there was no public source of revenue for the first two categories of institutions, little came of the plan except the opening of an Indiana seminary which later became Indiana University. One of the more interesting provisions was for 10 per cent of proceeds of town lots to go to the use of a library and for incorporation of a library company.

The next step taken was an act of 1824 to incorporate congressional townships and provide for public schools. Through a succession of laws up to 1849, the offices of county commissioners of education and county examiners were instituted, and the state treasurer was made superintendent of common schools. In the meantime, private groups were establishing schools and advocates of public education were busy. In proportion to their numbers, the Friends were the staunchest advocates of public schools, though they put their early efforts into their private schools because they could not send their children to schools supported by military fines and exemption monies.

Illustrative of the advocates of public education was Caleb Mills, born in New Hampshire, a Sunday-school organizer and theological student.

---

[62] Ethel Hittle McDaniel, "The Contribution of the Society of Friends to Education in Indiana," *Indiana Historical Society Publications*, vol. 13, no. 2, p. 140, 1939.

[63] Account of the development of a school system in Indiana adapted largely from Boone, *op. cit.*

On prompting of Mills via six papers signed "One of the People," the Legislature passed an act to ask the people whether they were in favor of free public schools. In October, 1848, in the fall elections, the legislators asked for a viva voce vote on the question: Are you in favor of public schools? The replies were "Yes," 78,523; "No," 61,887. Table 11-5 gives some pertinent statistics on the vote.

The explanation of the vote is varied, and reflects the people in many ways. Some of the lower classes feared the union of church and state in education. The denser counties, particularly the Southern ones, voted against free schools because seminaries and colleges had already been established through voluntary effort. Of the twelve counties that

Table 11-5. The 1848 Vote in Indiana on Free Schools

| Counties | No. of counties | Total vote | Vote | |
|---|---|---|---|---|
| | | | Yes | No |
| Northern............ | 47 | 64,850 | 41,560 | 23,290 |
| Southern............ | 43 | 75,560 | 36,963 | 38,597 |
| Total............ | 90 | 140,410 | 78,523 | 61,887 |

SOURCE: Richard G. Boone, *A History of Education in Indiana*, Appleton-Century-Crofts, Inc., New York, 1892, p. 107.

maintained the most prosperous seminaries, two-thirds voted against free schools.

On the basis of a majority vote for schools, the Legislature passed a law in 1849 which legalized public taxation for support of schools and authorized a levy of 10 cents on $100 of property. Boone says that in the period from 1848 to 1850, the tax probably yielded an annual income of not less than $250,000. In the distribution of the funds, the township was made the unit. All revenues, except for one, were distributed in the counties where the monies were collected. The vote on the 1849 law showed fifty-nine of the ninety counties in favor of the law: forty-six of them Northern with only one Northern county voting negatively; and thirty-one of them against, of which twenty were Southern and originally settled from the South. The law was to take effect only in those counties voting in the affirmative. Thereafter the counties were to be given an annual chance by ballot to change their vote.

*The Constitutional Convention.* The next drive for schools came in the constitutional convention of February, 1851. The success of the venture was probably due in no small measure to the efforts of J. R. M. Bryant, Edwin R. May, and John L. Morrison. Morrison had already demonstrated his keen interest in education. In 1835 he had built and established the Salem Female Academy. He had been principal of the Washington County Seminary in Salem, a professor of mathematics at Indiana, and was chairman of the committee on education at the convention.

Chief opponents of a comprehensive school system came from those interested in church-related institutions. Many genuinely believed that the state university should be abolished and the funds divided among the schools and colleges of the state. This view was subscribed to even by Caleb Mills, who later became the first state superintendent of public instruction.

Article 8 favoring schools finally became a part of the constitution. It called on the assembly to encourage by all suitable means moral, intellectual, scientific, and agricultural improvement, and to provide by law for a general and uniform system of tuition-free common schools which would be open to all. It established a common school fund, the principal of which was to be maintained intact to provide an income for schools. Through Morrison's interest, it also called for the election of a school superintendent who would hold office for two years.

*After the Constitution.* The auspicious start made with the constitution was halted by the law of 1852, which made a direct levy of 10 cents on each $100 of property taxable for state purposes as an appropriation for schools. The citizens at the local level fought over the tax, and a court decision finally had it that a tax for tuition was unconstitutional. Tuition in all public schools must be furnished by the state, and houses and appliances by the locality. Cities and towns alike found that they could not tax for tuition, and so many schools were closed and teachers and superintendents left.

The people again took over. There was a revival of seminary organizations. Earlier schools were revived, churches opened schools, and private individuals started seminaries. One of the more interesting of them was White's Indiana Manual Labor Institute, established near Wabash in 1852. White, colored, and Indian children were admitted from the beginning, but in the first thirty years, most of the youngsters were white. In the fall of 1885 the Indiana Yearly Meeting of Friends undertook, through contract with the government, to run the school. Indian children from the Quapaw, Sac, and Fox agencies were admitted.

In 1885, Judge Elliott of the supreme court reversed the decisions formerly held and said that because the Legislature must provide for common schools does not mean that the Legislature must directly levy taxes for each locality. The state shall provide through instrumentalities of government such as townships, towns, and cities. Judge Elliott pointed out that if local units of government could be given authority to tax for schoolhouses, then that authority could be extended to taxing for teachers' salaries. He felt no distinction could be made between the right to hire teachers and the right to provide facilities where children should be taught.

With favorable laws in 1866 and 1877 for the education of Negro youngsters, and with taxes available for instruction by 1885, the public school system of Indiana was finally on its way.

## SUMMARY

This case study of the impact of a population on school systems is particularly appropriate as the first in the series. The group that largely made the difference in schooling was made up of New Englanders, from whose subculture the dominant American culture has been built.

What can be learned from the way in which the men and the women of the Old Northwest went about the business of developing educational institutions? Perhaps the first, last, and only lesson to be learned about these frontier folk—incidentally members of the dominant culture—is that they were "self-moved." They were nostalgically American.

These pioneers of the Old Northwest behaved in ways termed ideally American. Initiative for the development of schools was taken by hundreds of obscure individuals. Schools were a part of grass-roots movements. Leadership in educational campaigns shifted from a "female" to a farm editor, to a preacher—all for the most part unsung in history books. The might of government was often ignored—except as it gave force to local decision making. Private and voluntary efforts and local consent to compulsory taxation provided the means through which educational enterprises were undertaken.

Out of this complex of meetinghouse, townhouse, schoolhouse, there emerged in the Old Northwest a series of substantial locally controlled public school systems, and equally substantial private and public higher-education institutions. Out of it also came a locally controlled system of education which had originated in New England and which was to spread throughout most of the United States.

# 12

# Establishing Schools for Negroes
# in Georgia

It is a mighty task, indeed, to reorganize the industry not
only of four millions of the colored race, but of five millions
of whites. Nevertheless, the vast progress you have made
. . . fills us with hope that every stain on your freedom
will shortly be removed, and that the erasure of that foul
blot upon civilization and Christianity—chattel slavery—
. . . will cause the name of Abraham Lincoln to be honored
and revered by posterity.[1]

ADDRESS TO PRESIDENT LINCOLN BY
THE CITIZENS OF MANCHESTER,
ENGLAND, JANUARY, 1863

The firing on Fort Sumter signaled the beginning of a process by which
several million Americans might become freemen. The term *process*
is used deliberately, for the most devastating war Americans have ever
fought did not automatically strike off the chains which bound their
Negro compatriots. Except for the brief period of the Reconstruction
government, these new citizens in former slave states have never participated fully, as did the freemen of ancient Athens, in the management of their government. Nor, until the present, have they bidden
fair to throw off the chains of ignorance—chains which determine any
people's slavery or freedom.

In the struggle for knowledge which these new citizens have made,
their success has been determined by their geographical location and
thus by the traditions of the area in which they have lived. Some
465,698—over 99 per cent of whom were slaves—made their homes in

---

[1] Frank Moore (ed.), *The Rebellion Record: A Diary of American Events, with
Documents, Narratives, Illustrative Incidents, Poetry, etc.,* G. P. Putnam and C. T.
Evans, New York, 1863, vol. VI, p. 345.

Georgia just prior to the Civil War.[2]  Georgia was one of the states which seceded—though only after a bitter fight—in the ante-Sumter period.[3]  It was largely rural, its population was almost equally divided between black and white, it still clung to the plantation economy of the Old South, and it had never developed a public school tradition.  Georgian society bore no resemblance to the neat New England culture of meetinghouse, townhall, and schoolhouse which had nurtured the so-called national school system.  It had few points in common with the rural milieu of Spanish-speaking New Mexicans (see Chapter 13), except for a commitment to a hierarchical society with an agricultural base. Georgians knew nothing of the process by which a heterogeneous people, as in Hawaii, might be unified (see Chapter 14).  Georgians of 1860 and of whatever color were largely native in the sense that their forebears had settled on farms and plantations in the 1700s.  Their one consuming problem in the postbellum period has been race relations.  This problem has conditioned a school system which is still another variation of the standard pattern but which, in the building, has repeated in distorted fashion the school building process of the Old Northwest.

This second case study is deliberately confined to the establishment of schools for Negroes only.  It typifies the efforts that have been made in many areas to develop schools for one-tenth of the American population.[4]

## ANTEBELLUM BACKGROUND

The hand of the past lay heavy in a state where, for absence of immigration, there was little change.  A rural economy resistant to modification, a tradition of private and pauper schools, and a largely illiterate and deprived Negro people were the heritages which partly determined the way in which education developed in Georgia.  The course of colonial and early national development probably played a more important role in postbellum Georgia's adjustment to a more powerful federalism than it did in the border states or even in other slave states.

### Status of the Negroes in Antebellum Georgia

One of the issues most difficult to resolve in the postbellum period was the right of former slaves to education.  Acceptance of this right

---

[2] *Preliminary Report on the Eighth Census, 1860,* 37th Cong., 2d Sess., *ex.* doc. no. 116, 1862, p. 131.

[3] Wesley M. Gewehr (ed.), *American Civilization: A History of the United States,* McGraw-Hill Book Company, Inc., New York, 1957, p. 253.

[4] For a history of education in Georgia, see Dorothy Orr, *A History of Education in Georgia,* The University of North Carolina Press, Chapel Hill, N.C., 1950.

was a long step for Southern whites to take, for in the antebellum period, the basic general assumption was that slaves were chattel (personal property) rather than persons. There were some exceptions to this viewpoint among members of the Northern churches, Roman Catholics, and Quakers, who believed that the Negro—like other men—possessed a soul. However, in Georgia—as undoubtedly in other Southern states —the issues of slaves as property versus slaves as people "remained an unresolved one."[5] The vacillation in policies respecting slaves and the markedly inferior status of freed slaves at the time of emancipation can be better understood against the historical background.

Negroes from the coasts of West Africa were first introduced into the colonies by Dutch traders. They were imported into Virginia in 1619, though slavery throughout the colonies did not become important until 1700 when England developed into the most substantial slave-trading nation.[6] Regardless of the development and growth of slavery, however, some abolition sentiment existed from early colonial days on, and some steps were taken to reduce or abolish the institution. The first known law against slavery was passed in 1652 in Rhode Island. The act read that all Negroes were to be freed after having given ten years of service. It is to Chief Justice Samuel Sewall, however, that the honor of the first written attack on slavery must go. In his *The Selling of Joseph* he said, "There is no proportion between twenty pieces of silver and liberty."[7] Even in Georgia there was no clear-cut commitment to the peculiar institution until the 1800s, though slavery was introduced there in 1749,[8] and in 1750 the colonists put pressure on the trustees of the colony to revoke an original ruling which had prohibited slavery.

Early slave laws were harsh. For example, before 1770, taking a slave's life was not a felony. By 1765, however, the most oppressive provisions were repealed, and in 1770 a slave code was developed. Among the provisions was one expressly forbidding "cutting, or wounding, or . . . cruelly and unnecessarily biting or tearing with dogs."[9] However, by an act of 1770, Negroes, Indians, mulattoes, and mestizos

[5] Milton Sydney Heath, *Constructive Liberalism: The Role of the State in Economic Development in Georgia to 1860*, Harvard University Press, Cambridge, Mass., 1954, p. 351.

[6] Gewehr, *op. cit.*, p. 27.

[7] Ullin Whitney Leavell, *Philanthropy in Negro Education*, George Peabody College for Teachers, Nashville, Tenn., 1930, p. 8; and Vernon Louis Parrington, *Main Currents in American Thought: An Interpretation of American Literature from the Beginning to 1920*, Harcourt, Brace and Company, Inc., New York, 1927–1930, vol. I, p. 95.

[8] Richard R. Wright, *A Brief Historical Sketch of Negro Education in Georgia*, Robinson Printing House, Savannah, Ga., 1894, p. 19.

[9] Kenneth M. Stampp, *The Peculiar Institution: Slavery in the Ante-bellum South*, Alfred A. Knopf, Inc., New York, 1956, pp. 18, 206, 218–219.

who were not free or living in peace with the government were "absolute slaves" and "chattels personal."[10]

In 1798 the importation of Africans was prohibited by law.[11] Both Georgia and South Carolina were opposed to closing avenues to sources of slaves. They preferred the imports from Africa to those from nearby states.[12] Georgians objected to the "villainous" Negroes being sent to her from other states, and particularly from South Carolina.[13] Some importation from other states was acceptable, for example, an immigrant to Georgia or a Georgia citizen could bring in slaves for his own use, but not for purposes of speculation.[14] Nevertheless, loud as were the complaints, slaves were important to the Georgian economy, and Negroes were brought into the state as merchandise up to the end of the confederate period.[15]

In general, the code of 1770 and state and local laws of 1833 governed the importation, management, and treatment of slaves up to the Civil War. The laws concerned a number of areas—the institution of slavery, traffic in slaves, the welfare and training of Negroes, as well as their employment, and competition between slave and white labor.[16] There were few regulations respecting separation of children and mothers through sale,[17] but the separation of husband and wife or parent and child would have been condemned by the public in general. The master usually dispensed justice on his plantation, both protecting and punishing his slaves. He was enjoined against murder or malicious killing, for which the punishment was the same as for attacks on white persons.[18] But despite injunctions against cruelty, for which fines or imprisonment were the punishments, the master's judgment prevailed in practice, and juries would not convict for, nor judges define the nature of, the master's crime.[19] The slave had little redress of grievance in law.

Manumission by lenient masters was hedged around with severe restrictions. Free Negroes were held in low regard, and less than 1 per

[10] Heath, *op. cit.*, p. 350.

[11] Stampp, *op. cit.*, p. 25.

[12] Heath, *op. cit.*, p. 351.

[13] Stampp, *op. cit.*, p. 243.

[14] Ulrich Bonnell Phillips, "Georgia and State Rights: A Study of the Political History of Georgia from the Revolution to the Civil War with Particular Regard to Federal Relations," *Annual Report of the American Historical Association 1901*, U.S. Government Printing Office, Washington, 1902, vol. II, p. 157-

[15] Stampp, *op. cit.*, p. 256.

[16] Heath, *op. cit.*, p. 350.

[17] Stampp, *op. cit.*, p. 252.

[18] Phillips, *op. cit.*, pp. 153–154.

[19] Heath, *op. cit.*, p. 352.

cent of the colored people of Georgia were free in the early national period.[20] Negroes were outside the pale of human intervention. They were "natural" slaves and "ordained by God to be forever the servants of man." Georgia law was powerless to transform slaves into "natural" free men.[21] As of 1801, manumission was illegal unless sanctioned by the Legislature, though the policy changed several times thereafter. Even in 1807, free Negroes in Louisville, Savannah, Augusta, and Milledgeville were subject to the same police regulations as were slaves. Renting a house to free Negroes brought penalty if done without official permission. In 1818 there was an act to prohibit entry into the state of free Negroes; if they ignored the law on immigration, they could be sold into slavery. As late as 1859, law decreed that vagrant free Negroes could be sold as slaves. Free Negroes had to have guardians and could not carry firearms. Neither could they own property, leave trusts, or secure profits through their labor.[22] By 1860, of the 465,698 Negroes in Georgia, only 3,500, or less than 1 per cent, were free.[23] Free persons who were colored were "peculiarly offensive to the institution of slavery."[24]

This outline of the Negro's status suggests the most devastating aspect of Negro society—an aspect that would determine the nature of the freedom colored people would have. These men and women probably had never been able to develop a cohesive culture which would give them security while making a transition to a new culture. It has been argued that there are remnants of an African past among Negroes in the United States. If so, these remnants could hardly have been knit into a consistent way of life when basic patterns, such as family and tribal organization, had been deliberately rent asunder by slave traders and slave holders. Yet these people, deprived of their own culture, had never been permitted—by reason of their status—to borrow the strongest elements of the white culture. Particularly had they not been allowed to develop a family system, which would have stood them in good stead as a stabilizing force. They came to freedom with a hybrid culture of dubious value.[25]

## Economy of Antebellum Georgia

It is probably impossible to assess the part which belief and sentiment, aside from economics, played in the attitude of Georgians toward their

[20] Phillips, op. cit., p. 155.
[21] Heath, op. cit., p. 354.
[22] Ibid., pp. 350–351; and Phillips, op. cit., pp. 155–156.
[23] Preliminary Report on the Eighth Census, 1860, p. 131.
[24] Heath, op. cit., p. 350.
[25] For a discussion of African heritages, see E. Franklin Frazier, The Negro in the United States, The Macmillan Company, New York, 1949, chap. I.

slaves, if, indeed, such separation existed.  So far as the economics of the situation were concerned, colored slaves were certainly considered particularly important to the cotton- and rice-growing enterprises.  On the other hand, a wave of humanitarian sentiment had accompanied economic reverses in Southern agriculture during the early national period.  There was even some sympathetic interest in a colonization society designed to help colored Americans settle in Africa.  The tide changed, however, and in 1827 the Georgia Legislature officially condemned the society.  Later a reward was offered for the discovery and conviction of the editors or printers of William Lloyd Garrison's *Liberator*.[26]

By the 1830s, Southern agriculture had recaptured the vitality which had characterized it in colonial days and Georgia was exporting cotton to the mills of Manchester and Lowell.[27]  The plantation system was being remade, and slavery was a settled—and growing—institution. Slaves were a source of labor both in the fields and in essential related enterprises.  Slaves had been chiefly responsible for building nearly 1,000 miles of roadbed in Georgia.[28]  Africans were considered essential on the rice, sugar, and sea-island cotton plantations where white workers were doomed by unhealthy working conditions[29]—all of them areas belonging to the Georgian aristocracy.[30]  There were variations in the slave-owning pattern from state to state and from region to region in a state.  In early nineteenth-century Georgia, two-fifths of the white families owned slaves.  By 1860, however, unfree Negroes were concentrated in the hands of only a few masters.  Only one-fourth of the slaves belonged to owners with fewer than ten Negroes.  Consequently, "Southerners measured their rank in society by counting their slaves."[31]

By the beginning of the Civil War, there was less profit from agriculture in Georgia and South Carolina than in the Southwest, yet the plantation system was still profitable.  By the 1850s, Georgia's exports had outstripped her imports,[32] and Louis Manigault, for instance, realized 10 per cent profit from his rice plantation.  The importance of slavery to the economics of the state is shown by the fact that by 1860, the taxable value of slaves in Georgia was $302,694,855—more than the value of all taxable land.[33]

[26] Phillips, *op. cit.*, pp. 158–160.
[27] Stampp, *op. cit.*, p. 27.
[28] *Ibid.*, pp. 27, 62.
[29] Phillips, *op. cit.*, p. 158.
[30] Stampp, *op. cit.*, p. 31.
[31] *Ibid.*, pp. 27, 30–31.
[32] *Ibid.*, pp. 238, 409–410.
[33] Willard Range, *The Rise and Progress of Negro Colleges in Georgia 1865–1949*, The University of Georgia Press, Athens, Ga., 1951, p. 19.

To the plantation aristocracy, the nearly 50 per cent of the population who were black and unfree had become, at the time of the Civil War, an indispensable labor supply and personal property, and possession of slaves was a mark of social status.

## Education in Antebellum Georgia

The slave was chattel property; he had few rights, he was not, even in the ordinary sense, a person. It is not strange, then, that he came to his "free status" in the 1860s with little preparation for constructive citizenship. So far as the Negroes' education was concerned, the lack of it was partly a result of the general attitude toward education—a free and poor white would have fared little better than a slave in Georgia in antebellum days. Georgia had not accepted the state's financial and moral obligation for the enlightenment of its citizens, an obligation that had been accepted in most of the states north of the Mason-Dixon Line in the period from 1820 to 1860. The compulsory and free common school for all the children of all the people was a New England concept, foreign to the thinking and practice of the Georgian dominant class. When it was introduced by Yankee teachers in the war and postbellum periods, it was a radical innovation.[34]

The pattern in antebellum Georgia was private education for children of the aristocracy and charity education for the children of paupers. For some years in private schools, there had been a fund for the education of the poor, and in 1843 a law was passed allowing counties to levy a tax for such education. By 1859, eighty-four counties were levying the poor tax, and some 82,800 white youngsters, out of a population of 107,825, ages eight to eighteen years, were in some kind of school.[35] Publicly supported efforts were local, voluntary, and stigmatized as promoting education for paupers.

The Legislature had indeed tried, but unsuccessfully, to set up a school system in 1845 and again in 1856. Failing to develop a state system, in 1858 the Legislature set aside for education the sum of $100,000 a year of the net earnings of the Western and Atlantic Railroad. Counties were allowed to establish free schools for which state funds might be used, but by 1860 only one county, Forsyth, had established such schools.[36]

[34] Louis R. Harlan, *Separate and Unequal: Public School Campaigns and Racism in the Southern Seaboard States 1901–1915*, The University of North Carolina Press, Chapel Hill, N.C., 1958, pp. 4–5.

[35] T. Conn Bryan, *Confederate Georgia*, The University of Georgia Press, Athens, Ga., 1953, p. 222.

[36] *Ibid.*

By 1860 there were some 1,752 public schools with 56,087 pupils. The latter constituted nearly 60 per cent of the total of 94,687 who were attending some kind of school. These youngsters were largely in elementary schools, probably primary, for only the larger towns supported secondary schools, which were generally private academies and seminaries rather than high schools. As a result of this very modest record of pauper rather than free public schools and a private school establishment, there were in 1860 some 44,257 white persons over twenty years of age who could not read or write.[37]

Even though thousands of whites were being schooled in antebellum Georgia, the absence of the free public school tradition would mean that postbellum Georgia would have a long hard road to travel in learning how to educate both Negro and white children.

With limited organized effort for the education of white citizens, it could hardly be expected that there would be a large group of literate slaves. An unfree Negro who could read and write was considered a menace to the safety and security of white Georgia. A literate person would have access to seditious ideas and might become a potential Nat Turner. Acts of 1755 and 1770 had forbidden teaching slaves to write. Later laws of 1829 meted out punishments of whipping, fines, or imprisonment to those who taught slaves to read or write and prohibited the use of Negroes in setting type.[38] Nevertheless, a few Negroes acquired the semblance of an education prior to the Civil War.

Earliest efforts to educate Negroes in colonial days and immediately after the Civil War are reminiscent of the process by which education got under way in the Old Northwest. The established church rather than the Congregational churches took the initiative. In 1701 the Society for the Propagation of the Gospel in Foreign Parts was chartered to serve the plantations, colonies, and factories overseas. It was considered that there were many lost souls in America, "abandoned to Atheism and Infidelity," and also to the "divers Romish Priests and Jesuits" who were perverting and converting "our said Loving Subjects to Popish Superstition and Idolatry." Between 1701 and the Revolutionary War, Negroes and Indians were of special concern to the society.[39]

The society had its ups and downs. Reverend Taylor's report, dated April 23, 1719, on teaching the catechism to slaves in North Carolina indicated only limited success, and he emphasized that his lessons were

[37] Ibid., pp. 222–223.

[38] Phillips, op. cit., p. 153.

[39] Edgar W. Knight, A Documentary History of Education in the South before 1860, vol. I, European Inheritances, The University of North Carolina Press, Chapel Hill, N.C., 1949, pp. 62, 64–65.

"without Book." The public's attitude may be inferred from the fact that he was informed by Esquire Duckenfield that he should baptize no more slaves until English law plainly stated that slaves were not to be free simply because they had been baptized.[40] Undaunted, the society in 1741 purchased Harry and Andrew, two Negroes, who were given a good education and established as schoolmasters of a Negro school in Charleston, South Carolina, in 1744. The school was recorded as having an attendance of sixty pupils,[41] among whom were children of a few Georgia slaves who had been privileged to receive money for their time.[42] At the same time, in Georgia, religious rather than educational efforts were being made and on December 20, 1750, the Rev. Bartholomew Zouberbuhler reported that he had baptized one woman of the two hundred Negro infidels.[43]

The first private endowment fund for Negro education was initiated by Rev. Thomas Bray, Commissary for Maryland of the Bishop of London. Charged by the Bishop with converting Negroes and educating their children, Bray interested M. D'Allone, private secretary of King William at the Hague. D'Allone gave Dr. Bray £900 for converting Negroes on British plantations. This money became the nucleus of an endowment administered on Bray's death by an organization called Associates of Dr. Bray and confirmed by a decree in chancery in 1731. The interest from the fund was used for some years to pay a catechist to instruct Georgia Negroes. This project did not go well. The account states that because of their commitment to superstition, resentment of slavery and hard labor, and ignorance of language adult Georgia Negroes were poor risks. The organization therefore turned to developing schools among Negro youngsters born and educated in the colonies. Two such schools were in operation in Philadelphia in 1760.[44] The schools and the society itself had some little impact on Negro education in general, but precious little on Negroes in Georgia.

Other missionary societies in the antebellum period were converting and educating the colored population in Christian knowledge. Robert Raikes' Ragged Schools for poor children were introduced in the United States. Soon after the schools were set up, the Methodist Conference recommended them for Negroes. These schools were later called Sunday schools, and were designed for teaching the three R's as well as religion. By 1857 the Methodist Episcopal Church had 172 missions for Negroes; by 1860 there were 335 missionaries in the field. Between

[40] *Ibid.*, pp. 87–88.
[41] Leavell, *op. cit.*, p. 6.
[42] Wright, *op. cit.*, p. 19.
[43] Knight, *op. cit.*, pp. 123–124.
[44] *Ibid.*, pp. 62, 139–140; and Leavell, *op. cit.*, p. 7.

1845 and 1860, the church spent $1,320,778.03 on missionary work among the colored population.[45]

In the early period, the Baptists tried little in the field of education. However, they did establish Negro churches, the first being at Silver Bluff, South Carolina, before 1778. Between that date and the Civil War, the founding of Negro churches went steadily forward in many places, including Savannah and Augusta, Georgia.[46]

In their own peculiar way, the Quakers may have made the greatest impact on the educational status of the Negroes. Their strength was in an assumption made by few of the other societies—that education was of value only to free men.[47] While a man was a slave, all that he did to improve himself was for his master's sake. When he became free, he had new needs and desires and his attainments would be for himself and his posterity.[48] The first task of Quakers was to exert themselves to free the bondsmen through manumitting their own slaves and persuading others to see slavery as sinful. Thereafter, they would educate the freedmen. From the time of George Fox, the founder of the Society of Friends, Quakers were enjoined to instruct Indians and Negroes as well as all others; for "He doth enlighten every man that cometh into the world, with His true light." Germans and Quakers together fought slavery in Pennsylvania. As early as 1770 the Friends established a Negro school in Pennsylvania. Where Negroes were too few for separate schools, Friends enrolled them in their white schools. They ostracized members who persisted in slaveholding, called on members to make regular reports on conditions among Negroes and the poor, and set aside meetings at which only the concerns of the colored were discussed.[49] Quakers worked in very few Southern states. One of them was North Carolina, where advocates of slaveholding attempted to prevent the Friends from affecting the slave institution. The gentle people persisted in their educational efforts, and were rewarded by the fact that as early as 1731, some Negroes could read and write.[50]

From the 1700s through the Civil War, the Friends established schools for Negroes or educated them in homes and schools with their own children in Delaware, Virginia, Maryland, Washington, D.C., and Indiana. In the last state, the only education provided for Negroes between 1834 and 1869 was given by Quakers. In 1861, some 318 colored

[45] Leavell, op. cit., pp. 18–20.
[46] Ibid., p. 21.
[47] Ibid., p. 9.
[48] Thomas Woody, Early Quaker Education in Pennsylvania, Teachers College Contributions to Education, no. 105, Bureau of Publications, Teachers College, Columbia University, New York, 1920, p. 238.
[49] Ibid., chap. XI, p. 234.
[50] Leavell, op. cit., p. 13.

children were in attendance at Indiana Friends schools; and Quakers maintained a college, the Union Liberty Institute, for those denied admission to public schools.

Even in New England they had to exhibit extraordinary courage. Prudence Crandall, Quaker, in 1832 admitted a Negro girl to her school in Canterbury, Connecticut. Miss Crandall brought on herself the wrath of parents of white children as well as the state Legislature, which acted to prohibit the school. Prudence Crandall was jailed and subsequently had to abandon her institution because it was almost totally ruined by a mob.[51]

Quakers persisted, occasionally with violence but most of the time quietly. They early were abolitionists, but believed in persuading slaveholders to undertake manumission activities voluntarily. When the more aggressive American Anti-slavery Society was begun in 1833, twenty-one Friends were among the sixty-two people present. From that time on, Friends were divided in their sentiments. The gradualists were scorned by abolitionists for being as sinful as slaveholders. Yet many Quakers of both groups participated in the Underground Railroad, and many suffered loss of property, imprisonment, and death for their heroic actions on behalf of slaves.[52] Throughout the period, they continued their educational endeavors, though most of them had little initial impact on the South and on Georgia in particular.

Though Quakers and some other missionaries did little directly in education for Negroes in Georgia in the antebellum period, there were desultory and clandestine attempts to educate. Masters were enjoined by law not to educate their slaves, but kindly masters, their wives, or their children occasionally taught favorite slaves to read and write. Poor whites made their living by teaching secretly. Underground schools are known to have been in existence in Savannah and Augusta in antebellum days. They had engaging names traceable to location or subterfuge. Some were called "old tailor shop schools"—probably because of their secret location in institutions manned by poor whites or Negroes. Others were known as "old chips schools"—a name taken from the saying that youngsters in attendance at a schoolmaster's house were going to pick up chips. If an officer chanced to come around on a police tour, youngsters would be found busily picking up chips.[53]

For thirty years a Negro woman named Deveau secretly conducted a school in Savannah.[54] The most noted clandestine school was opened

[51] Howard H. Brinton, *Quaker Education in Theory and Practice*, rev. ed., Pendle Hill Pamphlet no. 9, Wallingford, Penn., 1949, pp. 70–72.

[52] Thomas E. Drake, *Quakers and Slavery in America*, Yale University Press, New Haven, Conn., 1950, p. 140 and entire discussion.

[53] Wright, *op. cit.*, pp. 19–20.

[54] Range, *op. cit.*, p. 4.

by Julian Froumontaine, a colored Frenchman from Santo Domingo, in 1818 or 1819. Up to 1829, Froumontaine taught openly; with the prohibitive law of that year, the school went underground and stayed open for fifteen more years. Negro teachers in other schools were often found to have been trained in his institution.[55]

Through missionary activities, the illegal efforts of slaveholders and their families, the enterprise of a few Negroes who sent their children elsewhere to be schooled, and through clandestine institutions, some Georgian Negroes were educated in the antebellum period. The results of this thwarted education were understandably meager. It was said that, when the Civil War began, except for a modest number of Negroes in Savannah, Augusta, and Columbus, less than a dozen colored people in Georgia—none of them in rural areas—were able to read and write.[56] When it is remembered that Georgia was primarily rural and that nearly half the population was colored, the task confronting postbellum educators appears almost insurmountable.

## POSTBELLUM DEVELOPMENTS

The people of Georgia, like those of other Southern states, were catapulted from a mock feudalism to a modern scientific agricultural-industrial society in five years. The road they had to travel was paved with more than educational stumbling blocks. They had to transform a culture and, in the process, create institutions appropriate to their new society.

The agricultural base had been plantations, where there were slaves in lieu of serfs, and small and undeveloped farms. Could wage workers be substituted for slaves? Could scientific agriculture and diversified farming and an increase of free farmers be substituted for extensive plantation farming? Could former slaves and poor whites be transformed into industrial workers in a developing urban society?

The freeing of half the population of Georgia was of even greater social significance. Could slaves be developed into free citizens capable of participating in government and capable of becoming independent workers in economic enterprises? More important, could the white people of the South accept former bondsmen on a basis of equality with themselves?

It is quite apparent that a diversified and comprehensive system of education was the only expedient which eventually might solve the problem of transforming a society. At a time when states north of the Mason-Dixon Line had developed compulsory free school systems for

---

[55] Wright, *op. cit.*, p. 20.
[56] *Ibid.*, p. 21.

all their children and were ready to expand free secondary education in the 1870s, there were only the remnants of a pauper system of education for the one-half in Georgia who were white. For the one-half who were black, Georgia had no facilities at all except for purely clandestine institutions, and they were so meager as to be discounted entirely. Georgia's problem was to build an educational plant for probably as many as three-fourths of her children and to train teachers for the colored children as well as for many of the white youngsters. It is not surprising that progress was far from smooth.

## The War Years to 1871

A situation which perhaps not even the North anticipated developed when the Civil War was under way. As Northern armies began to penetrate the Southern states, hundreds of former slaves flooded the Union camps, seeking refuge. In May, 1861, Gen. Benjamin F. Butler of the Department of Virginia, declared that slaves who came to such camps were "contraband of war." A settlement of Negroes at Fortress Monroe was put under the supervision of Edward L. Pierce of Boston by General Butler on November 20, 1861.[57] In 1862, Gen. Ulysses S. Grant commissioned a chaplain, Rev. John Eaton, to take charge of Negroes flooding the Union establishments. By 1866 there were some 770,000 Negroes under Eaton's supervision.[58]

In Georgia, the sea islands and the coast for 30 miles inland were set aside for Negro refugees, who were put under the supervision and care of Gen. Rufus Saxton, whose headquarters were at Beaufort. The first necessities were relief and teaching Negroes how to use a minimum amount of freedom. The Union Army was most effective in teaching Negroes to work for money in the period from 1863 to 1865. The devastation of war, coupled with a population that was economically dispossessed, produced generally wretched social and physical conditions. Women and children in Atlanta had only the discarded canvas from Sherman's army with which to cover themselves. Negroes throughout Georgia were starving and destitute. Filth, crime, and fighting abounded.

The first schools were opened as a social control rather than an educational program, and were designed to provide occupation for idle freedmen.[59] Faced with this situation not only in Georgia, but wherever

---

[57] *Negro Education: A Study of the Private and Higher Schools for Colored People in the United States*, U.S. Office of Education Bulletin 1916, vol. 1, no. 38, p. 268. Prepared in cooperation with the Phelps-Stokes Fund under the direction of Thomas Jesse Jones, specialist in the education of racial groups.

[58] Leavell, *op. cit.*, p. 29.

[59] Range, *op. cit.*, pp. 5–7; and Wright, *op. cit.*, p. 23.

the Union armies penetrated a Southern stronghold, Union commanders, including Butler, Pierce, Dupont, and Sherman, appealed to Northern benevolent societies.[60]

These requests for assistance initiated a process comparable to the one begun some fifty years earlier in the Old Northwest. The long arm of New England, supported by people of the New England tradition, stretched out to give sustenance and light to the heathen. Only now the heathen were not lambs who had strayed (a New England euphemism), but a people of another race and a white people of another culture who had little in common with the public school, town-oriented folk of Massachusetts and Connecticut. Yet these missionaries, and later the foundations, would be a chief support of Negro education in Georgia until well into the twentieth century.

One of the first societies to organize was the Boston Educational Commission, dedicated to the general improvement "of persons released from slavery in the course of the war for the Union." The commission was founded on February 7, 1862; by March, 31 teachers and agricultural superintendents sponsored by the organization set sail for Port Royal in South Carolina. A development of 1863 was the formation of the United States Commission for the Relief of the National Freedmen, composed of freedmen's aid societies in Boston, New York, Philadelphia, plus the Western (Cincinnati), and the Northwestern (Chicago). This commission became the American Freedmen's Aid Union with another combination of constituents, and finally developed into still another national federation. The national group ended its work in 1869, but the New England society carried on until 1874.[61]

First to answer the calls for help from the Union armies was the American Missionary Association, a nonsectarian and New England–inspired society to do good. (The association had been formed in 1837 by a group of men who had come to the defense of the Negroes who had rebelled and captured the slave ship *Armistad,* which had put in at a Connecticut port.[62]) Before the end of 1861, the association had representatives in many areas of the South, and by 1864, 250 of its teachers and missionaries were in the Southern field. By 1865, the number of workers had increased to 320, and by 1866, with the help of the Freedmen's Bureau, there were 350 representatives in the several Southern states. The association, being nonsectarian, had gathered support from several church groups which used it as the agent for dispensing charity to Southern Negroes. Congregationalists, Free Will

---

[60] Leavell, *op. cit.,* p. 30.

[61] *Negro Education: A Study of the Private and Higher Schools for Colored People in the United States,* vol. 1, pp. 269–272.

[62] Range, *op. cit.,* p. 6.

Baptists, Wesleyan Methodists, and the Reformed Dutch contributed to the association's coffers. Later, aid for its work was forthcoming from abolition societies in Cincinnati, Cleveland, and Chicago. In 1867 the association dispensed clothing valued at $90,000 and spent $334,500 on education.[63]

Funds came from abroad as well. The workingmen of Manchester and other areas in Great Britain had longer memories and stronger convictions than did their countrymen in the House of Lords. Remembering the help Americans had given in the Irish famine of 1846 and in English and Scottish manufacturing areas in the year 1862–1863, British groups began to send aid for the freedmen. English Friends contributed through United States Friends. A London Freedmen's Aid Society was formed. In May, 1865, the English freedmen's aid societies met together to inform their member groups, to organize new groups, and to raise money. The member groups came from London, Birmingham, Midland, Manchester, Leicester, and Northhampton. They included a Congregational union, the Friends' Central Relief Committee, a workingmen's auxiliary, a Syrian Mission, and other groups. In 1866 the London Freedmen's Aid Society met to commemorate the passage of the thirteenth amendment to the Constitution. It was said that receipts in monies and supplies from Great Britain totaled $1 million.[64]

In Georgia, a modest but most auspicious first step to make use of the new funds was made through a conference on Negro education attended by both white and colored men in December, 1864. The conference was attended by Secretary of War Stanton as well as Gen. William T. Sherman. Colored representatives were ministers in Savannah; the Rev. Garrison Frasier made the presentation for his group. The decision was to open schools at once. The Rev. J. W. Alvord, secretary of the American Tract Society in Boston and representative of the American Missionary Society, who had come in with Sherman's Army, had charge of first schools. Alvord and the Rev. James Lynch of the African Methodist Episcopal Church (under Reconstruction, he became secretary of state for Georgia) were charged with the examination of teachers.[65]

The schools were then turned back to the American Missionary Association, of which Alvord was a member. In addition to the difficult job of securing teachers was the impossible task of finding housing. The Oglethorpe Medical College, the Wesleyan Church, and the First

---

[63] Leavell, *op. cit.*, pp. 31–33.

[64] *Negro Education: A Study of the Private and Higher Schools for Colored People in the United States*, vol. 1, pp. 278–283.

[65] Wright, *op. cit.*, pp. 16–18, 21.

African Baptist Church all saw service as primary schools for Negroes. One of the more interesting schoolhouses was the old Bryan slave mart in which stalls were knocked down to make room for benches.[66] Yet it was probably apparent that these wholly voluntary and unofficial missionary efforts were not going to be enough to cope with economic as well as educational problems.

With the end of the war, it became apparent that the Federal government must play a leading role in the education and rehabilitation of the some 4 million Negroes who had been given freedom of such dubious value. Although a bill was introduced into Congress in 1863, serious attention to a measure for relief of the colored was given only in 1864, following petition of the freedmen's aid societies. On March 3, 1865, Congress finally passed a bill creating a Bureau of Refugees, Freedmen, and Abandoned Lands. This agency was put in the U.S. Department of War, and came to be known as the Freedmen's Bureau. The Bureau was charged on the one hand with assisting loyal refugees and freedmen, on the other, with holding in the insurrectionary states abandoned lands to which title had been secured by confiscation, sale, or otherwise. The job of the Bureau was to relieve suffering, supervise workers who were for the first time learning the meaning of free labor, accept payment of bounties, administer justice, and establish schools. One of the economic tasks was to distribute land at the rate of not more than 40 acres per Negro farmer. The beneficiary was to have the use of the land for three years, at a nominal rental not to exceed 6 per cent of the value of the land.[67] This alone would seem a sufficient undertaking for a single government bureau, but the Freedmen's Bureau went ahead full scale on the educational as well as the economic and charitable tasks with which it had been charged.

On March 12, 1865, Gen. Rufus Saxton, who had supervised refugee affairs for the Union Army in Georgia, was relieved of his command. General O. O. Howard, Commander of the Army of Tennessee, was appointed Commissioner of the Freedmen's Bureau, and Gen. David Tillson was designated assistant commissioner for Georgia with headquarters at Augusta. Reverend Alvord of the American Missionary Association became the Bureau's inspector of schools in Georgia. From the Bureau's inception in 1865 until it ceased operation of schools in 1871, educational efforts for Negroes were made solely by the Bureau, colored people themselves, and the various missionary societies.[68]

Probably one of the most formidable obstacles faced by evangelists for Negro schools was the attitude of the white people. Some were

---

[66] *Ibid.*, pp. 18, 21.
[67] Frazier, *op. cit.*, pp. 115–116; and Leavell, *op. cit.*, pp. 48–49.
[68] Wright, *op. cit.*, pp. 22–24.

immediately able to see the relationship between education and the effective functioning of former slaves in a new order. Even during the war a few liberal planters had established schools to prepare their workers to live as free men and one such school had been discovered by General Sherman on his march to the sea. But to most white Georgians, "the idea of educating the ex-slave was as ridiculous as attempting to educate a mule."[69]  Being forced to accept the education of a presumedly inferior and less-than-human people was a bitter pill to swallow, and some Georgians acted accordingly. In the period from 1862 to 1872, enthusiasm waxed, then waned, then revived. The Rev. J. H. Caldwell kept a school for 600 Negro youngsters in LaGrange, Georgia. In 1866, mobs fired on the building. In Griffin, schools were burned. There was opposition in Thomasville, violence in Henry County, and in Columbus the ladies were heard planning to hang the Yankee teachers.[70]

The *Macon Messenger* in 1867 labeled the Northern teachers "fanatics or knaves." William J. White was shot at and threatened. Edmund Asa Ware, Northern educator working in Savannah, was denied permission to speak in a church for fear that he might address himself to politics. As early as 1865, J. W. Alvord, superintendent of schools for the Freedmen's Bureau, was inclined to believe that only military force could save the Negro schools in Georgia.[71]

The whites were not the only dissidents. Negroes showed something of the same cycle of sentiment as did their former masters. Initially they begged for education in Savannah and Brunswick and expectantly awaited the Northern teachers in Albany, Columbus, Lexington, Ellijay, Athens, and other centers. They offered for buildings a house in Calhoun and an old church in Sandersville.[72]  According to one Negro leader, "There was the emancipated Negro, an ignorant people, as it were, like a poor blind Samson, in quest of sight."[73]  Then, briefly the tide turned, even among the Negroes. In Columbus in 1868, the Northern teacher could find neither home nor school among the colored people. In 1870, the teacher in Hamilton advocated abandoning the school because parents were apparently not sending their youngsters. The pastor of the Negro church in Greensboro exhorted his congregation not to cooperate with Northern teachers. The causes of this disaffection are matters for speculation only. The hostility of the white

[69] Range, *op. cit.*, pp. 4, 19.
[70] Henry Lee Swint, *The Northern Teacher in the South 1862–1870*, Vanderbilt University Press, Nashville, Tenn., 1941, p. 118.
[71] Range, *op. cit.*, p. 16.
[72] Swint, *op. cit.*, p. 71.
[73] Wright, *op. cit.*, p. 18.

people, which made attendance at school dangerous, and the suppression of Negroes' political activity may have been involved. Probably more important was the general disillusionment with the power of education. In 1865, the editor of the *Freedmen's Record* said that Negroes looked at education as the "fetish" by which the white man achieved his power and status.[74] When a few months of the three R's failed to bring returns, the Negro turned against the white man's magic.

The tide turned again, however. As early as 1866 both Superintendent Alvord and the Rev. J. H. Caldwell, a Northern minister who visited Milledgeville, felt that sentiment of white Georgians was changing in a positive direction. Planters at Albany began to ask for schools for their Negro workers. In Atlanta, the idea of education for the colored gained in popularity.[75] The work of the benevolent societies and the Freedmen's Bureau would not be wholly lost.

The record of the Bureau in the whole South does not look impressive unless it is remembered that buildings had to be procured and teachers secured or trained before schools could be opened. In terms of the latter, the record of schools aided by the Bureau is impressive. Figures for two years, 1866, after the Bureau had operated for a year, and 1870, when it was about to close out its business, indicate some progress.

Expenditures for Southern Schools Aided by the Freedmen's Bureau

| Year | No. of pupils | Expenditures | |
|------|---------------|-----------------------|-------------------------|
| | | Freedmen's Bureau | Benevolent societies |
| 1866 | 90,778 | $123,650 | $ 82,200 |
| 1870 | 149,581 | 967,853 | 360,000 |

SOURCE: Ullin Whitney Leavell, *Philanthropy in Negro Education*, George Peabody College for Teachers, Nashville, Tenn., 1930, p. 50. Adapted by permission of the publisher.

Range indicates some of the aid given specifically in Georgia for one higher-education institution. In the period from 1869 to 1871, Atlanta University spent some $89,000. The American Missionary Society provided $19,000, and the state, through land-grant funds, $8,000 a year. The Freedmen's Bureau, however, gave $52,400.[76] Swint summarizes the activities of the Freedmen's Bureau by saying that between 1862

[74] Swint, *op. cit.*, pp. 72–73.
[75] *Ibid.*, pp. 118–119.
[76] Range, *op. cit.*, pp. 35–36.

and 1872, there were possibly $5 or $6 million used in supporting Yankee teachers, and in 1869, there were some 9,503 teachers in freedmen's schools.[77]

Housing remained primitive, but the fact that the Bureau was a Federal agency meant that army supplies could be commandeered and private housing could be solicited. A Negro educator, reminiscing about the first school he attended in 1865, recalled a frame structure not more than 20 by 30 feet, with scarcely one of the walls completely whole. For equipment, there were rough benches with no backs. The school was packed with students, aged six to seventy years. His next educational venture was in an abandoned boxcar. He remembered that some sites were even more informal. It was not uncommon for a Yankee teacher to tack up an old army blanket in some likely spot and open school. Between 1865 and 1871, of the $5 million or more spent in the South, the Freedmen's Bureau spent about $306,000 in Georgia. A part of the money went into buildings; benevolent societies and Negroes themselves assisted education in this way. The Bureau furnished 26 buildings, of which it owned 14; 10 were owned by Negroes; and 41 by others, presumably the missionary groups.[78] By 1867 the American Missionary Association alone had established schools in 15 of the 131 Georgia counties. Another report has it that of the 236 schools reported in 1867, 152 were completely or partially supported by the freedmen, who were recorded as owning outright 39 of the structures.[79] Probably few of these were impressive, yet their number and location indicate some movement in the direction of providing a school plant.

The most crucial problem was developing a corps of teachers native to Georgia. Teacher education through county institutes, lectures, and normal schools had begun some thirty-five years earlier in New England and the Old Northwest. It was highly improbable, however, that these educational institutions could supply enough teachers for all the Negro children of the South. Furthermore, some planters had indicated their willingness to set up schools, providing Northern ideas did not filter into them.[80] The task was to uncover or educate a sizable number of white and colored teachers.

The most natural assumption would be that colored adults should be trained for schoolwork. Yet it was said that not more than 100 Negroes in Georgia were able to teach primary school in 1865.[81] For most of

[77] Swint, op. cit., p. 3.
[78] Wright, op. cit., pp. 25–27.
[79] Range, op. cit., pp. 12, 14.
[80] Ibid., pp. 16–17.
[81] Wright, op. cit., p. 31.

them, ability to teach could probably be equated with elementary skills in reading and writing, for it should be remembered that, as of 1860, only twenty-eight Negroes in the entire United States had graduated from American colleges.[82]

Bureau officials, members of the missionary societies, and individual colored people busied themselves in the development of normal training. Three institutions were established: Ballard Normal School in Macon in 1865, Beach Institute in Savannah and Storr's School in Atlanta in 1867. Ballard was founded by the Freedmen's Bureau as the Lewis Normal School and was taken over by the American Missionary Association in 1868.[83] Both the Beach and the Storr's schools were founded by the association.[84] But the battle was hardly begun when the schools opened, as could be assumed from examination of the problems of institutions of higher education.

The meaning of higher education for Negroes began to take form, beginning with a proposal for education concentrated on practical training in agriculture and simple industrial skills. Faced with this educational proposition, members of the American Missionary Association agreed that, though the Negro knew little of modern agriculture and industry, he knew even less about the nature of family living and the meaning of civilized ways and of life itself. The lacks could be supplied only through an institution of higher education dedicated to the development of the higher abilities of Negroes, the education of well-grounded teachers, and the preparation of leaders who could provide inspiration for Negro communities. To these ends, the association established Atlanta University in 1867 under difficult circumstances. Money was hard to come by, and the association finally had to prevail on Negroes to dig the foundations for the first building.[85] But acquiring a minimum plant was only the beginning of the struggle to build a college.

The leading question at Atlanta, as at other colleges, was where to find a group of colored people who were prepared for college work. In the 1870s, admission to Atlanta was based on passing examinations in English, including composition, Latin and Greek, history and geography, and algebra and geometry. To secure a student body which could handle such examinations, the university had to open preparatory classes. It was only when Atlanta had graduated a preparatory class in 1872 that the college department opened with twelve freshmen. Succeeding college years were added as the original freshman group

[82] Range, op. cit., p. 5.
[83] Leavell, op. cit., p. 37.
[84] Wright, op. cit., p. 41.
[85] Range, op. cit., pp. 21–22.

advanced, and six were finally graduated from college in 1876.[86] The same process characterized the course of events at other institutions.

Prior to 1871, two other higher-education institutions were opened, both in Atlanta. Clark University started as a primary school in Clark Chapel in 1869. Bishop Gilbert Haven, New England reformer, secured grounds for the college, and students cut down trees and built roads leading to the building. In 1870 the institution was moved to a new building, and higher education was established as the ultimate goal. However, the first college student did not graduate until 1883.[87] The institution was eventually taken under the protecting wing of the Freedmen's Aid Society of the Northern Methodist Church.

Augusta Institute, later called Atlanta Baptist Seminary, was the brain child of an exslave, Richard C. Coulter, who had attended the National Theological Seminary. In 1866 he returned to Augusta with authorization to establish a school which was to be a branch of the Northern seminary. It was begun on a modest basis in a Baptist church. The American Baptist Home Mission Society offered to take it over. Its fortunes were mixed until 1871 when it showed signs of success, particularly through the persistence of the Negro Baptist "Father" Frank Quarles. The institution was moved from Augusta to Atlanta, where quarters were found near Atlanta University, and where it was renamed Atlanta Baptist Seminary. Thus three so-called colleges were begun in the first decade of freedom for Negroes in Georgia.

The term *college*, however, was used in the European sense to mean a secondary school which provided a semblance of liberal arts training and, until well into the twentieth century, normal or theological training which did not antipicate college graduation. In 1885, out of a total enrollment of 700 in these three higher-education institutions, only 28 were in the college departments, one-third of the students were in the normal departments, and the rest were elementary students. Having graduated its first college class in 1876, Atlanta University had by 1885 conferred only forty-one bachelor's degrees.[88] The inadequacy of normal training in the normal schools can be judged from the meaning of "normal" and "college" in Negro institutions of higher education.

Before 1871, the question remained as to where teachers were to be found when Yankee missionaries went home and until substantial numbers of Negroes could be prepared for the jobs. The postbellum attitude of whites was that it was a disgrace to teach "niggers," but times were hard as Georgia and the South recovered from devastation. A few poor whites had taught clandestine schools in the antebellum period,

[86] *Ibid.,* pp. 27–28.
[87] Leavell, *op. cit.,* p. 42; Range, *op. cit.,* pp. 23–24, 28.
[88] Range, *op. cit.,* pp. 24–26, 30, 31.

and they gradually signified their willingness to eke out a living in Negro schools. Economic circumstances prompted white professional and business people to do the same thing. By 1867, of the 147 white teachers in Negro schools, 83 were native Georgians.[89]

Two other educational developments are worthy of note in this early period: one was philanthropic, the other, state-supported. The record of the American Missionary Association has been referred to. A good number of other charitable and largely religious groups and abolition societies also began to operate in Georgia. By 1870 the St. Joseph sisters, who had had experience in African missions, and a few other Roman Catholic orders had established schools in Savannah, Washington, and Augusta. The Baptist Home Mission Society was active also. The Methodist Episcopal Church opened schools or theological institutions, as did the Presbyterian Board of Missions for Freedmen,[90] and a few other groups.

In 1867, a poor-school tax was levied, and for the first time some of the resulting money was given to Negro schools. Those particularly benefited were in the cities of Augusta and Macon and in Liberty County.[91] This was a temporary expedient and did not signal the immediate inclusion of Negroes in a public school system, for no provision for the education of colored children had been included in the constitution of 1865. In 1868 radicals were in control in both Washington and Georgia. The Georgian radicals managed to insert a clause whereby Negroes were to be given free education for at least three months every year.[92] In 1869 the state paid off its debt to Negro higher education by appropriating $8,000 to Atlanta University. The money was no gift from the state; it represented a part of the Negroes' share in the agricultural land scrip fund growing out of the Federal Morrill Act of 1862. The same appropriation was continued until 1887; at that time it ceased because the university had coeducation, which was contrary to state law.

In 1870, a public school system was established by law, and Gen. J. R. Lewis of the Freedmen's Bureau became the first superintendent. The plan was developed by teachers, a plan on which Georgia education was to be based some seventy-five years later. Public schools for colored children were opened in the summer of 1871, were suspended for lack of funds in 1872, and were resumed in 1873.[93] A new era was about to begin in the education of the colored population in Georgia.

[89] *Ibid.*, pp. 14–15.
[90] Wright, *op. cit.*, pp. 27, 41, 45.
[91] *Ibid.*, p. 29.
[92] Range, *op. cit.*, pp. 19–20.
[93] Wright, *op. cit.*, pp. 21, 39–40.

What had been accomplished in the first eight years (1863–1871) of Negro education?  In the area of finance, aid from national and charitable agencies was more impressive than that from the state.  Between 1865 and 1871, the Freedmen's Bureau had spent some $306,000 in Georgia.[94]  From comparative figures on Bureau and benevolent society expenditures,[95] it can be estimated that religious and charitable institutions may have spent anywhere from $100,000 to $200,000 in Georgia in the period.  A modest and probably undetermined amount had been contributed by Negroes.  Beyond the state's contribution of $8,000 a year, in the period from 1869 to 1871, a paltry sum from the poor fund had been donated.  In 1871, there were some 545,142 colored people in the state.  By 1870, there were not more than 17,519 colored youngsters in school; and by 1871, some 6,664 colored young people in public schools.[96]  Philanthropic agencies would continue for some years to be the solid prop of Negro education, for obviously, substantial sums of public money would be needed to give effective help to the uneducated in Georgia's large minority group.

## Philanthropy and the Educational Campaign (1871–1915)

The day of the public schools was dawning.  But the state's role in education for Negroes would develop so slowly in the period from 1871 to World War I that other agencies would be needed both to stimulate and to supplement education.  Thus the curious interweaving of public and private enterprises was continued, and a campaign for public education was initiated in the 1890s—a campaign which had occurred some sixty or seventy years earlier in the Eastern seaboard states above the Mason-Dixon Line.  The process is reminiscent of Frederick Jackson Turner's succession of frontiers in American history—life began over again on each new frontier.  But on this second or third educational frontier in Georgia, the life which began anew was not quite like that on earlier frontiers.  It was conditioned by the level of development which had been reached in the rest of the United States and by the fact that this was a different population from that in New England and the Old Northwest.  On this newest frontier, there were fewer among the white population to do battle for public education, and the one-half who were colored had been slaves so recently that they could not operate as effectively as had the housewives, farmers, and professional people of the Old Northwest.

[94] *Ibid.*, pp. 26–27.
[95] Leavell, *op. cit.*, p. 50.
[96] Wright, *op. cit.*, pp. 25, 32.

Although Yankee teachers began to go home as early as 1870, the churches of the North and of the South, and particularly the African churches, continued their activities largely in support of Negro education. In his study published in 1917, Jones listed some seven white Protestant denominational boards, a Catholic board, and four Negro denominational boards which, as of 1915 or 1916, were maintaining private and/or higher schools for colored people in Georgia (see Table 12-1).

Table 12-1. Boards Maintaining Private and Higher Schools for Colored People in Georgia, circa 1916

---

*White denominational boards*
    American Baptist Home Mission Society
    American Church Institute for Negroes (Episcopal)
    American Missionary Association (Congregational)
    Board of Missions for Freedmen of the Presbyterian Church
    Freedmen's Aid Society of the Methodist Episcopal Church
    Methodist Episcopal Church South
    Woman's Home Missionary Society of the Methodist Episcopal Church

*Catholic Board of Missions*

*Negro denominational boards*
    African Methodist Episcopal Church
    Colored Methodist Episcopal Church
    Baptist Conventions
    Baptist Local Conventions
    Seventh Day Adventist Church

---

SOURCE: *Negro Education: A Study of the Private and Higher Schools for Colored People in the United States*, U.S. Office of Education Bulletin 1916, vol. 1, no. 38, 1917, p. 368. Prepared in cooperation with the Phelps-Stokes Fund under the direction of Thomas Jesse Jones, specialist in the education of racial groups.

By 1915 these groups were of declining importance in elementary education, but they remained highly important in secondary and higher education. Jones contends that, for the Southern states as a whole, the private schools still provided nearly all the opportunities for Negroes above the elementary grade, and most of the instruction in agriculture, industry, teacher training, medicine, and religion. As of about 1915 in Georgia, there was still only one public high school with 321 pupils, of whom only 40 were of secondary grade. These 40 were less than 2 per cent of the 2,278 colored secondary pupils, and the latter group must have been a very small fraction of all pupils of secondary school age in a total Negro population of 1,176,987 in 1910.[97] At the time, the state

[97] *Negro Education: A Study of the Private and Higher Schools for Colored People in the United States*, pp. 8, 41, 66.

was maintaining only one institution designed to provide higher education: this was a land-grant school, and so far it had only elementary and secondary pupils. Genuine higher education was supplied solely by the twenty-one independent private schools and the fifty-seven maintained by denominational boards (see Table 12-2). It would take an

Table 12-2. Attendance in Private and Higher Schools for Colored People in Georgia, circa 1916

| Character of school | No. of schools | Attendance | | | |
|---|---|---|---|---|---|
| | | Total | Elementary | Secondary | College |
| Total schools in state..... | 79 | 11,970 | 9,592 | 2,229 | 149 |
| Land-grant............. | 1 | 390 | 280 | 110 | |
| Independent........... | 21 | 2,654 | 2,227 | 383 | 44 |
| Denominational........ | 57 | 8,926 | 7,085 | 1,736 | 105 |
| White boards......... | 39 | 7,037 | 5,560 | 1,382 | 95 |
| Negro boards........ | 18 | 1,889 | 1,525 | 354 | 10 |

SOURCE: *Negro Education: A Study of the Private and Higher Schools for Colored People in the United States*, U.S. Office of Education Bulletin 1916, vol. 1, no. 38, 1917, p. 368. Prepared in cooperation with the Phelps-Stokes Fund under the direction of Thomas Jesse Jones, specialist in the education of racial groups.

educational earthquake for the state, the status of Negroes, and educational institutions to come into some kind of reasonable balance in Georgia.

Religious and nonsectarian societies had begun their work on a propaganda level through abolition societies and had continued their efforts in relief and education during and after the Civil War. Before the postbellum period was fairly under way, that novel and benevolent invention of modern American capitalism, the foundation, was assisting both private and public schools. Paralleling the foundations, disciples of public education again were abroad on this new frontier, the Old South.

Since the Civil War, there have been five funds or foundations which have been influential in education for both Negroes and whites in the South. Their identity, with founding dates, is as follows:[98]

Peabody Education Fund .....................1867
John F. Slater Fund ...........................1882
General Education Board (Rockefeller) ........1903
Anna T. Jeanes Fund ........................1907
Julius Rosenwald Foundation .................1912

[98] Leavell, *op. cit.*, p. 58.

A sixth fund, which will not be discussed in detail, is the Phelps-Stokes Fund, begun in 1911.[99]

George Peabody was a New England banker and merchant who wished to give assistance to areas suffering from the Civil War. The extent of his benevolence was at the outset some $2,100,000, and he later added another $1,384,000. His fund, the earliest in the new field, was established in 1867, and by 1868, some $4,000 was being spent to hire Negro teachers in North Carolina and Georgia.[100] Though the amount of money was small, the way in which it was given was significant and indicated a new trend in private philanthropy. In Georgia, Dr. Barnas Sears, Peabody's agent, gave the first $2,000 through the state superintendent of schools, and this practice continued, with an eventual increase to $4,000 annually.[101] The long arm of New England in the person of George Peabody had stretched out to strengthen the public institution.

The stated purposes of the Peabody fund were to promote common (meaning public) school education, to provide scholarships for teacher trainees, and to promote the application of science by education in industrial pursuits. The fund's directors thought that education would be best served by acting through state authorities rather than by endowing private institutions. To this end, in 1871 they set up a scale of assistance; in theory, less was allotted for Negro than for white schools in view of cost differentials, but in practice, the amount was often the same for both. On March 8, 1880, the Peabody board sent Congress a memorial on the necessity for Federal aid to Southern states and especially for aid to the schools for Negroes, who would be "voters under the Constitution of the United States."[102] This new kind of philanthropy would set the pattern for succeeding funds which would assist private establishments and also would attempt to encourage public education—partly for its political usefulness.

Before an effective campaign was under way, the John F. Slater Fund contributed to educational endeavors. Slater was a Norwich, Connecticut, man who, stimulated by the success of the Peabody fund, set aside $1 million in 1882 for "uplifting" and providing a Christian education for persons lately emancipated. At the outset, the largest sums seemed to be put into private institutions. In 1883 the following schools for Negroes received money: two universities, Clark and Atlanta; Atlanta Baptist Female Seminary; and a private secondary school. As illustra-

[99] Edwin R. Embree, *Julius Rosenwald Fund: A Review to June 30, 1928*, Julius Rosenwald Fund, Chicago, 1928, p. 43.

[100] Leavell, *op. cit.*, pp. 59–84.

[101] Wright, *op. cit.*, p. 28.

[102] Leavell, *op. cit.*, pp. 61, 84–89.

tion of the emphasis of the fund, Leavell cites the year 1907–1908 as typical. In that year, $68,490 was expended: 74 per cent for private and denominational schools, 19 per cent for vocational training in public schools and state normal schools, and 7 per cent for an agricultural wagon in Alabama.[103] (Somewhat later, however, Slater funds would be used for an interesting innovation in public education which will be described in connection with another development.)

About 1829 a group of New England men had begun that organization of propaganda for the public schools, the American Institute of Instruction. Now in postbellum days it was time for such an organization to arise in the South, where the common school was not yet established. The educational campaign, sometimes called the Southern education movement, began with a tour of the South by Dr. Edward Abbott, Episcopal clergyman from Cambridge, Massachusetts, and brother of Dr. Lyman Abbott of New York. On his tour he stopped at the Capon Springs Hotel in West Virginia, where Capt. William H. Sale, former confederate officer, was proprietor. Dr. Abbott suggested to Captain Sale that he promote a conference on Southern education. Captain Sale concurred and, with Dr. Abbott's assistance in selection of guests, convened the first conference at his hotel on June 29, 1898.[104]

President of the first conference was the Right Rev. Thomas Dudley; other officers were the Hon. J. L. M. Curry and Rev. A. B. Hunter. A large part of this conference was given over to Negro education. So successful was the venture that Captain Sales invited over 100 men and women to a second conference in June, 1899. Still a third conference concerned largely with Negro education was held at Captain Sales's invitation, on June 27, 1900, with Curry as president.[105]

The guest whose influence was to be most telling was Robert Curtis Ogden, who, according to Harlan, was full of good causes. Ogden had interested himself in free pews, hungry Indians, settlement houses (he was from New York), flood victims, and Philadelphia Negroes. The stimulation he received at these conferences had been enough to set him off on another good cause. At Ogden's expense, a group of wealthy philanthropists took a trip to North Carolina in 1901. Out of a conference on Christian education, developed in 1901 the Southern Education Board, designed to give nothing but good advice on education in the South. The membership was made up of moderate Northerners and progressive Southerners who represented wealth on the one hand and

---

[103] *Ibid.*, pp. 62–65.

[104] Charles William Dabney, *Universal Education in the South*, vol. II, *The Southern Education Movement*, The University of North Carolina Press, Chapel Hill, N.C., 1936, pp. 3–5.

[105] *Ibid.*, pp. 5–7, 10.

education on the other. The New York contingent included Robert C. Ogden of Wanamaker's; George Foster Peabody, the Wall Street banker; and William H. Baldwin, Jr., who was in railroads. The transplanted Southerners, Walter Hines Page and J. L. M. Curry, acted as liaison with the Southerners, who were largely college presidents, Charles D. Mc-Iver, Edwin A. Alderman, Charles W. Dabney, and Edgar Gardner Murphy. By 1909 the board had seen to it that there was an educational campaign in every Southern state except Mississippi; main energies were expended in Georgia, North and South Carolina, and Virginia.[106] The work of the board was interwoven in clearinghouse fashion with the Peabody and Slater foundations, as well as with the Rockefeller General Education Board.

This last, the most pretentious of the foundations, was an extension of John D. Rockefeller's original interest in the American Baptist Education Society. With a catholic concern for the broad social field, Rockefeller set up the General Education Fund in such a way that trustees could promote educational endeavors of almost any character. Between 1902 and 1909, the founder deposited some $53 million. With this sizable sum at their disposal and carte blanche for educational planning, board members expended funds for many purposes, and for Negroes in particular, by assistance to private institutions established by Northern churches and Southern Negroes, and by stimulation of a good system of public education for Negroes in Southern states.[107]

Between 1902 and 1920, the General Education Board gave money for state agents (supervisors) for Negro schools, county training schools (to be described later), homemakers' clubs, and summer schools and scholarships for Negro teachers or trainees. It made grants also to the Slater and Jeanes foundations. On Rockefeller's request, grants to increase salaries were made to Negro colleges. This was in line with the founder's desire that able young people go into teaching and stay with it. Eventually the board had agents in twelve states, including Georgia. From 1902 to 1920, it expended some $1,770,264.85 on Negro schools and colleges, and from 1915 to 1920, made grants amounting to $674,255.65 to stimulate public education for Negroes.[108]

A delicate yet staunch little Quaker lady was the founder of one of the more practical organizations designed to benefit Negro education exclusively. Prior to the establishment of the fund, Miss Anna T. Jeanes had already made substantial contributions. She had given $10,000 to Hampton Normal and Industrial Institute and $200,000 through the

[106] Harlan, *op. cit.*, pp. vii, 75–77, 79–80, 83, 88–89.
[107] Leavell, *op. cit.*, pp. 66–71.
[108] *Ibid.*, pp. 100, 102, 105–106.

General Education Board for support of Negro private schools. In the course of her philanthropies, Miss Jeanes had come to know Dr. Booker T. Washington. Dr. Washington secured Miss Jeanes's undivided attention with his plans for improving small rural Negro schools. The tiny, white-haired Quaker lady decided that she would no longer shower gifts on the big, reasonably well-established institutions, but would give her "all for the little schools." She would make her contribution not to save her soul, but because she wanted to. Whereupon the delicate old lady in black taffeta and white lace shawl, who characterized herself as "just a poor woman," put $1 million in a fund for Negro rural education. Following the establishment of this fund, there were two unique educational developments: the Jeanes teachers, who have become justly famous, and the county training schools. The fund was put to a third use, hiring county agents to improve rural homes and schools and to create sentiment for better Negro schools.[109]

Rural Negroes, living on farms as tenants or owners, needed knowledge of handicrafts and simple skills with hand tools. Teachers were still inadequately trained, so a system of itinerant teachers responsible to the county superintendents was developed. These Jeanes teachers went from school to school in country districts, promoting or helping with what was called "industrial work."[110] The meaning of "industrial" becomes clear from Miss Virginia Randolph's report of her activities as a Jeanes teacher, beginning in Henrico County, Virginia, in 1908. The report will serve to indicate what a teacher would have faced in a Negro district in any Southern state including Georgia.

Miss Randolph pointed out that most of these children of her race would never be enrolled in a high school. Therefore, the school had to perform functions not expected of an elementary school.[111] Under her guidance, School Improvement Leagues were organized. Youngsters were expected to raise money to improve school and grounds and to help beautify the yards. Walks were put in, hedges and trees planted, fences whitewashed. Youngsters were introduced in school to sewing, needlework, simple carpentry, and the making of shuck mats. All of these activities were carried out with minimum materials. Old flour sacks and second-hand scraps and bits donated by Negro and white patrons were the stuff out of which the youngsters fashioned their

[109] *Ibid.*, pp. 72–74.

[110] *Ibid.*, p. 73.

[111] Lance G. E. Jones, *The Jeanes Teachers in the United States 1908–1933: An Account of Twenty-five Years' Experience in the Supervision of Negro Rural Schools*, The University of North Carolina Press, Chapel Hill, N.C., 1937, p. 127.

products.[112]   In several schools, youngsters developed a strong interest in school gardens.   Meager budgets were husbanded so that schools could install stoves and modest kitchen appurtenances.

The 1912–1913 report of twenty-three Jeanes teachers in Virginia suggests the breadth of their activities.   Some $26,020 were expended on 10 new and 15 enlarged buildings, an indication of the quality of structure with which they had to work.   The teachers reported that 46 buildings had been painted, 317 schools (out of 417) were using individual drinking cups, 428 improvement leagues were in operation, and 102 sanitary outhouses had been built.[113]

A taste of what an early Jeanes teacher endured is provided by Miss Randolph's 1908–1909 account.   Virginia Randolph was paid a monthly salary of $40, most of which went, at first, to hire horse, buggy, and driver.   When she felt familiar with her area, she purchased her own horse and buggy.   Her days began at 6:30 A.M. when she started for a country school which she hoped to reach by 9:30.   After working and visiting at the first school until 12:30 P.M., she departed for the second, and finally reached home  often not until 9 P.M.   Along the way, youngsters fed and watered her horse, but she was at the mercy of mud roads, her buggy was often stuck, and rain and snow often soaked her to the skin.[114]   She and many other Jeanes teachers worked in aching poverty to improve conditions so that Negro youngsters might be schooled more effectively.

Not only did rural teachers not have industrial skills, they had few others, being often themselves only eighth grade graduates.   In turn, Negro rural elementary schools were rarely eight-year schools.   In addition, some encouragement needed to be given for general improvement of elementary education.   So an idea was developed for a central school, located in the midst of a cluster of country schools and designated a "county training school."   In deference to the Slater foundation, which also contributed to these schools, education was to go through the eighth grade.   The function of the county training school was to supplement training received by youngsters in other rural schools, and to prepare some for teaching.[115]   The modest level of teacher training for rural schools is noteworthy.

The activities of the Jeanes fund interested trustees of other foundations, and additional funds became available for improvement of Negro education.   After 1912, some $921,764.68 had been given to the Jeanes

[112] *Ibid.*, chap. III, pp. 127–132.

[113] *Ibid.*, p. 134.

[114] *Ibid.*, pp. 45–46.

[115] Leavell, *op. cit.*, p. 73; *Negro Education: A Study of the Private and Higher Schools for Colored People in the United States*, vol. 1, pp. 37–38.

fund for Negro rural schools by the Phelps-Stokes Fund, the General Education Board, Keith Contributions, and the Julius Rosenwald Fund.[116] The last fund, set up in 1912, became closely involved with Negro education.

Julius Rosenwald's attention was called to small rural schools by Booker T. Washington, whom he knew through Tuskegee Institute. Dr. Washington felt that special personnel, working through county superintendents, should be employed in rural counties throughout the Southern states, to interest white leaders in securing adequate support for public education for colored people. Thus, funds would be relied upon initially only. Dr. Washington's argument was based in part on the discrepancy between the amount of support for education of white and Negro children. In one district, for example, the per capita cost of education per white child was $202, while that per Negro child was $3.12.[117] On the basis of this argument and others, the Rosenwald fund was set up. Between 1912 and 1920, Rosenwald agents contracted for 640 schoolhouses for the colored people. The contributions were as follows:[118]

|  | Amount | Per cent |
|---|---|---|
| Public (through public education) | $ 562,071 | 42 |
| Negroes | 456,597 | 34 |
| Rosenwald fund | 263,515 | 18 |
| Whites | 61,326 | 4 |
| Total | $1,343,509 | |

On January 1, 1928, the Rosenwald fund was reorganized with the stipulation that all the money was to be spent within twenty-five years after the founder's death. Rosenwald pointed out that future generations could well make provisions for their own needs, and that the most good could be done by spending money when it was needed on projects for which funds had been given.[119]

Jeanes teachers, Rosenwald school buildings, encouragement to public education, and support of private colleges—these were some of the contributions of the foundations to Negro education in the South. Monies came to Georgia as to other states. In 1929, of 2,766 Negro rural schools in Georgia, 203 or 7.4 per cent were Rosenwald schools.[120]

---

[116] Leavell, op. cit., p. 76.

[117] Ibid., pp. 76–79, 111.

[118] Ibid., p. 113.

[119] Ibid., p. 79–80. For a copy of the original Rosenwald letter see inside cover of Embree, op. cit.

[120] Leavell, op. cit., p. 181.

What was the effect of the benevolence of fund trustees and the Southern Education Board in the period before World War I?

## The Pattern of Discrimination Is Set

Between 1900 and 1915, white Southerners, so Harlan says, attempted to improve Southern schools. Aided and abetted by Northerners, they operated in such a fashion that the gap widened between rural and urban, Negro and white schools so that by 1915 "the pattern of racial discrimination in public schools was rather complete."[121] The story of how this situation came about is partly the story of the Southern Education Board, which was initiated to promote public education particularly for Negroes, but ended by supporting Southern conservatives.

The movement for reform began with the brief ascendancy of the Farmers' Alliance and the Populist party. These parties of small farmers controlled state governments in the 1880s and 1890s. After 1896, members filtered back into the Democratic party and thus lost their power to affect materially the course of educational or economic events. The effects of politics on education are illustrated by state appropriations. In response to populism in Georgia, in 1888 conservative Democrats put the state school fund for all schools up from zero to $1 million, and held it at this level until 1897. With populism weakened, the Governor in 1898 cut the fund in half. However, outraged educators managed to get it back to $800,000, where it was held for six years.[122]

Despite state aid, Negro schools were still in a bad way before the turn of the century. In 1896, 47.9 per cent of Georgia youngsters were Negroes, yet there were less than one-half as many teachers for Negroes as for whites, and salaries of teachers for Negroes were hardly one-third of those of teachers for whites. City schools were as bad as those in rural sections. In Atlanta at the turn of the century, there were schoolroom seats for two-thirds of the white youngsters, but for only one-third of the Negro children. The law sustained the *status quo*. In Cumming vs Board of Education in 1899, suit was brought to restore aid to a Negro high school. Aid had been discontinued on the premise that there was so little money that it should be given to the Negro elementary schools. Yet the same board had found money for the white high school. The board was sustained by the court.[123]

Two restrictions of the constitution of 1877 stood in the way of substantial improvement even in white schools. The original wording of the article setting up the public school system had restricted the system

[121] Harlan, *op. cit.*, pp. viii–ix.
[122] *Ibid.*, pp. 37, 213–214.
[123] *Ibid.*, pp. 212–213.

to "the elementary branches of an English education only."[124]   In the decade when Michigan and other Middle Western states were establishing the right to use public monies for high schools, Georgians were approving a constitution which eliminated consideration of a secondary school.   Technically, the board which had given money to the white high school and denied it to the Negro institution should have denied money to both.

A second restriction was inherent in what Harlan called the "simplest" financial system in any state on the Southern seaboard.   The state government was actually the only support of schools, except in "independent districts in cities and in four urban counties."[125]   The constitution of 1877 authorized counties and municipal corporations to maintain schools by local taxation, but such tax was to go into effect only if approved by two-thirds of the qualified voters and on recommendation of two grand juries.[126]   By 1900, educational progress was blocked by the constitution and because there was a draw in the battle between large taxpayers and educational reformers, and between citizens in predominantly white and predominantly black counties.   Both white and colored teachers were caught in the middle, although teachers in schools for Negroes fared the worst.   About 1900, the Negro child had spent on him for education about one-fourth the amount spent on a white child.   With money for salaries coming largely from the state, teachers were rarely paid on time, for legislators were dilatory in making appropriations.   The state superintendent warned that teachers, embittered as a result of financial policy, were not only disgusting but of no value to children.[127]

The educational campaign of the Southern Education Board, called "the Ogden movement," got under way in Georgia in 1901.   The first meeting was held in a Negro church with Booker T. Washington in attendance and the Governor conspicuously absent.   The board held a second conference on education in the South in Atlanta in 1902. Eugene C. Bronson, president of the state normal school, was its sponsor. There were no Southern educational reformers on the board to act as leaders, however, and members soon lost their influence and had to fall in with prevailing mores of dominant whites.   This latter group argued that a better education for whites would mean a better life for Negroes, because whites controlled the state anyway.   Educate the Negro for his place, an inferior one, for the answer to the problem is in the white

[124] Albert Berry Saye, *A Constitutional History of Georgia 1732–1945*, The University of Georgia Press, Athens, Ga., 1948, p. 307.

[125] Harlan, *op. cit.*, p. 210.

[126] Orr, *op. cit.*, p. 225; Saye, *op. cit.*, p. 307.

[127] Harlan, *op. cit.*, pp. 13, 214–215.

community—this was their argument. The less said about Negro education, the better. So the board agreed not to stress Negro education for a two-year period.[128]

There was one minor victory. In 1903 a Georgia Educational Campaign Committee was organized by Charles D. McIver, a member of the Southern Education Board. This committee met in the Governor's office and went on record for local taxation for schools.[129] An amendment extending provisions for local taxation to militia and school districts was finally ratified and put into effect in 1904.[130] But another amendment accompanying it restricted the amount of state taxation and counties failed to carry through with local taxation. In addition, the whole education movement suffered a severe blow by the untimely death in 1905 of Walter B. Hill, an honored Georgian of moderately progressive views.[131] Hill had been state campaign leader for amendments to allow taxation at the local level. After his death, there was no longer an organized drive for taxation.

The white supremacy movement in the South had been gathering force in the 1890s. With reverses of educational reformers, racism began to dominate affairs in Georgia. Robert C. Ogden and his fellow enthusiasts were dubbed "Pullman car philanthropists" and the "swell-belly parade." John Fletcher Hanson of Macon, a mill owner, railroad official, and publisher, stood for the most reactionary of white opinion. He charged that child labor legislation was socialism. He insisted that public schools represented paternalism run mad and anyone who came to school should be required to present a certificate showing that he had been to work.[132] In the face of such opposition, things went hard for the Southern Education Board.

The members of the Peabody foundation wished to crusade for Negro education. But the Southern Education Board was afraid that would alienate the whites and undo the campaign for universal education. The board tried to strike out in new fields, but once again was aligned with conservatives who wished to educate Negroes for their place. The local tax movement was in trouble also, since counties were laid off in districts and gerrymandering allowed some districts to lay claim to the wealthiest areas. Meanwhile, the foundations came into disrepute. Negroes were concerned that funds of philanthropic organizations were being used for white colleges but for Negro industrial institutes. Booker T. Washington stated bitterly that the foundations did little or nothing for Negroes. Ogden worried about the fact that Southerners

[128] *Ibid.,* pp. 78, 92–93, 216.
[129] *Ibid.,* p. 218.
[130] Saye, *op. cit.,* p. 307.
[131] Harlan, *op. cit.,* pp. 220–221.
[132] *Ibid.,* pp. 75, 97–98, 221, 230.

might divert funds to white schools and thus intensify racism.   In protest at conservatism, in 1906, Negroes began the Niagara movement which later developed into the National Association for the Advancement of Colored People.   Georgia deepened the distress by disfranchising Negroes through a literacy amendment to the constitution in 1908.[133]

In the meantime, there were two unfortunate developments in respect to school support.   First, schools were infinitely better supported in urban areas and counties than they were in rural areas, a situation duplicated in many places in the United States.   In the early 1900s, per capita aid for school children in five urban counties in Georgia was $594.75; aid in the remainder of the state, $153.48.[134]   Second, and even more distressing, was the fact that in few places did the Negro child receive even his meager share, particularly in a predominantly Negro area.

Table 12-3. Effect of Wealth and Race on Education in Georgia, 1913

|  | Fulton County | Randolph County | Cherokee County |
|---|---|---|---|
| True value of real property and improvements per school-age child (1904)................. | $3,287.00 | $516.00 | $427.00 |
| Expenditures per white child enrolled (1913).... | 35.96 | 19.84 | 6.63 |
| Expenditures per Negro child enrolled (1913)... | 3.66 | 2.15 | 3.02 |

SOURCE: Louis R. Harlan, *Separate and Unequal: Public School Campaigns and Racism in the Southern Seaboard States 1901–1915*, The University of North Carolina Press, Chapel Hill, N.C., 1958, table 13, p. 240.   Adapted by permission of the publisher.

A study of the situation in 1906 in respect to practices in white and black Georgia counties revealed the following interesting situation: In 13 counties in which less than one-tenth of the school population was Negro, expenditures per month per white child ranged from 75 cents to $1.14.   On the whole this was less than one-half the amount of money expended per white child in black counties.   In 21 counties in which names of Negroes were found on two-thirds or more of the school rolls, the monthly expenditures per white child ran from $1.50 to $4 and per Negro child, from 25 to 79 cents.   In 1908 in 5 counties where one-tenth or less of the population was Negro, $2.01 per child was received from the state and $2.02 expended per white child and $1.81 per Negro child.   In the same year in 5 counties where the Negro population was two-thirds or more of the total, counties received an average of $2.21 per child and spent $6.80 per white child and 99 cents per Negro child, a ratio of 7 to 1 in favor of the white child.

[133] *Ibid.*, pp. 40, 94–95, 97, 99, 223–224.
[134] *Ibid.*, pp. 237–238.

At least one side issue could be pointed up by such studies. The insistence of Southern whites that they did not wish to have their wealth used to educate Negroes could be answered by saying that they were not educating Negroes. Little more than was secured from Negro taxpayers was being used in Negro schools.[135]

Only modest success was achieved by law at the state level. In 1909, there was an attempt to get a mild compulsory education bill, but it failed. Such a bill was not made law until 1916 when compulsory attendance was set at eight to fourteen years or through fourth grade for a minimum of twelve weeks a year, "allowing any exemption acceptable to the school boards."[136] A drive to extend the schooling supported by public taxation was more successful but initially gave advantage to white children. An old charter gave the Senatus Academicus of the University of Georgia the right "to organize, direct, and supervise all the educational institutions of the state." With these powers, the university in 1899 had established the Georgia Normal and Industrial College at Milledgeville, designed to provide for girls who were not admitted to the university.[137] Under these powers, the board of trustees decided in 1903 to begin to encourage high schools. For this task they selected Dr. Joseph S. Stewart. With Stewart's urging, interest grew until in 1906 an agricultural high school was established in each of eleven Congressional districts.[138] An amendment was passed in 1910 and ratified in 1912, allowing state aid for high schools. By 1914 district agricultural high schools were being established. In 1914–1915, 11,167 youth were enrolled in 111 four-year schools,[139] but they were largely white youngsters. In about 1916, there was still only *one* public high school for Negroes in Georgia, and that enrolled only 40 secondary students in a population of 321, in a course of less than the traditional four years.[140]

Two simultaneous movements had occurred by 1915 to bring about a situation in which discrimination was fixed in Southern, and specifically Georgian, education. First, no protest had come from white Georgia counties, where white youngsters were educationally undersupported as compared with whites in predominantly black counties. Harlan suggests that even here finances were a factor. In all rural

[135] *Ibid.*, pp. 18–19, 235–236.

[136] *Ibid.*, pp. 231–233.

[137] Dabney, *op. cit.*, vol. I, 253.

[138] W. Carson Ryan, J. Minor Gwynn, and Arnold K. King (eds.), *Secondary Education in the South*, The University of North Carolina Press, Chapel Hill, N.C., 1946, pp. 72, 75.

[139] Harlan, *op. cit.*, p. 234; Ryan, Gwynn, and King, *op. cit.*, p. 119.

[140] *Negro Education: A Study of the Private and Higher Schools for Colored People in the United States*, p. 41.

counties there was a hatred of cities, where wealth was concentrated. Both white and black counties needed the state aid, which included monies from taxation of wealthier urban people. Therefore, county people were silent about inequities in education of whites and so helped to fix patterns of economic discrimination in schooling of whites as well as Negroes. In addition, the organization which could have been a power in promoting public education, the Southern Education Board, fell in with the Southern conservative tradition, and thus lost the initiative in promoting the welfare of Negroes as board members had originally wished to do.[141]

## The Plantation System Changes

Through the period up to 1915, when discrimination was being ensured as a way of life, still another factor was at work, a factor influencing the ability of Georgians at large and Negroes in particular to strengthen education. This was economic. Georgia's largely rural and unmechanized economy yielded a per capita income which in 1919 was 39 per cent below the national average.[142] This probably reflected both the long-term change to small-scale farming as well as the general poverty which had prevailed in Georgia from the time of the Civil War.

In the period from 1865 to 1868, for instance, there had been a crop failure so severe that in the fifteen months preceding September 1, 1866, the Freedmen's Bureau had issued rations to 847,694 people, of whom nearly 20 per cent were white. As conditions improved, there was an attempt to reinstate the plantation system and to take care of unoccupied Negroes. In 1866 an apprentice act was passed, binding out Negro minors to the age of twenty-one when parents were unable to support them, and charging the master with teaching his apprentices to read. Former slaves began to return to plantations they had previously inhabited.

But two developments complicated the reinstatement of the plantation system. No longer was the master in any position to handle petty misdemeanors as he had done when his farm workers were slaves. So courts were overloaded and penitentiaries overtaxed. Furthermore, free laborers had not yet got used to returning labor for money and food, and plantation owners found themselves unable to control their labor, which might disappear when it was most needed.[143]

[141] Harlan, *op. cit.*, pp. 97, 237–238.

[142] *Ibid.*, p. 35.

[143] Robert Preston Brooks, *The Agrarian Revolution in Georgia, 1865–1912*, University of Wisconsin Bulletin no. 639, History Series III, no. 3, University of Wisconsin, Madison, Wis., 1914, pp. 10–15, 19–20.

Simultaneously, several new farm systems began to go into effect. A share system was one of these. Here the laborer was paid the value of the cotton he raised, minus cost of food. Also, Negroes began to buy small plots and thus became independent farmers. Third, many farms with poor crops passed into the hands of town merchants who initiated the tenant system.[144] All of these systems meant that farms were being reduced in acreage, but they did not immediately bring an increase in acres under cultivation. The figures for 1860 and 1880 are revealing.

Changes in Land-holding Practices in Georgia (1860–1880)

| Year | Total farms | Average farm, size in acres | Farm acreage |
|---|---|---|---|
| 1860 | 62,003 | 430 | 26,650,490 |
| 1880 | 138,626 | 188 | 26,043,282 |

SOURCE: Robert Preston Brooks, *The Agrarian Revolution in Georgia, 1865–1912*, University of Wisconsin Bulletin no. 639, History Series III, no. 3, University of Wisconsin, Madison, Wis., 1914, p. 41.

Negroes increased their farm ownership only with difficulty, as will be indicated when the following figures are analyzed:

Increase in Land Holding by Negroes in Georgia (1874–1903)

| Year | No. of Negro landowners | Land owned by Negroes, in acres |
|---|---|---|
| 1874 | 2,974 | 338,769 |
| 1903 | 18,715 | 1,246,455 |

SOURCE: Robert Preston Brooks, *The Agrarian Revolution in Georgia, 1865–1912*, University of Wisconsin Bulletin no. 639, History Series III, no. 3, University of Wisconsin, Madison, Wis., 1914, p. 43.

In view of the fact that Negroes constituted nearly one-half of the population of the state and were primarily rural dwellers, the increase shown above hardly indicates a phenomenal growth in Negro ownership of Georgia farm land. In 1900 Negroes constituted 46.7 per cent of the total population and held taxable titles to only 4 per cent of the farm land. On the other hand, approximately every other white family owned land. Rather than reflecting an increase in landowning by Negroes, the figures indicate—indirectly—the growth of sharecropping

[144] *Ibid.*, pp. 34–36.

by Negroes. Thus, toward 1910, two-thirds of the way through the period in which Harlan says the pattern of educational discrimination was being fixed, the Negro farmer was also being fixed as a sharecropper or tenant rather than an independent farmer. The tenant farmer or sharecropper got no more than half of the value of the product raised.[145] Thus the money available in the Negro community was reduced. The following figures indicate this trend. Of the 291,221 farms in Georgia in 1910, 168,668 were operated by whites; 122,553 were operated by Negroes. Here is the pattern of operation:[146]

| Operator | White | Negro |
|---|---|---|
| Owner.............. | 50.0 | 13.0 |
| Cash tenant.......... | 18.9 | 41.1 |
| Sharecropper......... | 31.1 | 45.9 |

Thus when Range makes the statement that poverty among Negroes was the greatest drawback to development of higher education[147] there is indirect evidence to support the contention. Also there is evidence to indicate that poverty among all Georgians, not only the Negroes, affected the course of educational events.

## An Educational Summary
## of the Period to 1916

In view of economic circumstances, the truth of Jones's statement in a 1917 publication can be well attested. He said that Negro schools "undoubtedly form the most impoverished group of educational institutions in the United States." Dividing the total sum of teachers' salaries by the number of children in the six-to-fourteen age bracket, Jones came out with the summarizing statement that the per capita sum for teaching for each white child was $10.32 and for each colored child, $2.89—a barometer of the impoverishment of Negro schools. It was admitted that general poverty was at work; for in Northern states the per capita allotment was two and three times that for whites in Southern states. Yet the Southern states appropriated annually about $6,429,991 for "higher" schools for whites and only about one-third of a million for those for Negroes. The latter sum included monies for agricultural and mechanical schools, which were maintained largely at Federal expense, and six normal schools containing elementary and secondary grades.

[145] *Ibid.*, pp. 44–45, 47.
[146] *Ibid.*, p. 122.
[147] Range, *op. cit.*, p. 32.

Nearly all opportunities for Negro youth above elementary grades were being provided through private monies: one-half from white religious denominations, one-third from independent donors and churches, and one-sixth from colored donors.[148]

This generally impoverished situation was reflected in several aspects of education, no more so than in health. Yet the death rates in Georgia, though high for Negroes, were no higher than in certain northern cities (see Table 12-4).

Table 12-4. Death Rates in Selected Urban Areas, 1900 and 1910

| Place and date | Death rate, per thousand | |
| --- | --- | --- |
| | Whites | Negroes |
| Atlanta, Ga.: | | |
| 1900.............. | 18.6 | 27.3 |
| 1910.............. | 15.5 | 25.4 |
| Savannah, Ga.: | | |
| 1900.............. | 23.4 | 38.1 |
| 1910.............. | 19.4 | 34.1 |
| Chicago, Ill.: | | |
| 1900.............. | 15.2 | 23.6 |
| 1910.............. | 15.0 | 24.3 |
| New York, N.Y.: | | |
| 1900.............. | 20.4 | 32.1 |
| 1910.............. | 15.8 | 25.9 |

SOURCE: *Negro Education: A Study of the Private and Higher Schools for Colored People in the United States*, U.S. Office of Education Bulletin 1916, vol. 1, no. 38, 1917, p. 26. Prepared in cooperation with the Phelps-Stokes Fund under the direction of Thomas Jesse Jones, specialist in the education of racial groups.

Poverty was reflected in the statistic (1915–1916) showing that over 50 per cent of colored teachers in public schools had an education of less than six elementary grades. Jones and his colleagues, dealing largely with higher schools, reported another reflection of poverty—that of all Negro institutions surveyed, only Howard, Fisk, and Meharry Medical School had students, teaching force, equipment, and income sufficient to be called colleges.[149]

The picture which Jones and his associates painted for Negroes in the South in general was depressing; it was equally so in Georgia. The discrepancies in support for Negro schools in white and black counties,

[148] *Negro Education: A Study of the Private and Higher Schools for Colored People in the United States*, vol. I, pp. 7–8.
[149] *Ibid.*, pp. 12, 60.

links to this new institutional venture. Only by stretch of the imagination could it be said that the educational process in the Old Northwest, in New Mexico, and in Hawaii would be recapitulated in Georgia. Educational missionaries like those in Ohio, Illinois, and Indiana were to be found in the South; but in the Old Northwest they were largely of the body politic, whereas in the South they came almost entirely from the alien Yankee and industrial communities of the North.

The fact of minority was to be read in the records of both New Mexico and the South. But in the former area, those to be educationally freed were already politically free, whereas, Georgian freedmen would need to fight on to the middle of the twentieth century before they could begin to get the sense of political participation.

The educated missionaries of Hawaii and those of the South had much in common in their zeal to help their charges to a place in the American economic and social systems. But the New Englanders of the island empire could act and think about their people as potential equals and American citizens. The missionaries in Georgia could anticipate no such outcome and could only help their charges to operate within a framework marking them as inferior.

With these differences in educational process, the Negroes of 1917 found themselves burdened with separate and unequal educational facilities which would obtain well into the 1950s. The ideal curricula for Americans as initiated by national committees could have little meaning for those to whom such inadequate education was provided. The "poor blind Samson" would spend many years looking for light.

# 13

## Establishing Schools for
## Spanish Americans in New Mexico

It is well to bear in mind the entirely anomalous condition
of the people and Territory . . . and that the power has
not in all cases been vouchsafed to human wisdom to eradi-
cate the abuses of years in a day.[1]

W. G. RITCH, SECRETARY
OF NEW MEXICO,
DECEMBER 31, 1873

In a 1956 survey of bilingual education in Arizona, California, Colorado,
New Mexico, and Texas, it was found that approximately one-fourth of
the school population is of Spanish origin.[2]  Bilingualism as an educational problem has engaged the attention of educators in states of the
Southwest up to the present.  However, bilingualism is only a reflection
of an influence which runs deeper than language.  A church and a way
of life are the heritage of many people of the Old Southwest.  Residing
often in culture pockets apart from the main stream of the dominant
American culture, they develop their style of living around a set of
organizing principles strikingly different from those ordinarily termed
American.  A fascinating example of the way in which school business
has been sharply modified by cultural differences is to be found in New
Mexico.

This case study of the development of schools in a Southwest state is
broader in scope than the study of education in the Old Northwest and

[1] U.S. Office of Education, *Report of the Commissioner of Education for the
Year 1873*, 1874, pp. 458–459.  Letter from W. G. Ritch to the Commissioner.
[2] Fidel Garcia Baca, "Bilingual Education in Certain Southwest School Districts,"
unpublished doctoral dissertation, University of Utah, Salt Lake City, Utah, 1956,
p. 5 of Introduction.  (Microfilm.)

that of Negro education in Georgia. Like these two studies, it is concerned with the establishment of a common school system, a necessary adjunct of nationalism. But unlike them, the present work deals with attempts of educators to "Americanize" in terms of the dominant Anglo culture. Like the study of Georgia, it is concerned not with all education in a state, but only with education directed to a selected group. In the case of New Mexico, this selected group is made up of the Spanish-speaking peoples.

## PENITENTES OF THE OLD SOUTHWEST

One of the oldest groups in the United States is the Spanish-speaking people of New Mexico. Their identification with a mother country not ordinarily associated with America is symbolically reflected in the term *Penitentes*. Fray Angelico Chaves says that members of the society of New Mexico Penitentes had assumed that their organization came to New Mexico with the original colonists—it was erroneously assumed to have "degenerated from the Third Order of St. Francis." According to Fray Angelico, New Mexico Penitentes appear in the secular period with all the trappings of the Penitentes of Seville in their earlier phase. That this identification should have roots so many years back is the more remarkable in that Fray Angelico is inclined to believe the organization is no older than about 1800 and may be a New World innovation.[3]

Penitentes, symbolic Spanish-speaking people of New Mexico, came into the view of United States citizens only after 1848, when the United States government took over the Southwest territories from Mexico in the Treaty of Guadalupe Hidalgo.

Articles 8 and 9 of the treaty specifically concerned the status of Mexicans residing in the territories being transferred. They contained a statement to the effect that the native people might choose, within one year, whether they were to remain Mexican citizens or to become United States citizens. Those who declared no intention within the stated time period were to be considered to have elected to become citizens of the United States. Those who did not choose to keep their Mexican citizenship were, at the judgment of Congress, to be incorporated into the Union of the United States and[4]

---

[3] Fray Angelico Chaves, "The Penitentes of New Mexico," *New Mexico Historical Review*, vol. 29, no. 2, pp. 97–123, April, 1954.

[4] William M. Malloy (comp.), *Treaties, Conventions, International Acts, Protocols, and Arguments between the United States of America and Other Powers, 1776–1909*, U.S. Government Printing Office, Washington, 1910, vol. I, pp. 1111–1112.

. . . to the enjoyment of all the rights of citizens of the United States, according to the principles of the Constitution; and in the meantime, shall be maintained and protected in the free enjoyment of their liberty and property, and secured in the free exercise of their religion without restriction.

That these 1848 citizens are still an impressive group in the New Mexican society is evident from an estimate of 1940 which put the white Spanish-speaking population at 41.7 per cent of the total state population. Also, an estimate of 1950 established the white population with Spanish surnames at 248,880, or 36.5 per cent of the state population. That this Spanish-speaking group is an old population is apparent from the fact that, as of 1950, only 3.9 per cent of those having Spanish surnames were foreign-born.[5]

## Village Society

Despite their long stay in the United States, many of these people do not enjoy high status. Despite their nativity, members of the lower class are ordinarily referred to as "Mexicans" or "Mexican Americans." The older, wealthier, and best-established families are referred to politely as "Spanish Americans."

Village people, who constitute the bulk of Manitos, recognize three classes. The upper class consists of the old families who hold themselves apart from the rest of the villagers and exert political as well as economic control. They are businessmen, teachers, farmers, or ranchers. Some of them are now *patróns* or are descended from *patróns*, buffers between the villagers and the Anglos. The upper-class people do not question the superiority of Anglo culture. They send their children to school, live for the future, and concentrate on economic and political advantages rather than cultural amalgamation. In the state class system, they are apt to be middle class, though some from the very old and wealthy families are distinctly upper class.[6]

The second group in the village is the rural middle class of small farmers and day laborers. They retain many old Spanish values and customs, and are interested in family and village society rather than in social mobility. Their children ordinarily attend elementary school

[5] Lyle Saunders, *Cultural Differences and Medical Care*, Russell Sage Foundation, New York, 1954, pp. 286, 292.

[6] Account of the village system taken from John H. Burma, *Spanish-speaking Groups in the United States*, Sociological Series, no. 9, Duke University Press, Durham, N.C., 1954; and Donovan Senter and F. M. Hawley, "The Grammar School as the Basic Acculturating Influence for Native New Mexicans," *Social Forces*, vol. 24, pp. 398–407, May, 1946.

through the sixth or eighth grade and a few go to high school. However, many believe that Anglicization in high school leads to freedom of association between the sexes and immorality. "They live in the present and plan only for the immediate future." Their living standards are low and, as a substitute for better standards, they concentrate on good human relations.

The lower class, along with the rural middle class, constitutes a lower class in the state society. These people are very poor and often illiterate. Standards of cleanliness and health are below those of other villagers. They are prey to diseases contracted through lack of physical stamina. Medievalism is very apparent among them. They are believers in magic and witchcraft and in the powers of the Manito and Pueblo Indian *curanderos* or quacks.

Within this heavily structured village society, a devastating economic process has been going on. In the past the dons held sway over land and stock, and many of the jobs and villagers. Their influence and control have tended to disappear, though in some villages selected families still control much of the economic life. After 1848, however, as Anglos moved into New Mexico, the personal possessions of the natives began to disappear. Hispanos were not used to the monetary system and did not know land values. Anglos often got lands and made fortunes. Since 1854, says Burma, Hispanos have lost 2 million acres of private land, 1.7 million acres of communal land, and 1.8 million acres have gone to the state for education. The land that remains has undergone ruinous subdivision among succeeding generations. As a result, the typical Manito farm is 10 irrigated acres, plus a team, a milch cow, three or four beef cattle, twelve chickens, and two or more hogs. There are typically five or six members in the family, and they live in a four-room adobe house. The net yield of the farm is $20 per acre, so the farmer or his son must work off the farm, Burma states.

In consequence of impoverishment and isolation, electricity, telephones, window screens, and indoor water supply are rare or nonexistent. Houses are picturesque but rural slums of the first order. However, although the village pattern is indeed inefficient, it makes possible the development and integration of group life and institutions not possible in many other systems. Perhaps as a consequence of this last fact, the people cling tenaciously to their villages.

## Anglo- and Spanish-American Values

Limitations in viewpoint and a segmented approach to behavior change have characterized the efforts of many educators in New Mexico. This can perhaps best be judged by expanding on a description of this particular subculture by comparing Spanish-American values with the more familiar Anglo-American pattern.[7]

A difference in native language is quite obvious between the Anglo and the Spanish American. What is not so obvious is that in many areas in remote rural sections or in little "Mexicos" within cities, the Spanish-speaking person can get along quite satisfactorily without English. The Anglo-American expects, however, that his Hispano fellow citizen will either make the first move to learn English or will go back to his own country, quite forgetting that this is the country of many Spanish-speaking Americans.

It is quite probable that, despite schooling, the Hispano will cross the language bridge only when it becomes socially or economically necessary for him to do so. Whether he feels such a necessity probably depends on whether he endorses values alien to his subculture. The cultural step that he would need to take can be illustrated by describing other ways in which he differs from his Anglo brother.

For the Anglo-American, the clock runs. The Anglo is much preoccupied with fast-moving time. He carries a watch, he puts emphasis on being on time to work or school, he turns on the radio to get the right time, he watches the calendar. Saunders has said that one test of sanity in the Anglo culture consists in asking what day and year it is. The Anglo has his time scheduled days and weeks and often years in advance. He takes out insurance for the needs of old age. Time is of the essence because the Anglo lives in a present which is only a steppingstone to a future which he is attempting to control.

While the Anglo's clock runs, the Spanish American's clock walks. The latter's immediate past or even present is in a village agricultural society where the rhythms of life are seasonal rather than diurnal. The occupational life is simple. There is no need for careful intermeshing of activities as in an urban-industrial society. Tasks are not urgent. There is no pressure to develop any particular concern with time. The future, furthermore, will be much like the present. Let us live in the present and in terms of that which needs to be done now. If it is money to be earned, then take a job for a day; but if it is relatives to be visited, then the job can wait.

Intermeshed with any group's attitudes toward time are attitudes toward change. Anglo-Americans have deeply embedded in their value structure positive attitudes toward change. Newness is valued for its own sake. Note among Anglos the tendency to apologize for an outdated automobile and last year's refrigerator. Anglo consumers live

---

[7] Account of values taken from Saunders, *op. cit.*, pp. 104–140, with supporting comments of the author.

superficially in a world in which they are constantly bombarded via radio, television, and newspapers with the latest discoveries in miracle products and miracle power. The Sunday supplements are filled with stories of the house of the future or the airplane which will one day reach the moon—and invention of either will make today's conveniences appear to be by-products of the Old Stone Age.

The lure of new things is in their being better than the old, a concept quite congenial to the typical American, to whom the idea of progress is as old as his nation. Since the early 1800s European commentators have referred to the Anglo-American's extraordinary optimism which is never dimmed, however sharply the basis for hope may be belied by the reality of slums and drought-ridden farms. The American Dream is developed on the premise that there is nothing more certain than that the future will be better than the present, change is always progress, my children and my children's children will live in a better world.

Hispanos, on the other hand, who have lived in isolated villages, are used to an environment in which change is merely a familiar cycle consonant with the individual's biological life span and the circular flow of the seasons. A person is born into and dies among much the same kind of people and events as his father before him and his father before that. The future—to the degree that it is thought of at all—is thought of as being only an extension of the present. In a technologically simple society, furthermore, change may be dangerous. New health practices, new tractors, hybrid seed corn, and rainmaking—for the villager these may all be devices for courting disaster. The Spanish American fears change, or at least is confused by it to such an extent that he gains the reputation with Anglos of being backward and lacking initiative.

In the Anglo's hierarchy of values, industriousness is next to cleanliness and godliness, and laziness is a besetting sin. There is a fundamental lack of character in a man who does not like to work. A man is identified not by his family or his virtues, but by his occupation; he is not a good *man* (unless he is a good provider), but rather a good *carpenter*. Saunders points to several instances in which this identification with work has been in evidence. Note, says he, the dislike for retirement even when the individual will suffer no economic hardship. Recall the devastating effect on personality of losing a job in the Depression of the 1930s. "Psychologically traumatic" was the loss in status, coming with loss in income; almost equally so, according to Saunders, was the denial of something to do.

Work industriously pursued leads to success, and success is desired so much that the good parent is one who gives his child a good start toward some rewarding occupation. In some respects, the Anglo culture is so much one of a single goal, occupational success, that both women and, in turn, the family have been affected by it.[8] It is no longer quite proper for a woman to be a housewife. The woman who can successfully juggle a home, a family, and a career is the one who gets her picture in the rotogravure.

Coupled with the orientation toward success is a bent toward efficiency and practicality. The Anglo is interested in theories, but more so in what works. The college of education student always prefers practice teaching to history of education, and the typical college student can be persuaded to take a particular elective only if it is going to do him some *good*, that is, fill a lack that stands in the way of his achieving an occupational goal.

The ambition of the Spanish American, on the other hand, is to *be* rather than to *do*. A village has so few occupations that a man can hardly be distinguished for his occupational achievements. He is rather known by his family, his age, his sex. But opportunities for uniqueness in these terms are limited. There are other good sons, kind fathers, devout mothers. Thus no cult of success has ever developed among certain of the Spanish-speaking group, and hence work becomes something one does to meet the ordinary exigencies of living. Familiar techniques are at least predictable and therefore practical. Hence practicality and efficiency are not looked upon as values to be achieved. No unattainable or far-removed goals are embraced. Short-term goals of a simple technological order are usually reached. The mechanisms which motivate striving are nonexistent.

Anglo-Americans fight against circumstances. They raise huge sums of money to control devastating diseases. They dam up undammable rivers. It takes them a week to do the improbable, and a little longer to do the impossible. Their folk heroes are men who rose to high places through overcoming odds: Washington, the farmer, who became a great general; Lincoln, the rail-splitter, who became President; Franklin, the printer, who became the "First American." The so-called typical American reserves his deepest admiration for those who never say die.

Spanish Americans are resigned to fate and circumstances. They often irritate health workers because they will not willingly participate in campaigns to control disease. Employers describe them as docile, evidencing passivity toward those in authority. It is not that the Spanish American has no need for self-assertion, but his manifestations of assertiveness are unlike manifestations among Anglos—bursts of temper, oratory, and emphasis on masculinity. This kind of personal in-

---

[8] See comments in Florence R. Kluckhohn, "Cultural Factors in Social Work Practice and Education," *The Social Service Review*, vol. 25, pp. 38–47, March, 1951.

dividualism makes it often impossible for the Spanish-speaking person
to develop loyalty to an impersonal job. The Anglo can be loyal both to
a job and an organization, and expect no individual recognition. The
Spanish-speaking person can be loyal only to a person. "Impersonality
could hardly exist in a village where everyone was known to and shared
experiences with everyone else," says Saunders.

Imagine the lack of comprehension of a Spanish-speaking child when
a teacher asks him to be loyal to a flag, a constitution, and a form of
government—all abstractions which have meaning to Anglos but none
to those for whom persons are the only reality.

Of all the values of the Anglo, the one which most characterizes him
is his independence of other individuals. In the Anglo family, children
are encouraged early to find their own friends, to become independent
emotionally even of their parents. In times of depression, when Americans temporarily lose their independence and have to seek relief, social
workers concern themselves over the blow to character that comes from
dependent economic status. A large part of the social work movement
is oriented toward transferring the dependent person on relief to independent status. In recent years, educators as well as social workers
have been turning their attention to the trials of the elderly in an effort
to bolster their independence, apparently one of the sure roads to healthful living in the Anglo society. Among the aged themselves, one frequently hears "I do not wish to be a burden to my children."

In the life of the Spanish American, however, the only reality is the
village, which is often self-sufficient and independent. Within its
boundaries, however, interdependence and dependence flourish through
intermarriage, the extended family, the necessary reliance of the individual on personal assistance rather than on agencies in times of
trouble. Neither the orphan asylum nor the nursing home flourishes in
a Spanish-American village. Dependence is neither wrong nor dangerous, but an accepted way of meeting the problems of daily life.

Independence for the Anglo, however, does not mean independence
from the group; it means rather the freedom to join groups of his
choosing. By groups, one gets community jobs done and out of these
groups, leaders develop for the many emergencies of Anglo life. Having
used the group for some 200 years as an instrument for personal and
community welfare, Anglos have become familiar with collective enterprises. They are skilled both at setting up new organizations to fit
their purposes and utilizing them to attain personal goals.

In the Spanish village, most of the community problems can be
handled through informal personal relationships, often of kinfolk.
Spanish Americans cannot and do not wish to organize. The few organizations they have sponsored have usually died. However, there are

presently a few local and state-wide organizations which may well become a bridge to the Anglo culture—a culture which Spanish-speaking
persons need to embrace, at least in part, if they hope to improve their
status.

The same contrasting value systems as those described above can be
seen in studies of two groups in a drought-ridden area of New Mexico.[9] As geography remains the same, the effect of value systems on
ways of living and working can be judged. A total of five groups are
under study. Two groups have been selected for analysis here. Texan
homesteaders best typify the Anglo-American and provide best contrast with the other group selected, the Spanish American.

The Texans raise cattle and carry on commercial and largely mechanized farming. A principal crop is pinto beans. Individualism runs
strong. Homes are scattered over several townships, and social relations between families are competitive. There is competition for position and prestige. There is competition even in religion, for the 250
Texans belong to ten different Protestant denominations. Each man is
thought of as self-reliant and his own boss. Texans strive for mastery
over nature. They use the latest tractors and the most modern
farming techniques. They reject the past and use the present as a step-
ping-stone to the future. Their motto is "Progress." In times of
drought they may turn to prayer, but the majority are in favor of
artificial rainmaking. When doubts were expressed about interfering
with the workings of nature, a farmer was heard to remark that the
Lord would judge harshly people so ignorant as not to use the facilities
He had given them.

Spanish Americans living in the same drought-ridden area as the
Texans are livestock ranchers or wage workers. They put strong emphasis on lineality, that is, social relations are desirable when they are
appropriate to the hierarchy of their society. In their communities the
young people are subordinate to their elders, females to males, peons
to *patróns*—their secular structure "gears into the hierarchically arranged
Catholic church" to which they all belong. The Spanish Americans,
in tune with this hierarchy, say of the Texans that everybody tries to
be his own *patrón*.

The villagers have the normal-curve view of nature. One season will
be good, another bad; they accept the inevitability of nature's vagaries.
They do nothing about drought, neither soliciting nature by ceremonial
nor conquering her by science. Drought is a part of the normal curve.
They are interested primarily in a present in which they are secure in
a traditional familiar mold. It is ridiculous to work too hard, and even

---

[9] Account to follow taken from Evon Z. Vogt and John M. Roberts, "A Study of
Values," *Scientific American*, vol. 195, no. 1, pp. 25–31, July, 1956.

more outrageous to worry about the future. They have neither curiosity nor knowledge about the world at large. They live a rich and dramatic present in their fiestas, which are partly religious.

## THE SPANISH-AMERICAN GOES TO SCHOOL

As would occur in an analysis of any educational system, the New Mexican system must be viewed against the background of the particular responses to a social and physical environment which are stamped into its inhabitants from birth through old age. This background has been provided in the immediately preceding pages, and will be referred to in subsequent discussions as it allows for inferences respecting the unique elements in the New Mexican educational past.

### Attitude toward Schools

It is difficult to speak of the attitude toward schools without introducing Anglo value-charged terms. However, the phraseology carries no connotations of disapproval.

Under the Mexican regime, though attempts were made to institute schools, it can be said that there was on the whole a pervading indifference—if that word be understood correctly—on the part of the people who were later to be New Mexicans. The census of 1850, after two years of United States supervision, showed a population of 61,547 of whom 58,415 or 94 per cent had been born in the territory—a largely native-born population. Yet only a few were reported as attending school.

A memorial to Congress in 1854 indicated that 25,000 adult males could neither read nor write.[10] Yet clergy of the Roman Catholic church had been making sporadic efforts for two or more centuries at least to promote school enterprises. As a matter of fact, the first permanent educational institution was that of the Sisters of Loretta, who opened a Santa Fe school for thirteen youngsters in November, 1852.[11]

When the territory was taken over after the Treaty of Guadalupe Hidalgo, a promise was made to the inhabitants that schools would be instituted promptly. It is quite likely that the promise fell on deaf ears. A rural population living in an environment which no one wanted to change and a wealthy few who provided privately for their

[10] Here and in succeeding footnotes, reference will be made to Robert Arthur Moyers, "A History of Education in New Mexico," unpublished doctoral dissertation, George Peabody College for Teachers, Nashville, Tenn., 1941. It is to be understood that Moyers contains evidence for the facts cited, but that the interpretation of those facts is often the author's.

[11] *Ibid.*, p. 200.

children's education produced a situation in which there was no need for a system of publicly supported schools.

Despite the promise and undoubtedly because of the indifference of the people, succeeding census records showed a very slow change in the direction of a schooled population. The census of 1880 showed a total population of 119,565 with 35,695 school-age (five- to seventeen-year-old) children, of whom only 4,755, or about 13 per cent, were in school. Of the total population, 65 per cent (57,156) who were over ten years of age could still neither read nor write.[12] By the census of 1890, some change toward school going was apparent. The youth aged five to fourteen numbered 34,339, of whom 15,885, or about 46 per cent, were in private or public schools.

By 1910, the population in the six-to-fourteen age group had increased to 66,610, of whom some 72.9 per cent were in school. However, 48,697 of those ten years of age and over, or about 20.2 per cent, were still illiterate.[13] The percentage of illiteracy in the United States was only 7.7, even in the middle of the period of the heaviest immigration of people having high percentages of illiteracy.

There were other evidences, however, of general indifference to publicly supported schools. In the 1855–1856 legislative term, the territorial assembly decided to institute a school tax, provisions for which were cautiously worded in deference to a remembered tax rebellion of 1837. The subject of the tax was submitted to the voters in a special election. The vote was small. The decision, however, was not in doubt. There were 37 votes for the tax, 5,016 against it. United States Commissioner of Education John Eaton charged the lack of interest in schools to negligence of the United States government. However, he could not refrain from quoting a responsible writer on the territories:[14]

Parents either seem to have an idea that the propagation of children should return early profits, or to dread a little learning as a more dangerous thing for their sons and daughters than blasting in a mine, driving an ox team, taking in washing, and marrying early.

The depth of the indifference to education may be inferred from additional comments of John Eaton. The energetic New Hampshire–born

[12] U.S. Bureau of the Census, *Compendium of the Tenth Census: June 1, 1880,* rev. ed., parts I and II, pp. 4, 589, 1641, 1645.

[13] U.S. Bureau of the Census, *Compendium of the Eleventh Census: 1890,* part III, pp. 252–253; *Report on Population of the United States at the Eleventh Census: 1890,* part II, pp. 138–139; and *Thirteenth Census of the United States: 1910,* vol. I, *Population,* pp. 1106, 1205.

[14] U.S. Office of Education, *Report of the Commissioner of Education for the Year 1870, with Accompanying Papers,* 1870, p. 22.

commissioner was of the best tradition of democracy and progress. He had taught country school, organized the free school system of Tennessee, and been liaison officer between Gen. Ulysses S. Grant and President Abraham Lincoln in the interests of the Negro slaves from the South. In good bustling New England fashion, he took occasion to point out that the inhabitants of New Mexico lived in good circumstances for the development of schools. They were settled in plazas (villages) varying from fifty to several thousand inhabitants who were sustained by flocks and suburban farms. To a man used to the isolation of rural life in the Middle West or even the East, the New Mexican rural people appeared to be ideally situated for supporting schools. The United States Commissioner could not contain himself: "As if to show the world the most criminal example of how good opportunities may be neglected, here exists the most schoolless, ignorant and poverty-stricken people speaking a civilized though foreign language."[15]

The question might again be raised as to why the resistance to schools. The answer may be partially unfolded as the description of the New Mexican scene unfolds in the following pages. Suffice it to say here that a belief in the cyclical nature of change, the simple rural life, and the feudal concept of education for the elite combined to put the stamp of the unschooled on the New Mexican people.

## Organization of Schools

Spanish Americans made their mark in other ways on educational endeavors in New Mexico. One of these was that of the elite-motivated movements toward public and private education. No butcher, baker, or candlestick maker fostered the school movement in New Mexico as they had in the Old Northwest. Instead, a hard-working set of government officials, members of the Roman Catholic orders, and Protestant missionaries were the instigators of what schools there were in the early period.

One of the first moves of the Territorial Legislature was to write a memorial in 1854 to Congress requesting monies for schools. This kind of action was similar to actions of groups in other areas, but different in particulars. Other territorial groups requested lands and showed evidence of local initiative in developing schools, so that money from lands would constitute a supplementary fund. The New Mexican legislators were requesting Federal monies, presumably because none were forthcoming from the native population. Reliance on a higher authority for leadership and for finance was to be a pattern in establishing schools for some time to come. As a matter of fact, the first

[15] *Ibid.*, p. 326.

public school fund raised by taxation did not come in New Mexico until the year 1871–1872.[16]

Peculiarly Spanish in origin, too, is the early reliance put on judges in respect to school-board appointment and membership. A law of 1855–1856 created a county board of education of which the probate judge was to be president and to which he was to appoint at least one member. Through a law of January 27, 1860, justices of the peace were made responsible for general supervision of schools. Even as late as 1917, an act creating county boards with corporate powers put appointing powers in the hands of the district judge.[17]

A territorial board of education which reflected the Spanish and Spanish-Catholic backgrounds of the population was created by an act of January 28, 1863. Among members of the board were the Governor, judges of the supreme court, and the Bishop of New Mexico. The territorial board was recreated after 1890, and again reflected both a Spanish-Catholic outlook and confidence in an educational and official hierarchy. Members this time were to be, besides the Governor and the superintendent of public instruction, the president of St. Michael's College (Roman Catholic), and the presidents of the state university and the state agricultural college. The superintendent of schools was to be appointed by the Governor with the consent of the council.[18]

A change in the territorial board in 1901 brought some dispersion of authority, in that superintendents of four cities ranking highest in population were to be members. But still present on the board were, besides the Governor and the superintendent, five members who were heads of territorial institutions and the president of St. Michael's College. Centralization, a hierarchical concept, was evident in the organization, in that the superintendent had the authority to suspend a county superintendent.[19]

In 1909, when the board was empowered to pass on the qualifications of county superintendents, to prescribe their duties, and to control county institutes, centralization of authority, a typically Spanish-American concept, was further enhanced. Only in the constitution, which of course was affected by the United States Congress, were Spanish-Catholic backgrounds ignored. The board still remained structured, however, in terms of educational authority figures. In addition to the Governor and state superintendent were five members, to be appointed by the Governor with the consent of the Senate. Among the five were to be included the head of some state institution, a county superintendent, and one other

[16] Moyers, op. cit., p. 169.
[17] Ibid., pp. 154–155, 497, 693.
[18] Ibid., p. 699.
[19] Ibid., pp. 707–708.

person connected with educational work.[20]  Up to the writing of the first constitution, the idea of a board of education representing a lay public had not yet taken hold.

## Religious Participation in the Organization of Schools

As might be expected, members of the Roman Catholic clergy and orders have from time to time played significant and controversial roles in education.  In the 1870s, for example, Protestants charged that public schools were priest-ridden.  So strong was the protest that Governor Axtell spoke out strongly against the sectarian control of schools, and Governor Ritch carried on a long disquisition against sectarianism in his *Third Annual Report* to the National Bureau of Education.[21]  Whatever the nature of the participation, it was probably inevitable that there should be rather considerable Roman Catholic activity.  With a population organized in the form of a hierarchy and looking to higher authority in the form of church leaders, it would have been strange if the Roman Catholic church had not played a significant and controversial role in school affairs, including public school affairs.

Involvement of both Catholics and Protestants in the education of the Indians is clearly evident in many ways.  In 1849, James S. Calhoun, Indian agent of the Federal government at Santa Fe, met with Indians who recommended that schools be established for them.  In turn, Calhoun recommended that schools be set up, and that there be a press publishing in both English and Spanish, which some of the Indians could read.  A few months later Calhoun was referring to "wicked priests" who had changed the Indians' opinions in respect to schools.[22]

Following these first moves of the Federal government, missionaries were asked to establish schools.  Tribes were parceled out—the Pueblos to the Christian group, the Apaches and Navajos to the Presbyterians. Catholics, though assigned groups in other states, were not given any in New Mexico at first.  However, in 1872, Nathaniel Pope, superintendent of Indian Affairs at Santa Fe, reported that most of the Pueblo Indians were Catholics and asked for authorization to turn over funds for Indian education to Bishop J. B. Lamy at Santa Fe.

Confused and troubled years followed.  Mission groups, including Roman Catholics and Presbyterians, contracted for schools but with limited success in enrolling Indian children.  Protestants were accused

[20] *Ibid.*, pp. 709–711.

[21] W. G. Ritch, *Education in New Mexico: Third Annual Report to the Commissioner of Education*, as cited in U.S. Office of Education, *Report of the Commissioner of Education for the Year of 1875*, 1876, pp. 500–509.

[22] Moyers, *op. cit.*, pp. 739–741.

of proselyting Catholic Indians.   Whisky sellers were accused of creating trouble among Navajos and preventing them from working on schools. Day schools were changed to boarding schools in the hope that young Indians could be civilized and sent back to their tribes fired up to civilize their countrymen.   By 1890, among the Pueblo Indians, the most-favored group in respect to educational attention, only about 65 per cent (1,540 out of 2,050) of the school-age children were enrolled in Catholic, Congregational, other contract, or government schools.[23] By 1892, Catholics were receiving about $394,756 out of $600,000 of contract monies.   The Governor recommended the abandonment of contract schools.   His recommendation was accepted in 1900, when the contract fund ceased to exist.   At statehood in 1912, there were 2,085 Indian youngsters in government schools and 200 in mission schools. Of those of school age, 2,100 were not enrolled in school.   Two conflicting culture groups had boded ill for Indian education.

Religious workers apparently continued to be active in what should have been public school business.   The situation in 1950 in some areas must have roughly resembled that in some Latin-American countries where the Roman Catholic church is recognized as the state church. Whether in New Mexico or in a Latin-American country, the line between church and state schooling was so thin as not to exist at all.

In about 1948 to 1950, in Dixon, New Mexico, a community fairly equally divided between Protestants and Catholics, the matter of church-state relationships was brought to a head by action of Protestant parents.[24]   They objected to the teaching of religion in public school and to having the school housed in a church building.   On being told there was no money for a separate building, the group donated money and labor for a building and were rewarded with having a sister put in charge of the new school.   Through appeal to the state board of education, they finally obtained a lay principal and lay teachers.   But this situation finally provided a basis for a case, which was taken both to the district court and to the state supreme court.   The circumstances uncovered in New Mexico public schools are as fascinating as any to be found in the history of American education.

These circumstances were extremely complex, with such an interweaving of church and state in school business that no one generalization could cover the facts.   In some cases, teachers in religious garb were teaching in public schools and being reimbursed individually or through payment of public monies to their respective orders.   Religious pictures

[23] Ibid., pp. 749–758.

[24] Account to follow taken from L. O. Garber, "Supreme Court Defines Church-state Separation for Public Schools in New Mexico," Nation's Schools, vol. 49, pp. 69–71, February, 1952.

were to be found on the walls of some schools and religion (Roman Catholic) was being taught either in school time or immediately before or after school. In the latter case, bus schedules would be arranged so as to make allowance for time in religious instruction. In some instances, public school classes were being held in church buildings. On the other hand, school buses were being used to transport youngsters to parochial schools, and a separate list of books for use in Catholic schools was approved by state authorities. In some public schools, youngsters were released during school time to attend mass and confession; in others, sectarian texts were employed. It has been stated that often the teachers in public schools looked to the local parish priest rather than to the school board for directions, and that local boards had, in effect, given over their authority to superiors of religious orders.

In its ruling, the state supreme court defined church-state separation in much the same way that it would be normally defined in other states. However, there were three interesting exceptions to the judgment of the district court, which had previously addressed itself to sharp separation of church and state. For lack of evidence that they taught religion, some 6 or 8 of the 139 defendants (most of whom were members of religious orders) were not to be barred from teaching in public schools. In respect to wearing religious garb in public schools, the supreme court held that "the trial court should have granted an injunction." Finally, the court in effect dismissed the injunctions against the state department of education and the state educational budget auditor who had permitted the former practices to prevail.

## THE IDEOLOGICAL BATTLE
## —CULTURE AGAINST CULTURE

Meanwhile, an ideological battle has gone on at the practical level—a battle between those dedicated to the so-called Anglo concept of education and the often mute, but nevertheless powerful, people whose behavior has continued to be oriented in other directions. The battle began when the first Anglos moved into positions of power in New Mexico; it was heightened as recruits for school positions were drawn increasingly from Anglo groups. It is not strange that the number of Anglos in school positions was increasing. The Spanish population probably would have taken no steps to recruit lay teachers. They would have looked to priests, who were considered by Anglos as undesirable for nonsectarian school systems, though they were occasionally employed in public schools. In addition, there would have been few among the Spanish-speaking lay group who were prepared by attitude and training for educational service.

*Teachers and Administrators*

The most revealing story in respect to school people can be read in the *New Mexico Journal of Education,* which first appeared in January, 1905, and became, at different times, the official organ of the state department of education and of the New Mexico Educational Association. In this state of Spanish names, one is hard put to find other than Anglo names in the journal's annals. In an early issue, for instance, there is a list of 120 school people in the state; 105 of them are attending an educational convention. In the total list, only two Spanish names are to be found. One also looks almost in vain in an official organ for any indication that a particular culture might be the key to the educational problems of the state. Instead, the journal is filled with stories of teachers' reading circles, reports from the East and the nation at large on educational activities, detailed descriptions of new methodologies or techniques, with little hint as to their anticipated effect on a non-Anglo population.

Concerted drives, however, were made to enlist Spanish-speaking peoples in formal education, particularly as a preparation for teaching. The editor of a school journal took occasion to remark that it was good to see so many young Spanish Americans at summer institutes.[25] He went on to say that such young people—if patriotic, industrious, and honest—had a bright future in teaching. One wonders what meaning the value-charged words "patriotic" and "industrious" might have had to Spanish-speaking young people in whose vocabularies neither word would have carried a positive emotional charge.

A more significant gesture in the direction of interesting Spanish Americans in teaching had been made in 1909 with the opening of the Spanish-American Normal School at El Rito.[26] The preamble to the act establishing the school had indicated the necessity for the preparation of "a sufficient number of native Spanish-speaking teachers, in sympathy with their scholars." Furthermore, it had been found that in over 400 county schools, the language of the pupils was Spanish and this necessitated teachers who knew how to communicate with them. In deference to a group with limited schooling, students were admitted to the new normal school on the basis of a fourth grade education or passing an examination for entrance to the fifth grade. Students were required to guarantee that after training they would teach two years in the territory.[27]

For some years efforts to attract students yielded few results in spite

[25] *New Mexico Journal of Education,* vol. 7, p. 4, Sept. 15, 1910.

[26] Moyers, *op. cit.,* p. 456, and *New Mexico Journal of Education,* vol. 7, p. 23, Oct. 15, 1910.

[27] *New Mexico Journal of Education,* vol. 7, pp. 23, 25, Oct. 15, 1910.

of the fact that living expenses were $75 a year, tuition was free, and scholarships were available. The total number of students in the year 1910–1911 was only 75. By the year 1917–1918, only 123 were enrolled and many were pursuing primary and upper elementary education. Only 22 were actively engaged in special work for a teacher's certificate.

By necessity the school continued to have dual aims: to provide a general education for Spanish-speaking boys and girls, and to prepare teachers for Spanish-speaking communities. The second purpose could hardly have been achieved in view of the level at which the school must have operated. Prior to 1926, school officials were granting a diploma for completion of four years above the sixth grade. In 1926, there were four years of high school work, which included four units in agriculture and four in home economics, plus an industrial department or grammar school, and a training school. Plans were under way to offer college work in the year 1926–1927, but in 1930 the only professional work beyond the first twelve years was a course in psychology and one in pedagogy. It was not until 1939 that a college division was organized with three courses in education, two each in English, history, and Spanish, and one each in health education, music, and psychology.[28]

## Language as the Key to Americanization

The crux of the difficulties in recruiting Spanish-speaking teachers and in enrolling Spanish-American youngsters in school may well lie in the implied assessment of the educational problem. In order to Americanize these people, so the argument might have gone, we must get at them in their own language. Spanish rather than a culture thus became the implied key to Americanization.

Through a law of 1884, district directors were empowered to adopt texts in English or in Spanish. However, the wisdom of the directive might well be questioned when a county superintendent reported in 1910 that he seriously lacked teachers who could speak both English and Spanish.[29]

That something other than a language was involved was briefly recognized in 1910, when a note in the *New Mexico Journal of Education* pointed out a need for recognizing the non-English-speaking home. The writer indicated that a special effort must be made to invite parents in for Friday afternoon sessions.[30]

[28] Moyers, *op. cit.*, pp. 674–677.
[29] *Ibid.*, pp. 186, 326.
[30] Katherine Adams Hicks, "Co-operation of School and Home," *New Mexico Journal of Education*, vol. 7, pp. 10–11, December, 1910.

If language were indeed a key to good citizenship and education, then congressmen were determined to leave the educational door locked. In the 1910 enabling act, Congress directed that, in developing a constitution, provision must be made for a system of public schools open to all, free from sectarian control, and conducted in English.[31]

Again in 1911 language, as a key to education, if not to citizenship, was highlighted by C. F. Miller of Carthage, New Mexico, in an article, "Language Should Be Made the Leading Study in the Schools of New Mexico." Miller's concern was not for communication in Spanish but for intensive instruction in English. He listed several supporting pieces of evidence. The large majority of children did not speak English when they entered school, they continued to speak Spanish at home, and they left school early. Yet their parents wished them to learn English, which was an avenue to leading positions. "Consequently," said Miller, "there should be strenuous effort in the school room to counter-balance the negative influence of the home,"[32] this influence presumably being a commitment to the Spanish tongue.

Others were interested in the same language problem, as is evidenced by an article on the Spanish child in the reading class which appeared in 1913. Miss Jackson reported on her observation of the second grade in which she saw, so she said, three groups of children: those whose parents had a knowledge of current affairs and who directed the conversation whether the talk was in Spanish or English; the average youngsters (natural thinkers), who heard English only at school; and the indolent and dull from families of the first and second categories.[33] It is quite obvious that Miss Jackson was mixing quite a few ingredients in considering the Spanish-speaking child in the reading class. As a consequence, her advice to teachers of such children was equally diffuse: know the ability of the individual child.

Despite Miller's concern for the teaching of English, in 1915 it was directed by law that Spanish be taught as a separate subject in any public elementary or high school in the state if a majority of the board of school directors or the board of education in charge of the school so voted. Texts in English might be used if Spanish were employed in explaining the meaning of English words to pupils not understanding English. In 1917 it was made unlawful for a county superintendent to approve a teacher's warrant if the teacher refused on petition "to teach reading in Spanish and English by the bilingual method to all pupils

---

[31] Moyers, *op. cit.*, p. 486.

[32] C. F. Miller, "Language Should Be Made the Leading Study in the Schools of New Mexico," *New Mexico Journal of Education*, vol. 7, pp. 7–8, June, 1911.

[33] Alice A. Jackson, "The Spanish Child in the Reading Class," *New Mexico Journal of Education*, vol. 9, pp. 11–12, May 15, 1913.

in the first, second, and third grades." The law was repealed in 1923 but renewed in 1941 by a law requiring Spanish to be taught in grades 5 to 8 in schools with three teachers or more.[34] Directives respecting the teaching of Spanish solved few problems, least of all the language problem. In 1919 an article pointed out that teachers were still hard put to get the cooperation of parents because English-speaking teachers could not communicate at all and Spanish-speaking teachers had a tendency to promote the exclusive speaking of Spanish in the community.[35]

Meanwhile, other developments were under way, including giving status to study in and of Spanish. In 1917, H. D. Morrill published a series of articles on the Spanish child. He pointed out that "it should go without saying that the first task of the teacher of the Spanish-speaking child is to teach him to use the English language."[36] However, he commended the support that was given United States policy in respect to Spanish-speaking countries and concluded: "The educators and the schools that are teaching Spanish are doing the useful thing and the patriotic thing."[37]

In 1919 the first high school Spanish club was organized, and teachers of Spanish promoted a chapter of the American Association of Teachers of Spanish. In 1920 Spanish was defended against the charge of being a localism; its use in opening the doors to a great Spanish literature was pointed out. Indeed, competence in the language was a necessity for supporting United States efforts to improve commercial relations with Latin-American neighbors, and to ready New Mexico as a possible location for a proposed Pan-American university.[38]

No disaffection from English was probably intended, for so prominent a man as Governor Larrazolo said that the two greatest languages were English and Spanish, and they were not at odds. He agreed that there was no disagreement on every child's learning English; the question rather was how this might best be accomplished. As the Governor had been a teacher in Texas, he dared to advise New Mexican teachers that there must be a decided change in methods in the language arts. His own procedure had been to teach in Spanish for the first school

[34] Moyers, op. cit., pp. 496–497.

[35] New Mexico Journal of Education, vol. 16, p. 6, September, 1919.

[36] H. D. Morrill, "Teaching English to Spanish Children," New Mexico Journal of Education, vol. 14, p. 9, November, 1917.

[37] H. D. Morrill, "Spanish," New Mexico Journal of Education, vol. 14, p. 4, February, 1918.

[38] H. D. Morrill, "The Need of Teaching Spanish," New Mexico Journal of Education, vol. 15, pp. 6–8, December, 1918; New Mexico Journal of Education, vol. 15, p. 12, July, 1919; vol. 16, p. 13, Oct., 1919; and Edna Oakley, "New Mexico Spanish," New Mexico Journal of Education, vol. 16, pp. 3–5, May, 1920.

year and in English for the second year, which would be devoted largely to translation with the child copying both Spanish and English in his notebook.   Some of his former students who had been taught by this method were now holding responsible positions.[39]

Through succeeding decades, despite intermittent attention to the education of Spanish-speaking students, apparently the school made little impact in some communities.   In 1938 Ruth Miller-Martinez reported that of the 3,500 elementary school children in Taos County, less than 3 per cent spoke English.   The author pointed out that the approach to the Spanish child had been wrong.   Following—to the letter— one section of the state constitution, which said that all classes must be conducted in English, teachers had instituted a do-not-speak-Spanish movement which had made children ashamed of both their native language and their native arts and crafts.   School people forgot that the constitution also required giving attention to training teachers for Spanish-speaking communities.   In the spirit of this section, teachers in Taos County were developing a frankly bilingual program and were hoping for a grant which would enable them to carry on a genuine experiment.[40]

In the meantime, teaching Spanish was required in the grade schools. On the eve of another world war when tensions were already high and Americans were looking to their patriotic laurels, Antonio Rebollado took occasion to refer to Spanish teaching.   If teaching in Spanish in elementary schools was to be of enduring value, it must first give force "to the democratic enlightenment of the people . . . and secondly it must foster better relations between the two dominant races of the American continent."[41]

Although some young New Mexicans in self-defense must have learned English in the Armed Forces, the youngsters left at home apparently had little instruction.   In 1947 Lois Roquemore commented on the unsolved problem in the New Mexican schools; how to teach English to the Spanish-speaking children.   Her charge was that teachers were asking children to read English before they had English vocabularies and a comprehension of meanings in English.   Teachers had failed to teach reading precisely because they taught it too soon, using even the pre-first grade (an innovation for Spanish-speaking youngsters) for such purposes.

[39] *New Mexico Journal of Education,* vol. 15, pp. 12–13, July, 1919.

[40] Ruth Miller-Martinez, "Forecast of Language Instruction—both English and Spanish—in the Taos County Rural Schools," *New Mexico School Review,* vol. 18, pp. 16–17, September, 1938.

[41] Antonio Rebollado, "Spanish . . . in the Public Schools of New Mexico," *New Mexico School Review,* vol. 21, pp. 6–7, November, 1941.

School officials must recognize that teachers could not get all youngsters ready for the second grade by teaching reading in the first.[42]

That many school people were well aware of their record of failures was evidenced in 1952 by the title of another journal article: "New Mexico's Bi-lingual Problem Will Be Officially 40 Years Old on January 6, 1952."[43]    In the same year a story came out, "The Community Can Be Sold on Spanish."    In Las Cruces City, a concerted drive had been put on to improve and gain support for the teaching of Spanish, partially as a support for the United States in international affairs.    As a part of the program, Spanish teachers were offering their services to any teachers wishing to learn Spanish.    Another objective was also in evidence: developing security in the Spanish-speaking child.    Every teacher, according to the writer, must emphasize New Mexico's contribution to American education in the field of bilingualism.    The Spanish-speaking child should be made to feel how lucky he was to have an advantage in special skills "and in being an ambassador of good-will" for the United States.[44]

By the 1950s, new attitudes toward a subculture were possibly beginning to take hold; perhaps one could speak Spanish and still be a good American.    This new attitude might be one of the keys to solving the problem of the bilingual child.

## Making Good Americans
## Anglo Style

While the problem of educating the Spanish American was being described by reference to bilingualism, the task of building Americans was steadfastly pursued by means to which many young Hispanos must have been unresponsive.

By the 1890s, sixty-four important days were to be celebrated in schools—all to be observed by display of the flag and appropriate programs.    There was apparently little attempt to bridge the culture gap by devoting some of these days to persons and events with which Spanish Americans might have been familiar.    Neither Good Friday nor Easter appeared on the list, nor was any Spanish hero except Columbus acclaimed.    Rather, occasions were to be celebrated for persons and events familiar to the Anglos, such as Louisa M. Alcott, the first Con-

[42] Lois Roquemore, "Unfinished Business," *New Mexico School Review,* vol. 26, pp. 8–9, 37, May, 1947.

[43] "New Mexico's Bi-lingual Problem Will Be Officially 40 Years Old on January 6, 1952," *New Mexico School Review,* vol. 31, p. 13, November, 1951.

[44] Maria Gutierrez de Prieto, "The Community Can Be Sold on Spanish," *New Mexico School Review,* vol. 31, pp. 8–9, Apr. 1, 1952.

tinental Congress, Perry's victory on Lake Erie, Shakespeare, and the battle of the Merrimac and the Monitor. To reinforce the patriotic-symbol pattern, boards of education and school directors were required by a law of 1905 to provide schools with flagstaffs and flags not less than 5 feet long and the twelfth of February was designated Flag Day, although in 1909 it was changed to Lincoln's Birthday.[45]

In 1906 Clara Coulter had something to say about the role of the schools: "The problem before the public school is that of training and educating to good citizenship the mass of the people, which means that we must meet with an attempt to mould all classes of minds." In the interest of this goal, educators must emphasize the "meaning of the American flag" and the noble lives of great leaders.[46] Another writer recognized that there might be a reluctance on the part of some of the Spanish-speaking people to endorse certain aspects of American history, particularly the American Revolution, yet it was assumed that any citizen of New Mexico would be "glad that this great commonwealth is a part of the United States of America."[47] When it is remembered that in 1910 quite a few thousand New Mexican villagers did not speak English and were in a sense living in culture pockets at the foothills of mountain ranges, Mrs. Asplund's remarks seem a little overenthusiastic. She did not let the matter drop with a show of sentiment, however. She was in the midst of a movement to organize Children of the Republic clubs, an efficient medium of patriotic instruction. She said that youth must have "civic pride" and "love for New Mexico and love for the United States." These would be the most important concepts they could learn.[48]

World War I gave rise to statements such as this: Training for citizenship should begin with the child's first year in school and continue through the entire public school course. According to one writer, introducing a child at an early age to the Revolutionary period in American history "and the high purposes that gave rise to the Constitution" could not help but make a lasting impression on him. It could even develop him into "a patriot as loyal and ardent as were those who passed through that trying time."[49] When it is remembered that in the 1950s

---

[45] Moyers, op. cit., p. 320. See also compilations of New Mexico school laws.

[46] Clara E. Coulter, "Relation of Public Schools to Citizenship," New Mexico Journal of Education, vol. 2, p. 9, Apr. 1, 1906.

[47] Julia Brown Asplund, "New Mexico Day," New Mexico Journal of Education, vol. 6, p. 7, January, 1910.

[48] Julia Brown Asplund, "New Mexico Day—One Way to Observe It," New Mexico Journal of Education, vol. 7, p. 13, January, 1911.

[49] Clara E. Coulter, "Making Democracy Safe for the World," New Mexico Journal of Education, vol. 15, pp. 19–20, November, 1918.

writers still pointed to the Spanish American's indifference to abstract symbols and his attachment to a village, the value of the assessment of the roots of loyalty in New Mexico can be judged. It might be said here that whatever the judgment respecting the well-springs of loyalty, the patriotism of the New Mexicans should not be questioned. They have an enviable record for volunteering for service in World War II.

To return to the year 1919, the citizenship task of the schools was reemphasized by the new president of the University of New Mexico, Dr. David S. Hill. Giving his reasons for supporting universal education, he stated that every child born was a potential citizen, and that education of a proper kind was the rightful heritage of every child. "Our abiding platform . . . will be the ideals of universal education and of the American Republic."[50]

Through the years, legislators of New Mexico followed in the footsteps of officials in other states by requiring the teaching of various subjects assumed to contribute to the development of loyal citizens. Under the territorial government, public schools were required to include United States history in the curriculum. By legislation in 1912, New Mexican officials approved certain elements of the social studies in "An Act to Encourage the Instruction in the History and Civics of the State of New Mexico." This law required a history teacher to pass a satisfactory examination in United States and New Mexican history and civics before he might teach in the public schools.[51] These last requirements of legislators must have caused consternation among some teachers because in 1913 a review of a book which might solve the problem of the requirement of teaching New Mexican history appeared in the New Mexico Journal of Education. L. Bradford Prince had written A Concise History of New Mexico, which would be welcomed by teachers in public schools,[52] according to the review. After World War I, New Mexican legislators made effective immediately a law requiring such teaching because it was "necessary for the public peace and safety."[53]

By 1952, the citizenship task of the New Mexican schools had been put against a backdrop of the survival of democracy by no less a person than the state superintendent of schools.[54]

[50] David S. Hill, "A Message to The Teachers of New Mexico," New Mexico Journal of Education, vol. 16, pp. 3–4, September, 1919.

[51] Bessie Louise Pierce, Public Opinion and the Teaching of History in the United States, Alfred A. Knopf, Inc., New York, 1926, pp. 20–21, 51–52.

[52] New Mexico Journal of Education, vol. 9, p. 9, Feb. 15, 1913.

[53] Pierce, op. cit., p. 81.

[54] Tom Wiley, "Survival Comes High," New Mexico School Review, vol. 27, p. 5, December, 1952. From an address to the sixty-fifth New Mexico Educational Association Convention.

And by following the simple precepts of a proper home life, support of the churches of our choice, the right to work, a good education for every boy and girl, and active participation in government under our Constitution, we can and we shall survive as a great nation. We have every reason to be optimistic.

### Reinforcing a Changed
### Value Pattern

A good American salutes the flag, reveres the Constitution, and re- peats the most flattering facts of his national and state histories. He also exhibits certain other kinds of preferred behavior. He is clean, for cleanliness is next to godliness; he is healthy, for, as science advances, preventable disease is equated with dirt and sparkling health with clean- liness. The good American also has a reverence for work; useful work, preferably with his hands. He is a good provider who spends his days in honest labor that the present may be fruitfully used and the future secured. He cooperates with his fellows to further his own ends and those of the larger group.

To all these aspects of the good American, the teachers of New Mex- ico gave due attention and occasionally keyed in their teachings in sensi- tive fashion to the cues which have meaning for Spanish Americans. Health instruction, education in work, and the development of com- munity schools were all ardently pursued—often with the aim of ac- complishing several objectives at once.

The head of a school in Albuquerque titled an article of 1911 "Indus- trial Education for the Spanish-speaking People." Ross obviously in- tended that the education should accomplish more than its designation would imply. To be sure, the Spanish-American young people were going into industry and they needed training for future jobs but also the education must overcome the limitations of the children's homes— homes which were not inspiring. "The child must learn and the parent follow." That school might be an agency for changing a home environ- ment had been demonstrated by the noticeable change in home situa- tions of those youngsters who had attended boarding schools.[55]

At its inception, industrial education in a state which was largely agricultural had a special meaning. Industrial clubs for boys and girls promoted better growing of corn, kafir, milo, and peanuts, as well as better sewing and better making of bread. State contests were in full swing as early as 1912. Whether as an extension of such activity or as an independent project, school gardens made their appearance in rural and city establishments fairly early. In 1916, a director of school activi-

[55] J. C. Ross, "Industrial Education for the Spanish-speaking People," *New Mexico Journal of Education*, vol. 7, pp. 19–21, February, 1911.

ties, playground recreation, and school gardens was appointed to the Santa Fe school staff.[56]

Educators recognized the major outlines of a job which required changing a whole environment. So in 1911, the school journal carried an article on the schoolhouse as a social center. Here was an attempt to identify an institution as a total culture-changing agency, for the author of the article indicated that in this schoolhouse there should be enter- tainment and instruction for the whole family.[57] In 1912 a superin- tendent proposed that the school should be a rallying point of the community, a place where children could receive academic, industrial, and social instruction, and where parents could meet with teachers "to plan for greater progress." Indeed, the whole community should use the school as the place where discussions might go forward on issues important to the moral and material welfare of community mem- bers. Children should "be taught to love beauty of form, order, clean- liness, and harmony in everything." With such teaching, youngsters would not be satisfied with less than the best[58]—a projection of a change which might be brought about in a village environment by a dynamic school group.

Whether Spanish Americans who did not participate in voluntary activities and who had no commitment to the school as an institution ever rallied in great numbers to the community school is an open ques- tion. The educators' commitment to the approach was deep-seated, as is evidenced by an experiment in the Nambé community north of Sante Fe.[59]

Nambé village was founded in 1711 by Gaspar Ortiz y Pais who had come by oxcart from Tampico. The ditch which Ortiz built to bring water from the river to the fields is still used and exists for the com- munity, as is evidenced by its name, La Comunidad. With each new generation, the responsibility for caring for the ditch has passed from fathers to sons.

Up until 1850 there was plenty of land on which to maintain an agriculture that sustained the population adequately. However, as families grew and the community remained isolated, the land parcels

---

[56] *New Mexico Journal of Education*, vol. 9, p. 6, Nov. 15, 1912; vol. 13, p. 13, Sept. 1, 1916.

[57] *New Mexico Journal of Education*, vol. 8, p. 25, November, 1911.

[58] *New Mexico Journal of Education*, vol. 8, p. 13, April, 1912.

[59] Account of Nambé Community School taken from L. S. Tireman, "Discovery and Use of Community Resources in the Education of Spanish-speaking Pupils," *Community Resources in Rural Schools*, Yearbook of the National Education Asso- ciation, Department of Rural Education, Washington, 1939, pp. 72–85; and L. S. Tireman and Mary Watson, *A Community School in a Spanish-speaking Village*, University of New Mexico Press, Albuquerque, N.M., 1948.

per individual family became smaller, until some hardly sustained a family on a subsistence diet. In 1939 the largest holding was 65 acres; the smallest, 1 or 2; and the average, not more than 4 or 5. Up to 1929, approximately one person per family went out of the community to work so that his income was available to the family; but after 1929, income declined sharply. As of 1939, 60 to 70 per cent of the people were on relief and many of the others relied indirectly on relief for assistance.

In this community of 602 dirt farmers and their families the community school of Nambé was established, partly through outside beneficence and the assistance of the University of New Mexico, partly through effort of the villagers. This school was a projected rallying point for the community, where "needs"—as defined by observation of social habits— would take precedence over a formal curriculum. The subjects chosen for concentration became health and land management.

The school lunch was a first step in supplementing a diet judged to be prejudicial to good health. The county agent had already promoted the canning of corn, carrots, string beans, peaches, and apples, though popular foods remained pinto beans, potatoes, and chile. The county agent was called on to supplement canning activities with teaching schoolgirls to make salads (what so American as a salad!) which were sold to parents at a school exhibit.

Community members were induced to attach themselves to the school by being asked to teach. A jelly maker, a wood carver, and a deerskin tanner all found themselves a part of the Nambé school staff. The respectability of the special heritage of these villagers was in turn reinforced by celebration of Pan-American Day.

And what of the results of this venture? Reports are conflicting. On the one hand, average daily attendance in school rose to 95 per cent as compared with 75 per cent for the state—a positive evidence of the parents' commitment to the school, according to the director. In 1948, however, the school head remarked that he felt the school did not make as much impact as a high school would have made, for the small child, even though he learns new ways in school, cannot change an adult community.

Undoubtedly, many other attempts have been made in the state to make already established schools an integral part of the ongoing activities of the community. Two illustrations may indicate the nature of these attempts. One of these was made by a mathematics teacher who in 1943 reported success in developing a weaving class at the Española School.[60]

A second illustration is afforded by the activities of a school principal.

[60] Clara D. True, "A New Venture in the Española School," *New Mexico School Review*, vol. 22, p. 4, May, 1943.

After World War II, in the foothills of the Sandia Mountains and among some 1,800 people living in scattered groups, the principal developed a small pottery plant. The people had an average annual income of not more than $200 per capita. It seemed evident that the greatest need of the community was to increase this income by capitalizing on skills of community members. Through a series of meetings the principal explained the project. At first a group of women, then both men and women, joined the project. Instruments were primitive, but when the project was approved as a veterans' training program at the request of the veterans themselves, monies so secured were used to buy modern equipment. Personnel from the New Mexico School of Mines did analyses for the group, and the county agent helped. The plant is now producing commercially. The rationale was that the school is an agency of a new and better life—an agency through which the people were enabled to help themselves.[61]

### An Evaluation
### of the Making of Americans

For over a hundred years New Mexican teachers, with a missionary zeal and a deep conviction respecting their crucial role in United States society, have tried to standardize the Spanish-American children. They have fought against disease and dirt and have taught the flag salute and the principles of the United States Constitution. They have asked their charges to give attention to the glory of New Mexican history and of American heroes and events. They have labored at ways to promote good work habits and to reduce tardiness and absence. They have heralded the virtues of vitamins and scorned the vices of chile. They have promoted community schools and developed arts and crafts. All this they have done in the interest of making good Americans.

During these one hundred years, the educators have been forced to innovations not usually found in good American schools, and their nights have been haunted by the babble of foreign tongues. The pre-first grade, generally found in Indian communities in Latin America, has become a standard institution in Spanish-speaking communities. Teachers have wrestled with an off-and-on compulsory bilingualism, and some have memories of teachers and children who still communicate happily in remote villages in a foreign tongue. They battle with overage pupils, retardation, and early school leaving. And what of the results?

In the last two decades critics have been busy, both within and without the school system, assessing the errors—real or assumed—which

[61] Frank Angel, Jr., "Wheel of Fortune," *National Education Association Journal*, vol. 38, p. 585, November, 1949.

have been made by the school people in enculturating these long-standing Americans.

On the surface, the record of the New Mexican schools appears to be admirable in respect to sheer school going. As is indicated by Table 13-1, the ratio of pupils enrolled in public schools to the school-age

Table 13-1. Ratio of Pupils Enrolled in Public Schools to School-age Population (Five to Seventeen Years)

| Place | Years | | | | | | | | | |
|---|---|---|---|---|---|---|---|---|---|---|
| | 1870–1871 | 1879–1880 | 1889–1890 | 1899–1900 | 1909–1910 | 1919–1920 | 1929–1930 | 1939–1940 | 1949–1950 | 1951–1952 |
| United States........ | 61.5 | 65.5 | 68.6 | 72.4 | 73.5 | 77.8 | 81.3 | 85.3 | 81.6 | 84.7 |
| New Mexico......... | 4.4 | 13.3 | 42.3 | 61.4 | 59.3 | 75.4 | 80.2 | 86.7 | 83.2 | 86.4 |

SOURCE: "Statistics of State School Systems: Organization, Staff, Pupils, and Finances, 1951–52," chap. 2, U.S. Office of Education, *Biennial Survey of Education in the United States 1950–52*, chap. 2, 1955, table 12, pp. 48–49.

population has showed a phenomenal increase when thrown against figures for the United States at large. That the increase is not entirely the work of school people, however ardent their endeavors, may be assumed from the points at which the ratio shows significant increases. Note that after World War I, the ratio climbed from 59.3 to 75.4 and that as World War II approached and was left behind, the ratio surpassed and continues to surpass the United States figures. It might well be argued that the opportunity to observe the ways of the larger society afforded young people by the Armed Forces provided them with the meaning of and the desire for schooling.

The school people themselves, however, are less impressed by New Mexico's records. They are inclined to look more closely at differential figures by counties. An analysis such as that in Table 13-2 shows a distinct difference in school going between a largely Spanish-American and a largely Anglo-American population. Note that in the former, attendance at school has begun to drop off by fourth grade, and that only 35 out of 100 youngsters who started in second grade are left to finish the eighth grade.

One might ask what effect the various "Americanizing" measures have had on a youth group which remained so briefly in the acculturative institution. School people are apparently asking themselves the same question that is asked by those outside the system.

There are evidences that many learnings on which teachers spent so much time have not taken hold in so brief a period. Poor health as well as a fatalistic attitude toward illness are still characteristic of rural people. In explanation of a newly projected community health service financed by the W. K. Kellogg Foundation, Mrs. R. M. Overton pointed out in 1947 that the infant death rate for the past five years had been 94.8 per 1,000.[62] It was also reported that "in some counties from one-half to three-quarters of all deaths are registered as from unknown causes."[63]  The explanation of the latter is that there are no physicians

Table 13-2. Numbers of Students in Grade 2 Who Enroll in and Graduate from Succeeding Grades in Percentages (from Selected New Mexican Counties)

| Counties | Spanish descent (1938), % | Grade 2 (1937–1938) | Grade 4 | Grade 8 | Grade 9 | Grade 12 | Grad. (May, 1948) |
|---|---|---|---|---|---|---|---|
| Group 1....... | | 100 | 70 | 35 | 23 | 12 | 11 |
| Mora........ | 96 | | | | | | |
| Rio Arriba... | 93 | | | | | | |
| Sandoval.... | 83 | | | | | | |
| San Miguel.. | 83 | | | | | | |
| Group 2....... | | 100 | 100 | 86 | 78 | 47 | 42 |
| Curry....... | 6 | | | | | | |
| DeBaca..... | 26 | | | | | | |
| Luna........ | 57 | | | | | | |
| McKinley... | 38 | | | | | | |
| Roosevelt.... | ... | | | | | | |

SOURCE: George I. Sanchez, *Forgotten People: A Study of New Mexicans*, The University of New Mexico Press, Albuquerque, N.M., 1940, p. 30. "Where Did They Go? And Why?" *New Mexico School Review*, vol. 28, pp. 15–16, May, 1949.

available in rural areas. It may also, as some other accounts indicate, be a disregard for modern diagnosis and treatment of disease.

A low level of health has been evidenced in other ways. In a study done in the 1940s, it was found that the diet of New Mexican youngsters was shy of foods with high calcium, protein, and vitamin content. Children and youth suffered from general disability and had less mental energy than would be normal in a properly fed population. It was estimated that these youngsters were capable of only two hours of work a day.[64]  How was the impact of schooling on dietary habits to be manifested?

[62] R. W. Overton, "Community Health Service Project in New Mexico Schools," *New Mexico School Review*, vol. 26, pp. 13–14, April, 1947.

[63] Burma, *op. cit.*, p. 22.

[64] Reported in Baca, *op. cit.*, pp. 88–89.

A correspondingly indifferent attitude toward the utilization of the findings of agriculture is apparent in other accounts. In some rural areas, county agents have tried without success to introduce modern hybrid corn among a people whose diet consists largely of corn products.[65] Mary Austin said that she knew farmers who, at the urging of county agents, sprayed their orchards, "but in the same spirit of blind belief in which the Indian surrounds his fields with a magic spell."[66] Such a story would indicate that there has been little impact among New Mexican Spanish-American farmers of the typically Anglo farmer pattern of using knowledge to control nature.

Even the concerted drive over the years to establish an English-speaking population among Spanish-American youngsters has resulted only in an under-achieving group of pupils, according to the educators. Such results obtain even in experimental situations such as the one at the San Jose Training School. Two kinds of comparisons were made between achievement at this school and elsewhere: between San Jose pupils and those in control schools in other Spanish-speaking areas, and between San Jose pupils and youngsters in forty-five consolidated schools in the United States at large.[67]

The Gates Primary Reading and Silent Reading examinations as well as the New Stanford Achievement Test were used to measure progress. In the first and second grades, the norms for San Jose children were slightly above those for English-speaking children on the Gates and Stanford tests. "Beginning with the third grade, there was a divergence from the normal grade placement of about one and one-half years." This divergence continued through the eighth grade. What could be said for the San Jose experiment was that in the eighth grade there was a discrepancy of only 1½ years, whereas in the two control schools there was a discrepancy of 4 years.

When the performance and schooling of San Jose youngsters was compared with that of pupils in forty-five consolidated schools, there were several findings. First, whereas the greatest loss in school enrollment was in the seventh grade for the consolidated schools, it was found

---

[65] Burma, op. cit., p. 14.

[66] Mary Austin, Rural Education in New Mexico, Bulletin of the University of New Mexico, Training School Series, vol. 2, whole no. 205, Albuquerque, N.M., Dec. 1, 1931, p. 29.

[67] Account of the experiment at the San Jose Training School taken from Harlan Sininger, An Age-grade Study of the San Jose Training School and Its Two Control Schools, Bulletin of the University of New Mexico, Training School Series, vol. 2, whole no. 188, Albuquerque, N.M., Mar. 15, 1931; and Lloyd S. Tireman, Teaching Spanish-speaking Children, rev. ed., The University of New Mexico Press, Albuquerque, N.M., 1951.

to be in the fifth or sixth grade for San Jose pupils. Overageness ended "in the elimination of larger numbers of Spanish-speaking pupils at lower grade levels than that shown for other pupils." Of the several measures used, only the fourth grade median in arithmetic reached the appropriate grade norm. A selective process was also in operation, for as grade levels increased at the San Jose school, excepting the arithmetic score, so also did medians and Q1 and Q3. Nevertheless, the San Jose experiment, effective as it was, had not completely solved the acculturative problem in respect to the school subjects.

In the meantime, serious question has been raised respecting the wisdom of segregating Spanish-speaking children either through special classes or special schools. Quite apart from the question of discrimination is the question of the acculturating effect on the children. The proportions of the question are substantial. In a study completed in 1956, Fidel Garcia Baca stated that of thirty-six New Mexican school systems reporting, 12, or 33⅓ per cent, had segregation of Spanish-speaking youngsters. This percentage approximated that of the Spanish-speaking school population (31 per cent). Three systems segregated through the first grade only; six, through the third; and three, through the sixth. In the thirty-six systems, twenty-four used some form of adapted or special course of study.[68] What were the effects of this segregation?

Baca's study concerned bilingual education in five Southwestern states. Baca's findings were several. His conclusions as to segregation alone were not heartening. The practice of separating Spanish-speaking youngsters from other children contributed to social maladjustment and promoted feelings of inferiority and apathy. It also prevented wholesome vocational and political adjustment.[69]

Educators and anthropologists have indicated other ways in which the schools have failed and proposed remedies for their failures. One of these has to do—as inevitably—with money: there are poorly paid rural teachers and inadequately supported classroom units. As an example, in the county of Lea, only 9 per cent of the population were of Spanish descent in 1938, and in the same school year $2,974 was available per classroom unit. On the other hand, the county of Rio Arriba, with 93 per cent of its people of Spanish descent, was spending only $831 per classroom unit. This is the mirage of equalization, said Greiner, for over 80 per cent of school monies come from the state. In 1949 he pointed out that Rio Arriba had only $5.08 on a per capita

[68] Baca, op. cit., pp. 52, 59, 66, 92.
[69] Ibid., pp. 67–68.

average-daily-attendance basis while Lea had $81.50 on the same basis. There was state aid but not state equalization.[70]

Another critic was not so sure that finance was at the root of school difficulties. Backgrounds and economic troubles might account for the lack of holding power in part, but political domination of schools was the principal deterrent to school attendance in selected areas. This critic referred to situations in schools in Group 1 counties as noted in Table 13-2. In these counties there had been constant representation from teachers on tenure and contractual problems, dismissals for political reprisals, transfers to less desirable positions, late employment and assignment.

Conversely, there were no known teacher-employment problems in counties of Group 2. "Neither the people nor the teachers would tolerate political interference with schools in that area." Method of selection of county boards and superintendents brought about political domination in the Group 1 school systems. These "pseudo-school" people who had fought against change in policy-making and administrative posts could undoubtedly get "much satisfaction from knowing they have made a contribution to this continuous erosion of human resources."[71]

Whatever the validity of the analysis of school problems, the facts of difference in the way school government operated in two sets of counties recalls a cultural difference between Anglos and Hispanos which has existed for at least a hundred years. Anglos typically look on government as a means by which independent people can achieve their ends through direct participation in controlling that government. Hispanos who have been acclimated to a hierarchical society typically ignore or actively distrust government and apparently have neither been educated to nor inclined to participate in its control. If the facts of the difference in government operation are correct, then the school patrons in counties of Group 1 have still not learned, in over a hundred years of Americanization, the meaning of free government.

Some critics say that the adjustments which schools should have been making and which were made sporadically should have been carried through consistently. There should have been systematic and radical revisions in the aims of schooling in the first few years. The endeavor to teach a foreign tongue in these years has been largely wasted because

[70] Per cents of Spanish descent from George I. Sanchez, *Forgotten People: A Study of New Mexicans,* The University of New Mexico Press, Albuquerque, N.M., 1940, p. 30; school costs from Bright E. Greiner, "The Mirage of Equalization," *New Mexico School Review,* vol. 29, pp. 9, 27–28, December, 1949.

[71] "Where Did They Go? And Why?," *New Mexico School Review,* vol. 28, p. 16, May, 1949.

the effect of a meager language skill is lost when the child slips back into a Spanish-speaking community. In the meantime, teachers have missed a valuable opportunity to instruct in Spanish in health practices, food selection, land management and use. Teacher training has been at fault. Though education of rural teachers has been steadily on the increase, additional years of teacher training are of little avail when they are not concerned with skills needed by teachers in rural areas.[72]

How can schools re-form their forces? One way has been suggested in the work of an individual rural teacher. David Salazar, son of a Colorado circuit rider, has established himself and his family in a home adjacent to his one-teacher school in Juan Tomas. Salazar has utilized community resources by asking the county agricultural agents to help him with a curriculum in sewing and agriculture, and he has endeared community members to him by seeking their help in his own farming enterprises. He owns a battery radio set which helps to keep the community in contact with the outside world, and he runs a truck with which he takes youngsters on trips around the state. He comes from a Spanish-speaking background, yet he is a veteran who has seen the outside world and been a part of it. He can inspire confidence in both community members and pupils.[73] This is only one example of what sensitive teachers are doing in rural communities.

Another way in which the school can re-form its forces is by mobilizing all the government agencies in rural communities in a cooperative effort, with the school as a focal point for that mobilization and with a needed adjustment in the curriculum of the first few years.[74]

Superintendents have recently charted a five-year program for all the New Mexican schools: enforcing school attendance and taking a census every four years; increasing the school term; extending the program in the areas of health, vocational training, music, art, homemaking, library facilities, and guidance; securing a change in teacher-pupil ratio and in teachers' salaries as well as extending the range of teachers available; reorganizing county administration and improving supervision. These, so the superintendents say, are the answers to the dropout rate in schools and the illiteracy, which have been caused by the traditional curriculum, excessive teaching loads, lack of enforcement of compulsory school laws, inadequate teacher supply, and inadequate remedial work.[75] Whether

[72] See Sanchez, *op. cit.*

[73] E. R. Harrington, "Teaching a One-room Mountain School," *Nation's Schools,* vol. 55, pp. 62–64, April, 1955.

[74] See Sanchez, *op. cit.*

[75] "The Five-year Program for the Public Schools of New Mexico," *New Mexico School Review,* vol. 24, pp. 14–15, September, 1944. Report of outcomes of a superintendents' study conference.

these standard answers, which might have been developed by any group of superintendents in the United States, are really answers, remains to be seen.

The answer is certainly not in supporting all kinds of cultural differences, as would be advised by cultural relativists, says Dr. Kluckhohn. The melting-pot concept should not be discarded, but rather the way of preparing people for it should be changed. If educators cheerfully accept and reinforce differences, they are also reinforcing lack of mobility and general lower-class status.[76] In the same vein, another commentator points out that it may be a downright disservice to rural groups to improve techniques which tie rural people to an insufficient land base when there is already an excess of labor.[77]

Groping toward a solution for the schools are other critics who take account of culture difference and the ways to overcome such difference when it prejudices the welfare of the minority group. Senter and Hawley propose a three-point program for the schools in Spanish-speaking areas: (1) training in how to compete, (2) development of a daily environment in which children divide themselves into associative groups, and (3) a program of Americanization, "a concept referring to acquisition of the culture symbols characteristic of the majority group rather than to citizenship per se."[78]    The teachers of New Mexico do not equip Spanish-speaking children with competitive skills nor with adequate Anglo culture symbols.   The Hispano child must acquire an arsenal of cue-producing responses in English.  So inadequate are the schools that those who turn to education are met in the villages with social disapproval.   Grooming learned in the school is turned to account not for advantage in family and vocational situations, but as a prelude to illicit relationships.   In Manito suburbs close to Anglo towns, teen-age girls are pickups for soldiers.   When Manito children go to high school, they are discriminated against.   The Manito boy who tries to rise above the farm is hampered by a large family to which he owes allegiance.   In view of all these circumstances, it is hard to convince parents that high schools where children learn only undesirable behaviors are anything but a luxury.   Parents often prefer subsistence status to the breakup of tradition.   Nevertheless, the school is the one place where Spanish-American children can most effectively learn Anglo culture symbols and how to respond to them.[79]

[76] Kluckhohn, op. cit.
[77] Burma, op. cit., p. 16.
[78] Senter and Hawley, op. cit., p. 398.
[79] Ibid., whole article; and Donovan Senter, "Acculturation among New Mexican Villagers in Comparison to Adjustment Patterns of Other Spanish-speaking Americans," Rural Sociology, vol. 10, no. 1, pp. 31–47, March, 1945.

## SUMMARY

Is there any answer to effective integration of this native group into the larger society—without disastrous disorganization of the old village culture—before the new culture has taken root? The question is still open-ended. The process is occurring over the world and neither New Mexicans nor the world's peoples probably yet know what they are working with.

In connection with this case study, however, two matters are of especial interest. First, the way in which school development went forward and the way in which schools teach Americanism in New Mexico are very different from those same processes in the Old Northwest. Here in New Mexico there was no folk movement; rather, there was stimulation for education from a new population (Anglo) which moved into, or in a sense took as charges, the Spanish-speaking population. Here also the symbol and value systems of people in the Old Northwest would have little meaning unless they could somehow be translated into concepts which would have meaning for a people oriented to another culture.

A second outstanding phenomenon is the extended and extensive role proposed for the school, as that role is seen through the cross fire of criticism and approval of school practices. Whether the problem is considered an economy to be organized, a people to be rehabilitated, or a set of culture symbols to be taught, it is the schoolteacher who must take the task in hand. Here in microcosm is a demonstration of the peculiarly extensive and intensive role of the school as it has developed in extending the meaning of "Americanization."

# 14

## Establishing Schools in Hawaii

> Americanism is not, and never was, a matter of race or ancestry.
>
> FRANKLIN D. ROOSEVELT,
> THIRTY-SECOND PRESIDENT
> OF THE UNITED STATES

Some time during World War II, a twenty-four-year-old American was photographed sitting cross-legged on a bed in the Memphis General Hospital. He smiled as he reminisced to a reporter about his days in McKinley High School in Honolulu. The twenty-four-year-old was Pfc. Yoshinao Omiya, affectionately called "the Turtle" by his comrades. The Turtle smiled even though bandages covered the holes where his eyes had been—the eyes that had been blown out by a land mine.[1]

The Turtle is a symbol of the 100th Infantry Battalion, which was made up of Hawaiian National Guardsmen, and the unit in which the battalion was incorporated, the 442d Combat Team. He stands for the 3,915 individual and 10 unit citations given to the 442d Nisei unit that moved into the Italian campaign in 1944. He represents the group of outstanding Americans that, after the war, marched down the streets of Washington to the cheers of other Americans.[2] The Turtle also represents Hawaii, an island universe.

As a symbol of Hawaii, the Turtle stands for more than the brave Nisei of the 442d Combat Team. He is one of a substantial minority of a varied people. If the watchers at a postwar parade had seen a representative sample of the Turtle's territorial compatriots pass in review, they would have been impressed with the number of races repre-

[1] U.S. Department of the Interior, War Relocation Authority, *Nisei in Uniform in Collaboration with War Department,* n.d.

[2] Orville C. Shirey, *Americans: The Story of the 442d Combat Team,* Infantry Journal Press, Washington, December, 1946.

sented among Americans.  That members of such a varied group could achieve recognition as outstanding *Americans* would be attributed by many to one of the more interesting experiments in Americanization.

The school system of Hawaii has put its mark on as diverse a population as is to be found anywhere in the world.  As a result of that educational enterprise, one people has emerged—one, that is, in the general dedication to the welfare and some of the ideals of the United States. The story of making one people out of Orientals, Polynesians, Europeans, and descendants of the Puritans is a fascinating story of the fusion of cultures as unique as any in the United States.

## ISLAND BACKGROUNDS

The nature of the problem of schooling in the Hawaiian Islands must be seen in the context of missionaries and sugar, sailing ships and

Table 14-1.  Origins of the School Population in the Hawaiian Islands

| Origin | Years | | |
|---|---|---|---|
| | 1910 | 1920 | 1930 |
| Hawaiian | 4,354 | 4,030 | 3,873 |
| Part Hawaiian | 3,718 | 6,119 | 10,518 |
| Portuguese | 4,890 | 6,678 | 7,981 |
| Spanish | ...... | 441 | 305 |
| Japanese | 7,262 | 20,651 | 43,910 |
| Chinese | 2,872 | 5,068 | 8,092 |
| Filipino | ...... | 1,126 | 4,120 |
| Puerto Rican | 350 | 1,143 | 1,276 |
| Korean | 270 | 729 | 2,047 |
| Other Caucasians | 1,469 | 2,492 | 5,331 |
| Others | 585 | 446 | 1,124 |
| Total | 25,770 | 48,923 | 88,577 |

SOURCE: Territory of Hawaii, Department of Public Instruction, *Biennial Reports.* Liberties have been taken with the tabulations by combining certain categories for 1910 and 1920.  In the former year, figures for Americans, British, and Germans have been put in the classification "Other Caucasians," and so also with Scandinavians and Anglo-Saxons for the year 1920.

Hawaiian nobility, defense and the Japanese Imperial Rescript.  An analysis of school population origins indicates the reconciliation of these phenomena and forces (see Table 14-1).

The gradual disappearance of the original population will be noted in the drop in figures for the Hawaiian group.  But the respect for that culture, engendered by the people and their early missionary friends, can be noted by the persistence of the category Part Hawaiian, as well as its decided increase. Hidden in this category are some Caucasian Hawaiians, but a larger number of Asiatic Hawaiians. Perhaps the way to acceptance in this particular American society has been through intermarriage with the Hawaiians, who, as early as the 1820s, voluntarily accepted United States educational ways.

An industrial agriculture centering in sugar and pineapples is reflected in the presence and sharp increases of other groups. The earliest importation of agricultural workers was from China. They were followed by Japanese and Portuguese, and then by Filipinos, as well as Puerto Ricans and Koreans. Members of each of these groups intended to stay only long enough to earn a little money. Instead of returning to their homelands, however, they found themselves raising families and becoming established. In turn, their progeny were reflected in the school census.

The category Other Caucasians, if broken down for the year 1910, would have shown persons of British, German, and American origins; for 1920, it would have shown Scandinavian origins as well. In other tabulations there will be a few Russians. These groups have been vying for power in the islands, though some are of missionary stock.

The racial picture is more complex than the table would indicate. In the regular census, some who are listed as Hawaiian are actually of mixed blood. Persons of Chinese-Caucasian origins are known as Chinese, and those who are Chinese Japanese are classified as Chinese or as Japanese according to race of father. Mixed bloods of other combinations are obscured in the same way by census classifications.[3] It is reasonable to assume that the school census in the same way provides an oversimplified picture of race in Hawaii.

What Table 14-1 and the census do not reveal is the size of the public school problem—in the year 1930, for instance, 86 per cent of the 88,577 youngsters were in public school. Nor do the table and the census really indicate the small amount of help which teachers received from Caucasian children, who might be assumed to represent the dominant culture in the United States, for most children of this group were enrolled in private schools. In the absence of such "Americanizing elements," Americanization of these youngsters of many backgrounds was accomplished, and the usual symbol system was acquired. However, in the process, the American school system in Hawaii became something different from what it would have been in Mississippi or Kansas. The school adapted to its environment in such a way that it incorporated

[3] See Romanzo Colfax Adams, *Interracial Marriage in Hawaii: A Study of the Mutually Conditioned Process of Acculturation and Amalgamation,* The Macmillan Company, New York, 1937. See particularly chap. II.

elements of the cultures it embraced and communicated a large tolerance which emerged in a nonawareness of race.

## Origins of a Polyglot School Population

The twenty islands of Hawaii were annexed in 1898 by the United States and at the behest of the original citizens of the islands. The territory was established in 1900, but American-style schooling goes back to the 1820s, when American missionaries first arrived on the islands.[4]

Prior to the coming of New Englanders, however, the Polynesians, who had lived in the islands since at least 500 A.D. and probably earlier, had established an educational system with objectives for their society. Character education with an emphasis on bravery, respect for religious ceremonies and forms of worship, and temperate living—all these were part of this informal education, according to David Malo. Knowledge of the principles of government, preparation in the art of war, and acquisition of personal skills were among the other objectives. These objectives were probably very informally expressed, if stated at all, for the Polynesians had no written language and, as a consequence, no schools in the formal sense.

These people had many accomplishments to their credit when the white men first found them. They had developed a language rich in poetry, they used simple mathematics, had devised a calendar, and utilized 300 different herbs in medical practice. Their culture, however, had undergone some modifications by the time the missionaries first came, for, after Capt. James Cook's discovery of the islands in 1778, a flourishing sandalwood trade—at its prime in the period from 1810 to 1830—began to bring foreign adventurers to the island shores.

Following the introduction of the world at large to the islands, Hawaiians began to explore the outer world, including the United States, and so inadvertently introduced themselves to another culture. In 1809, Opukahaia from the islands landed at Yale College. He was found by the Rev. E. W. Dwight, who thereupon established the Foreign Mission Training School at Cornwall, Connecticut. In Dwight's first school were twelve pupils, seven of whom were Hawaiians.

Following Dwight's discovery of the Hawaiian mission field, the Prudential Committee of the American Board of Commissioners for Foreign Missions organized a party of missionaries who took up their new work in 1820. From the time of their landing, the island people were influenced

---

[4] Historical account adapted from Benjamin O. Wist, *A Century of Public Education in Hawaii, October 15, 1840–October 15, 1940,* Hawaii Educational Review, Honolulu, Hawaii, 1940.

in their educational patterns, even though the American board gave up its supervision of the missions in 1863.

Apparently the efforts of the missionaries went forward on two fronts. One concerned the propagation of their religion and the education of the people and was carried on through the mission schools. The other concerned peaceful and systematic changes in the government and economic system designed to foster trade with the nations of Western Europe.

The first task of the missionaries, Christianizing and educating the Polynesians, began with development of a written form of the language, printing texts in the language, and teaching the rudiments of the written language. This phase of the program covered the period from 1820 to 1831. The pupils, who were numbered in the thousands, were largely adult. In the next decade, the missionaries put their efforts into improving the training of teachers, organizing special schools, and switching the clientele from adults to children. Whether or not there is approval for the Westernizing and Christianizing of alien populations, it might be interesting to speculate on whether the acculturation of these Polynesians did not go forward more rapidly and more peacefully because the missionaries first worked with adults rather than with children.

The second task, governmental and economic change, went forward swiftly. Contacts with the outside world had continued from the days of the sandalwood trade, and Hawaii had become a center for outfitting whaling vessels. Consequently, there had been an increase in the foreign population in Honolulu and an increase in exports, which by 1840 included hides, salt, sugar, tobacco, candlenut oil, arrowroot, and ships' supplies. The topography seemed ideally suited for the development of the sugar industry, but the landholding system, reminiscent of that among the Inca Indians, stood in the way. All land was held by the king, who periodically distributed it to his chiefs; in turn, his chiefs distributed it to the commoners or serfs. This last group undoubtedly paid tribute for the use of the land to both the chiefs and the king. The system had been a handicap to the development of the sugar industry because a man who wished to use his properties for sugar raising was never sure how long he could hold his land. Developments in the 1840s, however, weakened this system and paved the way for a new economy.

With the help of Protestant missionary personnel, a bill of rights was developed in 1840, and the government was changed from an absolute to a constitutional monarchy. The organic acts of 1845–1846 became the basis of the legal structure throughout the monarchy. Along with this new government came a Minister of Education. Under new land divisions of the constitutional monarchy, lands were divided so that chiefs, the commoners, and foreigners might now hold title to land.

In some instances, the resulting confusion harmed the native Hawaiians. Unused to having to secure title to land, the small peasant would often neglect to secure title to the piece which his chief had given him, or would sell his plot, assuming that there would be more forthcoming in the next land division. Unfortunately, many of the native group lost any share in their geographical inheritance in this way.

The shift to a new economic system brought with it the development of the big sugar plantations; these, in turn, brought economic maladjustments as well as a new population. Descendants of Europeans, including American and Norwegian farmers, proved to be unsuccessful in working on the plantations. Because of the inadequacy of white workers, some 293 Chinese were imported in 1852; in 1859, laborers were brought from the South Seas; and in 1868, the first Japanese were brought in. Portuguese were first imported in 1878 and proved to be so well adapted to farm work that in 1882 Portugal and Hawaii concluded a treaty which opened the way for a steady flow of laborers from the Azores and the Madeira Islands. With the beginning of the pineapple industry in 1892, when the first cannery was opened in Honolulu, the destiny of the islands as a melting pot of many nationals employed as farm workers was assured.

In the meantime, trade relations with the United States had improved. The islanders had found their best market on the mainland, but they were competing with United States and West Indies sugar. In 1876 a reciprocity treaty between Hawaii and the United States was signed; sugar could come into the States duty free in return for certain goods being allowed in Hawaii on the same basis. Industrial agriculture under a representative government was now firmly established.

## Education Developments under
## the Republic of Hawaii

Public education continued to develop under the monarchy, but it was public education only in its financing. In actuality it had been two systems of parochial education under Catholic and Protestant auspices. Within these "public" systems, elementary education as well as some secondary education had been developed. With the cooperation of prominent Hawaiians, lands had been granted for several kinds of schools. For example, vocational education, including crafts education, had been under way. However, strains and tensions had resulted from the two parallel and competing systems, and with the inauguration of the Republic of Hawaii in 1894, changes were introduced. The educational system became a department of government, from which it had been excluded in one of the past changes. English was made the language of instruction over the protests of some of the missionaries who still believed in communication in the Hawaiian language. Public secondary education was inaugurated, and aid for any schools except those under public auspices was abandoned. James L. Dumas, graduate of the Oswego Normal School, became head of the teacher training department of the newly organized Honolulu High School, and in 1896 the department was separated from the high school and became the Honolulu Normal and Training School. In 1893 the Woman's Board of Missions organized kindergartens for Japanese, Portuguese, and Hawaiian children, as well as children of other nationalities.

The education system under Hawaiian auspices approached the American system so closely in outward form that it met with the unqualified approval of the commission appointed to look into the annexation of the Hawaiian Islands to the United States. The commission noted that the law already called for compulsory education and instruction in English. The effect of the law, according to the commission, was[5]

. . . to break up the racial antagonisms otherwise certain to increase, and to unite in the schoolroom the children of the Anglo-Saxons, the Hawaiians, the Latins, and the Mongolians in the rivalry for obtaining an education. No system could be adopted which would tend to Americanize the people more thoroughly than this.

To be sure, the main outlines of something that looked like an American education system had been instituted voluntarily by the Hawaiians with the help of the American missionaries. Whether this system would automatically Americanize—if the commissioners envisioned making prototypes of New England youngsters—is highly doubtful. Subsequent developments would show that problems of schooling were to be very different from those on the mainland; that adaptations were to be made in the "typical" American pattern; that a different rationale was needed, even when educators were trying to institute educational practices like those on the mainland. In other words, Hawaiian education would have to adapt itself to the people so that they could accommodate themselves to the necessity of becoming American citizens. This story—of the people and the schools—is essentially the story of the 442d Combat Team and how it came to be marching down the streets of Washington after World War II.

## BACKGROUND OF SCHOOLING
## UNDER THE AUSPICES OF THE UNITED STATES

The backdrop for the problems of the educators in the islands is provided by the nature of the school population and the teachers them-

---

[5] Quoted in *Ibid.*, p. 142.

selves, as well as by the nature of the economy, which has retained a character somewhat different from that of the United States as a whole.

## Population: Pupils and Teachers

In respect to population, the islands are indeed a topsy-turvy world. This is the only area in the United States where people of North European origins are not predominant—in fact, they are a relatively insignificant minority. Yet it is their largely middle-class culture—predominant in most of the United States—which the schools had to communicate to a diverse group of pupils.

The majority of Hawaiians were members of what Americans would ordinarily call a minority group. There were other wide differences between most Hawaiians and the average American of European descent. Not least among the differences was language. Japanese, Chinese, Hawaiian, and Portuguese—all were commonplace on the islands, but relatively rare on the mainland. The difficulties imposed on children who spoke Japanese at home and English at school can be noted only by the development of pidgin English, a lingo which was neither English nor an Oriental language. It is interesting to speculate on the impact that the differences between Oriental and Occidental languages may have had on habits of thinking. As if the difficulty of reconciling two such dissimilar languages as Japanese and English were not enough, it is said that, through the mixing of races, children were often exposed not to one but to two foreign languages at home.[6]

However, language is only one thread of the warp and woof of culture —an important thread, to be sure, one which communicates meanings. What might have been communicated is suggested by the fact that in a population of 368,336 in 1930, some 137,000 were Buddhists.[7] To someone who assumes that an American is of North European descent and of the Christian (preferably Protestant) faith, the religious commitments of 37 per cent of the Hawaiian Americans might well appear to be an insurmountable barrier to assimilation.

Another possible barrier, though one Americans had met on other occasions, was class origin. Americans, it might be said, are peasants, and a significant portion of the Hawaiian group had origins similar to the American. In the 1920s, 56,000 of the 92,000 adult aliens were Japanese, and the great majority came from the backward areas of Japan "where the people differed little from the Japanese of pre-Meiji days."[8]

[6] Katherine M. Cook, *Public Education in Hawaii*, U.S. Office of Education Bulletin 1935, no. 10, 1936, p. 46.

[7] Frederick E. Bolton and Miles E. Cary, "Going to School in Hawaii," *The Nation's Schools*, vol. 8, no. 4, p. 41, October, 1931.

[8] Henry Butler Schwartz, "The Foreign Language Schools of Hawaii," *School and Society*, vol. 23, no. 578, p. 99, Jan. 23, 1926.

To these sons of the Emperor of Heaven were added an old Polynesian group, many of whom had been serfs as late as the middle of the nineteenth century. To them were added agricultural workers, probably many of them illiterate, from Portuguese territories and from China, and migrants from the Philippines, another United States territory. The last group bore the traces of another ancient crossroads of the world. Added to this motley group have been a scattering of white missionaries from the United States and, in the twentieth century, military personnel.

Probably unique in United States annals is the character of the migrations—particularly the migrations of Orientals—to Hawaii. Except for the very early explorers, most American immigrants have been refugees from restrictive regimes. They have intended to stay in the United States for economic advantage or for political or religious freedom. Furthermore, many of them migrated in families or, soon after their arrival and the establishment of homes, they sent for their families. Few of these characteristics were to be found in migrations to Hawaii. Even according to sympathetic writers, most of the male agricultural workers brought into the Hawaiian Islands never expected to stay. When they found that the money for the return to their homelands was not forthcoming, they sent to the home country for brides, picture brides. With some like the Japanese, nostalgia for the old country remained; and though probably after a while, most of them did not wish to return to Japan, they still wished to keep the possibility alive by bringing up their children in the language and customs of the homeland.[9] In the very circumstances of their migration, the cultures of other lands were bound to be living realities even in an American Hawaiian present.

Such a rich and varied people called for a school system which, through the graciousness of the early Polynesians and through the grace of the early missionaries, had indeed got under way. But a school system needs teachers. Where were they to be found but among people who, according to the strict constructionists, could hardly be called American? Race has been so close to the surface of concern that, until the 1930s, the school census classified teachers and children by origin. In 1902 the superintendent of public instruction reported a table on the comparative nationality of teachers. In this table, he listed Hawaiians, Part Hawaiians, Americans, Chinese, Japanese, and members of other national groups.[10] It is significant that a separate category is given to

[9] For one interpretation, see *ibid.*

[10] *Biennial Report*, Territory of Hawaii, Department of Public Instruction, 1902, p. 10. Titles of superintendents' reports vary slightly in wording for the period 1900 through 1943–1944. To obviate the necessity of multiple listings, the title *Biennial Report* which approximates title for 1943–1944 will be used to refer to all reports for the period 1900 through 1943–1944. In footnotes the designation *Biennial Report* is followed by the years the report covers and page reference.

Americans, presumably people whose immediate origins were on the mainland. And this is despite the fact that most—if not all—the people in other categories were also Americans, probably at least second- or third-generation Americans and holding American citizenship.

For some years, Americans continued to be a dominant group in the teaching force. In 1902, they constituted well over 50 per cent of the public and private school teachers. However, even in 1902 the normal school was reported as having eight nationalities represented in the student population; of the 92 then enrolled, 60 were Hawaiian or part Hawaiian and 10 were Chinese.[11] Up to and including the year 1919, students of European extraction outnumbered any other group, being 287 as against 255 for the Hawaiian, the next highest group.[12] But the handwriting was on the wall; among the 1920 enrollees, those of Hawaiian extraction were first with 57, followed by those of European extraction with 19, followed by those of Chinese extraction with 17. As the twentieth century wore on, the teachers became even more diverse in their origins, and properly so if they were to communicate adequately and to represent a varied population. But their diversity, along with their recent affinity to other cultures, introduced the problem of language in respect to teachers as well as to pupils, and it was occasionally hinted that teachers did not, after all, necessarily speak "good English."

## The Economy: Rural but Industrial

When the sandalwood trees had been cut down and the whaling ships had largely disappeared over the horizon, the chief sources of income for the people of Hawaii were sugar, pineapples, livestock, and tourists. Industrialization of a sort came in the last of the nineteenth century with the necessity for processing fruit for shipment. The chief sources of wealth, nevertheless, were to be found in an agriculture which called for large numbers of semiskilled and unskilled workers.

Moving up and out of the category of farm worker was difficult in an economy which remained rooted in hand labor. When parents, as is their custom even in Hawaii, would equate schooling with social and economic mobility, their hopes would be largely disappointed. Plantation owners, in the meantime, would try to counteract the movement of farm youth. As their supplies of workers were reduced because of restrictive immigration quotas, they would attempt to retain on the farm the children of their original farm workers. The children, on their part, would find their hopes of work on the mainland frustrated by an unaccustomed prejudice against Orientals and Polynesians. The nature

[11] *Ibid.*, p. 18.
[12] *Biennial Report,* 1919–1920, p. 68.

*of the economy made more difficult the problem of assimilating into an American culture a group which, at best, would have presented problems to educators.

In this context of an unusual school population and an atypical economy, school officials moved forward to adapt and to interpret in special ways practices to be found in all systems. In the adaptive process, they introduced a few content items to be found only in this Hawaiian-style American school system.

## EDUCATION FOR ALL HAWAIIAN YOUTH

The commissioners who had studied the problem of the annexation of Hawaii had referred to the Americanization potential of the schools. Some forty years later, in 1937, senators and representatives who visited Hawaii in connection with a request for statehood were particularly interested in the school system for the same reason. "The public schools of Hawaii," they said, "are the foundation of good citizenship." They noted the presence of children of foreign or alien parentage and the necessity which this implied for a program of Americanization, which the schools had been most successful in instituting. "Through the schools, more than by any other means, the people of Hawaii are being molded together into the American pattern and philosophy of life."[13]

There was a more subtle task of Americanization which is rarely stated and cannot be described through reference to specific school practice. It can only be mentioned here in passing. Its rationale must be put within the philosophy of the American form of government.

A cornerstone of democracy, as of most world religions, is the fundamental equality of human beings one to another. This equality might be taken inferentially to mean amalgamation as well as assimilation and, in reference to schooling, integration as well as desegregation. As can be well supported by fact, the American philosophy of government and American practice have been often at odds. Intermarriage across religious and racial lines has been fraught with peril. Many minority peoples have from time to time suffered in the extreme from outgroup status. A dual school system has flourished in seventeen states and the capital city, and segregation by design or prejudice has existed in classrooms throughout the nation. Though the record of Americans in respect to prejudice is not bad considering the mammoth proportions of the problem of enculturation, the record of the Hawaiians is infinitely better than that of the dwellers on the mainland.

One of the refreshing aspects of the story of Hawaii is the oft-stated acceptance of and rejoicing in the fact of amalgamation. As far back

[13] Quoted in *Biennial Report*, 1939–1940, p. 2.

as 1914, Ernest J. Reece looked forward to the development in Hawaii of a new stock which would have the excellences of all the parent races.[14] Adams's 1937 study of interracial marriage in Hawaii leaves one with the impression that the author gives it the highest sanction.[15] Lind, whose study is partially concerned with bringing an earlier study by Adams up to date, seems to accept as a final conclusion the fact that Hawaii's people will become one through both spiritual and biological fusion.[16] Although observers note tension and difficulties in racial fusion, most of them look on its eventual achievement with optimism and hope.

The evidence that the process of fusing is more real and less painful than on the mainland is substantial. The very fact that Hawaiians of Oriental extraction have been rebuffed in California when accepted on the islands is one piece of evidence. Another is the behavior of Chinese in Hawaii as contrasted with that of Chinese on the mainland. Fighting tongs which may be a function of "rigid exclusion of the social relations with whites" have flourished in San Francisco and in other mainland cities, but never on the islands. Chinese living in Hawaii have been so fully accepted that they enter with freedom into politics, office holding, and typical American sports—all of which alleviates the necessity for perpetuating negative aspects of their homeland culture. There is a noticeable freedom from constraint among them as contrasted with the reserve which characterizes the Chinese in California.[17]

The reality of the easy acceptance of racial difference can be seen in another light with the violent reactions of the Hawaiians to the prejudices of the mainlanders who occupied Hawaii during World War II. American servicemen had a habit of calling "any non-Caucasian 'gook,' 'nigger,' 'slant-eyes,' and 'yellow-belly' . . . ." The Hawaiians replied with " 'white trash' or 'damn haole.' "[18] Evidences such as these can be multiplied many times.

The conditions for establishing a pattern of unstrained race relations in Hawaii are probably many. "You can't tell what will happen on an island," said Adams, quoting J. M. Barrie. The original Polynesians looked with favor on marriage of their women with white men—this may have been one of the conditions. Their king often sanctioned such marriage by giving land to white traders, who thereupon settled

---

[14] Ernest J. Reece, "Race Mingling in Hawaii," *The American Journal of Sociology,* vol. 20, p. 116, July, 1914.

[15] Adams, *op. cit.*

[16] Andrew W. Lind, with the technical assistance of Robert Schmitt, *Hawaii's People,* University of Hawaii Press, Honolulu, Hawaii, 1955, chap. 5.

[17] Adams, *op. cit.,* pp. 318–320.

[18] Lind and Schmitt, *op. cit.,* pp. 11–12.

down in Hawaii and began mixed-race families that were accepted as being of high status. The Polynesian women were glad to accept these husbands, who were better providers and more generous than their own countrymen. They had much the same attitude toward the Chinese.

The early missionaries, for their part, were antislavery advocates from New England. They could hardly have done justice to their Christian cause and to their stand on slavery if they had done other than accept the Polynesians and racial fusion with equanimity.[19] This general acceptance of the equality of peoples, as manifested partly in intermarriage, probably provided a firm base for the continuing acceptance of other groups as they came into the islands. The effect has been so widespread that even the Chinese, who ordinarily feel the pull of family and racial ties, are affected. In 1950, 41 per cent of the Chinese grooms and 42.5 per cent of the Chinese brides married persons outside their group.[20]

A persistent theme, however, is that the schools have contributed to easy enculturation in Hawaii. In 1914 education was listed as an influence encouraging fusion.[21] Adams speaks of developing a community morale, which the schools have a significant part in creating. This the schools have done by encouraging youngsters to discuss and intellectualize school and home problems.[22] Whether as effective as other social forces in Hawaii in promoting amalgamation and integration and thus enforcing the democratic ideal, the schools have certainly been concerned with this subtle aspect of Americanization. Whether this more delicate meaning was implied in the 1937 commendation of the schools by the congressmen is a moot point.

For public purposes and whatever the meaning, the essential task of the schools was and still is Americanization. What the schools have done in that regard can be dimly seen through the congressmen's words, which characterize the efforts as molding these young "into the American pattern and philosophy of life." Such a task meant not only teaching a language in which to communicate, but changing the habits attendant on family and vocational life, shifting the value pattern respecting the nature of government, introducing a prescientific people to the uses of science, particularly in connection with health and diet—and doing all this among a population and in an economy more than ordinarily resistant to Americanization.

Though the story of how the schools promoted tolerance must be left unexplored, limited aspects of how the schools Americanized can be

---

[19] For a discussion of intermarriage and role of missionaries, see Adams, *op. cit.*
[20] See table in Lind and Schmitt, *op. cit.*, p. 104.
[21] Reece, *op. cit.*, p. 111.
[22] Adams, *op. cit.*, pp. 307–308.

shown through a description of kindergartens and school gardens, bilingualism and retardation, 5-cent lunches and toothbrush drills, rural high schools and agriculture in the fifth grade.

## English versus Pidgin English

In 1892, six years before the territory was annexed, a course of study for the public English schools of Hawaii called particular attention to the course in English. "All teachers are agreed as to the importance of this branch in our mixed population," said the preface to this manual, written prior to the decades when the population would become even more mixed.[23]

Since this statement on English, which may well have been preceded by others, the importance of English in the curriculum and the difficulty of teaching it have been continuously stressed in practically every superintendent's report up to the 1940s at least. Other subjects have often been justified because of their use as media for teaching English, and new school facilities have been defended as necessary for teaching the language or for their general efficacy in the Americanization process.

The report for 1900 on the work of the schools contained a statement on the contributions of manual training to language work. It (manual training) afforded the "most natural means of acquiring and using the English language." Other agencies were noteworthy as they contributed to this main aim of teaching English. The Chinese mission, for example, was doing good work in educating Chinese boys and girls in both English and Chinese.[24]

In the biennial report for 1913–1914, it was noted that entrants to McKinley High School in Honolulu were most seriously deficient in English. What youngsters did to the tenses of verbs appeared to be most disturbing. On the basis of these findings, various recommendations for ratings in English in entrance examinations were given.[25] However, the report for 1919–1920 noted as an achievement of the schools that department examinations had been abolished in all grades except the eighth, and that promotions were based on daily work and spoken English.[26]

The high schools were continuing the English emphasis begun in the elementary school. The report on the Kauai High School indicated that stress was being put on English and citizenship, for decisions could not be made by public opinion unless all citizens knew the language of their

[23] Honolulu Board of Education, *Course of Study for the Public English Schools of Hawaii*, R. Grieve, Book and Job Stream Print, Honolulu, Hawaii, 1892.
[24] *Biennial Report*, 1900, pp. 34, 44.
[25] *Biennial Report*, 1913–1914, p. 28.
[26] *Biennial Report*, 1919–1920, p. 39.

country. The principal of the McKinley High School reported in the same vein, but in more specific terms, on the training which was given in learning to think clearly and quickly through contests on such subjects as "My Ideal of Character and Civic Improvement in Honolulu." He noted with pride that in the contest on "The American Meaning of Thanksgiving," first place in the senior class was taken by a Japanese boy; in the junior class, by a Chinese girl; in the sophomore class, by an American; and in the freshman class, by a Chinese-Hawaiian girl.[27]

The concern for English continued to be so great that Prof. Percy M. Symonds of the University of Hawaii could couple his plea for the introduction of measurement with the necessity for improving English. In the 1921–1922 report on schools, Dr. Symonds pointed out that habits of thought and action, presumably executed with reference to English, were essential to Americanism. Yet educators did not know which language group in the schools was the most defective in English, or who the most successful teachers of the new native language were. Symonds was in the process of developing instruments for the measurement of language facility, and offered to find investigators who could do an analysis of pidgin English, that bugaboo of the schools.[28]

In line with the spirit of Dr. Symonds's suggestions, Katherine Murdock was pleading for a bureau of educational research. At the request of the principal of the McKinley High School, she had been trying to assess the native intelligence of the freshmen. In order to get a fair measure of ability, she had devised a test which called for a knowledge of English in only two of its parts; in the other two parts, it called for a response by gesture, with a measure of nonverbal intelligence.[29] At the same time, the principal was worried about the teacher-pupil ratio which was larger than that on the mainland; yet it should be even smaller because of the language handicap of the pupils.

During the same year, problems of English were particularly acute at the Maui High School. Over 60 per cent of the youngsters had failed their English at the end of their first six weeks in the school.

For several years, the superintendents regularly included in their biennial reports a statement on problems as well as on achievements. So, as was usual, the superintendent in the 1923–1924 report stated that teaching English was still the greatest problem confronting the elementary schools. Unfortunately, before children ever got to school, they had talked not only in a foreign language, but in pidgin English "of the cane fields, the ranches and the street, frequently mixed with profanity. A whole set of wrong speech habits are thus reinforced be-

[27] *Ibid.*, pp. 48–49, 61.
[28] *Biennial Report*, 1921–1922, p. 20.
[29] *Ibid.*, p. 28.

fore the children ever attend school." One valuable aid in this severest of teaching problems was the new socialized recitation, which should take the place of older systems of conducting recitations.[30]

In the 1927–1928 report, the superintendent pointed out that better English usage was, as always, one of the primary aims and problems of the schools. This was reiterated under his discussion of problems of the high schools, which he reported as emphasizing activities and courses using oral language, including oratory, debating, and dramatics. All departments in the high school had been pressed into the service of improving English. Educators at the normal school had also been working with teachers in training with a view to analyzing speech problems. The school had employed specialists in linguistics and phonetics for special work with the preservice group.[31] This same report contained a new aspect of the English problem. In connection with a report on schools on the island of Kauai, where parents and the general community were giving support to the schools, it was pointed out that parent-teacher associations were not developing as they should. The barrier to their development was the variety of languages spoken by parents. "Attempts to conduct meetings in several different languages have proven tiresome to the visitors." It was concluded that community educational councils rather than parent-teacher associations might be the key to appropriate cooperation between school and community.[32]

By the next biennium, 1929–1930, the English problem had become more critical. The need for careful supervision was increasing because schools were continuously using a higher percentage of island teachers who themselves had probably come up the pidgin English route.[33]

Though superintendents continued to report on the crucial problem of English teaching, few new ramifications were introduced in its discussion in succeeding reports. However, in the year 1939–1940 it was reported that the elementary schools in the last two years had been concentrating on English,[34] and the 1941–1942 report mentioned a "Speak English campaign." The community had at last approved of speaking English in everyday discourse.[35] The islands were beginning to feel the stress of impending war. Approval of English did not make the English problem dissolve in thin air. In the fall of 1946, a sys-

[30] *Biennial Report*, 1923–1924, pp. 17–20.
[31] *Biennial Report*, 1927–1928, pp. 93, 108.
[32] *Ibid.*, p. 54.
[33] *Biennial Report*, 1929–1930, p. 52.
[34] *Biennial Report*, 1939–1940, p. 9.
[35] *Biennial Report*, 1941–1942, p. 28.

tematic, territory-wide program for the improvement of English was inaugurated. In 1949 the Legislature directed the Department of Public Instruction to raise the standards of all public schools to those of the English standard schools.[36] As late as 1950, Marian Wauke, tenth grader, was declaring that she and her peers could help the younger generation by speaking good English. With such a program, pidgin English would in a few years cease to be a problem "and the future generation will be speaking English of which everyone can be proud."[37]

The whole population may, in a few years, as Miss Wauke predicts, be speaking acceptable English, for, in an area where promoters of school going have had to fight a peculiar economy and an imported peasant population, the educational record is nothing less than remarkable. School attendance of sixteen- and seventeen-year-olds, who are just beyond compulsory school age, is a barometer of the effectiveness of compulsory education. In 1910, 35.9 per cent of this age group were in school; by 1950, 85.8 per cent. Particularly outstanding was the record of Japanese youngsters (94.1 per cent in school) in view of the fact that the Japanese are of more recent immigration.[38] If going to school will settle the English problems, Hawaiians will have one academic battle won.

*Foreign Language Schools.* Even though the problem of the Hawaiian schools, like that of New Mexico schools, lay in a competition of cultures rather than in language, one might well ask why the schools were not more successful than they reported in teaching English. Compulsory education had worked well on the islands. Though the level of schooling was below the average for the mainland, youngsters had been kept in school in large numbers until their fourteenth birthdays, and truancy was at a surprising minimum for such a varied population.

Many Hawaiian educators were apt to accuse the foreign language schools of being one of the roots of their difficulties. Whether they were or not, they loomed large in a description of the handicaps under which the schools labored. They were evaluated by the 1920 Federal Survey Commission, which pointed out that there was nothing comparable to them in the States and that they had "grown to formidable proportions, particularly among the Japanese."[39]

It will be remembered that the agricultural laborers who had been imported for work in the sugar and pineapple fields had not expected to

---

[36] Ethel S. Hoeber, "Every School an English Standard School," *Hawaii Educational Review*, vol. 38, pp. 3–4, September, 1949.

[37] Marian Wauke [Grade 10, W. R. Farrington High School], "Better Speech," *Hawaii Educational Review*, vol. 38, p. 227, May, 1950.

[38] See table in Lind and Schmitt, *op. cit.*, p. 87.

[39] Cited in Wist, *op. cit.*, p. 170.

remain in the islands. Neither had other groups coming for other reasons. All wanted their children to be prepared for the homeland, whether it was in Europe or in Asia. Consequently, most groups had opened language schools for the children, and some of these schools had persisted through several decades. The Lihue German Schools had been opened in 1882 on the island of Kauai, but they had gone out of existence in 1918. Portuguese language schools were opened in 1889, but were out of operation by 1920.[40] In 1891 a Portuguese language class was organized in the Portuguese Mission School, and in 1905, the Portuguese Benevolent Society began a school which included an evening division. This institution continued until 1913. In 1917, Portugal sent Prof. Euclides G. Costa to Honolulu to conduct a school in the Portuguese language and Portuguese history. This school was soon discontinued but reopened in the Catholic Mission.[41] The Chinese and Koreans developed schools that persisted through the decades of the 1920s and 1930s. The numbers of children enrolled were never very large. In 1924, for instance, 225 Korean and over 1,100 Chinese youngsters were reported in these schools.[42] The Japanese schools were by far the most formidable from the standpoint of the public school teachers. The first reason for distress was that there came to be a large number of schools which, in a sense, blanketed nearly the whole of the child population of Japanese origins. The second reason was that the Japanese came rapidly to be the dominant group in educational institutions.

The first Japanese laborers began to arrive in numbers in the 1880s. At first there were few children, and some of them were sent home. For those who remained but were expected to return, the first school was opened in 1896. This developed into a school called the Central Institute. By 1920, each plantation and every community center had one or more schools. Pupils numbered about 20,000; the schools, 160; and the teachers, 440.[43] In 1932, when there were some 46,352 youngsters of Japanese origin in a few private and the many public schools, there were 40,017 of the same group in the Japanese language schools.[44] If one wishes to understand the effect of the dual system on the Hawaiian teachers, one has only to imagine himself a teacher in Kansas, with 87 per cent of his youngsters learning Bantu in anticipation of returning to South Africa.

These foreign language schools did indeed create dual systems, for no

---

[40] *Ibid.*, p. 171.
[41] *Biennial Report*, 1919–1920, pp. 26–27.
[42] *Biennial Report*, 1923–1924, p. 116.
[43] *Biennial Report*, 1919–1920, p. 27.
[44] *Biennial Report*, 1931–1932, pp. 99, 101.

child was excused from attendance in regular public or private English-language-oriented institutions, and few youngsters were excused by their parents from attending foreign language schools. Before the 1920s, hours of these special schools were 7 A.M. to 8:30 A.M., and 3 P.M. to 5 P.M. in the afternoon.[45] The original aim of these schools had been to duplicate the primary schools of Japan. For that purpose, they offered work in ethics and in Japanese language, history, and geography. For some twenty years of the twentieth century, they had used the same texts as those used in Japanese schools. In these texts, the mythological history of Japan was related as fact and the political leader to whom the youngsters were asked to give respect was "Our Emperor." The sixth book of the series began with the Imperial Rescript on Education, which was usually read in Japanese schools on all national holidays. The rescript was considered the highest authority in the field of morals.[46]

Whether the rescript and the history lessons had any effect on the children was a matter for debate and some doubt on the part of educators. One authority was inclined to think that the children of Oriental parents preferred public school to the language school. Regardless of birthplace of parents, in 1926, 99 out of every 100 children enrolled in the Japanese-language schools had been born in Hawaii. The boys, so Dr. Schwartz said, were often sullen about going to language school.[47] The superintendent in office in 1920 said that there was even a difference of opinion among Japanese adults as to the value of the schools. They had called for shorter hours and had asked for a limitation of the curriculum to language study only.[48] But the schools had continued to be richly supported, for "the annual expense for their upkeep and for teachers' salaries," said Dr. Schwartz in 1926, was "not far from ten dollars per annum for every male Japanese wage-earner."[49]

The educators were inclined to discount the character-shaping influence of the foreign language schools and to confine their lamentations about them to their effect on the learning of English—not so the Hawaiian legislators. In the upsurge of patriotism following World War I, they decided to react forcefully to the threat of foreign influences. They had available the Federal commission's recommendations that the schools should be outlawed and that the several foreign languages should be taught by teachers in public schools. But the

[45] *Biennial Report*, 1919–1920, p. 27.
[46] Schwartz, *op. cit.*, pp. 100–101.
[47] *Ibid.*, pp. 99, 103.
[48] *Biennial Report*, 1919–1920, p. 27.
[49] Schwartz, *op. cit.*, p. 100.

Hawaiian legislators, in 1920, chose to develop their own plan for the schools.

The act passed by the Legislature put the foreign language schools under the Department of Public Instruction, their operation to be contingent on permission from the department. Control by the department extended to teachers, who were to secure permits to teach and denied permits if they were found to be unfamiliar with American history and institutions, or unable to read, write, and speak the English language. The teacher-applicant was to sign a pledge to abide by the regulations of the department and to teach in such a fashion as to develop his charges into good American citizens. Attendance at language schools was to be restricted to one hour daily, after the close of the public schools. Authority of the department extended finally to courses of study and texts to be used in the schools.[50]

Following this act to control the language schools, the Department of Public Instruction appointed a director to supervise them.[51] The department also named a committee to evaluate the schools. Members found in practice what legislators presumably had been trying to control through the act, for the committee reported that the courses of study were poorly suited to efficient teaching and wasteful of time and energy; in addition, they tended "to lay the foundations of alien ideals in the mind of the child and retard the teaching of American ideals and institutions."[52]

The matter of the language schools was so crucial to the lawmakers that in 1923, the Legislature amended the 1920 act by creating a Division of Oriental Language Schools in the Department of Public Instruction. In the meantime, the officials in the language schools had taken a cue from persons involved in the closing of foreign language classes in the States. They had chosen to fight the legislation. The superintendent reported in 1924 that many of the schools were in litigation.

Before the fate of the language schools would be settled for the decades of the twenties and thirties, the Department of Public Instruction had taken further steps for their improvement and control. A first step was the development of new texts in the Japanese language. These were edited from the standpoint of the American child. "My country" in these books became the United States, and lessons on American history and biography as well as on Japanese life were included. American manners and behavior, sanitation and personal hygiene were also a part of the new text material. According to the

---

[50] Wist, *op cit.*, p. 172.
[51] Schwartz, *op. cit.*, p. 102.
[52] *Biennial Report,* 1921–1922, p. 5.

superintendent, these books were well received but the department could not mandate their use because some schools were in litigation.

The department's obligation to the Americanizing of the teachers was in part carried out. It held an institute attended by seventy teachers from the language schools. The institute was primarily for the purpose of instruction in American history and ideals.[53]

In the end, the litigation was temporarily successful. In 1927 the Supreme Court of the United States declared the Hawaiian laws on the foreign language schools unconstitutional. Within three years, enrollment in the schools was over 41,000 pupils.[54] So momentous was the decision on the schools that editors of the *New York Times* took occasion to comment on the situation. To the extent that the Hawaiian law on the language schools had been construed by the Japanese government as discriminating against Japan, said the article, the Supreme Court decision would reduce the friction between the governments. But, the writer pointed out, the youngsters in the school who were born in the United States were American citizens by law, and the Supreme Court's decision would not make easier a solution of racial problems. These citizens, as all others, needed a knowledge of English and a general acquaintance with subjects taught in American schools.[55] To some educators in the Hawaiian schools, too, the foreign language schools would continue to be "an anachronism and an obstacle to the full assimilation of the Japanese into the American culture pattern."[56]

The *coup de grâce* was finally administered to the schools under the pressure of the crucial position of Hawaii during World War II. In the biennial report for 1943–1944, the superintendent reported that the Legislature had passed a law forbidding the teaching of modern languages below the fifth grade. This act had eliminated the foreign language schools which had apparently enrolled the elementary school child. It was reported, however, that there was a desire to offer Chinese, Japanese, and Korean in public schools, beginning with the seventh grade. But the only youngsters who would be eligible were those who had passed a rigid English examination.[57]

*Kindergartens.* To combat the assumed influence of the foreign language schools, particularly on the Oriental youngsters, the public schools moved in many directions. One of the ways in which they tried to improve language facility was through kindergartens.

[53] *Biennial Report*, 1923–1924, pp. 84–87.
[54] Wist, *op. cit.*, p. 173.
[55] "Hawaii's School Problem," *The New York Times*. Reported in *School and Society*, vol. 25, March 5, 1927, p. 289.
[56] Wist, *op. cit.*, p. 173.
[57] *Biennial Report*, 1943–1944, p. 8.

Kindergartens had come to America in the middle of the nineteenth century. Their rationale had been based on the new-found discovery of the child as an independent and important being, or of the natural unfolding of a human being who was to become one with God, as Froebel, originator of the movement, thought.

The rationale for this institution in Hawaii, however, was somewhat different and, it can be construed, infinitely more practical. In 1893 the Woman's Board of Missions organized four kindergartens: one for the Japanese, a second for the Portuguese, a third for the Hawaiians, and a fourth for the youngsters of other races. The kindergarten was to become an arm of Protestantism and also an instrument of Americanization, which probably was indistinguishable from the former. Wist reported that these early kindergartens affected the public school by helping the non-English-speaking children and preparing them for first grade. In 1896 the Free Kindergarten Association opened a school enrolling children of several racial groups. This proved to be highly successful.[58]

By the year 1919–1920, the establishment of free public kindergartens as part of the school system was listed as one of the achievements of the Department of Public Instruction. Furthermore, the department was cooperating with local kindergarten associations in a campaign to secure more kindergartens "as a most potent agency for Americanization." However, only four of some twenty-two kindergartens were actually being maintained by the department, with the help of local organizations. They enrolled some 250 children. About 1,600 more youngsters were being cared for in eighteen or more free kindergartens run entirely by private funds. As there were 12,000 children in first grade, Miss Frances Laurence, supervisor, reasoned that there were at least 10,000 children for whom there were still no kindergartens.

The department, so Miss Laurence said, planned to advance the cause of kindergartens, for only 2 to 3 per cent of the school children came from English-speaking homes. First grades were clogged with repeaters. Sometimes children could not go to school until they were eight years old because there was no room for them. Kindergartens could actually cut the cost of elementary schooling through reducing the numbers of repeaters; for "the earlier a language is learned, the more at home one feels in its use." Furthermore, "any adequate Americanization plan must start with kindergartens." The kindergarten child learns not only a language, but "our standards of behavior, our attitude toward the essential facts of life, learning at this early age to love their country, so different from the one their parents hold dear."[59]

---

[58] Wist, op. cit., pp. 134–135.
[59] Biennial Report, 1919–1920, pp. 36, 156–158.

For their assistance in teaching English, kindergartens continued to merit some mention in the succeeding decades. For instance, in 1921–1922 it was noted that the Hilo Free Kindergarten had been discontinued for a period, but The Japanese Women's Society had been instrumental in erecting a building and equipping the school in time for its opening in the fall of 1921.[60]

There continued to be a concerted drive for the opening of more public kindergartens, for probably "nowhere in the United States are kindergartens so badly needed as in Hawaii." The magnitude of the English problem faced by the schools and the sharply increased need for socialization, including Americanization, demanded that the islands increase the numbers of their kindergartens. Improved education in Honolulu was already showing the effects of the greater number of kindergartens located there.[61]

Kindergartens continued to be a need rather than a regularly budgeted item for community schools. In the year 1939–1940 it was stated that the widespread establishment of kindergartens would be more effective in speech improvement than any other device the schools might use. The same plea for the urgency of their need was continued in the 1941–1942 report.[62] Finally, by an act of 1943, the Legislature laid the foundation for public kindergartens, and in 1943–1944, twelve kindergartens were officially opened.[63] Some twenty-five years of special pleading and efforts by voluntary associations had finally resulted in a specific institutional response not for a simple extension downward of the school system, but to a language and Americanization problem.

### Americanization
### in a Special Kind of Economy

At first, agriculture—then agriculture, tourists, and the military—have constituted the basic props of the Hawaiian economy. The peculiar kind of agricultural economy that was developed and the way it was developed laid the basis for another set of problems for the Hawaiian schools.

These problems had to do with the people who were imported (aside from their need for English instruction) and the occupations into which they needed to be inducted. A simple, hard-working folk not far from feudalism needed more than language to become Americans, according to the Hawaiian educators. They needed instruction in modern health and dietary practices, in how to develop a new and different family

---

[60] *Biennial Report*, 1921–1922, p. 124.

[61] *Biennial Report*, 1927–1928, p. 146.

[62] *Biennial Report*, 1939–1940, p. 22; and 1941–1942, pp. 53–54.

[63] *Biennial Report*, 1943–1944, p. 8.

life. They most certainly needed help with scientific agriculture and with the development of modern trade skills. When they were still enrolled in large numbers in the language schools and the school day was thereby extended unduly, the younger children needed rest and all of them needed food. In response to these needs, a fundamental education, American style, developed in Hawaii. Long before the term was invented for the mainland, Hawaiian educators were addressing themselves to "life adjustment" education on a simple, straightforward, practical basis.

A basic point of view, adopted very early in the Hawaiian school system, helped to foster the adjustment of the schools to an agricultural economy manned largely by persons of foreign and prescientific ways. This point of view was that every child, regardless of circumstances, was to have available the same educational resources that the richest community could command. Along with this proviso was a compulsory education law with teeth in it, and the compulsory feature of the school system dated back to pre-United States days. To be sure, children did not always progress in school as far as educators would have liked, but they all secured an education in the first years of the elementary school, regardless of how remote the plantation on which they lived.

That there was an equality of sorts between the rural and urban systems of education in Hawaii had been a matter of note for some years. In the 1919–1920 report when he was commenting on how the Hawaiian education system compared with systems on the mainland, the superintendent took occasion to note that opportunities for education were available to rural and urban children alike. Even salaries for teachers were comparable. Rural teachers were occasionally paid above the territorial schedule.[64] In a U.S. Office of Education bulletin for 1936, it was again pointed out that there was an equitable distribution of opportunities between rural and urban schools. There was no discrimination in facilities or salaries, though often tuition charges had to be exacted in the higher grades.[65] As late as 1950, it was still said with pride that Hawaii had an enviable record in equalization of rural and urban education. The situations in the two kinds of areas were comparable in length of school year, in teacher requirements and salaries, in curricular offerings, in distribution of funds, and in other respects.[66] A point of view had been maintained steadily in practice for most of the twentieth century, and had been the foundation for other developments.

*Health.* A fascinating study would be what the reports of superintendents tell of the preoccupations of educators in state and local school

[64] *Biennial Report,* 1919–1920, p. 6.

[65] Cook, *op. cit.,* p. 48.

[66] W. Harold Loper, "Educational Opportunity," *Hawaii Educational Review,* vol. 38, p. 141, February, 1950.

systems. Very properly, the reports of the Hawaiian superintendents do not look like those of any other system in the United States. Aside from the statistics on pupils, teachers, and plant, there is little similarity between these reports and those to be found in the States.

A reporting of pupils by origin up to the 1930s is in itself unique. A listing of teachers by name and origin, as well as school, is another unique feature of these reports. The preoccupation of the Hawaiian educators is clearly evident from the way human beings are tabulated.

A complex of activities are reported rather continuously, which indicates another preoccupation, the health of youngsters of foreign origin and prescientific backgrounds. The complex includes fairly extensive reporting on health and the activities of the health officer, concentration on home economics at several levels, a continuous interest in the development and expansion of a special kind of cafeteria service, and the institution of required rest periods in elementary schools. As the concept of what an American is expands, most of these activities become rationalized as a part of the making of the good American.

In 1922 in the Konawaena Junior High School, an elaborate home economics program was in progress among the girls, who were learning ways to prepare foods, how to make suitable school dresses, and how to incorporate wholesomeness and cleanliness into their living. It was necessary to teach these skills and values in the school because the homes from which the girls came had such very different standards from ordinarily accepted ones. "That their home surroundings become typically American is just as important in the process of Americanization as that they should learn American history and study the American form of government."[67] Again in 1928 it was stressed that, in a system where youngsters come from so many different types of homes, "a great deal of very effective work in citizenship can be given by effective training in home ideals." About this same time under a new division of research a committee was formed to study the Hawaiian environment.[68]

Home economics programs were apparently supplemented in senior high schools by home projects, as reported in 1932. High school youngsters undertook such tasks at home as training a younger sister to go to bed regularly, helping children to get rid of sores, making toy cupboards and teaching younger brothers and sisters to keep their playthings in the cupboards, remaking clothes, and cleaning and planting yards.[69]

In the fall of 1925 evening courses in homemaking were offered for the first time in Honolulu. These included classes in foods, clothing,

[67] Biennial Report, 1921–1922, p. 115.
[68] Biennial Report, 1927–1928, pp. 125–126, 138.
[69] Biennial Report, 1931–1932, p. 38.

and child care.[70]  This program continued to flourish and was reported
by the superintendent in 1940 as being an extensive program in adult
homemaking.[71]  In 1944 the superintendent recommended a division of
adult education which would promote classes designed to help adults
improve their English and secure an understanding of the customs of
the American home and the nature of American institutions.  A widespread adult education program could assist in developing a better
family life and an improved civic life.[72]

Each practice introduced into the Hawaiian school system served
many purposes, as in other systems.  This was true of the special
cafeteria service introduced somewhat earlier perhaps and on a wider
scale than on the mainland.  Many Hawaiian children came to school
from poor homes on remote plantations.  They might have started out
at six or six-thirty in the morning in order to attend a foreign language
school.  They possibly might have walked several miles to the public
schools, and because of their obligations to the foreign language school
in the afternoon, they would not arrive home before six in the evening.
Feeding these children became an obligation.  They needed a hot noon
lunch, not only because they would otherwise not have had any food
for a ten- or twelve-hour stretch, but because the dietary practices of
foreign homes would have been suspect.  According to educators, the
school lunch often constituted the child's major food for the day.[73]

When the lunch program first began, there were no funds for hiring
cafeteria help, particularly as the program had to be instituted in a
great number of schools, some of which were one-room affairs.  Teachers
and older children were responsible for the lunch program, and it was
customary for teachers and youngsters, particularly in rural areas, to
dine together.

The program must have gained support through activities such as that
of a woman's committee on child welfare in 1920.  The committee had
found many undernourished children and the women were providing
food for them.  They followed this by weighing youngsters regularly and
watching their growth.  They urged the necessity of racial standards.
The Bowditch standard developed in connection with children of European ancestry was obviously unfair to youngsters of Oriental descent,
so they reported.[74]  By 1927–1928, the development of an efficient
system of school lunches was reported—lunches which were particularly

[70] Adelaide S. Baylor, "Home Economics in the Territory of Hawaii," *Journal of Home Economics,* vol. 18, no. 9, p. 515, September, 1926.
[71] *Biennial Report,* 1939–1940, p. 14.
[72] *Biennial Report,* 1943–1944, p. 7.
[73] Cook, *op. cit.,* p. 55.
[74] *Biennial Report,* 1919–1920, pp. 162–163.

beneficial to plantation children who had breakfasted at five-thirty or six in the morning.[75] In 1924 there had been only 30 cafeterias. By 1932, 106 were operating and serving 29,000 five-cent lunches daily along with 500 penny lunches for children who did not have five cents. This was the Depression, and, in addition to making the accommodation of the penny lunches, the cafeterias were stressing the use of local foods so that good eating habits could be developed at home.[76]

The Depression required more stringent measures. Oatmeal mush and cod-liver oil were being furnished at cost in the schools, and milk was being distributed extensively in order to teach its use as a part of the diet. Rest periods had been instituted for all children in the first four grades. One-half an hour a day for rest was compulsory. Youngsters in the upper grades were often also being granted the privilege of rest periods.[77]

Beyond supplying food, the need for which was quite obvious, the cafeterias were also promoting other health measures and general social customs. Youngsters were learning to wash their hands before eating and to eat slowly and in orderly fashion while sitting at their desks or tables. They were also discovering the pleasures of conversation with meals and the proper use of tableware and mealtime courtesies.[78]

By 1940 there were 147 school cafeterias in operation, and by 1950–1951, hot lunches were being served to 60,550 youngsters or 67 per cent of the total school population. The number served had been an increase of 3 per cent over the figure for 1949–1950.[79] In the meantime, the program had long since been so well established as to justify hiring special personnel for manning the cafeterias. Whether youngsters were still in such desperate need of food as they had been in the 1930s was in a sense beside the point. A practice developed to meet the needs of a special population had become an institution.

*Education for Employment.* Mainland educators have from time to time foreseen the crises which might arise in American economic life caused by graduating an increasing number of young people from both high schools and colleges. If educational level is to be equated with vocational opportunity, then where are these youth to be placed? This has been a perennial question, particularly in time of depression. The mainland economy, however, whether in response to the educational pressure or independent of it, has expanded in so many directions that

[75] *Biennial Report,* 1927–1928, p. 126.
[76] *Biennial Report,* 1931–1932, p. 24.
[77] *Ibid.,* p. 43.
[78] Cook, *op. cit.,* p. 54.
[79] *Biennial Report,* 1939–1940, p. 15; and *Hawaii Educational Review,* vol. 40, p. 47, October, 1951.

in the long view it has absorbed all who could be educated and is constantly demanding more education for present employees and future prospects.

High school and college teachers in mainland schools have been fortunate in the placement of graduates, in comparison to their Hawaiian colleagues. To the latter, no happy multiplication of jobs or expanding industrialism has appeared to be imminent. Although they could educate a limited number in the professions and in the business occupations, their occupational training task has always been overwhelmingly to make agricultural and semi-skilled pursuits acceptable to youngsters to whom occupational doors on the mainland were closed and for whom the only opportunity was to be found largely in six or seven agricultural islands.

School people early recognized their task as unique, as is indicated by the superintendent who in 1914 reported having studied vocational education on the mainland and having come to the decision that it might be best for Hawaiian educators to chart their own course.[80] By 1918 it was suggested that one "of the most serious tasks placed upon the schools is that of developing in their graduates a tendency towards agricultural and mechanical employment." Academic standards as an aim of schooling were all well and good for some situations, but Hawaiian educators needed to put foremost another aim, training for work. The territory would not long be able to sustain the "wasteful policy" of importing laborers for agricultural work. To forward the vocational aim, training in agricultural work had been given over the last four years in the normal school. Until four years ago, teachers for the schools had been in short supply, being limited to four instructors; but now that normal graduates were equipped with special skills, instruction in carpentry, agriculture, and domestic science was in process in nearly every large school in the territory.[81]

Another emphasis in practice was the school garden, which was attached to many of the elementary schools in the rural areas. The garden had many functions; one of them might have been to provide science instruction or opportunity for nature study. It might also have been used to encourage growing proper foods or as a device for improving home landscaping; probably it was intended to impress youngsters with the importance of agriculture as an occupational aim. By 1930, twenty-seven special garden teachers were already employed, and a total of 30,526 elementary school youngsters were receiving instruction in nature study or gardening.[82] By 1952 the school garden had become a relic

[80] *Biennial Report*, 1913–1914, p. 10.
[81] *Biennial Report*, 1917–1918, pp. 6–7.
[82] *Biennial Report*, 1929–1930, pp. 116–117.

but it could still be used as an aid in many other kinds of programs. Social studies, language arts—almost any of the school activities—could be enriched by the garden, which had otherwise lost its function.[83]

In the meantime, other devices had been used to interest children in various forms of manual labor. In 1920 the schools had distributed 5,000 copies of farm-craft lessons and exhibits of handwork, and shop and garden products had been encouraged—activities which owed their beginning in part to World War I. On the island of Maui all boys from the fourth grade up were taking shopwork. The university was making itself felt throughout the territory by concentration on agricultural extension and adult education courses. Not only were the vocational aspects of the program and particularly in arts and crafts valuable for their occupational orientation, they also were important as Americanization devices. The manners and customs of Americans differed from aliens, according to Hawaiian educators, precisely because their activities were different.[84]

It was noted again in 1931 that prejudice on the mainland and the economic situation had produced a saturation point "for desirable occupations, and for high school graduates." A governor's committee was studying the problem. One outcome of the committee's work was to eventuate in arranging school activities so as to give emphasis to activities for youngsters whose formal schooling would end with high school graduation. Another outcome was the initiation of a new plan in September, 1931, in McKinley High School. One feature of an otherwise individualized curriculum was a core based on out-of-school activities and needs of pupils. Youngsters would be in school part time and working in the community the rest of the time. Shifts in school would be scheduled up to 9 p.m. to accommodate students when they were free. Full-time attendance in high school would be denied youngsters over eighteen years of age.[85]

By the 1950s, training in agriculture was included in many programs. Young-farmer projects, partly financed by Federal monies, were a settled development in Hawaiian schooling.[86] A people who lived on agriculture were becoming sensitive to the need for conservation of soil, as reported by Shizuto Kadota, trainer in agriculture at Hilo and instructor at the Hawaiian Vocational School in commercial floriculture.[87]

[83] L. Canaday and C. R. Ferdun, "The Elementary School Garden . . . An Educational Experience," *Hawaii Educational Review,* vol. 41, pp. 94–95, December, 1952.

[84] *Biennial Report,* 1919–1920, pp. 38, 71, 82, 116.

[85] Bolton and Cary, *op. cit.,* pp. 46–48.

[86] Clarence R. Ferdun, "Young Farmer Programs," *Hawaii Educational Review,* vol. 41, pp. 10–11, September, 1952.

[87] *Hawaii Educational Review,* vol. 40, pp. 42–43, October, 1951.

Agriculture and shopwork for persons from the fourth grade through adulthood; school cafeterias on remote plantations as well as in city areas; home economics and arts and crafts, through which adaptation to social customs might go forward—these were some of the ways in which the Hawaiian education system sought to assist the children of alien and peasant backgrounds to live as Americans in Hawaii.

## Other Americanization Tools

Hawaiian educators have used practices and ideas which are common to mainland educators. Music and physical education, toothbrush drills and physical examinations have been a part of island education. Hawaiian teachers, like their American colleagues in the states, rediscovered the whole child in the late 1920s. Outwardly, the Hawaiian school system might appear much like any system in the United States. The difference has been in the perspective from which the Hawaiians judged each of the innovations in turn, and the peculiar and special uses to which they put them.

Music has had some place in American education for at least one hundred years. Its place in Hawaii is so special that in 1900 it was pointed out that Tonic Sol-fa notation had been introduced in grades 1 to 3 and children in third grade were singing simple two-part songs. Why this concern with Western music? Because the "cosmopolitan character" of the schools created "peculiar difficulties for the music teacher." Students were unsure of themselves in the English language, and Chinese and Japanese youngsters had "untrained" ears—they were unused to the sound of Western music.[88]

Despite the difficulties attendant on the teaching of music, the struggle continued. In view of the way Hawaiian educators saw their central problem it must be assumed that singing could serve several functions. It was quite obvious that an important part of Americanization was learning the scale used typically in the United States and so foreign to Japanese or Chinese ears. Singing was also a group activity in which all nationalities could blend their efforts, and in which students' deficiencies would not be noticeable. Furthermore, singing patriotic songs would be one way to impress these children with where their loyalties really ought to lie. Shifting attention from Fujiyama to "America, the Beautiful" and from the Emperor to "The Star-spangled Banner" could be carried on quite smoothly through choruses and daily "song fests." A special concentration in a taken-for-granted field led in Hawaii to a statement by the superintendent that "Hawaii is notable for the excellence of its public school singing."[89]

[88] *Biennial Report*, 1900, p. 80.
[89] *Biennial Report*, 1919–1920, p. 7.

Physical education, likewise, became a special kind of Americanization device, though it has perhaps been unconsciously used for this purpose in many different school systems in the United States. Willard E. Givens, principal of McKinley High School, Honolulu, reported in 1920 that the outstanding achievement in his school was the introduction of physical education on a regular basis. "We are also teaching many children how to play and play fairly, a thing that many of them do not know when they come to high school." Through group efforts on the athletic field and through being asked to maintain high standards, youngsters were learning much that was essential to the good American, Givens felt. Mrs. Mary S. Close reported in the same year that organized play, a necessary adjunct to exercise, appealed to Hawaiian children but not to Chinese and Japanese youngsters.[90]    By 1928, members of the teaching staff of the Konawaena High School were using physical training and clubs and student organizations to impress their young people with the importance of playing the game fairly, having strong, healthy bodies, and leading clean lives.

A frontal attack on character education in the high school was made in 1927–1928. Character marks had been added to students' report cards. Youngsters were to be graded on industry (perseverance and effort), attitude (cooperation, cheerfulness, courtesy, friendliness, attention), and dependability (punctuality and trustworthiness). Character education and citizenship were mentioned in the same breath. Possibly physical education and character education, as they related to citizenship, were considered a bulwark against dance halls and dance-hall girls, both mentioned in the 1930 report, and gambling, which was mentioned in other reports. So serious had the jitney-dance evil become that educators were hoping the Legislature would help in the fight against it.[91]

Although the missionaries who had begun their educational work in 1820 had worked with adults, a formal public school adult education program was begun only about 1944. This, too, has proved to be an Americanization tool. In the school year 1948–1949, elementary English was taught to more than 2,000 individuals, and high school courses enrolled 2,100 with over 1,000 receiving high school diplomas. In the same year, Dr. Harry Overstreet and Dr. Bonaro Overstreet conducted community meetings designed to assist in enforcing the "solidifying of community desire to create a new sense of responsibility."[92]

By the school year 1956, some 9,178 adults were enrolled in citizenship, elementary and high school, and community-interest programs,

[90] *Ibid.*, pp. 48, 91.

[91] *Biennial Report,* 1927–1928, pp. 81, 94; 1929–1930, pp. 52–53.

[92] Territory of Hawaii, Department of Public Instruction, *Annual Report,* June 30, 1949, pp. 12–13.

and other classes. The problem of English instruction as an Americanization device had now shifted to the adult level. Two items pointed out by the director, Frank J. Drees, were that the English language course of study had been revised and that naturalization training had been stressed. Out of an adult enrollment of 10,997 in 1957, some 1,774 were engaged in citizenship courses. It is interesting that the number of students enrolled in elementary education is the same as the number enrolled in English-language development.[93] It is clear that Hawaiian educators are still tussling with a problem which concerned them in 1896.

*Reaching for Roots*

While the mainland educators were groping, along with Hawaiian schoolteachers, for the meaning of an American, the latter were looking for a more tangible and meaningful tradition than that of the Pilgrim Fathers, whose home had been some 2,000 miles away. Every people needs a past, and the educators no less than the people of many races were looking for one.

In the Hawaiian school environment, the educators found a past. It is one which came to them quite naturally, for it was enshrined in the names of their schools and islands, in the grants of land of the Hawaiian nobility, and in the remnants of ancient arts and crafts. That past was probably always recognized, as it may be today, as a lure for tourists, but it has a far deeper meaning than the dollars which visitors bring to the islands. Its meaning was probably not recognized by the missionary educators who were still operating in Hawaii in 1902. They had been promoting the art of mat weaving and of *lau hala* and bamboo work as natural activities for their largely Polynesian clientele. Miss Lucy Adams must have had the same thought when she told of thirty-five girls who were learning torchon lace work under the direction of native teachers. Miss Adams looked forward to the time when various kinds of lace should be offered for sale, including a distinctly Hawaiian pattern with a taro leaf design.[94]

By 1920 the original Polynesians who were needed for the American past in Hawaii had already given way to the influx of Orientals. As a consequence, they were ripe for glorification. They were already innately intellectual, spiritual, and civic in their leanings, according to commentators, and had withal a splendid physique, kindly disposition, beautiful hospitality, and delightful physical traits. All of these traits which had enabled them to make a genuine racial contribution had also

[93] Territory of Hawaii, Department of Public Instruction, *Annual Report,* June 30, 1957, pp. 9–10, 66.

[94] *Biennial Report,* Supplement to 1902 report, pp. 7, 83.

enabled them to embrace rapidly both popular education and Christianity. In deference to this recently found past, Hawaiian handicrafts
were being revived and emphasized as a part of the industrial arts
curriculum; and a department of Hawaiian handicrafts had been inaugurated at the normal school. But the revival was not without its
drawbacks; apparently, few of the teachers then in service knew the
art of *lau hala* weaving which had such great possibilities for rural
schools. Perhaps teachers might be found in the old Hawaiian settlements.[95]

By 1922 there was a report from the weaving department of the Territorial Normal School, and the superintendent was finding it necessary
to ask why handicrafts should become an integral part of the primary
curriculum. The answer was that the skill and efficiency developed in
the school could be exploited in the home. Through employing leisure
hours, handicrafts might benefit the family as well as the child.[96]

The high schools began to do their part to develop a past. In 1928
they were reported as offering several foreign languages, among them
Hawaiian. Chinese, Korean, and Japanese were given, too, but there
was a function in their offering. They might serve as a counterbalance
to the lure of the foreign language schools. Polynesians, however, had
been for some years now in the habit of attending English-speaking
schools, their numbers were decreasing, and they were not in possession
of one of the great world languages. That Hawaiian should now be
offered in high schools must bear another interpretation, the excavation
of a past. This item in the curriculum was bulwarked, furthermore, by
one in Hawaiian art.[97]

In the 1930s, the Legislature took a step which resulted in an observance not unlike the period of silent prayer. They decreed that in every
public school "conducted in any settlement of homesteaders under the
Hawaiian Homes Commission" courses in the Hawaiian language must
be given for at least ten minutes daily. Whether stimulated by this
religious observance or as a part of the same wave of sentiment, adults
were reported as having increased their demand for classes in Hawaiian
crafts.[98]

By the postwar period the past had become well established in its
appropriate role. Old Hawaii had returned in story, song, and dance to
the eighth grade class of the laboratory schools at the University of
Hawaii. The youngsters had learned from Hawaiian folk artists the
uses of old Hawaiian instruments. They had learned Hawaiian songs
and the hula and the dance with sticks. Their performances had been

[95] *Biennial Report*, 1919–1920, pp. 7, 38, 129.
[96] *Biennial Report*, 1921–1922, pp. 78–79, 166.
[97] *Biennial Report*, 1927–1928, pp. 76–77.
[98] *Biennial Report*, 1935–1936, pp. 12, 27.

embellished with block designs from the old Hawaiian art.  Their contributions to Hawaii's traditions had been made into recordings by the University of Hawaii which was prepared to lend them to schools throughout the islands.[99]  Melvin Yamachika, fourth grader, who had been studying the early Hawaiians, had made his own contribution to his new Polynesian-American past.  He had painted the coat of arms on which was inscribed in Hawaiian, "The life of the land is perpetuated by righteousness."[100]

In righteousness indeed was this past founded.  May Kato, an eleventh grade student, writing on what "aloha" meant to her, said that it symbolized a melting pot in which it was possible to break down prejudice.  More than that, it was spiritual power by which peoples of different backgrounds might live harmoniously together.  In this power was America's greatness—equal opportunity regardless of race, color, or creed.[101]  The past of the people of many races had merged, through the gracious Polynesians, with the emergent tradition of the mainland.

## SUMMARY

This description of a universe on nine islands completes the fourth case study on establishing schools in the United States.  It underscores once more the role of schools in supporting nationalism, but more than that, how adaptable a state or territorial school system must be in order to carry out its main task when it is confronted with still another "atypical" American population.

Hawaiian educators used all the culture items of mainland school systems.  They established kindergartens, instituted school lunches, developed vocational education, put in music and physical education and home economics.  But all of these typical American devices had to be employed uniquely as Americanization instruments among a school population which was not familiar with the dominant Anglo symbol system.  How successful the descendants of New England missionaries and the new "native" Hawaiian teachers have been is attested to by the high level of race relations in Hawaii.  An assumption of many Americans is that "Americanism is not, and never was, a matter of race or ancestry."  Hawaiians may have come closer to realizing this assumption in practice than have Americans on the mainland—thanks in part to the Hawaiian educational system.

[99] Naomi St. Denis, "Old Hawaii Returns in Story, Song and Dance," *Hawaii Educational Review,* vol. 41, pp. 35, 42, October, 1952.

[100] Melvin Yamachika, "The Hawaiian Coat of Arms," *Hawaii Educational Review,* vol. 38, p. 236, May, 1950.

[101] May Kato, "What Aloha Means to Me," *Hawaii Educational Review,* vol. 38, p. 229, May, 1951.

# 15

## Education in Retrospect
## and Prospect

> I know, indeed, that some honest men fear that a republican
> government can not be strong, that this Government is not
> strong enough; but would the honest patriot, in the full tide
> of successful experiment, abandon a government which has
> so far kept us free and firm on the theoretic and visionary
> fear that this Government, the world's best hope, may by
> possibility want energy to preserve itself?[1]
>
> THOMAS JEFFERSON, FIRST INAUGURAL
> ADDRESS, MARCH 4, 1801

Certainly few if any Americans would abandon their government, as
Jefferson once implied they might. But as in the past, Americans are
raising questions about the strength of republican government and
whether it wants the energy to preserve itself. If Americans can find
answers, they will undoubtedly be found embedded somewhere in the
schools—kindergarten through university and adult education.

Whether this nation would survive depended on whether the people
were enlightened, according to early leaders. An intelligent and virtuous
citizenry and an incorruptible group of public servants would be developed only if a common school system and colleges were founded and
maintained. If the language of the early 1800s be taken as symbolic,
then neither the premises of the leaders nor the tasks of the schools have
changed fundamentally. The overriding purpose of American education
has been and is to support republican government.

---

[1] James D. Richardson (ed.), *A Compilation of the Messages and Papers of the
Presidents,* Bureau of National Literature, Inc., New York, 1908, vol. I, p. 322.
Prepared under the direction of the Joint Committee on Printing of the House
and Senate.

RETROSPECT

The task of making Americans has been anything but simple. It has been as complex as inventing, nearly every generation, a new educational pattern to shape an American needed for a changed age. Yet the basic concept of the American has changed little; rather, the job of developing the ideal American has been complicated by social and economic forces modifying the American society.

In the early national period the chief task was to forge a school system and to describe the ideal America and American. The latter task was in part the work of New England middle-class intellectuals, who patterned the American in textbooks and through propaganda after some New England prototype. This American was Protestant, ambitious, a respecter of work, equalitarian, a supporter of private property and economic individualism, and highly competitive. He was properly respectful of cleanliness, which was next to godliness, and he bore with Spartan-like firmness the vagaries of the present in order that the future might be secured to his children.

However, forces were at work in the United States to confuse the task of shaping this intelligent and virtuous ideal American and ideal public servant judged proper for a republican society. The first was the nature of the "people." Far from being blank tablets on which educators might write an ideal pattern, the people who have come to America in the decades since 1776 or who have been incorporated into the society, as in the Old Southwest and Hawaii, have had cultural heritages unlike those of the dominant culture pattern. Throughout the 185-year history of the United States there has never been a decade or a generation in which there has not been, in some culture pocket or diffused throughout the society, a foreign language press, a foreign church, and foreign schools—foreign, that is, to the dominant culture.

Added to diversity in cultural expectation and behavior has been diversity induced by social and economic movements. Freedom was a heady wine for Americans to drink, and as they indulged, they tried out ideal communities of religious or ethical bent. Many of these groups flourished only in the period from 1820 to 1860, but many remain with us, as evidenced by the Mormons of Utah, the Mennonites of Pennsylvania, and Jehovah's Witnesses.

Freedom also put emphasis on equalitarianism, which meant that class lines (except for Negro and white) were not and are not rigidly drawn. When interrogated, Americans will be found to be middle class regardless of sociologists' classifications. The movement of rural peoples from old farms to new frontier lands and from rural to urban areas has fed the feeling of equalitarianism and complicated the task of adjusting people to new social and economic environments. Freedom and equalitarianism dictated that there should be no designated group of public servants, that they should come out of the whole society. Since Jackson's day it has been common to assume that the mantle of public office could well be worn by any citizen ambitious enough to go after it.

With no groomed leadership, with no established church to set the moral tone of the republican society, with equalitarianism, religious freedom, and competition feeding a restless upward mobility of the population, with a steady influx of new peoples to be assimilated, and with social and economic ills to be combated, where should Americans turn for stability? The common school, said early leaders. And ever since, the common school, the high school, the college, and the university have been the institutions on which Americans have depended to develop loyalty and to adjust their children to their peculiarly fluid and complex national state.

The connection between schools and society from the time of the founding fathers and through World War II has been premised on a more glorious future, which has helped Americans to bear their misfortunes and has served as a guide for current action. That thirteen underpopulated and underdeveloped states were the hope of the world might have appeared ridiculous to a sophisticated observer—not so to the starry-eyed leaders of the late eighteenth century. Supported by schools which were to inculcate intelligence and virtue, and bulwarked by an expanding frontier, progress and an impossibly rosy future dangled before the confident eyes of those who lived through the re-forming decades from 1800 to 1860. Through a properly developed school system, crime, disease, and poverty would be rooted out. Through carefully planned colleges, a group of incorruptible public servants would be developed. But always, if the means were at hand, the future would be infinitely perfectible.

When the shock of the Civil War was subsiding, the school people came face to face with the 100 per cent common school system which earlier advocates had said was urgently needed. Before they had got used to the 100 per cent in the grades, educators were confronted with expanding high schools and junior colleges aborning. In the wake of human devastation left by an uncontrolled expansion of industry, and faced with increasing numbers of native- and foreign-born youngsters, with the help of laymen, school people developed during the period 1900 to 1918 the ideal of the socially efficient American and of the schoolhouse as social center. Educators through national committees also developed a series of curricular devices by which to make both elementary and secondary education meaningful for all the children of all the people. This first national curricular movement culminated in the 1918 report on the reorganization of secondary schools.

Despite the social disorganization of the first fifteen years of the twentieth century, the world's best hope saved the world for democracy in 1918. In the aftermath of war, patriotic hysteria had a field day, but the economy was expanding, old tyrannies had fallen, peace was stretching indefinitely ahead, and the future was more alluring than ever.

The Depression of the thirties gave the American Dream one of its severest jolts, and the schools took stock. Educators began the curricular innovations which would eventuate in general education and life adjustment, which, in turn, would ensure the continuance of an expanding and secure America. A Federal alphabet system and subdued bankers worked to quell the rebellions among workers and farmers alike. The future was not so clearly in perspective, but at least the present was made endurable.

In the meantime, there had been no simple way of instituting common schools, or national curricula, or social centers, or general education among a diverse people dedicated to locally controlled school systems. If loyalty rests on the efficiency of the school system, then that efficiency in turn rests and rested on the shifting interests of state and local leaders and on voluntary groups. Wherever New Englanders went and wherever were to be found such populations as the German freethinkers, there the people went to work to build their own school systems and their own loyalties. Where there were populations out of harmony with the dominant American culture, as in New Mexico and much of the Old Southwest and in Hawaii, as well as in little pockets in cities, there appropriate schools and patriotic symbols would be developed, often by outsiders, that is, those outside of the unique culture groups. In these areas, schools and teachers adapted their practices and techniques to local idiosyncrasies. Some educators would say that their job in these areas is not yet done to their satisfaction; but despite the perfectionist attitudes of the educators, schools in at least one area, Hawaii, have been successful in developing a United Nations out of a heterogeneous people.

The one-tenth of the nation, many of whom were of slave origins and even now are often second-class citizens, still pose problems to schools and make a blot on the American society. The educational fate of Negroes who were freed by the Civil War was for several decades largely in the hands of voluntary groups and still is a function of folk sentiment, which is gradually being aroused to public duty.

Because Americans are now in a crisis in which their world leadership is called into question does not mean that enduring problems have been solved.  Individual and group differences still characterize the society and the eternal question of how much difference can be allowed is still being fought out in courts and in newspapers.  Many youngsters in the society still do not have that equality of educational opportunity to which Horace Mann looked forward.  American educators are still not sure of their ground when adjusting individuals to patterns of conformity, and making room for desirable individual differences.  The educators are still engaged in a great moral enterprise.

## PROSPECT

Yet has education for nationalism shifted ground in the immediate past?  Is it possible that America has reached the end of an era?  From 1776 to 1957, Americans had a future.  That future comforted them in a poverty-stricken present, and served to gloss over the social ills in any of the intervening decades.  Yes, there were crime, poverty, discrimination, disease, Teapot Dome scandals, and maudlin mediocrity.  But somehow, if Americans all worked hard, expanded the suffrage, built more schools, and developed more trade abroad, the American Dream would be realized.  Democracy would triumph at home and peoples abroad would applaud and be persuaded.

Despite war and periodic depressions, the technique of keeping eyes trained on a future did indeed appear to guarantee an improved and improving life nearly every decade.  An expanding economy, followed by an increasing number of persons whose homes had inside plumbing, served to gloss over the fate of those who were economic camp followers.  An improved food supply and an increasing control of disease for the fortunate majority served as cover for mental illness and juvenile delinquency.  A gadget-happy America, enticed by the argument concerning the necessary expansion of the economy, ignored gross waste of raw materials and the consequences of their procurement from less fortunate people in the underdeveloped countries.  A school system that managed to enroll all the children who were sent to it served to deaden the effect of the educators' warnings as to its financial and other inadequacies.  A bit of progress toward a material dream whitewashed the feet of clay.

America had always had a future in which she was a world leader showing the way toward prosperity and liberty to the unfortunate all over the world.  Has America had her future?  Has she achieved her brief moment as most powerful nation and is she now in a decline toward a minor role among the nations of the world?  If she is, as some would have us think, then Americans through their schools must do something which they have not been called upon to do for 180 years—they must either learn to live without a future, or they must forge a different future from that which has served them so well in the past.

This new future may well require a searching stock taking followed by moral reformation. The enemy may be neither the Russians nor the Chinese, but Americans themselves. It may be that their strength to preserve themselves in the foreseeable future will come solely from their success in doing those things which were envisioned by their forefathers, developing incorruptible public servants and a people whose characteristics are intelligence and virtue. It may include entering into cooperative and equalitarian relationships with free and neutral peoples—this same relationship which has served them so well in welding one people out of many in their own country.

If this different future they must forge is grounded in moral reformation, then the plea for more mathematics and science in the schools is a puny answer. Can laymen and educators forge an answer for the new era in American life? Does this government "in the full tide of successful experiment . . . want energy [and, one might add, the intelligence and moral integrity] to preserve itself"?

# Index

505